# Theory and Explanation in Archaeology

## The Southampton Conference

*EDITED BY*

### Colin Renfrew

Department of Archaeology
University of Cambridge
Cambridge, England

### Michael J. Rowlands

Department of Anthropology
University College
London, England

### Barbara Abbott Segraves

Museum of Anthropology
University of Michigan
Ann Arbor, Michigan

 1982

**ACADEMIC PRESS**
A Subsidiary of Harcourt Brace Jovanovich, Publishers
New York   London
Paris   San Diego   San Francisco   São Paulo   Sydney   Tokyo   Toronto

ACADEMIC PRESS, INC.
111 Fifth Avenue, New York, New York 10003

*United Kingdom Edition published by*
ACADEMIC PRESS, INC. (LONDON) LTD.
24/28 Oval Road, London NW1 7DX

Library of Congress Cataloging in Publication Data
Main entry under title:

Theory and explanation in archaeology.

Papers presented at the 2nd open conference of the
Theoretical Archaeology Group, held in Southampton,
England, Dec. 14-16, 1980; sponsored by the Dept. of
Archaeology, University of Southampton, and the Dept.
of Prehistory and Archaeology, University of Sheffield.
Includes index.
1. Archaeology--Philosophy--Congresses. 2. Archaeology
--Methodology--Congresses. I. Renfrew, Colin, Date.
II. Rowlands, M. J. III. Abbott Segraves, Barbara.
IV. Theoretical Archaeology Group (England) V. University
of Southampton. Dept. of Archaeology. VI. University of
Sheffield. Dept. of Prehistory and Archaeology.
CC72.T47        930.1'01        81-17613
ISBN 0-12-586960-6              AACR2

PRINTED IN THE UNITED STATES OF AMERICA

82 83 84 85    9 8 7 6 5 4 3 2 1

*For Leo S. Klejn*

# Contents

# 12
# Catastrophe and Continuity in Social Evolution                          175
*JONATHAN FRIEDMAN*

# 13
# The Polanyi Paradigm and a Dynamic Analysis
# of Archaic States                                                       197
*JOHN GLEDHILL AND MOGENS LARSEN*

# 14
# "Civilization," "Society," and "Anomaly" in Amazonia                    231
*STEPHEN L. NUGENT*

# 15
# The Formation of Tribal Systems in
# Later European Prehistory: Northern Europe,
# 4000–5000 B.C.                                                          241
*KRISTIAN KRISTIANSEN*

# III

## MORPHOGENETIC CHANGE IN COMPLEX SOCIETIES 281

# CONTENTS

# List of Contributors

*Numbers in parentheses indicate the pages on which the authors' contributions begin.*

P. M. ALLEN (347), Service de Chimie Physique II, Code Postal 231, Campus Plaine U.L.B., Boulevard du Triomphe, 1050 Brussels, Belgium

JIM BELL (65), Department of Philosophy, University of South Florida, Tampa, Florida 33620

LEWIS R. BINFORD (125), Department of Anthropology, University of New Mexico, Albuquerque, New Mexico 87131

JAMES DORAN (375), Department of Computer Sciences, University of Essex, Wivenhoe Park, Colchester CO4 3SQ, England

MANFRED K. H. EGGERT (139), Archäologisches Institut, Universität Hamburg, Johnsallee 35, D-200 Hamburg 13, West Germany

JONATHAN FRIEDMAN (175), Institute of Ethnology, Frederiksholms Kanal 4, 1220 Copenhagen K, Denmark

ERNEST GELLNER (97), Department of Philosophy, Logic, and Scientific Method, London School of Economics and Political Science, Houghton Street, London WC2A 2AE, England

JOHN GLEDHILL (197), Department of Anthropology, University College, Gower Street, London WC1E 6BT, England

JOHN HALL (147), Department of Sociology, University of Southampton, Southampton SO9 5NH, England

GREGORY A. JOHNSON (389), Hunter College, City University of New York, New York, New York 10021

KRISTIAN KRISTIANSEN (241), National Agency for the Protection of Nature, Monuments and Sites, Ministry of the Environment, Amaliegade 13, 1256 Copenhagen K, Denmark

MOGENS LARSEN (197), Institute of Assyriology, Kajsergade 1, 1155 Copenhagen K, Denmark

D. H. MELLOR (57), Department of Archaeology, University of Cambridge, Downing Street, Cambridge CB2 3DZ England

DANIEL MILLER[1] (83), Department of Archaeology, University of Cambridge, Downing Street, Cambridge CB2 3DZ, England

STEPHEN L. NUGENT (231), Department of Anthropology, University College, Gower Street, London WC1E 6BT, England

FRED PLOG[2] (25), Department of Anthropology, Arizona State University, Tempe, Arizona 85281

KLAVS RANDSBORG (423), Institute of Prehistoric Archaeology, University of Copenhagen, Vandkunsten 5, DK-1467 Copenhagen K, Denmark

COLIN RENFREW (5, 459), Department of Archaeology, University of Cambridge, Downing Street, Cambridge CB2 3DZ, England

ROBERT ROSEN (301), Department of Physiology and Biophysics, Dalhousie University, Halifax, Nova Scotia, B3H 4H7, Canada

M. J. ROWLANDS (155), Department of Anthropology, University College, Gower Street, London WC1E 6BT, England

MERRILEE H. SALMON[3] (35), Department of Philosophy, Building 27, University of Arizona, Tucson, Arizona 85721

WESLEY C. SALMON (45), Department of Philosophy, Building 27, University of Arizona, Tucson, Arizona 85721

BARBARA ABBOTT SEGRAVES (287), Museum of Anthropology, University Museums Building, University of Michigan, Ann Arbor, Michigan 48109

BRUCE D. SMITH (73), National Museum of Natural History, Smithsonian Institution, Washington, D.C. 20560

S. E. VAN DER LEEUW (431), Institute voor Prae- en Protohistorie, Universiteit van Amsterdam, Singel 453, Amsterdam C, The Netherlands

E. C. ZEEMAN (315), Mathematics Institute, University of Warwick, Coventry CV4 7AL, England

[1]*Present address:* Department of Anthropology, University College, London WC1E 6BT, England.

[2]*Present address:* Department of Sociology and Anthropology, New Mexico State University, *Box 3BV, Las Cruces, New Mexico 88003.*

[3]*Present address:* Department of Philosophy, University of Pittsburgh, Pittsburgh, Pennsylvania 15260.

# PREFACE

Archaeology today is an ambitious discipline, seeking to apply the rigor of the sciences to the surviving material evidence of the human past. This aim of employing scientific explanation within the broad field of human history, and thus of exploring systematically the organization of culture and the dynamics of its change, requires for its fulfillment a firm basis in theory. One of the great achievements in archaeology over the past two decades has been the widespread development of a keen awareness of this requirement. That awareness, which the late David Clarke aptly termed "the loss of innocence," is indeed one of the principal features both of what came to be called the "New Archaeology" in the United States and of its equivalent in Britain together with Scandinavia and the Low Countries.

The present volume is a product of that awareness, and of the growing realization that the task of developing a sound explanatory framework for the study of sociocultural organization and change was far from easy: It is by no means simply a matter of borrowing some of the models developed in other disciplines, or taking some of the concepts and procedures currently employed by philosophers of science, and applying them directly to the available data relating to man's past. For while the cultural realm is no less amenable to scientific investigation than, for example, the biological or the physical, it comprises a distinct analytic unit or area of inquiry, and the development of its theories and explanations must reflect this essential integrity while at the same time recognizing those homologies of form and process, and similarities of methodology, shared with other areas of scientific inquiry. This suggests a number of very basic questions for the discipline and its students. This book arises from the papers presented at the conference of the Theoretical Archaeology Group in Southampton in December 1980, at which many of these problematic issues were discussed. All the contributions are directed toward the theoretical problems that archaeologists encounter in seeking to explain the past and in understanding its changing patterns over time.

The first theme, considered in the first section under the rubric "Explanation Revisited," is the search for an explicit methodology. What is the appropriate form for the explanation of the human past? How shall the validity of explanations be evaluated by bringing them into effective contact with the data? That there is as yet no straightforward and widely accepted answer to these questions is rapidly apparent. The discussion clarifies a number of current issues, however, many of them arising from the special position of archaeology as a discipline that aspires to develop the formal precision of the harder sciences and apply it to what has traditionally been the subject matter of the humanities.

Several different approaches toward the problem of change may be discerned in contemporary archaeology. Underlying the chapters in the second section, "The Dynamics of Change," is an appreciation of the unity of social systems and how their form at any moment in time can be understood only by explaining how they came into being. In their study of large-scale historical social change, all the authors have derived inspiration, to a greater or lesser extent, from current Marxist debates in the social sciences. Their approach is also resolutely theoretical in happy disregard of conventional distinctions among archaeology, history, and anthropology. Thus they do not all necessarily share the somewhat positivistic approach of many of the authors in the first section. Nor would they subscribe to the reified categories and typologies that came to characterize traditional forms of "evolutionism" and that underlie some of the more recent mathematical approaches to the study of complex systems in general.

The chapters in the final section, "Morphogenetic Change in Complex Societies," focus on the potential utility for archaeology of the examination of certain theoretical advances in scientific disciplines as diverse as sociology, biology, and nonequilibrium physics. One strong current of interest here is the progress being made in evolutionary studies, where the application of mathematical approaches (including bifurcation and catastrophe theory, as well as information theory) together with a basic systemic perspective offer the hope of understanding some of the more general characteristics and processes of complex systems, certain of which are not necessarily restricted to human societies alone.

The contributors to this volume, and we as its editors, would claim to have raised important questions rather than to have disposed of them, to have clarified rather than resolved. The questions center around three significant themes: (a) the nature of explanation and the kinds of explanation appropriate to the investigation of man's past; (*b*) the behavior of societies on a long time scale, giving due weight to socioeconomic systems that may transcend the boundaries of individual polities; and (*c*) the organization and behavior of societies seen in the wider context of complex systems in general.

These are fundamental issues for the understanding of human societies. Indeed, the societies themselves and the changes they undergo cannot properly be understood until we have examined more carefully the nature of our own attempts at understanding. That is why theory and explanation are currently such important subjects of study in themselves, if we are to make real progress toward an understanding of the human past.

C. R.
M. J. R.
B. A. S.

# Acknowledgments

The chapters in this volume were first presented at the second open conference of the Theoretical Archaeology Group, held in Southampton in December 1980, although Robert Rosen and Jonathan Friedman were not able to attend in person. The editors wish to thank the co-organizers of the conference, C.S. Gamble, S.J. Shennan, J.A. Riley, and Sarah Colley, for that work, together with Mrs. Susan Stephenson and Mrs. Anke Elborn for undertaking the heavy burden of secretarial and administrative work involved. Thanks are due also to the many other members of the Department of Archaeology in Southampton whose cooperation and assistance made the conference, C.S. Gamble, S.J. Shennan, J.A. Riley, and Arah Colley, for that Archaeology in Sheffield by which the conference was jointly sponsored.

# I

# EXPLANATION REVISITED

The contributions to Part I of this volume together constitute a multifaceted review of the nature of explanation in relation to archaeology. They are therefore not so much contributions to archaeological general theory as explorations and clarifications of what such theory might be like—of what form it might take. Their diversity is striking, and the disparate nature of the positions taken concerning explanation in archaeology is an evident measure of the timeliness of the review. Although the discussion is inevitably an abstract one, the issues are central to the whole of archaeology. For if our goal is explanation, as many workers today unhesitatingly agree, what form will these explanations take?

The last wide-ranging review of the theme of explanation in archaeology on such a scale was undertaken a decade ago at the Sheffield Conference and was published under the title *The Explanation of Culture Change* (Renfrew 1973). That conference itself came roughly a decade after "the great awakening," which is described in the first chapter of this part. As indicated there, several workers, including Lewis Binford, saw the need to make the processes of reasoning that we use in archaeology more explicit, and to reach a clearer view of the nature of explanation. This inevitably led to the serious consideration by archaeologists of the philosophy of science and the application of the thought of such prominent philosophers of science as Sir Karl Popper, Carl Hempel, and Richard Bevan Braithwaite to the processes of archaeological reasoning.

Twenty years after that awakening, and 10 years after that last major review,

**1**

THEORY AND EXPLANATION
IN ARCHAEOLOGY

the position has grown more complicated. The direct application of the deductive–nomological (D–N) method of Hempel and Oppenheim, which was advocated to archaeologists by Fritz and Plog (1970), has not proved immediately successful, notwithstanding the useful debates and clarifications that may have resulted. Moreover, the discussion has now been enriched by the contributions of a number of philosophers of science who are not primarily archaeologists or anthropologists. The Sheffield volume had one such contributor—Mellor (1973). This first part of the present volume has five.

In the chapters that follow, at least three positions may be distinguished in response to the very widespread realization that the mechanical application of the Hempelian D–N procedure is not directly successful. The first may be described as *reactionary,* although with all the risks of misunderstanding that accompany that term. Here I imply no more than a reaction against the formal procedures set out by Hempel and others, and indeed a movement away from theory. The contribution by Bruce Smith at times moves in that direction, as does the "Comment" by Manfred Eggert. Despite the undoubted sophistication of their approaches, there is a feeling here, as I see it, of "enough talk: Let's get back to the job."

The second response is of a very different kind. It recognizes the difficulties that the broadly *positivist* approach of Popper and his successors have encountered in archaeology and in the social sciences and seeks instead a new epistemological basis. In this part, only the contribution by Daniel Miller (Chapter 8) takes this line, although a number of the contributors to Part II, "The Dynamics of Change," would share some of his criticisms of positivist procedures while not necessarily adopting his proposed solution. As John Hall indicates in his "Comment," a very wide range of epistemological positions are now held by various workers in the social sciences (see Keat and Urry 1975). The most influential of them in the field of anthropology is of course the *structuralist* one, whose application to archaeology was predicted to the Sheffield Conference by Edmund Leach (1973). Ernest Gellner, in his brilliantly lucid chapter (9), makes the useful distinction between what he identifies as the two main conceptions of causation, which he distinguishes as *emanation* and *covering law.* His not unsympathetic analysis of the *structuraliste* position greatly illuminates aspects of the current debates in the field of social anthropology and perhaps some of those in archaeology that are yet to come.

The third response, recognizable in the contributions, to the difficulties of the mechanical–positivist approach is essentially to be much less mechanical. That is to say, it recognizes the difficulties and seeks to overcome them without either turning away from theory like the first group, or seeking a new, perhaps "emanationist," basis like the second. The chapter by Merrilee Salmon very helpfully stresses the different expectations that archeologists and philosophers of science have of their theoretical frameworks. Wesley Salmon develops further, with a commentary by D. H. Mellor, his probabilistic approach to explanation, which elaborates and refines ideas arising from his statistical–relevance (S–R) model of explanation. Jim Bell, our fifth professional philosopher, offers a useful and constructive exposition of the *refutationist* approach. There is no suggestion here, like those of the first two responses, that the Popperian position be abandoned, but rather some helpful advice as to its application in a flexible way in the course of research. Such is also the objective of Lewis Binford in the final chapter of this part, which formed the text of his Conference Address. The concern here is for what he has labeled "middle-range theory," whereby the archaeological data may be brought to bear on the wider theoretical issues under discussion by means of explicit interpretive or theoretical procedures. These will, in many cases, be special to archaeology because of the special problems that attend the archaeological data. As I see it, the concern of this third response, despite the variety of personal positions within it, remains with theory building, albeit with a greater awareness than previously of the pragmatic concerns of the archaeologist in the field, about which Schiffer (1976) has written illuminatingly.

Few easy conclusions can be drawn from these 10 very varied chapters, and the two Comments that follow them. One, however, is that there are no ready theoretical formulations that prescribe the "right way" to undertake archaeological research: There is no royal road to success. Archaeological theory, and indeed archaeological epistemology, are relatively new as explicit subjects of discussion, although by recalling the work of R. G. Collingwood (1946) and Glyn Daniel (1962) we can avoid the mistake of imagining that all the current theoretical questions are new ones. I personally share the view of Lewis Binford and those whom I have identified as the third group that a clear theoretical awareness is indispensable for contemporary archaeology and that theory building is one of our most urgent tasks. But I think we should heed also the advice of our philosopher colleagues that our concern, albeit theoretically aware, should be primarily with the substantive issues that are the special subject matter of archaeology. We shall use the philosophy of science and the advice of these colleagues to the best advantage when we direct it systematically to this end.

—A.C.R.

# REFERENCES

Collingwood, R. G., 1946, *The Idea of History,* Oxford, University Press.
Daniel, G. E., 1962, *The Idea of Prehistory,* London, Watts.
Fritz, J. M., and Plog, F., 1970, The nature of archaeological explanation, *American Antiquity* 35, 405–412.

Keat, R., and Urry, J., 1975, *Social Theory as Science,* London, Routledge and Kegan Paul.

Leach, E., 1973, Concluding address, in Renfrew, C. (ed.), *The Explanation of Culture Change: Models in Prehistory,* London, Duckworth, 761–771.

Mellor, D. H., 1973, On some methodological misconceptions, in Renfrew, C. (ed.), *The Explanation of Culture Change: Models in Prehistory,* London, Duckworth, 493–498.

Renfrew, C. (ed.), 1973, *The Explanation of Culture Change: Models in Prehistory,* London, Duckworth, and Pittsburgh, University of Pittsburgh Press.

Schiffer, M. B., 1976, *Behavioral Archaeology,* New York, Academic Press.

# 1

# Explanation Revisited

*COLIN RENFREW*

A recurring theme in the thinking and writing of most contemporary archaeologists—indeed perhaps the single dominant theme—is the need for archaeology to go beyond the mere reconstruction and description of the past and to seek insights enabling us to *explain* how that past came about. An essential characteristic of what is today called "processual archaeology" is the intention to seek explanations for the archaeological record of the past in terms of valid general statements, which manage to avoid the particularism of some schools of historical explanation. Yet despite these widely acknowledged aims, there is very little agreement about explanation itself, about what constitutes a meaningful explanation, or about the appropriate ways of validating or testing explanations that have been offered.

Twenty years ago, at the beginning of the critical reexamination of our discipline that some were to label the "new archaeology," this was understandable. Today it is quite unacceptable, and the present confusion manifestly works to the disadvantage of the discipline, when many students are constrained to structure their work into some supposedly logical format for which there is in reality no good theoretical basis. If explanation is the ultimate goal, as many of us would argue, is it not time that we were able to point to at least a few explanations—of *something*—whose content we can respect as apparently valid and whose form we can recognize as methodologically sound?

The absence of agreement on acceptable explanatory forms and the dearth of

5

THEORY AND EXPLANATION
IN ARCHAEOLOGY

instances of what most would agree to be "good" explanations occasions the
present volume and makes it a particularly timely one. In this short chapter, I
should like to outline some of the recent history, as I see it, which leads up to our
present state of intellectual disarray. This I shall do first by sketching the recent
past, followed by a survey of the "isms" of our time, and a brief consideration of
some of the explanations that are currently on offer. No conclusions are
vouchsafed: My hope is that this volume will clarify some directions and resolve
some of the confusion.

## EXPLANATION IN ARCHAEOLOGY

### The Early Ferment

There was little explicit treatment of the nature of explanation in archaeology
or of the central issues of archaeological theory between the early ferment of the
third quarter of the nineteenth century and the great awakening of the 1960s.
Between the two came the long sleep of archaeological theory.

In the two decades following 1859, the impact of Darwin's *Origin of Species*
was felt and reflected in the writings of Pitt-Rivers (1875). At about the same
time, the fathers of anthropology were tackling the fundamental problems of the
origins of society in a fresh and original way (Tylor 1870, Morgan 1877). The
application of ethnographic ideas to archaeology (Lubbock 1865, Wilson 1876)
resulted, without any great controversy, in a framework of thought in which it
was apparently possible for scholars to work without much methodological
heart-searching. Many of the key issues that remain unresolved today had been
raised, but they declined again into uncontroversial obscurity.

### The Long Sleep

The succeeding 80 years saw astonishingly little theoretical discussion—
discussion that was about basic questions of principle. Naturally there were
many developments of methodology: The refinement by Montelius of his
typological method was one of these. Gordon Childe was responsible for many
innovations in archaeological thought, and in works like *Man Makes Himself*
(1936) he was already putting forward what one can recognize today as
processual explanations. But there was at this time little direct reference to
explanatory methodology. Even the rebuttal of the hyperdiffusionist views of
Elliot Smith and his followers was undertaken more by a fresh rehearsal of the
evidence than through a close examination of the basic underlying principles
that were at the root of the divergence. In the United States also, archaeologists
continued to practice normal science under the existing paradigm, and the

challenge of Walt Taylor's *A Study of Archaeology* (1948) was not taken up at once.

## The Great Awakening

The great awakening in archaeology came, as in several other disciplines, in the 1960s. Its origins, I suspect, lay outside archaeology—in the field of the philosophy of science. Certainly there was a widespread new awareness of the need to examine more carefully the logical basis for statements made about the past and to examine the nature of the purported explanations put forward to account for the data pertaining to the human past. This was seen as demanding explicit and objective (i.e., interpersonally valid rather than purely individual and hence subjective) procedures of reasoning of the kind already clearly formulated for the natural and, especially, the physical sciences.

Certainly I remember—coming fresh to archaeology in 1960 from the sciences—the acute and pressing obviousness of the need, in the confused state of archaeological thought of that time, for some of the clear and explicit reasoning well exemplified by R. B. Braithwaite's *Scientific Explanation* (1960). I expressed that view later in a short note entitled "Models in Prehistory" (Renfrew 1968, see also 1962). David Clarke's *Analytical Archaeology* (1968) was a major and sustained attempt to bring some of the necessary clarity and rigor to archaeological thinking, and his preferred philosopher of science was also Braithwaite.

In the United States, Lewis Binford had already (1962) argued for fundamental rethinking in archaeology in his paper "Archaeology as Anthropology," and later (1968a, 17) he made explicit reference to the American philosopher of science Carl Hempel (1965). The theoretical issues had been raised at last. They soon provoked controversy: The first, and perhaps the best, reassertion of historiographic primacy came from Jacquetta Hawkes in her article "The Proper Study of Mankind" (Hawkes 1968, 255) when she spoke of "preventing the scientific and technological servant from usurping the Throne of History."

## The Full Weight of the Law

It was both inevitable and desirable that Binford's aspiration for the "laws of cultural development" (Binford 1968a, 9) and the generally acknowledged need for explicit theorizing, should be met by an attempt to formulate clear explanatory procedures. But it was unfortunate, perhaps, that it was specifically to Hempel that the lawgivers should turn. Fritz and Plog (1970) and Watson, LeBlanc, and Redman (1971) turned for guidance to a paper by Hempel and Oppenheim (1948) that I had read and found (no doubt like other archaeologists) difficult to refute but impossible to use. It may or may not be desirable to formulate all archaeological explanations in the form of general laws. But it had certainly never been done before, and it has not been undertaken successfully since. With a few doubtful exceptions, mostly of so consummate a triviality that they have been termed "Mickey Mouse laws" by Flannery (1973, 51), no laws of culture process of such global generality have yet been put forward. Some of the exceptions (e.g., Plog 1973) appear to risk entering tautology when they depart from triviality.

These attempts have been criticized on several sides (e.g., Tuggle, Townsend, and Riley 1972), and my own view is that the "law-and-order" group (following Flannery's 1973 terminology) put archaeology in a paradoxical situation by prescribing as obligatory an explanatory form so little appropriate that vanishingly few good explanations already accepted in the field could be found to conform to it.

### The Present Confusion

The present confusion results largely from the derailment of the deductive–nomological (D–N) bandwagon. Flannery (1973) has identified a second group of theorists he calls the "Serutan" or "Ex-Lax" group. Unfortunately American medicinal brand names are not well understood east of Cape Cod, and these students are better characterized as the "natural regularity" archaeologists, who advocate a systems approach. But self-regulation, or homeostasis, and the other elements of systems thinking do not of themselves constitute an explanatory mode (see Renfrew 1981). The present diversity of thinking is in reality not much wider than Flannery insisted. There is, indeed, a risk that archaeologists are beginning to think in terms of "isms," of supposedly new frameworks of thought, each superseding the defects of the recent but ultimately unfashionable framework or ism, now to be rejected. We had a foretaste of this at the Sheffield Conference on Explanation in 1972 when Leach (1973) castigated the archaeological community for being functionalists. Social anthropologists, it was explained, had recently been functionalists and had now mercifully escaped from that error. He prophesized that in a few years we would follow the social anthropologists into their latest neologism—structuralism. The archaeologist, like the geographer (Bird 1977), may perhaps be skeptical of a notion of scientific procedure that sees development in a discipline as a rapid succession of mutually contradictory "paradigms." Their various claims are nonetheless worth examining.

### ISMS OF OUR TIME

The aims of explanation may be described, without initial reference to any explicit methodology, as *to make intelligible*. This must imply making the events or processes to be explained seem natural, plausible, or predictable to a specific observer in terms of a framework of thought that is familiar to him. The experience of a feeling that something has been explained generally seems to arise from the revelation of a conformity, or of a coherent relationship, between the explanandum and the framework.

To the biblical fundamentalist it may be sufficient to show how the events in question can be regarded as the will of God. E rly explanations for national origins relied heavily upon similarities in names Trojan Brutus, for instance, was claimed as the ancestor of the ancient Brit ns, whose place in a larger scheme of things was thereby assured. Prehi toric monuments have been explained as the work of extraterrestrial agencies, and here again the element of explanation lies in the fitting of the data into some wider and (to the specific observer) familiar framework.

The requirements that the explanation be *scientific*, or at least *scholarly*, are more demanding but, at least for a subject like archaeology, remarkably ill defined. It is upon these that discussion will focus in this book. The criterion of testability is not always easy to exercise in practice when the potential data are finite and the available data set difficult to enlarge. The related criteria of generality and simplicity, while much in harmony with the "process" school, are not stressed by those preferring historical arguments.

It is possible at present to distinguish at least five different approaches to the past, each of which implicitly rests upon a rather different notion as to what form a good explanation will take.

## Historiographic

Historical explanation is already a subject so extensively discussed that the main themes cannot be encapsulated in a few words. It is, however, probably fair to say that it is often felt to require an exceedingly detailed analysis of antecedent circumstances. The explanation for the historical events that constitutes the explanandum will arise from a very thorough knowledge of the context in which the event occurred. The motivations of the actors can only be approached by an informed act of creative imagination whereby the commentator–explicator can "put himself into the shoes" of the actor. This I take to be the position of Collingwood, and it is the essence of idiographic explanation (Trigger 1978, 25) that it seeks to explain the individual event by the analysis of its particularity rather than by a nomothetic approach that would emphasize rather its generality. There are of course very different kinds of explanation employed in history, with generalizations of an economic and a social nature. Yet Gordon Childe, who sometimes pioneered much more general formulations, was speaking very much in the historiograhic tradition in his "Retrospect" (Childe 1958, 70) when he wrote of his book *The Dawn of European Civilisation* as aiming at "distilling from archaeological remains a preliterate substitute for the conventional politico–military history with cultures instead of statesmen, as actors, and migrations in place of battles." Many archaeologists today proceed on this basis, seeking the key to the understanding of events as the more thorough analysis of their antecedents.

## Hypothetico–Deductive

At the other extreme to the historiograhic mode is the hypothetico–deductive or deductive–nomological approach. The most rigorous (and rigid) version of the H–D approach is that of Hempel and Oppenheim (1948), which was clearly set out for archaeologists by Fritz and Plog (1970) and Watson, LeBlanc, and Redman (1971). Here the thing to be explained (the explanandum) is to be deduced from the joint application of general laws and the antecedent conditions pertaining in the case in question. But whereas in the historiographic mode the antecedent conditions are stressed and the inferences from them often regarded as so evident that no general laws need be adduced, here it is the *laws* that are important. And it is these laws that, ideally, may be arranged in a hierarchy, as in the physical sciences, with more specific laws derivable from higher-order laws of greater generality.

The difficulties in applying this model in practice have been indicated above. The "law of cultural dominance," for instance, and the "law of evolutionary potential" (Plog 1973) appear to be based on a possible circularity, in that in one case the recognition of the culture that "most effectively" harnesses energy sources seems to depend upon a knowledge of the outcome. The outcome can therefore hardly be used as an independent test of the law.

An influential and informative recent work, M. B. Schiffer's *Behavioral Archaeology* (1976) makes repeated reference to the need for laws in arch-aeology and indeed purports to proceed upon such a basis. But although the work has much to teach us and has added greatly to the systematic con-sideration of formation processes, it appears to contain very few nontrivial formulations that can be seen as clear examples of Hempelian nomothesis. I find it difficult to escape the conclusion that, however persuasive the appeals to analytical rigor, these authors have not succeeded in constructing real or substantial archaeological explanations within the framework that they advocate.

## Systems Behavior

Systems thinking pervades much current archaeological work. It does not generally carry with it any explicit body of theory, but it draws upon a vocabulary that many find useful, involving such terms as *system state, system parameters, trajectory, open system, positive feedback, negative feedback, homeostasis, energy flow, information flow, entropy, requisite variety,* and *morphogenesis.* The political unit, or the region and its population, is seen as a system whose perpetuation is ensured by homeostatic processes and whose growth is viewed by some (e.g., Hill 1977) as a homeostatic response to exogenous change, and by others (e.g., Renfrew 1981, Klejn 1973, 703) as essentially endogenous, arising from interactions within the system.

This general-systems approach does not usually have the precision of the system paradigm set out by Tuggle, Townsend, and Riley (1972, 8), following Meehan, where the system is a *formal, logical structure*—an abstract calculus. The complexity of interactions is much the same, and in fact the system dynamics modeling of Jay Forrester (1971), exemplified in archaeology by Hosler, Sabloff, and Runge (1978) and perhaps by Cooke and Renfrew (1979), employs a formal, logical structure of the kind envisaged by Meehan.

In general, however, explanation using some general systems model tends to be very much less clear -cut, resting on the supposed propensity or tendency of the system of the subsystems to behave, under certain circumstances, in a given way. While these are, in intention, statements of some generality, they are rarely framed with any rigor. There appears to be the underlying assumption, or hypothesis, that system behavior is intelligible and predictable, but the precise conditions (which are obviously crucial, when so many interactions operate) are rarely stated.

## Neo-Marxist

Recently several scholars have sought to reject the "vulgar materialism" that they see accompanying the frameworks of thought employed in the hypothetico–deductive and systems-behavior approaches. While some of the language of systems thinking (e.g., "trajectory") has crept into the vocabulary, the analytical framework (e.g., Friedman 1974) is derived directly from Marx, and discussion is in terms of modes of production, relations of production, and forces of production. Care is exercised, however, with the terms *superstructure* and *infrastructure*, since the primacy of economic over social or symbolic structures and processes, formerly thought to be the direct legacy of Marx, is now a matter of debate. Examples of neo-Marxist argument in archaeology and anthropology may be found in a recent work edited by Friedman and Rowlands (1978). Precisely what constitutes the desired *form* of an explanation is not entirely clear. In many cases it consists in showing how the events and processes, appropriately analyzed and interpreted, can be seen as operating in conformity with the general model as set out by Marx in the Preface to *A Contribution to the Critique of Political Economy.* A key element in the dynamics of change is the emergence of *contradictions* (Marx 1968, 181–182):

> At a certain stage of their development, the material productive forces come in conflict
> with the existing relations of production, or—what is but a legal expression for the same
> thing—with the property relations within which they have been at work hitherto. From
> forms of developments of the productive forces these relations turn into their fetters.
> Then begins an epoch of social revolution.

It is my impression that the explanatory force of many discussions in the neo-Marxist mode springs largely from bringing the circumstances of the specific case into harmony with this somewhat vague general model. If this perception is correct, the force of the explanation rests ultimately upon the authority of Marx. Any deeper epistemological underpinnings remain implicit, if they exist. These observations do not apply to the very different tradition of Marxist thought current in Eastern Europe, whose theoretical and methodological foundations, despite the useful publications of a few authors, both Eastern and Western (Klejn 1977; Gellner 1973, 1977; Moberg 1980), remain little examined in the West.

## Structuralism

The principles of structuralist thought have not yet been extensively applied in archaeology, although Leach (1973), influenced by Lévi-Strauss, has prophesied their adoption. In the field of anthropology, structuralist explanations are applied primarily to structures of a figurative kind, pertaining to the symbolic or projective field (Renfrew 1972, Chapter 19). They relate, that is, to categories and to mental constructs that the archaeologist will sometimes be unable to observe directly. He must therefore infer such categories from the arrangement of design elements, for instance, or the spatial organizations of settlements, houses, and other structures, or the configuration of jewelry or body decoration, or other material expressions and reflections of inferred mental constructs. The archaeologist observes the material world and lacks direct access (available to the social anthropologist through direct discussion with his informant) to thought categories. His explanations have tended to be "etic" rather than "emic" (Harris 1968, 571–576), his models "operational" rather than "cognized" (Rappaport 1968, 237).

Explanation, in such cases, is likely to proceed by showing that the phenomena or structures observed conform, in some way, with more general structural principles that can be seen at work in other societies and in other aspects of the same society. Thus when Sir Edmund Leach asks in the title of a lecture, "Why Did Moses Have a Sister?"—we may confidently predict that the answer will not lie in the physiological or genetic field nor in a detailed analysis of the motivations of the parents of the siblings. I predict—not having heard the lecture—that the answer will lie within the structure of myth, that the Moses story will be seen as one of a larger class of stories sharing structural affinities and that the siblinghood of Moses will be "explained" by reference to this larger class. Structuralist explanation in archaeology will likewise lay stress upon correspondences of this kind. The precise logical content of such explanations has yet to be carefully analyzed: Some may prove to be, in Binford's pejorative phrase, "post hoc accommodative arguments."

These five isms certainly do not exhaust the range of explanatory modes adopted in contemporary archaeology, but they summarize some of the most explicit of them. Most processual archaeologists would prefer not to ally themselves definitively with any one of these camps. Yet they share a desire to explain the past by means of generalization of some kind. This does not imply the construction of lawlike formulations of the hypothetico–deductive school. But it does involve the recognition that the explanatory principles adduced for one society will be applicable to certain other societies in appropriate circumstances. To refine and define these ideas into some more coherent notion of "explanation" must be seen as a major objective of archaeological theory.

## SOME ARCHAEOLOGICAL EXPLANATIONS

One remarkable feature of most discussions of the nature of explanation in archaeology is that, with few exceptions, they focus on the form that explanation *should* take rather than the form that it *does* take in practice. In a postinductive era it perhaps seems natural to proceed from analysis rather than from the data. Yet, in seeking to understand what are the logical elements of a good explanation, it may be more fruitful to study some explanations that are felt by various workers to be good, rather than to prescribe, on a priori principles, the criteria for goodness.

At this stage in the development of the discipline it might well be worthwhile to collect numerous examples of what pass for useful explanations in the various fields of archaeology and to analyze them with care. To do so, however, would be a very lengthy exercise, and what follows is only a preliminary initiative.

### Explanation of What?

As soon as one begins to think of specific cases, it becomes clear that explanations are sought in very different instances. It is by no means clear that comparable forms of explanation will be appropriate in each case.

#### The Specific Event

This is the most obvious and usual subject for explanation, from Collingwood's "Why Did Caesar Cross the Rubicon?" to the study, to take a more recent example, of the Classic Maya collapse (Culbert 1973).

The Class of Events

Although generalization is still rare in archaeology, some of the most interesting recent explanations have set out not merely to discuss one event, even as an instance of a hypothetical more general class, but to consider the class itself. Two of the major foci of research in recent years have been widely conceived in these terms.

*The Origins of Food Production.* Although most field projects and the explanations that accompany them are generally restricted to a single region (e.g., Iraqi Kurdistan, the Tehuacán Valley of Mexico, the Ayacucho region of Peru), this is one of the instances where the "neolithic revolution," although perhaps originally conceived by Childe as a single, specific case, is seen as a general phenomenon. The problem thus becomes the development of an explanation that will be relevant to a number of independent cases. Lewis Binford's paper "Post-Pleistocene Adaptions" (Binford 1968b) offers the best-known example.

*The Origins of the State.* The problem of the development of complex societies has been increasingly seen by archaeologists in recent years as a general one, under which specific instances might be subsumed. Childe's original exposition of the "urban revolution" (Childe 1936, 141–142) was formulated in a form referring specifically to Mesopotamia, but it will be shown below that much of its explanatory force came from the generality of the expression, so that it might conceivably be applied to other instances. Most serious fieldworkers have restricted themselves to explaining the rise of their particular civilization or state (e.g., Rathje 1973), and very few workers have deliberately set out to apply the explanation that they have developed in that specific context to other potentially analogous contexts in such a way as to test the hypothesis deliberately on a wider basis.

At the same time, however, this is one field where there have been more general theorists, from the early days of Rousseau and Marx. In more recent times, Wittfogel's "irrigation hypothesis" and Carneiro's "circumscription theory" (Carneiro 1970) have been formulated with considerable generality (see also Flannery 1972). There is a tendency also for workers concerned with a specific instance to frame their explanations deliberately in very much more general terms (e.g., Wright and Johnson 1975).

It should be noted that these general classes of events may be regarded as transitions between system states—from hunter–gatherer to food producer, from chiefdom to state, or whatever. The recognition of such a class of events must therefore logically follow upon the recognition of categories, such as *food production* and *the state*, by means of which the specific instances may be likened. Without some taxonomy or classification of static forms or system states there can be no classification of transitions or "allactic forms" (Renfrew 1979a, 16) and hence no general explanation.

The Process

The phenomenon to be explained does not need to be restricted to a specific range of time, as does an event, or to an assemblage of limited ranges of time, as does a class of events. Instead, insight may be offered into processes at work in society, which may be of a continuous and long-enduring nature. Many discussions of trading mechanisms, for instance, are of this kind. A good example is offered by Wright and Zeder (1977) in their paper "The Simulation of a Linear Exchange System under Equilibrium Conditions."

The Pattern

Often the archaeologist perceives some pattern in the archaeological record. The concept of pattern implies order, and to explain the record it may be sufficient to elucidate the mechanisms underlying that order. Processual explanations will usually do so within a dynamic framework—that is to say, showing how the pattern was built up over time. But an appeal to dynamical process is not the only possible form of explanation for pattern: Certainly a structuralist explanation might appeal to quite different principles. Ammerman and Cavalli-Sforza (1973) offer an elegant explanation in terms of the "wave-of-advance" model for the pattern of radiocarbon dates obtained for early farming settlements in Europe. The "down-the-line" model (Renfrew 1972, 465–466) sets out to explain the phenomenon of exponential falloff of quantity with distance for certain traded commodities.

There may be other classes of phenomena that the archaeologist seeks to explain. In general, however, it should be appreciated that the very nature of archaeological fieldwork, rooted in any given project in the stratified levels of a certain date at a definite place, leads naturally to a desire to explain specific events, circumstances, and patterns. A deductive strategy may indeed lead the archaeologist to excavate a particular site to contribute information on some more general problem, but the course of his work will inevitably produce new and *specific* problems at that site. The considerable current investment in rescue or salvage archaeology works in the same direction, since the initial impetus arises from the threat of destruction of a particular site or area of sites. The destruction threat is thus area specific, not problem specific, although intelligent project design can partially overcome this constraint.

## The Classic Maya Collapse

A recent volume on the collapse of lowland Classic Maya civilization around A.D. 900 offers a most interesting review of previous explanations for the collapse. They are classified by Adams (1973, 23) as follows:

1. Ecology (interrelations between man, his cultural systems, and natural systems)
   Soil exhaustion
   Water loss and erosion.
   Savanna grass competition
2. Catastrophism
   Earthquakes
   Hurricanes
3. Evolution
4. Disease
5. Demography
6. Social structure
7. Invasion

Several of the explanations discussed depend upon agencies understandable outside the Maya system itself. Thus the incidence of disastrous earthquakes, the onset of destructive hurricanes, the appearance of a virulent strain of yellow fever, and the arrival of hostile military agencies could be regarded as externally determined events. Most of the other explanations do, however, appeal to some general principle.

Thus, the soil exhaustion argument is summarized by Adams (1973, 23–24):

> *Milpa* agriculture is inherently destructive to the soil and encourages various deleterious effects including encroachment of grasses. . . . Once a population dependent on a slash-and-burn system has grown enough to make necessary the reduction of the minimum rest period, then a rapid and disastrous decline in soil fertility will take place.

In many ways this is not in practice a satisfactory argument, but it does depend upon a generalization. It is, however, typical of most or all of the general arguments advanced—that they are considered only in the context of the specific case under study here, the Maya civilization. Their potential relevance or applicability to other instances is nowhere considered. Adams (1973, 23–24) notes at the conclusion of his discussion that "explanations of the collapse have generally moved from the 'prime mover' category to the multifactor approach." He adds, disquietingly for nomothetic explicators, that "finally I reiterate that which I have said elsewhere: the circumstances of the collapse were probably different, perhaps unique, from region to region and even from site to site."

## The Urban Revolution and State Formation

Gordon Childe's concise explanation for the urban revolution in Mesopotamia was set out in his *Man Makes Himself* (Childe 1936, 141–142). It is worth quoting his words, which are amplified elsewhere in his book:

On the large alluvial plains and riverside flatlands the need for extensive public works to drain and irrigate the land and to protect the settlement would tend to consolidate social organization and to centralise the economic system. At the same time, the inhabitants of Egypt, Sumer and the Indus basin were forced to organize some regular system of trade or barter to secure supplies of essential raw materials. The fertility of lands gave their inhabitants the means for satisfying their need of imports. But economic self-sufficiency had to be sacrificed, and a completely new economic structure created. The surplus of home-grown products must not only suffice to exchange for exotic materials; it must also support a body of merchants and transport workers engaged in obtaining these and a body of specialized craftsmen to work the precious imports to best advantage. And soon soldiers would be needed to protect the convoys and back up the merchants by force, scribes to keep records of transactions growing ever more complex, and State officials to reconcile conflicting interests.

This is an instance of a form of explanation now very common. Although it refers to a specific instance, it is framed in a rather more general manner. Moreover, a whole series of general statements are linked together to form what almost becomes a narrative. The interrelationships of the various factors are stressed. This formulation could certainly be put forward as a precursor for much contemporary neo-Marxist explanation, which likewise often consists of linking together statements that, if interpreted specifically, form a kind of idealized narrative, but if interpreted in a more general sense seem to constitute some form of general model whose logical relationships are not examined in detail.

It is interesting to compare this with one of the mechanisms of multiple variable interaction proposed by Wright and Johnson (1975, 285):

There could be interaction between variables. Two regulatory processes which, when they operate alone, have a damping or negative feedback effect, could have a positive effect when they operate simultaneously. For example, suppose the internal prosperity of the society is signalled by the amount of goods redistributed from the center to smaller communities. When lesser amounts of these essentially symbolic commodities are given out, rebellion becomes more likely, producing a more effective leadership or smaller, more manageable social units. Also suppose that regional population is in part regulated by raiding. These two devices would operate at different organisational levels and perhaps at different times as well. If, however, raiding thoroughly fragmented existing social units to the point where goods were being distributed to units which might in fact raid in return, then redistribution becomes a payment rather than a signal, and a constant flow of goods requiring a reorganization of production would be needed. Reorganization of some productive tasks could lead to complementary specialization and reorganization of others, with consequent specialisation of task control, increased information flow, and subsequent increased hierarchical complexity.

Making allowance for a more sophisticated vocabulary in this case—and some elements of the explanation, such as hierarchical complexity, are defined and considered earlier—there are similarities in the form of explanation offered here with that from Childe quoted above. The similarities in content however are notably few. In both cases what we are offered amounts to a scenario in which a number of fairly general events or processes are related, partly in temporal sequence and partly by feedback linkages.

Wright and Johnson (1975, 288) follow this outline mechanism with a sort of disclaimer:

> These brief sketches are not intended as testable propositions. They do not formally define either the variables that might be involved or the principles that relate these variables. They only suggest patterns or mechanisms by which variables might be related. These . . . suggestions do serve to indicate the approaches to field research which will be needed if any multiple variable explanations are to be tested.

But the disclaimer cannot reflect our attention from the absence of any firmly stated general propositions whatever. As in the case of Childe, the scenario, although clearly conceived with the Near East in mind, has a vague generality that would allow it to be applied to societies in similar environments. Embedded within it, and perhaps not difficult to extract from it, lie a series of implied general propositions. But they are certainly not spelled out in such a way as to lead us to seek to test them by applications to other instances, perhaps outside the Near East.

In making these observations I am not seeking to deny the interest of the article in question or the richness of the insights that Childe and Wright and Johnson have to offer: I have chosen this article for discussion because it is, in my view, one of the best statements on the theme currently available. My own treatment of the emergence of Aegean civilizations could certainly be criticized in analogous terms. There, two alternative scenarios are offered—the subsistence–redistribution model and the craft-specialization–wealth model— as instances of a more general matrix of interactions. Growth is discussed in terms of the "multiplier effect" (Renfrew 1972, 486), but the demonstration of a complex of positive feedback processes is not in itself an adequate explanation. Both these examples illustrate the methodological disadvantages of the multiple variable or systemic perspective: The very undertaking of building a model or explanation of sufficient complexity to cope with the multiple variables involved results in a construct so elaborate that its explanatory simplicity and force is diminished.

## Explaining Classes of Events

Part of the complexity observed in the foregoing cases may arise precisely because they address themselves to specific events: the Maya collapse and the rise of complex society in the Near East (Childe, Wright, and Johnson) and in the Aegean. My brief review of the literature suggests that explanations that concern themselves with classes of events may avoid more readily the excessive concern with circumstantial detail—although, in consequence, they are not able to "explain" with the same wealth of detail.

By way of example, the following passages have been taken from successive pages of Binford's chapter dealing with worldwide emergence of food-producing groups after the Pleistocene period (Binford 1968b, 328–334).

> With the recognition that equilibrium systems regulate population density below the carrying capacity of an environment, we are forced to look for those conditions which might bring about disequilibrium and bring about selective advantages for increased productivity.
>
> Change in the demographic structure of a region which brings about the impingement of one group on the territory of another would also upset an established equilibrium system, and might serve to increase the population density of a region beyond the carrying capacity of the natural environment. Under these conditions manipulation of the natural environment in order to increase its productivity would be highly advantageous.
>
> Under conditions of increased sedentism we would expect population growth.
>
> Therefore where there is a marked contrast in degree of sedentism between two sociocultural units within a relatively restricted geographical region, there would be a tension zone where emigrant colonies from the more sedentary group would periodically disrupt the density equilibrium balances of the less sedentary group. Under these conditions there would be strong selective pressure favoring the development of more effective means of food production.
>
> It is proposed here that it was in the selective context outlined above that initial practices of cultivation occurred. Such selective situations would have been the consequence of the increased dependence on aquatic resources during the terminal and immediately post-Pleistocene period. Not all portions of rivers and shorelines favor the harvesting of fish, molluscs and migratory fowl; it is with the systematic dependence on just these resources that we find archaeological remains indicating a higher degree of sedentism in both the Archaic of the New World and the terminal Palaeolithic and Mesolithic of the Old World.
>
> The shift of the exploitation of highly seasonal resources such as anadromous fish and migratory fowl did not occur until the close of the Pleistocene. This shift, probably linked with worldwide changes in sea level, with attendant increases in sedentism, established for the first time conditions leading to marked heterogeneity in rates of population growth.

The clarity and generality of this exposition mark it out as one of the most satisfying explanations, from a formal standpoint, available in the literature, whether of either a single event or of a class of events. It is with disappointment, therefore, that one must note that fresh data bring out limitations in its content. For instance, changes in sea level, with consequent potential for coastal and riverine sedentism, cannot have much bearing on early food production in inland zones that are far from the resulting migratory fowl and anadromous fish. Yet it is now clear that food production existed as early in such inland zones as in coastal ones. But in *form*—which is what we are primarily considering here—it is both clear and general.

Carneiro's circumscription theory for state origins (Carneiro 1970) has some of these qualities, starting from a very general perspective. Unfortunately, however, after a concise general statement, he develops his ideas with reference to two specific instances—the coastal valleys of Peru and the Amazon basin. This development then follows the scenario mode of explanation, which we have seen earlier in relation to state origins in the Near East and the Aegean.

A third instance of a very general explanation would be my own formulations for systems collapse (Renfrew 1979b), which in fact subsumes the case of the Classic Maya. Use is made of the "cusp catastrophe" to model the abruptness of the decline, but in the present context the attempt to formulate a general explanation for a whole class of events is of more interest than the precise form of the formulation.

Other instances of explanations for classes of events can be found (see Flannery 1972). They are in fact relatively few in number, perhaps partly because contemporary archaeology has found itself cautious of classes or categories of any form. The polemic for and against the use of the term *chiefdom*, for example, illustrates the reluctance with which such taxonomic constructs are sometimes used. The terms *band, city, state, hunter–gatherer, food production, ranking* or *ranked society*, and *stratified society* now seem accepted as constructs to be used without self-consciousness, but there are few others of which this could be said. *Chiefdom, tribe, culture,* and *civilization* are terms whose use is, for various reasons, deplored in different quarters. Further generalization in this area may be a prerequisite for the production of general explanations.

## CONCLUSIONS

In the foregoing discussion I have stressed the much greater awareness that has developed over the past two decades of the need for a more adequate understanding of the nature of explanation in archaeology. This realization has had, as one result, the development of a number of explanatory paradigms or isms, some of them mutually exclusive in their assumptions. In the second part of this chapter I have sought to show that there is a considerable disparity between the forms of explanation advocated by the partisans of the various isms and those actually employed and found effective by working archaeologists.

As a result, the theorists lack credibility, and their formulations sometimes seem irrelevant to the actual development of contemporary archaeological theory. But, on the other hand, that theory, as it developed by those working firsthand with the data and with a real sense of problem, often seems lacking both in logical form and in any clear awareness of what would (if found valid, after further investigation in relation to the data) constitute a good explanation.

Those who have tried to construct explanations in conformity with a notional hypothetico–deductive or deductive–nomological pattern have often found themselves formulating as a general "hypothesis" some statement of very limited generality. Frequently this is then "tested" solely with the context where it first arose. Testing the hypothesis thus becomes a charade, without any attempt to investigate the wider implications of the supposed explanatory generalization or to explore it in relation to societies in other places and times. It is difficult to see how a general "law" formulated in relation to the pueblos of the American Southwest, for instance, and applied solely in that region, can make any serious claim as a hypothetico–deductive explanation.

A very preliminary review of the literature suggests that a very common form of explanation is the *scenario form*, where processes of some generality are described, with linkages that are partly temporal and partly of feedback type, so that a general plausibility is generated for a sequence of related processes and events. One interesting feature of the scenario form is its quasi-generality: While the propositions are not restricted to the specific context, they are clearly formulated in relation to it and are not in fact applied to other contexts.

Only a few explanations can be found currently that apply to general classes of events rather than simply to specific cases. While they are more satisfying in their formal properties, none of those examined actually ranks as a "good" explanation in terms of its content. None, that is, inspires the feeling that something has been satisfactorily explained. This is the rather strange situation that I feel merits further discussion.

One possible conclusion is that archaeology needs to be more willing to generalize. There is some measure of agreement that good processual explanations must consist of propositions that are more widely applicable than to the single case in hand. It would seem to follow then that there should be a systematic attempt to formulate and apply propositions to a wide range of cases. This would imply a willingness to make cross-cultural comparisons of a kind that in practice may impose difficult demands on the factual knowledge of archaeologists who, for understandable, practical reasons, are familiar primarily with the material of a single area.

I am aware, of course, that this conclusion runs counter not only to the historiographic and structuralist schools of thought, but to others who seek "hermeneutic" explanations. It must simply be recognized that there are two different paths here—one toward the general and hence the comparative; another toward the specific analysis of context and hence ultimately to the unique.

My own preference is for the former, and it is no coincidence that we have in this book contributors who have developed a facility in other fields, notably in mathematics and mathematical biology, for dealing with complex interactions and with that emergence of complexity that we have come to call *morphogenesis*. A number of the works that I have cited, for instance that by Wright and Johnson (1975), show the same aspiration toward the elucidation of morphogenesis in its different forms that we see in the work of Rosen, of Zeeman, or of Nicolis and Prigogine (1977). Our perception of what is an adequate form for archaeological explanation is thus likely to be such as to recognize as appropriate in form the generalizations and formalizations that they have produced and will produce. This then is an aspiration that may itself be categorized by those of hermeneutic preference as subjective. Be that as it may, the aspiration leads one to seek to develop *scientific explanation* within archaeology. It should be clear from the foregoing that such development is thus far incomplete, inadequate, and in some cases, unsound.

## REFERENCES

Adams, R. C. W., 1973, The collapse of Maya civilization: A review of previous theories, in Culbert, T. P. (ed.), *The Classic Maya Collapse*, Albuquerque, University of New Mexico Press, 21–34.

Ammerman, A. J., and Cavalli–Sforza, L. L., 1973, A population model for the diffusion of early farming in Europe, in Renfrew, C. (ed.), *The Explanation of Culture Change: Models in Prehistory*, London, Duckworth, 343–358.

Binford, L. R., 1962, Archaeology as anthropology, *American Antiquity* 28, 217–225.

Binford, L. R., 1968a, Archaeological perspectives, in Binford, L. R. and S. R. (eds.), *New Perspectives in Archaeology*, Chicago, Aldine, 5–32.

Binford, L. R., 1968b, Post-Pleistocene adaptations, in Binford, L. R. and S. R. (eds.), *New Perspectives in Anthropology*, Chicago, Aldine, 313–341.

Bird, J. H., 1977, Methodology and philosophy, *Progress in Human Geography* 1, 104–110.

Braithwaite, R. B., 1960, *Scientific Explanation*, Cambridge, University Press.

Carneiro, R. L., 1970, A theory of the origin of the state, *Science* 169, 733–738.

Childe, V. G., 1958, Retrospect, *Antiquity* 32, 69–74.

Childe, V. G., 1936, *Man Makes Himself*, London, Watts.

Clarke, D. L., 1968, *Analytical Archaeology*, London, Methuen.

Cooke, K. R., and Renfrew, C., 1979, An experiment on the simulation of culture changes, in Renfrew, C., and Cooke, K. L. (eds.), *Transformations: Mathematical Approaches to Culture Change*, New York, Academic Press, 327–348.

Culbert, T. P. (ed.), 1973, *The Classic Maya Collapse*, Albuquerque, University of New Mexico Press.

Evans, J., 1875, The coinage of the ancient Britons and natural selection, *Proceedings of the Royal Institution of Great Britain* 7, 476–487.

Flannery K. V., 1972, The cultural evolution of civilizations, *Annual Review of Ecology and Systematics* 3, 399–426.

Flannery, K. V., 1973, Archaeology with a capital *S*, in Redman, C. L. (ed.), *Research and Theory in Current Archaeology*, New York, Wiley, 47–53.

Forrester, J. W., 1971, *World Dynamics*, Cambridge, Mass., Wright-Allen.

Friedman, J., 1974, Marxism, structuralism and vulgar materialism, *Man* 9, 444–469.

Friedman, J., and Rowlands, M. J., (eds.), 1978, *The Evolution of Social Systems*, London, Duckworth.

Fritz, J. M., and Plog, F. T., 1970, The nature of archaeological explanation, *American Antiquity* 35, 405–412.

Gellner, E., 1973, Primitive communism, *Man* 8, 536–542.

Gellner, E., 1977, Class before states: The Soviet treatment of African feudalism, *Archives of European Sociology* 18, 199–222.

Harris, M., 1968, *The Rise of Anthropological Theory*, London, Routledge.

Hawkes, J., 1968, The proper study of mankind, *Antiquity* 42, 255–262.

Hempel, C. C., 1965, *Aspects of Scientific Explanation*, New York, The Free Press.

Hempel, C. G., and Oppenheim, P., 1948, Studies in the logic of explanation, *Philosophy of Science* 5, 135–175.

Hill, J. N. (ed.), 1977, *The Explanation of Prehistoric Change*, Albuquerque, University of New Mexico Press.

Hosler, D., Sabloff, J. A., and Runge, D., 1978, Simulation model development: a case study of the Classic Maya collapse, in Hammond, N. (ed.), *Social Process in Maya Prehistory,* New York, Academic Press, 553–590.

Klejn, L., 1973, Marxism, the systemic approach and archaeology, in Renfrew, C. (ed.), *The Explanation of Culture Change: Models in Prehistory*, London, Duckworth, 691–710.

Klejn, L. S., 1977, A panorama of theoretical archaeology, *Current Anthropology* 18, 1–42.

Leach, E., 1973, Concluding address, in Renfrew C. (ed.), *The Explanation of Culture Change: Models in Prehistory*, London, Duckworth, 761–771.

Lubbock, J., 1865, *Pre-Historic Times,* London, Williams and Norgate.

Marx, K., 1968, *Karl Marx and Frederick Engels: Selected Works,* London, Lawrence and Wishart.

Moberg, C.-A., 1980, Vers une analyse sociologique en archeologie, in Schnapp, A. (ed.), *L'Archeologie Aujourdhui,* Paris, Hachette.

Morgan, L. H., 1877, *Ancient Society,* New York, World Publishing.

Nicolis, G., and Prigogine, I., 1977, *Self-Organization in Non-Equilibrium Systems,* New York, Wiley Interscience.

Pitt–Rivers, A. H. L. F., 1975, On the evolution of culture, *Proceedings of the Royal Institute of Great Britain* 7, 496–520. (under the author's signature A, Lane-Fox).

Plog, F. T., 1973, Laws, systems of law, and the explanation of observed variation, in Renfrew, C. (ed.), *The Explanation of Culture Change: Models in Prehistory*, London, Duckworth, 649–662.

Rappaport, R., 1968, *Pigs for the Ancestors,* New Haven, Yale University Press.

Rathje, W. L., 1973, Models for mobile Maya, in Renfrew, C. (ed.), *The Explanation of Culture Change: Models in Prehistory*, London, Duckworth, 731–760.

Renfrew, C., 1962, Comments of Dr. Daniel's, seminar on G. R. Lowther, Epistemology and archaeological theory, *Current Anthropology* 3, 504.

Renfrew, C., 1968, Models in prehistory, *Antiquity* 42, 132–134.

Renfrew, C., 1972, *The Emergence of Civilization: The Cyclades and the Aegean in the Third Millennium B. C.,* London, Methuen.

Renfrew, C., 1979a, Transformations, in Renfrew, C., and Cooke, K. L. (eds.), *Transformations: Mathematical Approaches to Culture Change.* New York, Academic Press, 3–44.

Renfrew, C., 1979b, Systems collapse as social transformation: catastrophe and anastrophe in early societies, in Renfrew, C., and Cooke, K. L., (eds.), *Transformations: Mathematical Approaches to Culture Change,* New York, Academic Press, 481–506.

Renfrew, C., 1981. The simulator as demiurge, in Sabloff, J. A. (ed.), *Simulating the Past,* Albuquerque, University of New Mexico Press, 283–306.

Schiffer, M. B., 1976, *Behavioral Archaeology,* New York, Academic Press.

Taylor, W. W., 1948, A study of archaeology, *American Anthropologist Memoir* 69, Washington, D. C.

Trigger, B., 1978, *Time and Traditions,* Edinburgh, University Press.

Tuggle, D. H., Townsend, A. H., and Riley, T. J., 1972, Laws, systems and research designs: a discussion of explanation in archaeology, *American Antiquity* 37, 3–12.

Tylor, E. B., 1870, *Researches into the Early History of Mankind,* London, John Murray.

Watson, P. J., LeBlanc, S. A., and Redman, C. L., 1971, *Explanation in Archaeology: An Explicitly Scientific Approach,* New York, Columbia University Press.

Wilson, D., 1876, *Prehistoric Man,* London, Macmillan.

Wright, H. T., and Johnson, G., 1975, Population, exchange and early state formation in southwestern Iran, *American Anthropologist* 77, 267–289.

Wright, H. T., and Zeder, M., 1977, The simulation of a linear exchange system under equilibrium conditions, in Earle, T. K., and Ericson, J. E., (eds.), *Exchange Systems in Prehistory,* New York, Academic Press, 233–253.

# 2

## Is a Little Philosophy (Science?) a Dangerous Thing?

*FRED PLOG*

During the late 1960s and the 1970s a small but significant portion of the collective attention of archaeologists was devoted to an exploration of the history and philosophy of science. While the percentage of this effort reflected in the published literature is high, the actual effort to delve and to counterdelve is certainly much higher. This chapter addresses two questions: *Why?* and *Did It Matter?* In answering the first question, I will attempt to identify some of the factors that led to the interest on the part of a number of archaeologists in the literature of the history and philosophy of science. In addressing the second, I will be concerned with identifying tentatively—a qualifier that will certainly be forgotten—some of the effects of this epoch of exploration on the manner in which archaeologists do archaeology and whether these effects are of any importance for the practice of our profession.

### WHY THE INTEREST?

There is perhaps no behavior more suspect in current archaeology than the initial efforts on the part of some members of the profession to understand more completely and more deeply the literature dealing with the questions of how and why scientists and scholars come to know what they know. Perhaps the only alternative not currently considered is that stated at the time—that a number of

THEORY AND EXPLANATION
IN ARCHAEOLOGY

archaeologists felt it important to essay the state of knowledge reflected in the literature dealing with the *wherefores* of obtaining knowledge in general. Presumably the activity was undertaken in the hope that such an exploration would be of utility to us in attempting to understand the past.

Yet, one must not be content with explanations that operate in terms of individual motives, since the worst information on one's own motives are behaviors, but instead look for broader trends within the discipline to which such behavior might be related. The first candidate is a diffusionist one. It is difficult to avoid noting that during the 1950s and early 1960s—during the period just prior to our experience of, or infatuation with, the philosophy of science—archaeologists began to concern themselves with literature in the natural and life sciences in which philosophical issues loomed somewhat larger than had been the case previously in archaeology itself. Such an explanation is unsatisfactory for the usual reasons: Principally, cause and effect are confused.

A second candidate is the oft-cited "religious" one—that the surveyors of the literature did so in an effort to prove their absolute rectitude in the face of infidels. While such claims abound—particularly those written by archaeo-politicians and philosophers of science—the argument can be sustained only at the expense of ignoring the qualifying words, sentences, and paragraphs written by almost everyone. Of course, the accusation that the arguments of others are attacks on straw men are especially useful when one is doing so oneself.

At the same time, it is difficult to characterize the "ethos" of discipline at a particular point in time without risking the accusation that "no archaeologist ever did or believed such a thing." Risking such an accusation, I want to suggest that a number of characteristics of the discipline during the 1950s and early 1960s led to the reaction that occurred during the late 1960s and the 1970s. If my characterizations are in fact caricatures, they were much discussed among the students of the period, even those who would now deny participating in such heresy.

First was the perceived view that "truth" was measured in direct proportion to the consensus of professionals, that good archaeology was what made archaeologists happy. That a few individuals chose to state this conclusion in print poorly reflects the extent to which the attitude was pervasive. I have heard that one archaeologist, widely cited as an example of a proponent of the H–D method in archaeology, has claimed that a good explanation is "whatever the archaeologists who matter accept as one." While such statements admittedly identify a sociological truth, they hardly help in setting standards that will result in improved research at any level. Many other archaeologists never verbalized such a belief, precisely because it was a fact of life. Underlying this belief is, of course, a basic commitment to ad hominem argument—that whoever makes the argument is more important than the logical and empirical justification for it—that politics supersedes reason. This circumstance is, and continues to be, a fact of life.

The "idle-speculation" model of generalization was a second factor. While we have been assured by philosophers of science and archaeologists that "all archaeologists want to go beyond description," those of us who suffered through the dreary enterprise of reading site report after site report, the only generalizable element of which was the section on "conclusions" or "summary" or "interpretation" at the end, find such a claim empirically difficult to accept. The standard routine monograph once consisted of pages and chapters of description with a relatively minor section on synthesis or generalization at the end, the relationship of which to the data that had been described was at best unclear.

I suppose that such idle speculations sufficiently approximate generalizations so that one can call them "early examples of generalization" if one chooses. However, I submit that the majority of attributes of generalization, by any definition, were absent. It should also be clear that, in commenting on idle speculation, I do not intend to treat it as trivial. Given a clear distinction between discovery and insight, some important general theory, some broad orienting statements, will come from intuition and speculation. This circumstance should be neither frightening nor hopeful. That some discoveries result from applying less than the best scientific methods is of little utility to the majority of us who need devices and concepts to guarantee any productivity at all, since we are not gifted with intuition.

A third factor was the equation of material culture with culture, MC = C. Description was satisfactory not simply because it was description, but because material culture *was* culture. That the task of describing cultural patterns involved inference was not widely admitted by the practitioners of sociocultural anthropology. Therefore, why should archaeologists have behaved in a manner other than arguing that they also merely described what was general, that inference was not a necessary activity?

Fourth, the "accretional" model of generalization was beginning to fail. This model assumed that the site reports were to be summarized into local prehistories or chronologies, which would themselves be summarized first into regional summaries, then into continental ones, and finally into worldwide syntheses. (This model was, of course, also a personal one that presumed the integrity and the skills of the synthesizer.) Unfortunately, the model did not prove to be a very useful one. Syntheses attempted without pertinent attention to the manner in which data would be used failed. Uncoordinated tasks of data collection proved difficult to synthesize—even by the most brilliant of grand synthesizers. Out of this failure grew a recognized need for more explicit efforts to evaluate generalizations that pertained to spatially large areas, at least to areas sufficiently large that an uneven distribution of either survey or excavation data was likely.

In the final analysis, all of these changes are probably best explained as a response to the increasing number of archaeologists. Deciding "truth" or validity in a face-to-face group has been a simple undertaking throughout human affairs. Deciding the same matter with a cast of thousands has been, and will be, problematical. Agreeing to defer to the expertise of others quickly proves to be a problem. Agreeing to their objectivity, equally so. Eventually, nonpersonal standards, such as the rigor of argument and testing, prove necessary.

None of the preceding discussions is intended as a denial of the substantial element of "true believerism" that pervaded much of the writing of this period— even that which did not deal with the philosophy of science or with "new archaeology". However, it is worth recalling that there was substantial, if rarely published, opposition to the entire enterprise by many archaeologists of older generations.

## WAS ANYTHING LEARNED?

I suspect the primary lesson learned from archaeologists' collective experience with the literature of the history and philosophy of science is the same as that learned in our explorations of most every other literature: Don't expect to find agreement among the experts. Those issues that are germane, if peripheral, to our daily activities, but for which we would seek clear-cut advice, are precisely the topics over which the practitioners of the disciplines to which we turn spend hours arguing. (Ask one statistician for advice, and one receives clear direction. Ask two, and the conflict begins. Don't ever ask three.) Thus, it should have come as no surprise (but it still did) that the Hempel–Oppenheim model could be described almost simultaneously by different philosophers as the only way of formulating an explanation and as an extremely dubious philosophical doctrine. Similarly, while some philosophers regard the statistical–relevance model as an alternative to H–D, or at least a meaningful modification of that thesis, others, including diehard anti-Hempelians, classify it as a footnote. Finally, one reads expressions of shock that articles have been written by archaeologists combining the ideas of philosophers whose approaches have generated armed and competing camps within philosophy—Hempel and Kuhn, for example. Admittedly, one can carry eclecticism too far. However, archaeologists are under no obligation to maintain the ritual purity of particular philosophical doctrines—however sacred. Useful *advice* can and often does come from colleagues who hold little other than contempt for one another's ideas.

A second, anthropologically interesting discovery is the manner in which at least some philosophers of science choose to defend their conclusions on the grounds that they are, in essence, the ethnographers of the scientific community. Of course, in many respects they are, especially when their task is identified as constructing a parsimonious model of how scientists go about the task of discovering, analyzing, confirming, and so forth. However, like some ethnographers (the bad guys, of course), some commentators on archaeology have proven remarkably capable of telling the "natives" (us) that they know more about *why* and *how* we undertake our activities than we do ourselves. In some respects they are right, but in others they are dead wrong.

It makes little sense to read claims that archaeologists cannot possibly be correct in their belief that particular literatures provide stimulation or insight in approaching some of the issues with which we deal. For a philosopher of science to claim that a particular set of ideas or theories cannot be useful in the manner in which users have found it useful is a failure to investigate precisely what one would assume to be the most interesting question. Arm-twisting—trying to convince a group of practitioners that what they believe is a useful "literature" for dealing with archaeological problems should not, from a philosophical perspective, be useful to them at all—is counterproductive.

Perhaps even more devastating are efforts that attempt to assume out of existence problems that are basic to the issues. We have been told, for example, that if archaeologists are not sufficiently precise, it is because they do not know how to be more precise. However, such a position ignores the obvious effort on the part of many archaeologists over several generations to find argument after argument for maintaining an atmosphere of imprecision (one in which the opinion of experts holds sway, of course): Archaeological data are not amenable to quantification; the sampling literature is irrelevant because archaeologists do not sample—they simply decide what data to collect, etc. The presumption that archaeologists have always sought precision in the generalizations they attempted to formulate is flawed by its very assumption that all archaeologists either cared about generalizations or whether or not they were well formulated.

Viewed from this perspective, there is clearly great utility in the literature of the history and philosophy of science to the extent that it is used for exploring the question of how outsiders believe we do what we do. I do not intend to belittle in any way the importance of such an investigation. To the extent that we are able to increase self-awareness and explicitness in the task of generalizing, concluding, formulating, we will do more precise and sounder research—most importantly, research in which it is clear why particular conclusions were reached and not others, and in which the level of believability that can be attached to particular results is, at least, clearer.

Clarity of argument and precision of analysis are not simply general changes that I would attribute to archaeologists' experience of the literature under discussion. I argue that specific changes in the manner in which archaeologists invest their time and behave have resulted. These changes are perhaps best described in regard to what I previously defined as three contexts of explanation: the formal, the substantive, and the operational (Plog 1974).

## The Formal Component

Explanation in a formal context refers to *the process of constructing clear and at least testable arguments*. Greater archaeological attention to this effort is reflected in a number of areas.

Laws

I do not intend to argue that the profession as a whole has been persuaded of the desirability or utility of attempting to formulate, evaluate, and use laws. I do believe, however, that the average level of awareness of general (and even middle-range) theory has increased dramatically in recent years. Two decades ago, the major "generalists" and theoreticians in American anthropology were sociocultural anthropologists, and the major methodologists were physical anthropologists. Today, general theory in graduate departments of anthropology is far more typically controlled by faculty and students in archaeology, sociocultural anthropology having lost itself in a period of malaise and particularism. Similarly, I suspect that the average level of statistical competence and facility with the computer found among archaeology faculty members and students is at least equal to that characteristic of physical anthropologists, and that exploration of the cutting edges of the statistical and mathematical literature is far more characteristic of archaeologists. In summary, while I do not wish to represent general theory as any equivalent to laws, the collective attention of archaeologists has shifted dramatically toward more general issues.

Alternatives

A second change is a tendency toward the clear statement of alternative hypotheses and arguments and the simultaneous use of alternative methodologies. The "idle-speculation" model or, more kindly, models that involve no more than an archaeologist's "best-bet" interpretation of the prehistory of an area are no longer acceptable. Such attempts are identified for what they are—just-so stories. It is difficult to find examples of archaeological interpretation that are given much credibility in the absence of clear indications of the alternatives that were explored—although, certainly, discovery through blind insight will always be a part of our activity. I do not intend that this argument be interpreted as a claim that archaeologists have widely adopted the philosophy of multiple working hypotheses. That literature has, however, had a considerable influence.

Grant Proposals

Typical grant proposals, at least the ones that are funded, are based more and more frequently on well-developed and clearly stated arguments and hypotheses. This change is a dramatic one. The earliest grant proposals that I read followed a style of argument that might be characterized as: *This is a very important site, and I am a very important archaeologist.* As archaeology became more "scientific," proposals had as a central theme: *This proposal will utilize every environmental, ecological, chemical, physical, and statistical innovation known to archaeology.* More and more routinely today, proposals identify alternative arguments, and the means for choosing among the one that is primary.

This discussion has not, of course, addressed these two most crucial formal questions: (*a*) Are there laws of human behavior and culture process? and (*b*) Will you state one for us? While the early literature may have naively envisioned the immediate generation of a multitude of laws, its overall emphasis was on slow, systematic, and thorough evaluation of the host of lawlike generalizations in the existing literature. Most effort to date has been invested in conceptual clarification and the development of new measurement techniques, which are both badly needed for the evaluation of any generalization—indeed, for the formulation of a solvable problem.

That many proposed laws and lawlike statements are problematical is true. However, they are tautologies only to the extent that we fail to identify adequate measurement devices for the concepts–variables that they embody. They are trivial to the extent that we fail to note their applicability to the most mundane of archaeological tasks, and the dependence of interpretation on their successful application. They become the basis of our efforts to generalize to the extent that we overcome triviality and tautology, although for a time this task will undoubtedly continue to prove to be a difficult one.

## The Substantive Component

In its substantive context, explanation is *accounting for observed variation.* The changes in this area are straightforward. First, the use of statistics and other quantitative techniques in the published literature of archaeology appears to be increasing exponentially (G. Clark, personal communication). I would not argue that the use of quantitative–statistical procedures automatically increases the attention of the investigator to variation, but that it tends to do so, especially as analyses of variance and attention to residuals, for example, become a more routine aspect of what we do. Second, archaeologists have become collectively more familiar with theoretical literature that emphasizes explanation as articulated diversity and rely less on past discussions where norms and commonalities were most basic. Finally, we have to consider routinely additional sources of variation in accounting for patterning in archaeological data, cultural and natural transformation processes for example.

I certainly do not intend to conclude this section with the claim that all the preceding issues are now resolved—only that progress has been made. If we have learned, for example, that statistical samples are not "unbiased," as was once claimed, and now correctly state that such samples allow biases to be described, there is much to do before these statable biases are routinely explored in our analytical results. Similarly, if *robustness* (I would prefer to add *rigor*) appears preferable to the unattainable and unenjoyable standard of objectivity, we have far to go before our efforts are routinely robust or rigorous.

## The Operational Component

In its operational context, explanation is *the activity of designing research and of attempting to ensure that the variation under study is, in fact, observed.* Perhaps the most basic change in this area is the almost universal attention to the question: What is a good research design? At least most younger archaeologists have a sense of what they regard as an ideal research design, and they are prepared to defend it. That these research designs differ in specifics is neither surprising nor problematical. The effort involved in thinking about generating them represents a major shift in concern over the question of how we know and there is considerable attention to keeping "thinking" as well as field notes so as to maximize the opportunities for discovery as systematic plodding—an activity I have defended previously—proceeds.

Perhaps more important is the increasingly detailed evidence of the manner in which our research strategies have interfered in major ways with our understanding of the past. For example, we know that as much as 80 to 90% of the apparent variation in site densities across the southwestern U.S. is attributable to differences in survey techniques. Similarly, in the case of laboratory analyses, differences of 20 to 30% in the classification of lots of sherds by individuals trained in the same typology have been documented. Finally, multivariate statistical techniques have proven capable of discriminating between sherds separated by the same individual on different days. Clearly, if so high a percentage of the variation with which we deal is the product of observer differences, patterns that are not, in point of fact, prehistoric may have formed a major segment for some time of what we take to be our data base.

## CONCLUSION

There are certainly occasions on which doubt about the utility of experiencing the philosophy of science has arisen. These occasions are typically ones when philosophers of science manage to impress the archaeological community through the use of more sarcastic and acidic words than are common to archaeological writing, or when archaeologists seem committed to impressing their colleagues with their skills as philosophers of science—the past and archaeology momentarily forgotten. Thus, I have never felt the "devastation" that Michael Levin (1973) is said to have wrought on the article John Fritz and I (Fritz and Plog 1970) wrote because, while Levin's article contains a number of important points, it is also one of the most outstanding examples of a word game to have appeared in *American Antiquity* in the history of that journal. Similarly, I have been unable to achieve the appropriate degree of horror over the thought that the hypothetico–deductive method actually required the use of (God forbid!) induction. The need for a careful blending of induction and deduction was described in the earliest pertinent archaeological writings.

Finally, I am unconvinced by efforts to add additional modifiers to H–D or to replace the first or second of these terms with alternatives so that the newly found and true nature of archaeological inference—as opposed, I suppose, to inference in general—can be correctly identified.

Of course, the ultimate utility of our efforts to "do" explanation in any of these contexts is their importance in understanding the past. Whatever philosophy, whatever theories, whatever methods may be used, the business of prehistorians is to try to make sense of the poverty–stricken record that we have of 99% of the human experience. I see no way of offering an argument that on a worldwide basis the quality of our understanding of the past has increased as a result of our efforts to explain. However, in the literature with which I am most familiar, that of the American Southwest, this has clearly been the case at many different levels of generalization. We have learned, for example, that typical sites during most time periods had 3 rooms, not the 30 indicated in many syntheses. We have learned that facile assumptions of village-level ceramic production are almost impossible to support. And we have learned that when the assumptions and inferences—many of both—that necessarily underlie every chronology are not carefully tested, the merit of chronology is likely to be minimal, as are reconstructions based on it.

While I recognize that none of the preceding represents a convincing case for a causal relationship between any particular model of explanation and change in archaeology, I believe that the investment archaeologists made in that literature did have a considerable impact. The issues raised by our exploration of that literature are, to me, far more important than tortured arguments over the precise meaning of particular concepts—theory, law, validity, etc.—and their precise applicability to scientific behavior. I suspect that archaeologists will continue to benefit far more from casual exploration than from attempting to become miniphilosophers of science.

## REFERENCES

Fritz, J. M., and Plog, F. T., 1970, The nature of archaeological explanation, *American Antiquity* 35, 405–412.

Levin, M., 1973, On explanation in archaeology: A rebuttal to Fritz and Plog, *American Antiquity* 38, 387–395.

Plog, F., 1974, The study of prehistoric change, Academic Press, New York.

# 3

# Models of Explanation: Two Views[1]

*MERRILEE H. SALMON*

New archaeologists have said that explanations offered by their predecessors and colleagues are scientifically inadequate. In support of this claim they have cited works in which philosophers of science analyze the structure of scientific explanation and attempt to set standards of adequacy. After an initial period of hope that philosophy of science could be enlisted to help reform archaeological explanation, many archaeologists have become disillusioned. While philosophers had laid down standards, such as the requirement that explanations use laws, by which explanations in archaeology were judged inadequate, they had little to offer in the way of guidelines for constructing successful explanations in archaeology. Some archaeologists, pointing to the scarcity of suitable laws in related disciplines, such as history, raised doubts that explanation in archaeology could meet the scientific standards put forth in the standard philosophical models. Others turned their efforts to the formulation and testing of possible explanatory laws. Along with these retreats from and advances

[1]This chapter is based upon work supported by the National Science Foundation under Grant No. SOC 78–15726. The University of Arizona Committee on Foreign Travel provided funds to attend the meeting of the Theoretical Archaeology Group at which this chapter was first presented. I gratefully acknowledge the hospitality of the Theoretical Archaeology Group during my stay in Southampton.

THEORY AND EXPLANATION
IN ARCHAEOLOGY

toward nomothetic goals, there has been a growing awareness that some of the problems may lie with inadequacies in the philosophical accounts of scientific explanation rather than with explanation in archaeology.

Thus, interchanges between philosophers and archaeologists have served to stimulate research on the possibility and nature of archaeological laws and also on alternative models of explanation. This has opened doors to a deeper understanding of the complexity of the problems of explanation in archaeology, a point underscored by the contributions to this volume. One important theme that emerged from the early, somewhat rancorous exchanges between archaeologists and philosophers (Levin 1973, Morgan 1973, Watson, LeBlanc, and Redman 1974) was that the two disciplines conceived the problem of explanation in rather different ways. Philosophers were interested primarily in the formal structure of scientific explanation, although a few, like Michael Scriven (1959), have always rejected purely formal analyses. Archaeologists were, and are, interested in more substantive aspects of the problem. Although philosophers who constructed formal models of explanation addressed minimum requirements of empirical adequacy, far less attention was paid to these than to the formal requirements. These different approaches to explanation and the fact that the differences have not always been explicitly recognized have been sources of confusion and disappointment in the dialogue between archaeologists and philosophers. A focus of much of this confusion is the expression *model of explanation*, which has two distinct, equally standard meanings—one favored by archaeologists and the other by philosophers.

In the philosophical vocabulary, "model of explanation" refers to a set of criteria of adequacy for any scientific explanation, regardless of subject matter. Models of explanation, in this sense, are not concerned with any but the most general empirical considerations, such as truth of explanatory claims. Instead, they focus on formal features of explanation, such as the logical relations between descriptions of events to be explained and explanatory claims. A particular set of criteria might be proposed and then "tested" by trying to see whether explanations that seem intuitively satisfactory meet these criteria. The superiority of a particular set of criteria is thus decided by a priori considerations, by argument, and counterexample. We have a preanalytic conception of "good explanation," and we try to construct models that capture the good-making features. Some of the questions that have arisen in trying to devise adequate models are the following: Are explanations *arguments* to the effect that an event or pattern that is to be explained was certain (or likely) to occur in light of the explanatory information? Can there be explanations that invoke statistical generalizations? Is it possible to present a good explanation in the absence of any law statements? Exactly what role do law statements play in explanations? Can the same explanatory information be offered to explain both the occurrence and the nonoccurrence of some type of event?

It should be obvious that empirical research and factual information can be of little use in answering questions of this sort. In order to develop an adequate theory of explanation, a philosopher must have enough empirical information to recognize and understand explanations that are regarded as successful by practitioners of various scientific disciplines. But this is only the starting point. The principles in virtue of which these explanations are deemed successful are not easy to discern, so philosophical work of a nonempirical sort must be done to uncover them.

Except when they are specifically discussing philosophical works, archaeologists who talk about models of explanation are not at all interested in questions of the sort just mentioned. The expression *model of explanation* can also be used to refer to an empirical structure that provides some framework or context in which an incompletely understood phenomenon may be placed. This is the way the term is most frequently used by archaeologists. In this sense one can contrast a climatic change model of explanation of Pleistocene extinctions with an overkill model. Different models allow one to explain by fitting available information into different intelligible patterns. The term *model* is used partly to suggest that a proposed explanation is tentative. One recognizes, at least implicitly, that other patterns or models may be constructed to accommodate the data with some degree of plausibility.

Thus when archaeologists talk about selecting a model of explanation, they are concerned with a substantive issue: What general empirical framework provides the best way to represent, organize, understand, and correctly describe some phenomenon? Archaeologists believe that such questions will be answered, if they ever are answered, by the careful accumulation and interpretation of empirical data, not by a priori considerations of the type employed by philosophers. Even when the choice is between such general models as a systems model of the development of agriculture and a diffusionist model of the same phenomenon, important factual issues are involved. The two models disagree about what kinds of generalizations are relevant in explaining the data. Are the appropriate laws those of cultural diffusion or the laws of natural selection? They further disagree about the sorts of evidence that should be sought in order to fill in details of the models. Searching for the first corn cob is silly if a diffusionist model has been discarded and replaced by a systems model.

This is not to say that the choice among several models, particularly when they are very general, is based entirely on straightforward empirical criteria. In the absence of any compelling physical evidence, one model may be selected over another because of its superior "fit" with other well-established theories, or because it can generate an interesting research program. Such has been the story of the abandonment of diffusionist models in many areas of archaeology. It was not so much that diffusionism was conclusively falsified by the data in every case, but that researchers were left with the feeling that there was nowhere to go with the models and that systems models offered promising new paths to explore. Systems models were also perceived as resembling successful explanatory theories in other disciplines. Such considerations are certainly important and relevant when one is trying to select among models. Once a given model is chosen and becomes the focus of a research program, there is little chance that any evidence favorable to a competing model will develop. At this stage evidence in support of alternative hypotheses is not what one is looking for, and so it is unlikely that such will be found. Research efforts will be directed toward filling in details of the chosen model. Nevertheless, in spite of nonempirical aspects in the choice of a model, the final acceptance of one model over another is closely tied to empirical considerations in a way entirely absent in choosing among rival philosophical models.

The expression *systems model of explanation* has been particularly troublesome because some writers use it to refer to a model of phenomena (as in "a systems model of the development of agriculture") or to a general class of such models (as in "systems models have been more successful in accounting for all kinds of archaeological phenomena than diffusionist models"). Other writers use the expression *systems model of explanation* to refer to a general set of criteria for scientific explanations, i.e., a philosophical model. Still others use it in a way that indicates unawareness of the ambiguity. Systems models of the phenomena usually emphasize one or more of the following features: (*a*) multiple interacting causes that jointly contribute to produce the phenomenon; (*b*) feedback of either a negative or positive sort; (*c*) mechanisms that promote equilibrium in the face of pressures for change; and (*d*) the development of the phenomenon as a result of internal rather than external factors (M. Salmon 1980). Colin Renfrew (1969) and Kent Flannery (1968) are clearly concerned with some of these features in recommending systems models of the phenomena in preference to diffusionist models and/or invasion models for explaining cultural change. Eugene Meehan (1968), in presenting his systems models of explanation, makes it clear that his is a philosophical model, an alternative to the deductive–nomological model (Hempel 1965), which he believes is inadequate for social science explanation. But commentators are not always clear about the distinction between models of the phenomena and philosophical models of explanation. One finds references to Flannery's systems model as an alternative to Hempel's deductive–nomological model (LeBlanc 1974). Since these writers are dealing with entirely different sorts of problems, the solutions that the two offer can in no sense be considered alternatives to one another. Furthermore, no one has succeeded in showing that those who pursue systems models of the phenomena adopt explanations that conform to the pattern suggested by Meehan. Meehan himself does not offer a single example of an explanation in the social sciences that conforms to his model.

In spite of the fact that commitment to systems models of the phenomena does not in itself demand or preclude acceptance of a particular philosophical model of explanation, archaeologists who are convinced of the value of the systems approach should be concerned that philosophical models they endorse provide an adequate account of *functional explanation*. The whole point of characterizing certain interrelated phenomena as parts of a system is usually to *explain* the behavior of the various components in terms of their contributions to the system as a whole. Such explanations are, of course, functional explanations. To call them "systems explanations" is simply to rename them. Functional explanations are as pervasive in archaeology as they are in biology. In light of this, it is reasonable for archaeologists to demand—as biologists have done—an account of functional explanation before accepting any philosophical model.

Providing such an account has posed a serious challenge to philosophers, and there is no consensus about the success of proposed analyses. One stumbling block has been the inability of functional explanations, when they are understood as arguments whose conclusions state the existence of the feature to be explained, to show why a particular item occurs rather than some "functional equivalent" (Hempel 1965, pp. 311–314). For example, the functional explanation of the presence of hearts in humans, which appeals to the heart's role of pumping blood, necessary for maintenance of human life, leaves unanswered the question of why *hearts* do this and not some other mechanism for pumping blood. Some accounts, such as Nagel's (1977), bring functional explanations into conformity with the deductive–nomological model by insisting that the system that includes the item whose presence is to be explained and the goal that the item supports be specified in a careful and detailed way, using all our knowledge of laws of nature, evolutionary processes, etc., so that the problem of "functional equivalents" is eliminated. This approach has some plausibility when we are looking at some clearly defined biological system, such as the human body. It is less plausible to say that our understanding of the laws of nature rules out functional equivalents when we are considering less well-defined systems, such as Flannery's food-procurement systems, which typically interest archaeologists.

Another price to pay with Nagel's analysis of functional explanation is the forfeit of causal analysis, since the laws invoked in these explanations do not have proper temporal order. Any law that says, for example, that *plants of a given type in particular circumstances are propagated only if they have limp pods* is not a causal law, because success at scattering and nurturing seeds is not an antecedent condition of any given plant's having a limp pod. Nagel simply accepts this consequence of his analysis and says that explanations that are noncausal are appropriate in these circumstances. He believes that formal considerations (i.e., conformity with the deductive–nomological model) outweigh causal ones in presenting a satisfactory account of scientific explanations and in certifying certain sorts of explanations as legitimate.

Larry Wright, another philosopher and a former student of Scriven, rejects all attempts to characterize explanations in terms of their formal characteristics. An explanation's ability to expose causal factors is his sole criterion for its success. Functional explanations occupy a special category in Wright's scheme because they refer to a special kind of cause. According to Wright (1976), when the fact that some mechanism has a particular effect is causally relevant to the very existence of that mechanism, then that mechanism is a functional cause or function. The mechanism of limp pods on certain plants is causally relevant to the continued existence of that type of plant and thus to the existence of the limp pods themselves, so limp pods are a functional cause or function. Wright tries to bring out the similarity between cases of natural functions, such as limp pods, and cases of conscious functions, such as artifacts or other features designed for a particular purpose. An example of the latter is smoke holes in houses, since a consequence or effect of such holes is the reduction of smoke in dwellings, and the fact that smoke holes have this effect is causally relevant to the construction of smoke holes in houses. The legitimacy of this close analogy between cases of conscious design and the process of natural selection is a matter of great controversy among biologists and philosophers of biology (Nagel 1977, 287).

Whatever the overall value of Wright's account of functional explanation and regardless of its correctness in matters of detail, Wright's insight into the *causal* implications of saying something is a *function* is extremely valuable. Functions have always been recognized as effects or consequences, but Wright manages to distinguish these effects from other, merely "accidental," effects (e.g., the difference between the pumping effect of hearts and their heartbeat-sound effect) by appealing to the causal relation between a thing's having some particular effect and that thing's existing or being where it is. Wright's priorities in doing this offer a sharp contrast to Nagel's. Nagel views logical structure or form as the crucial element in explanation, and tries to preserve formal similarity between functional explanations and deductive-nomological explanations at the expense of causality. Wright sees concern with causality as the sine qua non of explanation, and regards the shared ability to expose causes as the unifying feature of satisfactory explanation, while dismissing questions about formal structure as irrelevant.

While I agree with Wright that any philosophical account of explanation must take causal considerations seriously, I do not see that this means the rejection of all formal considerations. I also believe, though this cannot be argued in detail here, that the statistical–relevance model of explanation (W. Salmon *et al.*, 1971) can be developed to incorporate causal considerations along with important formal elements. However, the formal requirement that explanations be arguments that show that the event to be explained must have occurred or was very likely to have occurred on the basis of the explanatory information is *not* a feature of the statistical–relevance model. This requirement has made it difficult to accommodate functional explanations within the deductive–nomological model, but there are other objections to regarding explanations as arguments as well (W. Salmon 1977). The statistical–relevance model does try to come to grips with one of the most desirable features of the "systems approach" to archaeology, i.e., recognition of the importance of multiple, relevant, interacting explanatory factors. The model recognizes that there may be serious problems in sorting the ways in which various statistically relevant factors operate when they are jointly present, and the "screening off" condition (W. Salmon *et al.*, 1971, 55) handles some of these problems, though not by any means all of them.

Statistically relevant factors are not always causally relevant to the occurrence of an event. But statistically relevant factors are often useful in narrowing our search for causes. In their attempt to explain different survival patterns of anatomical parts of dead sheep on sites exposed to free-ranging dogs, Binford and Bertram (1977) found that the season of occupation (winter or summer) was a statistically relevant factor. The authors used this information, along with information about the breeding habits of sheep and relative densities of bones in adult and juvenile animals, to find the relevant causal factor: the different degrees of resistance that bones offered to scavenging dogs (M. Salmon and W. Salmon 1979). Current work on the statistical–relevance model is directed towards explicating relations between statistically relevant and causally relevant factors in explanations. This work takes full cognizance of the importance of causal considerations in any adequate model of scientific explanation.

In addition to confusion because of the ambiguity in "model of explanation," many archaeologists have been disappointed with philosophical accounts of explanation because these do not give sufficient attention to a problem that especially concerns archaeologists—confirmation of explanatory statements. Much of the criticism that has been directed at archaeological explanation simply points to an absence of reasons for believing some claim that forms part of an explanation. Martin and Plog (1973, 324–325) are unhappy, for example, with the explanation that attributes the abandonment during the thirteenth and fourteenth centuries of many major pueblo sites in the southwestern United States to attacks of Athabaskan invaders. This statement has little claim to truth, they say, because there is no direct evidence that Athabaskans were even in the region before 1600 A.D..

Now hardly anyone would disagree with demands that there be some good reasons to regard as true the claims made in a satisfactory explanation. The most die-hard, antiscientific humanist would be reluctant to accept an explanation based on statements that were regarded as unfounded or false. Unless an explanatory statement has some claim to truth, it cannot explain anything. The point, it seems, on which reasonable persons might disagree is on the nature of evidence required to support the truth of the explanatory claim. As a defense of the Athabaskan-invader account of the abandonment of pueblos, for example, a person might appeal by "inference to the best explanation" to the reasonableness of such a claim, given our general background knowledge. A critic might say that we must and can do better than this in our explanations, and simply forbear offering one if there is no positive evidence for an explanatory claim.

All the standard philosophical models of explanation include some concern with truth of the explanans as one of their nonformal requirements. Hempel's (1966, 49) formulation is widely regarded as acceptable: the statements constituting an explanation must be capable of empirical testing. In order for the explanation to be accepted, the explanatory statments must not only be testable, but they must also be true, or at least strongly confirmed. An explanation that is satisfactory in other respects, but that depends upon a testable, though as yet untested, claim would be characterized by Hempel (1965, 338) as a "potential explanation." If this approach is accepted, then the "explanation" that involves Athabaskan invaders to explain pueblo abandonment could at best be only a potential explanation. It would be incumbent upon those who offered such a potential explanation to test and support their hypothesis before asking anyone to accept that explanation.

At one important level of disagreement then, discussion of the problem of explanation in archaeology is a dispute about differing standards of evidence for the truth of explanatory claims. At this level the problem is one for the *logic of confirmation,* which can be treated without regard to any particular philosophical model of explanation. Requiring true, or well-confirmed, explanatory statements is a characteristic of the deductive–nomological model of explanation, but it is not a distinguishing characteristic by any means. Reducing a problem of archaeological explanation to that of confirmation does not constitute a solution to the problem, of course. It just changes the focus. But with the new focus it may be possible to pursue a solution without the added baggage of other sorts of problems that belong specifically to explanation.

One recent discussion of the unsatisfactory character of certain explanations in archaeology is that of Donald K. Grayson (1980). In this work Grayson is clearly concerned with inadequate *confirmation* of claims made in various explanations of Pleistocene extinctions. In discussing explanations that appeal to climatic changes and those that appeal to the effects of man's hunting prowess, Grayson (1980, 391) bemoans the fact that these alternative claims have not been subjected to "the kind of scrutiny one usually associates with the scientific method." This method, as Grayson perceives it, consists in arranging competing hypotheses alongside one another and drawing mutually exclusive test implications from them in order to eliminate those that do not meet the tests. In other words, Grayson seems to want some crucial experiment or observation that can lead to the rejection of one alternative while strongly supporting the other. Grayson says that this has not been attempted in the case of Pleistocene extinction explanations and that the advocacy method has been used instead. Grayson, who borrows the term *advocacy method* from E. Wilson (1975), characterizes this method as one that involves providing data to show that an opponent's hypothesis is incorrect and then presenting an alternative together with a body of supporting evidence. Grayson, again following Wilson, says that the advocacy method precludes falsification, though given *his* characterization of it, it is not clear why this should be so. If data are presented to show a hypothesis is incorrect, this appears to be a method that involves falsification. Falsification would be precluded only if no refuting data were presented, and hypotheses were not rejected on the basis of evidence, but were forgotten or allowed to slip out of favor from lack of advocate action.

In any case, Grayson's main concern is not with standards of explanation (as philosophers conceive the problem) but rather with correct standards and procedures for acceptance or rejection of hypotheses. In a philosophical theory of explanation, something will be said about the confirmation of explanatory statements, but this will not be sufficiently detailed to settle issues of what must happen if a statement is to be considered confirmed. The hypotheses about the causes of Pleistocene extinctions are very complicated. It is not at all clear in cases like this that a crucial experiment—or set of such experiments—can be devised to choose among hypotheses. Grayson seems to assume that it is always possible to set up mutually exclusive test implications, but when hypotheses one wishes to test are enmeshed in a network of other hypotheses, this assumption is doubtful. Philosophers have interesting and useful things to say about such problems, but one won't find them in the literature on explanation. These are problems in confirmation.

Because archaeologists' and philosophers' concerns about the nature of explanation are so different, discussion of explanatory problems break down at crucial points. In spite of this, I believe that each discipline can learn something from the other. Philosophers, when confronted with archeological explanations, should see that they must pay attention to nonformal aspects if their accounts are to be adequate, and they should also see that functional explanations cannot be ignored. Archaeologists may come to see some of the benefits of philosophical analysis, such as the increase in conceptual clarity that can come from isolating and separating issues in a complex problem. At the same time archaeologists should see that it is unreasonable to expect a philosophical model to provide a basis for choosing among various substantive models in archaeology or to provide a method to discover the correct explanation of some archaeological phenomenon.

# REFERENCES

Binford, L. R. (ed.), 1977, *For Theory Building in Archaeology,* New York, Academic Press.
Binford, L. R., and Bertram, J. B., 1977, Bone frequencies—and attritional process, in Binford, L. R. (ed.), *For Theory Building in Archaeology,* New York, Academic Press, 77–153.
Butts, R., and Hintikka, J. (eds.), 1977, *Basic Problems in Methodology and Linguistics,* Dordrecht, D. Reidel.
Flannery, K., 1968, Archaeological systems theory and early Mesoamerica, in Meggers, B. J. (ed.), *Anthropological Archaeology in the Americas,* Washington, D.C., Anthropological Society of Washington, 67–87.
Grayson, D. K., 1980, Vicissitudes and overkill: The development of explanations of Pleistocene extinctions, in Schiffer, M. B. (ed.), *Advances in Archaeological Method and Theory,* 3, New York, Academic Press, 357–403.
Hempel, C. G., 1965, *Aspects of Scientific Explanation,* New York, The Free Press.
Hempel, C. G., 1966, *Philosophy of Natural Science,* Englewood Cliffs, N.J., Prentice–Hall.
LeBlanc, S., 1974, Two points of logic, in Redman, C. L., (ed.), *Research and Theory in Current Archaeology,* New York, Wiley, 199–214.

Levin, M., 1973, On explanation in archaeology: A rebuttal to Fritz and Plog, *American Antiquity* 38, 387–395.

Martin, P. S., and Plog, F., 1973, *The Archaeology of Arizona*, Garden City, N.Y., Doubleday–Natural History Press.

Meehan, E.J., 1968, *Explanation in Social Science: A System Paradigm*, Homewood, Ill., Dorsey Press.

Meggers, B. J. (ed.), 1968, *Anthropological Archaeology in the Americas*, Washington, D.C., Anthropological Society of Washington.

Morgan, C. G., 1973, Archaeology and explanation, *World Archaeology* 4, 259–276.

Nagel, E., 1977. Teleology revisited: The Dewey lectures 1977, *The Journal of Philosophy* 74, 261–301.

Redman, C. L. (ed.), 1974, *Research and Theory in Current Archaeology*, New York, Wiley.

Renfrew, C., 1969, Trade and culture process in European prehistory, *Current Anthropology* 10, 151–169.

Salmon, M. H., 1980, Reply to Lowe and Barth, *American Antiquity* 45, 575–579.

Salmon, M. H., and Salmon, W., 1979, Alternative models of scientific explanation, *American Anthropologist* 81, 61–74.

Salmon, W. C., 1977, A third dogma of empiricism, in Butts, R., and Hintikka, J. (eds.), *Basic Problems in Methodology and Linguistics*, Dordrecht, D. Reidel, 149–166.

Salmon, W. C., Jeffry, R., and Greeno, J., 1971, *Statistical Explanation and Statistical Relevance*, Pittsburgh, University of Pittsburgh Press.

Schiffer, M. B. (ed.), 1980, *Advances in Archaeological Method and Theory*, 3, New York, Academic Press.

Scriven, M., 1959, Explanation and prediction in evolutionary theory, *Science* 130, 477–482.

Watson, P. J., LeBlanc, S., and Redman, C., 1974, The covering law model in archaeology: Practical uses and formal interpretation, *World Archaeology* 5, 125–131.

Wilson, E., 1975, *Sociobiology*, Cambridge, Mass., Belknap Press.

Wright, L., 1976, *Teleological Explanations*, Berkeley, University of California Press.

# 4

# Causality in Archaeological Explanation[1]

*WESLEY C. SALMON*

If I were an archaeologist—which I am not—I imagine I should be seeking explanations for various phenomena and that the desired explanations would be causal. In asking for the explanation of the abandonment of the Grasshopper Pueblo at the end of the fourteenth century, I should be looking for the factors that caused the inhabitants to leave. In asking why a scarlet macaw was buried with the body of a child at that site, I should want to know what causal processes led to the presence of a bird of that species so far north of its current natural habitat. Additional examples come readily to mind, but the point seems almost too obvious even to be worth mentioning. The reason for raising it is that archaeologists have been widely influenced by Hempel's treatment of scientific explanation (1965, 1966), and his theory leads to a radically different conception.

It will not be a primary aim of this chapter to go into the details of Hempel's well-known deductive–nomological (D–N) or inductive–statistical (I–S) models of explanation, nor my statistical–relevance (S–R) model. Instead, I intend to

[1]The material in this chapter is based upon work supported by the National Science Foundation under Grant No. SES–7809146. I wish to express my gratitude to the NSF for this support of research, to the University of Arizona Committee on Foreign Travel for providing a travel grant that enabled me to attend the meeting of the Theoretical Archaeology Group at which this chapter was first presented, and to the Theoretical Archaeology Group for its kind hospitality during the meeting.

**45**

examine certain general conceptions of scientific explanation that have motivated the construction of such formal models. As it turns out (see W. Salmon
1978), two basic intuitions have guided much of the discussion of scientific
explanation during the last few decades. According to one of these—*the
inferential conception*—to provide a scientific explanation of a phenomenon is
to construct an argument that shows that the event to be explained was to be
expected on the basis of the explanatory facts. This is the conception that
Hempel—along with a number of other leading philosophers of science,
including R. B. Braithwaite (1953), Ernest Nagel (1961), and Sir Karl Popper
(1959)—has advocated and elaborated. According to the second basic
intuition—*the causal conception*—to provide a scientific explanation is to
identify the causal factors that produced the event to be explained. This
conception has given rise to some of the sharpest criticisms of Hempel's models
of explanation (e.g., Scriven 1975, Wright 1976), and to certain criticisms of
my S–R model as well (e.g., Cartmill 1980, King 1976, Lehman 1972). In her
contribution to this book, M. H. Salmon (Chapter 3) discusses the fundamental disagreement between Nagel and Wright on the subject of functional
explanation—a difference that emerges rather patently from the fact that
Nagel adheres to an inferential conception, while Wright embraces a causal
conception.

The main purpose of this chapter will be to explore the divergence between
these two conceptions in the hope of illuminating certain fundamental problems
concerning scientific explanation that have, I believe, proved troublesome to
archaeologists. In order to address the issue, permit me to take a short historical
detour back to the beginning of the nineteenth century—the heyday of Laplacian
determinism. In expounding his deterministic outlook, Laplace made reference
to his famous demon—the hypothetical superintelligence that (*a*) knew all of the
laws of nature; (*b*) knew the state of the universe in complete detail at some
particular moment; and (*c*) could solve any mathematical problem. For it,
Laplace remarked that, "Nothing would be uncertain and the future, as the past,
would be present to its eyes" (1951, 4). It seems evident that this demon would
be able to subsume any actual occurrence under basic universal laws in
conformity to Hempel's D–N model and would be able also to discern the
causal mechanisms leading to any such occurrence. Indeed, within the Laplacian
framework, it is not clear that there is any point in distinguishing the two
conceptions, for Laplace gives the distinct impression that he views the basic
laws of nature as both *universal* and *causal* (cf. Salmon 1978, 685–686).

When we shift our framework from classical physics, with its deterministic
outlook, to twentieth-century science, where we must take seriously the
possibility that the world is in some respects indeterministic, we find a sharp
divergence between the two fundamental conceptions. Given our current state
of physical knowledge and the fact that the statistical interpretation of quantum
mechanics is the received interpretation, it seems to me that our philosophical
theories of scientific explanation *must* take account of the *possibility* that some

phenomena are in some respects undetermined, and therefore not amenable, even in principle, to D–N explanation. Consider radiocarbon dating. Radioactive decay is an ineluctably statistical phenomenon; it is, at best, highly probable that about half of any given collection of $^{14}C$ atoms will disintegrate in 5730 years. Moreover, leaving aside altogether the current status of microphysics, we can surely see that in most sciences the only *available* explanations of some phenomena are probabilistic or statistical. In evolutionary biology, for example, we can say that a given trait raises or lowers the probability that a particular organism will survive and procreate, but physical necessity is not involved. Evolution is a statistical phenomenon.

Although the classic Hempel–Oppenheim (1948) essay explicitly acknowledged the fact that there are legitimate scientific explanations of the statistical sort, the first serious attempt to develop a systematic theory of statistical explanation was, to the best of my knowledge, offered by Hempel (1962a). A sketch of this theory was presented in Hempel (1962b), and the theory was significantly refined by him in 1965. A sketch of the newer version was given in the elementary textbook (Hempel 1966). The leading proponent of the inferential conception of scientific explanation recognized the existence of statistical explanations, and he provided a philosophical account of this pattern. The inductive–statistical model is the result. He *never* maintained that all acceptable scientific explanations must conform to the D–N schema.

The transition from deductive–nomological to statistical explanation brings out the fundamental differences between the inferential and causal conceptions. If one adheres to the inferential approach, it is natural (as Hempel clearly recognized) to regard statistical explanations as inductive arguments—analogous to the deductive arguments that characterize D–N explanations—and to require that the inductive argument render its conclusion highly probable in relation to the explanatory facts. The obvious result is that events can be explained only if they are highly probable with respect to some suitable explanatory conditions, and that events that are simply improbable in relation to all available information are not amenable to scientific explanation. The inexplicability of improbable occurrences leads to difficulty on two scores. First, it appears that we *do* regard improbable events as explainable. An archaeological example is given in Salmon and Salmon (1979, 70). Ring-built and coil-built pottery can usually be distinguished from single-lump, wheel-thrown ceramics by traces of junctions between the rings in the finished product. However, in a small fraction of cases the junctions are totally obliterated during shaping and firing. Although this happens far less frequently than not, when it does happen, the shaping and firing explains the absence of such traces. A variety of other, nonarchaeological examples is furnished in the same place and in W. Salmon (1977, 151–155).

Second, it seems to me, we *should* consider some improbable occurrences just as explainable as certain highly probable occurrences. Hempel (1965, 391) mentions an example taken from Mendelian genetics. In a certain population of pea plants, there is a probability of ¾ for red blossoms and a probability of ¼ for white blossoms. If we take ¾ to be a high probability (and if we don't, it is easy enough to cook up another example with a higher value), then we can explain the occurrence of a red blossom, but we cannot explain the occurrence of a white blossom in the same population. This represents a strange lack of parity, for it seems to me that we understand the occurrence of a white blossom in that population exactly as well as we understand the occurrence of a red blossom. (In a 1976 postscript, Hempel [1977, 98–123] appears to have agreed with this point.) When we consider carefully the nature of statistical explanation, we find that the inferential conception of scientific explanation encounters serious difficulties; these have been more fully elaborated by me elsewhere (1977, 1982).

The statistical–relevance model was originally motivated by an intuitive sense of dissatisfaction concerning the high-probability requirement associated with the I–S model (Salmon *et al.* 1971, 10–12). In Salmon and Salmon (1979 67–68), examples are offered to show that putative explanations that fulfill all of the conditions for correct I–S explanations, including the high-probability requirement, cannot be considered acceptable, while other examples that do not satisfy the high-probability requirement are bona fide explanations. Reflection upon these and a host of other similar examples convinced me that the relation of statistical relevance, not the relation of high probability of the explanandum relative to the explanans, was the *fundamental* explanatory relation. Strangely, it seemed to me, Hempel and other proponents of the inferential conception of explanation never seemed to appreciate the explanatory significance of statistical relevance relations. It is now easy to see why. In the first place, as the arguments of Cartmill (1980), Lehman (1972), and King (1976) have shown, it is simply incorrect to suppose that the relation of statistical relevance has explanatory import in and of itself; rather, it is at best a *symptom* of a bona fide explanatory relation.

If we find a higher incidence of lung cancer among heavy cigarette smokers than we do in the population at large, this positive correlation suggests that a causal relation exists, but the relation of positive relevance in and of itself does not explain anything. If one holds the view that furnishing an explanation consists in constructing an argument that shows that the event to be explained was to be expected—either with deductive certainty or with high inductive probability—on the basis of explanatory facts, then statistical relevance relations will not seem very important from an explanatory standpoint. At best, they will appear as pale substitutes for the desired relations of high probability required in strong inductive arguments. Statistical relevance does not say much to a proponent of the inferential conception of scientific explanation. If, on the other hand, one holds the view that furnishing a scientific explanation consists in locating and displaying causal mechanisms, then relations of statistical relevance will be precisely the kinds of clues we need to ferret out the underlying causal relations that can be used in constructing scientific explanations. To the advocate of the causal conception, relations of statistical relevance are beacons guiding our way to crucial explanatory relations.

If it is acknowledged that the inferential conception encounters severe difficulties in providing a satisfactory account of statistical explanation, then we must ask how the causal conception will fare if indeterminism is admitted. If we think of causality in the usual deterministic way—sticking rigorously to the principle *same cause, same effect* (Hempel, 1966, 53)—then the causal conception will be incapable of coping. It seems to me, however, that we need not saddle a contemporary philosophical theory of scientific explanation with a Laplacian deterministic or Humean constant-conjunction notion of causality, and consequently we can save the causal conception, even in the face of events whose occurrences are not fully determined in every respect. To make good on this claim obviously requires the development of a theory of probabilistic causality, as attempted, for example, by Suppes (1970). I should like to say a little about probabilistic causality, partly because the notion is so unfamiliar that people are likely, I suspect, to consider it an incoherent concept. These issues are pursued in more detail in W. Salmon (1980) and in my forthcoming article on causality (in press).

Almost every morning, it seems, the newpaper carries a story about some causal claim. Cigarette smoking causes lung cancer; saccharine causes bladder cancer in laboratory rats; and recently, the use of a certain brand of tampon causes toxic shock syndrome. In each case, the *evidence* for the causal claim comes in the form of a relation of positive statistical relevance. In his introductory text, Giere (1979, Chapter 12) spells out the details of several interesting examples. If we compare investigations of this sort with the Humean constant-conjunction conception of causality, we are immediately struck by an enormous discrepancy, for in virtually every case we find nothing remotely approaching constant conjunction. The typical example usually involves a *small* increment in a *minute* probability. Last spring, for instance, there was a suspicion that such substances as epoxies and resins to which workers in the General Motors' woodshop are exposed are carcinogens. The evidence that led to this suspicion was that during a 10-year period, 14 cases of cancer of the rectum or colon developed in a population of more than 1600 woodworkers (less than 1%), while the normal rate for a sample of this size would be 6 cases. For another example, among the 2235 soldiers who witnessed an atomic blast at close range in Operation Smokey in 1957, 8 (approximately ⅓ of 1%) subsequently contracted leukemia. Nevertheless, in the opinion of the medical investigator who examined the evidence, there was "no doubt whatever" that the radiation had caused the leukemia (W. Salmon 1978, 688–689 and Note 15). The crucial issue in all such cases is not any pretense of constant conjunction, but whether a significant positive relevance relation exists.

The standard answer to these considerations is to maintain that the discovery of positive relevance relations, while providing *evidence* for the claim that we have located a *causal factor* in a complicated situation, does not enter into the *analysis* of the causal relation itself. In cases of the foregoing sort, it may be said, it is possible in principle to locate numerous other causal factors, and when we have collected all of them we will find a constant conjunction between a complex set of causal conditions and a given effect. In this way we can save the general principle "same cause, same effect" and hang onto our cherished deterministic prejudices. The basic objection to this approach is, in my opinion, that there is no reason to believe that it is true.

Consider a couple of examples. Suppose that an ice cube is placed in a glass of tepid water and melts. I think we would not hesitate to say that being placed in the water is the cause of the melting, though we know theoretically that being placed in lukewarm water is neither sufficient nor necessary for the melting of the ice cube, merely rendering the result highly probable. This is true, by the way, even in classical statistical mechanics based upon deterministic laws of motion for the molecules, because the initial condition—that the water be tepid—is not sufficient under that theory for the melting of the ice cube.

Or take the case of a simple type of laser. A large number of atoms are pumped up into a relatively stable excited state for which the average decay time by spontaneous emission is fairly large. If, however, radiation of the appropriate frequency impinges upon these atoms, there is rapid decay by stimulated emission, resulting in a burst of radiation from the laser. The acronym *LASER* stands for "light amplification by stimulated emission of radiation." There is no doubt, I believe, that the impinging radiation *causes* the emission of radiation by the laser, but it is neither necessary nor sufficient for the occurrence. There is an admittedly minute nonzero probability that the atoms would all decay rapidly by spontaneous emission, and an admittedly minute nonzero probability that they would not decay rapidly even in the presence of incident radiation of a sort suitable to stimulate emission.

The preceding examples are cases in which the effect follows the cause with such a high probability that the nonoccurrence of the effect has so low a probability as to "make no odds." Let us look at an example that is less extreme. Some children are playing baseball, and one of them hits a long fly ball that shatters a neighbor's window. Suppose, for the sake of argument, that we can specify rather precisely the position and momentum of the ball as it strikes the window and that we can specify quite precisely the type of glass that shattered. Suppose further that a window pane of that particular sort will break in 95% of all cases in which it is struck by a ball of just that type traveling with the same momentum and striking the pane in the same spot. If someone were to say that it would be possible, if we knew further details about the internal structure of the glass and other relevant features of the situation, to ascertain exactly which collisions would result in breakage and which would not, I would remain skeptical.

Classical physics, from which we derive much of our deterministic inspiration, notoriously failed to provide any satisfactory theory of the structure of matter, and hence would be at a loss to deal with the preceding example. Contemporary solid-state physics, which may or may not have an adequate theory of the structure of glass (I don't happen to know), is not fundamentally deterministic. The basic point, however, is this. We may fuss as much as we like about the details of this example, and argue ad nauseam whether a deterministic account of the breaking of the window is possible in principle. It would make no difference how the argument came out. Either way, we would all readily agree, under the conditions stipulated, that the baseball *caused* the window to break. I cannot see why anyone should fear that such a judgment would become false or nonsensical if the supposed deterministic underpinning turned out to be absent. Such metaphysical baggage is completely dispensable to a satisfactory account of causality, and can play no useful role in the understanding of archaeological explanation.

My primary thesis, in the foregoing discussion, has been the inadequacy of the inferential conception of scientific explanation and the superiority of the causal conception. Implementation of the causal conception, it has been noted, requires a probabilistic concept of causality if it is to be able to deal with statistical explanations. Although there are, admittedly, serious difficulties involved in the full elaboration of a theory of probabilistic causality, the problems do not seem insuperable (see W. Salmon 1980, in press).

Having sketched these claims, I should now like to apply them to some archaeological examples that are not altogether trivial. In each of these cases, several alternative potential explanations will be mentioned, but I shall make no attempt to decide which explanatory accounts, if any, are correct. That is the kind of question that can only be answered by the professional archaeologist who is in full command of the relevent empirical data. I shall, instead, point to general features of all of the various alternatives that deserve to be taken seriously.

Consider, first, the case of a piece of worked bone found in Alaska that has a radiocarbon date of approximately 30,000 B.P. (Dumond 1980). This object has obvious bearing upon the problem of how early there were human inhabitants in Alaska. Let us assume for the sake of argument that the radiocarbon date is correct—that the bone is indeed about 30,000 years old. The question is how to account for the presence of this object at an Alaskan site. According to one potential explanation, there has been continuous human habitation in Alaska for at least 30,000 years. According to another, there was a brief period of human habitation about 30,000 B.P., followed by a long period during which no humans were there. On either of these theories, the presence of the worked bone is explained by human production (a causal interaction between the worker and the piece of bone) in Alaska 30,000 years ago. A different potential explanation is that the bone had existed, preserved frozen in an unworked state for about 20,000 years before it was discovered and made into a human artifact about 10,000 years ago. This is a very different causal story. As noted above, I have no intention of trying to say which, if any, of these potential explanations is correct, but I do want to emphasize the fact that any satisfactory explanation will involve a complex of causal processes and interactions leading to the presence of the worked bone in Alaska.

It should be explicitly remarked that no assumptions about causal determinism need be taken to underlie any of the explanations. On the third alternative, it may have been a matter of sheer chance that an ancient artisan came across a piece of frozen bone suitable for working—indeed, it would be gratuitous to assume that it was even probable in the circumstances that the bone would be found, picked up, and worked. Furthermore, the recent presence of the worked bone in Alaska involves causal processes that account for its preservation for 10,000 years after it had been worked. Who knows the vicissitudes such an object might have suffered or escaped, and who can say that its endurance over 10 millenia was causally determined in a nonstatistical sense or even that it was highly probable in the circumstances? These considerations seem to me to render dubious at best the claim that we could ever hope to construct a D–N or I–S explanation of the presence of the worked bone in Alaska. They do not seem to militate in the least against a probabilistically causal sort of explanatory account.

As another example, let us consider the problem of Pleistocene extinction of large mammals over large regions of the earth. I am aware of two main types of explanations that have been offered (Grayson 1980). One kind of explanation appeals to a radical climatic change, which in some accounts led to a loss of habitat to which the various species had become adapted and which in other accounts led to the birth of the young out of season. On this sort of explanation, the extinction is a result of evolutionary processes that resulted in the non-survival of many species. As I remarked before, evolution is a statistical affair, and it might be added, there is no reason to presuppose a deterministic foundation. If an organism, born into a given environment, has a certain characteristic, that fact may raise or lower the probability that it will survive and procreate, but whether it does or not is a chancy affair. A baby mammoth, born out of season, may have a lessened chance of survival, but there is no basis for claiming that its failure to survive was wholly causally determined. Nevertheless, while causal determinism is no part of the story, we are all clearly aware of the kinds of causal mechanisms involved in the relationship between an organism and its environment that have a bearing upon survival and procreation.

A rather different sort of explanation attributes the extinction to human overkill. The superfluousness of deterministic underpinnings are obvious in this case as well. Whether a particular animal escaped notice by a human hunter might well be a matter of chance. Given that the hunter has spotted the animal and thrusts a weapon with a Clovis point into its body, there might be a chance of only 95% that the animal will die as a result. The matter of death due to the penetration of a Clovis point appears to me entirely parallel to the case of the window shattered by the baseball.

What I have said about the preceding two examples applies quite generally, I suspect, to explanation in archaeology. If, for example, any adequate explanation of the abandonment of Grasshopper Pueblo can ever be found, it will, I imagine, involve appeal to a complex set of factors that, taken together, account for the phenomenon. Some factors, such as a moderately severe drought, which would tend to cause people dependent upon agriculture for food to move elsewhere, will be positively relevant to the occurrence. But such droughts do not always result in abandonment. Perhaps the existence of a fairly large and complex pueblo would tend to make people remain—even under circumstances of physical hardship. Factors of this kind would be negatively relevant. Again, a recent rapid growth in population, which led to the agricultural exploitation of marginal land, might be positively relevant to departure, since production on marginal land would be affected more drastically by drought than would production on land better suited to agriculture. This kind of approach to the explanation of the abandonment of Grasshopper Pueblo clearly involves a search for contributing causes (positively relevant factors) and counteracting causes (negatively relevant factors). In this way, we hope to be able to exhibit the complex causal mechanisms that produced the event we are trying to explain.

In the period of about two decades since Hempel's work began to exert a wide influence upon archaeologists, there have been developments of fundamental importance within the philosophical theory of scientific explanation. It is easy to see the powerful appeal of an account of scientific explanation that demands deductive subsumption of the event to be explained under universal laws of nature—as is schematized in the D–N model. In 1960, as I mentioned previously, no systematic theory of probabilistic or statistical explanation existed. It must have been clear to many archaeologists, however, that the demand that every explanation conform to the D–N pattern was an unrealistic goal for archaeology. Since then, we have seen the emergence of at least two models of statistical explanation—the I–S model and the S–R model. Both have been subjected to severe criticisms. The major criticism of the former model is that it imposes a high-probability requirement; the latter model overcomes the basic problem by shifting emphasis from high probabilities to relations of statistical relevance. The S–R model has, in turn, been criticized for failure to take adequate account of causal considerations—a criticism that applies equally to the other two models. When we attempt to repair this difficulty, we find ourselves facing another fundamental philosophical problem, because cause–effect relations have traditionally been construed as cases of constant conjunction. This conception of causality leads to the principle "same cause, same effect," which implies that causal laws are universal laws. On this view of causality, the problem of finding causal explanations is just as insuperable as is the problem of deductive subsumption under universal laws demanded by the D–N model. It appears that we have come full circle.

The way out of this difficulty, I have been suggesting, lies in the development of a different conception of causality—a probabilistic concept, along the lines suggested by Suppes (1970) and myself (1980, in press). Relations of statistical relevance play a crucial role in any theory of probabilistic causality. Thus, the theory of causal explanation that emerges when we employ probabilistic causality is an extension or enrichment of the S–R model. However, in order to implement the probabilistic theory of causality, we must relinquish the time-honored principle "same cause, same effect." We must be prepared to admit that a given cause may on one occasion produce one sort of effect, but the same kind of cause may on another occasion produce a different sort of effect. If, as contemporary physics suggests, indeterminism actually obtains in our world, that is exactly what we must expect. For example, in the famous Stern–Gerlach experiment, an atom of a given type may be deflected upward when it enters a certain magnetic field, while another atom *exactly similar to the first in all physical respects* may be deflected downward by the *same* magnetic field. If the world has this sort of indeterminacy at the level of fundamental physics, we should not be dismayed to encounter indeterminacy in other domains as well. In order to have any hope of developing theories of explanation adequate to the contemporary sciences—including archaeology—we must be prepared to re-examine critically some of our most cherished philosophical concepts.

## REFERENCES

Braithwaite, R. B., 1953, *Scientific Explanation*, Cambridge, Cambridge University Press.
Cartmill, M., 1980, John Jones's pregnancy: Some comments on the statistical–relevance model of scientific explanation, *American Anthropologist* 82, 382–385.
Dumond, Don E., 1980, The archaeology of Alaska and the peopling of America, *Science* 209, 984–991.
Giere, R., 1979, *Understanding Scientific Reasoning*, New York, Holt, Rinehart & Winston.
Grayson, Donald K., 1980, Vicissitudes and overkill: the development of explanations of Pleistocene extinctions, *Advances in Archaeological Method and Theory* 3, 357–403.
Hempel, C. G., 1962a, Deductive–nomological versus statistical explanation, in Feigl, H., and Maxwell, G. (eds.), *Minnesota Studies in the Philosophy of Science* 3, Minneapolis, University of Minnesota Press, 98–169.
Hempel, C. G., 1962b, Explanation in science and in history, in Colodny, R. (ed.), *Frontiers of Science and Philosophy*, Pittsburgh,University of Pittsburgh Press, 7–33.
Hempel, C. G., 1965, *Aspects of Scientific Explanation*. New York, The Free Press.
Hempel, C. G., 1966, *Philosophy of Natural Science*. Englewood Cliffs, N.J., Prentice–Hall.
Hempel, C. G., 1977, *Aspekte wissenschaftlicher Erklärung*. Berlin, Walter de Gruyter.
Hempel, C. G., and Oppenheim, Paul, 1948, Studies in the logic of explanation, *Philosophy of Science* 15, 135–175. (Reprinted in Hempel (1965).)
King, J. L., 1976, Statistical relevance and explanatory classification, *Philosophical Studies* 30, 313–321.
Laplace, P. S., 1951, *A Philosophical Essay on Probabilities*, New York, Dover.
Lehman, H., 1972, Statistical explanation, *Philosphy of Science* 39, 500–506.
Nagel, E., 1961, *The Structure of Science*, New York, Harcourt, Brace and World.
Popper, K. R., 1959, *The Logic of Scientific Discovery*, New York, Basic Books.
Salmon, M. H., and Salmon, W. C., 1979, Alternative models of scientific explanation, *American Anthropologist* 81, 61–74.
Salmon, W. C., 1977, A third dogma of empiricism, in Butts, R., and Hintikka, J. (eds.), *Basic

*Problems in Methodology and Linguistics*, Dordrecht, D. Reidel, 149–166.

Salmon, W. C., 1978, Why ask, "why?"?—an inquiry concerning scientific explanation, *Proceedings and Addresses of the American Philosophical Association* 51, 683–705.

Salmon, W. C., 1980, Probabilistic causality, *Pacific Philosophical Quarterly* 61, 50–74.

Salmon, W. C., 1982, Comets, pollen, and dreams—some reflections on scientific explanation, in McLaughlin, R. (ed.), *What? Where? When? Why?* Dordrecht, R. Reidel.

Salmon, W. C., in press b, Causality: production and propagation, in Asquith, P., and Giere, R. (eds.), *PSA 1980*, 2, East Lansing, Mich. Philosophy of Science Association.

Salmon, W. C., Jeffrey, R., and Greeno, J., 1971, *Statistical Explanation and Statistical Relevance*, Pittsburgh, University of Pittsburgh Press.

Scriven, M., 1975, Causation as explanation, *Nous* 9, 3–16.

Suppes, P., 1970, *A Probabilistic Theory of Causality*, Amsterdam, North–Holland.

Wright, L., 1976, *Teleological Explanations*, Berkeley, University of California Press.

# 5

# Probabilities for Explanation

*D. H. MELLOR*

I agree with Professor Salmon that the explanations he cites are causal and that they can dispense with determinism. Causal explanations of phenomena need only make them more or less probable, even if at some other (e.g., microscopic) level the phenomena are also in fact determined by "hidden variables." Causal explanation is thus a special kind of statistical explanation, deductive–nomological explanation being simply an extreme case that gives the explained phenomenon a probability of 1. The dearth of deterministic laws in the human sciences generally, and in archaeology in particular, makes this extreme case of little practical interest. And excessive emphasis on it by the "new archaeologists" has only served to discredit the idea of archaeological explanation as being either causal or lawlike. In fact it is both, although the laws may only be statistical, and it is not necessary to specify them in giving causal explanations, so long as the explanation clearly gives the phenomenon to be explained whatever probability is required.

There is of course more to causal explanation than probability, but I shall not discuss the other requirements, e.g., that causes precede their effects, nor why they matter. I wish only to make two points about the probabilities involved: one about the *kind* of probability, the other about the *level* of probability, that causal explanation demands.

Explanatory probabilities must be objective. There is a subjective theory of probability, which treats it merely as a measure of how confident people are of

**57**

THEORY AND EXPLANATION
IN ARCHAEOLOGY

whatever they think probable, but that theory is clearly inadequate to this application. It is not the business of explanation to make us more, or less, confident that the phenomenon to be explained has occurred. Usually we were already quite confident about that, and in looking for an explanation we are not looking to have our degree of confidence in it increased, or reduced, or confirmed. In explanation we are not concerned, as subjective probability is, with establishing to our satisfaction that the phenomenon to be explained has actually occurred. The idea that we are is the widespread misconception of explanation as a kind of argument or inference, a misconception that Salmon has notably and rightly combated.

By the same token, however, not all objective probabilities are explanatory. In particular, merely inductive probabilities are not. However objective they may be, merely inductive probabilities are still only measures of confidence: not of how confident we would be, but how confident we *ought* to be, of the occurrence of the phenomenon to be explained if all we knew was the proposed explanation of it. That is not at all what explanation is about.

The quickest way to see how merely inductive probabilities differ from the probabilities causation needs, without going too far into current philosophical controversy about probability, is by means of a simple instance of probabilistic decision making. Suppose the statistics suggested probabilities of .4 and .1, respectively, for smokers and nonsmokers getting cancer, and that (in some suitable units) I attach relative utilities of 10, 9, −10, and −11, respectively, to not getting cancer with and without smoking, and to getting it with and without smoking. This means in particular that I would prefer to smoke whether I had cancer or not. So the so-called "dominance principle" of decision theory tells me to carry on smoking. But the principle of maximizing my expected utility tells me to quit, since my expected utility if I smoke is 2 $[10 \times .6 - 10 \times .4]$ and if I don't it is 7 $[9 \times .9 - 11 \times .1]$. Which principle should I follow—should I quit, or not?

It all depends on whether the probabilities involved are merely inductive or are what I shall call "causal probabilities." If whether I smoke or not actually *affects my prospects* of getting cancer, the probabilities are causal, and I should quit. But smoking might, for example, be just a statistical symptom of a genetic predisposition to get cancer whether I smoke or not, just as a falling barometer is only a symptom of ensuing rain. All the higher probability of cancer among smokers would show then is that smoking is some evidence for the presence of this predisposition. That is, the probability would be a perfectly good inductive probability, but my giving up smoking would not affect my prospects of getting cancer in the slightest—any more than putting a falling barometer under pressure will stave off rain. So, since I prefer to smoke in any case, I should follow the dominance principle and carry on.

I will *define* causal, as opposed to merely inductive, probabilities as *the objective probabilities that make the principle of maximizing expected utility rational to follow even when it conflicts with the dominance principle.* (I say "as opposed to *merely* inductive" because causal probabilities are inductive all right, i.e., they are a good measure of the confidence one should have in the occurrence of whatever has them. But that is not all they are.) Now it is obvious in the smoking example that probabilities must have this property if they are to support causal explanations. If smoking were only inductive evidence for the presence of incipient cancer, a man's smoking would no more cause or causally explain his getting the disease than a falling barometer causes or causally explains the subsequent rain for which it likewise is inductive evidence. Only if the probabilities of cancer among smokers and nonsmokers are causal in the sense just defined can a smoker's habit properly be said to cause or causally explain his getting cancer.

Now when searching for probabilistic causal explanations, one cannot expect to read the relevant probabilities straight off the statistics, in this case the proportions of actual smokers and nonsmokers getting this or that disease in some limited population. A correlation might be a freak statistical accident in a small population. Even in a large one, the statistics might just reflect inductive probabilities. Or they might be a mixture of inductive and causal probabilities, with different sorts of smokers having different causal probabilities of getting cancer. Here, as in the interpretation of statistics in archaeological examples, it is by no means straightforward to extract whatever causal probabilities there may be. Basically, it demands a theory to suggest possible causal mechanisms and means whereby their presence or absence can be tested for. That is a complex subject that I cannot embark on here: I only want to emphasize that it takes more than a statistical correlation to show the presence of causal probability. What more it takes is well illustrated in the successive reports on smoking and health put out by the Royal College of Physicians. The tobacco companies' objections to a causal interpretation of the statistics are certainly untenable now; but while there was only a correlation to go on, they had a case.

As in this simple and familiar case, so mutatis mutandis in the archaeological and other cases cited by Salmon. The explanatory force of the statistics appealed to rests in every case on the probabilities involved being causal rather than merely inductive, as a little reflection will reveal. Take the climatic explanation of Pleistocene extinction. The relative probabilities of survival of species in different climates must be taken to be causal for this to be an explanation. That is, by definition, it must be rational for an agent with a sufficient interest in wiping the species out and able to control the climate to alter it to do so, even though he would himself prefer a milder climate, whether the species survived or not. It must not for example be that extinction and climate are alike merely statistical effects of some independent cause, as rain and a falling barometer are of a lowering of atmospheric pressure. For then there would be no more point in altering the climate to wipe out the species than there is in trying to prevent rain by pressurizing a barometer; so the altered climate would no more explain species extinction than a rising barometer explains sunshine.

Which brings me to the second point I want to make—about the *level* of causal probability required for causal explanation. The phenomenon to be explained must be made more probable by the factors cited to explain it than in the circumstances it would have been had they not obtained. I need to make this point and to defend it because in the course of developing his statistical–relevance model of explanation Salmon was led to deny it, and the increasing influence of his model among archaeologists may mislead them on the matter. In particular, since the point is both true and important, I should not like Salmon's denial of it to discredit probabilistic theories of causal explanation and inhibit their acceptance by theoretical archaeologists.

Now I do not dispute the considerations that led Salmon (e.g., Salmon *et al.* 1971) to deny that causes must raise the probability of their effects. I merely think he was misled by them. First, he rightly observed that Hempel's reason for demanding high probability in statistical explanation—namely that high probability of the conclusion is a self-evident virtue in statistical inference— is no reason at all, because explanation is not a kind of inference. Just because the phenomenon to be explained would be more safely predictable if it were more probable doesn't mean it would therefore also be better explained.

But disposing of a bad reason for requiring causes to raise their effects' probabilities does not dispose of the requirement itself. Salmon, however, also has a positive reason for denying it. This is his observation that probabilities used in causal explanation must be relative to all statistically relevant causal factors (at the level of explanation involved—excluding for instance possible microscopic causes). A statistically relevant factor is one that affects the causal probability either way, whether raising or lowering it, and of course Salmon is right to insist that causal probabilities must be relative to all such factors. That is a precondition of the probabilities concerned being causal in the first place, rather than merely inductive. It is no use trying to raise the probability, and so beef up the explanation, of someone's getting cancer by suppressing the fact that he never smoked.

But this precondition, that causal probabilities must be relative to all relevant causal factors, does not mean that all causal probabilities provide equally good causal explanations. If it did, it would mean that a probabilistic causal explanation of a phenomenon occurring would serve just as well to explain its nonoccurrence, which is absurd. Someone's smoking would have to be as good an explanation of his not getting cancer as it is of his getting it, which it is not. Climatic changes that make the survival of a species less likely would have to be as good explanations of its survival as of its extinction, which they aren't. Take any of the examples Salmon cites, or any others seriously considered in archaeology or anywhere else. To practitioners not already brainwashed by the statistical–relevance model it will be quite plain that their acceptability as explanations depends on the causal factors they cite being not only statistically relevant but (in Salmon's terminology) positively relevant.

I suppose Salmon might protest here that our intuitions about this have been distorted by years of exposure to the Hempelian misconception of explanation as inference and need to be retrained. I doubt it: I reckon the intuition that causes need to raise their effects' probabilities predates Hempel and will be found flourishing among scientists who have never exposed themselves to contamination by the philosophy of science. But however that may be, Salmon would also remark at this stage that since improbable events are bound to occur occasionally, and their low causal probability nonetheless provides as good an explanation of them as there is, my requirement condemns some events to being absolutely inexplicable. So it does, and so they are . Of course, the fact that very improbable events occur from time to time is entirely explicable, since it is very probable that they will. But to the extent that each individual event is improbable, its occurrence remains unexplained. The fact that the proposed explanation is as good as there is does not mean that it is good enough, i.e., good enough to satisfy the original desire to know why the event occurred rather than not. Making hell inescapable does not make it heaven, and I see no a priori reason to expect the universe to scratch our every itch to understand it.

It may be tempting to conclude at this point that Salmon and I are quibbling as to which of two marginally different concepts has the better right to the title *explanation*—a terminological squabble of no serious interest to archaeologists or anyone else. The temptation should, however, be resisted for three reasons, of which the second especially has immediate application to a proper understanding of archaeological method. And although the first may seem rather abstract, it is worth mentioning because it helps to explain what may have appeared a bizarre invocation of decision theory to characterize causal probabilities.

What makes decision theory pertinent is that human action is the very paradigm of causation: Whatever else causation is, it is the mechanism that links the bodily movements we directly perform to other events and states of affairs we act, for whatever reasons, to influence or bring about. I do not mean that causation depends on human action—there could be plenty of causation in a world wholly devoid of agency—merely that our concept of causation has inter alia to make sense of action, including human action, as a phenomenon of the natural world. And that means in particular that it must always make sense to act in order to bring about an effect of that action. But only if causes make their effects more probable than in the circumstances they would otherwise have been will that be so, since otherwise the action would not make the effect desired more likely to occur.

This principle may be put in decision theory terms as follows. The effect of an action is the outcome of it that, if most desired, makes that action maximize expected utility when the action itself has no intrinsic utility, i.e., when the utilities of the outcomes are the same whether the action is performed or not, so that it must be done entirely for the sake of its effects. Suppose for example that smoking as an activity has no intrinsic utility for me in this sense, so that I must base my decision whether to go on smoking entirely on the utilities I attach to outcomes such as getting or not getting cancer. Then because as things are the probability of cancer is greater if I smoke than if I don't, maximizing my expected utility in this case means smoking if I would prefer to get cancer, and not smoking if I prefer not to. That makes cancer an effect of smoking and noncancer an effect of not smoking, and it does so because my smoking raises the causal probability of my getting cancer above the level it would have if I didn't smoke.

That is the fundamental reason causes have to raise their effects' probabilities, to make sense of causation's being the mechanism of action. But there is another reason as well, of more immediate interest to archaeologists, namely to make sense of their applications of the principle of inference to the best explanation. This is the principle that data that could be explained by several incompatible hypotheses give reason (*ceteris paribus*) to accept the hypothesis that would if true explain the data best. I cannot go here into the rationale, force, and limitations of this principle, but appeals to it occur all the time in everyday life, in law, in history, and in sciences and technologies, both natural and human. Archaeologists especially should be aware of it, since it provides their main reason for being interested in explanation in the first place. Very little of the archaeological record, after all, is interesting enough to be worth explaining for its own sake. Most archaeologists are prehistorians, interested in the record chiefly as evidence for the prehistoric happenings that caused it. They look for good prehistoric explanations of it because the better the explanation would be if it were true, the more likely it is to be true, other things being equal.

But how, in order to apply this principle, does one assess the comparative quality of putative causal explanations? Clearly there are many factors—simplicity, for one—that I cannot go into here. But there is also the causal probability that a proposed prehistoric explanation would, if true, bestow on the archaeological data it explains. The higher that is, other things being more or less equal, the more likely the explanation is to be the true one, i.e., the higher its *inductive* probability relative to the data it purports to explain. That is the so-called "maximum likelihood" principle of statistical inference. Now, is this principle really entirely independent of the principle of inference to the best explanation, as it would have to be if the level of causal probability supplied by causal explanations made no difference to their quality as explanations? If so, assessments of prehistoric hypotheses as prospective explanations, and by how probable they would if true make the data, must be entirely separate processes leading, if they conflict, to a further process of adjudication between them. And obviously they are nothing of the sort. Comparing the causal probabilities rival prehistoric hypotheses invest the archaeological record with is all part of finding out how good they would be as explanations if they were true: The higher the probability, the better the explanation, and so the more likely it is to be true.

The best possible causal explanation then is one that inter alia raises the causal probability as far as it can go, namely to 1. That is, it is a deterministic causal explanation conforming to the deductive–nomological model. And that is my final reason for requiring causes to raise the probability of their effects. It explains, what is otherwise a complete mystery, why we would obviously always prefer a deterministic explanation (other things being equal) if we could get it—so obviously that until the pioneering work of Salmon and others, indeterministic causal explanation was, as he says, thought to be a contradiction in terms. But in showing that it isn't, it is important not to get carried away and weaken the concept of causation so much that the appeal of deterministic causal explanation is lost sight of, the principle of inference to the best explanation mysteriously separated from the maximum likelihood principle, and the rationale destroyed of acting for the sake of the action's effects. That cannot be right, and it is in no way necessary to a probabilistic theory of causal explanation.

## REFERENCES

Jeffrey, R. C., 1980, How is it reasonable to base preferences on estimates of chance?, in Mellor, D. H. (ed.), *Science, Belief and Behaviour*, Cambridge, Cambridge University Press, 179–187.

Mellor, D. H., 1976, Probable explanation, *Australasian Journal of Philosophy* 54, 231–41.

Salmon, W. C., Jeffrey, R., and Greeno, J., 1971, *Statistical Explanation and Statistical Relevance*, Pittsburgh, University of Pittsburgh Press.

# 6

# Archaeological Explanation: Progress through Criticism

*JIM BELL*

There is an expanding interest in the scientific status of archaeological explanations. Science, at least physical science, is considered the paradigm of empirical knowledge. Formulating theories in accordance with the criteria of the physical sciences has thus become a major objective in archaeology. This is a mixed blessing, in my view. It seems beneficial if it leads to improved solutions to old problems or radically new solutions to old problems or even to new problems. On the other hand, the numerous and inconsistent views of good science are confusing enough to physical scientists and even more so to social scientists. One or some combination of the various interpretations of scientific method must be selected. That method must also be applied correctly to explanations. Furthermore, the desire to be scientific can become so dominant that work on important problems is relinquished if they do not seem amenable to scientific analysis. Trivial problems that do seem open to scientific investigation can steal the show. This last danger always lurks behind the scenes, and especially in the social sciences.

Despite these problems, are there signposts that are beneficial to archaeologists who are trying to improve their explanations by making them scientific? I believe there are. The path may lead across some potholes, but it should skirt the land mines. Controversy surrounds some of the recommendations. The pros and cons should become evident in this and other chapters in this book.

THEORY AND EXPLANATION
IN ARCHAEOLOGY

**65**

## CRITICIZABLE THEORIES

The preliminary comments (to be discussed first) will be followed by a section on the physical sciences, which will provide a framework for an analogous section on archaeological explanation. The conclusion will summarize the main points and give bibliographical references.

By now it is commonly accepted that identifying weak points in explanations is valuable for improving them or replacing them by different explanations. Theories ought to be criticizable—open to the risk of being incorrect, incomplete, or inadequate. Weaknesses motivate the search for alternative explanations. They also provide desiderata for progress: A better explanation overcomes at least some of the weak points of a given theory.

The primary role of facts is to help find weak points in theories. A factual test corroborates a theory, if it is correct at test points, or refutes it, if it is mistaken at test points. Showing a theory to be incorrect is the more important of those two alternatives. Although people expounding a theory might be crestfallen, for the advancement of knowledge, discovering weaknesses is irreplaceable.

A scientific theory should *not* be perfect. It should be open to error. In this view, science is *not* truth, but movement toward the truth by superseding error. The history of science is interpreted as a succession of false theories replaced by other false, but better, theories. It is hoped that the future of science will be an extrapolation of the same process.

Scientific theories should be formulated such that they are prone to error. Theories without possible weakensses are often too vague, and they make it tempting to turn anomalies into confirmations. Furthermore, there are popular views of science that endorse techniques to ward off criticism or diminish its bite. One technique is to limit the range over which a theory is to apply. Another is to use purely correlative relations and a probabilistic convention for the acceptance of them. Such qualities of theories or strategems of method are highly undesirable.

It is time to make my philosophical "colors" explicit. The view of science and scientific method recommended here is close in hue to *refutationism*—the method of conjectures and refutations. Refutationism was systematically formulated by Sir Karl Popper in his *Logik der Forschung* (1932; published in English as *The Logic of Scientific Discovery* in 1959). Popper exhorts scientists to work on significant problems, even if difficult and baffling, rather than on trivial but easy problems. Proposed solutions to problems are not ends in themselves, but should contain theories that are testable—refutable—and hence improvable. Refutationists are not just interested in science and the types of theories that will lead to progress there. Similar techniques and the same attitude should be applied to all types of explanations in all fields. It is recognized that there are many important problems, the proposed solutions to which do not contain clearly refutable theories. This is true in the physical sciences, social science, and many other areas, such as in personal ethics, social theory, and so forth. Nevertheless, a critical spirit should reign: One's eye ought to be focused principally on the weakness in explanations, and those weaknesses should be exploited for progress.

## REFUTABLE THEORIES IN THE PHYSICAL SCIENCES

A salient logical property of theories in the physical sciences is vulnerability to error. Theories can be interpreted in such a way that some conceivable statement(s) of fact could refute them. After testing, they can be regarded as corroborated at those point(s) where fact(s) show them right, but where they risked being wrong. Theories can be considered falsified when tested and shown to be incorrect. There are two basic reasons why theories should be refutable. First, they become empirical at those points where they risk being wrong but turn out to be right. Second, erroneous point(s) provide desiderata for improvement and motivate the search for alternative explanations. At least some failure point(s) ought to be corroboration point(s) for a modified theory or a new theory. Some crucial guides for generating refutable theories in the physical sciences are outlined in what follows.

Refutability of theories is enhanced by formulating causal explanations. Causal explanations can be interpreted as universal statements—statements such as "whenever $x$ happens, so will $y$"—and these statments, because of their universality, leave their flanks most open to potential conflict with the facts.

Unlike causal relations, purely correlative relations are normally confined to application over a given range of data and, if they are also statistical, allow for improbable but possible exceptions. Both factors tend to weaken, rather than increase, the refutability of theories. Putting boundaries on the application of a correlation excludes potentially refuting facts, and statistical allowance of exceptions can permit refutations to be acceptable. Correlations may be helpful by suggesting possible causal explanations, but it is not desirable to allow them to substitute for causal explanations.

In the physical sciences, mathematical formulations of theories can increase refutability. They give theories more precision and hence make them more refutable. They can also trace the implications of theories, by deduction, into areas not readily apparent and thus expose theories to more potential refuters. It is very important to remember, though, that the mathematization of theories does not in itself guarantee refutability. Statistical correlations provide a good example. They can be very complex mathematically, yet be very weakly refutable, if refutable at all, for the reasons previously discussed. Identifying science with sophisticated mathematics is unfortunate when it disregards the functions of math.

Despite the experimental precision sometimes achieved when testing theories, physical scientists must make many interpretative decisions about their theories, background assumptions, and experiments. If an experiment yields what seem to be refuting facts, should it be considered veridical? It can be repeated, but the question will still have to be answered by making a decision. Further, if a refuting experiment is considered veridical, then what is refuted? Theories are complex, and in simplest form can be considered as a long string of conjuncted statements. But which of the statment(s) is to be regarded as mistaken? Should auxiliary hypotheses be added to explain away possible error if it is decided that the theory is itself correct? If so, it may be difficult to avoid an ad hoc reformulation. Perhaps there are mistaken assumptions in the background. If so, how can those assumptions be tested?

These types of questions force many conventional decisions on physical scientists. Elements of subjectivity cannot be avoided. Throughout the morass of these decisions, however, when scientists must use their noses as well as their intellects, there is a guiding light—a critical attitude. Its role is of paramount importance.

With a critical attitude, one views all theories, background assumptions, and experimental input as tentative, and hence open to possible change and even rejection. This attitude also implies that alternative explanations always should be seriously entertained, an extremely important point.

One reason for considereing alternative explanations is that they are candidates for replacing present theories. If not given a thorough hearing, a potentially fruitful new explanation might be lost. I emphasize that any and all alternative explanations ought to be honestly explored, regardless of whether they are acceptable by scientific standards or not. Let me explain.

It is commonly believed that all important debates over competing theories in the physical sciences involve clearly testable explanations and that the debates can be decided on the basis of tests. This is not the case. Some of the most significant controversies in the history of physical science have been over theories that were not testable or became testable only after the debate had been completed. One example revolved about the differences between Newtonians and Leibnizians concerning the nature of forces and matter. Newton's universe was made of atoms and empty space. A serious problem for Newton, his proponents, and his critics was to explain how a force like gravity could act through space. Leibniz's views did provide an answer. For him the universe was constituted of forces. They were everywhere and everything. "Matter" is a more concentrated force: It is a force that resists. There were no clear tests that could decide between these two views. Newton did prevail—his physics had captured the day after all. But ultimately Leibnizian force fields took over, first with the development of electrical theory and then with the establishment of Einstein's relativity theories.

The Newton–Leibniz controversy was metaphysical. If Newtonians and/or Leibnizians had attempted to argue only clearly testable theories, there would have been no debate. One of the most significant and fruitful exchanges in the history of the physical sciences would not have occurred.

Another reason for considering alternative theories of all sorts is that they help one see the errors and inadequacies in other explanations. Weaknesses are especially difficult to recognize in established theories. It is not important whether another explanation is strong or weak, acceptable or unacceptable. If it sheds light on weaknesses of alternatives, it has served a very important function.

Before moving on, a brief summary is in order. The refutationist veiw of science and the refutationist method have been presented and supported. Science is viewed here as a continuous replacement of false theories by other false, but better, theories. The most important quality of scientific explanations is that they are vulnerable to error, which is essential for progress. A finished, "true" theory is not desirable. Vulnerability to error is enhanced by postulating causal explanations. Strategems that tend to weaken vulnerability, such as setting boundary conditions or using statistical conventions, are to be avoided. Finally a critical attitude is crucial. It requires concentration on weaknesses in theories, which implies that one be open to all alternative explanations. Alternative explanations might eventually become established, but even if not, they may illuminate weaknesses in competing explanations.

## CRITICIZABLE EXPLANATIONS IN ARCHAEOLOGY

Explanations in archaeolgy normally contain human variables that make testing for error more difficult than in the physical sciences. Archaeological explanations are focused on past societies, and while many tests can be made retrodictively, repeating them under both similar and different conditions is not always possible. Values and beliefs, which are very significant motivating factors among humans, also render many explanations less accessible to empirical testing. Add these factors to the considerable number of subjective elements and conventional decisions necessary for evaluating theories in the physical sciences, and it might seem that to pinpoint weaknesses in archaeological theories would be to expect the impossible. When compared to the physical sciences, however, differences in searching out and exploiting lacunae seem to me much less important than the similarities. Criticizing theories and improving them in archaeology need not be distant in technique or spirit from the physical sciences.

I first want to consider what is diversionary and harmful. It is counterproductive to be compulsively "scientific." If, in the name of "science," time and energy are drained away from considering the most interesting problems or from considering insightful but "nonscientific" theories as possible solutions to those problems, then one is being inconsistent with good science. As in the physical sciences, many significant explanations will not be readily refutable, and many important problems may not be amenable to analysis according to some preconceived view.

Lack of clarity about the problem(s) to be resolved by explanations is also a detriment. It seems obvious that problems should be lucidly conceived. They are not always well formulated, however. The result is confusion concerning the function for which explanations are to serve. If the function(s) of explanations are not clear, evaluating them for weaknesses is difficult, as is comparing them with alternative explanations.

Clarifying problems is not always easy. But effort spent honing them is always worthwhile and usually results in either sobering or exciting surprises. Sometimes one discovers that there is no clear problem. Energy can then be directed elsewhere. At other times the problem that was thought to be significant is really quite trivial, but an important problem is discovered underneath. Attention can then be focused on that problem. On other occasions two or more problems will be found conflated together. Separating them will normally be productive. The reverse also occurs. What was thought to be separate problems turns out to be the same problem. Reducing them to one is usually fruitful.

As preliminaries, then, do not be preoccupied with the scientific status of explanations, but do be meticulous about clarifying the problem(s) for which they are to function. Now let me turn to some rules of thumb that should help in making archaeological explanations more criticizable.

As in the physical sciences. it is better to conjecture causal explanations than be satisfied with correlating data, except where correlations shed light on causal explanations. The reasons are the same as for searching out causal explanations in the physical sciences. Causal explanations can be interpreted as universal statements and can be exposed to many potential errors. Furthermore, causal explanations can include value parameters—they are not limited to physical or measurable parameters. Value mechanisms can sometimes even be quantified, and can become part of a multicausal explanation consisting of both physical and value inputs (see Bell 1981).

Correlations are not a desirable substitute for causal explanations. Data correlations are usually expressed statistically, and acceptance is normally judged by a convention, such as the 95% rule. The trouble is that statistical correlations allow for improbable, but possible, counterevidence. Instead of regarding such anomalies as serious weaknesses, an explanation can be considered sound. There is no obligation to search for alternatives. An opportunity for progress can be lost. Even if a correlation is not expressed statisitically, boundary conditions on the data range can have a similar effect: Anomalous input can be excluded, blunting the force of error and crippling the search for alternative explanations.

In the section on the physical sciences it was argued that mathematizing an explanation can be helpful in tracing its implications and in rendering it more precise. Both factors make an explanation more vulnerable to error, in the former case by finding new and sometimes distant points to test, and in the latter case by making the tests more exacting. Explanations in archaeology are not generally as accessible to quantifications as in the physical sciences. This is certainly reason to be even more careful about the function to be served by math, but it is advisable to use mathematics whenever it can help put theories to more tests, or more demanding tests.

For example, if a theory about the spiritual beliefs of a past society, along with other factors, implies that the size and/or elegance of religious artifacts should increase substantially over a given period, and they do not, then a rather straightforward analysis of the archaeological evidence would be helpful in finding weaknesses in the theory. Very little formalization would be needed. It is only necessary to do enough to test the theory against the record. Another example. Suppose a theory about ritual organization in temples implies a precise geometrical arrangement of religious symbols. One might in such a case generate a highly formalized mathematical model of the theory and then check for weaknesses against the archaeological data in the temples. Here, the precision of the ritual theory rendered it much more vulnerable to error than the theory in the prior example. A discrepancy of a few degrees in the position of a figure might be at odds with the theory.

Both examples above are caricatures, to be sure. An archaeologist in the process of formulting, testing, and evaluating theories would have to devote much attention (as would a physical scientist) to the factual record and to background assumptions. In any case, however, he or she should be very clear as to how any mathematical formulas are to function. They should be used to help find possible weaknesses in theories. If mathematics is employed so that an explanation only can be confirmed without running the risk of error, then the mathematics may obscure rather than help.

Finally, it is the critical attitude held toward explanations and not just the logical properties of explanations that is all important in recognizing weaknesses and exploiting them for progress. This attitude serves the same purposes and provides the same guidelines in archaeology as in the physical sciences. First, keep an open mind to all possible explantions. Consider them seriously. Even if alternative explanations seem ridiculous, they may highlight weaknesses in even the most acceptable explanations. Further, one never knows if an alternative theory might actually replace a present theory. Second, focus on the weaknesses of theories rather than on the strengths. Remember that tests that might reveal flaws are the most important for progress. Third, when weak points in theories are found, try not to "ad hoc" them by turning the weaknesses into confirmations. Take anomalies seriously. Do not be so attached to an explanation that lacunae are treated flippantly or even ignored. Fourth and finally, remember that more progressive explanations should account for at least some weaknesses of competing theories. Even if new theories are assessed and considered preferable, explore them with the same critical attitude so that progress can continue.

## CONCLUSION

Most archaeologists want their explanations to meet scientific standards. In turning to philosophers of science for standards, however, they have received a set of inconsistent views. The mixed signals were inevitable. There are numerous and sometimes sharply contrasting theories about the nature of science and the standards by which explanations are to be assessed (see Bell and Bell 1980, 3–22, and Popper 1963, 97–119). In this chapter I have outlined and argued for a version of the refutationist view of science. According to it the goal is progress. Its method is aimed at formulating vulnerable theories, searching out the weaknesses, and then exploiting them for improvement. The appropriate attitude is the critical one, an attitude that encourages admission of error and discourages defensive strategies in face of it. If the refutationist view of science has perked your interests I have listed here several sources with which to launch further exploration.

1. Karl R. Popper: *The Logic of Scientific Discovery.* This is an English translation of Popper's systematic formulation of the refutationist view. The original German edition was published in 1933. At times it is complicated, but almost always clear. For a thorough understanding of refutationist method and the arguments supporting it, this is *the* book.
2. Karl R. Popper: *Conjectures and Refutations.* This collection of papers by Popper includes discussions of the refutationist view of science, its implications for scientific communities, and its place in the theory of knowledge. There are essays devoted to the implications of the refutationist method on social and political theory. Some essays focus on the history of the scientific method and Popper's own life.
3. Paul Schilpp (ed.): *The Philosophy of Karl Popper.* The two volumes composing this work begin with an intellectual autobiography of Popper. The remainder consists of essays written by prominent supporters and critics of refutationism, with rejoining comments by Popper.

## REFERENCES

Bell, J. A., and Bell, J. F., 1980, System dynamics and scientific method, in Randers, J. (ed.), *Elements of the System Dynamic Method,* Cambridge, Mass., M.I.T. Press.

Bell, J. A., and Senge, P. M., 1980, Methods for enhancing refutability in system dynamics modeling, in Legasto, A. A. (ed.), *Studies in the Management Sciences* (Vol. 14: *System Dynamics*), New York, North–Holland.

Bell, J. A., 1981, Scientific method and simulation modeling, in Sabloff, J. (ed.), *Simulations in Archaeology,* Albuquerque, University of New Mexico Press.

*Popper, K. R., 1959, The Logic of Scientific Discovery,* New York, Harper and Row.

Popper, K. R., 1963, *Conjectures and Refutations,* New York, Harper and Row.

Schilpp, P. A., (ed.), 1974, *The Philosophy of Karl Popper,* LaSalle, Ill., Open Court.

# 7

## Explanation in Archaeology[1]

*BRUCE D. SMITH*

In their impatient search for a logical model of explanation, a number of archaeologists managed to stumble upon, and subsequently champion, the deductive–nomological model of Carl Hempel. This was unfortunate, since Hempel's D–N model is clearly not appropriate for archaeology. I think that even the most hard-line of the Hempelian archaeologist "Imams" will now begrudgingly acknowledge that no universal archaeological laws have been documented. Since Hempel's D–N model requires at least one such universal law per explanation, it simply will not work in archaeology. A second unfortunate aspect of these misguided attempts to sell Hempel to archaeologists involved the condescending and confused nature of the sales pitch, which understandably alienated a large percentage of the potential audience. There is in fact a persistent, lingering distaste on the part of many archaeologists for any form of logical model of explanation or any mention of laws or lawlike statements. This widespread aversion for logical models and laws is all the more disturbing because, while it is possible to rule out those logical models that require universal laws, it is at the same time apparent that laws of some sort are a necessary ingredient in any explanatory model that is to be acceptable in terms of logical structure.

[1]Support for participation in the second conference of the Theoretical Archeology Group and the writing of this chapter was provided by a Smithsonian Institution Fluid Research Award.

THEORY AND EXPLANATION
IN ARCHAEOLOGY

Judging from the characterization of laws and lawlike statments recently provided by Salmon and Salmon (1979, 62–63), however, this need for laws does not represent the serious and mysterious burden that a number of archaeologists have described. A law, according to the Salmons, is simply a statement of regularity concerning the observed "linkage" or cooccurrence of an event and the circumstances surrounding that event. If such an event and its surrounding circumstances always cooccur, are always linked, then the statement of regularity is a universal law. If the cooccurrence of the event and its surrounding circumstances is anything less than 100%, the statement describing their linkage is a statistical or probabilistic law. Statistical or probabilistic laws do not necessarily have to be expressed in terms of numerical percentages—it is acceptable to use rather unspecific phrases such as "more likely," "normally," or "frequently" in characterizing or presenting statistical laws (Salmon and Salmon 1979, 67). If such statements of regularity, either universal or probabilistic, cannot be certified and stamped as being true, and they often can't, then they are referred to as "lawlike statements" rather than laws.

One of the most basic and automatic activities carried out by archaeologists involves the search for, and recognition of, patterns in the archaeological record—regularities in the spatial cooccurrence of tool types, for example, or regularities in the temporal cooccurrence of designs on ceramics. It would thus appear that archaeologists have been intent on discovering and documenting statistical lawlike statements pertaining to the archaeological record for over 100 years.

Taking the Salmons' clear and straightforward description of laws into consideration, it is evident that archaeological explanation will continue to involve "statistical lawlike generalizations," and that the attachment in effect of this descriptive label to a long established archaeological practice will not be at all difficult for archaeologists to accept. All that has been needed, really, is a statement like the one recently provided by the Salmons—clear, concise, and devoid of the convoluted heavy-jargon overtones that shroud the various archaeoprophetic pronouncements on the subject.

In addition to providing archaeologists with a much needed clarification of the role of laws and lawlike statements in explanation, the Salmons have also proposed the statistical–relevance model of explanation as being more appropriate for archaeology than either Meehan's "systems approach" (Meehan 1968) or Hempel's covering-law models (Salmon and Salmon 1979, 67). Constructed by Wesley Salmon (Salmon *et al.* 1971) to overcome a fundamental logical difficulty in the D–N and I–S (inductive–statistical) models, the S–R model is based on the idea that the explanatory facts or surrounding cicumstances should make a difference to the occurrence or nonoccurrence of the event to be explained, rather than making the event highly probable, as in the D–N and I–S models. More specifically, Salmon and Salmon state (1979, 69):

According to the statistical–relevance model of scientific explanation, *an explanation is an assemblage of factors that are statistically relevant to the occurrence of the event to be explained,* accompanied by an associated probability distribution.

Thus, under the S–R model, an event is "explained" through the controlled comparison of those situations along with their surrounding circumstances in which the event occurs, on the one hand, and those situations along with their surrounding cicumstances in which the event does not occur. The explanatory facts are those that *"make a difference* to the occurrence or nonoccurrence of the event to be explained" (Salmon and Salmon 1979, 68).

This S–R definition of what constitutes an explanation is appealing because it is simple and logically straightforward. An S–R explanation does not entail a logical argument format. It avoids the problems of irrelevance associated with the D–N and I–S models. It can accommodate events with a low statistical probability, since it is based on observed differences between controlled comparison situations. A final advantage of the S–R model that the Salmons have quite correctly identified as being of great importance to archaeologists is its ability to accommodate situations of functional equivalence—where the same event or result can be functionally linked to different surrounding circumstances in different situations. The S–R model of scientific explanation should also be appealing to archaeologists for yet another reason—it should sound quite familiar.

Archaeologists seek out and document repeated patterns of cooccurrence in prehistoric material culture. This activity appears to constitute the formulation of statistical lawlike statements. This process of observing, describing, and comparing different situations of patterned cooccurrence and non-cooccurrence of artifact types, design motifs, etc., also qualifies as "explaining" each of the component parts of such patterns in terms of the other "surrounding" cooccurring components.

It is important to emphasize at this point that such an "internal artifact-based explanation," even though appearing to conform to the S–R model of explanation, would not constitute, in and of itself, a fully satisfactory scientific explanation. This is because S–R explanations in general suffer from causal insufficiency (Salmon and Salmon 1979, 71):

> Although we believe that the S–R model of explanation has certain virtues, we do not believe it can provide a fully adequate account of scientific explanation. In order to have any hope of achieving a satisfactory treatment of this notion, we must supplement the concept of statistical relevance with some kinds of causal considerations.

If the foregoing is in fact an accurate and correct characterization of the S–R model, it leads to a number of interesting conclusions. First, quite a few of the "new-wave" and "punk-rock" archaeologists will rise in indignant outrage: "This is ludicrous," they will say. "You can't explain patterning in the archaeological record in terms of the artifacts themselves—why that's what archeologists were doing back in the 1930s." Back in the 1930s—what a frightening revelation! Can it possibly be true that those crusty old fogeys with their burned out normative paradigm, their Midwest taxonomic system and their disgusting trait lists, were actually operating under the statistical–relevance model of scientific explanation? Although I am sure that contrasting viewpoints will be presented, I would argue that much of the pre-1960s archaeology in the United States will fit very comfortably into the S–R model of explanation, even though the model was not formally described until the 1970s. I certainly invite the Salmons and other interested philosophers of science to look over some of this archaeology of the not too distant past, because I have the feeling that some rewriting of the "new-arch" or "arch-bark" gospel is in order. It will indeed be ironic if the "traditionalist" archaeology of the pre-1960s, so viciously attacked as being unscientific and inductive, turns out to have been operating under a model of scientific explanation that was, in terms of logical form or structure, clearly superior (if admittedly incomplete) to the "more scientific" deductive models proposed to take its place.

Such noncausal explanations have a number of attractive attributes. First, it appears that the S–R model of explanation can accommodate noncausal archaeological–material culture cooccurrence explanations. So noncausal archaeological explanation of this type has a satisfactory if incomplete framework in terms of logical form. Second, the demands made on the archaeological data base by this type of explanation are not beyond its capabilities. This kind of archaeological explanation can be done. Archaeologists have in fact been doing it for quite some time and are becoming better and better at it everyday. On the negative side, this kind of noncausal explanation is in some quarters of the discipline viewed as being "blue-collar dull and boring," and oh, so pedestrian. This condescending attitude of smug derision has unfortunately limited to a surprising degree the opportunities for material–culture explanationists to attain the trappings of success in our field. It is clearly more advantageous at the present time, in terms of short-term career goals, to talk about causal explanation even if you can't deliver, than to limit yourself to explanations of the noncausal type.

It is important to remember, however, that such carefully detailed descriptions of patterning in the archaeological record and their inherent explanations are a necessary prerequisite to any successful attempts at causal explanation. The degree to which any archaeologist can hope to eventually construct a causal model of explanation that necessarily must link patterns of human behavior and patterns in recovered material cultural assemblages will in part depend on her or his ability to discern and extract patterns of information from those scattered bits and pieces of garbage that constitute our data base.

In turning to a consideration of the *pro's* and *con's* of causal explanation, I should first emphasize that I am not against efforts to construct such causal frameworks in archaeology. I freely admit, in fact, that I am one of the eager fluttering moths trying to touch the elusive causal flame. What I do object to are the cavalier and obviously inept attempts at causal explanation that have been produced. We can do better than "just-so" stories.

The most obvious attraction of causal explanation involves the intrinsic human drive to understand, to comprehend in some manner the reason, the cause, for observed events—both prehistoric and present day. Noncausal explanations just do not satisfy this need. At the same time, to state the obvious, such causal explanations in archaeology represent the ultimate in available puzzles. Because very few satisfying causal models have been constructed, this makes the challenge even more fascinating and irresistible.

The fact that convincing causal explanations have in most part so far eluded even the best of the discipline's puzzle-solvers and storytellers makes the challenge attractive for another reason. Even the least-gifted member of our discipline can pass the jargon entrance exam and radiate self-importance as he or she joins the game, secure in the knowledge that he or she is not doing that much worse than anyone else, and that the game will continue for some time to come.

Causal explanations in archaeology are also attractive because they more obviously involve direct consideration and explanation of human behavior, thus bringing the archaeologist into the same arena as the cultural and social anthropologists, as well as the numerous other behavioral social scientists.

The most obvious negative aspect of attempting causal explanations in archaeology is that we don't seem to have been able to carry it off in any convincing manner. While this is no reason to fold up our tents and withdraw, it is an indication that too much time and effort is being focused on some aspects of the problem, while others are being largely ignored. To be more specific, I think that too much time has been spent in excitedly searching for and describing substantive models of explanation. I think that enough models have already been identified to provide a broad enough spectrum of choice, without having to undiscriminatingly add to the backlog of ones already proposed as having archaeological potential. This is particularly true since very few of these substantive models of explanation have acutally been applied to any archaeological situation. The continuing craze seems only to involve finding such models and speculating about their great potential for providing insight into the prehistoric past, not actually determining their applicability. A particularly disturbing recent trend in the find-yet-another-substantive-model contest involves the apparent misconception that if the models proposed so far have not been successfully applied to archaeological situations, then they must necessarily be inadequate, so let us find others. This has produced an ever-expanding search pattern that has now reached beyond the fringes of the possible into the realms of the bizarre. Within the past year, for example, I have seen substantive models of explanation that likened prehistoric cultural process to the successional sequence of deciduous forest ecosystems, the geomorphological processes of erosion and sedimentation, and the sequential digestive processes of ruminants. Satisfactory models of causal explanation will not of necessity be found only by an ever-expanding random search for substantive principles and theories. They are far more likely to emerge from the difficult and tedious process of overcoming the obvious obstacles that are keeping those substantive models of explanation already in our arsenal from being deployed and successfully used.

First, and probably most importantly, there must be a much more concerted effort on the part of both philosophers and archaeologists to master the structural problems inherent in the logical construction necessary to bridge the gap between causal patterns of human behavior and the resultant patterning in the archaeological record. Without an understanding of how such logical bridges can be constructed and what kinds of substantive models they can be expected to support, little real progress toward causal models can be expected.

In working on such logical bridging-structures, an effort should be made to make them compatible with, and logical supplemental extentions of, the statistical–relevance model of explanation, since the S–R model appears to be the most appropriate logical model to employ in noncausal explanations on the material culture side of the gap.

I might also tentatively propose that, until someone comes up with something better, it would be worthwhile to supplement the S–R model with the hypothetico–analog (H–A) method of bridging this causal gap (Smith 1977).

Second, there is an obvious and serious need for a more accurate and broader understanding of the patterning of human behavior on the one side and material culture on the other that we hope to link through such logical and substantive models of explanation.

Although rapid improvements in recovery techniques and quantitative methods for pattern recognition and description are certainly adding important new depth and detail to our noncausal artifact-based explanations, there is still a long way to go on the archaeological side. The simple question of temporal control, for example, still looms as a major obstacle. Until it is possible to place sites and artifact assemblages within a tighter temporal framework than the 5–10 generation slices most of us still have to work with, we cannot really assume that our observed archaeological patterns are accurate, representative reflections of prehistoric reality that in turn can be used to construct either diachronic or synchronic models.

On the human behavior side of the problem, there is an obvious need for a broader and more detailed descriptive base of human behavior patterns at all levels of specificity, particularly in terms of resultant material culture patterning. I won't belabor this point, since it has been made numerous times over the past 20 years. What has been mentioned much less frequently in the last two decades, however, is the parallel need to develop logical and explicit guidelines for both defining and partitioning appropriate reference classes and for choosing between alternative behavioral analogs. The sin that archaeologists seem to commit most often (at least in print) is the cavalier and careless selection of behavioral analogs to go with observed patterns of material culture.

Under the general heading *causal explanation* in archaeology, two distinct categories of explanatory models can be distinguished. The first of these two categories can be termed *human behavior–material culture* causal explanations. This type of explantion represents a logical extension of *artifact-based noncausal* explanation in that a necessary first step involves documenting patterns in the archaeological record that are identified as explanatory facts or surrounding circumstances of the events to be explained. These patterned explanatory facts in the archaeological record are then linked by logical argument to their corresponding causal human behavior patterns.

This familiar type of causal explanation, discussed briefly in the preceding paragraphs and in more detail in previous publications (Smith 1977, 1978), is commonly attempted in archaeology with varying degrees of specificity and success. Such human behavior–material culture explanations are often constructed to explain a fairly isolated and specific class of events (e.g., Binford's 1967 smudge-pit and hide-smoking explanation). They can be and sometimes are formulated, however, to explain a number of related patterns in the archaeological record, with their causal patterns of human behavior susequently forming a *human behavior noncausal* explanation.

A brief consideration of prehistoric and historically described chiefdoms along with their defining characteristics should serve to clarify what I mean by human behavior noncausal explanations.

Although there is still active debate concerning how best to define chiefdoms and how chiefdoms emerge out of egalitarian-level societies, there is some general agreement concerning the basic attributes of chiefdoms. A number of scholars, including Renfrew (1973), have enumerated and discussed these attributes that characterize chiefdoms.

A human behavior noncausal explanation (within an S–R framework) for a present-day or historically described chiefdom would involve the controlled comparison of cooccurrence of these various attributes or explanatory facts in appropriately partitioned reference classes of ranked and unranked societies.

At least some of these chiefdom attributes, such as the presence of ceremonial centers, high-status élite, craft specialization, and monumental architecture, can be linked through human behavior–material culture explanations to specific correlate patterns in the archaeological record. In this manner, archaeological chiefdoms can join their more recent counterparts and be explained in terms of a human behavior noncausal model.

The second category of causal explanation in archeology can be termed *human behavior causal* explanation, and it is a logical extension of human behavior noncausal explanatory models. This category of causal explanation involves taking the various attributes or explanatory facts identified and described in a human behavior noncausal explanation and arranging them in a causal sequence or network (e.g., arranging the attributes of a chiefdom into a model that describes chiefdom emergence).

Satisfactory high-probability explanations of this type appear to be quite often out of reach of archaeologists at the present time unless they are dealing with a very unusual situation, and are able to come to grips successfully with a number of quite different problems involving both logic and substance.

The most obvious problem facing an archaeologist intent on causal construction of this type involves establishing temporal precedence in the change in value of the variables that are being considered in the model. This necessity of establishing which events are antecendent exists, whether the substantive explanatory model is of either a linear or systems variety (Salmon and Salmon 1979). To do this the archaeologist needs better control of time in the archaeological record than now exists in most situations, as well as a better ability both to identify artifactual reflections of relevant variables and to measure change in those variables.

A second obvious difficulty in constructing causal explanations in archaeology involves the lack of good quality analog situations to fill the needed reference classes. How many good ethnographic descriptions of chiefdom emergence exist, for example?

A third obvious difficulty in causal frameworks that is often conveniently overlooked is the logical possibility of quite different causal networks producing the same end result. At the same time, it is certainly possible for apparently quite similar causal networks to produce quite disparate end results.

It is unfortunately necessary to reiterate these obvious inherent problem areas in human behavior causal explanations because all too often over the past 20 years archaeologists have constructed causal scenarios through the simple expedient of identifying a set of potentially relevant variables or factors, and then plugging them into the abstract causal network that happens to be enjoying popularity at that point in time.

## DISCUSSION

I have attempted to outline and briefly characterize a sequence of four logical categories of causal and noncausal explanation in archeology:

1. Material culture or artifact-based noncausal explanations
2. Human behavior–material culture causal explanations
3. Human behavior noncausal explanations
4. Human behavior causal or processual explanations

These four categories of explanation form an inescapable explanatory progression in that each successive category by necessity must incorporate explantions of the foregoing types. One of the obvious preliminary steps in developing any sort of processual human behavior causal model involves identifying and accurately describing the relevant factors or variables to be employed in the model. This, in essence, is what is being accomplished in a human behavior noncausal model. The factors that are statistically relevant to the event to be explained are presented and characterized but are not arranged in any sort of causal network. These final two steps or categories of the explanatory progression are not unique to archaeology. They are a necessary part of any attempt at causal explanation in other scientific disciplines.

Any attempt to identify and describe relevant human behavior vairables (to formulate a human behavior noncausal model) in an archaeological context, however, necessitates the prior construction of human behavior–material culture causal explanations that link artifact patterning with the human–behavior variables to be employed. Such human behavior–material culture explanations in turn rest upon artifact-based noncausal explanations. Thus any archaeologist intent on formulating an explanation that falls into any one of these categories must begin by observing and documenting patterns in the archaeological record.

It could be argued that two of the four categories of explanation listed previously do not really represent acceptable, satisfactory explanations, since they are noncausal in form. Human-behavior noncausal explanations, at least when attempted in an archaeological context, do contain a causal step in the form of inherent human behavior–material culture explanations, and thus they would appear to contain at least some redeeming causal attributes. It is perhaps worth pointing out in this regard that the "explanations" of Longacre (1970) and Hill (1970), hailed as causal paradigms of the new archaeology, clearly fall into the human behavior noncausal category of explanation. On the other hand, artifact-based noncausal explanations do not constitute, in and of themselves, a satisfactory form of archaeological explanation, since they contain no redeeming causal attributes.

These four categories of explanation in archaeology form an exceedingly lengthy and complex explanatory sequence or progression. Each successive phase or step in the sequence involves additional assumptions, extensions of logical models, and demands on the data base. Formulating plausible noncausal and causal models within the realm of human behavior is in itself a difficult and often frustrating task. Archaeologists must face the additional prerequisite task of identifying and analyzing patterns in the archaeological record that can be linked to relevant causal variables of human behavior. This arduous obstacle course that faces any archaeologist intent on explanation is made even more frustrating by the present-day expectation of universal attainment of human behavior causal explanations.

In measuring the relative merits of any archaeological explanation, the prevailing current yardstick appears to involve an assessment of how far along the sequence one's explanatory efforts have progressed. Processual models are better than noncausal ones, which in turn are better than simple human behavior–material culture causal models. This emphasis on attainment of "process peak" at any cost has resulted in a large number of scenario explanations (see Renfrew, Chapter 1 this volume) that are imaginative explanatory frameworks unsupported by either logical arguments or by factual information. How far along this progression of explantion an archaeologist can successfully and justifiably advance depends on many things—personal perceptions of what constitutes a satisfactory explanation, the relative strength of the logical and substantive models employed, knowledge of relevant reference classes, etc.—but to an important extent, it will depend upon the nature of the event to be explained.

More specifically, it has to do with clear and undisturbed material-culture patterning and detailed and unequivocal analog reference classes. The utimate key to successful formulation of explanatory models in archaeology, then, rests with an archaeologist's ability to select an event for which there is sufficiently clear patterning in both the archaeological record and relevant analog situations.

## REFERENCES

Binford, L. R., 1967, Smudge pits and hide smoking: the use of analogy in archaeological reasoning, *American Antiquity* 34, 376–384.

Hill, J. N., 1970, Broken K Pueblo: prehistoric social organization in the American Southwest, *Anthropological Papers of the University of Arizona* 18, Tucson, University of Arizona Press.

Longacre, W. A., 1970, Archeology as anthropology—a case study, *Anthropological Papers of the University of Arizona* 17, Tucson, University of Arizona Press.

Meehan, E., 1968, *Explanation in Social Science—A System Paradigm,* Homewood, Ill. The Dorsey Press.

Renfrew, C., 1973, Monuments, mobilization and social organization in neolithic Wessex, in Renfrew, C. (ed.), *The Explanation of Culture Change: Models in Prehistory,* London, Duckworth, 539–558.

Salmon, W. C., Jeffrey, R., and Greeno, J., 1971, *Statistical Explanation and Statistical Relevance,* Pittsburgh, University of Pittsburgh Press.

Salmon, M., and Salmon, W., 1979, Alternative models of scientific explanation, *American Anthropologist* 81, 61–74.

Smith, B. D., 1977, Archeological inference and inductive confirmation, *American Anthropologist* 79, 598–617.

Smith, B. D., 1978, *Prehistoric Patterns of Human Behavior: A Case Study in the Mississippi Valley,* New York, Academic Press.

# 8

# Explanation and Social Theory in Archaeological Practice

*DANIEL MILLER*

The major proposition of this chapter is a somewhat surprising one. It is to argue that cetain ideas of an eighteenth-century philosopher on ontology (the nature of the world) and epistemology (the process by which we may come to have knowledge of the world) are responsible for unreasonable explanations of the variability in material remains of past societies given by archaeologists working in the latter half of the twentieth century. This relationship is not direct, being mediated by several factors, of which the most important is the social theory that has been found campatible with these philosophical principles and that has implicitly guided both the form and acceptability of archaeological explanations. The emphasis here will not, however, be on the critique of contemporary archaeological explanation, but rather on the provision of alternative models. It will be suggested that current developments within the philosophy of science provide models of explanation and verification that are not only more reasonable in themselves, but are far more appropriate to the needs of the archaeologist as a social scientist. By releasing archaeology from the grip of epistemological dogmatism, we may also be able to provide a clearer picture of what, in archaeological practice, are the main criteria by which explanations are deemed more or less acceptable.

Although there have been occasional moves to relate the insights of archaeology and philosophy, most noticeably in the writings of Collingwood (1946), the attempt at a consistent integration of archaeological reasoning

**83**

THEORY AND EXPLANATION
IN ARCHAEOLOGY

within a particular epistemological tradition is relatively new. It took the form of an espousal of a current version of a strain in epistemological thought that stemmed from the writings of Hume in the eighteenth century. The selection was from certain of the writings of Hempel and Popper, and the theory espoused may be termed "deductivism," standing for both deductive–nomological and hypothetico–deductive accounts of explanation (Hill 1972, Spaulding 1968, Watson, Leblanc, and Redman 1971). According to Habermas (1978, 308), the principles of deductivism provide

> the frame of reference that prejudges the meaning of possible statements, establishes the rules both for the construction of theories and their critical testing. Theories comprise hypothetico–deductive connections of propositions, which permit the deduction of lawlike hypotheses with empirical content. The latter can be interpreted as statements about the covariance of observable events; given a set of initial conditons they make prediction possible.

Deductivism may be regarded as the dominant ideology in current archaeology. That is to say, its main purpose has been to provide legitimation for certain kinds of archaeological practice and to condemn others as invalid. Thus, stress has been laid less on models of explanation than on criteria for verification. It may also be termed "ideological" in that it has effected a shift in discussion away from problems of social theory, which may be the main practical basis for choosing between proferred explanations, to problems of espistemology that provide the legitimation for such choice. The central concern of this chapter will therefore be less with the question of coherence in theory construction than with the problems of correspondence—that is, the way in which the prescriptions of our model of explanation are given meaning in archaeological practice.

If we wish to assess the impact of deductivist principles on archaeological practice, the obvious place to begin is with the original justification for their incorporation. Do they, as predicted, aid in discriminating between valid and unacceptable analysis and interpretation? I would suggest that the answer is clearly *no*, especially when the attempt is to explain social change or processes of human behavior. While over the last two decades certain inductive procedures, such as statistical inference, have become embedded in our general evaluation of whether a study is plausible and scholarly, it seems likely that it would still be words such as *plausible* that would characterize our judgments of archaeological work. If this is the case, then, as Renfrew suggests elsewhere in this volume, (Chapter 1) there is still a massive gulf between epistemological theory and archaeological practice.

It does not follow, however, that the adoption of these principles has had no profound effect. On the contrary, a sufficient number of archaeologists have been influenced for a major shift to have taken place within the discipline. Deductivist principles demand that explanation should include reference to lawlike propositions. While archaeological practice has shown that lawlike generalizations might be found with relative ease in the study of the physical context, for example the ecological background to human behavior, only rather dubious examples could be found in the study of human behavior itself, despite early attempts to apply these ideas to the reconstruction of kinship patterns. It is therefore no coincidence that this period has seen a marked concentration on the properties and processes that characterize natural phenomena. These range from the very valuable work on site-formation processes to important studies of the properties of stone, rock, and bone, and the reconstruction of past environments—all of which have led to marked refinements in archaeological methodology. Today these natural processes and their implications are no longer relegated to specialist reports at the end of excavation reports, but have become the central reference point for many self-consciously "theoretically minded" archaeologists (Binford 1978, Schiffer 1976).

The problem is that archaeology is a social science and not a natural science. Some link must be made between these studies and the human behavior expressed in material variability that we are concerned to explain. There are two major elements in the linkage that is made at present—the notions of "adaptation" and "system." *Adaptation* may be taken as the key word in modern archaeological attempts at explanation. Some have gone so far as to define culture as "man's extrasomatic means of adaptation" (Binford 1965 following White 1959). Adaptation can be used to predict and thereby explain human behavior in terms of its relation to its environmental context following the principles of deductivism. This is the reason why, despite Hempel's 1959 critique of functionalists–systems approaches, these have become a crucial part of such explanations. Systems analysis can be used to postulate linkages between disparate aspects of social behavior, such that they in turn become linked into relations of adaptation. Under deductivist principles, systems can only have some pretension to explanation if they are used together with explicit reasons for the connections made between different elements of the system, these being made up of lawlike propositions. Steadman (1979) has recently provided a history of the use of the terms *adaptation* and *system* in evolutionary models of culture change. He shows how the social basis of "needs" that are adapted to is consistently ignored, and that there is a general abuse of the notion of "system."

Since deductivist principles provide legitimation, and adaptive relations are the only forms that have been found compatible with them, we find in modern archaeology a tendency to claim explanation, only insofar as one can claim to have shown adaptation, and all other "cultural" bases for explanation are resorted to only in the last instance. Binford's Introduction to his book *Nunamiut Ethnoarchaeology* (1978) provides a clear example of the desire to remove cultural considerations from explanatory models. Adaptive relations are virtually ubiquitous in archaeological studies in the American Southwest, but other examples range from Gunn's systems approach (1975) to the use of human biogeography to explain the distribution of cultural variability in

Melanesia (Miller 1980a, Terrell 1977), or even why the Tasmanians stopped eating fish (Jones 1978).

Although it is never explicit, there is indeed a social theory implied in these explanations of human behavior. Its closest analogy lies in behaviorism, where adaptation has become the link between stimulus and response. That is, if we know enough about the external factors that bear upon human activity, we can predict and thereby explain that activity (Skinner 1972). Deductivist principles therefore have resulted in an essentially passive conception of man. This is the social theory that is implied in what Binford (1977, 4) has proposed as a typical hypothesis: "Other things being equal, dependence upon stored food will increase as the diversity of the subsistence base decreases in environments with less than 365-day growing seasons." The example is unusual only in the explicit caveat *all other things being equal.* It may be noted how the notion *falsifiability* is about the only element of Popper's extensive writings to have been included in the deductivism ascribed to by archaeologists, an approach that has led to a degree of determinism that he would strongly reject (Popper 1966). The roots lie rather with Hempel and the underlying positivist tradition.

In my present work, in which I am concerned to explain the variability in material forms in Melanesia and South Asia, I find much evidence to suggest that this variability cannot be reduced to adaptive behavior, and we may ask whether this framework of adaptation and systems analysis could provide a convincing explanation for the variability of material forms in our own society. If this is not the case, when we are faced with a situation in which the more "epistemologically pure" (in deductivist terms) we have attempted to become, then the less reasonable have been our explanations. In response to this problem, we may examine three alternatives. The first of these represents changes within the same tradition of the philosophy of science; the second, the adoption of a realist theory of science, based upon a rejection of the Humean ideas that form the basis of the first tradition. The third looks beyond the notion of archaeology as a science to investigate other factors that bear upon our explanations.

The first alternative is exemplified by the book *Naturalism and Social Science* by David Thomas (1979). This is representative of an argument that accepts the flaws found in deductivism, but suggests that the changes within that tradition have been so drastic that current views on the nature of explanation in the natural sciences provide a plausible basis for models of explanation in the social sciences. Although deductivism attempts to reduce the opposition between theory and observation in contrast to previous empiricist traditions, nevertheless it still retains the belief that theory can be tested against direct experimental evidence and that theoretical language is essentially parasitic on observation language.

Mary Hesse (1974) has argued against these assumptions and proposed what has become virtually a linguistic analysis, in which the emphasis is no longer on the immediate reference of a term within a theory, but more on the way the meaning of a term is derived from its relationship to other terms within that theory. Thus we will not get very far in understanding or applying Marxist theory if we use a concept of value that is derived from an alternative theory. Moreover, if we do use a term such as adaptation, it is important to state whether we are implying a Darwinian model or a Lamarckian model, since the latter implies the possibility of a more active role for the subject (Steadman 1979). Futhermore, by an extensive examination of the use of models, analogies, and metaphors, Hesse has shown the pervasive influence of linguistic criteria and the tendency to relate to the unfamiliar through a translation into familiar categories in the interpretation of explanations (Hesse 1966). She (1974, 33) has commented on her results that "the present account amounts to a denial that there is a fundamental distinction between theoretical and observation predicates and statements, and implies that the distinction commonly made is both obscure and misleading." Thus the relationship between theory and observation is now characterized as reflexive, with theory and our notions as to what the empirical evidence itself represents developing alongside each other.

This is only one of a number of problems confronting the idea of testing or falsifiability. We find that, at least in the social sciences, it has become implausible to claim that we can sufficiently isolate the relevant factors that bear on a hypothesis, for that hypothesis to be tested. Alternatives range from Lakatos's and Musgrave's (1970) attempts to dilute the original notion of falsifiability to Hesse's (1974) characterization of the mutual constraints of theory and empirical evidence as a learning process.

Deductivist approaches also affirm a fact–value dichotomy that has been subject to increasing criticism. Thomas (1979) argues for a value metaphysic in the social sciences on a par with metaphysics in the natural sciences as a basis for our choice of theory, our decision as to the relevant factors, and our assertion of the validity of the scientific process. Value is a relativistic factor in the consideration of theory, and Thomas rejects Kuhn's notion of a paradigm. While Kuhn's discussion (1962) of the sociology of science is clearly of interest, the term *paradigm* is easily subject to abuse. In particular, we might be tempted to remove all the relativistic problems intrinsic to the construction of theories and place them in a separate category called "paradigm", thus apparently obviating the need to take them into account when assessing theories. Although Thomas would reject the extreme conventionalism of Feyerabend (1975), we must note the major importance that anthropologists have had to attach to this question of relativism. The understanding of another culture must in some sense be analogous to the act of translation in which the terms and behaviors observed are communicated through the terms and categories that derive meaning from the social conventions of our own society (Wilson 1970). While contra Winch (1958) the success of translation may serve as a model for the possibility of such understanding, the relativistic problems intrinsic to the act of translation must be considered.

The qualifications to deductivist principles provided in the modern philosophies of science are legion, and the preceding may stand as a sample. The important point is that these are not used by Thomas to argue against the use of models deriving from the natural sciences. But rather, because they are held to apply to the natural sciences as well, they represent an argument *for* the continued adherence to these principles in the social sciences. Furthermore, the criteria of verification that have become familiar may still be applicable—that is, the tendency toward generalization, precision, and prediction—but the crucial term here is *tendency*. Thomas argues that such criteria in the strongly prescriptive form advocated in deductivist approaches are neither necessary nor applicable to the social sciences. As long as there is a tendency toward such ideals, then the study can be classed as scientific as opposed to everyday discourse. In the same way, Marxist theory, where it is revisionist or potentially revisionist, is scientific, but where, as with some of Althusser's studies, it reduces to mere tautology, it is no longer scientific.

There proposals present two major advantages to archaeologists. First, while virtually nothing in archaeological practice could accord with the strong prescriptions of deductivism, precisely because some, but not all, archaeological studies might be classed as scientific by Thomas's definitions, the gulf between epistemological theory and archaeological practice might be bridged. Second, the term *explanation* itself has been freed from the narrow definition it had taken within the positivist tradition to become closer, although by no means identical, to its colloquial usage.

It will be evident that Thomas's account amounts to a constant dilution of the major tenets of a given tradition in the philosophy of science. This suggests that the relationship between the proposed principles of social science and the principles of ontology and epistemology on which they were based have become tenuous. The alternative, therefore, represents a direct challenge to those very principles that spring from the writings of Hume. This alternative may be termed a "realist" approach to science, and variations in this approach may be represented in the work of Rom Harre (Harre 1970; Harre and Madden 1975), Roy Bhaskar (1978, 1979), and in part by Wesley Salmon (1971, in press, Chapter 4 this volume). The realist view stands in direct opposition to the Humean "fictionalist" stance, in that it is prepared to postulate real mechanisms and structures that are taken as giving rise to observable phenomena, and these include structures that are not themselves observable. Second, they stand in direct opposition to the Humean reduction of causation to the constant conjunction of events, and they insist upon a genuine causal input in explanations, the nature of which is a central concern. Thus relations, of necessity, may be real relations and not just logical ones. Structures and mechansims may be related through generative processes and not just through absolute processes to observable phenomena, and they may be intrinsically statistical. It may be noted that all three of the cited authors are philosophers of the natural sciences, and their examples are taken from the natural sciences, although the first two also have been specifically concerned with the implications of their ideas for the social sciences.

Harre, Bhaskar, and W. Salmon all stress different aspects of the realist approach. Bhaskar is concerned with its foundations in the rebuttal of the Humean notion of ontology that provides the basis for the critique of epistemology. Not only is the constant conjunction of events upon which Hume depends unavailable in the social sciences, but even within the natural sciences it is most often procured by the scientist creating, through the laboratory, an interaction between only the relevant factors. Harre provides the most systematic elaboration of the critique of Hume and introduces the notion of causal powers based in the generative potential of mechanisms (Harre and Madden 1975). Harre's work should be referred to for a detailed account of a realist theory, but since it is the work of Wesley Salmon that has been projected recently as providing a possible basis for archaeological attempts at explanation (M. Salmon 1975, 1976), it may be more useful to concentrate on how his work may be considered within a realist theory.

Salmon has not himself emphasized any such commitment to a realist ontology but his rejection of the Humean approach to explanation through the constant conjunction of events and his recent discussion of the nature of causative processes suggest at least a related base (in press, Chapter 4 this volume). Salmon's analyses of causal processes are perhaps harder to translate into terms relevant to the social scientist than Harre's, at least in part because he is not himself concerned with those aspects of causality of specific concern to, for example, the archaeologists. Salmon's analyses are, however, also part of a generative rather than an absolute framework, in which processes that are not in themselves in direct interation can nevertheless be explained by reference to their common causal basis—what Salmon calls a "conjunctive fork" (in press). A major contribution of Salmon's work has been to the statistical characterization of such processes, and this, together with the causal emphasis, is used to show how an unlikely process may still be held within an explanatory framework by reference to its causative base. Overall, this is a major departure from the Humean demand for constant association as the basis for explanation.

We can see more clearly why it is important to locate Salmon's ideas within a realist rather than a deductivist stance, by reference to a problem raised by Renfrew (Chapter 1 this volume) on the need to make more generalizations as a key to archaeological understanding. If we were to retain an essentially deductivist position we would interpret Salmon as arguing as follows:

*We begin with a theory that consists of higher-level generalizations from which we deduce lower-level hypotheses that predict specific generalizations in terms of the materials that we are studying.*

Thanks to Salmon, we can now see that this generalization should be of a statistical and not an absolute form, which presents difficulties but not insoluable problems for the notion of testing, which is the main criterion by which we know our hypothesis to be scientific. Anyway, we are using statistical characterization rather than absolute laws because we are unable to isolate the factors that would allow us to see the true nature of our correlations (which are ideally absolute), statistical generalizations being a heuristic second-best approximation. Reinforced by these ideas, the archaeologist might then go off looking for statistical correlations in the human relations file as a basis for contructing hypotheses.

I submit that this is a fundamental misreading of the ideas suggested by Salmon (as incidentally, is Chapter 7 in this volume by Bruce Smith, with his conception of noncausal explanations). If, on the contary, we locate the statistical–relevance model within a realist approach, it then demands a causal input in which mechanisms are held to generate observable phenomena, and our concern would be rather with the nature of this causal relationship. Statistical techniques provide a genuine rather than a best-fit characterization of such processes, within which an unlikely event is understood in terms of the probability of its being generated by a causal process. The relationship between theory and observation would have to be reflexive rather than being based on the construction of definitive tests. Under this approach the archaeologist would have to understand his observations on ancient societies as possibly representing different realizations of certain causal processes. This is an important point, because under the deductivist approach we can only explain the similarities between all societies with our generalizations, reducing differences to their correlations with external factors. Under a realist approach, however, we can explain the differences between societies as well as the similarities by relating them, often using statistical techniques, to transformations of causal processes.

The flexibility of a realist approach allows it to be compatible with a number of approaches in the social sciences. If we examine Gellner's characterization of structuralism (Chapter 9 this volume), we can see that it depends upon a realist base, with structural mechanisms, genuine causal inputs, and statistical relations. Wylie (1982) has argued that realism can provide a base for a structural approach to archaeology. I have argued elsewhere (in press a) that there are severe problems in utilizing structuralist ideas as such in the study of material culture, but by an emphasis on the pragmatic relations that lead to the realization of categories in everyday variability, rather than on the more formalistic approaches common to structural studies, and by attempting to locate the causal mechanisms that generate variability in the process of categorization, we may be able to to explain much of the variability in material forms that eludes us at present.

Clearly, a realist approach is predicated on our ideas about what is acceptable as a causal input in our attempts at explanation, and since we are concerned with archaeology as a social science, the causal processes that will be of most interest are those that relate to human behavior and social processes. It is fortunate that the major exponent of realist approaches, Rom Harre, is also a key figure in the development of social theory, and his recent work *Social Being*

(1979) may provide a convenient starting point for a translation of these ideas into archaeological concerns. Harre's interest is with what he terms the "expressive" aspect of human behavior, which he suggests often dominates the practical nature and concerns of human life. One of his main themes is the pursuit of reputation and its manifestation in different societies. We may take the pursuit of reputation as a social strategy. Within the context of Harre's work, it may be considered part of a social theory. I suggest the concept of social strategy is a useful basis for the postulation of causal processes in the social sciences.

A problem with Salmon's account of causality is that his terminology tends to relate to human behavior only insofar as that behavior is observed as a physical process. It is possible (though unlikely) that we could reduce a social strategy to description in terms of physiological processes, energy exchange, or even atomic theory. The question is whether, even if these were to provide a stronger deterministic basis, they would thereby be more satisfactory as causal mechanisms. I submit that the statement *John picked up the ruler* would be better explained in terms of some form of purposive causal process than by any analysis of physiological processes as pertain to John, or physical processes as pertain to the ruler, and their interaction. Purposive explanation, though it may have teleological implications, is not reducible to individual rationality or solely psychological theory (Harre 1979, Taylor 1970). The pursuit of reputation is meaningless unless it is considered as a social process in terms of social conventions. Nor is social strategy the sole input of the notion of causality's being used. Popper's notion of "World Three" (1972, 106–153) provides an essential corrective to the reduction of all material patterns to human purposive behavior, by pointing out the autonomy of the material results of human actions with respect to those purposes. The intrinsic properties and potentials of material artifacts thereby find a place in archaeological explanation.

The emphasis on social strategy is not to deny that some social theory is implied in alternative approaches. As we have seen, deductivist approaches employing the concept of adaptation have such an implied theory, although a minimalist one. Equally, the problems with the use of some forms of systems analysis, game theory, and catastrophe theory (Renfrew 1978) are most pronounced precisely when we try and delve into the social theory that is implied in their use. This tends to depend upon the form of rationality embedded in modern economics. The extent to which this has failed to provide a convincing model of "value," "consumer," and "production choice" in modern industrial societies, especially when we come to consider material artifacts (Doulas and Isherwood 1979), does not bode well for use in the analysis of societies where "function" and "value" are even less abstractable. We can see here why the problem of relativism must be faced in archaeological explanation. Our notion of "social rationality," that which we suggest we may reasonably project backwards into the archaeological record, is inevitably a core notion in social theory whether explicit or implicit, and it is obviously predicated on our understanding of our own society. It is often only in the analysis of discourse, that is, the implications of the terms we use and the contexts in which we use them, that our essential principles of social rationality become clear (e.g., Godelier 1972).

How a social strategy may work in terms of the social manipulation of material forms, an area with which the archaeologist has a particular interest, may be exemplified in a particular form of the pursuit of reputation—the process of emulation (Miller 1982b). This process may be used to show how, where a material-culture set is used to express socal hierarchy, this may result in a dynamic force generating continual change in the material forms without any corresponding change in social structure. Thus, if a society has several ranks and a particular form is associated with a high rank, then the lower ranks may wish to raise their status by copying this form. Now since it is the contrast that is of importance and not the actual forms, the simplest response from the high rank is to ensure a change in the form that becomes associated with them. Thus by the time the lower ranks have copied the form, those associated with the high rank have also changed, and the contrast is thereby maintained. The relationship between emulation and fashion, or consumer choice, in our own society has been well studied from Thornstein Veblen (1970) to Quentin Bell (1976). Labov, from whom the above example is taken, illustrates its importance in accounting for continual linguistic change in New York (1972), while I have used it to investigate the acceptance of new pottery forms in a modern ethnographic context and to discuss changes in eating utensils in north India over two millennia (Miller 1982b).

Emulation has been recognized by archaeologists, but it and discussions of artifacts as expressive media have been subsumed within a systems–functionalist description that attempts to obviate the need for a direct consideration of the nature of the human agency (Schiffer 1976). Several points emerge from the brief account of this process. Our knowledge of the physical properties of the forms is irrelevant, since it is their symbolic property—status set against social hierarchy—that may bear no relation to any intrinsic property that is of importance here. Second, change in the material form cannot be correlated with change in the medium being expressed, since the dynamics of one acts alongside stability in the other. The relations between the social groups remain constant. Emulation is not lawlike. We cannot predict the extent of hierarchy within a given society, nor can we predict that hierarchy will be manifested in a given medium, such as stone tools; and if hierarchy is so expressed, we cannot predict that emulation will be employed as a social strategy with respect to that medium.

It may be that, as in the Indian villages I am studying, we can place emulation against the alternative strategy of prohibition, which is to prevent the copying of higher-status forms. This has the same effect as emulation on relations between the social ranks (though obviously not on the material forms). The question then becomes, can these two alternatives be related to any other differences in social relations, such that one strategy would be more likely than the other in a given circumstance? While this may be the case in other areas, in the Indian context it seems unlikely that such a correlation could be found. Indeed, emulation may be in a cyclical relation with prohibition—the former employed when the latter has become too blatant, and the latter used when emulation is taken to extremes. The occurrence of emulation is then inherently probabilistic and not deterministic. We can see how quite a rare strategy may still be understandable in terms of its being one of a number of possibilities to be generated by a given social structure of categories. The archaeologist is thereby bound to include an element of search procedures, as exemplified by Clarke's notion *key attributes* (1968) and found recently defended on practical rather than theoretical grounds by Redman *et al.* 1978, 159–192). But statistical relevance derives from our models of social strategy and the pragmatic transformations through which strategy is expressed in material patterns.

Before concluding, I would like to advance one stage further beyond presently discussed notions of explanation in archaeology. All the approaches dealt with so far lie within the corpus of naturalism. That is, they claim to provide frameworks for explanation and verification that apply to both the natural and the social sciences. It may be, however, that our understanding of science does not exhaust all those considerations that bear upon the acceptability of archaeological explanations, and indeed our emphasis on science may have prevented a proper examination of some of these additional elements. Outside of naturalism, there are arguments emerging from hermeneutics and critical theory that some have said replace positivistic science and its central criterion of instrumental success. Here, however, these will be considered merely as additional elements in the discussion, which holds that many of the relativistic problems raised in these approaches may be subsumed within a reformed naturalism.

The example of these approaches used here is that presented by Habermas in his *Knowledge and Human Interests* (1978), and the additional element being considered is the social context within which archaeology is practiced. Habermas argues that beyond scientific methodology, there are questions of interpretation that cannot be subsumed in the criterion of instrumental success. Interpretation is seen rather as being modeled on consensus, where this is held to result from discourse outside of external pressures. This caveat demonstrates the consensus model to be an idealized normative criterion, rather than mere description of academic debate. In a consideration of the practice of archaeology in a developing country (Miller 1980b), I try to relate my concept of the meaning of the past in the present and my commitment to a science of archaeology to the concept of the past held by the Solomon Islanders among whom I worked in order to show that the practice of archaeology can be interpreted as an attempt to transform the concepts held by the subjects—in this case the Solomon Islanders.

The point of such a study is to show that the goals to which we subscribe as

archaeologists, including our commitment to scientific method, represent values
that we hold by reason of our membership in the society from which they derive,
but which members of other societies may not neccessarily share.To this extent,
then, the practice of archaeology must be seen as an attempt to change people's
values, and it is neither neutral nor objective in the ways it has sometimes been
projected. I suggest that for any archaeologist concerned with the social
implications of his own discipline,the traditions represented by critical theory
make up an essential component of his consideration of the nature of archaeological explanations.

This chapter by no means exhausts the current debate about the relationship
between epistemology and acceptable explanations. There has been no discussion of the conventionalists (Feyerabend 1975), nor the emergence of an
argument that philosophy cannot of itself provide the kinds of criteria that we
are attempting to obtain from it (Rorty 1980). Although there has been an
emphasis on the realist approach, the intention here has not been to proclaim
any one philosophy of science as potentially able to provide a strongly
prescriptive formula for explanation in archaeology. It has rather been to show
that we can dispense with the deductivist approach, and not thereby leave
ourselves open to anarchy. Most contemporary philosophers of science would
not support the rigid deductivist model, and there are many alternatives, undergoing continual development, that can provide criteria for verification. By
freeing ourselves of a particularly rigid and oppresive model of legitimation, we
may be able to consider more thoroughly the problems of social theory and the
nature of material patterns as expressive of categorization processes, which may
be far more important in our actual choice between proffered explanations in
archaeological practice.

# REFERENCES

Bell, Q., 1976, *On Human Finery*, New York, Schoeken Books.
Bhaskar, R., 1978, *A Realist Theory of Science*, Sussex, Harvester Press.
Bhaskar, R., 1979, *The Possibility of Naturalism*, Sussex, Harvester Press.
Binford, L., 1965, Archaeological systematics and the study of culture process, *American Anti-
quity* 31, 203–210.
Binford, L. (ed.), 1977, *For Theory Building in Archaeology*, New York, Academic Press.
Binford, L., 1978, *Nunamiut Ethnoarchaeology*, New York, Academic Press.
Clarke, D., 1968, *Analytical Archaeology*, London, Methuen.
Collingwood, R., 1946, *The Idea of History*, Oxford, Blackwell.
Douglas, M., and Isherwood, B., 1979, *The World of Goods*, Middlesex, Penguin Books.
Feyerabend, P., 1975, *Against Method*, London, New Left Books.
Godelier, M., 1972, *Rationality and Irrationality in Economics*, London, New Left Books.
Gunn, J., 1975, An envirotechnological system for Hogup Cave, *American Antiquity* 40, 3–21.
Habermas, J., 1978, *Knowledge and Human Interests*, London, Heinemann.
Harre, R., 1970, *The Principles of Scientific Thinking*, London, Macmillan.
Harre, R., 1979, *Social Being*, Oxford, Blackwell.
Harre, R., and Madden, E., 1975 *Causal Powers*, Oxford, Blackwell.

Hempel, C., 1959, The logic of functional analysis, in Gross, L. (ed.), *Symposium of Sociological Theory*, New York, Row, Peterson, 271–307.
Hesse, M., 1966, *Models and Analogies in Science*. Indiana, University of Notre Dame Press.
Hesse, M., 1974, *The Structure of Scientific Inference*, London, Macmillan.
Hill, J., 1972, The methodological debate in contemporary archaeology: a model, in Clarke, D. (ed.), *Models in Archaeology*, London, Methuen, 61–107.
Jones, R., 1978, Why did the Tasmanians stop eating fish?, in Gould, R. (ed.), *Explorations in Ethnoarchaeology*, Albuquerque, University of New Mexico Press, 11–47.
Kuhn, T., 1962, *The Structure of Scientific Revolutions*, Chicago, University of Chicago Press.
Labov, W., 1972, *Sociolinguistic Patterns*, Oxford, Blackwell.
Lakatos, I., and Musgrave, A. (eds.), 1970, *Criticism and the Growth of Knowledge*, Cambridge, Cambridge University Press.
Miller, D., 1980a, Settlement and diversity in the Solomon Islands, *Man* 15, 451–466.
Miller, D., 1980b, Archaeology and development, *Current Anthropology* 21, 709–726.
Miller, D., 1982a, Artifacts as products of human categorisation processes, in Hodder, I. (ed.), *Symbolic and Structural Archaeology*, Cambridge, Cambridge University Press.
Miller, D., 1982b, Structures and strategies: an aspect of the relationship between social hierarchy and cultural change, in Hodder, I. (ed.), *Symbolic and Structural Archaeology*, Cambridge, Cambridge University Press.
Popper, K., 1966, *The Open Society and Its Enemies*, London, Routledge and Kegan Paul.
Popper, K., 1972, *Objective Knowledge: An Evolutionary Approach*, Oxford, Blackwell.
Redman, C., 1978, Multivariate artifact analysis: a basis for multidimensional interpretation, in Redman, C., Berman, M. J., Curtin, E. V., Langhorn, Jr., W. T., Versaggi, N. M., and Wanser, J. C. (eds.), *Social Archaeology*: Beyond Subsistence and Dating. New York, Academic Press, 159–192.
Renfrew, C., 1978, Trajectory discontinuity and morphogenesis: the implications of catastrophe theory for archaeology, *American Antiquity* 43, 203–222.
Rorty, R., 1980, *Philosophy and the Mirror of Nature*. Oxford, Blackwell.
Salmon, M., 1975, Confirmation and explanation in archaeology, *American Antiquity* 40, 459–463.
Salmon, M., 1976, Deductive versus inductive archaeology, *American Antiquity* 40, 376–380.
Salmon, W., 1971, *Statistical Explanation and Statistical Relevance*, Pittsburgh, University of Pittsburgh Press.
Salmon, W., in press, Causality: production and propagation in Asquith, P., and Giere, R. (eds.), *P.S.A. 1980*, 2, East Lansing, Mich., Philosophy of Science Association.
Schiffer, M., 1976, *Behavioral Archaeology*, New York, Academic Press.
Skinner, B., 1972, *Beyond Freedom and Dignity*, Middlesex, Penguin Books.
Spaulding, A., 1968, Explanation in archaeology, in Binford, L., and S. R., (eds.), *New Perspectives in Archaeology*, Chicago, Aldine, 33–39.
Steadman, P., 1979, *The Evolution of Designs*, Cambridge, Cambridge University Press.
Taylor, C., 1970, The explanation of purposive behaviour, in Borger, R., and Coiffi, F. (eds.), *Explanation in the Behavioural Sciences*, Cambridge, Cambridge University Press, 49–95.
Terrell, J., 1977, Geographic systems and human diversity in the North Solomons, *World Archaeology* 9, 62–81.
Thomas, D., 1979, *Naturalism and Social Science*, Cambridge, Cambridge University Press.
Veblen, T., 1970, *The Theory of the Leisure Class*, London, Unwin Books.
Watson, P., Le Blanc, S., and Redman, C., 1971, *Explanation in Archaeology: An Explicitly Scientific Approach*, New York, Columbia University Press.
White, L., 1959, *The Science of Culture*, New York, Farrar, Strauss.
Wylie, A., 1982, Epistemological issues raised by a structuralist archaeology, in Hodder, I. (ed.), *Symbolic and Structural Archaeology*, Cambridge, Cambridge University Press.
Wilson, B. (ed.), 1970, *Rationality*, Oxford, Blackwell.
Winch, P., 1958, *The Idea of a Social Science*, London, Routledge and Kegan Paul.

# 9

## What Is Structuralisme?

*ERNEST GELLNER*

A specter is haunting Europe, or at any rate Cambridge: "Structuralisme." But what is it? Or perhaps: What the devil is it? Popular explanations of it fluctuate between the unintelligible and the obvious, with a heavy list toward the former. Communism at least had a Manifesto that articulated its central ideas with vigor, lucidity, and authority. To my knowledge, there is no corresponding "structuraliste manifesto" that could tell us just what it is that is haunting us, or some of us. On an occasion that most impressed them, archaeologists were advised to embrace structuralisme by Sir Edmund Leach. But what exactly is it they are to embrace?

I was once involved in translating what is probably the most theoretical and synoptic work by the best-known structuraliste. This exercise on my part was not due to any ambition to set up as a translator in order to make money that way or to test or refute theories about the indeterminacy of translations. Not at all. It happened quite differently. The original translator, after submitting a couple of sample chapters to the top structuraliste and exchanging some amiable letters or letters that perhaps began as amiable, soon came to illustrate the "indeterminacy of translation thesis" by getting involved in a flaming row with the author and ceasing to be on speaking, or indeed writing or translating, terms with him. The publishers had already paid an advance and wanted to see the translation completed, and they commissioned a conceptual go-between, a

THEORY AND EXPLANATION
IN ARCHAEOLOGY

tertius quid, to mediate between the two warring parties. Unfortunately, far from becoming a *tertius gaudens*, he rapidly became a *tertius perdens*, if there is such an expression, as the chain reaction continued and he too ceased to be on speaking, writing, and translating terms with the original translator. There was indeed no reason whatever why the chain reaction should ever cease. At some $n$th stage I was sucked into the recursive process, more for reasons of personal friendship with the $(n-1)$th victim than by virtue of any competence or qualification. Instead of fumbling into the abyss to join the others, I managed to terminate the regress, by means largely of abject humility: This series at any rate was not allowed to follow out its rule to infinity. I humbly stressed to the aggrieved original translator that I had no pretensions to authority in this matter, and I underlined, as indeed is the case, that I had actually failed my O–levels (school certificate as it was called in those distant days) in the language in which the work had originally been composed—which is quite an unusual distinction in itself. I then worked on completing the translation. When the work was done, the original translator threatened to sue if his name appeared on it, but likewise to sue if anyone else's, notably mine and that of $n-1$, was credited with it. So the translation appeared without any name or names to which credit or blame might be attached—as if it had sprung into being, unaided and spontaneously. One friendly reviewer described it as execrable, but several others, and I think the majority of those who commented on it at all, praised it.

The work in question is probably the main succint theoretical summary of his own position by the leading structuraliste, and as I say, I put in a lot of work on the translation of it. It might well be the nearest thing we have to a structuraliste manifesto. Yet I must confess that, at the end of all that work on the correct rendering of single sentences and paragraphs, I still had no idea of what its overall argument was meant to be. In this I do not appear to be alone: Noam Chomsky has commented on the work in question, saying that all it seems to amount to is the idea that men generally classify things. This, though evidently true, would not, on its own, amount to any kind of new illumination, so one supposes there must be more to it. But what is it and where is it to be found? This is the moral of my story: There is no facile rosy path to the central ideas or tenets of structralisme.[1]

If indeed there is no such key text for the identification of structuraliste doctrine, some other method must be used for locating it. I shall attempt to use a kind of generative method—the construction of a model of structuralisme, consisting of a set of ideas or themes. Such a model then has some claim to be considered a correct rendering, if the observed activities and positions of people normally described as structuralists follow from them, and activities repudiated or conspicuously avoided by them do not follow from them; and there is a

---

[1]I know of one admirably lucid essay that sets out to clarify the principles of structuralisme, but it is not easy to locate. It is Jean Pouillon's contribution to *Soviet and Western Anthropology* (Pouillon 1980).

reasonable amount of evidence to suggest that this set of ideas did operate in the minds of such people. Such evidence can be sought in their writing, but it can also be sought in the problem situations in which they are known to have been involved.

I believe that the philosophical roots of structuralisme are deep. One problem to which it is, I believe, related, is that of the general nature of explanation and of causation. There are two main conceptions of causation: what might be called "emanation," and what is customarily called "covering law." The idea underlying the former conception can be best conveyed, at least initially, in a kind of pictorial or suggestive way, which may leave philosophers feeling uneasy and seem to them sloppy, but which nevertheless does, I think, capture the central intuition that inspires this view. The idea is this: Things have deep natures or constitutions or structures or inner essences, or whatever you wish to call them. These are normally, or perhaps permanently, hidden from view, but the regularities we discern in the phenomena that are open to view emanate, or flow frm, those hidden, permanent inner forms. Once those inner forms are perceived or understood or conceptually seized, all else follows and is clear. But without such understanding, any attempt to bind the visible phenomena under generalizations is bound to remain superficial, and will probably be abortive, even if it restricts itself to surface classification and prediction.

Very often, this conception of knowledge is also very satisfying morally: Those inner forms tend to be not merely potent in their explanatory force but also gratifying aesthetically and ethically. They reveal a moral as well as an ontological order; in fact, these various orders converge. Truth, beauty, and goodness are one. From the viewpoint of someone interested only in the philosophy of science and explanation of course, this blessed convergence of the axiological and cognitive realms is a kind of optional extra: The emanation view of causation can be held on its own, without these moral and aesthetic overtones or associations. They are not entailed in the emanation view of causation as such. Nevertheless, the elective affinity of these views is relevant to the understanding of the appeal of this vision. Similarly, the *rejection* of the fact–value convergence, or if you like, the cagey insurance against disillusion should it fail to hold, itself also constitutes a clue to the appeal of the *rival* view of causation.

Over the recent centuries, the "emanationist" view has been, on the whole, in decline. The main logical reason for this has been the increasing reluctance to rely on inherently hidden, inaccessible entities for purposes of explanation. This might be called the empiricist or positivist trend. (It is a nice question to ask: Have we lost faith in the fact–value convergence because we have become more empiricist, or have we become empiricists because we have lost faith in that convergence?) It may well be that one of the roots of this new vision itself is, ironically, ultimately theological—that antiquity lacked the notion of natural law (evidence to the contrary being at least in part due to mistranslations and conceptual retrojections) and was implicitly emanationist; and that the "law" conception of natural order and explanation is a consequence of the doctrine of a hidden, austere, orderly, and voluntarist deity, which reveals neither its own designs nor the hidden essences of things, but obliges its creatures, if they are smitten by the desire to know, to content themselves with the tabulation of mere regularities in the surface phenomena, which alone are available to their inspection. Such a deity does not stoop to any brazen signaling of its meaning or to self-display.[2] In any case, whatever its historic roots, this empiricism foreswears the reduplication of the world into hidden essence and visible emanation, which seems inherent in emanationism. Emanationism explains the visible world in terms of entities and forces of another world. But the only access to that other world, we now realize is through its alleged manifestation in this world. Is this not a circular or vacuous procedure? Is it not better to be honest and treat the explanations merely as shorthand, as summaries of the regularities found in the phenomena, rather than endowing them with a "realist" status and treating them also as simultaneously descriptive characterizations of another realm, underlying ordinary events? Positivists, given to epistemological Machismo, see them as mere shorthand abbreviations of descriptive accounts of events in *this* world. So a powerful epistemological tautology—what you cannot observe, you cannot observe—comes to reinforce a spirit that was perhaps initially inspired by the faith in a very hidden, mysterious, yet austere and order-loving deity.

It was of course David Hume who, starting from the premises that the world we think is bounded by what we can sense, ended with an early form of the covering-law theory of causation. His inference was *from* radical empiricism *to* the "law" theory. I am not clear whether the reverse inference holds formally, though it is a rather natural step to take. The affinity between the two positions—an empiricist reluctance to countenance experience-transcending entities, whether for explanatory purposes or any other, and the law theory of causation—arises as follows: If there is nothing other than experiences, then the causal link between experiences cannot be anything either between or beyond them (there not being any such things), and therefore what else could it be, other than the pattern of similar experiences, the regular association—in other words, the observed law? Conversely, if the notion of law or regularity captures the essence of causation, then there is nothing to it other than that law and the elements that is connects or binds. Nothing else being required, it would seem to follow that nothing else is relevant. Hence experience-transcending entities, even if they exist (which this argument on its own cannot exclude), have nothing to do with causation.

It is a striking fact about the world we inhabit that at the phenomenal level, there are few good regularities (though there are some). The heavenly bodies are one sphere where regular behavior is conspicuous; with a little less

---

[2]For this fascinating historical speculation, I am indebted to a brilliant paper by Dr. John R. Milton of Imperial College, London (1981).

precision, there are the tides and the seasonal rhythms of nature. (It is interesting to note that of two great theories of religion, Hume's and Durkheim's, one links religion to the fear of the irregular, the other to the confirmation of the regular.) In all those extensive spheres where regularity is absent at the immediate level of phenomena, it can only be sought (and is frequently found) at higher levels of abstraction, i.e., in terms that relate to experiential ones only indirectly, in some complex way. The two theories of causation—the emanative and the covering-law one—then lead naturally to quite opposed assessments of the status of those more abstract terms, which figure in the causal laws. For the emanationists, they are names of real things, somehow responsible for the order specified in the law and providentially discovered through that very order. For the covering-law theories, it is natural to think of them as simple shorthand. But it is interesting to note that Sir Karl Popper, for instance, is simultaneously a warm adherent of the covering-law theory of explanation and a passionate realist and anti-instrumentalist. I am not suggesting that the two positions are in formal contradiction, but it would be interesting to know how the strain between them is resolved.

Although a hidden, austere, and orderly deity may be historically a crucial source of the descriptive–covering-law view of science and cognition (by simultaneously denying the prospect of the mind's penetrating to the heart of things, while at the same time holding out the promise of regularity and order, unlike earlier, more capricious and manipulable spirits), yet theism and emanationism can also be combined. Descartes did fuse them; he had the intuition, which most of us share, that all the various states of the world do not "really" have the power to produce their successor situations, so that talking of one of them "causing" the other is but shorthand. "Really" what happens is that the deity directly generates both succeeding stages, and only their orderly continuity produces the illusion that one of them causes the other. Descartes was in effect an emanationist both with respect to the deity and the mechanical and extended realm, which persisted only because it was perpetually renewed by God. The only things that escaped this emanationism were the clear and distinct links of logical thought, whose validity had to antedate even the existence of God (though they were thereafter underwritten by God), because they alone established the existence of that God, and which were consequently independent of any emanationist core, so to speak. Just as in the movements on a watch dial, successive positions of the hands do not really cause each other, but are, all of them, caused by the central and hidden mechanism, so the successive states of such a natural system all flow from the hidden deity, rather than being "really" linked to each other. Mechanical and theistic emanationisms have a certain resemblance to each other and were indeed fused by Spinoza. In a sense, the covering-law view of causation, which amounts to saying that there is no link, no "power" connecting elements in a causal chain, that the only connection is in an extraneous law not intrinsically part of either of the connected events, is itself the consequence of an extreme emanationism: The perception that the links following each other are not really connected with each other but both emanate from a hidden core, when followed by an amputation of that core (because we realize that, being inherently hidden, it is never accessible to us and hence irrelevant), leads to a Humean view of causation. First, God absorbs all causal potency into Himself, making nature so to speak inorganic, inert. Then God is abstracted from this picture, and what is left is an inert, inorganic world in which connections can only be contingent regularities, noted ex post, but devoid of any inner necessity accessible to reason. In other words, Hume's account.

The repudiation of vacuous "reduplication," the use of a transcendent realm that is merely a hidden way of referring to *this* realm that it purports to "explain," is perhaps the most powerful philosophical motive for preferring the descriptive view of science and the associated law view of causation. But there is one region in which the reduplication of the world, the supposition of an independently existing substrate, somehow responsible for surface phenomena, is not absurd, presumptuous, circular, and unwarranted—an area in which we really are allowed to peep behind the veil of Maia, and habitually do so; where the "other" reality is accessible and really *is* known to exist. That area is the area of human performance.

In the human sphere, external experience of reduplication, contact with a second reality behind appearance, occurs in, at any rate, two forms: through the multiplicity of persons and through the passage of time. Let us take time as an example. A strict empiricist, nonreduplicationist, positivist attitude to the past, for instance, is to treat it simply as equivalent to the evidence about "what we call the past" in the present, which alone is now eligible for experience. But we do not really believe that the past is merely the marks of the past in the present. (A. J. Ayer attempted at one stage to persuade himself of this and asserted such a view in print, but he admits now that he cannot sustain this heroic piece of positivist puritanism.) The past was once present, as *the present*, and it was real. The acts of historical personages that explain certain marks in the present are not merely summaries of those marks. They "really" existed, and they explain those marks in this philosophically "realist" way. Their being,is not exhausted by their role as premises from which current data follow. They have a true reality of their own, transcending their explanatory instrumentality. And we believe the same, whether or not we can prove it, in connection with the independent existence of other selves.

Our faith in the independent existence of our own selves in the past gives us a kind of precedent for a similar kind of positivism—defying hubris with respect to other people.

And it is not merely the sheer existence of the reduplicated, transcendent, independently existing that is confidently affirmed in this sphere. Those transcendent objects do not merely exist; they are plausibly allowed to have purposive structures. So, at least in some measure, they are allowed to exhibit that fact–value, *Sein–Sollen* convergence that otherwise scandalizes the empiricist conscience. Nature may not be allowed to be a language; but language at least *is* a language. Irrespective of whether it was designed by a creator or by the play of chance and natural selection, it is allowed to constitute a purpose-adjusted system. Whatever mechanism it is that generates all the sentences of a given language and excludes noise-sequences not acceptable in it, does not merely "exist" independently, but is allowed to be a purpose-serving system. As a system, it operates in a way to satisfy, in some measure, some specifiable requirements. The study of language, for instance, is the study of linguistic *competence*. In other words, it is the study of how a range of performances manages to satisfy certain criteria, which define competence within their realm. So, it is not merely legitimate, but actually inherent in the very inquiry, to assume that there is a system and that what it emits or generates satisfies a range defined by certain norms. A similar assumption in the study of nature might seem anthropomorphic; in the study of human competence, it is entirely appropriate. *Some* measure of anthropomorphism may be allowed in the study of man. But if this is so, then not merely the independent existence of the explanatory core structure but also its systematic and norm-satisfying nature may legitimately be assumed. So, in this field, we are not merely allowed to indulge in philosophic realism (the independent existence of external objects), but in, so to speak, morally saturated and heart-warming realism, which postulates that those extraneous realities form systems and satisfy norms.[3]

To sum up: In the human sphere, emanationism is alive and moderately well. At any rate, it is well enough to have some prospects of survival. The emanationist assumptions of the independent existence of systems that are more than mere shorthand summaries of the data and that which are in some measure purpose-bound, or norm-satisfying, seem permissible, or perhaps mandatory, in this sphere.

This is one, but one only, factor underlying structuralisme: For structuralisme is a form of emanationsim. But this is only one root among a number. We would misunderstand structuralisme if we thought this was all there is to it.

Let the scene now shift from the heady, stratospheric abstraction of explanation and causation in general (and the distinction between a nature that does *not*, and a culture that *does*, make reduplicationist purposiveness thinkable) and descend to the more concrete sphere of research into societies, and in particular into fairly small-scale societies, within the tradition of inquiry known as social anthropology. This tradition has for a long time had its own kind of humdrum

---

[3]Watkins (1952) triggered off that record-breaking series of philosophical articles on "methodological individualism" (philosophy's answer to *The Mousetrap* and still running strong). He argued, interestingly, for reduplication license in human studies, invoking the authority of Lionel Robbins's views on the methodology of economics—we know man twice over, from inside and out. But he used this for a "unity of science" conclusion, i.e., a view that does not radically distinguish methods in natural and social sciences (unless perhaps the obligation to attribute rationality, sometimes held obligatory in human studies, distinguishes them from natural ones). I am here arguing that it is the plausibility of reduplication in the human sphere, constrasted with its philosophic offensiveness in nature, which encourages structuralistes to return to an emanationist view of causation and explanation.

structuralism—solid, earthy, blokey, and without any of that scent of the Left Bank that is forever attached to structuralisme. Within social anthropology, the old-fashioned, homely structuralism meant roughly this: a stress on groups, their organization, and the constraints this imposed on the conduct of individuals. The idea was that a tribal society has a certain structure or organization, each part of which imposed such pressures and sanctions on the individuals within it so as to ensure that they behaved in a way that in turn sustained that structure, and so on forever, or at any rate for quite a long time. Structure was important, a matter of serious concern for men (inside the society or among investigators). Culture, on the other hand, was relatively ephemeral, accidental, epiphenomenal, and altogether suitable for women (inside the society or among investigators). Structure was, for instance, whom one could marry; culture was what the bride wore. Marriage restrictions or prescriptions were an important element in how the society actually worked; but the specific *tokens* or *symbols* by means of which categories of people were identified as marriageable, unmarriageable, eligible for political status, objects of aggressions, etc.—that was a fairly trivial, superficial, and accidental matter. A token was required to identify this or that category of people, this or that ritual occasion. The classification or the ritual was important, but *which* token was used to mark it off was a matter of chance. *Structure* dictated where tokens were needed; accident or history (if indeed those two could even be distinguished) determined which concrete object was to serve as token. The deployment of tokens mirrored solid structure, but the specific nature of the tokens themselves mirrored nothing. No reason could be given why, let us say, the color *white* should be a sign of rejoicing in one society and of mourning in another. That could only be an historical accident and was barely worthy of the attention of a serious scholar, especially when it occurred in illiterate milieus in which historical accidents could not be established for lack of records.

This kind of anthropology was seriously concerned with structure, the organization of groups for the serious ends of the maintenance of order and production, the allocation of roles and of obligations and of brides; and it was implicitly somewhat dismissive of culture—the set of symbols by which groups, roles, statuses, and so forth, were identified and recognized in a given society. Its implicit theory of culture was half an accident theory, half of echo theory. Cultural elements mirrored and thereby reinforced and sanctioned "real" constellations of people on the ground. Culture was the decoration, often important for information or reminder, but without a direct structural role. The echo and the accident aspects of this theory of culture complement each other: It is an accident that this token signals this or that structural feature, but it is the structural features of the society that determine how many kinds of echo, roughly speaking, there are to be. I may be exaggerating or overstating a little this rather dismissive, somewhat philistinical attitude of the old structuralism to culture—but basically this was it.

It is significant that this kind of earthy structuralism was associated with the declared aspiration to turn anthropology into a natural science of societies. Structure was that part of society best amenable to this. Hence there was order and regularity to be found, and these were not to be expected in the sphere of culture. There is a striking analogy between the use made by this kind of old structuralism of the distinction between structure and culture, and the Lockian distinction between "primary" and "secondary" qualities. It was primary quality that explained, and the secondary that *was* explained. The primary quality was the central concern of science. Primary qualities like inpenetrability resemble the economic and power relations of groups—in other words, structure. And just as secondary qualities are thought of as merely engendered by the interplay of primary ones and our senses, so cultural traits—the sartorial, gastronomic, linguistic, and other indicators of structure—are merely a kind of surface illusion produced by the contingent forms of the sensibility of the culture in question.

The ambiance of *structuralisme* could hardly be more contrasted to that of *structuralism*. Its favored areas are precisely in the realm of culture: symbolism, mythology, ritual, literature, art—the erstwhile secondary qualities of culture, and also, a little less congruently, kinship. Kinship may be the odd man out in the list; it may or may not be significant that in his study of Lévi-Strauss, Edmund Leach (1970, 9) singles out his celebrated work on kinship as the field in which he was least successful. But concentrating for the moment on the mainline concerns of structuralisme, it could be said that it has put culture into the very center of anthropological concern, when it had previously been a kind of epiphenomenal echo. Whereas, by contrast, Lévi-Strauss for instance has on occasion vaunted his lack of interest in politics. Culture, it now appears, has its own structure of which the political system knows nothing.

It is not just the epiphenomenality of culture that is being denied (and that is being replaced by an implicit doctrine of the autonomy of culture or even an assertion of its centrality). It is the echo theory of culture that is firmly destroyed. Structuralisme has a theory of meaning that is, above all, a denial of the echo doctrine: The essence of a symbol is not its relationship to the thing symbolized. (In the empiricist theories of meaning, the symbol is a kind of shadow of what is meant or, in Hume's case, the concept is simply the aftertaste of the thing.) Its essence is its place in a wider system of symbols. *John* is given its meaning not by its relation to John but by its place in a system also containing *Peter, Paul,* etc. The system is assumed to have its central set of rules, which generates everything that can occur within it. Any relationship to anything outside, one might add, is almost accidental. As in the case of old-fashioned structuralism, the actual token doesn't matter much; but whereas previously, what gave it life was its relation to the bit of reality that "controlled" it or to which it referred or which it symbolized, now it has the breath of life infused into it by the core-generating mechanism that assigns a place to it. It should be said also that the new structuralistes can be found handling both meanings and the tokens that are their carriers: Both are equally grist to this mill.

Empiricism was essentially an echo theory of knowledge. As Hume put it:

> "all our simple ideas . . . are derived from simple impressions . . . which they exactly represent.

Not surprisingly, when Radcliffe-Brown hoped to further an empirical science of society, he tended also to adopt an echo theory of culture. But Hume had to qualify his theory concerning the invariable origin of our ideas in our impression. There was the famous exception—the Blue Patch.

> Suppose . . . a person to have enjoyed his sight for thirty years, and to have become perfectly well acquainted with colours of all kinds, excepting one particular shade of blue . . . which it had never been his fortune to meet with. Let all the different shades of that colour, except that single one, be placed before him, descending gradually from the deepest to the lightest; it is plain that he will perceive a blank, where that shade is wanting, and will be sensible that there is a greater distance in that place, betwixt the contiguous colours, than in any other. Now I ask, whether it is possible for him . . . to supply this deficiency, and raise up to himself the idea of that particular shade, though it had never been conveyed to him by his senses?

Hume answers his rhetorical question with an emphatic Yes, but discounts the counterexample to the echo theory as "so particular and singular, that it is scarce worth our observing."

Evidently, because the "missing shade of blue" is part of a spectrum we work with and comprehend, it generates a curious exception to the echo principle. The structuraliste approach, in a way, stands Hume on his head. This is no exception; on the contrary, this is the very paradigm of how we acquire ideas! It is only because our minds are sensitive to given spectra or polarities that impressions can provoke ideas in us. Our mind would be incapable of echoing anything not already found within the span of its sensibilities. So structuralisme seeks out the polarities that define our sensibilities.

So at the very center of stucturalisme, there is a preoccupation with culture— the set of concepts, symbols, etc., that men use—and a firm determination not to see it merely as a set of echoes (whether of things or of social groups and statuses), but instead, as a system that has its own rules, the manner in which its visible elements are generated, laid bare.

A version of structuralisme was already implicit, for instance, in Wittgenstein's concept of a "language game." The point of that notion was to draw the reader's attention to the wide variety of such games, of systems of rules and elements, within which a given expression could have a role and hence a "meaning." What he was concerned with denying was the assumption that in language there was but one game, or only one game that mattered, namely that of matching linguistic units (sentences) with real-world units (facts). He held, rightly, that many theorists of language has assumed this; and he also held, quite wrongly, that what are known as philosophic problems are only or generally engendered by the failure to see this point. With the old view there also went a corresponding distinction between primary and secondary qualities, or a kind of logicians' and linguists' variant therof: There was logical form—hard and solid—and its filling—ephemeral and secondary.

With the insistence on the diversity of games, or of structures as we can say in the present context, this belief in such a neatly two-tier structured reality automatically vanished. There is no list of generic primary qualities, or secondary ones, holding over the entire variety of diverse language games. Games draw quite different distinctions between the solid–substantial and the ephemeral, and some of them perhaps don't have such a distinction at all, or they have a multiplicity of them. There is a parallel here with structuralistes who also believe in a plurality of structures and who also do not look down on culture as secondary. There is also a striking similarity between Berkeley's assault on the primary–secondary distinction, through his attack on the notion of "abstraction," and Wittgenstein's erosion of a neatly stratified world, through his attack on the notion of an underlying homogeneity of language. This assumption had played a part in the view he was destroying, entriely analogous to that attributed by Berkeley to "abstration." If we could abstract, we could reach a generic substance–substratum; and if there was but one real kind of language use, its form gave us the general nature of reality—its primary qualities.

But there is also a difference between the structuralistes and Wittgenstein here. They do also seem to think that the various structures formally resemble each other and are rooted in some generically shared structure of the human mind. For Wittgenstein, the whole point of language games was their irreducible diversity.

The outlook known as structuralisme really emerges through the super-imposition of these two insights, or switches of vision. In two distinct spheres, an echo or reflection theory is denied: Any set of human or cultural products are seen as really emanating from a persistent core system, emanating from it rather than merely consisting of linked elements in a sequence, and culture specifically is saved from being seen as a mere set of frills, pale shadows of true substance. The meanings that constitute it, again, are seen as systematically generated. On the one hand, epistemological realism takes over from the notion of "explanation as shorthand and fiction," with its attribution of a merely instrumental, illusory status to the entities cited in an explanation; and on the other, an implicit sociological reductionism of culture, which had seen it as a mere set of reflections, in language, ritual, mythology, or whatnot, of the serious, weighty, substantial, structural relations in, as it were, masculine areas such as politics and the economy, is rejected. Henceforth, culture was to have its own structure, its own laws, emanating from its own persisting central core. Given all this, it is odd that there should have been a Marxist–structuraliste rapprochement, given the Marxist view of the derivativeness of the super-structure. In part, the Marxist–structuralist syncretism was indeed also associated with doctrines conferring autonomy on theorizing and intellectual activity, by treating it as one further form of *practice*. In part, I fear that those who operated this syncretism were not unduly fastidious logically. The Marxist–structuraliste union reminds me of the story of the celebrated head of a famous and very enlightened and liberal Cambridge college, who was heard to remark at a wedding, nodding at the happy couple: "I have slept with both of them, and can recommend neither to other other."

But the influence is richer still. There were other considerations and influences contributing to the sense that the correct or fruitful mode of explanation in human, social, or cultural studies is not subsumption under an extraneous law, but generation or emanation from a permanent core structure.

There are areas in which the pursuit of covering laws is fairly unpromising or outright hopeless, whereas the attainment of generative or emanative explanations, so to speak, is a perfectly reasonable prospect. As stated, some realms of human activity tend to be like this, but not only human realms. In fact, covering-law and generative explanation can on occasion be related inversely. Take as an example a system that is more natural than human–namely, the roulette wheel.

The operation of the roulette wheel generates a sequence of numbers, usually between 0 and 32, also classifiable (but for the eccentric 0) as *odd* and *even, red* and *black,* etc. Now the sequence is not merely not subsumable under any law governing the pattern of numbers; the system is so designed as to ensure that this is not possible. And not merely is it not possible at the ground or phenomenological level, it is also not possible by means of that favored strategy of covering-law theorists, i.e., by means of concepts at some remove from the ground-level phenomena. In other words, not merely is there no law saying that after a 3, we are to expect such and such a number, but equally, there are no subtler laws, of the form, let us say, of something like this: After $n$ even numbers, expect an odd one. This is of course the main strategy of inquiry of the covering-law school: If, as is generally the case, no good laws are to be found in a given realm at the level of our initial and observational categorizations of objects or events in that field, we must reconceptualize the realms in "deeper" terms that do lead us toward powerful generalization. We do not talk physics in daily life, and few if any powerful generalizations can be stated in terms of the categories employed in daily life. But the language of chemistry and physics, while referrring indirectly to an important proportion at least of the kind of event we deal with in daily life, does it in more abstract terms, not referring directly to the familiar objects of daily "lived" experience, but making the formulation of laws possible.

But this strategy, which is the very essence of successful science as conceived by the law theories, is not applicable to a well-built roulette wheel. Does, then, the sequence of a roulette wheel escape all explanation? If we were provided with such a sequence from within a society whose manner of operation we did not yet understand, should we be obliged to give up in despair? Not in the least. Suppose an archaeologist from a society totally ignorant of roulette came across a partly decipherable document that in fact is the record kept by a croupier at a table in Monte Carlo. We'd better make our imaginary archaeologist a structuraliste, for we can then imagine him to be a very happy archaeologist indeed. As the language in which the croupier kept his record has not yet been mastered by the scholars of our structuraliste–archaeologist's culture circle, he does not know what those signs, like *odd* and *even* or *red* and *black*, actually mean. But that does not worry him one little bit. In fact, it give him pleasure. He is, after all, a structuraliste. Extraneous reference of a symbol is not a thing of great moment. It is the system of which it is a part that matters. The *structure* is the thing.

And here the *structure* is very plain. In fact it has that binary polarized quality that brings joy to his heart. Here is a system oscillating neatly between the polarities *red* and *black, odd* and *even.* Whatever these terms refer to (and to hell with that), they clearly were the polar concepts entering into the construction of that world, indicating its limits, expressing its vital tensions. And what was more, this world had a number of such polarities and tensions, which combined and recombined with each other in all possible ways, thus neatly teaching the denizens of that world the limits and the dramas of their existence! And there was even, on occasion, an entry in the record, namely zero, that apparently eluded those polarities. No doubt it was specially significant, indicating the ambiguous fusion, sublation, and temporary transcendence of the binary oppositions that make up that world. Clearly, the occurrence of zero was a kind of climax in the series, an apex of the semantic triangle, an orgiastic suspension of the customary oppositions and of the law of the excluded middle, which like the famous suspensions of logic in central religious doctrines, simultaneously signals the sacredness of the occasion and yet, by containing the suspended oppositions in an explosive, unstable, transient unity, reminds the believer of the bounds, oppositions, and tensions of the world over which the faith presides and on which it confers its conceptual structure. (As you can see, I too can write structuraliste prose when I set my mind to it, though I daresay this is a mediocre and derivative specimen of it.)

Let us leave the example of the roulette wheel. A roulette sequence is produced by natural, not social or conceptual, causation, though of course the significance of the series is social. I introduced the example because of its simplicity and because it shows how plausible, and in this case indeed fully valid, structuraliste explanations can be used in an area in which the searcher after covering laws is forever doomed to disappointment. But lest the example misleads someone, a point needs to be made. The shift from the search for covering laws to the pursuit of generative structures is not the same thing as the shift from causal to statistical explanation. In the case of the roulette-produced sequence, if our hypothetical archaeologist had a penchant for probability theory rather than for structuralisme, he would of course quickly have spotted that, though there seemed to be no causal order in the sequence, it was admirably amenable to calculations of probability. But this option, evidently open and indeed correct in this particular example, is not always available and, more important, is not always relevant. And that brings us to the other, more realistic precedents for the adoptions of the emanationist–generative approach.

Take the case of linguistics. Here, once again, as in the roulette case, the sequences of sounds as such are barely susceptible to causal covering laws or any covering laws. As Chomsky observes, the probability of any one sentence being uttered at a given point of time is extremely small, so small as to be negligible. Probabilities of course attach to given sounds and sound patterns (if only because the number of phonemes in any language is finite, and indeed not very large). But these probabilities hardly exhaust linguistics.

On the contrary, revolution in linguistics of some decades ago consisted precisely in the abandonment of the search for causal sequences, which would link linguistic sound patterns with antecedent situations in the extralinguistic world. *That* was the behaviorist program, which simply confused the (plausible) doctrine that all assertions must be experientially tested with the (absurd) view that all mental performances, including assertions, must be uniquely tied to experiential antecedents. As Chomsky pointed out, the causes in the world that allegedly "controlled" the utterances had to be invented ad hoc and ex post. In retrospect, this behaviorist search for the elements in the world of experience "under the control of which" given linguistic utterances came to be made (a search so effectively ironized by Chomsky) does indeed seem absurd. The new "generative" strategy consists of attempts to specify the formal features of the core structure, form which the actual range of utterances recognized in a given language, as it were, emanates. It doesn't even try to show why a particular utterance occurred at a given time and given circumstance. It can only show how that utterance comes to lie within the bounds of the generative power of a given language. This powerful precedent no doubt provoked attempts at emulation in other areas of the human and social sciences. Whether indeed this strategy is as appropriate in other fields, whether their problems and circumstances are relevantly similar to linguistics, is something that needs to be examined.

Take the case of phonetics. As a matter of historical fact, certain developments in phonetics did indeed stimulate the efforts to develop a structuraliste method in anthropology. If I understand those advances in phonetics properly, they amount to this: The sounds emitted by the human throat can be characterized by a set of binarily opposed characterizations, such that only one, but at least one, of each pair of opposites applies to any sound. Thus if the characterizations are $A$ and $-A$, $B$ and $-B$, $C$ and $-C$, and so on, then every sound will be characterizable as simultaneously either $A$ or $-A$, $B$ or $-B$, and so on. Languages construct their "phonemes," i.e., units of sound such that within the limits of one phoneme all sounds—despite whatever further subtle differences there might be between them—are interchangeable and make the same contribution to the meaning or role of an utternace. If the number of these opposed pairs is finite, as is the case, the number of possible phonemes is correspondingly finite. Languages do not exhaust all the possible phonemes available to them: They leave some of them unused, or they lump together classes of sounds that, in another language, are subdivided into a number of phonemes.

The influential precedent in phonetics has at least two very important features. One of them is what might be called its binarism. The generative mechanism is simple and really relies on the principle that each entity in the "generated" realm must have one of two attributes, drawn one each from a finite set of pairs. Whether binarism can indeed be transferred from phonetics (without prejudice to the question concerning whether it works to perfection in that sphere, an issue on which I am not competent to speak), if so why so, and if not why not, is a question that deserves ample discussion. I see no reason why it should be true, though of course any finite set of distinctions can be presented as a series of nested binary ones.

Phonetic structuralisme, in this sense, achieves a kind of pleasing transcendence, or if you like, ontological penetration of reality. This is seldom given us, and we must be grateful when we come across an example of it. As indicated at the beginning, part of the appeal of structuralisme is that it links us with the old emanationist tradition, the hope that explanations give us not just shorthand summaries of surface patterns, but reveal for us a deep, permanent, morally saturated, and satisfying reality, qualitatively different from and superior to the ephemeral and amoral connections observed on the surface of things. Now it would be an exaggeration to say that phonetics propels us into some noumenal and moral realm. But, at a more modest level, phonetics does significantly bridge disparate regions and explains one in terms of another, and thus it does provide a very profound kind of explanation. The point is this: The binary characterization of sounds, which provide the basic material, as it were, from which the bricks of language are made, are defined in *phonetic* terms, i.e., in terms of physically indentifiable and definable properties, definable in neutral, interlinguistic, intersocial, physicalist, and operational terms. They are, so to speak, part and parcel of physics and not necessarily of any culturally specific perceptual space. But they generate phonemic elements, i.e., the bricks of individual languages, and these bricks—phonemes—notoriously are not the same in diverse languages.

Now this is very important. It shows how elements drawn from (or definable in terms of) the physicalist world generate the elements used for the inner phonetic world of distinct cultures—of specific linguistic communities. Given the shared and universal properties of sounds, the capacities of the human throat to produce varieties of them, and of the human ear to receive and discriminate between these sounds, we can see how nature's material is turned into cultural bricks. The generative prototype in phonetics, which has so much inspired structuralisme in anthropology, is a good if simple specimen of a genuine, illuminating explanation. It is of course noteworthy that all this has inspired an important piece of terminology in current anthropology, notably the distinction between *etic* (from phonetic) and *emic* (from phonemic).

By etic, an anthropologist means the characterization of some social activity in terms appropriately used by an outsider, employing neutral, "scientific" terminology; by emic, the characterization of an activity in terms employed from the inside, by the natives themselves. If, in any given field of activity, we can identify the mechanisms by which etic materials are turned into emic meanings, we have achieved a great deal. There is of course no guarantee whatever that any given piece of emic significance can be explained as a transformation of etic materials at all. No doubt cultures possess "private meanings," so to speak, which are not etically explicable at all; which, from the viewpoint of a scientistic philosophy, we could say the culture in question simply "makes up" from its own head, as it were. Relativism could be redefined, I suppose, as the view that there aren't any etic concepts at all, really; that the soi-disant etic is merely somebody's emic (say that of members of twentieth century Western scientific communities), and that it wrongly and presumptuously claims a special, intercultural, or rather transcultural, privileged status. Whether this is so is an issue that can hardly be pursued here. Suffice it to say that while some anthropologists claim to hold such a relativistic, etic-denying view in their working life, in practice they behave like normal members of the Western scientific community, speak "etic" to each other most of the time or indeed all the time, and most or all of the theories and accounts they offer would simply make so sense unless this were so. In a world in which only "emic" speech existed, anthropology and comparative social studies simply would not make sense.[4]

Now let us consider logic and metamathematics. This important and active

---

[4]Some adherents of this modern form of relativism actually welcome this consequence, and are pleased that intersocial generalizations should be impossible. It enables them to treat all cultures as cognitively equal and exempt from rational criticism purporting to stand outside local cultural custom. Extending this then to their own culture (or whichever culture they favor), this then enables them to endorse what would otherwise seem to be archaic and logically indefensible beliefs.

field seems to have shifted in this century from a Cartesian to a generative or emanationist paradigm. When logic was revived around the turn of the century as part of an attempt to provide a firm basis for mathematics, the idea present in the minds of at least some of the practitioners was that the "logicization" of mathematics would lead to a science exemplifying the Cartesian ideal—a firm base, providing a kind of risk-free, or at least minimally risky, foundation, giving virtually no hostages to cognitive fortune and transmitting this security by means of rigorous reasoning to the entire edifice erected on it. Partly, but only partly, for technical reasons that undermined the faith in the feasibility of this exercise, this ideal no longer seems to haunt the subject. The picture is now quite different. The general strategy seems to be the exploration of the generative power of an artificially invented or postulated   core and mapping it against the actual practices of mathematicians.

In substantive or empirical fields, the contrast is between emanative or generative power of an artificially invented or postulated core and mapping it other. In formal fields such as mathematics, emanation is constrasted not with any kind of causation (which is absent) but with deduction. The background picture in this field now seems to be this: The working mathematician does indeed work by a kind of natural deduction, employing principles of inference that he does not formalize. But mathematical logic is concerned with constructing formal systems within which the elements (axioms, inference rules, etc.) of the central structural core are strictly specified, and where the practitioner is concerned, precisely, with understanding the limits of what this system can or cannot generate. The logical understanding of mathematics then consists of mapping the relatively intuitive, naturally deductive work of mathematicians onto such formal generative models. If I am right in supposing that this is the pervasive spirit of the subject now, then this in turn provided a precedent and model for the endeavor to practice structuralisme in other regions of inquiry. I have little doubt but that this persuasive and prestigious exemplar did indeed exercise such an influence.[5]

---

Holders of this view have received a curious reinforcement from the philosopher W. V. Quine, who affirms the relativity of meanings under the name of the "indeterminacy of translation." His reasons are not however the usual ones (which are a kind of Herderian reverence for the privacy and dignity of each and every culture). Instead, his view follows in part from his exclusion of meaning from his own ontology, which in turn entails the impossibility of asserting identities of meaning (within as much as between languages), and hence excludes confident, or any, translations. This is all rather odd in as far as for other purposes operative within his philosophy he welcomes a rather physicalist–evolutionist account of the general role and manner of operation of those incommensurate clusters of ideas, allegedly debarred from communicating with each other owing to the absence of a shared, universal conceptual currency. Yet they are all described in terms of building world pictures as extrapolations from their own sensory stimuli with a view to predicting the pattern of further such stimuli—an account of cultures and world views that not only leaves out a large part of what interests anthropologists and other philosophers but that also seem to presuppose that there is a single world and an optimal, if not uniquely correct, idiom for describing it, after all (see Quine [1962, 139] and Gellner [1979, Chapters 11 and 12].

[5]See Musgrave, A. [1977].

The "generative" paradigm stands contrasted with *both* causation *and* deduction, when either of these is conceived as God-given or nature-given, to be accepted and simply explored for the connections that they just bring with themselves. Instead, the notion *generativeness* contains the key insight that whatever connections emerge on the surface are there as manifestations of the permanent core, and it is the core and the rules that link it to the surface that must be understood. The surface connections on their own have no explanatory power.

Structuralisme is basically a shift back to an emanative or generative model of explanation, from a linear or covering-law model. It is inspired partly by the consideration that when we handle cultural products, systems that men make even if they are not conscious of so doing, we believe that the central generative core or structure really is there, and our faith in this is not eroded by the empiricist interdict on inventing reduplicative and inaccessible "other realms" when explaining the patterns of this, our accessible world. The shift is further reinforced by a transfer of attention to systematic cultural productions such as mythology, away from spheres that are not so much cultural products as they are the result of an interplay of social and natural forces—notably, economic and political life. The shift is reinforced further still by apparently successful implementations of a similar strategy in linguistics, phonetics, and mathematical logic, and possibly other areas.

This is itself, so to speak, the generative core of structuralisme—the elements present in the minds of actual structuralistes that manifest themselves in their actually visible, surface productions. Hence, this is the point at which it is appropriate to sketch out the overall syndrome of structuralisme.

Structuraliste work tends to exhibit the following traits:

1. It operates with a theory of meaning that is systematic rather than representational. The meaning of a sign is its place in a system of signs, rather than its relationship to a special bit of the world of which it should be the *Doppelgänger* or shadow.
2. The system is assumed to be generated by a kind of core set of elements or structure, persisting independently, and at least ideally located in a realm of being other than that of its own generated manifestations.
3. A society or culture is assumed either to be, or at least to be very intimately linked to, such a system, comprising both core and manifestations.
4. It is generally assumed that the core elements occur in contrasted pairs, or if you like, that each of them splits into a pair of polar opposites. This might be called "Binarism."
5. The core not merely genuinely exists—this approach involves a realist not an instrumentalist theory of explanation—but also persists unchanged over time. Otherwise it could hardly extend its explanatory cover over manifestations occurring at diverse and successive dates.

6. Structuralisme either actually favors cultural products (myths, rituals, literature, gastronomy), or at the very least treats them as equal in importance to the "hard" elements of social life (order-enforcement, production). It is quite free of that anthropological equivalent of the distinction between primary and secondary qualities that is the old distinction between structure and culture, where the latter is assumed to be both accidental and largely epiphenomenal.

7. When contemplating cultural products, be it say an epos or a menu, a structuraliste will seek out the opposed extremes on or in it and assume them to be the limits of the world in question *and* to be parts of the generative core that produced it. This might be called the method of "beating the bounds."

8. For structuralistes, meaning is the very material of their inquiry, not merely something that accompanies, precedes, or possibly helps explain or characterize conduct.

All these various traits are of course not fully independent. For instance, the preferences for cultural products and for meaning are clearly connected and overlap. If I have separated these in effect intertwined strands, it is simply because one aspect or another of structuralisme may be more manifest from various angles, and it is worthwhile including them all. Also, it should not be assumed that all these elements are necessarily consistent. For instance, the timelessness of the explanatory core structure does not tally with the indentification of such a structure within a society, given that societies notoriously have a habit of changing over time. Or again, is it really plausible to equate the polar extremes found in the manifestations of a culture with the core-generating elements, given that, in a well-constructed generative explanation, core explanans and surface explanandum may be expected to be articulated in different idioms, to be made of different materials?

These are some of the inner strains that may be expected to appear in structuralisme, if I have identified its essence correctly. But I shall concentrate on some of the main weaknesses or doubts one may have about the unqualified or uncritical application of the structuraliste approach to the study of human societies.

The structuraliste approach is not interested in surface or linear sequences; it is assumed that the full range or potential, as it were, of the generative core in question will play itself out, and that the precise order of appearance of the cast, so to speak, does not matter. The pack has a certain number of cards; all of them will sooner or later be played; and we work out the nature of the pack from the run, whatever its order. This assumption has to hold if the structuraliste approach is to make sense.

Does it? It does in certain spheres. No wonder structuralisme has been influenced by linguists, and no wonder that areas such as mythology, ritual, and symbolism are favored by it. The point about the symbol tokens used by systems such as language is that they are *cheap*, that opportunity-cost of using them is virtually zero. Sounds, marks on the paper, symbolic gestures, all cost virtually nothing in terms of effort or any other price involved. That, no doubt, is one of the reasons why they came to be used as such.

To appreciate the significance of this, imagine a contrary situation. Imagine, for instance, that the letters of the alphabet constituted an economically scarce resource, which had to be secured by production or trade. Think of the following articles in the financial sections of the press:

> *The Polish economy is in dire straits owing to the continued shortage of Ls, without which it cannot function. The only unexhausted high-yield L-ore is now found in central Asia, and the Soviet government has shamelessly used this as a means of pressurising the Poles. The recent patented process for extracting Ls from the sea has proved uneconomical, and the Polish government now places hopes in its deep L-drilling in the Carpathians. If this fails, L-rationing will be imposed both on the Polish press and on private correspondence. The town council of Łodz has offered a large prize for the most suitable renaming of the city.*

Or again:

> *A question is to be asked in Parliament about the alleged continued dumping of Hs in the British market by both the Russians and the French, neither of whom has any uses of Hs. This is however ruining what is left of the old Lancashire H-industry. Several Lancashire MPs of both parties are planning both to approach the Chancellor of the Exchequer with a view to introducing import restrictions on Hs, and the Minister of Education with a request that elementary schools be asked to redouble their efforts against the dropping of Hs, a habit that continues to have a severely adverse impact on the H-market.*

Or again:

> *Following an initiative by the Swedish Ministry of Trade, the Scandinavian countries have agreed to set up a joint board for the supervision of the trade and production of øs, without which the Scandinavian economies cannot operate. The Danish parliament has approved the setting up of a commission that is to investigate the compatibility of this board with Denmark's obligations under EEC rules.*

Now the whole point is this: In fact, the entities used in symbolism and communiation operate under a rather special economy, without scarcity. Or rather, one should put this the other way round: Symbolic systems choose as their units, their vehicles of communication, elements whose cost approaches zero. Because this is so, but *only* because this is so, or in as far as it is so, we can expect symbolic systems to play out their full inner potential, so to speak; and for this very reason, we can infer from the range of their production the nature of the core mechanisms that produces them. The range of surface phenomena produced is not distorted by shortages, not affected by rising and falling prices. The zloty may not be worth much, but the Ł is free, and the Polish government can print as many Łs as it likes without fearing that the resulting inflation will make them unusable. Their use is already predicated on the assumption that they are to be had for free. A very, very tired and exhausted Pole may on occasion be too weary to utter even an Ł, but the majority of members of the Polish speech community can expand or contract their simultaneous production and consumption of Łs without batting an eyelid. In fact, as far as speech is concerned, we are *already* in that realm of plenty in which, as Marx foresaw, the distinction between work and self-expression lapses. It is a pity that no philosopher has noticed this intriguing fact sooner. It could have been used to cheer us up.

But large segments of social life—need we be told?—do not operate under such blessed conditions. The economy is in effect defined by economists in terms of *scarcity*. Politics, again, is a realm that seems to be a zero-sum game; power for some means less power for others. The same holds true of prestige and status. (Some must lose, and somehow or other be constrained to accept their loss. In the telling of a story, neither narrator nor listeners need to be losers; and in *such* a situation, it is plausible to suppose that an *un*constrained code plays itself out to the full, freely relasing all its potential. But other aspects of life are not so free of constraint, conflict, and painful choice of incitable loss *somewhere*.) In brief, there are extensive aspects of human life, alas including those that seem essential for our survival, where the actual sequence of events is determined not merely by the free play of some underlying core mechanism (if indeed it exists at all), but by the blind constraints and shortages and competitions and pressures of the real extraneous environment. A large part of the social sciences has been rightly concerned with an attempt at understanding how that kind of extraneous and straight–causal constraint can be fused with the emanative, unconstrained free play of a generative mechanism. Are we justified in trying to apply the structuraliste paradigm here?

Frazer would have had us believe that the priest at Nemi suffered himself to be killed, victim to nothing more than the association of ideas. I find it just as hard to believe that he should perish merely because his death was a message in the generative code of a culture. Pace the structuralistes, although society does use codes, society is *not* a code. What happens in a society cannot be inferred from even a successful working-out of the range-potential of its code, whether that code be conceived as (literally) a language or a "tradition" or even a set of persisting institutions.

Closely related to this objection is another one. The generative or emanationist model of explanation makes sense in contexts in which there reason to suppose that there is indeed a persisting, reasonably stable core structure, responsible for the emanations or surface phenomena. In the case of human language, this is indeed so. Notoriously, the best-known and most provocative thesis associated with the emergence of the idea of generative grammar is precisely the existence of an invariant, universal and innate linguistic human potential, activated into being and given its superficial phonetic and other traits by the experience of a specific language. but possessing a basic form manifested equally in any human language and not dependent on any. This ultimate core is assumed to be located in human neurophysiology in a manner that is as yet quite beyond the power of neurophysiologists to locate. Even if we think of the more specific generative core of a single language (as opposed to that ultimate core shared, according to this theory, by all languages), the existence of such a permanent and stable core structure is perfectly plausible. The corpus of phonetic, syntactical, and any other rules that define a given natural language can be assumed to be built into the customs of an ongoing community of the users of that language, rather in the way some heavy object can be carried by a large number of bearers, and remain unaffected by the perpetual dropping out of some bearers and their replacement by others. This is evidently how languages do perpetuate themselves. They do of course change, but they change rather slowly: Compared with the speed with which single concrete utterances follow each other, languages change so slowly that they are stable for all practical purposes. They do flow, but so do glaciers; the flow of a glacier does not prevent a mountaineer or skier from treating the glacier as a fixed object.

But what is true of glaciers and languages is *not* generally true of societies and institutions. Above all, though a language is in a sense "made up" of the utterances that occur in it, the utterances do not modify it (or only very seldom and trivially). There is no feedback from utterances to language—from *parole* to *langue*. Very, very occasionally, an earth-shaking political speech, a brilliant witticism by a man of letters or a comedian, may from the moment of its utterance introduce a new turn of speech into the language. But this is rare, and even when it happens, it does not modify the language in any very serious way. But does this hold of institutions and communities?

Some may indeed approach this kind of stability—but even then, it must be said, they only do so rather precariously, and the distance between *parole* and *langue* is, in their case, incomparably smaller than is the case for (literal) languages. It might be said, for instance, that in a relatively long-lived and fairly stable institution such as the British parliament, the rules of parliamentary procedure, the core structure that limits the pattern of activities in parliament, change rather slowly and are not effects by individual performances within parliament. But even in this rather exceptional and privileged case, which might perhaps be paralleled in the rituals of stable and long-lived religions, the ratio of structural, dispositional change to episodic performance is far greater than is the case in language. If one multiplies the few hundred parliamentarians by an estimate of the number of parliamentary speech acts performed by them per generation and relates the resulting figure to the amount of deep change occurring as a result of new political situations in a generation, the resulting ratio must be far, far smaller than the ratio of speech acts performed by even small linguistic communities per generation, related to the amount of changes in a language per generation.

But in any case, whatever the result of such calculations (which would of course depend on how we decided to count acts and changes), the procedural rules of stable institutions such as the British parliament are not, for better or for worse, typical of human institutions and societies in general. In many political and economic activities, important events and decisions modify the core itself. To put it another way, there is no stable and independent core that is reasonably insulated from events in the sequence on the surface. Or to put it another way still, changes in the core are parts of the surface sequence itself. Or to put it another way still, no useful distinction can be drawn between a core-generating structure and a generated surface sequence. For better or for worse, that is our condition, at least in very many of our activities. This may or may not make life more interesting; but one price paid for it is that the activities for which this observation holds are not easily amenable or are not amenable at all to the structuraliste paradigm. All this is merely another way of saying something that others have noted previously: It is puzzling how structuralisme could cope with basic change. It can really only cope with diachronic phenomena by treating them as syncronic—as accidentally successive manifestations of a stable, permanent core.

Another aspect of this point is that in some of the fields that structuralistes try to impose it, one has some difficulty in imagining just where the central core could possibly be located. With language, we have no such difficulty: Neurophysiology plus the disembodied, diffused, collectively carried rules of a natural language, spread out over the perpetually repeated language use of an entire community, are perfectly reasonable candidates for the locus or carrier of the core. In other spheres, no such candidate-loci seem to be easily available. This does not seem to bother structuralistes too much, but it seems to me wrong on their part not to worry about this question, for it deserves serious consideration. There is an irony in the structuraliste–Marxiste flirtation or rapprochement: Marxism is supposed to insist on a material base and on change. As far as I can see, the whole bias of the structuraliste model favors the assumption of timelessness, and its practitioners do not seem to mind too much when the base–core is allowed, in what would seem to be a somewhat idealist spirit, to float in thin air.

One could put the matter as follows: Structuralisme is a bit like reconstructing a pack of cards from the record of a run of dealt cards. This method works, if indeed there *is* a stable, permanent pack; and also, if there is nothing that systematically interferes with the dealing out of the cards. But suppose some censoring mechanism inhibits the dealing of certain cards? If there is some such interfering mechanism, it too must be understood; or perhaps we should say, it must be understood *first*. In the life of real societies, some of these mechanisms have familiar names—such as coercion or economic constraint.

This analogy also breaks down or is incomplete. The operation of dealing cards from a pack is easily understood. The mechanisms by which visible, surface elements emerge from a permanent cultural core are *far from* being self-evident or transparent. Cards are the same whether they sit in the pack or whether they are dealt. No such manifest identity can be assumed in cultural "generation." On the contrary, one may suspect that the materials used in the deep and surface structures are *not* identical, and a good explanation must show just *how* the one "produces" the other.

Just this constitutes another and, once again, related objection to the practice of structuralistes. The method is valid if we are, so to speak, shown the generation of one world from materials drawn from another, above all, independently identifiable world. In the priviledged case of phonetics, it was apparently shown that, drawing on the realm of physically identifiable noises, the range of socially significant noises, i.e., phonemes, could be extracted. Given the phychologically established competence of the human ear to distinguish the available combinations of those paired opposites, and given the sociolinguistically established capacity of speech communities to carry appropriate subsets of the available usable potential phonemes and to bring them effectively to the attention of children who are being socialized into them—given all that, it really has been shown how the phonemic world of given cultures is constructed out of the phonetic world kindly provided by nature. The elements of the surface are explained in terms of the rather different elements of the core structure.

In the actual work of structuralistes dealing with phenomena such as mythologies or works of literature or rituals, I often fail to detect signs of any such achievement. There does not seem to be even any attempt to locate some deeper level so as to explain the surface in terms of it. Instead, elements plucked by some mysterious process from the surface text—usually the alleged polar extremities occurring in it—are attributed a kind of double status, marking both the limits of the emic world in which they occur and being somehow mysteriously credited with also being the (etic?) bricks out of which that inward world of the culture in question has been constructed. Can they really be both?

Now this particular objection could not be raised against those two great proto-structuralists—Immanuel Kant and Emile Durkheim. I am not defending either the former's *Critique of Pure Reason* or the latter's *The Elementary Forms of Religious Life* from other criticisms that can be raised against them. But they are, both of them, gloriously free of this particular blemish. In the great *Critique*, Kant endeavors to show how the emic world of all men (strictly, all being endowed with our kind of reason), who for him formed but one single culture, was inevitably generated from the combination of certain core elements. Given that we are beings with sensibility (receiving sensations with spatial and temporal dimensions), and given that we had "reason and understanding," by which he meant basically the capacity to group individual objects under generic concepts and the capacity to combine concepts into judgments and to erect pyramidal systems of concepts and judgments—given all that, he thought he could show how a certain world, containing substances, causal order, a single deity, and even Newton, inevitably emerged. A kind of minimal epistemological receptor is postulated with only the equipment specified in the *Critique*, and a habitable *Lebenswelt* tumbles out as a consequence—a world fit for Newtonian scientists and Pietist Protestants to live in. I am not suggesting that the execution of this program was flawless, and I do not wish to defend Kant against the charge that the generated world bears little resemblance to *some* human worlds and at the same time a suspicious excess of resemblance to one special world—that of conscientious, orderly, unitarian, and science-oriented Protestants. But at least the program itself satisfied an important criterion for a genuine structuraliste explanation. It led us from one level to another. The items used at the explanans level were very economically, nonarbitrarily chosen; and the elements in the generated explanadum would bare some resemblance to a world actually inhabited by some of us.

The same can be said of Durkheim. There is an irony about this, given Durkheim's expressed preference for explaining the social by the social. In a sense, the reason why the *Elementary Forms* is such an interesting achievement is precisely because he did not follow this precept in it. The distinctively social and human (the possession of shared, compulsive, categorical concepts) is explained in terms of something that could be presocial—namely ritual. *Ritual maketh man.* This seems to me analogous to the phoneticians' achievement of explaining the phonemic in terms of the phonetic. I am not saying that Durkheim's theory is actually true, only that it satisfies the requirement that the explanans and the explanandum be at different levels (rather than at the same level and presupposing each other), and that it is plausible. Bertand Russel ironized the "social-contract" theory of the origin of language, which would have an assembly of hitherto speechless elders solemnly agree henceforth to call a cow a *cow*. Durkheim's version would have a group of hitherto behaviorist, associationist, conceptless elders, persistently indulge in common rituals, which would *eventually* imprint and impose shared, compulsive concepts on them, thus rendering them human and beyond the reach of a merely stimulus–response (S–R), behaviorist model of conduct, and thus also propel them into the realm of thought proper. And this theory is not absurd—whether or not it is accurate.

For Kant, the generative core was not accessible to observation, but could be inferred by reasoning that locates the presuppositions of our world, our cognitive and moral judgments. For Chomsky, the core is only contingently unobservable; we infer it, but one fine day neurophysiologists may actually locate it. For Durkheim, the core was *already* observable by anthropologists. Ritual conduct had for him a kind of double ontological status: On the one hand, accessible to observation by the field researchers, and on the other it constituted at least part of the core that engendered our conceptual powers. Durkheim seemed to think (erroneously, I suspect) that a Humeian–behaviorist–S–R psychology might work for animals, but failed with us because it could not account for the *compulsiveness* of categorical and moral concepts.

In the realm of sound, we can go to the *sub* or basement world of physics in order to explain the ground-level phonemic world of the sounds we perceive; and the same is possible in the sphere of colors, and indeed Edmund Leach (1970, Chapter 2) chooses this realm to explain what structuralisme is about. But when it comes to our *entire* cultural–conceptual world, the world we live in, do we have any subworld, some neutral base, the combinations of which would explain the bricks on our world? We have not. In practice, structuralistes then explain our world or the world of a given culture in terms of itself—of (arbitrarily?) selected polar elements within itself. Finally there is also in structuralisme a certain ambiguity concerning whether each culture has a single generative core from which its myths and rituals emanate or whether the hunt is one for a universal, panhuman core, manifested by the cultural products of *all* societies.

But our latter-day structuralistes seldom seem even to try to emulate Kant and Durkheim and locate a sub-basement that would explain the range of output of a culture or of mankind. They are content to stay at the same level, explaining a cultural world in terms of itself, merely underlining its alleged salient polarities. Admittedly, it would be appallingly difficult to do the other thing: The world of meanings of any one culture is no doubt infinitely more complex than its phonemic world. And we have little indication where on earth (literally) we could look for those pre-semantic elements that would explain the semantic to us. We have no other world to supply the bricks of this one.

This failure to be fastidious about the logic of their program or the precision of its execution seems to me closely associated with another habitual failing. Not only are the polar extremes of a text simply plucked out and then treated as somehow explanatory of the world that the users of the said text live in, but no criteria are offered for how one is to identify the crucial polarities of a world from any old contrast that a willing and imaginative observer may locate in it. The structuralistes seem to be far too willing simply to trust their intuitions in this matter and to expect their readers to extend this trust to them. Polar extremities no doubt abound in many texts, but has anyone ever put it to the test by locking diverse structuralistes in insulated cubicles with the same text, and seeing whether they all emerge with the same binary opposition at the end? And if they do not, as I suspect would be the case, how do we know which one of them got it right? Answer comes there none. If these suspicions are well founded, the conclusion could be that in these fields, the structuraliste method consists of a somewhat arbitrary extraction of polar patterns at the whim of the individual structuraliste virtuosos. As for Binarism, I see no reason for even suspecting it to be true, any more than the Aristotelian doctrine of virtue as a "mean" between two extremes, which it resembles. Admittedly any linear spectrum must point toward two extremes, but I seen no reason for supposing that such spectra are the only ultimate constituents of our cultural worlds.

A number of cautions should be borne in mind. A descriptive account of the spectra or polarities a given society or language works with is *not* the same as a generative account of how these spectra are produced. In other words, one should not confuse, so to speak, descriptive or phenomenological structuralisme with a genuinely explanatory kind. (Often, the former is presented as if it were the latter.) Moreover, a sheer highlighting of our polarities is not even a proper description of a world: It does not tell us how they mesh into each other or whether they are exhaustive. And is there necessarily only one unique way of distinguishing the polarities of a given cultural world? These questions do not seem to be faced seriously when the structuraliste fireworks are being let off.

All these doubts do not amount to an indiscriminate rejection of structuraliste ideas and methods.They merely amount to a recommendation of caution in the application of these ideas to fields other than those in which they were originally fruitful, and likewise, a recommendation of greater thoroughness and fastidiousness in working out the implications of those ideas even in the fields in which they may indeed be applicable.

# REFERENCES

Gellner, E., 1979, *Spectacles and Predicaments,* Cambridge, University Press.
Gellner, E. (ed.), 1980, *Soviet and Western Anthropology,* London, Duckworth, and New York, Columbia University Press.
Leach, E., 1970, *Lévi-Strauss,* London, Fontana.
Milton, J. R., "The origin and development of the concept of 'law of nature' ", *Archives Européennes de sociologie,* XXII, 1981, No. 2.
Musgrave, A., "Logicism Revisited," in *The British Journal for the Philosophy of Science,* vol. 28, No. 2, Jan. 1977.
Pouillon, J., 1980, Structure and structuralism, in Gellner, E. (ed.), *Soviet and Western Anthropology,* London, Duckworth, and New York, Columbia University Press, 275–282.
Quine, W. V., 1962, in *La Philosophie Analytique,* Paris, Cahiers de Rougemont.
Watkins, J. W. N., 1952, Ideal types and historical explanation, *British Journal for the Philosophy of Science,* May 1952.

# 10

## Objectivity—Explanation—Archaeology 1981

*LEWIS R. BINFORD*

Albert Spaulding once said that archaeologists reminded him of a stately minuet with lots of twirling and pirouetting and nobody going anywhere. This impression of archaeology is nowhere more evident than at conferences where individuals posture and present their paradigmatic suggestions in strongly polemical phrases.

For instance, Hodder (in press) has stated that "the dangers of the ecological functionalism rife in prehistoric archaeology are first that ranking in, for example, burial is seen as directly reflecting social hierarchy, whereas, in fact, burial patterns are meaningful transformations of social differentiation."

Another charged statement was recently issued by Gledhill and Rowlands (in press): "Over the past few years a growing number of archaeologists have begun to move away from explanations derived from functional ecology, system theory, and the more naive forms of cultural materialism towards a focus on specific social and political processes and their economic functioning within defined historical circumstances."

These are statements of posture or paradigmatic bias. They advocate the wearing of a particular pair of glasses through which to view the world. The implication is clear that one pair of "glasses" will permit us to see the world more clearly than when we wear, for instance, a "naive-materialist's" or even an "ecological-functionalist's" glasses. Such statements have their place, and it is acknowledged that change of paradigm is one source of change within scientific

**125**

THEORY AND EXPLANATION
IN ARCHAEOLOGY

disciplines. However, such statements do not fulfill functions other than purely sociological ones within the discipline to which they are addressed, unless they are coupled with rather fundamental ideas concerning the nature of science and with a full acceptance of the responsibility that we have to evaluate ideas scientifically once they are proposed.

## PARADIGMS ARE NOT EXPLANATIONS

You may think of our cognitive frame of reference or paradigm as forming the ideas and concepts that give meaning to experience. These condition what one considers relevant to describe or what one chooses to discuss as of interest. One's cognitive frame of reference may be thought of as the culture of science. It consists of the concepts or terms in which experience is intellectually assimilated. In spite of the definitional controversy (see Masterman 1970), I follow Kuhn (1977) in viewing a paradigm as the intellectual terms upon which one meets experience. In short, it is what we expect the world to be like. Things become complicated when we recognize that we cannot gain a direct knowledge of the essential properties of the world. Our cognition is not direct nor objective, but it may be indirect and subjective relative to our beliefs about the world, i.e., our paradigm.

We generally defend our knowledge claims about the world with inferential arguments. I prefer to call these *warranting arguments*: They are arguments advanced that tend to *warrant to others* the beliefs that one has about the world. If done in a robust manner, they make one's knowledge claims appear plausible and acceptable to others. Rarely are such arguments formalized in that the premises are rarely explicit, so conclusions are warranted by appeal to a "common body of knowledge or belief." The more comprehensive the alleged knowledge or more widespread the belief serving as the intellectual context for a warranting argument, the more plausible it appears and therefore the greater likelihood it has of being accepted.

Working within a frame of reference is similar to participation in any other culture: We accommodate experience through our shared cognitive devices. The fact that they facilitate this accommodation appears to us as proof that the world is in fact the way we expect it to be. We may be astonished that others do not see the world the way we do. Cultural man has for all time felt that his beliefs were given by "reality" and were therefore "right," while those of other cultures were clearly misguided or "stupid" for not having seen the "truth" inherent in experience.

Everyday arguments of accommodation—where models of the world are merely fitted to experiences through conceptual devices—form the normal method whereby individuals are enculturated to varying points of view or differing cultural conventions for seeing the world. Contrasting paradigmatic understanding is the basis for all forms of conflicting belief. It is the form of reasoning used to justify or warrant every belief system that man has ever invented outside of the culture of science. The criteria used for justifying one's belief are generally that: (*a*) it accommodates experience in terms of a broader, more comprehensive view of nature; and (*b*) it appears plausible. These are the criteria that cultural man has used ever since he has enjoyed a reasoning capacity. These are the criteria around which argument centers when the pros and cons of contrasting religions, political views, or other culturally variable systems of belief and value are discussed.

There is an unfortunate misconception regarding explanation that is current today, namely that a paradigm provides a useful explanation. Science has been an experiment in developing ways of going beyond the epistemologically unsatisfactory approaches and forms of evaluation already outlined. The history of science describes a long series of investigations in search of criteria for evaluating ideas that go beyond the everyday cultural bias of whether a proposal appears to be a "good or satisfying idea to think." I discussed this problem previously in the following manner (Binford 1977, 3):

> Science is a method or procedure that directly addresses itself to the evaluation of cultural forms. That is, if we view culture as at least referring to the particularly human ability to give meaning expediently to experience, to symbol, and, in turn, view experience through this conceptual idiom, science is then concerned with evaluating the utility of the cultural tools produced.

What is being asserted is that the production of a paradigm with the accompanying warranting arguments may be sufficient to justify its serious consideration, but the warranting arguments—citing a close accommodation between the argument and experience, numerous, seemingly convincing arguments from example, as well as the subjective criteria that it appears to be a good and satisfying idea to think—are unsatisfactory epistemological criteria in any endeavor that seeks to evaluate cultural forms of thought.

## OBJECTIVE EVALUATION

Scientific investigation is the conscious and designed attempt to obtain an *objective* evaluation of the utility and accuracy of proposed ideas and propositions. The reader will immediately recognize that the crucial word in the above sentence is *objective*. What constitutes objectivity? How can we achieve it, given the recognition that *we* in fact design the scientific procedures? Perhaps the first place to begin is to say what objectivity is not. It is not the view of an "outsider" seeing nature in its true form from some privileged observation platform outside of nature. It is not the "pure observer" frequently discussed during the nascent days of science. This change in perspective has been well summarized by Amsterdamski (1975, 169, italics added):

Characterizing by one, shortened formula the intellectual revolution of the 16th and 17th centuries, *it is possible to state that God, as the measure of all things, was replaced by man.* Man, however, as a knowing subject was provided with at least some divine attributes. *He was to be an ideal observer external to the universe under study, and he was to be capable of achieving the absolute truth about this universe.* Beginning with Descartes and Bacon, and ending with Kant and Hegel, this concept of man, variously justified in all philosophical terms as being capable of cognitive procedures, co-determined the style of thinking of modern science. This may be discerned within both empiricists' as well as rationalists' epistemology. . . . By including the knowing subject more and more into the world of nature, by depriving it of its privileged, outside status within nature, modern science steadily undermined its own epistemological basis. *Now not God, not man standing beyond nature and confronting it as a perfect knowing subject, but nature itself was to become the measure of all things.*

In short, man as the creator of his own destiny and man as the observer, outside of nature, capable of *seeing* truth directly, has fallen. We have turned to the study of the causes of human action itself and the evaluation of the effects of our own ideas and actions on how we view the world and what appear to be "facts." Man, both as a subject of study and as observer, has been returned to nature instead of being seen as standing above or outside it.

As suggested above, the growth of knowledge within science gradually undermined early ideas about the world and about the epistemology used. This does not mean that science had rendered itself obsolete, as many alleged social scientists would like to suggest. Quite to the contrary, another and more useful view of "objectivity" developed within the sciences. That was the view that it was not the status of the observer that yielded objectivity *but the status of logical or intellectual independence between the ideas being evaluated, on the one hand, and the intellectual tools employed in the evaluated investigations, on the other.* Under this view, objectivity now rested with the design characteristics of a methodology and the procedures of its implementation rather than with the characteristics of a particular observer. It was something that could be differentially achieved and could be evaluated quite independently of ad hominem arguments or allusions to subjective manipulations by different observers. This linkage between ideas and observations, which suggests that ideas be evaluated by objective means, pinpoints the need in any science for developing such means and further emphasizes the *fact* that the testing of theory is dependent upon the availability of robust methods. I have designated development of such means as "middle range research." It is not middle range because it is unimportant. Quite to the contrary, it is middle range because it links observations and experiences as to what the world is like to ideas— theories (if you will) that seek to tell us why the world is the way it appears to be.

## MIDDLE RANGE RESEARCH

Middle range research results in the production of knowledge and under-standing that may grow, serving as the research-based paradigmatic underpinning of science. This point has been well presented by Amsterdamski (1975, 86) with regard to developed sciences.

> The distinction between "empirical" and "theoretical" . . . may be only a relative one. It is relative historically. A scientist who undertakes the study of a particular problem, for example of a biological one, and who uses various scientific instruments constructed on the grounds of different physical theories, is quite aware of the fact that together with the equipment he uses he accepts also these theories. In spite of this fact, however, he will treat the statements he will formulate by means of these instruments as observational. The observational language is, for him, something already present and historically given by the development of science and common knowledge.

Archaeology is perhaps in a fortunate position in that while there is much contemporary "culture" or paradigmatic bias regarding the nature of man or concerning the causes of history, there is very little folk "knowledge" regarding the formation of the archaeological record. This means that there is little explicit prior development of cognitive devices and frames of reference—paradigmatic development—regarding archaeological phenomena in the literal, "static" sense of the word. For the further development of archaeology the growth of a paradigm, developing cognitive means for identifying properties of the past, or diagnosing the archaeological record and thereby giving meaning in terms of the past, is crucial.

An observational language is at present essentially nonexistent in archaeology. I believe the concepts and hence paradigmatic characteristics of traditional archaeology are essentially useless for modern archaeology. As was suggested in the preceding quotation, the instruments that permit and facilitate unambiguous, meaningful observations must be developed, demonstrated, and tested, using scientific means. Later, as the science of archaeology becomes more mature, these "instruments for measurement" may be taken for granted, and the results of their utilization treated as direct observations on the past. We are a long way from this level of maturity today. We need to recognize very explicitly the current "state of the art" and address the growth of a scientific paradigm as basic and fundamental.

What we are seeking through middle range research are accurate means of identification and good instruments for measuring specified properties of past cultural systems. We are seeking reliable cognitive devices. We are looking for "Rosetta Stones" that permit the accurate conversion from observations on statics to statements about dynamics. Put another way, we are seeking to build a paradigmatic frame of reference for giving meaning to selected characteristics of the archaeological record through a theoretically grounded body of research, rather than accepting "folk" knowledge—let alone implicit folk knowledge—as the basis for describing the past.

My view is that we cannot know the past until we first address the problem of how we go about giving meaning to the archaeological record (see Binford 1968a). *Meanings are carried by concepts and arguments, and the archaeo-*

*logical record contains only arrangements of matter.* We assign concepts to different arrangements of matter or offer arguments regarding the sources or conditions that brought into being particular arrangements of matter. All such propositions are inferences from static to dynamic states that are no longer available for observation.

Given that we have made observations on the archaeological record, offered some generalizations about its properties, and gained considerable experience with the record, we must now ask the question that is crucial to paradigmatic growth: Why is the archaeological record constructed and patterned the way it appears to be?

## THE ARCHAEOLOGICAL RECORD

The direction of attention to the archaeological record itself, rather than the continuation of the self-deceit that we study the past directly, seems central to progress. We not only have to seek knowledge of the archaeological record, we have to seek explanations for its many forms. Explanations (Hempel 1977, 244, italics added) presuppose theories or statements as to why the world is the way it appears to be.

> Theories are the key to the scientific understanding of empirical phenomena, *and they are normally developed only when previous research has yielded a body of information, including empirical generalizations about the phenomena in question.* A theory is then intended to provide deeper understanding by presenting those phenomena as manifestations of certain underlying processes.

During the early 1970s it became clear that my views on archaeological theory were not generally shared. For instance, one view (Watson, LeBlanc, and Redman 1971, 164) equated "theory" with arguments about the explanations for "what happened in history": "There is in a sense an 'archaeological theory' although it might be better characterized as evolutionary anthropology . . . human and cultural evolution is of such scientific and intrinsic interest that there is certainly an essential nomothetic role to be played by archaeologists."

I saw the development of archaeological theory as necessary for the making of reliable statements about the past. Others seemed to see this task as a simple matter of paradigm growth where "constructing" the past was assumed to "flow" naturally from the interaction between a good archaeologist and his experience with the archaeological record. We "did" archaeology, it was felt, to investigate interesting problems, such as the origins of the state, the shift to agriculture, and so forth. Under the latter approach, "doing" archaeology was viewed as the experimental phase of investigating the causes of the past. In my view, we had to conduct another type of experimental research in order to use our observations on the archaeological record for making statements about the past. As stated earlier, *the principles used in making inferences from observations on the archaeological record could not be adopted from other "sciences" since no other science addressed itself to the study of the properties of the archaeological record.* Second, in the absence of reliable inferential procedures for describing the past, there was no way of using the archaeological record either to explicate the past or as "data" for evaluating models or arguments as to why the past was the way it appeared to be.

I saw as a necessity the development of the science of the archaeological record—theoretically independent of the "science of cultural evolution" or other nomothetic approaches that made use of the history constructed by archaeologists. This view addresses directly what Michael Schiffer (1972) has called the formation processes of the archaeological record. We seek to understand the dynamic conditions that brought into being the static forms and arrangements of matter remaining for us to observe. To be useful for developing a picture of the past that is accurate and germane to our curiosity and to ideas about the past, we must develop a theoretical understanding of certain properties of the archaeological record that will *have unambiguous referents in the past and will be uniformly relevant to the past.* If the conditions that brought into being a particular fact are unique and restricted to a particular time period, we cannot make meaningful statements about such phenomena directly. We must derive meaning with reference to some sets of facts that we do not understand. This implies that the intellectual means that serve the functions of a paradigm within a science must largely refer to the unchanging characteristics of human sociocultural organizations of behavior. We must be able to establish intellectual "anchors" in the past before we can explore characteristics that may differ from our current understandings of our current ideas of the past. We can only evaluate differences with reference to some known and stable factors. The latter must be developed for use in inference before we can make meaningful statements about the character of the past. Researching such uniform and regular patterns of relationships between static and dynamic conditions is research directed toward the elucidation of *functional relationships.*

The study of functional relationships is central to the development of well-grounded middle range understanding of the archaeological record, and hence it constitutes the very basis for making statements about the past. From this point of view I find it difficult to understand critics who decry "functionalist" propositions (see Hodder in press). Basically I subscribe to many of the criticisms of functionalism as it was practiced in the social sciences. I fully concur that functional arguments cannot offer explanations for differences between systems, nor explain a system's change, although they may be essential to its useful description. On the other hand, they must, in my opinion, be the basic form of argument used by us in the development of methods for inferentially referring observations on the contemporary archaeological record to active dynamic conditions in the past. Any statement that confers meaning in historical terms to observations made on the archaeological record is an inference. The justifications for such an inference must be robust arguments that link the properties observed (*static matter*) to the properties inferred (*dynamic conditions*). These linkages refer to organizational properties within socio-cultural systems, and by definition they are therefore functional arguments. Those who discourage research of such linkages would have us remain wallowing in opinionated paradigmatic debate forever.

## SOME MISUNDERSTANDINGS

While addressing criticism I cannot fail to mention those critics who decry the reconstruction of the past! Those who seek some knowledge of the past from the archaeological record are labeled "reconstructionalists" (Dunnell 1978, 194–195), or berated with the claim that their approach is the *"fallacy of prehistoric archaeology as cultural anthropology* (Eggert 1976, 57). Such critics fail to realize the central role that methodology must play in our field. We seek to know the past through the investigation of contemporary phenomena, and we seek to describe the past in dynamic terms, having only "statics" to provide the clues.

For instance, critics freqeuntly attempt to characterize the methodological challenge associated with gaining a knowledge of the past as misguided reconstructionism (see Dunnell 1978, 194–195)—overly influenced by "cultural anthropology." These critics suggest that those who seek reliable means for making inferences from the archaeological record to the past are attempting to "reconstruct" an ethnography as might be done by some half-cocked, contemporary ethnologist or even by a more traditional one, for that matter. There has never been any suggestion by myself or my colleagues that we should seek to reconstruct prehistoric "lifeways" in terms of criteria dictated by cultural anthropology. I did suggest that there seemed to me to be every reason to suspect that we could develop ways of extracting from the archaeological record information regarding properties of cultural systems, including social and ideological components, since they were organizationally integrated with the matter remaining in the archaeological record—the relic of an ongoing system in the past. I never proposed or seriously considered the idea that we should attempt to use the archaeological record to investigate limited subject interests as dictated by various cultural anthropologists. I did maintain that insofar as we sought to know something about the past based on our observations in the present, then we shared with cultural anthropology a common subject matter—the dynamics of cultural systems.

I further suggested that the causes of variability observable in the archaeological record could be expected to refer to the dynamics—both functional and evolutionary—of past cultural systems. I saw no reason to expect that the statics remaining could be understood solely in terms of coincidentally preserved components of the archaeological record. The archaeological record was conditioned in its completeness by largely postdepositional processes of decay, displacement, and mixing. The properties surviving are, quite literally, remnants relative to the dynamics of the past and could have been conditioned both in their form and patterns of association by many factors that have not left direct material by-products. Stated another way, the reality of the present archaeological record cannot be viewed as limiting the reality of past dynamics or the realities of history. Because something was not preserved does not mean that it may not have been a crucial factor in the operation of a past system. It was this situation that prompted me to encourage students to seek operational means for monitoring aspects of social organization or ideology through the study of archaeological remains.

Those offering the reconstructionist criticism appear to deny the need for inferences to the past and to be willing to take the archaeological record at face value. This is an old apologist's view held by traditional archaeologists. In 1968 I (1968b, 15) wrote:

> Rouse (1964, 1965) has offered archaeologists an "out" and his ideas undoubtedly have great appeal for those who would like to study cultural processes but lack the methods for doing so. He states that since we recognize a difference between the processes of evolution and the products of evolution, that the study of process should properly be the domain of ethnologists, "who are able to observe change as it is still going on" (Rouse 1964, 465). He suggests further that the archaeologists might more appropriately study the products of evolution in systematic terms—by descriptive taxonomic and distributional schemes.

Rouse is not alone in this perspective, and it certainly represents the view of many dedicated and thoughtful archaeologists. For example, Wauchope (1966, 19) has written:

> One reason for archaeology's continued lag as a contributor to culture theory, in spite of great strides in the last ten years, is that we continue to see our main goal as the reconstruction of ancient ethnology. Since we have so great a handicap to begin with here, where speculation and inference mix too confusingly for the student who likes to keep his lines of reasoning clean cut, most archaeologists if they are concerned are fighting a very uphill battle indeed. I think we are overlooking another order of interpretation which is in some ways much better suited to our data, for it is less dependent on inference; one can manipulate the artifacts statistically without much concern whether one understands precisely what they originally were, exactly how they were used, and just what they meant to the ancients.

This rather dismal view seems to be the very basis of recent criticism by Dunnell (1978, 195). He states:

> Two general notions ... have prevented ... development ... (2) a belief that the appropriate subject matter is behavior rather than the hard phenomena of the archaeological record. This belief, inherited from the reconstructionists, forces us to manipulate inferences instead of phenomena, and thereby deprives us of the full use of performance standards.

While some, like these critics, would have us manipulate the archaeological "phenomena" directly, others would have us treat archaeological remains as manifestations of unseen, past mental phenomena. Since mental conditions are only "reflected" in material things, they are knowable only by accommodative post hoc arguments as to what appears consistent with material patterning. A defense of argument through accommodation is often presented, alongside a quest for labored exceptions to more substantial arguments, as the justification for the mentalist paradigm. In fact the strict empiricist view and the strict mentalist view both neatly sidestep the basic issues: How do we justify the relationship of empirical materials to ideas? The empiricists claim that our paradigm derives from common sense and is drawn "in an unstructured fashion from common experience" (Dunnell 1978, 196). Advocates of a "contextual approach" require a concern with the "implementation and reconstitution of beliefs in practices, the ideological manipulation of beliefs . . . and the development of models concerning such inter-relationships" (Hodder in press).

In one case the link between ideas and empirical properties of the archaeological record is taken as direct and unambiguous, while in the other the link is simply viewed as one of plausible accommodation. Both deny the need for scientific objectivity and hence for a battery of robust middle range means for making inferences to the past. But posturing gets us nowhere. Even good ideas, which could explain or provide explanations for many basic questions about the past and about the central issues of why things happen as they do, will remain in the area of opinionated debate until we develop the methodology for evaluating ideas in objective terms. *Objective* is here used in the sense introduced earlier—namely, that the arguments used for warranting the meanings given to observations must be intellectually independent of the arguments being evaluated through an appeal to the meanings of observation.

## THE LINKING PROCESS

Radiocarbon methods provide a good example of what is meant by scientific objectivity. We can all recognize the importance of knowing the "date" of events indicated archaeologically. We may, for instance, have some theory regarding the rates of change in agricultural intensification relative to political growth. Clearly, one way of obtaining a partial evaluation of such a proposal would be by measurement of the rates of change by dating sequent archaeological materials, referable to both agricultural and political growth. In order to achieve objectivity, our methods of dating must be intellectually independent of the arguments being evaluated. Radiocarbon techniques are admirably suited to the task, since the justification for inferring a period of elapsed time—from observations of radioactive emissions as measured by some device similar to a Geiger counter—derive from observations regarding the distribution of radiocarbon relative to stable nonradioactive isotopes in nature, from a knowledge of decay rates of radiocarbon, as well as from a knowledge of processes that lead to the fixing of radiocarbon in living tissue. In short, the theory that permits the inference of elapsed time treats the interaction between biological and physical processes, processes that are in no sense dependent for their characteristics or patterns of interaction upon interactions between agricultural intensification or political growth.

Since the warranting arguments for inferring elapsed time from archaeological charcoal or other organic debris refer to causal or interactive conditions totally independent of the arguments being evaluated with the method of inference, it constitutes an objective measure relative to the argument being evaluated by dating methods. We must generate such methods, and only with the growth of objective paradigmatic means can we proceed realistically to the task of evaluating alternative explanations and ideas advanced as to why the world is the way it appears to be. Why is there patterning in history? Why are there apparently regular sequences of events leading up to the development of agriculture. Why do power-based sociopolitical forms in the history of culture change differentially in different regions? We all may have ideas—some may even be good ideas—but we will never know until we have objective means for linking the conceptual domains, which we are so skilled at creating, to the existential characteristics of the world of nature in an evaluative manner. The linking process is the true foundation of science, and we must seek to develop the skills required.

Those who do not place critical emphasis upon the development of middle range theory are forced into the strange position of generating theories with pitifully few objective means to use in their evaluation, or conversely, into making many observations on the archaeological record that are naive to the possible conditions in the past that were responsible for the properties observed. Theories generated about the past in the absence of middle range theory have little hope of being related to relevant observations on the archaeological record in a reliable manner. Discussions of the past in such a situation remain idle speculations, and suggestions regarding the meanings to be attached to observed archaeological phenomena likewise remain intuitive insights to be accepted or rejected in terms of one's subjective biases. In short, given an absence of a robust body of well-founded middle range knowledge and understanding, general theory remains in the air, adrift from the empirical phenomena with which it could be profitably evaluated. Similarly, observations of patterning within sets of the empirical materials serve only as stimuli for intuitive insight, itself remaining in the domain of opinion and subjective evaluation and guided by generally inconclusive inductive argument.

It has been the failure of the social sciences to develop a robust body of principles serving the methodological needs of the fields in question. This failure has doomed those alleged sciences to endless paradigmatic debate and endless stylistic replacements of one "theory" by another, largely in response to sociological characteristics within the discipline and in step with simple rates of generational replacement within the academic community. The result of these conditions is pseudoscience, operating with exactly the same intellectual tools that cultural man used in ethnocentric debate since the beginning of conceptual thought. I use the term *pseudo* because the practitioners of simple paradigmatic debate in the modern academic world, while commonly denying the epistemological basis of science, claim to be generating knowledge of general utility! Science is the only strategy thus far developed for evaluating the general utility of ideas generated in a paradigmatic context. It is the search for ways of using experience as the arbiter of ideas that renders some measure of utility. As we achieve increased understanding, that is, as we develop theories as to why the world is the way it appears to be and seek objective means for evaluating such ideas, we stand in the exciting position of contributing to the growth of knowledge. This position has reference both to our theories as to why the world is the way it appears to be and to our paradigms that condition for us the way the world appears. Progress must proceed through both growth of theoretical understanding and paradigmatic accuracy.

Thomas Kuhn (1977) argued that the very process of scientific growth was the patterned replacement of one paradigm by another. I take strong exception to such a view, while fully recognizing the paradigmatic character of our conceptualizations of experience. Science grows as a consequence of the development of means for objectively monitoring experience in its myriad forms. As our skill at objective evaluation of ideas grows, there is a growth with continuity, or pattern of accumulative development of knowledge. Kuhn's view of change by paradigm replacement could only be true in the absence of objective means of evaluating experience. It may be the normal pattern for prescientific intellectual change, but within science orderly growth and accumulative development of knowledge are the patterns to which the scientific method is dedicated. Paradigm change may give the appearance of revolutionary change when poorly developed areas of a science become increasingly developed and there is a shift from the general cultural paradigm to a more objective, scientific one. Such realities of life are in no way valid justifications for abandoning scientific goals and returning to prescientific forms of debate. Similarly, the argument against the logical positivist's position, questioning the role of theory testing, is misguided.

For instance, we may all acknowledge that if our paradigm leads us to consider the earth as flat, we may nevertheless proceed to ask the question, Why is the earth flat? We may then develop a body of theory that seeks to explain our "observation" of a flat earth. It should be clear that given that the earth is round, we could waste considerable time and energy in testing our theories as to why the earth is flat. More likely, however, we could just as well learn, through our search for objective means of evaluating our ideas, that the world was round. We would therefore gain knowledge and simultaneously a good reason to modify our paradigm. Paradigms are routinely modified as a consequence of scientific research. It is true that they may be modified or conditioned by factors outside the domain of science per se, but it is the regular growth of knowledge and modification of both paradigm and theories toward which scientific effort is directed. The recognition that science can be affected by extrinsic factors or even fail to succeed at times is not justification for abandoning the goal of achieving an orderly pattern of accumulative growth in knowledge and understanding through scientific endeavors.

As long as our reasoning remains "paradigmatic" in character, we are doomed to the endless polemical debate, laced with emotionalism, that also typifies other arguments about alternative cultural beliefs or values. The self-deceit that social scientists can observe cause and therefore study directly why the world is the way it appears to be (see Leach 1973) lies at the root of the ill-founded belief that man is too complex and that human sociocultural phenomena are by nature unsuited for study by scientific means. It is a false paradigm that treats as extranatural the human sociocultural experience and that already claims as a failure those scientific methods that, in general, have never been implemented or indeed in most cases have not yet been developed.

## REFERENCES

Amsterdamski, S., 1975, Between experience and metaphysics, *Boston Studies in the Philosophy of Science*, 35, Boston, D. Reidel.

Binford, L. R., 1968a, Archaeological theory and method, in Binford, L. R., and Binford S. R. (eds.), *New Perspectives in Archaeology*, Chicago, Aldine, 1–3.

Binford, L. R., 1968b, Archaeological perspectives, in Binford, L. R., and Binford, S. R. (eds.), *New Perspectives in Archaeology*, Chicago, Aldine, 5–32.

Binford, L. R., 1977, General introduction, in Binford, L. R. (ed.), *For Theory Building in Archaeology*, New York, Academic Press, 1–10.

Dunnell, R. C., 1978, Style and function: A fundamental dichotomy, *American Antiquity* 43 (2), 192–202.

Eggert, M. K. H., 1976, On the interrelationship of prehistoric archaeology and cultural anthropology, *Praehistorische Zeitschrift* 51 (1), 56–60.

Gledhill, J., and Rowlands, M. J. in press, Materialism and socioeconomic process in multi-linear evolution. (Paper delivered at the Annual Meeting of the Society for American Archaeology, Philadelphia, 1980.)

Hempel, C. G., 1977, Formulation and formalization of scientific theories, in Suppe, F. (ed.), *The Structure of Scientific Theories* (2nd edition), Urbana, Ill., University of Illinois Press, 244–265.

Hodder, I., in press, The identification and interpretation of ranking in prehistory: a contextual perspective. (Paper delivered at the Annual Meeting of the Society for American Archaeology, Philadelphia, 1980).

Kuhn, T., 1977, Second thoughts on paradigms, in Suppe, F. (ed.), *The Structure of Scientific Theories* (2nd edition), Urbana, Ill., University of Illinois Press, 459–517.

Leach, E., 1973, Concluding address, in Renfrew, C. (ed.), *The Explanation of Culture Change: Models in Prehistory*, London, Duckworth, 761–771.

Masterman, M., 1970, The nature of a paradigm, in Lakatos, I., and Musgrave, A. (eds.), *Criticism and the Growth of Knowledge*, Cambridge, Cambridge University Press, 59–89.

Rouse, I., 1964, Archaeological approaches to cultural evolution, in Goodenough, W. (ed.), *Explorations in Cultural Anthropology*, New York, McGraw-Hill, 455–468.

Rouse, I., 1965, The place of "peoples" in prehistoric research, *Journal of the Royal Anthropological Institute* 95 (1), 1–15.

Schiffer, M. B., 1972, Archaeological context and systemic context, *American Antiquity* 37 (2), 156–165.

Watson, P. J., LeBlanc, S. A., and Redman, C. L., 1971, *Explanation in Archaeology: An Explicitly Scientific Approach*, New York and London, Columbia University Press.

Wauchope, R., 1966, Archaeological survey of northern Georgia, with a test of some cultural hypotheses, *American Antiquity*, Memoir No. 21.

# Comment I: On Form and Content

*MANFRED K. H. EGGERT*

*Fortunately, anthropologists can take comfort in the knowledge that the construction of good explanations in anthropology need not wait upon solutions to these problems about models. The lack of an adequate model of scientific explanation is no more a problem for anthropologists than it is for physicists or chemists.*

M. H. Salmon and W. C. Salmon

## SOME MODES OF EXPLAINING THE PAST

At this juncture it seems appropriate to pause for some stocktaking. I do not propose, however, to assess the totality of the accomplishments brought about by the new archaeology as I recently attempted for its first phase (Eggert 1978). I should like to concentrate instead on the current state of concerted efforts to set down the rules of an archaeological model of explanation conforming to what is perceived as the natural sciences model. The question to be addressed can be phrased as follows: How far have archaeologists or, for that matter, new archaeologists succeeded in prescribing for their discipline a formula that combines both methodological soundness and workability?

At a conference that offers a symposium on "Explanation Revisited" our question might pass for nothing but some sort of the most common denominator of an array of much more elaborated queries both of a general methodological as well as a distinct archaeological nature. In his impressive *tour d' horizon*, Colin Renfrew (Chapter 1 this volume) has convincingly outlined the discipline's various phases of addressing or, as the case may be, not addressing the crucial issue of explanation since "the early ferment" of the last decades of the nineteenth century. He has shown, by way of carefully chosen examples, that those intent on assessing the differing approaches over time are indeed prone to be dissatisfied with what it all finally amounted to. Concentrating on what

**139**

THEORY AND EXPLANATION
IN ARCHAEOLOGY

Renfrew terms "the great awakening," we should be able to come up with an answer permitting us to see more clearly into what kind of cul-de-sac the discipline has maneuvered itself and how to proceed under these circumstances.

For the sake of convenience, we may start by considering Renfrew's preliminary classification of "isms of our time," i.e., contemporary approaches to the past embodying more or less drastically differing notions of our concept of explanation.

Of the five approaches distinguished by Renfrew, the historiographic and the neo-Marxist approach are neither basically new nor in any sense characteristic of what today has to pass for the mainstream of nontraditional archaeology. Quite to the contrary, Renfrew's historiographic mode of conceptualizing the past was and still is very much the pivot of the (more or less) silent majority's archaeology. Structuralism, another of Renfrew's "isms," can likewise be ignored here because of its up-to-now very limited application in archaeological reasoning. Systems thinking, though certainly of major importance after the break in the early 1960s with the "traditional" framework of thought (for a review see Plog 1975), still seems to operate mainly at the terminological level of analysis (Eggert 1978, 69–86, M. H. Salmon 1978). The great potential ascribed to it has not yet been demonstrated other than in purely heuristic terms, and one cannot escape the notion Merrilee Salmon (1978, 181–182) has detailed elsewhere that as yet there is very little in the way of explicit explanatory systems models (see also Lowe and Barth 1980, Renfrew 1981, M. H. Salmon 1980). The only exception I am aware of is that of the political scientist Eugene Meehan's (1968) "system paradigm" whose application in archaeology has been advocated by H. D. Tuggle, A. H. Townsend, and T. J. Riley (1972). As the Salmons (1979, 65–67) have demonstrated, the Meehan model has to be classed together with the deductive–nomological (D–N) model of explanation in that both need laws in their explanans and both imply a deductive relation between explanans and explanandum. That is to say, the criticism to be leveled against the D–N model applies to Meehan's system paradigm as well.

The foregoing leaves us with Renfrew's second ism, which he labeled "hypothetico–deductive." As this approach is indeed an important element of what we have come to think of as the new archaeology, it will be the focal point of the following comments.

## DEDUCTIVE–NOMOLOGICAL MODEL OF EXPLANATION VERSUS HYPOTHETICO–DEDUCTIVE METHOD

Since the very beginning of applying an analytical philosophy's conceptual framework to archaeology (Fritz and Plog 1970, Watson, LeBlanc, and Redman 1971), a basic misconception as to the mutual relationship of the D–N model of explanation and Carl G. Hempel's (1966) "method of hypothesis" pervades the literature. As has been detailed elsewhere (Eggert 1978, 29–37, 39–50), the method of hypothesis, or as British philosophers (e.g., Braithwaite 1968, 9) used to call it, the hypothetic–deductive (H–D) method, is an ideal model of how to test hypotheses, while the D–N model offers a logical account of how to explain under certain prevailing circumstances. That is to say, the H–D method pertains to the context of confirmation, whereas the D–N model spells out the logical structure of a specific kind of scientific explanation. Necessarily, both accounts are structured according to the particular procedures within the context of scientific reasoning they are intended to model. It follows that, whereas the D–N model is of no use to the empirical testing of hypotheses, the H–D method does not provide a model of scientific explanation. Consequently, citing the method of hypothesis in connection with conceptualizing the logical structure of explanation, as has been done repeatedly up to the present day, seems rather awkward, to say the least.

Having clarified this point, there is not much to add to what has been said here (Renfrew, Chapter 1 this volume) and elsewhere (Eggert 1978, 32–37, 47–49, 67–69) on the D–N model of explanation. With as yet no "general laws of cultural dynamics" (Binford 1968, 268) at our disposal, it hardly makes sense to insist on applying this model to cultural anthropology, or, for that matter, to archaeology.

## STATISTICAL–RELEVANCE VERSUS INDUCTIVE–STATISTICAL MODEL OF EXPLANATION

In an earlier article, written in 1975–1976, I directed attention to Carl G. Hempel's less well known (in archaeological circles) work on statistical explanation in pointing out that what Hempel (1965, 381–412, see also 1962a, 1962b, 1966, 58–69) calls "inductive—statistical" (I–S) explanation was much more appropriate to the cultural sciences (Eggert 1978, 37–39). I advocated developing the necessary means for this model to be employed in archaeology. At that time I did not know of Wesley Salmon's (1971) work on statistical explanation. Having familiarized myself with it in the meantime (see also W. C. Salmon 1975, 1977, 1978), I no longer saw fit to speak up for Hempel's I–S model. On the contrary, it seemed to me that Salmon had convincingly demonstrated the superiority of his statistical–relevance (S–R) model over that advocated by Hempel. So I felt confident that here at least we had the kind of logically satisfying account of scientific explanation adequate for the anthropological sciences. Evidently, there were (and still are) others who shared in that feeling (e.g., Smith, Chapter 7 this volume).

As several critics (Cartmill 1980, King 1976, Lehmann 1972, see W. C. Salmon, Chapter 4 this volume) have pointed out, however, and as the Salmons (1979, 71–72) themselves have frankly admitted, the S–R model, though being superior to the I–S model in several important respects, does not provide a totally satisfying account of statistical explanation either. There are furthermore, as Wesley Salmon has outlined elsewhere in this book (Chapter 4), some rather fundamental difficulties with the concept of causality. These difficulties, so we are informed, can only be overcome by replacing the now dominant deterministic conception of causality with a probabilistic one. However, the development of a theory of probabilistic causality itself faces serious problems (W. C. Salmon 1980, in press, and Chapter 4 this volume).

Now, it seems to me that all this should have come as some kind of a shock to all of us who felt certain that it was the S–R model of explanation we were looking for all along. At this juncture, I am afraid, we can no longer escape drawing some general conclusions from the constant breakup of our serial monogamy with the explanatory models of analytical philosophy already mentioned.

## LOGICAL FORM VERSUS ANTHROPOLOGICAL CONTENT

The current state of philosophical debate of scientific explanation, deplorable though it might be for those professionally engaged in it and, perhaps to a lesser extent, for the scientific community as a whole, need not be utterly distressing for archaeologists. The Salmons (1979, 72) quite rightly assured us that in the final analysis it is the professional, the archaeologist say, who is in command when it comes to deciding which kinds of propositions are to qualify as adequate explanations of the problem at hand and which definitely are not.

As has been noted repeatedly (e.g., Eggert 1978, 43, 147, Salmon and Salmon 1979, 63), the archaeologists so far have concentrated almost exclusively on the logical form they feel an explanation should exhibit. There can be little doubt, if I may dare to say so, that archaeologists usually are pretty bad philosophers. So perhaps we should abandon trying to force our explanatory efforts into the Procrustes' bed of some more or less poorly understood philosophical model. Rather, it would be wise to leave the philosophical part of our attempts at explaining the past to those philosophers who have developed a keen awareness of the critical issue of explanation in anthropology and, specifically, in archaeology. This, I understand, is exactly the position of the Salmons (1979, 72) and, I am sure, of the philosophical community at large.

What I am advocating here amounts to giving up on pseudophilosophical reasoning and to concentrate instead on exploring the anthropological dimensions germane to our discipline and, as for that, to the specific problems we are concerned with here. To phrase it somewhat differently, you might say that archaeologists should substitute logical form for *anthropo*logical content. The following remarks are intended to briefly outline this rather general recommendation.

Under the prevailing circumstances, the path to be followed in implementing the preceding recommendation can hardly be expected to have anything fundamentally new to it. As a matter of fact, the proposals that follow are not even new in a more limited sense for those who conceptualize archaeology, as most of us do, as the "anthropology of the dead": For these archaeologists there is nothing new at all to the notion that we should direct our efforts at systematically studying the relationship of cultural behavior and its potential material correlates, i.e., material culture per se as well as the tangible results of secondary processes of materialization recoverable through contextual in situ analysis. As the thriving of ethnoarchaeological studies demonstrates, an ever-growing number of anthropologically minded archaeologists are aware of the fact that to broaden our understanding of the complex interplay of sociocultural behavior and material culture we have to initiate systematic research on the interface of the living and the dead. In this respect, the value of a more technically oriented subfield of archaeology—experimental archaeology—need not be especially outlined here.

Considering the current state of generalization in archaeology, one cannot but realize that we are a far cry from having at our disposal a body of firmly established empirical generalizations—let alone statistical laws. Although there are some who argue the constant, if largely implicit, use of laws on the part of archaeologists (e.g., Reid, Schiffer, and Rathje 1975, Schiffer 1975, 1976), the generalizations proposed so far can hardly be said to have been tested, in a rigorous manner, either ethnographically or archaeologically. What we need most urgently then is a body of cross-culturally tested ethnographic hypotheses (see Eggert 1976a, 51–54 on this) to be confronted with and applied to the archaeological record.

## ON COVERING THE MIDDLE GROUND: MIDDLE RANGE VERSUS GENERAL THEORIES

In the last few years earlier claims as to the seemingly unlimited possibilities of explaining or, for that matter, "predicting" (in case you do not prefer "postdicting") the past have given way to a more adequate notion of what can be accomplished through archaeological reasoning. By discarding most of what in 1975–1976 had to be castigated as "exaggerated," "unrealistic," and "pretentious" (Eggert 1978), the discipline gave up on rhetoric and instead concentrated effectively on exploring more immediate avenues of basic research.

In Chapter 10, Lewis Binford has emphasized the growing need of the discipline for the development of middle range theories as indispensable means for successfully relating the contemporary static data base to the dynamics of past sociocultural systems. Being an adherent of middle range reasoning myself and having recommended its development in the context of European ethnology (Eggert 1972, 1974) and, specifically, archaeology (Eggert 1976b), I most emphatically endorse Binford's position. I think it very important and timely indeed to develop what Binford calls "the science of the archaeological record." This is, in fact, exactly what I demanded when in 1975–1976 I argued for a "theory of archaeological data" (Eggert 1978, 148).

There are, however, some minor but nonetheless basic objections to be leveled against Binford's notion of theory and theory-building. Adhering to what I would call a rather rigid frame of reference (see Binford 1977), he conceives of theory as integrated concepts of "how the world works, why man behaves the way he does at different times and places, and how we may understand recognized patterns of changes and diversity in organized human behavior" (Binford 1977, 6). At the same time, however, he tends to downplay the role of empirical generalizations in the process of theory-building. According to him, strategies aiming at empirical generalizations "will not move us in the direction of explanation" (Binford 1977, 1). This seems to me a counterproductive or, at best, unrealistic stance toward scientific progress. I maintain instead that empirical generalizations play a crucial role in the context of theory formation, for they are building blocks relating higher-order concepts of integration, i.e., theories, to those phenomena of the empirical world that these concepts are said to account for.

Also, it appears to me that Binford (1977, Chapter 10 this volume), in stressing the need for developing a "science of the archaeological record," neglects the equally important necessity of using the potential of ethnographic data in the context of theory-building. Evidently, this particular imbalance stems from the fact that he is especially interested in Paleolithic studies. Establishing "intellectual anchors," to use his phrase, with regard to understanding the behavior of populations other than the species Homo sapiens, necessarily has to go beyond the range of behavior documented ethnographically. What we need in addition, however, are middle range theories based on ethnographic (including historical) data relating to Homo sapiens.

The ethnographic hypotheses derived from this particular body of data are to be converted, relative to the degree of cross-cultural testing performed, into generalizations of a differential order of confirmation. These generalizations will then serve as important elements in theories accounting for the *ethnographic* record. Having thus established what you might call the first level of ethnographically oriented middle range reasoning, we are prepared to proceed to the second level, which is constituted by relating the theoretical accomplishments, or parts thereof, to the *archaeological* record. Ethnoarchaeological studies obviously crosscut, as it were, the two levels distinguished here.

In view of the procedural differentiations proposed here, Binford (1977, Chapter 10 this volume) has offered but a partial or, as for that, somewhat imbalanced account of the integrated field of middle range theorizing and explanation. Let me finally add a point Binford (1977, 7) emphasized—namely not to divorce the formulation of middle range theories from parallel development of general theory. The reason offered to bolster this suggestion is strictly pragmatic in that Binford argues that middle range reasoning unguided by criteria of relevance springing from general theory may be "a waste of time." Though not totally unwarranted, such arguments are not particularly convincing when it comes to conceptualizing research strategies. Nevertheless, the development of middle range theories should indeed be coupled with a constant effort at integrating what has been accomplished already into an increasingly more general framework of thought.

## CONCLUSION

Summing up, I should like to note my impression that, after heavy turbulences, the discipline, more vigorously than before, has initiated a process of sifting the chaff from the wheat. In 1975–1976, the situation looked quite different, and my analysis of what then represented the state of the methodological and theoretical debate of the field had to be unsparingly critical indeed. I now feel, however, that the gap between the prevailing conditions of that time and the position I thought (and still think) reasonable to support has been rapidly narrowed down by the down-to-earth tendency, observable since the mid-1970s, of approaching the crucial issues of archaeology. Consequently, I am quite confident that the further development of what, *horribile dictu*, Francis Bacon conceptualized as *axiomata media* will lead us a long way toward replacing logical form with anthropological content in our concerted efforts to "explain" the past.

## REFERENCES

Binford, L. R., 1968, Some comments on historical versus processual archaeology, *Southwestern Journal of Anthropology* 24, 267–275.
Binford, L. R., 1977, General introduction, in Binford, L. R. (ed.), *For Theory Building in Archaeology,* New York, Academic Press, 1–10.
Braithwaite, R. B., 1968, *Scientific Explanation,* Cambridge, Cambridge University Press.
Cartmill, M., 1980, John Jones's pregnancy: some comments on the statistical–relevance model of scientific explanation, *American Anthropologist* 82, 382–385.
Eggert, M. K. H., 1972, Kommentar zu "On the concept of cultural fixation" by Sigfrid Svensson, *Ethnologia Europaea* 6, 144–147.
Eggert, M. K. H. 1974, Zur Theoriebildung in der Europäischen Ethnologie, *Zeitschrift für Volkskunde* 70, 58–63.
Eggert, M. K. H., 1976a, "Archaeology as anthropology" and its case: remarks on reasoning in prehistoric archaeology, *Western Canadian Journal of Anthropology* 6, 42–61.
Eggert, M. K. H., 1976b, On the interrelationship of prehistoric archaeology and cultural anthropology, *Praehistorische Zeitschrift* 51, 56–60.
Eggert, M. K. H., 1978, Prähistorische Archäologie und Ethnologie: Studien zur amerikanischen New Archaeology, *Praehistorische Zeitschrift* 53, 6–164.
Fritz, J. M., and Plog, F. T., 1970, The nature of archaeological explanation, *American Antiquity* 35, 405–412.
Hempel, C. G., 1962a, Deductive nomological versus statistical explanation, in Feigl, H., and

Maxwell, G. (eds.), *Minnesota Studies in the Philosophy of Science* 3, Minneapolis, University of Minnesota Press, 98–169.

Hempel, C. G., 1962b, Explanation in science and in history, in Colodny, R. G. (ed.), *Frontiers of Science and Philosophy*, Pittsburgh, University of Pittsburgh Press, 9–33.

Hempel, C. G., 1965, Aspects of scientific explanation, in Hempel, C. G., *Aspects of Scientific Explanation and Other Essays in the Philosophy of Science*, New York, The Free Press, 331–496.

Hempel, C. G., 1966, *Philosophy of Natural Science*, Englewood Cliffs, N.J., Prentice–Hall.

King, J. L., 1976, Statistical relevance and explanatory classification, *Philosophical Studies* 30, 313–321.

Lehman, H., 1972, Statistical explanation, *Philosophy of Science* 39, 500–506.

Lowe, J. W. G., and Barth, R. J., 1980, Systems in archaeology: a comment on Salmon, *American Antiquity* 45, 568–575.

Meehan, E. J., 1968, *Explanation in Social Science: A System Paradigm*, Homewood, Ill., Dorsey Press.

Plog, F. T., 1975, Systems theory in archeological research, *Annual Review of Anthropology* 4, 207–224.

Reid, J. J., Schiffer, M. B., and Rathje, W. L., 1975, Behavioral archaeology: four strategies, *American Anthropologist* 77, 864–869.

Renfrew, C., 1981, The simulator as demiurge, in Sabloff, J. A. (ed.), *Simulating the Past*, Albuquerque, University of New Mexico Press.

Salmon, M. H., 1978, What can systems theory do for archaeology?, *American Antiquity* 43, 174–183.

Salmon, M. H., 1980, Reply to Lowe and Barth, *American Antiquity* 45, 575–579.

Salmon, M. H., and Salmon, W. C., 1979, Alternative models of scientific explanation, *American Anthropologist* 81, 61–74.

Salmon, W. C., 1971, Statistical explanation, in Salmon, W. C., Jeffrey, R. C., and Greeno, J. G., *Statistical Explanation and Statistical Relevance*, Pittsburgh, University of Pittsburgh Press, 29–87.

Salmon, W. C., 1975, Theoretical Explanation, in Körner, S. (ed.), *Explanation*, Oxford, Blackwell, 118–145.

Salmon, W. C., 1977, A third dogma of empiricism, in Butts, R. E., and Hintakka, J. (eds.), *Basic Problems in Methodology and Linguistics*, Dordrecht–Holland and Boston, Reidel, 149–166.

Salmon, W. C., 1978, Why ask, "why?"?—an inquiry concerning scientific explanation, *Proceedings and Addresses of the American Philosophical Association* 51, 683–705.

Salmon, W. C., 1980, Probabilistic causality, *Pacific Philosophical Quarterly* 61, 50–74.

Salmon, W. C., in press, Causality: production and propagation, in Asquith P. D., and Giere, R. N. (eds.), *PSA 1980*, 2, East Lansing, Mich., Philosophy of Science Association.

Schiffer, M. B., 1975, Archaeology as behavioral science, *American Anthropologist* 77, 836–848.

Schiffer, M. B., 1976, *Behavioral Archeology*, New York, Academic Press.

Tuggle, H. D., Townsend, A. H., and Riley, T. J., 1972, Laws, systems, and research design: a discussion of explanation in archaeology, *American Antiquity* 37, 3–12.

Watson, P. J., LeBlanc, S. A., and Redman, C. L., 1971, *Explanation in Archeology: An Explicitly Scientific Approach*, New York, Colombia University Press.

# Comment II:
# Too Many Cooks Spoil the Broth

*JOHN HALL*

Let me begin masochistically by telling you something about the theoretical exuberance that has characterized the recent history of my own special subject—namely sociology. Early social theorists, such as Marx, Comte Spencer, Durkheim, and Weber, all concentrated their efforts on trying to understand and explain the broad set of historical changes that led to industrialism. This interest in the substansive philosophy of history, with the establishment of patterns in history, has not been much in evidence recently. Instead, a concern with formal questions in the philosophy of history has led to the unfettered creation of new theoretical approaches. I cannot name all recent contenders in sociology, but you can get some idea of the state of play if I mention the existence of exchange theory, phenomenology, Gramscian Marxism, structuralist Marxism, phenomenological Marxism, hermeneutics, critical theory, symbolical interactionism, linguistic sociology, and structuralism. As it happens, I am firmly of the party believing that a concern with patterns of history should define sociology. But even those disagreeing with me on that point would accept that this multiplication of theoretical standpoints has scarcely helped sociology become a cognitive giant. Professor Bell (Chapter 6 this volume) seems to me far too sanguine in his advocacy of "anything goes." Indeed his recommendation would seem likely to encourage a sort of relativist morass. There seem to be two reasons why too many cooks tend to spoil the broth. Most immediately your energy is needed in constructing positions, given

147

THEORY AND EXPLANATION
IN ARCHAEOLOGY

the continuing ability of Paris and Frankfurt to flood us with their intellectual débris. But perhaps I am too pessimistic here, and the rousing advice of the Hemingway among modern archaeologists—Professor Binford (Chapter 10 this volume)—to use theories to investigate the world, rather than as safe houses to live in, may be taken. But I doubt this for the second reason. Some of the positions mentioned above are epistemologically sophisticated. Thus we have recently been graced with an antiempiricist argument from two structuralist Marxists insisting that "theoretical praxis" is far more important than misguided research. An analysis of Marx's concepts leads these thinkers to assert that Marx's "Asiatic mode of production" *could not* have existed—the empirical record is examined as a mere afterthought so that the reader can be assured that it did not *in fact* exist (Hindess and Hirst, 1975). In these circumstances Professor Binford's appeal for "robustness" is not sufficient. It become necessary to argue for empiricism–positivism as one paradigm among many, since we can no longer take it for granted that all red-blooded individualists think alike.

This picture will probably increase Professor Renfrew's gloom (see Chapter 1 this volume). He would perhaps feel still worse were he to realize that more sophisticated Marxists now reject the 1859 Preface to which he refers on the grounds that it is hasty and innaccurate and no proper guide to the deeper structure of Marx's thought (see, for a recent example, Levine and Wright 1980). However, the point of the parable is exactly opposite to this: Compared to how bad things could be, archaeology looks rather healthy. I suspect that a runaway inflation of theory in archaeology is held back by hidden agreements on a shared data-base. Whatever the case, I detect no sophisticated epistemological arguments capable of undermining the desire to use theory to investigate the archaeological record. Given this, the presence of competing theories—oh! but *so* few—matters little. I have no final word to add to the Kuhn–Popper debate that has proved so influential in the recent philosophy of science. Sometimes theories are indeed criticized and hopefully replaced (Wittfogel's hydraulic hypothesis, for example, looks done for, once and for all), but more often they are refined. The latter process should not worry us just so long as the theories continue to breed investigation while growing old gracefully.

There are perhaps technical problems of archaeologists that will lead them to theories not generally held attractive in the rest of the social sciences. Hence I would only like to comment on some of the theories on offer, about which I have some specialized knowledge. Very great scepticism needs to be shown to the critical or hermeneutic theory of Habermas that Daniel Miller now advocates for archaeology (Chapter 8 this volume). The tradition of the *Geisteswissenschaften* on which Habermas draws stresses that (*a*) humans, unlike atoms, make meanings; (*b*) the social world is made up of such meanings; (*c*) the experts of such *Weltanschauungen* are those who participate in them; and (*d*) social science has no choice but to accept the accounts offered by such experts. Such a theory seems designed to cripple archaeology. There are many good reasons to reject such rampant idealism (see Hall 1981). Most important, belief systems are not harmonious wholes but ragbags containing different options that can be activated by different social groups as interest requires—and the investigation of such interest is, of course, thoroughly materialist and thus in line with traditional practices in archaeology. The historiographic approach outlined by Professor Renfrew (Chapter 1 this volume) seems to be based on something of a misunderstanding. In a famous essay, Max Weber made abundantly apparent that the true specification of the unique depended upon a sense of social structure precisely so that it could be shown why a single event proved to have such influence (Weber 1949). Many contemporary historians would agree with this: They continue to see narrative history as their greatest ambition, but feel that it can only be written on the basis of a proper understanding of social process. The Marxism offered by Dr. Rowlands (Chapter 11 this volume) makes me slightly suspicious for three reasons. Firstly, I do not think that a theory in which the economic seems unable to determine any of the other spheres deserves to be called Marxist—but perhaps this is a quibble, and one should instead welcome the realization of these Marxists that the economy does not always determine (not even in the last instance). Second, I am not at all sure that the emphasis is firmly on using the approach in research, rather than on redescribing the research of others in Marxist terms: Time will tell, and I look forward to having my fears proved groundless. Finally, structuralist Marxism as a whole is justly coming to be seen as having many parallels with systems theory. The functionalism of such Marxism is to be regretted the more since a conflict-based Marxism needs advocacy in order to keep systems theory on its toes.

Finally, I would like to record my amazement that Professor Renfrew has been able to get away with his assertion that we have no decent explanations of anything. This nonspecialist reader found the generalizations in *Before Civilisation* illuminating (Renfrew 1978). Unless he now denies the theses of that book—and I hope vanity will prevent his so doing—he must withdraw his blanket accusation. And to make him happier still, I will offer another generalization that could be expanded variously. This is that the obvious difference in social structures of river vallys and, say, Mediterranean hills is simply explained: the ability of pastoralists to run away leads to equality, while peasant immobility leads to stratification (Lattimore 1962, especially Part IV).

## REFERENCES

Hall, J. A., 1981, *Diagnoses of Our Time,* London, Heinemann Educational Books.
Hindess, D., and Hirst, P. Q., 1975, *Pre-Capitalist Modes of Production,* London, Routledge and Kegan Paul.
Lattimore, O., 1962, *Studies in Frontier History,* Oxford, Oxford University Press.

Levine, A., and Wright, E. O., 1980, Rationality and class struggle, *New Left Review* 123, 47–68.

Renfrew, A. C., 1978, *Before Civilisation,* London, Penguin Books.

Weber, M., 1949, Objectivity in social science and social policy, in Weber, M., *The Methodology of the Social Sciences,* translated and edited by Shils, E. A., and Finch, H., New York, The Free Press, 50–112.

# II

# THE DYNAMICS OF CHANGE

## INTRODUCTION

It is becoming commonplace, as part of a general reaction to positivistic philosophies, to claim that the social sciences will in future become more historical in character. If this means that historians and archaeologists have become more sophisticated users and creators of sociological constructs and sociologists and anthropologists more critical of synchronic–diachronic dichotomies in their work, then such a rapprochement can only be welcomed.

However, complex issues are involved in understanding how these disciplines came originally to define themselves in opposition to each other. It is for example a paradox of social theory that antifunctionalist critiques are an enduring feature of all new theoretical innovations. The paradox of why tautology should be a constant lurking shadow in any social theory debate rests on a basic premise that the present as an area of study can be separated from the past. Both Durkheim and Weber accepted that this was so in order to construct a synchronically defined comparative social theory that might be used subsequently to develop more sophisticated historical explanations. Only recently have we seen a limited tendency for this ideal state of affairs coming about. But the social history that made the acceptance of such a dichotomy an appropriate procedure for research was itself only part of a more general discourse structured by conflicts between social and political theories within Europe at this time.

THEORY AND EXPLANATION
IN ARCHAEOLOGY

A perception of rapid social change in Europe came to be contrasted with a belief in the relative timelessness of other non-European societies and with those of Europe of a premodern age. This acceptance of a modern–traditional rupture implied that a special status could be given to the analysis of modern society while the traditional was something to be worked back into at a later stage, and subsequently was relegated to be the province of the historian and the prehistorian.

This essentially Eurocentric view of a history of the world continued into twentieth-century social thought. In anthropology it was exported in the study of non-European societies that were perceived as static and timeless. Acculturation theory, for example, was based on the premise that change in traditional societies could only come about as a result of the impact of external forces. Contemporary social change could be limited to a particular conception of the modern and the short-term and opposed to the traditional where change was essentially cyclical and reversible in historical time.

To its credit, archaeology has been the most vehement critic of received anthropological wisdom concerning the static and atemporal nature of the "traditional" societies that were studied. But empirical criticism will not in itself expose many of the fallacies of social models that seek to explan development without referring to longer time ranges than what is perceived to be immediately historical and relevant. The archaeology of so-called ethnographically rich areas can, for example, take on the role of modern history although the coarse-grained nature of the evidence is even here likely to result in the detection of patterns only over fairly long-time periods. But the value of archaeological data depends in the long run on the specification of historical processes that require models that seek to explain developments occurring in distant time ranges.

The chapters in Part II seek to concentrate therefore on what might be termed macrohistorical processes operating at a level of systemic organization that may be neither planned, programed, nor within the conscious control of social actors that may be encompassed by it. An implicit contrast can be drawn therefore between system behavior and system dynamics, with the former viewed as short-term, cyclical changes that are potentially reversible and noncumulative and the latter as the irreversible effects of the resolution of internal contradictions leading to structural transformation. Although starting from different theoretical standpoints, there are a number of convergences in papers of this section and part III. For example, they share a similar view of human social systems as essentially contradictory in nature and tending constantly toward instability and change rather than to equilibrium and stability. Hence explanations of change in both parts tend to focus on the limits of system functioning and on perturbations that promote increasing instability, transformation to a new order, and renewed instability on a long time-scale. The chapters in Parts II and III are opposed therefore to gradually unfolding models of social change and explanations that assume homeostasis and goal-oriented behavior as the characteristics of systematic organization.

But the concern of the chapters in Part II is with the specific properties of certain categories of human social systems. As social models, they are historically relativistic in that they aim to define the specific laws of reproduction that determine the cumulative development of internal contradictions within a specific social formation. Jonathan Friedman (Chapter 12) outlines a general model of reproductive systems that defines the appearance of local social forms by the roles they play within larger systems of interaction and exchange. He applies this general model to a historical and ethnographic survey of Oceania, explaining variation in these local societies by the particular conditions and constraints imposed upon them by their function within larger regional systems. The results of his analysis should be relevant to archaeologists working on the Later Neolithic of Western Europe and other cases where Asiatic states function on the periphery of expanding prestige good organized exchange networks.

John Gledhill and Mogens Larsen (Chapter 13) present a comparative analysis of archaic states as exemplified by the case studies of Mesoamerica and Mesopotamia. Taking Polanyi's work as a starting point, their intention is to demonstrate the limitations of the essentially static formulation of the Polanyi paradigm and to reanalyze part of this material from a materialist perspective. They show that an inherent tendency exists in both cases for phases of centralization and increasing control of the economy by a bureaucratic state apparatus to be followed by phases in which failures in political control stimulate private commercial activity and decentralization of state control. However, these cyclical phases are not repetitive, and they generate irreversible changes in structure and regional and interregional organization that underlie a long-term tendency toward monarchically organized forms of empire.

Kristian Kristiansen (Chapter 15) applies Friedman's concept of a system of social reproduction to an analysis of the transformation of tribal systems in the Neolithic period and Bronze Age of northern Europe. The chapter outlines a long-term sequence of "tribal" systems that go through definite cycles of irreversible change, and permits the usefulness of these concepts to be assessed within a purely archaeological context. Stephen Nugent (Chapter 14) demonstrates how the different models used by archaeologists and social anthropologists working in the same area produce markedly differnt perceptions of "traditional" Amazonian society. He proposes an historical reconstruction, based on archaeological evidence, suggesting that formerly a complex set of interrelations linked lowland Amazonia to the highland "civilizations"—a fact that has been entirely obscured by ethnographic concern for the local society. He argues persuasively that the isolated Amazonian Indian society is a product of anthropological myopia, and as a distorted image it directly influences contemporary attitudes and government policy. Part II begins with a general essay (Chapters 11) in which I discuss various convergent tendencies in the study of long-term processes of change in archaeology and the other social sciences.

— M. J. R.

# 11

## Processual Archaeology as Historical Social Science

*M. J. ROWLANDS*

Historical consciousness no longer occupies, as it once did, the central stage of intellectual activity in the modern world. Under the aegis of a nineteenth-century idea of progress, it was easier to believe in the vital importance of history's linking past and present. The current widespread belief that there is no stability in systems—whether natural or social—reverses a previous wish to view the world as a harmonious, self-regulating system for which cybernetics perhaps marked a sophisticated culminating point. All major trends in the social and natural sciences over the last 50 to 60 years share an antihistorical bias. Many would and indeed have claimed synchronic analysis to be prior to diachronic analysis, structure to be a determinent of process, and links with the past to be discontinuous rather than continuous. Recent claims may be correct that a synthesis betwen these opposing tendencies is imminent, but a disillusion with history is not merely an academic concern. As many have noticed, it reflects a profound sense of despair, in the light of twentieth-century events, at being able to predict or control any future event and with the value of history for our understanding of the human condition (Hawthorne 1976, Megill 1979).

Those who saw history as a source of knowledge were less affected by this development than those who believed that past events could only be explained by their place in some larger developmental process. One could argue that those philosophies of history that emphasized the imaginative or empathetic understanding of the past shared with the other social sciences a reaction to

THEORY AND EXPLANATION
IN ARCHAEOLOGY

**155**

historicist traditions, positivist or otherwise, that emphasized progress and a natural unfolding of a process in social evolution that was both teleological and optimistic about the human condition. Reaction in the social sciences to causal analysis and historicist explanation was accompanied by the formalization of an already existing plurality of views about the nature of social reality that had in common only a distaste for historical speculation. Hence, it was not so much that evolutionism (or the weaker notion of development) was refuted in the social sciences, as that it was abandoned as ideologically blinkered, speculative and incapable of proof, and perhaps what is more important, as no longer desirable as an account of how social reality came to be.

Disconnection with history was also entailed in the process by which social anthropology and sociology established themselves as autonomous disciplines. Sociology's identification with the building of theory through synchronic comparison was achieved by defining-out history as the analysis of unique sequences of events over time in a particular region. This included a bias for the essentially "nationalistic" forms of history that predominated at the end of the nineteenth century, rather than what were seen as its speculative predecessors in Hegel, Comte, and Marx and that overgeneralized ragbag of "historicism." The problem of how historical knowledge came to be defined cannot in turn be disassociated from the attacks on historical materialism made among others, by the neo-Kantian school associated with Simmel, Rickert, and Weber. Weber's position in particular, involved no rejection of historical knowledge as such, but made a distinction between sociology as a general theory of society and its application in explicating concrete and unique sequences of historical development (Roth and Schluchter 1979, Zaret 1980, for Durkheim see Bellah 1959). A secular theory, in Weber's sense, causally relates a series of events over a given period of time; "events" as such are not facts but are constituted by the mental activity of the empirical investigator. Weber's ideal types are intentionally selective and do not constitute a total theory for a given historical society. More significantly he rejected the claims of evolutionists and materialist alike for a unified history of mankind with its regular stages of development—a view of history that most Marxists would now reject as well (see Banaji 1977) and proposed instead that history should concern itself with the precise definition of causal relations between sequences of events.

Building on Dilthey's distinction between the sciences that seek to explain (i.e., generalize) and the humanities that seek to understand (*"wie es eigenlicht gewesen war"* as the manifesto of modern empirical historiography), the social sciences came to appropriate the role of generalizer. As has happened before in the institutionalization of other disciplines, sociology violently rejected its antecendents and formalized various theoretical positions that have in common a hostility to what were seen to be speculative (i.e., historicist) generalizations about the past. The collapse of this consensus within the social sciences in the postwar period is perhaps the major reason for the regular appearance of programmatic statements concerning the need for rapprochement between history, sociology, and social anthropology (Braudel 1980, Burke 1980, Evans-Pritchard 1961, Giddens 1979, Smith 1962). However the history that most authors have in mind is clearly the conceptions of modern empirical historiography or Weberian causal analysis rather than any willingness to contemplate the existence of historical process as such (see Teggaert 1941 for the survey of the tensions between these two "views" of history.) There is an obvious reluctance to return to that other conception of historicism that may be summarized as a belief that a thing can only be properly understood in terms of the place it occupies within some larger process of development (Mandelbaum 1968).

Whatever their differences, both modern historiography and the various interpretations of nineteenth-century historicism took as axiomatic what Hexter has called the "reality rule," i.e., historians cannot just tell any old story of the past but must "interrogate" evidence in order to reconstruct the past as it really was (Hexter 1967). This does not deny that what is known about the past is largely contingent upon our perception of the present, but it does deny that our knowledge of the past is simply a figment of the present. There are good grounds for agreeing with Lévi-Strauss that history is a Western preoccupation and to follow him in distinguishing between "hot" and "cold" societies, i.e., those societies that perceived themselves to be in a permanent state of change as opposed to those that believe that they exist in a timeless present and for whom the past has no relevance (Lévi-Strauss 1966). But the "relativist" or phenomenological thesis that perceives all history as myth, as a figment whose production varies with contemporary need or hunger for history, is confronted in a more profound manner by the archaeological record than by historical documents since the objective reality of the former (but not its meaning) is less disputable than the observations of the latter. In either case, perceptions of change in a profound sense affect all societies at certian periods, and the way in which individuals experience the effects of such transformations can be separated from the objective conditions for observing what actually happened. It may well be the case that, in this sense, archaeology will have a more profound affect on those societies for whom an "ethnographic present" has been ordained by outside observers, often in collusion with the internal world of views of the same societies (Groube 1977).

## PROCESSUAL ARCHAEOLOGY AND THE REJECTION OF HISTORY

Archaeology seems to be risking a great deal in its continued loyalty to the cause of historical process and evolutionism. Indeed, the whole enterprise has been dismissed as an absurd form of intellectual neglect by archaeologists of what everyone else has known for over 50 years (Leach 1977, 164). To a certain extent, the subject has also become a victim of its own courage in holding fast to the investigation of remote periods of prehistoric time in the "core areas" of the Old and New Worlds.

Disillusion with "laws of cultural development" suited academic historians who were able to concentrate on being vigorous in their own particular speciality and on increasing the adequacy of the evidence available for empirical investigation. Many archaeologists were affected in a similar manner. What Renfrew (Chapter 1 this volume) calls the "long sleep of archaeological debate" is also a period (1920s to 1960s) during which archaeology left synthesis aside and concerned itself with developing techniques of excavation and field survey and with working out solutions to basic problems of spatial and temporal coordination of archaeological assemblages (mostly within a nationalistic historiographic framework; hence the plethora of "cultures" in European prehistory, for instance.)

It is of interest that the development of field methods contrasted with the study of museum-based collections that had been considered sufficient for evolutionistic purposes and that a tension between these two forms of empirical investigation in archaeology still exists today. Simple notions of culture, innovation, diffusion, etc. were clearly adequate rubrics for such activities. Moreover, subsumed by a particular form of historiography, archaeology took as its primary concern the understanding of particular sequences of events in particular regions over long periods of time. In the context of a philosophy of history that stressed the knowledge of the past, in as much detail as possible, as valuable in itself, knowledge of the remote past had as much justification to exist as that of recent times. Collingwood's [1946] dissemination of certain tenets of German post-Kantian idealism was of critical importance here. Attempts at synthesis were few and far between and, when attempted, were clearly intended for popular consumption and were preceded by disclaimers as to the complexity and detail of the archaeological record and the difficulty of presenting any simple generalizations. Of course, there were some exceptions. Gordon Childe retained a belief in certain tenets of evolutionism, comparative methodology, and an orthodox Marxist theory of historical process (i.e., primacy of the productive forces thesis). He still believed in laws of historical progress although never in a simplistic or dogmatic manner.

What some would see as a rupture or "epistemological break" in archaeological thinking by the mid-1960s was brought about by those practitioners (particularly in the United States) who wished to move their interests in the subject out of history, which was then universally condemned as narrow and particularizing (e.g., Flannery 1967 Trigger's defense of history 1968). It was claimed that archaeology should approach as near as possible the ideal of a generalizing, comparative, positivist natural science. This was in part for overt political and ideological reasons. Politically, as exact an antithesis to existing practice as was possible had to be sought in order to define an explicit polemical position. The ideal of hard, rigorous "science" appears well suited to play such a pedagogic role: It was used in a similar ideological manner in the founding of Comtean sociology in the mid-nineteenth century and in the debates leading to the founding of British social anthropology in the 1920s. This "rupture" was due also to the lack of sympathy for the aspirations of some archaeologists in disciplines such as British social anthropology where—as we have seen—any concern with history was very much of the short term and encapsulated in the speciality of social change. The fact that this was not the case in the United States, where for peculiar national historical reasons a different kind of archaeology–anthropology interface had evolved, resulted in a neoevolutionist–cultural materialist–functional ecology fusion to form the American "new archaeology."

The renewal of archaeology in the United States under the banner of "hard science" also depended on the availability of a positivistic world view commensurable with American political aspirations in the postwar era. Similar but very different intellectual reorientations in British archaeology would likewise have to be located in a social context stressing a radically changing world role and aspirations for a unified "European" world view. How one views the various debates of this period in archaeology, including abstract questions about what should form adequate objects of knowledge for a prospective science of archaeology and what should constitute adequate bases for explanation— depends on one's particular view of what science is about (e.g., Hempel–Nagel neopositivism). Kuhn's view of science as an essentially revolutionary activity with periods of "normal science" being interrupted by crises and disorganization served as a legitimation of what was supposed to be going on in archaeology at that time. (For alternative views of how "science" works, see Lakatos 1971, Feyerabend 1975, Chalmers 1978). The Lakatos research program for instance, denies falsificationism and favors a more partial and provisional conception of scientific activity. His criteria for adequate research requires coherence in initial assumptions and novelty in the discovery of new phenomena. Proliferation of ingenious conjectures will lead to progress as long as some of the predictions prove eventually to be successful. The definition of successful is a result of new insights and stimuli for future understanding rather than the immediate ability to satisfy "hard" scientific rules of verification (Lakatos 1971). This is not to deny that empirical confirmation of a prediction must at some stage be possible. However, it does deny that there are any certain rules by which this can be achieved, and asserts that intellectual "pluralism" is a surer guarantee for progress in research.

Methodological considerations were also a major preoccupation. This conceded a deep unease about the adequacy of the archaeological record and an increased sensitivity about it in the face of scepticism that archaeology could be a science when its data base was widely regarded as not open to any rigorous testing and verification procedures. Moreover, the aspirants of a revitalized archaeology had to confront both the scepticism of hoped-for supporters in other, "harder" sciences as well as that of the adherents of an older form of historiographic archaeology, for whom the acknowledged poverty of the archaeological record was a justification for the application of intuition and personal skill in the evaluation of limited remains and a reason for rejecting reliance on "number-crunching" machines.

What some now wish to see as disarray in archaeology—a threatening disorder of competing paradigms and "isms"—is of course nothing new. Such plurality of views has been the case all along. But when any sober assessment of the actual practice of archaeology is made, one comes to the conclusion that while a varieity of differing theoretical postures have been adopted, the aims are still markedly historiographic, namely, the pursuit of particular sequences over a period of time in a particular region. Nobody doubts that specialist knowledge is a particular constraint of practical work. However, the extent to which practitioners are concerned with emphasizng the uniqueness of an historical subject rather than it being illustrative of some more general principle defines the extent to which the product of their work is capable of contributing to further comparative generalization. But it does not determine in practice that a marked gulf should exist between "idiographic" and "nomothetic" goals, nor that choices have to be made between delivering lawlike statements or offering only particularistic detail. The question of "Mickey Mouse laws" is a common enough problem in any discipline that purports to produce generalizable statements. If specificity is lost altogether, any generalization becomes so general as to be useless, and if too much specificity is retained, then establishing its meaning by relating it to events or cases of a similar class becomes impossible. The problem for many archaeologists is knowing what class of general propositions they might contribute to.

The most consistent answer to this question in recent years has been that archaeology is concerned with processes of change. More specifically, its concern is with the way different types of societies react to changes in their immediate environment (physical and social) and the internal mechanisms that both stimulate and provide the solutions to the internal stresses that precede social transformation. A difficulty arises in knowing the kind of process on which an archaeological or a wider historical perspective can throw light, when the existing conceptual repertoire consists of discredited nineteenth-century evolutionary propositions or sociological constructs from which the temporal setting is deliberately shed in order "to take them out of the flux of time and achieve a conceptual stability as a sociological proposition" (Evans-Pritchard 1961, 4). (This perspective casts some doubt on the validity of Weber's justification of sociology as a preparation for historical analysis. E. P. Thompson's (1978) repudiation of the coupling of static sociological formulations to the motor of history are very much to the point here.)

In biological evolution, a breakthrough was achieved when the mechanisms of genetic mutation and natural selection were found to underlie processes of variation and change. Similarly, in linguistics, little success at the formal level of comparison was achieved prior to the specification of the general rules that could be used to generate all language forms. In other words, it is almost certain that archaeology is not going to get very far if it relies on comparisons of formal sequences as the source of its generalizations. Lévi-Strauss's famous dictum—"in anthropology as in linguistics . . . it is not comparison that supports generalization, but the other way around"—is equally apposite for archaeology (Lévi-Strauss 1963, 21).

It has been claimed that Marxist theory can play the vital intermediary role in a synthesis of history and the social sciences (Goldelier 1977). Apparently this is true in spite of the obvious difficulties presented by the essential ahistoricism of much of the neo-Marxist theory and its implicit acceptance of the limiting assumptions of existing social science (Kahn and Llobera 1980). As Banaji has observed, much of the recent obsession with mode-of-production analysis in contemporary Marxism has resulted in turning away from dynamics and the reproduction of static formulations of social totalities that seem incapable of forming any coherent attack on contemporary social theory (Banaji 1977). Moreover, recent trends in contemporary Marxism would appear to prove only too clearly that no salvation is to be found in any dogmatic return to Marx as a guideline (Llobera 1979). Many debates in Marxist anthropology appear to have foundered on the attempt to apply a body of principles—assumed to form the core of a general theory of historical materialism—to social formations that clearly bear little relation to the forms of nineteenth-century capitalism that Marx orginally set out to analyze (Harbsmeir 1978).

All of this may in retrospect be seen to be unduly pessimistic. Whatever its successes and failures, it is undeniable that French Marxist anthropology has helped to revitalize the subject and has opened to question assumptions that were threatening to drift into established anthropological "facts" (e.g., the separation of social practice, kinship as cultural idiom, symbolism as an autonomous domain, the reality of isolated social units, etc). The adequacy of the concepts derived from Marx and Engels is, after all, answered by their own insistence on the historical specificity of all concepts and on the view that concepts and evidence are themselves the products of contradictions and movement in their own historical circumstances. For an archaeologist to admit to having derived inspiration from Marx's contributions to historical investigation is one thing, but the significance of that contribution is not to be valued in terms of the eternal "correctness" of his results. What Marx had to say on precapitalist formulations was limited, and much of it would not stand up to modern empirical research. The same could be said of his use of particular concepts such as the separation of base–superstructure, organic totality, class, exploitation, etc. In fact, the principles of investigation that he developed to create such notions in the first place ought to be of more enduring value for the construction of new concepts in changing historical circumstances.

As others have shown, the tendency after Marx's death was to superimpose his ideas upon a range of then current modes of thought in order to give substance to a new orthodoxy of historical materialism. This is not to say that his ideas were never along these lines but rather that subsequent political contingencies led to the rapid closure of a set of flexible and constantly changing categories of thought into a fixed system of ideas (Llobera 1979). Nor was the result a particularly coherent whole. Darwinism and Spencerian evolution were strong influences on Engels and Kautsky. Plekhanov dabbled with Darwinism combined with environmental determinism and Ratzel's anthropogeography. Bukharin and, to a lesser extent, Lenin evolved a pure form of technoeconomic determinism that became the more well-known Marxism of the twentieth century (Samuel 1980). The various codifications of historical materialism that had evolved by World War I cannot therefore be clearly segregated from preceding evolutionist and diffusionist traditions, nor can their formation be separated politically from their need to defend themselves against the polemics of Durkheim, Weber, and others against what was to become an increasingly justifiable characterization of Marxism as simplistic economic determinism.

It cannot be said that archaeology has no theory. Rather, it was the various complicated strands of these formulations and their overlaps with the more neutral evolutionist and diffusionist traditions that were and still are most influential. Also, in a diluted form, the primacy of nature over culture (the materialism–idealism disjunction) maintained a strong influence in archaeology, colluding with an assumption that the nature of its data provided the most evidence on technology and the least on culture. In other words, while Gordon Childe was the only explicit "Marxist" in British archaeology, his ghost will not lie down for the very good reason that in their historicist assumptions and their often implicit acceptance of the complicated interweavings of historical materialism, Darwinian and Spencerian evolutionism, Morganian anthropology, technoeconomic determinism, and biological reductionism, current perceptions of the subject of archaeology are not all that different from Childe's. In a curious manner, therefore, archaeology is in the position of never having gone through the rupture with historicism (unless now belatedly) or, at least, not as radically as the other historical and social sciences. This is probably for the good reason that there can be little justification for the investigation of remote periods of time unless one adheres to some notion of historical process as a constraint upon or determination of social facts. But to accept the epistemology is not necessarily to go along with the conceptual baggage that might be carried at any point in time. For archaeology to recognize what this is and to recognize its derivation and conceptual status is perhaps of greater importance now than it was 20 years ago.

## ARCHAEOLOGICAL "HOLISM" AND THE SOCIAL-TOTALITY MODEL

It could be argued that the strength of archaeology as a discipline—in addition to its technical expertise in data recovery—lies in the investigation of aggregated units and the conditions that lead to their transformation over time. If one meant by this little more than the notion that entities larger than the individual existed in the past—entities that formed the social field in which the individual operated—then archaeology would share a view of society held by functionalists, structuralists, and Marxists alike.

Archaeology has borrowed from Marxist analysis, systems theory and functionalism—a conceptualization of a social totality that is to be understood by the way its constituent elements are interrelated. Marxist analysis differs from functionalist analysis both in terms of its conception of what these parts are and in an attempt to show that contradictions exist in the complex determination of the structures that go to make up the whole. Analysis proceeds from the abstraction of the whole to that of its parts and back to the whole again and from the abstract to the concrete at each of these levels (Marx 1973, Introduction). Such a view is always partial in the sense that some things are always left out, and the whole may or may not correspond to what may be isolated empirically as a concrete "society." The totality is therefore a conceptual entity that has reality only in the sense that it forms a mental appropriation of a real world that exists separate from thought process (Marx 1971, 207). In this sense, population, society, or a mode of subsistence could all be totalities and abstractions at the same moment, the validity of their application depending on how they relate to each other in the analysis of concrete situations.

But the real force of the totalizing effect is not the argument that the "whole is greater than its parts," but the fact that to reject it leads to analyses that depending on dualistic assertions (culture–nature, materialism–idealism, facts–values, concepts–reality, etc.) and the selection by the researcher of finite segments of reality abstracted from a social context that is either unknowable or a chaotic "stream of events" (Weber 1949, 117–118). Both Marxist and Weberian analyses, for instance, can be said to contain value-loaded notions. Such preconceptions can be said to dictate the abstraction from reality of certain variables against others for empirical analysis (e.g., prestige variables versus power relations in regard to the manipulation of resources of various kinds). However, a Marxist perspective would assume that such variables can only be explained in terms of how their function is determined by being part of some large whole (e.g., why mercantile forms of accumulation are found in many different types of social formations but with very different effects) and the position that whole occupies in some larger process of historical development.

For Weber, on the other hand, because only the individual can produce meaningful action, history is the product of individual actions, the cultural significance of which can be assessed statically but explanation of which depends on detecting causal sequences in the free flow of historical events (hence the inevitable tensions between structural history and histories of the event). Archaeologists have generally, if unwisely, dismissed the latter enterprise as impossible or inappropriate, assuming insuperable difficulties in detecting individual action in the archaeological record. But to do so would be an unfortunate act of intellectual evasion. If archaeology cannot justify its adherence to the existence of aggregated units as theoretical entities, then they have no right to continue to adopt the attitude that they do exist as objects of analysis simply because of an assumption that the "coarse-grained" nature of archaeological data allow only broad patterns to be detected. Again, this brings us back to the premise that the development of archaeological theory depends on the reexamination of its own inbuilt and often implicit assumptions and obliges us to ask why—as almost a matter of reflex—such loyalty has been shown to its historicist and holistic origins. It may well be the case that "the widespread assumption in Western sociology that historicism has been laid to rest is premature" (Zaret 1980, 1199), and if so, archaeology may finally be rewarded for its perseverence. Yet any development is also likely to be impeded by further reliance either on holistic categories that are assumed to have a universal significance or on methodological assumptions about invariable laws of human nature. The notion of society, for example, has led to attempts to find the equivalent of bounded units in the archaeological record within which discrete sets of activities can be said to have occurred. Recent archaeological experience indicates that such entities do not exist (e.g., Shennan 1978). The material culture record also does not appear to exist as a unity that can be correlated with any discrete behavioral activity. It forms a category only because archaeologists classify it as such, as part of the taxonomic space within which they operate and as part of the definition of their own discipline. "Society," as a construct, is also used freely in anthropology to refer to named units that are supposed to exist in geographical space. But we have only to look at cases such as the Nuer–Dinka debate to see that problems of classification stem from the initial assumption that cultural identity equates with differences in social structure and with adaptations of discrete populations to environments in a given territory (Glickman 1972, Newcomer 1972, Southall 1976).

This debate also raises more fundamental theoretical questions of how "societies," defined in this way, come into being. Ethnic categories, for example, emerge as "states of mind" in concrete political and historical circumstances. Such categories take on increasingly fixed proportions as groups maintain and reproduce themselves in opposition to each other. These in turn may coincide with divergent tendencies in social structure from what may have been a previous common tradition. However, if there is homology between the two results it is not because of some general rule but as part of a concrete historical process. Understanding such processes archaeologically and historically will not be helped by starting with borrowed unitary notions of society, the derivation of which must be sociology's own starting point–the emergence of nation–states in Western Europe in recent times.

## POLITICS AND ECONOMIC DETERMINATION

The classical Marxist notion of social totality and its Althusserian reformulation have recently been exposed to a number of critiques that radically alter the perspective they provide for the analysis of percapitalist social formations (Friedman 1976, Harbsmeir 1978, Hindess and Hirst 1977, Kahn and Llobera 1980, Levine and Wright 1980; for an orthodox reaction see Cohen 1979).

Western Marxism has developed more or less in opposition to the classic historical materialist thesis of the primacy of the forces of production and its five-stage theory of social evolution. The Althusserian purpose in saving the historical materialist thesis required the rejection of the economic determination of history in order to save its valuable aspects, in particular the concept of contradiction and "social effect" as the result of the articulation of relations of dominance and determination within a larger system (Althusser and Balibar 1970). Hence for Althusser the difference between capitalist and precapitalist societies is essentially that while "economic" relations are dominant and determinant in the former, other social relations (religion, politics, and kinship) can dominate in the latter, although in the last analysis there must be an economic reason for why this should be so.

The central concern however is to retain a privileged role for the economic in causal analysis. The *economic* is defined as a set of productive forces and relations of production that form the core of a social system. Analysis of the form this can take would then in turn provide insight into the particular representational form of the social system as well as its conditions for change. In fact, as a number of authors have pointed out, both these formulations are teleologically functionalist, and their claims to a theory of social change are logically suspect anyway (Friedman 1976, Hindess and Hirst 1977, Kahn 1978). If one cannot show that any particular set of productive forces necessarily corresponds to any particular set of relations of production, then to talk in terms of dominance and determination in their relationship seems unwarranted. Friedman (1979, 19) concludes a critique of Althusser and Goldelier by saying that "I consider the basic notion of structural causality— that the economy determines which instance or social structure will dominate its organisation—to be a kind of static functionalism that has no explanatory power."

As it stands, we are left with the theoretically thin notion that the social totality is composed of a dialectical interplay of "definite social relations and practices, relations and forces of production, law, and so on, but there is no necessary form in which these concepts must be articulated into the concept of the essential structure of a social formation" (Cutler *et al.* 1977, 229). We are left with no conception of hierarchy, determination, or abstract definition of causality. Instead, the precise articulation of the relations making up the whole is explained "by laying bare the structural transformation by which it came into being, i.e., by accounting for its genesis" (Friedman 1979, 19).

We appear to arrive at another instance of theoretical problems that are being generated because of an initially inadequate conceptualization of the problem in historical terms. But to pass the problem to history and to leave the social totality as an undifferentiated set of relations vaguely articulated in the determination of temporal process would place an extraordinary load on duration as the explanatory variable. Without some specification of what generates movement, the explanation of particular social forms is left to the accidential conjuctures of historical events. It was, after all, Marx's intention to specify the laws of motion of capitalism as an historical formation and not as a synchronically defined totality. Moreover, it was precisely the need finally to reject the economism of the orthodox Marxist theory of history and his rejection of historicism in general that led Althusser to reincorporate determination by the economy in the last instance into a functionalist and static conception of the social totality. By rejecting the Althusserian formulations of the social totality and in the face of the present inadequacy of any formulation of historical process to replace it, we arrive at a particular impasse as far as the possibility of a general theory of the social totality is concerned.

One important result of this apparent stalemate has been the emergence of a number of more thorough reexaminations of the development of historical materialism. On the basis of this, a number of authors have independently stressed the primacy of the political over the economic and have emphasized the central importance of "class struggle" in social change (in history Brenner 1977, in anthropology Seddon 1978 and Kahn and Llobera 1980, and in sociology Laclau and Mouffe in press).

As we have seen, an orthodox Marxist theory of history developed in the political context of the systematization of Marxism as a party doctrine in Europe. Inexorable laws of progress due to the inherent tendency for productive forces to expand formed the scientific bases for predicting the inevitability of social change against which the reality of political dissent and discord could be unified and subsumed as mere flotsam on the surface of history. The movement of history was reduced to a single contradiction between the forces and relations of production, and social change was thought to occur at a point in time when this contradiction had reached its highest point, irrespective of particular political circumstances. Combining elements derived from various evolutionist and biological theories and by reducing Marx's multilinear scheme to a unilinear five-stage theory of human history, historical materialism came to possess a coherent theory of history with explicit predictions to organize political action around. As Laclau and Mouffe, among others, have demonstrated recently, Leninism represented a critical point in the disintegration of this reductionist model of history, and a new move to redefine Marxism centered on the primacy of the political (Laclau and Mouffe in press). For if—as in the case of Russia—a new critical conjuncture could come about due to political forces set up by the integration of a country into the capitalist world system, then the place where a new balance of forces between classes emerged could not be said to coincide with a situation in which the contradiction between the forces and relations of production were said to have reached their highest point.

The break is seen most clearly in the reaction of Lukacs and particularly of

Gramsci to the political events of this period. The development of the political instance in Gramsci's work and his elaboration of concepts such as relations of force, hegemony, historic bloc, and his rejection of narrow class interests as the sole basis of political action, acknowledged the importance of political relations that were more than relations of production. In Gramsci's work, politics encompasses the whole domain of social relations. History, in a concrete sense, emerges as a result of the resolution of continuous antagonisms existing between social subjects. What defines the social whole, therefore, is the form of political articulation that constitutes the totality of social relations, and in the sense that Gramsci uses the term (as an ensemble of relations of forces), it has no particular locus (in the state, for example) ("The Modern Prince" in Gramsci 1971). It follows that politics is not definable in any institutional form but refers more generally to power struggle and to the idioms, symbols, and other means used to define relative status and position.

If politics cannot be defined as a special category of social relations, then it must also be assumed that it does not exist in opposition to "economics," and one must assert instead the primacy of politics within the economy itself. Far from forming a homogeneous field with a production logic of its own, the "economy" itself becomes a complex relation of forces between different social agents, and the productive forces are themselves subject to a rationality imposed on them by these relations. What constitutes the problem of the "economic" therefore in this framwork would be the manner in which political relations and antagonisms impress themselves on the productive forces. In other words, it is how differentiation of political relations determines—however indirectly—specialization and intensification in the exploitation of material resources, the developement of new production processes, divisions of labor, modes of circulation and exchange, and the symbolic–ideological means available for the reproduction of these patterns. The fact that the latter are not simply products of the former, but exist as elements to be grasped, implies the existence of constraints on the elaboration of these categories. Moreover, those production and exchange categories that exist as functions of certain political relations are realized ultimately in a given set of environmental conditions that constrain freedom of material reproduction.

## PROCESS AND DYNAMICS IN PRECAPITALIST SOCIAL FORMATIONS

For the study of precapitalist social formations, this implies agreement with the now-widespread rejection of the economistic arguments of a Marxist anthropology and a reformulated notion of the social totality which gives greater weight to the political determination of material processes.

It is well known, for example, that one of the striking features of many precapitalist societies is the way in which blocks or constraints are placed on the acquisition of status and on free flows of wealth (see Douglas 1967 for an illuminating discussion on this point). Leadership and the political structure appear to be set apart from subsistence, from control of the means of production, from commerce, from the alienation of property, and from wealth accumulated directly through the exchange of local products. Historically, we know of numerous examples where abstract wealth in a money from and agents of trading for gain were viewed with deep suspicion by incumbent power holders and were isolated by mechansims such as "ports of trade" (see Polanyi 1957), where their activities could be regulated. The implications are that uncontrolled sources of wealth, particularly from outside parties, threaten the monopolies imposed by power holders on the acquisition of positions within the status hierarchy. In other words, as status hierarchies differentiate into increasingly rigid internal divisions, a similar hierarchy of rights emerges to control certain resources, to produce certain items, or to maintain the craftsmen to do so, and to direrct certain production processes. This segregation also tends to be cumulative as higher-status positions incorporate some of the resources and functions of lower-status categories but on an expanded scale.

The essence of these types of society is, therefore, monopoly in the means of achieving political power and the creation of highly differentiated sets of political relations to achieve this. Increasing monopolization of rank and power and control over the resources needed to maintain them is achieved by those who define degrees of eligibility to position. Douglas argues that the main function of status insignia and prestige items is to legitimate access to high-status positions, to maintain rank, and to hinder attacks on status (Douglas 1967). For status positions to remain defined and to prevent open competition for access to such positions, the distribution of such items must be controlled and used to manage access to resources and "not bring about a pattern of control over goods and services which is at variance with the pattern of ascribed status" (Douglas 1967, 133). Thus, the status hierarchy establishes as many sets of productive forces as there are status positions that need to be defined relative to each other. These in turn define by default, a separate sphere of "subsistence production," and mechanisms for the local exchange of domestic surpluses that must be common to all status categories and cannot be directly implicated for exclusive possession within the status hierarchy. Since local resources and wealth acquired through local exchange are common to all, it must follow that access to higher status cannot be defined in terms of local wealth and the latter must in some way be constrained from being too easily converted into the categories of wealth that define lower status position. Hence, the definition of local political status and the maintenance of controlled competition must be regulated by the distribution of items gained through larger systems of ceremonial exchange. Equally, the "value" of the items circulated is determined by their political functions and the status of the participants and not by any qualities intrinsic to the items themselves. In the absence of abstract labor, inequalities in labor time or other such measure cannot be used to determine exchange values directly. Shares of surplus products will depend upon social status and not on the amount of labor contributed to production (see Bradby 1977, Kahn 1978, Rowlands 1979).

However, *this is not to argue for simple primacy of the political over the economic in precapitalist societies.* It is quite obvious that status hierarchies often experience considerable difficulties in maintaining blocks on the disruptive effects of free flows of wealth. In other words, conditions develop that do bring about patterns of control over resources that are at variance with the traditional pattern of ascribed status. It is because of this that "commerce" cannot exist within the "primitive community" but must always exist on its boundaries. Systems have broken down in the past into increasingly fragmented, competitive, and individualistic universes, as political structures have failed to maintain ordered hierarchies and patterns of control over goods and services that are at variance with the established status hierarchy. It would be lower-ranking groups that would be particularly likely to collude with outside agents (e.g., rivals to those agents that had already established monopoloy advantage in trade with, for example, the incumbent elite). In so doing they would try to gain control over local and external sources of demand. This would serve to destabalize an existing hierarchy in the expectation of establishing a new hierarchy with themselves as power holders.

It would be tempting to recognize here the forcefulness of the argument that conditions for the material reproduction of local systems rarely coincide with the limits of local political control, and hence the reproduction of the latter must always depend ultimately on the conditions of the former (e.g. Wallerstein 1974, Friedman 1976). But we find instead that, at whatever level of social complexity in precapitalist societies (chiefly elite exchange, archaic-state gift exchange, or empire expansion transforming trade into tribute), power holders attempt to maintain their control over the mechanisms by which materials circulate, over free flows of wealth, and over the agents that for political and logistical reasons achieve a certain autonomy of action (specialist trading groups, organizers of trading expeditions, foreign commercial agents). Also, this is not a matter of political controls that are being extended over previous, independently defined economic flows. The latter never appear to exist. At whatever level of social complexity, the economy is "embedded" depending on the degree of unity and competition that exists within and between status hierarchies, on forms of international gift exchange, alliance formation, and foreign diplomacy, and in a very general sense, on the degree to which these mechanisms are used by different interest groups within weak or strong "states" to maintain their control over the functioning of material flows. (For an extended discussion of such principles applied to the Aztec case and Meso-potamia, see Gledhill and Larsen Chapter 13 this volume.)

For example, in Mesopotamia, it has been recognized that (*a*) transforma-tions from early, competing city states to one-ruler empires to monolithic, bureaucratized empires were always preceded by periods of apparent fragmentation and decline (so-called "Dark Ages") indicative of the failure of existing hierarchies to maintain such controls; and (b) periods of unification are associated with high degrees of coherence in the organization of the political landscape, allowing little room for the actions of free agents (Larsen 1979). A significant element of foreign diplomacy at such times is concerned with mutual support of kings, including military cooperation, and the strengthening of local political position through the formation of coalitions, and regulations on the movements of population and certain categories of materials (see for instance Munn-Rankin 1956). Further elucidation of these processes can only contribute further empirical confirmation of recent criticisms of Wallerstein and would help develop the orientation that he and others have developed within the world-system framework (Brenner 1977, Skocpol 1977).

To what extent do these considerations affect our understanding of the more long-run dynamics of the various kinds of precapitalist systems that have existed in history? Some models of these processes have already been offered elsewhere (e.g. Ekholm and Friedman 1979, Friedman and Rowlands 1977, Frankenstein and Rowlands 1978, Gledhill 1978). In Marx's analysis of capitalism, the genesis of one system is explained by the devolution of another, and both effects are explained by the same process—the development of internal contradictions within the previous system, the resolution of which requires both its movement and transformation into a new configuration. Elaborating upon these principles to explain the origin of capitalism, Marx emphasized contradictions between new forces of production and old relations of production as the moving force (i.e., transition from feudalism to capitalism).

However, there is no reason to assume that even if this were a complete argument for the origins of capitalism, the specific content of the thesis could be applied to other social formations. For example, in many so-called "tribal systems," significant constraints are imposed on conversions between different "spheres of exchange," the rigidity of which appears to vary according to the velocity of circulation within the higher-ranked systems. Constraints appear to function both as a "licensing system" to use Douglas's phrase (1967: 131), and as a kind of pump that controls the velocity of circulation by making wealth flows pass through valves in the system. (This assumes that it was mainly European contact that either rigidified such systems, i.e., hierarchized them, or broke them down into completely individualistic and competitive systems. See Damon 1980 for the conversion mechanisms existing in the *Kula* case.) A basic contradiction appears to lie therefore between production for use and pro-duction for exchange in such systems, where the latter plays a primarily political role. Such constraints serve to buffer what are essentially antithetical tendencies between local subsistence production and exchange relations and "politically defined" circulation spheres.

Similar forms of contradiction occur in more elaborated systems where the reproduction of political hierarchies as a social process is dependent upon material flows that are administered by distinct groups that may be coresidential with, but not socially defined as part of, an incumbent hierarchy. The genesis of such systems appears to lie in a progressive separation of functions linked to internal competition and differentiation within the ruling groups of previously more unified structures (Gledhill and Rowlands in press). Where production for exchange takes on an overtly commercial aspect, the organization of trade becomes differentiated from the sector that controls the production of surpluses for exchange. The latter, represented as an automous set of political institutions, becomes increasingly disembedded from subordinate strata which may retain the autonomous "community aspect" described in the Asiatic mode of production model. While there are numerous conflicting tendencies in such systems, constraints on the possibility of mercantile accumulation's having any direct impact on traditional status hierarchies and contradictions arising from intensified controls by the latter over material resources (tribute, corvée, personal ownership of land, and the generation of various servile forms of labor, etc.), assume a dominant aspect (see Gledhill and Larsen Chapter 13 this volume).

As many others have already noted, the development of mercantile accumulation and the precise manner in which it is constrained by older forms of status hierarchy has more long-term implications for the evolution of complex societies (Weber 1976, Wittfogel 1957, Wallerstein 1974). Without going into detail, a strong antithesis exists between two sets of processes. One, to be found in the formation of many early state systems, encourages differentiation of political structure and the economy into state and private sectors and the elaboration of constraining mechanisms to prevent the easy transfer of resources and personnel (mobility in a sense) between them. The other encourages intervention by incumbent power holders to control other sectors of the political economy in order to regulate their functioning in support of political processes at the center. Increasing differentiation therefore finds its negation in increased political centralization as the tendency which underlies the transformation of early states into empires.

## CONCLUSION

We have been concerned in this chapter to relate some of the tendencies that exist in archaeological theory and objectives with what appears to be a growing awareness for the need for an historically situated social science that avoids some of the abstracted and overgeneralized notions of contemporary social theory. In a sense, both trends represent a move back to a position implicitly or explicitly held by the founding ancestors of both the historical and social sciences. For Durkheim to say "it is necessary to go into the past to discover the deep lying forces, which so often unconscious, are determinative of the social process" was no idle aphorism from the founder of modern functionalism but a deeply held conviction that he believed could only be satisfied when further theoretical and empirical research had been done (Durkheim 1899 quoted in Bellah 1959, 450).

Having said this, the perspectives available to understand these processes do have a number of weaknesses. Durkheim, concerned with a particular view of the social whole, emphasized constraining elements that would explain the deeply conservative and unchanging nature of social systems. Inherited by French historians of the *Annales* tradition (and some French Marxist anthropologists as well), this resulted in the work of Marc Bloch and in particular that of Fernand Braudel focusing not on the explanation of change but on what prevents change from occurring. This appears to be largely a matter of geographical, climatic, and demographic factors (see Hexter 1973). It is possible to understand therefore the necessity for this tradition to dismiss the "political event" as superficial surface turmoil and of little significance for the study of duration (a point that may come to affect current emphases on the primacy of the political in recent Marxist debates). It was precisely the "superficial event" that was most appropriate for the causal analysis of sequential change that most influenced Weberian sociology. Often misrepresented to fit political events in the twentieth century, historical materialism retained only a superficial respectability as a theory of social change, the usefulness of which to prehistory might best be sought in the stimulus to thought of its original principles rather than adhering rigidly to any one of the distorted categories that exist at present. Current conceptualizations of ideological relations of reproduction, social relations of production, attendant power relations and their technical and environmental requirements form an arena for theoretical debate that has already provided new insight into the nature of the archaeological record and prehistoric social change.

## REFERENCES

Althusser, L., and Balibar, E., 1970, *Reading Capital*, London, New Left Books.

Banaji, J., 1977, Modes of production in a materialist conception of history, *Capital and Class* 3, 1–44.

Bellah, R., 1959, Durkheim and history, *American Sociological Review* 24, 4, 447–461.

Bradby, B., 1977, The non-valorisation of women's labour, *Critique of Anthropology* 9–10, 131–138.

Braudel, F., 1980, History and the social sciences, in Braudel, F. (ed.), *On History*, Chicago, University of Chicago Press.

Brenner, R., 1977, The origins of capitalist development: a critique of neo-Smithian Marxism, *New Left Review* 104, 25–92.

Burke, P., 1980, *Sociology and History*, London, Allen and Unwin.

Chalmers, A. F., 1978, *What Is This Thing Called Science?*, Milton Keynes, The Open University Press.

Cohen, G. A., 1979, *Karl Marx's Theory of History*, Oxford, Clarendon Press.

Cutler, A. et. al. 1977: *Marx's Capital and Capitalism Today*. Ross RKP, London.

Collingwood, R. G., 1946, *The Idea of History*, Oxford, Clarendon Press.

Damon, F. H., 1980, The Kula and generalised exchange, *Man* 15, 2, 267–292.

Douglas, M., 1967, Primitive rationing: a study in controlled exchange, in Firth, R. (ed.), *Themes in Economic Anthropology*, ASA Monographs 6, 119–145.

Evans-Pritchard, E. E., 1961, *Anthropology and History*, Manchester, University Press.

Feyerabend, P. K., 1975, *Against method: outline of an anarchistic theory of knowledge*, London, New Left Books.

Flannery, K., 1967, Culture history versus culture process, *Scientific American*, August,

Frankenstein, S. M., and Rowlands, M., 1978, The internal structure and regional context of Early Iron Age society in south-western Germany, *Bulletin of Institute of Archaeology, London* 15, 73–112.

Friedman, J., 1976, Marxist theory and systems of total reproduction, *Critique of Anthropology* 7, 3–16.

Friedman, J., 1979, *Structure, System and Contradiction*, Copenhagen, National Museum.

Friedman, J., and Rowlands, M. J. (eds.), 1977, *The Evolution of Social Systems*, London, Duckworth.

Giddens, A., 1979, *Central Problems in Social Theory*, London, Macmillan.

Gledhill, J., 1978, Formative development in the North American Southwest, in Green, D., Haselgrove, C., and Spriggs, M., (eds.), *Social Organisation and Settlement*, Oxford, British Archaeological Reports. pp. 241–290.

Gledhill, J., and Rowlands, M. J., in press, Materialism and socio-economic process in multilinear evolution, in Renfrew C., and Shennan, S. (ed.), *Ranking, resources and exchange*, Cambridge, Cambridge University Press.

Glickman, M., 1972, The Nuer and the Dinka; a further note, *Man* 7, 4, 586–594.

Godelier, M., 1977, *Perspectives in Marxist Anthropology* Cambridge, Cambridge University Press.

Gramsci, A., 1971, *Selections from the Prison Notebooks*, London, Lawrence and Wishart.

Groube, L., 1977, The hazards of anthropology, in Spriggs, M. (ed.), *Archaeology and Anthropology*, Oxford, BAR Supplementary Series 19, pp. 69–90.

Harbsmeir, M., 1978, Critique of political economy, historical materialism and precapitalist social forms, in *Critique of Anthropology* 12, 3, 3–37.

Hawthorne, G., 1976, *Enlightenment and Dispair: A History of Sociology*, Cambridge, Cambridge University Press.

Hexter, J., 1967, The rhetoric of history, *History and Theory* 6, 3–13.

Hexter, J., 1973, Fernand Braudel and the monde Braudellian, *Journal of Modern History* 44, 480–539.

Hindess, B., and Hirst, P., 1977, *Mode of Production and Social Formation*, London, Macmillan.

Kahn, J., 1978, Perspectives in Marxist anthropology: a review article, *Journal of Peasant Studies* 5, 4, 485–496.

Kahn, J., and Llobera, J., 1980, French Marxist anthropology: twenty years after, *Journal of Peasant Studies* 8, 1, 81–100.

Laclau, E., and Mouffe, C., in press, *Hegemony and Socialist Strategy*, London, New Left Books.

Larsen, M., 1979 (ed.), *Power and Propaganda*, Copenhagen, Akademisk Forlag.

Lévi-Strauss, C., 1963, *Structural Anthropology*, New York, Basic Books.

Lévi-Strauss, C., 1966, *The Savage Mind*, London, Weidenfeld and Nicholson.

Lakatos, I., 1971, Falsification and the methodology of scientific research programmes, in Lakatos, I., and Musgrave, A. (eds.), *Criticism and the Growth of Knowledge*, Cambridge, Cambridge University Press.

Levine, A., and Olin, Wright E., 1980, Rationality and class struggle, *New Left Review* 123, 47–68.

Llobera, J., 1979, Techno-economic determinism and the work of Marx on precapitalist societies, *Man* 14, 2, 249–270.

Mandelbaum, M., 1968, *The Problem of Historical Knowledge*, New York, Harper and Row.

Marx, K., 1973, *Grundrisse*, London, Penguin Books.

Marx, K., 1971, *Critique of Political Economy*, London, Lawrence and Wishart.

Megill, A., 1979, Foucault, structuralism and the end of history, *Journal of Modern History* 51, 451–503.

Munn-Rankin, J. M., 1956, *Diplomacy in western Asia in the early second millenium B.C., Iraq* XVIII, 68–92.

Newcomer, P. J., 1972, The Nuer are Dinka: an essay on origins and environmental determinism, *Man* 7, 1, 5–11.

Polanyi, K., 1957, in Ahensberg, C., and Pearson, H. (eds.), *Trade and Market in the Early Empires*, New York, The Free Press.

Roth, G. and Schluchter, W., 1979, *Max Weber's Vision of History*, Berkeley, University of California Press.

Rowlands, M. J., 1979, Local and long distance trade and incipient state formation on the Bamenda Plateau, *Paideuma* 25, 1–19.

Samuel, R., 1980, Sources of Marxist history, *New Left Review* 120, 21–96.

Seddon, D., 1978, *Relations of Production*, London, Cass.

Shennan, S., 1978, Archaeological "cultures": an empirical investigation, in Hodder, I. (ed.), *The Spatial Organisation of Culture*, London, Duckworth.

Skocpol, T., 1977, Wallerstein's world capitalist system: a theoretical and historical critique, *American Journal of Sociology* 82, 5, 1075–1090.

Smith, M. G., 1962, History and social anthropology, *Journal of the Royal Anthropological Institute* 92, 73–85.

Southall, A., 1976, Nuer and Dinka are people: ecology, ethnicity and logical possibilities, *Man* 11 4, 463–491.

Teggaert, F. J., 1941, *Theory and Processes in History*, Berkeley, University of California Press.

Thompson, E. P., 1978, *The Poverty of Theory*, London, Merlin Press. ·

Trigger, B., 1968, Major concepts of archaeology in historical perspective, *Man* 3, 4, 527–541.

Wallerstein, I., 1974, *The Modern World System*, London, Academic Press.

Weber, M., 1976, *The Agrarian Sociology of Ancient Civilisations*, London, New Left Books.

Weber, M., 1949, *Methodology of the Social Sciences*, New York, The Free Press.

Wittfogel, K., 1957, *Oriental Despotism*, New Haven, Yale University Press.

Zaret, D., 1980, From Weber to Parsons and Schutz: the eclipse of history in modern social theory, *American Journal of Sociology* 85, 1180–1200.

# 12

## Catastrophe and Continuity in Social Evolution

*JONATHAN FRIEDMAN*

Evolutionary anthropology–archaeology has not changed significantly since the later work of Steward and his followers. Multilinear evolutionism has continued to dominate archaeology, at least in the United States, in spite of minority protests such as those by Marvin Harris (1979). The changes that have occurred have been more of technique than of substance. From the early and rather vague ecological and technological determinism of Steward's core–superstructure formulation, we have moved through a variety of systems theoretical reformulations—*Homo cyberneticus*—to the extremes of Harris's vulgarization of vulgar Marxism (1979). In general, we have moved from a model of technological determinism to a population pressure model of social evolution. There are two apparently different families of models that dominate at present—the cybernetic and the cultural materialist.

The cybernetic model is best represented by Rappaport (1971, 1977, 1979) and Flannery (1972), but it owes, of course, a great deal to the work of Bateson (1972). The unit of analysis is the society, structured as a control hierarchy in which highest-order "sacred" general programs set guidelines for more specific political and economic programs that direct lower-order activities all the way down to immediate production. This model is an explicit reaction against the strict causality of cultural materialism. Rather than lower levels determining the form and function of higher levels, the reverse is the case. Organization flows down, and output flows up. Evolution here consists in a change in the highest-

**175**

THEORY AND EXPLANATION
IN ARCHAEOLOGY

order regulators of the social system. These highest-order programs are always sacred, in order to remove them from the sphere of ordinary political discourse and action. This is necessary if a society's basic adaptation is to be maintained. According to Rappaport, primitive society has ritual regulation of environmental and social relations as its highest-order program. This program is, moreover, a general purpose program, i.e., one whose goal is merely continued survival (1977, 1979). Ritual regulators are thus negative feedback mechanisms that maintain primitive society within its ecologically adaptive limits. For Rappaport, evolution consists essentially in the promotion of lower-order specific-purpose programs to the highest orders of regulation. Chiefs, kings, industrial monopolists, impose their low-order goals of expansion and accumulation upon the system as a whole through the sanctification of their programs. For Rappaport, the process is of a maladaptive nature, insofar as it destroys the original ecological equilibrium of ritual regulation. For Flannery, this development is more neutral, and for both him and Rappaport, the emergence of new programs of regulation are not the products of a social process but are responses to external conditions, such as population growth, or to an excess of information generated ultimately by responses to environmental factors. Thus, while evolution is not necessarily considered to be a simple process of ecological optimization, society is still defined as a static organism-like entity that responds functionally to external pressures. The motor of evolution is external to society.

The cultural materialist approach maintains a more strictly causal–functionalist approach to evolution. It accepts the cybernetic assumptions of the ecologists but does not accept Rappaport's and Bateson's theories of runaway social development and increasing maladaptation. In the current version we have, instead, a constant "natural" population growth anticipating diminishing economic returns, crises, and the development of new social organizations that are better adapted to more intensive forms of extraction of energy from nature and higher population densities. Social evolution is seen primarily as an adaptation to the disorder reaped by increasing population pressure. Thus, "big-man" systems, chiefdoms, and states are all progressive responses to man's biological propensity to have children (Harris 1977).[1]

Common to these two models is a single general conception of the relation between social transformation and external (environmental) conditions. The latter determine, by way of internal response, the nature and development of

---

[1] The recent attempt (Price 1977) to wed cultural materialism to regional system analysis is hampered by the fact that cultural materialist causality does not need "higher levels" of intersocietal organization to account for local social structure. This is clear in Price's failure to come to any clear conclusion concerning the nature of systemic determination. It would appear that in her model regional systems are the result of standard evolution rather than the reverse. While she insists that the "cluster" of societies is the evolutionary unit, the causality continues to operate in one society at a time.

social forms. Functionalist causality and cybernetic explanation are identical in this respect.

Three assumptions appear to underlie neoevolutionary, cybernetic, and materialist theories. First, social, like biological, evolution is essentially a smooth process characterized by moving equilibrium. This is implicit in an adaptationist approach. Second, social evolution is a regular and continuous process. This is also the general neo-Darwinian view. Third, biological and social evolution as directional, negentropic processes are anomalous in an otherwise steady-state universe in which equilibrium is the rule. Negative feedback, adaptive structure, and ecological functionalism in general are correctives for this anomaly. Biological nature is also basically stable.

## THE END OF EQUILIBRIUM

Stability, continuity, and moving equilibrium are concepts that are slowly being undermined by recent developments in the natural sciences. There is mounting evidence that biological evolutionary changes can no longer be accounted for by natural selection. On the contrary, it seems that genetic change per se is largely irrelevant for evolutionary process (Kimura 1968) and that "the lack of natural selection may be a pre-requisite to major evolutionary advance" (Ho and Saunders 1979, 589). The paleontological record reveals an alternation of long stable periods and rapid transformation rather than a continuous development (Lewen 1980).

The biological model that has served as the basis for ecological and materialist anthropology is the homeostatically functioning organism. In biology; Waddington has done much to replace this physiological framework with a focus on the morphogenetic life cycle. Here, apparent stability is always part of a larger morphogenetic process. Using the catastrophe theory of Thom (1972), Waddington has suggested that biological growth and evolutionary change are best analyzed in terms of thresholds and discontinuous change, where stability is shifted from the level of homeostasis to that of homeorhesis (stability about a trajectory) (Waddington 1974). It might also be suggested that stability is not the result of stabilizers, such as negative feedback devices, but it is an aspect of all structured process—the combination of directional developmental processes combined with external constraints leading to particular canalizations or "chreods." Thom replaces the notion of homeostatis with the mathematical concept of "attractor" to account for stability.[2]

---

[2]Applications of catastrophe theory to the social sciences have been singularly unenlightening in almost all cases. While congruent with a framework constituted by concepts such as contradiction, crisis, morphogenesis, discontinuous change, the model remains a metaphor for processes that have either already been accounted for or which remain in the dark. While catastrophe models may have some pedagogical value, their properties are usually far too general to tell us anything specific about the reality to which they refer (Bennet 1978, Mees 1975, Parijs 1978 for an absurd example, Zeeman 1974, 1976, Renfrew 1978 for a general survey).

**Figure 12.1.** A general model of thermodynamic evolution. (After Prigogine *et al.* 1972, 25.)

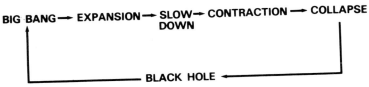

**Figure 12.2.** Model of the life cycle of the universe.

The work of Prigogine and associates (especially 1972) on nonequilibrium thermodynamics and on the thermodynamics of evolution has led to the introduction of the notion of dissipative structure—an open system maintained by a flow of energy at a state far from thermodynamic equilibrium. Such open systems characterize both the living and nonliving. They can be described thermodynamically as "giant fluctuations stabilized by exchange of matter and energy" (Prigogine *et al.* n. d., 46) at states far from thermodynamic equilibrium. The general model of thermodynamic evolution is shown in Figure 12.1. The principal characteristic of this evolution is the movement from order to instability to new order.

Finally, current views of the "evolution" of the universe are also characterized by the phenomena of instability and rapid transformation. The universe's life cycle, from big bang to gravitational collapse, is far indeed from the steady-state universe of the recent past (Hawking 1977, Wheeler 1974). The original big bang marking the birth of our universe leads to an expansion forming the galaxies and smaller complexes, including life. As the expansion phase reaches its limit, gravitational force overtakes the centrifugal movements, resulting ultimately in total collapse into a universal black hole.[3] Now it has been suggested that black holes may be both the beginning and end of expansion (Hawking 1977), which implies a cycle of the sort shown in Figure 12.2.

It might be noted here that the universe emergent from a new big bang could have physical laws very different from our present universe. This implies not only a finite universe but a notion of so-called universal laws that only apply to our present universe.

Living systems and their human social derivatives emerged in some cooling corner of an expanding universe. In terms of universal processes, life is a

[3]Black holes, formed by the gravitational collapse of stars, are so dense that their gravitational force prevents the escape of light (photons).

marginal negentropic phenomenon within a cosmic fluctuation of matter and energy.

## REPRODUCTION AND TRANSFORMATION

For a number of years an alternative framework has been emerging. Several works by myself and others have suggested a focus of analysis that is significantly different from the evolutionary approach.

1. The unit of analysis is neither society nor a particular institution, but the total process of reproduction, the system of cycles connecting production–appropriation by way of differential consumption with new production–appropriation. These cycles form a structural totality in which smaller cycles are embedded in larger cycles. Thus, there are intersocietal cycles of exchange, intrasocietal exchange cycles, life cycles, and production cycles. These cycles are socially determined. Their combination is equivalent to the social reproductive process. Cycles are not reducible to internal social processes. They are regional and are often crucial for the very definition of the local social identity units. This has been discussed for social forms from the capitalist nation state (von Braunmühl 1976) to tribal society (Friedman 1979, Ekholm 1977, Leach 1953). Warfare, which may be conceived as the absence or even the disappearance of exchange, is traditionally acknowledged as a powerful identity-building phenomenon.

2. Social reproduction is governed by social operators. The latter are structures that organize the dynamic properties and direction of social activity and thus determine the nature of the reproductive process. The structures of big-man activity, of capital accumulation, and of escalating trade monopolies (prestige-good systems) impose specific directions on social systems. It is, of course, possible for social systems to be relatively stable. This occurs often in cases of isolation where expansion is blocked. The stability of modern hunter–gatherer societies, for example, may be a relatively recent phenomenon resulting from integration or marginalization in the larger system. The particular tendencies generated by social operators are equivalent to Thom's notion of attractor, stable, or homeorhetic trends. These tendencies are not strictly deducible from the operators themselves, since they are also "canalized" by their conditions of existence. In my analysis of tribal reproduction in northern Southeast Asia (1975, 1979) I suggested that the cycles of political hierarchization and collapse had different shapes depending on the general conditions of agricultural production (where there was no access to external wealth) and the local kinship structure (which was itself a product of previous development). In conditions of increasing population density, produced by the social system itself, the resultant two conditions determined the steepness or flatness of the cycles as shown in Figure 12.3. This development leads from a cycle of theocratic chiefdoms to one that is more feudal in character (where scarce land

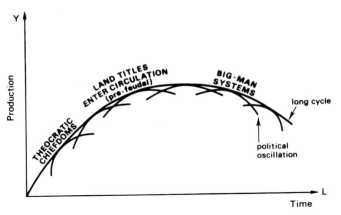

**Figure 12.3.** Evolutionary–devolutionary cycles in the reproduction of tribal systems.

enters the sphere of circulation of valuables) to an increasingly warfare-ridden big-man cycle where prowess in battle and skill in headhunting may be the only basis for the minimal hierarchy that periodically emerges.

3. The social space within which reproduction occurs can and must be divided into that part that is directly organized by social operators and that part that is beyond social control and intentionality. This division is extremely important in spite of the fact that it is often overlooked in the social sciences. The social categories of a social system do not contain the totality of the system. Generalized exchange of women produces circular tendencies in an alliance structure, but circles are not an organizing property of the system. Similarly, the categories and structure of the accumulation of capital generate business cycles. The latter are nonintentional aspects of the system and not part of its social organization. It is here that the notion of "fetishism" is applicable (Friedman 1974). Fetishism can be defined as *the noncorrespondence between the internal goals defined by the categories of a social structure and the material effects of that structure.* This is equivalent to the distinction between the directly organized and nonintentional sectors of a system. Insofar as the directly organized activities of social operators have a structure different from the operators themselves, they too belong to the nonintentional sector of the system—hence Marx's use of the concept. The distinction between social operators and the larger process of reproduction has not been generally acknowledged in anthropology. On the contrary, the general trend has been to develop reductionist models that rationalize rather than explain. In cultural materialism, social operators are simply reduced to adaptive mechanisms— functional responses to their own effects. Among structuralists, poststructuralists, and structural Marxists there is a tendency to incorporate different orders of reality with entirely different types of structure into a single all-encompassing generative model. Recent attempts to reduce the totality of social existence to an

"idéo—logique" (Augé 1977, 1978, Godelier 1978) is the most extreme form of this activity. While poststructuralism (Ardener 1978) seems also to be primarily concerned with the construction of single homogeneous models, "world structures," and "$p$ structures," from which all of social reality might be generated, Lévi-Strauss himself has apparently begun to suggest some of the shortcomings of this approach, at least implicitly. In reference to his early attempt to "explain" the combination of symmetry and asymmetry in Amazonian social structure in terms of a single abstract model containing both forms (1958, 147–180), he now seems to suggest that such structures are the product of the collapse or devolution of former chiefdoms (1973). The former model, which may be a correct ideological representation (Crocker 1969), is in fact a translation of diachrony into synchrony.

4. The evolutioary process implied in the above model is one characterized by crisis and sudden transformation. The nature of the process is determined by the nature of the variables of the systems involved. A social reproductive system is constituted by a number of interlocking dynamic processes that are functionally necessary to one another and, at the same time, possess properties that diverge from one another. The latter phenomenon is expressed by so-called contradictory tendencies of a system that threaten its very existence. Thus, the character of social evolution has little to do with a notion like adaptation or the classical model of biological evolution. On the contrary, it is closer to Waddington's model of morphogenesis and catastrophe or to Prigogine's and associates' (1972) and Eigen's (1971) models of prebiological evolution. The principal difference between the model presented here and neoevolutionary anthropology is that the object is of a different nature. For neoevolutionism, the object is society as a quasi-organism or control hierarchy. It is a stable entity that does no more than react to external environmental or demographic (also external) changes. In the present model, the object itself has directional tendencies. It does not respond to environmental pressures, but, rather, challenges its environment, uses it for its own ends and, finally, comes into contradiction with it.

## THE DIRECTION OF EVOLUTION

The kind of model I am suggesting here is concerned with the nature of tranformational processes and not so much with replicating biological evolution that, as I have said, is a different kind of phenomenon. Those notions of recent evolutionary biology and thermodynamics that appear to be similar are *canalization, homeorhesis, epigenesis, dissipative structure, catastrophe*, etc. These concepts refer to the formal properties of dynamic nonequilibrium systems and not to any specific biological entity. Insofar as social systems are dissipative structures like the living beings that inhabit them, the above concepts can be applied, and social evolution will bear some resemblance to biological evolution.

While the accumulative nature of human social systems implies a tendency for growth and the intensification of energy extraction, there is no continuous developmental process in human history. There are, instead, morphogenetic developments in which initial systems are transformed by means of continued accumulation, involution, or collapse in ways that are determined by the conjunction of initial system properties and their constraining conditions of existence. While one might at least admit that there has been an evolution of technology, it has been neither a continuous nor a cumulative process. There have been repeated developmental thrusts and declines, but it is only with the modern industrial revolution that a qualitative leap occurred with respect to the earliest civilizations. Furthermore, as technological development is driven by the accumulative goals of social systems, what we are referring to as evolution may be no more than a case of intensification that, from the point of view of the human dominated ecosystem, is devolutionary in the long run.

Our approach is clearly different from the usual adaptive ordering of bands, tribes, chiefdoms, states—egalitarian, ranked, stratified, or whatever variation there may be on this theme. It has been suggested elsewhere (Ekholm and Friedman 1980) that this stage theory is very much an ideological reflection of the general center–periphery–margin structure of our civilization as of previous ones. It has also been argued (Friedman 1975, 1979, Ekholm 1977, Coquery–Vidrovitch 1969) that the traditional stages of neoevolutionism are better understood as phases in a partially reversible continuum where the basic operators are constant. It has, finally, been suggested (Ekholm 1980, Ekholm and Friedman 1980) that while there is clearly an epigenetic or evolutionary process of formation of states and civilizations, there is no obvious continuity of social evolution after the emergence of civilization. It would appear that the regional systems of civilizations, with their commerical centers, peripheral chiefdoms and tribes, and marginal bands, have been stable organizations until the modern period. While centers of accumulation have shifted, there has been no fundamental change in form, only differences in dominant economic sectors—state versus private—and the form of exploitation—peasant, serf, slave, or wage labor—that have been prevalent. It is not until industrial capitalism that the geographic size of world systems changed radically and a dominant wage-labor sector emerged. The two phenomena are, of course, closely related.

## OCEANIA: A CLASSICAL EXAMPLE

Oceania is certainly the classical area for the application of the neo-evolutionist scheme. The general view is that there is a gradual evolution from egalitarian big-man systems to more hierarchical Melanesian societies to the increasingly ranked chiefdoms and stratified quasi-states of West and East Polynesia (Sahlins 1958, 1963, Goldman 1955, 1970, Harris 1977, Kirch 1980). All of these models—whether technological or demographic determinist, or, as in the case of Goldman, based on a general social phenomenon such as status rivalry—have one crucial characteristic in common. Instead of starting from the nature of the social systems (Goldman comes close in some of his discussions), they abstract general traits from the societies that can be translated into the evolutionary classification in use. The evolutionary categories themselves are abstracted from individual societies. As such, the possibility that the dynamic of Oceanic societies, even their development, might be best understood as a regional system phenomenon is made inaccessible (Schwartz 1962).

In the following sketch, I shall attempt to provide an alternative model of Oceanic developments that takes as its starting point a reconstruction of the specific regional systems.

The notion that societies evolved from Melanesian to Polynesian types is contrary to what we know about the relative age and conditions of production and demography of the two areas. Melanesia, by far the oldest area, ought to have the most, not the least, devolved structures. Furthermore, no adaptationist argument is applicable here. Melanesia has some of the most densely populated areas of Oceania, and clearly affords conditions for very high agricultural productivity. There is, thus, no reasonable argument to explain why it should be at the bottom of the evolutionary scale when the most recently settled areas of East Polynesia, often in conditions of lower productivity, should be at the top. An evolutionary model must be compatible with the historical record.

Recent linguistic work (Blust 1980a, 1980b) and archaeology (Allen 1977, Ambrose 1976, 1978) indicate the following:

1. That proto-Malayo–Polynesian society was based on some form of generalized exchange (MBD marriage) and some form of asymmetric dualism. This is a phenomenon widespread in Indonesia, central Africa, and the Americas, and it associated with what we shall discuss as prestige-good systems (Ekholm 1972, 1977).
2. That Melanesia was characterized earlier by long-distance trade similar to the more recent trade of West Polynesia and Micronesia, and that it may have "evolved" to the more fragmented, specialized short-distance trade of the recent past.

There is also evidence that some areas of southern Melanesia (New Hebrides) that are today characterized as big-man societies were in the past highly ranked or stratified societies showing evidence of trade with Polynesia (Garanger 1972).

Those areas of northern Melanesia that have maintained political hierarchies, such as the Trobriands, apparently based themselves on a monopoly over highly valued imported goods that were passed down from high-ranking monopolists to lower-ranking groups in exchange for service, tribute, and wives. It has been suggested that monopoly over external trade as the basis for hierarchy in the Trobriands could only be maintained under conditions of trade scarcity (Brunton 1975, Persson in press). Thus, the Trobriands on the periphery of the *Kula* had a well-developed hierarchy, while Dobu in the center had, instead, intense big-man type competition. In the New Guinea highlands, the classic big-man area may have developed as the result of European-organized increase in access to valuables. Early reports from the Mt. Hagen area (Vicedom and Tischner 1943–1948, Vol. II) report a relatively stable hierarchy that was apparently based on a monopoly by "chiefs" over the shell trade to the coast. The hierarchy collapsed into the present-day more egalitarian big-man system as a result of European distribution of formerly scarce valuables.

It might well be argued that the characteristic small-scale intensive short-distance trading of big-men typical of much of Melanesia is a long-term result of the increase in trade density. In such systems, lack of monopoly over external exchange leads to a situation where trade wealth is converted into competitive feasting (Harding 1970).

When trade thins out or when individual societies are cut off, there is a corresponding intensification of the feasting side of the local system in order to build or maintain status. This leads to the characteristically pure big-man model without trade, where status is a function of the intensification of production leading to "fighting with food" (Young 1972) and "struggle for land" (Brook-field and Brown 1963). The big-man society without trade is similar in many ways to the society with "too much" trade insofar as there are similar conditions of competition and control.

On the basis of the new reconstruction of Austronesian (including Malayo–Polynesian) asymmetrical marriage and dualism, it is possible, I think, to suggest that a general model of prestige-good systems can render the historical distribution of Melanesian social types comprehensible within a larger model for the transformation of Oceanic social systems.

Prestige-good systems can be characterized in their most elementary form in terms of the following elements: (*a*) generalized exchange; (*b*) monopoly over prestige-good imports that are necessary for marriage and other crucial payments, i.e., for the social reproduction of local kin groups; (*c*) bilineal tendency in the kinship structure (asymmetrical); and (*d*) tendency to asymmetrical political dualism: religious–political chiefs, original people–newcomers, etc.

The preceding elements are organically linked in a process of expansive hierarchization. The control of prestige goods implies an exchange situation in which wives move toward monopolistic centers, and valuables and men move in the opposite direction. This model implies a tendency to the formation of localized matrilines and dispersed ranked patrilines whether or not they are cognized as such (Ekholm 1977). The general dualistic structure of such systems is the result of women moving up and/or men moving down, creating a local asymmetrical dualism: low = female/high = male (see Figure 12.4). In the usual case where men move down (politically speaking), the local group represents ritual power, and control of fertility, while the incoming group represents political power. If we assume that religious status, defined as descent from local ancestors, is logically primary, then the control of prestige goods may be said to emerge in opposition to the former ritual control.

Evidence of prestige-good systems is found throughout western Polynesia, Micronesia, southern Melanesia, and parts of northern Melanesia. In the latter area, characterized by a high degree of political fragmentation and competition, the Trobriands represent a tendency, however temporary, toward the kind of structure outlined above. Here the existence of matrilineal clans is combined with dualistic tendencies: the division of society into four totemic clans, the reciprocal alliance between the two highest-ranked subclans (patrilateral cross-cousin marriage), combined with an apparently asymmetrical form of generalized exchange between the paramount lineage and its vassals. Malinowski notes the apparent opposition between "the patriarchal and matriarchal principle" (1966, II, 360), i.e., between the passage of power from father to son as opposed to mother's brother to sister's son, which is the usual form. He (1966, II, 364) points out the tendency for higher-ranking men to marry into lower-ranking subclans: "Operating through the wife and allowing sons of high rank to settle in an inferior village . . . the doctrine of rank brings about the permanent shifting of authority and sovereignty to new territories."

Subclans of low rank tend to remain localized, while high-ranked subclans are dispersed and are associated with immigration from a distant source (Malinowski 1966, II, 365): "The correlation between high rank and mobility, on the one hand, and, on the other, low rank and territorial permanence, is clear."

By combining the two preceding quotations, we can deduce a pattern of localized matrilines and high ranking in marrying dispersed patrilines that are the result of the movement of sons to new lower-ranking areas. This may, of course, be represented by the unity of a local and an in-marrying matrilineage.

| Local lineage | In–marrying lineage |
|---|---|
| MBW | MB |
| MBD | EGO |
| D | ZS |

Thus, whether or not a patriline is recognized, and this is not of course necessary at the local level, the ranking of matrilineal local groups can be traced through the relationship between F, S, and SS.

There is, finally, an indication of a partially defined dual power structure expressive of the same pattern. The chiefly Tabalu subclan is dispersed over a large part of Kiriwina district. In-marrying, high-ranking clans are ceded land by the local "original inhabitants." According to Malinowski: "In Vakuta, the

Tabalu own most of the garden fields, but garden magic is still in the hands of the original sub-clan" (1966, II, 368).

There is, thus, a tendency for power to be divided between high-ranking political and local clan leaders who control rituals of gardening (Uberoi 1962, 40)—a dualism of political versus religious functions common to prestige good systems.

There is evidence of hierarchically organized prestige-good systems in both the Trobriands and the Admiralties in northern Melanesia. Southern Melanesia, especially New Caledonia, is characterized by chiefdoms well into the modern period. It is known that the area was linked to the Tongan "empire" and the early sandalwood trade (Guiart 1963, Ralston 1978). Here, we again find evidence of diarchy—political chiefs versus earth priests ("*maître du sol*" versus "chef"):

> "Kavu—le maître de la terre. Celui qui détient les droits du premier occupant, sacrifie à l'ancêtre (Léenhardt 1935, 140).

> Ainsi la différence entre le maître et le chef apparaît en quelque sort une différence de forme. Le chef est là pour parler, pour agir à la vue de tous; mais il ne peut rien sans l'appui discret des vieux dignitaires qui lui donneront le signal d'aller de l'avant. Le chef . . . est là pour manifester l'honneur et le prestige du clan. Mais les anciens du pays . . . gardent la réalité d'une puissance qu'il est difficile de ne pas qualifier de politique, quoique les justifications en soient apparues de prime abord d'ordre religieux (Guiart 1963, 41).

As is usual with prestige-good systems (Ekholm 1972, 151–165), this dualism is interpreted as a relation between an original population and invaders. Guiart (1963, 37) speaks of "*une complementarité des fonctions, non pas entre le chef et le maître de la terre, qu'entre les chefferies anciennes qui ont su conserver pour elles l'autorité du à leur presence première.*"

Southern Melanesia, contrasting as it does with the typical New Guinea big-man organization, provides an empirical basis for the argument that the simple dichotomy *Melanesia–Polynesia* is incorrect and that the same kinds of tendencies may crosscut the supposed cultural and/or evolutionary boundaries. This should be evident in the following discussion of West Polynesia.

West Polynesia represents a classic example of the full-blown prestige-goods systems (Hjarnø 1979–1980). Even Goldman, who is not terribly concerned with such problems, notes the contrast with East Polynesia on this point. Where exchange in East Polynesia is characterized by competitive reciprocal feasting and taxation in kind, in West Polynesia valuables move against food. The Samoan chief, by giving *toga* (fine mats), can obtain "foodstuffs for feasting from the lower orders of rank" (Goldman 1970, 507) that he in turn uses to obtain more *toga* by feasting external allies. The pattern is essentially the same as that in the Trobriands.

Tongan oral history explains that at one time there was only a single high chief, the *Tui Tonga*, who was a sacred ruler. In a period of political crisis he delegated political power to his son while retaining religious power. While the Tongan system developed three or four titles,[4] there is a pervasive political–religious dualism throughout Tonga. Interestingly enough, genealogical traditions place this development at the same period as Tongan expansion to surrounding islands and Samoa, i.e., the formation of the Tongan "empire." This expansion has been described in terms of the extension of the leading chiefly lineages by the establishment of junior branches in the dominated areas. The partilineage—*haa*—appears to have a local basis, for Guiart (1963, 669) says that "*quoique non strictement localisé puisque disperse le plus souvent sur plusieurs îles.*"

This image of a ranked partilineage extending from a center of power in Tonga Tapu, the capital, is, again, typical of prestige-good systems.

Tongan society features an emphasis on matrilateral cross-cousin marriage. Wife-takers rank higher than wife-givers, and the male line ranks higher than the female line. This is all strikingly similar to Samoa and Fiji. By listing the main features of this pattern we can discover the kinship structure that generates them:

$$
\begin{array}{lll}
\text{Wife-taker} & > & \text{Wife-giver} \\
\text{Male side} & > & \text{Female side} \\
\text{B} & < & \text{Z} & > = \text{ranks higher than} \\
\text{Bch} & < & \text{Zch} & < = \text{ranks lower than}
\end{array}
$$

This pattern is predictable from a bilineal structure of generalized exchange where women marry up and/or men marry down. There is evidence that men of the highest lineages went to rule parts of islands so that the pattern, at least among the aristocracy, might have been like that described for the Kongo kingdom (Ekholm 1977, see Figure 12.4). Besides generating the structure of Tongan kinship  and political dualism, this model accounts for the Tongan origin myth that describes how chiefs come from outside and marry indigenous women. This analysis should also shed some light on the recent reinterpretation of Tongan kinship as bilineal instead of patrilineal (Goldman 1970, Kaeppler 1971, Rogers 1977).

The paramount chiefs of Tonga, Samoa, and Fiji were linked by a marriage circle. Tonga was wife-giver to Fiji and wife-taker from Samoa. The former really amounts to husband-taking. The logic of external relations fits the internal structure. As sister ranks higher than brother, the paramount chief's sister is unmarriageable inside the society. In Samoa, such women remained sacred virgins unless external connections could be found. High-ranking Samoan women could be sent to Tonga. In Tonga, the taking of Fijian chiefly men

[4]The fourth title, *Tamaha,* is not really a lineage, but the ZD of the *Tui Tonga,* highest in rank in the kingdom and unable to marry in theory since her children have the status of bastards. The actual marriage of the *Tamaha* to a Fijian lineage creates a real fourth line, but one whose status is clearly ambiguous in Tonga.

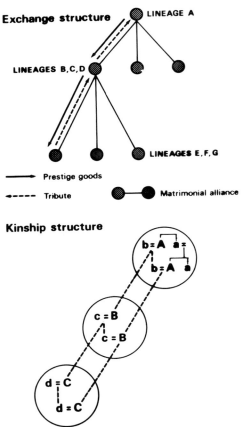

**Figure 12.4.** Generalized model of a prestige goods system. (From Ekholm 1977.)

created a new lineage, *Fale Fisi,* which while theoretically of higher rank than the *Tui Tonga,* was no threat as a foreign lineage.

The evidence for the prestige-good systemic nature of West Polynesia is rather clear. For example, Samoan fine mats are necessary elements in Tongan funerals and as gifts (Kaeppler 1978, 250) Large numbers of Samoan mats, *kie hingoa,* are given at marriages. Imported Tongan red feathers are essential in Samoan marriages and other exchanges, and it has been argued that the control over Tongan trade contacts was essential in the short-lived political centralization of Samoa (Hjarnø 1979–1980).

Sahlins (1976), following Hocart (1952), has found in eastern Fiji the kind of dualism that we have discussed. In his reanalysis of Moala social organization he finds the following kinds of asymmetric dualism:

Male > Female
Sea people > Land people
Outside > Inside
Chiefs > Commoners
Elder > Younger

At the same time, Moalans practice bilateral second cross-cousin marriage, which would seem to contradict our model of generalized exchange. Sahlins shows, however, that this apparently restricted exchange contains a seed of asymmetry, since at any one time, MB < ego < FZ. He (1976, 42) goes on to consider the Tongan structure and concludes, falsely, I think, that Fijian dualism "contains the embryo of another cultural order," i.e., the hierarchic system of Tonga. I would argue that it is more likely that Fijian asymmetrical dualism is the product of integration of this area into the Tongan system and that the breakdown of that system led local Fijian societies to close in on themselves. As local exogamy became impossible, it was converted into local endogamy, but with the same categories as before (see Figure 12.5).

Without embarking on a further discussion, it can simply be suggested that Micronesia, especially the western and central areas, shows clear resemblances to western Polynesia, from large-scale regional exchange systems (the Yap "empire") to asymmetrical dualism in both kinship and politics.

West Polynesia consists of a relatively limited number of variations of the prestige-good system. Many variants are the result of decline, such as Ontong Java, Tikopia, Futuna, Pukapuka, and Niue. The same kinds of transformations may have occurred here as those described for eastern Fiji and the Lau Islands. We are not in a position to analyze all the variation in this chapter, but it can be noted that a great many of the features of the prestige-good system are preserved in transformation. The situation is completely different in eastern Polynesia.

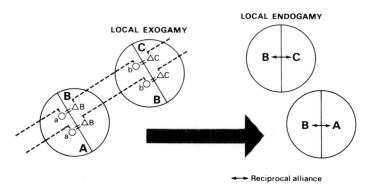

**Figure 12.5.** Breakdown of the Fijian social system.

In eastern Polynesia, it is possible to argue that the prestige-good system of the western area broke down very early. The earliest-known settlement to date, the Marquesas, represents a minimal link to western Polynesia. It maintains cross-cousin marriage to some extent. In the earliest archaeological period we find pottery reminiscent of western styles, something that is otherwise entirely absent from eastern Polynesia. Handy (1923), in his reconstruction of the social structure of the island of Ua Pou, which was politically more developed in the past, describes a situation reminiscent of western Polynesian dualism in decline. There are male and female chiefs, and the land is divided into chiefly and commoner sides. It also appears that the male and female chiefly lines were linked in some kind of asymmetrical dual-marriage structure. This kind of dualism is very rare in the east. There are traces of it in Mangaia and Easter Island.

While western Polynesia is characterized by exogamy and external exchange, eastern Polynesia is typified by endogamy and warfare. Dualism tends to disappear, especially in the more developed societies such as the Society and Hawaiian Islands. The bilineal character of kinship and ranking disappears as well, and seniority becomes the dominant principle. While the sacredness of chiefs is well developed in the stratified societies of western Polynesia, this is taken to extremes in Tahiti and especially Hawaii. Chiefs are both religious and political. There is no political dualism. There is apparently an enormous intensification of agricultural production wherever possible, and it would appear that the lack of external monopoly leads to increasing competition within the aristocracy and an accompanying intensification of production, which unlike West Polynesia becomes a crucial factor in the accumulation of power and status.

The argument for the transformation of western into eastern Polynesian structures runs as follows: The breakdown in the prestige-good system may be related generally to the quantum increase in distance between island groups. The loss of monopolistic control must have led to increased competition—the escalation of competitive feasting and warfare. This in itself would have led to a rapid intensification of agricultural production by means of irrigation. In such a situation it is also likely that the alliance system would break down. In the absence of monopolies, marriage strategies, in the effort to maintain status, will tend toward endogamy combined with selective alliances with distant lines of at least equal rank (Valeri 1972). Genealogically based hierarchies could easily be overturned by warfare and conquest. Unification tended to lead to a redistribution of titles and land by and for the new central lineage, but political centralization was normally short-lived. This is in sharp contrast to Tonga where the exchange hierarchy tended to stabilize political relations. The emergence of cognatic kinship in eastern Polynesia is largely the product of the randomization of the former bilineal structure. While there are still, in Hawaii, examples where "priestly" lineages are the wife-takers of chiefs as in western Polynesia, this is in no way a systematic phenomenon. The same changes in the conditions of social reproduction lead to an amplification of chiefly sacredness, a multiplication of taboos and severe punishments for "wrong doers." When the prestige-good system breaks down, the entire power structure becomes dependent upon its religious or theocratic aspect, i.e., the material force of supernatural dictates.

It seems that where agricultural intensification fails in eastern Polynesia, there ensues a long devolutionary trend. This is most clearly evident in the Marquesas and Easter Island where hierarchy had declined significantly, where famine was common, and where warfare was endemic and without political issue. There is some indication that even Hawaii may have reached a peak of intensification sometime before the arrival of the Europeans and that it was suffering from declining productivity (Kirch personal communication). Societies that Goldman characterizes as "open" in eastern Polynesia— Mangaia, Easter Island, and the Marquesas—were all plagued by intense warfare and unstable political hierarchy. While Goldman suggests that open societies are generally on the way to stratification, it is, perhaps, more likely that these societies represent devolution. They are all characterized by relatively high population density and relatively poor ecological conditions, often themselves the result of overintensification.

It can, thus, be argued that the general condition of eastern Polynesia is political fragmentation, competitive in-kind exchange systems, and warfare with a cycle of conquest, political centralization, and new fragmentation. It is clear that none of the wide areal integration of western Polynesia occurs here, while on the inside of any chiefdom there may be a harsher form of social control than occurs in the west. No stable centralized polities emerge in East Polynesia comparable to Tongan dominance. In fact, it is not until the advent of the European arms trade and direct intervention that real state structures emerge in Hawaii and Tahiti.

## SUMMARY

I have attempted in this chapter to hint at some of the transformational processes that might account for the different kinds of social structures that are found in Oceania. The following diagram (Figure 12.6) is a hypothetical model of broad transformational processes that might account for the general characteristics of the main classes of Oceanic societies.

The development of Oceanian societies can thus be represented as a series of "bifurcations," thresholds at which rapid transformations of the systems occur. The major tendencies or "attractors" in the social systems are localized to three separate sets of reproductive conditions in which the major factor is relative trade density (see Figure 12.7).

By considering systems of social reproduction, we can, I think, offer different kinds of solutions to the variation of social forms in history. The model I have

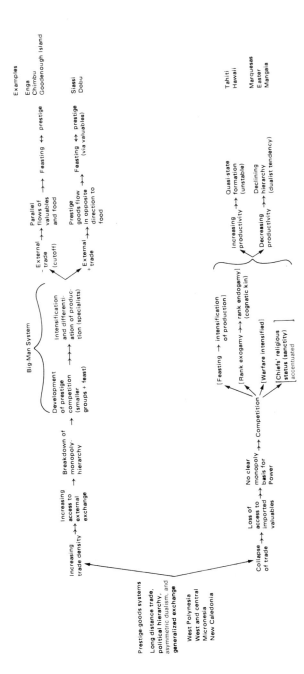

**Figure 12.6.** Multilinear trajectories of prestige goods systems.

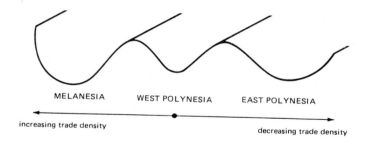

Figure 12.7. Three attractors in Oceanic history.

discussed here represents an attempt to account for the historical differentiation of social structures in Oceania, the differences in local cycles of reproduction, and the differences in the kinds of rank and stratification. The usual evolutionary model cannot account for the devolution of Melanesian societies from more hierarchical to more egalitarian political structures at the same time as the economy becomes more intensive and elaborate. It might, in fact, be argued that Melanesia is more developed than Polynesia in terms of economic elaboration and specialization. Rathje has made a similar argument for the Mesoamerican development from Classic to Postclassic Maya (1975), and Ekholm and myself have suggested a similar political fragmentation as part of the process of commerical civilization in Mesopotamia (Ekholm and Friedman 1979). The decline in political centralization is the general threshold effect of an increase in trade density. At the other end of the scale, the evolutionary model cannot help us understand that western and eastern Polynesian developments are the results of two very different kinds of processes and not part of a single continuum.

## CONCLUSION

I have tried to suggest a view of social evolution that breaks with the traditional anthropological interpretation of biological evolution. This is a view that is, I think, gaining increasing support from recent developments in the natural sciences. Once we break with functionalism and the model of continuous moving equilibrium, we are able to confront the specifics of the essentially blind history of our species. The opacity of social goals with respect to their conditions of existence lays the foundation for the literally catastrophic development that we call social evolution, for lack of a more accurate, if perhaps more incriminating, term. The acceptance of this critical property of human social systems is, perhaps, a necessary starting point for the understanding of the process of evolution.

# REFERENCES

Allen, J., 1977, Sea traffic, trade and expanding horizons, in Allen, Golson, and Jones (eds.), *Sunda and Sahul*, London, Academic Press.

Ambrose, W., 1976, Obsidian and its prehistoric distribution in Melanesia, in Barnard, N. (ed.), *Chinese Bronzes and Southeast Asian Metal and Other Archaeological Artifacts*, Melbourne, National Museum of Victoria.

Ambrose, W., 1978, The loneliness of the long distance trader in Melanesia, in Specht, J., and White, J. P. (eds.), *Trade and Exchange in Oceania and Australia, Mankind* 11,3.

Ardener, E., 1978, Some outstanding problems in the analysis of events, in Schwimmer, E. (ed.), *Yearbook of Symbolic Anthropology*, I, 103–122.

Augé, M., 1977, *Pouvoirs de vie, pouvoirs de mort*, Paris.

Augé, M., 1978, Vers un refus de l'alternative sens-fonction, *L'Homme* 18, 3–4.

Bateson, G., 1972, *Steps to an Ecology of Mind*, New York, Chandler.

Bennet, J. P., 1978, Imperialism on a swallowtail: applications of catastrophe theory to international relations, *Quality and Quantity*, 12 (1)

Blust, R., 1980a, Early Austronesian social organization: the evidence of language, *Current Anthropology* 21, 2.

Blust, R., 1980b, Notes on Proto-Malayo-Polynesian phratry dualism, *Bijdragen tot de Land-, Taal-, en Volkenkunde* 116.

Brookfield, H. C. and Brown, P., 1963, *Struggle for Land*, Melbourne, Oxford University Press.

Brunton, R., 1975, Why do the Trobriands have chiefs?, *Man* 10, 544–588.

Coquery-Vidrovitch, C., 1969, Recherches sur un mode de production africain, *La Pensée*, 144.

Crocker, C., 1969, Reciprocity and hierarchy among the Eastern Bororo, *Man* 4, 44–58.

Ekholm, K., 1972, *Power and Prestige: The Rise and Fall of the Kongo Kingdom*, Uppsala.

Ekholm, K., 1977, External exchange and the transformation of Central African social systems, in Friedman, J., and Rowlands, M. J., (eds.), *The Evolution of Social Systems*, London, Duckworth.

Ekholm, K., 1980, On the limitations of civilization: the structure and dynamics of global systems, *Dialectical Anthropology*, 5, 155–166.

Ekholm, K., and Friedman, J., 1979, Capital, imperialism and exploitation in ancient world systems in Larsen, M. T. (ed.), *Power and Propaganda: A Symposium on Ancient Empires*, Copenhagen, Akademsk Verlag.

Ekholm, K., and Friedman, J., 1980, Towards a global anthropology, in Blusse, Wesseling and Winius (eds.), *History and Underdevelopment*, Leiden, Centre for the History of European Expansion.

Flannery, K., 1972, The cultural evolution of civilizations, *Annual Review of Ecology and Systematics*, 3, 399–426.

Friedman, J., 1974, The place of fetishism and the problem of materialist interpretations, *Critique of Anthropology*, 1, 26–62.

Friedman, J., 1975, Tribes, states, and transformations, in Bloch, M. (ed.) *Marxist Analyses and Social Anthropology*, London, Malaby.

Friedman, J., 1979, *System, Structure and Contradiction in the Evolution of 'Asiatic' Social Formations*, Copenhagen, National Museum of Copenhagen.

Garanger, J., 1972, *Archéologie des Nouvelles Hebrides* (Société des Oceanistes, 30), Paris.

Godelier, M., 1978, La part idéelle du réel, *L'Homme*, 18.

Goldman, I., 1955, Status rivalry and cultural evolution in Polynesia, *American Anthropologist*, 57, 680–697.

Goldman, I., 1970, *Ancient Polynesian Society*, Chicago, University of Chicago Press.

Guiart, J., 1963, *Structure de la chefferie en Melanésie du Sud*, Paris, Travaux et memoires de l'institut d'ethnologie 46.

Handy, E.S.C., 1923, *The Native Cultures in the Marquesas* (Bernice Bishop Museum, 9), Honolulu.

Harding, T. G., 1970, Trading in Northeast New Guinea, in Harding, T. G. and Wallace, B. J., *Cultures of the Pacific,* New York, Random House.

Harris, M., 1977, *Cannibals and Kings: The Origins of Cultures,* New York, Random House.

Harris, M., 1979, *Cultural Materialism. The Struggle for a Science of Culture,* New York, Random House.

Hawkins, S., 1977, The quantum mechanics of black holes, *Scientific American* 236, 1, 34–49.

Hjarno, J., 1979/80, Social reproduction: towards an understanding of aboriginal Samoa, *Folk,* 21–22, 72–123.

Ho, M. W. and Saunders, P. T., 1979, Beyond neo-Darwinism—An epigenetic approach to evolution, *Journal of Theoretical Biology,* 78, 4, 573–592.

Hocart, A. M., 1952, *The Northern States of Fiji,* London, Royal Anthropological Institute, 11.

Kaeppler, A. L., 1971, Rank in Tonga, *Ethnology* 10, 174–193.

Kaeppler, A. L., 1978, Exchange patterns in goods and spouses: Fiji, Tonga and Samoa, in Specht, J. and White, P. (eds.), *Trade and Exchange in Oceania and Australia (Mankind,* 11, 3).

Kamakau, S., 1961, *Ruling Chiefs of Hawaii,* Honolulu, Bernice Bishop Museum.

Kamakau, S., 1964, *The People of Old,* Honolulu, Bernice Bishop Museum.

Kimura, M., 1979, The neutral theory of genetic evolution, *Scientific American* 241.

Kirch, P. V., 1980, Polynesian prehistory: cultural adaptation in island ecosystems, *American Scientist* 68.1, 39–48.

Leach, E. R., 1954, *Political Systems of Highland Burma,* London, Athlone Press.

Léenhardt, M., 1935, *Vocabulaire et grammaire de la langue Houailou* (Travau et Memoires de l'Institut d'Ethnologie, 9) Paris.

Levi-Strauss, C., 1958, *Anthropologie Structurale I,* Paris, Plon.

Levi-Strauss, C., 1973, *Anthropologie, Structurale II,* Paris, Plon.

Lewen, R., 1980, Evolutionary theory under fire, *Science,* 210.

Malinowski, B., 1966, *Coral Gardens and Their Magic. Vol. I: Soil Tilling and Agricultural Rites in the Trobriand Islands,* London, Allen and Unwin.

Mees, A., 1975, The revival of cities in Medieval Europe, *Regional Sciences and Urban Economics,* 5.

Persson, J., in press, Cyclical change and circular exchange: a re-examination of the kula ring, *Oceania*

Price, B., 1977, Shifts in production and organization: a cluster-interaction model, *Current Anthropology,* 18, 209–233.

Prigogine, I., Nicolis, G. and Babloyantz, A., 1972, Thermodynamics of evolution, 2 parts, *Physics Today* 25, 11, 12.

Prigogine, I., Allen, P. and Herman, R., n.d., The evolution of complexity and the laws of nature, ms.

Ralston, C., 1978, *Grass Huts and Warehouses: Pacific Beach Communities in the Nineteenth Century,* Honolulu, Bernice Bishop Museum.

Rappaport, R., 1971, The sacred in evolution, *Annual Review of Ecology and Systematics,* 2.

Rappaport, R., 1977, Maladaptation in social systems, in Friedman, J. and Rowlands, M. J. (eds.) *The Evolution of Social Systems,* London, Duckworth.

Rappaport, R., 1979, *Ecology, Meaning and Religion,* Richmond (California)

Rathje, W. L., 1975, Last tango in Mayapan, in Sabloff, J. and Lamberg-Karlovsky, C. (eds.) *Ancient Civilization and Trade,* Albuquerque, University of Mexico Press.

Renfrew, C., 1978, Trajectory discontinuity and morphogenesis: the implications of catastrophe theory for archaeology, *American Antiquity* 43, 2, 203–222.

Rogers, G., 1977, The father's sister is black: a consideration of female rank and powers in Tonga, *Journal of the Polynesian Society* 86, 2.

Sahlins, M., 1958, *Social Stratification in Polynesia,* Seattle, University of Washington Press.

Sahlins, M., 1963, Poor man, rich man, big-man, chief: political types in Melanesia and Polynesia, *Comparative Studies in Society and History* 5, 285–303.

Sahlins, M., 1976, *Culture and Practical Reason,* Chicago, University of Chicago Press.

Schwartz, T., 1963, Systems of areal integration: some considerations based on the Admirality Islands, *Anthropological Forum,* 1.

Thom, R., 1975, *Structural Stability and Morphogenesis,* Reading, Massachusetts, W. A. Benjamin.

Uberoi, J. P. S., 1962, *Politics of the Kula Ring,* Manchester, Manchester University Press.

Valeri, V., 1972, Le système de rangs à Hawaii, *L'Homme* 12, 1, 29–66.

van Parijs, P., 1978, Théorie des catastrophes et matérialisme historique, *Revue française de sociologie,* 19.

Vicedom, G. and Tischner, H., 1943–48, *Die Mbowamb,* Hamburg.

von Braunmühl, C., 1976, The bourgeois nation state within the world market, in Picotto, S. (ed.), *State and Capital,* London.

Waddington, C. H., 1974, A catastrophe theory of evolution, *Annals of the New York Academy of Sciences,* 231.

Wheeler, J. A., 1974, The universe as a home for man, *American Scientist* 62, 6, 683–691.

Young, M. W., 1971, *Fighting with Food: Leadership, Values and Social Control in a Massim Society,* Cambridge, Cambridge University Press.

Zeeman, E. C., 1974, On the unstable behavior of stock exchanges, *Journal of Mathematical Economics* 1, 39–49.

Zeeman, E. C., 1976, Catastrophe theory, *Scientific American* 234, 4, 65–83.

# 13

## The Polanyi Paradigm and a Dynamic Analysis of Archaic States

*JOHN GLEDHILL AND MOGENS LARSEN*

## INTRODUCTION

Karl Polanyi's scholarly work has its background in a passionate concern with the crisis that he found engulfing his own world. His books and articles were meant to contribute "to world affairs in a period of perilous transformation" (Polanyi 1977, xliii). His aim was not to present a clear program for political or economic action, but was instead to create a new analytical framework that went beyond the tradition of classical economy, breaking out of what he termed "our obsolete market mentality." A general theory of the place of economy in society, based on the recognition that the market economy and market society of our own age is a historically transitory phenomenon, constituted for Polanyi a necessary condition for enlarging "our freedom of creative adjustment, and thereby improving our chances of survival" (Polanyi 1977, xliii).

Traditional economic theory had little use for ancient civilizations or primitive cultures, which were seen as irrelevant for a proper understanding of the problems of our own age. Polanyi's position was the opposite one—that history and social anthropology had shown that man as a social being was basically changeless and that "the necessary preconditions of the survival of human society appear to be immutably the same" (Polanyi 1944, 46). All societies prior to the rise of Western capitalism show the economy as

**197**

THEORY AND EXPLANATION
IN ARCHAEOLOGY

"submerged" or "embedded" in the social relationships, and a theoretical framework must accordingly set out the various ways in which the economy can become instituted at different times and places. Such a theory will be necessary for a realistic evaluation not only of the past but of the options available to modern societies in crisis.

Polanyi's analysis was based on the premise that there are three fundamental forms of socioeconomic integration: reciprocity, redistribution, and exchange. His understanding of the first two forms was based to a large extent on his reading of Malinowski and Thurnwald, and his systematization of anthropological observations led to the creation of descriptive categories that have come to play a highly influential role in subsequent economic anthropological writings. Exchange as an integrative mode is a unique feature of the market economy, an "utterly new type of economy," which developed in Europe in the nineteenth century. In a slightly ambiguous way, this scheme, which is expressly said not to represent an evolutionary historical interpretation, is linked to a developmental set of sociopolitical categories: *tribal, primitive, archaic,* and *modern* societies.

Our concern in the present chapter will be an evaluation of the *archaic* paradigm with special reference to ancient societies in Mesopotamia and Mesoamerica. It is clear that limitations of space must prevent us from a general discussion and evaluation of Polanyi's theories, but it should be pointed out that even a limited investigation is ultimately of more fundamental significance than simply proving Polanyi right or wrong in a special case. Advancing alternative accounts of the empirical data of necessity leads to problems of theory and conceptualization, and our observations consequently must both underpin and be selected for by an alternative analytical framework. At the same time it is essential to avoid the pitfalls of the primitive dichotomy established by the "formalist–substantivist" debate and to retain the basic realization—shared by substantivism and Marxian theory—that there is no autonomous category *economy* as a separate sphere of social life in precapitalist societies; we must insist on the historical relativity of economic categories and in fact the category *economic* itself.

Polanyi's "archaic" institutions are linked with the emergence of what he calls "state societies" out of the tribal, kinship organized societies. A set of economic institutions make their appearance in the early states, and the essential difference between tribal and archaic conditions is the development of transactions that refer to and concern wealth and the disposal of land, rather than to the status of the individual participants. Polanyi was particularly concerned with the difference between the Greek states and Mesopotamia, where transactional and dispositional methods were introduced into the redistributive economy of the palace and temple.

The archaic equivalents of trade, market, and money are to be found within Polanyi's framework of "administered treaty trade," ports of trade, and equivalencies. His specific analyses of the Mesopotamian institutions, hailed by

Wheatley (1971, 282) as "a classic example" of treaty trade, will be critically examined in a following section. This critique, in conjunction with the alternative interpretations suggested for the Mesoamerican trade patterns points to fundamental weaknesses in Polanyi's and his collaborators' empirical analyses. In this introduction we shall indicate briefly some basic theoretical flaws that only partly spring from the specific interpretations of historical situations.

One such weakness is the static and descriptive nature of the basic conceptual framework that therefore does not lend itself easily to a discussion of dynamics. A fundamental difficulty arises from the account Polanyi gives of the relationship between the different "forms of integration" and their supporting societal structures. He noted himself that the forms of integration can be conceptualized in terms of diagrammatic representations of the locational and/or appropriational movements of goods and services, but that such a representation would serve only a formal purpose. An explanation of movements and their integrative effects cannot be given without specifying definite structures in society that may be seen as "symmetrical" with such material flows. So an explanation of the "mix" or changes in the mix of different integrational forms that characterize a given economy must accordingly entail a theory of change in the "embedding" institutions of the whole social system.

On occasion Polanyi does provide illuminating ad hoc explanations for particular institutional developments, such as the rise of the Athenian retail food market, which is seen as the product of a political strategy pursued by the "democratic" faction of the oligarchy (Polanyi 1977, 164–166). However, his conceptual starting point predisposes him to a static, institutional, and functional analysis, and since his analyses are essentially descriptive, the problem of the explanation of the "embedding institutions" is not broached directly. Therefore, unanalyzed concepts such as "moral order" or "custom" are introduced into the analysis as ultimate explanations. Polanyi's scheme has thereby become open to general critiques of anthropological functionalism (e.g., Schneider 1974). Moreover, his inability to offer an adequate theory concerning the dominance of an integrational form in a given social system has ironically led to the adaptation of his work in the hands of the neoevolutionist writers to the service of an economism that he would clearly have found repugnant. The growing "needs" of an autonomous material-provisioning system teleologically determine changes in the supporting structures.

A common critique leveled against Polanyi is that substantivism focuses on categories of exchange rather than production. It is important, however, to note two points here. First, for Polanyi, the dominance of market exchange as a form of integration is premised on the transformation of land and labor into commodities. That Polanyi saw this principle as "the rational kernel" of the Marxist classification of economic systems in terms of the "status of labor," while insisting that the "integration of land into the economy" is "hardly less vital" (Polanyi 1977, 43), is significant. It shows Polanyi's limited grasp of

Marx's arguments and concepts, as well as his own empiricism. The same empiricism, however, characterizes the simple "start-from-production" rubric that motivates many criticisms of Polanyi advanced from a supposedly Marxist viewpoint, as a perusal of the Introduction to the *Grundrisse* might indicate (Marx 1973).

Polanyi did attempt to model economic systems of different types as totalities. But his concept of "totality" merely amounted to aggregation. Marx insisted that the nature of the elements of a totality could not be determined in isolation in a dialectical sense, as his discussion of the genesis of capitalist ground rent demonstrates particularly clearly (Marx 1959, see also Gledhill 1981a). For Marx, the functional role of a system element is determined by the effects of the dominant production relations of the whole system, but in a quite different sense to that version of a "holistic" perspective enshrined in organicist functionalism. Marx encourages us to try to go beyond the formal labels attached to superficially identical, isolated phenomena in otherwise fundamentally different totalities (Banaji 1977). Polanyi's discussions of, for example, the differences between the "capitalism" of Rome and modern industrial capitalism share a similar broad objective. But we must submit that their success is very limited, precisely because of these initial conceptual limitations. Our case will be elaborated in the discussion that follows.

## POLANYI'S IMPACT ON NEAR EASTERN STUDIES

If we were to judge the extent of Polanyi's influence on the study of the societies of the ancient Near East simply on the basis of the direct references to his writings found in the scholarly literature, we would have to describe it as negligible. The Assyriological conference held in 1976 had as its theme "Trade in the Ancient Near East," but in the published proceedings we find only one or two passing references to Polanyi (*Iraq* 39, 1977). Another conference held in 1978 had as its title "State and Temple Economy in the Ancient Near East," and in the published proceedings (Lipínski 1979), we can find only one reference to Polanyi.

In view of the fact that Polanyi himself took a great interest in the civilizations of the Near East and even wrote whole chapters that dealt explicitly with Mesopotamian matters, this apparent lack of interest on the part of the Assyriologists is somewhat surprising—and a little disconcerting. The fiercely antitheoretical bias of much of traditional Assyriology undoubtedly provides part of the answer, and Marxist scholars have clearly not found Polanyi's theoretical framework worth more than a passing blow (see for instance Liverani 1978, 191). However, other scholars have also exhibited some unease with Polanyi's conceptual framework. Even Oppenheim, who was clearly deeply influenced by Polanyi and who contributed a chapter to *Trade and*

*Market,* was engaged in a subtle modification of Polanyi's theories, reacting against the exaggerations and overhasty generalizations (cf. Humphreys 1978, 43).

Where Polanyi described Mesopotamia as a paradigmatic case of a society dominated by a redistributive mode of integration, centering of course on temple and palace, Oppenheim instead spoke of a social structure with *two* components: on the one hand the city, defined as "the community of persons of equal status bound together by a consciousness of belonging, realised by directing their communal affairs by means of an assembly"; and on the other hand the two redistributive "great organizations," which derived their income from agricultural holdings and redistributed it by way of a system of rations (Oppenheim 1964, 95). Oppenheim (1964, 89) made it clear that in his view Mesopotamia shows us a "coexistence of divergent systems of integration, storage versus private economy," but he also stressed that economic integration was effectuated "to a large extent in terms of a storage economy." Although he appears deliberately to avoid the phrase *dominant mode of integration,* his position is in fact rather close to Polanyi's. He too maintained that different forms of integration "occur side by side on different levels and in different sectors of the economy . . . it may often be impossible to select one of them as dominant so that they could be employed for a classification of empirical economies as a whole" (Polanyi *et al.* 1957, Chapter 13, 1968, 149). There is a real danger, however, that these descriptive categories serve simply to isolate the various elements without providing any framework for an analysis of how they relate to each other. And furthermore, Polanyi's position is somewhat ambiguous in view of the fact that the societies that were in fact discussed in detail in *Trade and Market* "were presented as dominated by one type of economic organization" (Humphreys 1978, 67).

Oppenheim's (1964, 89) insistence on a kind of regional specialization in the near East introduces another modification of Polanyi's scheme, even though it can be seen as a development of the concept *port of trade.* In a somewhat obscure passage, Oppenheim (1964, 89) suggested that the storage system of the southern Mesopotamian alluvium "originally lacked the means of contacting the world around it," leaving it to the groups "outside the magic circle of the storage system" to provide the alluvium with essential raw materials and to be paid for their services. This refers to the pattern noticed by Oppenheim of a corona of transit centers around the southern Mesopotamian plain, which functioned as markets and terminals for long-distance trade (cf. Larsen 1979, 99, Leemans 1977, 5–6). Oppenheim directly described the city of Sippar in northern Babylonia on the periphery of the main urbanized region as "probably a port of trade between the sheep nomads of the desert and the inhabitants of the urbanized stretches along the Euphrates" (1964, 116). This regional variation is related to Oppenheim's views concerning the market. Whereas he always claimed that the market was of "limited and marginal importance" in the cities on the alluvial plain, he did accept the existence of markets in the peripheral societies (see Veenhof 1972, 352–353).

Oppenheim's comments point to three main areas of disagreement with Polanyi's general theoretical formulations:

1. –Oppenheim stresses that symbiotic nature of different patterns of integration rather than isolating one as dominant. Any theory that is based on such dominance runs the risk of obscuring the interplay of the various sectors in the socioeconomic structure and of failing to explain change except in terms of external stimulus.
2. –Oppenheim expresses a concern for systemic regional patterns, rather than a frame of reference where the society is the basic unit.
3. –We find already in Oppenheim's own chapter in *Trade and Market* a stress on the discontinuity in the long-term pattern of Mesopotamian history, as opposed to Polanyi's static paradigm.

Oppenheim referred to "shifts in emphasis which brings now one and now another form of economic integration to the foreground without the others disappearing at any time" (1957, 29). The extreme position that sees a continuity of the same socioeconomic patterns through historical sequences spanning three millennia is hard to defend, and it has in fact been a basic weakness in much of Polanyi's writing on the ancient Near East. It is exemplified in his treatment of the question of the market, where the postulated absence of any market mechanism in the Persian period is taken to indicate that it could not have existed previously either. And Polanyi's concentration on institutions, such as for instance the "status trader" (*tamkarum*), tends to lead to a transfer of elements in the socioeconomic, political, or cultural system from one millennium to another. It is true that the linguistic continuity and the extreme conservatism of certain areas of terminology make such a procedure more tempting. Also, we do not have any serious study of the complexities of the patterns of continuity and discontinuity, but we should nevertheless realize that the static, unchanging world of the ancient Near East is no longer a viable paradigm.

Oppenheim's reluctance to frame clear theoretical statements and his constant concern with the understanding of the ancient Near Eastern past within the traditional framework of philological practice explains the absence from his works of a clearly expressed evaluation of Polanyi's theories. It is indeed remarkable, that apart from a bibliographical reference to *Trade and Market,* Oppenheim's celebrated synthesis *Ancient Mesopotamia* (published only seven years later) does not contain a single mention of Polanyi. This must not lead us to forget, however, that Oppenheim's modified version of Polanyi's theories has been highly influential in the field of Assyriology, even though explicit references to the original books and articles are relatively rare.

## Markets, Merchants, and Accumulation

Even though Polanyi emphasized repeatedly that his basic conceptual scheme involving three modes of integration—reciprocity, redistribution, and exchange—must not be seen as representing an evolutionary pattern, there is a clear tendency in some of his writings to link these modes with specific stages of societal development. In the book *The Livelihood of Man* this comes out clearly in his discussion of the emergence of economic transactions. The transition from a tribal or clan "level" to what he termed "the archaic conditions so general at the outset of civilized society" (Polanyi 1977, 57) was marked in some societies at least by a beginning separation of status transactions and economic transactions. He devoted a great deal of attention to the emergence of market activities in the Greek cities, and it was of particular importance for him to contrast this development with the pattern that he found in Mesopotamia. Here, in spite of a redistributive economy, he saw the introduction of "transactional and dispositional methods of great economic significance," and he asked these questions: How did the differences between conditions in Greece and Mesopotamia arise and what determined them? (Polanyi 1977, 59).

The answer provided was relatively simple in the case of Mesopotamia: "Exchange, the most precarious of human ties, spread into the economy when it could be made to serve the validation of the community. In effect, economic transactions became possible when they could be made gainless." This is based on the contention that the Mesopotamian state was able to control exchange by way of the declaration of equivalencies for goods to be bought and sold, thereby removing the "peril to solidarity involved in making selfish gain at the expense of the food of one's brother" (Polanyi 1977, 61). From this programmatic statement springs Polanyi's detailed interpretation of such features as administered trade, equivalencies, special-purpose money, and ports of trade, and it constitutes his explanation for the alleged absence of the market in Mesopotamia.

It may be in order to point out very briefly that Polanyi's claim that markets never existed in Mesopotamia simply does not stand up to closer scrutiny. The absence of large open spaces in Mesopotamian cities must necessarily remain a postulate as long as no city has been uncovered in toto. In fact, the ancient city hiding under the ruins of Tell Taya, where the existence of stone foundations visible on the surface makes it possible to establish a nearly complete town plan, could very well have contained a quite substantial marketplace (cf. Reade, 1973). Furthermore, the market in an economic sense could exist without a large open space, and here one would immediately think of the city gates that often seem to have functioned somewhat like a Greek *agora*.

The further claim that the texts contained no references to marketplaces and that in fact no word for such an institution existed in Akkadian must also be rejected. At least three words can be given this meaning, and a recent investigation of this problem concluded that the ancient Near Eastern towns as a rule had marketplaces where goods for everyday consumption were traded and where money transactions were carried out (Röllig, 1976). On the other hand, it is clear from the quite few textual references that this market trade in foodstuffs was of no great concern for at least the ordinary textual corpus, and this may indicate that Oppenheim was right in regarding the market in the towns of southern Mesopotamia as of "marginal and limited importance.

Humphreys (1978, 49) has pointed out that Polanyi's emphasis on a system of fixed prices or equivalencies as constituting the essential difference between primitive and modern markets cannot be maintained and has indeed been modified by Dalton and Bohannan (1962). The claim made repeatedly by Polanyi that "the proclamation of equivalencies is one of the main functions of the archaic king" (1977, 74) was based on a number of references in law codes—(Hammurapi's Code, Eshnunna Laws, and the Hittite Laws)—and in Old Babylonian royal inscriptions, where we find lists of prices and rules concerning wages and rent. Such references have often been understood as royally promulgated tariffs, and there is no doubt that they represent attempts to exercise control over aspects of the economic life. However, as pointed out by Edzard (1976), actually attested prices are often not in agreement with these "tariffs," and it seems probable that such statements represent ideological descriptions of the flourishing economic life created by the excellence of the king's rulership.

Farber's study (1978) of the prices and wages of the Old Babylonian period shows a pattern of quite substantial fluctuations in prices of basic commodities, and these fluctuations over the long term can undoubtedly be related to developments in the economic pattern of the region as a whole. A very interesting interpretation of the social and economic consequences of a crisis in the economy of the city of Nippur in the middle of the eighteenth century B.C., based primarily on a study of the prices of land, houses, and temple offices, provides a relatively clear picture of a situation where a group of wealthy private landowners could manipulate conditions created by  some disaster to gain control of most of the land through purchase (Stone 1977). It is worth mentioning that the royal "tariffs" never refer to the well-documented short-term fluctuations in the prices of for example, grain (see Farber 1978). These are probably to be related to references to "current prices." These features cannot be studied in a meaningful way unless they are related to considerations about the economy as a whole, and in particular to the questions of production and accumulation.

The traditional interpretation of Mesopotamian history posits a development from a monolithic redistributive system, the "temple–city" (cf. Falkenstein 1954, Adams 1966), to an economy where individual ownership of land and other resources became a strong factor. With a few exceptions (e.g., Renger 1979), scholars now agree that some kind of private landownership always existed alongside temple and palace, even in the Sumerian city-states of the southern alluvium. The private sector appears to have changed character from a domination of what Gelb (1979, 68–71) calls "large ownership" of land and houses, to a system where we find individual owners rather than family or clan ownership. Gelb sees the major change in this pattern beginning in the Akkadian period and individual ownership dominating from the Ur III period onward.

This change is apparently accompanied by a real growth of the private sector, but most scholars tend to see this development as typical of the Old Babylonian period (cf. Klengel 1971, 51–52). It is also in this period that a large private sector in foreign trade can be described in some detail. Some publications have indicated that even this modified picture should be viewed with some caution. Foster (1977) has presented a detailed picture of commercial activity as early as the Akkadian period, and he suggests that private entrepreneurs participated in numerous business enterprises where they cannot be described as agents for the state. He contrasts the *tamkarum,* "a business agent who sought profits in cash or commodities for his clients" (among whom we find the palace or temple as well as private individuals), with another kind of trader known as *ga-raš* or *gaeš*, "a purchasing agent who acquired commodities the state needed."

For the following Ur III period Powell has presented a similar picture, based on an observation which is vitally important to his argument, that "the merchant operated *primarily* on the basis of profit and loss and that the state or temple *never* undertook systematically to underwrite his losses" (1979, 24). Without mentioning Polanyi directly, he states that the evidence from the third millennium (going back even to the Early Dynastic period) bears "witness to a type of economic structure that corresponds more closely to a model of market economy than to a model which posits some kind of central redistributive agency such as the temple or state."

Although these statements will undoubtedly be regarded as extremist by many Assyriologists, Powell's strictures underline the need for a flexible theoretical framework that can accomodate both synchronic and diachronic diversity. Furthermore, we need to reexamine the commonly held view that fundamental changes took place between the Ur III period, described by Diakonoff as a time of an "exemplary police order" under "one of the worst totalitarian régimes known to history" (1971, 20), and the following Old Babylonian period with its much more chaotic political history. It is essential to keep in mind that the textual evidence that is available to us necessarily suffers from serious distortion: Not only is it terribly fragmentary; it changes character from one period to another; and it is heavily concentrated on the activities of the major bureaucratic agencies in the society. This is not helped by the traditional archaeological obsession with monumental architecture, for temple and palace archives tend to provide us with very little information about trade, and practically all of the relatively well-known phases of foreign trade activities are illuminated by texts found in private houses.

For the "state" sector, trade conforms well with Polanyi's definition as "a method of acquiring goods not available on the spot" (1977, 81). The imports to the cities on the alluvium were of course essential for the maintenance of civilized life, not only luxuries such as silver, gold, and precious stones, but metals, wood and stone for weapons, tools, and ceremonial buildings. Imports of slaves seem never to have been substantial. The traders of southern Mesopotamia must at all times have been heavily involved in these activities on behalf of the great organizations. As late as the Old Babylonian period it seems clear that the state to a large extent controlled the production of wool and of textiles, and these commodities were always among the most prominent export articles from the alluvium. Another field where the state may have played a decisive role was shipbuilding, providing transport facilities for the copper trade over the Persian Gulf (cf. Butz 1979, 371). It seems that shipments consisting of at least some 20 tons constituted the joint investment of a large number of individual traders.

For the Old Babylonian period, Polanyi's concept of the status trader, for which he chose the Akkadian designation *tamkarum,* does not seem to be of much help. As pointed out earlier, it is open to doubt whether the trader in Mesopotamia was ever an "official" in the sense of a person who as a member of a bureaucratic organization acts for the state, drawing a salary and/or receiving a grant of land. According to Polanyi, only small gains could be made on transactional trade in archaic societies, so "he who trades for the sake of duty and honor grows rich, while he who trades for filthy lucre remains poor—an added reason why gainful motives are under a shadow in archaic society" (1977, 84). At least for the Old Babylonian period this definition cannot be substantiated. Rather, it is flatly contradicted by our evidence, which shows us how private individuals invest in commercial ventures and how foreign trade is carried out by independent entrepreneurs.

The clear-cut contrast between the trader as an official and as a private entrepreneur may be misleading, as pointed out by Humphreys (1978, 56–57), who regards such a distinction as potentially anachronistic. Polanyi himself suggested that the status trader (*tamkarum*) developed into a merchant when he was able to carry out private trade while still retaining his original functions, and such a combination has been suggested many times   by various scholars: Falkenstein was willing to consider this even for the traders in the Sumerian temple–city (1954, 804), and Zaccagnini suggested that private enterprises "were carried out as a side-activity by merchants going abroad on behalf of the palace" in Nuzi of the fifteenth century B.C. (Zaccagnini 1977, 180). The inadequacy of our categories is brought out very clearly by the profusion of terms used (*officials, commercial agents, employees of the administration,* etc.), and in particular by the difference in emphasis that we find in the analyses offered.

*For the Old Babylonian period it is essential to bring the concept of the karum,* or "harbor," into this discussion. This word originally denoted a mooring place and came to mean a harbor area and finally the community of merchants living in such a harbor. It has been suggested that the harbor was a feature of all major Mesopotamian towns, but that it was a separate unit located outside the town proper. It is one of the words that may be translated *market* in certain contexts, and it is clear that the harbor played some role in the exchange linking town with agriculture hinterland. No such *karum* in the Mesopotamian area has yet been excavated (although Butz has suggested tentatively that the suburb of Ur known as Diqdiqah could have been the harbor), but in Anatolia large sections of an Old Assyrian *karum* located as a suburb of the ancient city of Kanesh have been uncovered. The evidence from Babylonia, indicates that it was typically a settlement of private houses and shops inhabited and onwed by merchants.

The Old Babylonian *karum* also was, however, the community of merchants of the town, i.e., it had a corporate character and even a separate administrative and judicial apparatus. The best-known Babylonian *karum* is the one located at Sippar, and it should be kept in mind that it may not have been typical of Babylonian harbors since it clearly had a vitally important strategic location on the border between the urbanized areas and the steppe. We can see here that the official in charge of the harbor served for one year. He appears to have been selected by lot from among a group of wealthy men, and he even came to function as a kind of mayor of the town of Sippar itself (Larsen 1976, 215–217). Oppenheim suggested that the mayorship should be compared with the institution of liturgies in the Greek city–states, so that these men carried a fiscal responsibility vis-à-vis the royal administration in Babylon (Oppenheim 1969, 10–11).

The precise nature of the *karum* as a corporate unit is hard to define, but several texts show that it was through the medium of this institution that the state usually organized its contact with individual traders. In their capacity as members of a *karum*, however such membership was defined, the Old Babylonian traders may perhaps be referred to with the phrase *licensed merchants* or the traditional German phrase *Gildenkaufmann* (cf. Landsberger 1925, 12).

A royal edict issued in the late old Babylonian period contains some illuminating references to the relationship between *karum* and palace. Kraus has shown that one paragraph contains the revealing rule that the palace might invest only one half of the capital in any commercial operation that the *karum* carried out. The merchants moreover could be charged with the collection of dues from taxpayers (peasants, shepherds, etc.) to be used directly in commercial activities. The *karum* as such, or presumably the individual traders who become involved in the transaction in question, had accordingly, in each case to put up an investment that equaled the one submitted by the palace. Kraus drew the inevitable conclusion that the palace made use of the *karum* as agent precisely because it consisted of *independent businessmen* (Kraus 1979, 428–429). This principle was valid for all spheres of the Old Babylonian economy, according to Kraus, and its aim was to reduce or avoid direct state management of production, trade, and supervision, and to force the various independent agents to carry the risks involved in the transactions. These agents were free to amass private wealth. Indeed, it was a condition for this system to work that they did so and were capable of shouldering the risks.

For a proper understanding of the dynamics of such a socioeconomic system it is obviously essential to be able to describe the process of private accumulation in more detail. Given the present state of affairs in the field, such an analysis is beyond our reach, but it is clear that wealthy men did have the option to buy land, as is known both for certain traders (cf. Leemans 1950, 65) and for groups of persons in Nippur, as mentioned earlier. Moneylending was an activity that was clearly commonly practiced by merchants, and the Hammurapi Code contains paragraphs that regulate such affairs, using the term *tamkarum* with the meaning of "creditor."

It is unclear whether all towns in southern Mesopotamia had a special *karum* quarter, but there was doubtless a high degree of commercial specialization in the area. It is furthermore not clear whether the *karum* was in fact always located outside the town proper. Oppenheim was clearly inspired by Polanyi when he suggested that intracity and intercity economies must be kept separate "in order to maintain the specific economic and social climate of the community" (1964, 114). He saw the *karum* as a port of trade—a buffer between the redistributive system of the city and thes shady dealings of the market place. The dual-city phenomenon in Mesopotamia is poorly understood, and it is uncertain whether it is to be interpreted in the same way as the urban complex of Tenochtitlán and Tlatelolco discussed in a later section.

The potentially disruptive character of the relations between the commercial sector and the traditional political apparatus was mentioned by Rowlands (Chapter 11 this volume), and the analysis of Ur III trade by Neumann has in fact led to the suggestion that a steadily growing private sector, where commercial capital was invested in moneylending, was a major factor in the breakdown of the centralized bureaucracy of the Ur III state (Neumann 1979). The marginalization of merchants in a special city quarter may in part have been due to the conflict between a status elite whose wealth was bound up in land and the upredictable and volatile commercial capital. It is interesting to note that the city of Assur, which was a major commercial center in the Old Assyrian period, does not appear to have had a *karum* at all; like Genoa it was a city of merchants and the saying *Genuensis ergo mercator* is equally meaningful for Assur (cf. Larsen 1976, 227–236).

### The Old Assyrian Trade

To illustrate his concept of risk-free, marketless trade, Polanyi chose to present a detailed analysis of a corpus of documents stemming from around 1800 B.C., which have been found at a site known as Kültepe in central Anatolia. In his reconstruction of the society described by these texts, we find all the key elements in Polanyi's theoretical framework: an absence of markets and trade that consisted in selling and buying goods for cash at equivalency rates where the trader's revenue was derived from commissions on the exporter—the city of Assur itself. Equivalencies were established by treaty and since revenue accordingly resulted entirely from the turnover of consigned goods, participation in business meant participation in profits. The trader, while remaining a free agent, had to operate within the framework of a governmental organization. Apart from goods on consignment from the state, he could trade in so-called "free goods" to a limited extent, but such activities were strictly regulated. The traders were not *tamkaru,* for this title was restricted in use for special public trustees who had the duty to facilitate the trade in various ways and who derived no revenue from the businesses but had their living ensured through a landed property given by the state.

Somewhat disconcertingly, Polanyi ended his discussion with the observation that "when all is said, this type of organization of trade and business was probably unique in history" (Polanyi *et al.* 1957, 25). This statement is strange in view of the fact that he chose precisely the Old Assyrian trade as his one well-documented example of a system of administered, marketless trade. In fact, with a different interpretation it becomes possible to draw numerous parallels to other well-known systems of foreign trade such as the medieval Jewish trade reflected in the Geniza and the early Italian trade in the eastern Mediterranean. Also, it is really rather unlikely that the Old Assyrian trade should be without parallels in other periods and areas within the ancient Near East.

The available textual documentation stems nearly exclusively from early illicit diggings by local peasants at the site of Kültepe—the ruins of the ancient city of Kanesh. During the first centuries of the second millennium B.C. Kanesh was a capital city in one of the many small territorial kingdoms that were scattered over the Anatolian plateau. At the foot of the mound itself, which shows a concentration of elaborate public buildings, was a large suburban settlement protected by walls and consisting of well-built, substantial houses. In these have been discovered a large number of private archives containing letters, contracts, accounts, bills of lading, legal texts, verdicts issued by various authorities, notes, and memoranda. The total number of excavated texts is assumed to be at least 20,000 now, and between 3000 and 4000 of these are available for study.

This suburb was known as *karum* Kanesh, i.e., "the Kanesh harbor" (in spite of the absence of any navigable waterway), and the archives reflect the activities of a large number of Assyrian traders. These men and women had their home-base in the relatively small city–state of Assur located on a cliff above the river Tigris. The Kanesh harbour or "colony" was the main Assyrian establishment in Anatolia, but some nine other harbors plus an unknown number of smaller settlements known as "trading posts" were scattered over a large area in northern Syria and eastern and central Anatolia as shown in Figure

13.1. Kanesh was the administrative center for this entire network of commercial establishments. Its governmental structure included a "council" composed of "great men," a primary assembly composed of "great and small," a secretary of the colony, and a special official who held a weekly, eponymic position. The Kanesh harbor was directly subordinated to the assembly of the city of Assur, and envoys from there apparently always assisted the Kanesh assembly in its diplomatic dealings with the many Anatolian kingdoms with which the Assyrian traders had treaty agreements (Larsen 1976, Part Three).

The political structure of the mother city itself shows a delicate balance between a king, an aristocratic assembly that was apparently presided over by the king, and an eponymic office held for a year by members of the aristocratic elite and exercising control over the main administrative bureau of the city, known as either "City Hall" or "the office of the eponym" (Larsen 1976, Part Two).

On the private level we find a reflection of this governmental structure. In the mother city we have a number of merchant houses that we may describe as family firms and that were directed by men who clearly formed part of the elite of the city. The men and women in Kanesh and the other commercial

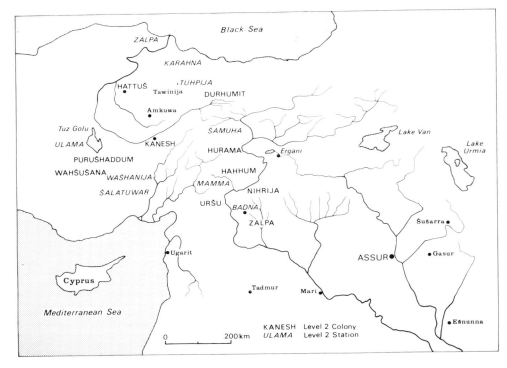

**Figure 13.1. Colonies and smaller trading posts in northern Syria and eastern and central Anatolia during the Old Assyrian period.**

establishments functioned basically as *factors* or agents for the merchant houses in Assur, even though in time they established very close ties to their new homes in Syria and Anatolia. The documentation from the Kanesh harbor covers a period of 50–70 years, during which time we can follow the activities of three generations of traders. At least during the first decades of the period in question, most firms had their main office abroad in Kanesh. Here we find the men who were in charge of the Anatolian activities—important traders in their own right whose archives we now have to study. The great men of Kanesh were normally sons or nephews of the bosses in Assur, and they were surrounded by a staff of family members—brothers, sons, nephews, who were charged with special tasks such as representing the family in one of the other harbors, leading caravans between Assur and Kanesh, or traveling around the Anatolian area.

Cutting across this pattern of family ties we find a special investment or partnership contract, which gave a fund of money (in the best-known case a capital of no less than 120 pounds of silver) to an individual trader. He administered this over a period of a number of years (in one case 12 years), and the contracts contained rules concerning the division of profits accruing currently, reinvestments in the fund, and the withdrawal of money from it. At least in some cases, up to 15 investors would contribute to such a partnership, and the entire contractual relationship amounted to something close to a general commercial company, akin to the institutions known from the Italian cities (Larsen 1977).

The pattern of the trade as reflected in the documents from Kanesh is represented by the model (see Figure 13.2). With respect to the wider international ramifications of the trade, two basic points should be made. First, a comparison between the model and the map of the Assyrian expansion clearly indicates that two elements in the trade are nearly entirely undocumented by the texts from Kanesh. The trade in copper appears to have been of interest to the Assyrians in Kanesh only as an import from the mines in eastern Anatolia to the kingdoms of the central plateau. (Polanyi's contention that the whole basis for the existence of the Assyrian settlements in Anatolia was the procurement of copper for Assur can therefore be flatly rejected.) The concentration of Assyrian harbors and trading posts in the north Syrian area is likewise very poorly reflected in the texts from Kanesh. These establishments must clearly have been engaged in large-scale commerce that involved contacts with the Syro–Palestinian region, and casual references to men coming from or going to such places as Tadmur–Palmyra or Ebla give us just a glimpse of this different world.

The second basic point is that the trade in Anatolia can be observed to have constituted only one leg in a vastly more expanded system of international trade. The two categories of commodities exported from Assur—tin and textiles—did not originate there. Tin came from the east exported from Assur—tin and textiles—did not originate there. Tin came from the east, maybe from mines in northern Afghanistan (personal communication from Diakonoff), and the

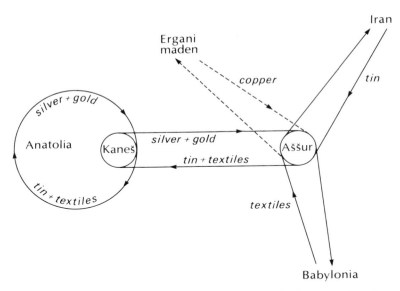

**Figure 13.2.** A model for Old Assyrian trade as reflected in the documents from Kanesh.

majority of the textiles exported from Assur were sent there from the production centers in southern Mesopotamia. The market in Assur was a transit point where a number of commercial circuits intersected.

The pendulum trade linking Assur with Kanesh involved the transportation of vast amounts of tin and textiles by way of donkey caravans. Directly attested in our small published corpus are some 600 assloads of textiles (circa 15,000 pieces) and about 200 loads of tin (corresponding to about 13,500 tons) (Veenhof 1972, 79). We may safely assume that at least five times as much is represented in the texts already excavated in Ankara, so about 100,000 textiles and some 80 tons of tin may be posited as a conservative estimate for the exports from Assur to Kanesh over a 50-year period.

The texts allow us to describe the caravan transactions in great detail, and there can hardly be any doubt that the investments were made by private individuals and firms. Goods bought in Assur are in all cases that can be documented by the texts paid for with private funds—often silver sent back from Kanesh as the proceeds from the sale of previous shipments. When we hear of substantial amounts of silver arriving in Assur that was not reinvested in goods for a new caravan, they are regularly said to be spent on the purchase of houses in the city or as payments to cover debts. Caravan accounts written from Assur provide detailed information about the purchase of goods, and typically between 85 and 90% was invested in the caravan as such, while the remainder went to cover transport expenses. The export tax levied by the office of the eponym on all caravans amounted to only 1/120 of the silver value of the shipment (Larsen 1967, 141–155).

A close analysis of the Old Assyrian trade therefore flatly contradicts Polanyi's picture of an administered or dispositional trade, and instead reaffirms the interpretations suggested by such scholars as Julius Lewy and B. Landsberger. Polanyi's claims concerning the absence of a market and the function of silver as "money" in the Old Assyrian trade have been subjected to detailed scrutiny by Veenhof (1972, Part Five), and his conclusions likewise contradict Polanyi; markets did exist and silver did in fact function as money. The Assyrian trade cannot be properly understood in terms of the concept *import interest* once it has been shown that its rationale was not the procurement of copper, but rather the accumulation of enormous wealth in the form of silver and gold. Substantial fluctuations in prices can be observed, and these can be related to textual references about specific market situations where goods are said to be "in short supply" and "expensive." The supply-and-demand mechanism was clearly the basis for the trade in the markets both in the Anatolian cities and in Assur itself, but it must be kept in mind that in the latter city the large merchant houses somehow controlled the purchases and charged a fee of 5/120 for their services. The relationship between these houses and the market in the city remains to be elucidated. Another feature that should be mentioned is that losses—contrary to Polanyi's statement about a risk-free trade—are in fact referred to many times. It therefore seems highly unlikely that Polanyi's analysis or his theoretical framework in general will provide much help in our further attempts to understand this society—and this is true also for the discussion that follows concerning the precise meaning of the term *tamkarum* in the Old Assyrian texts (Garelli 1977, Larsen 1977, Veenhof 1972, 356).

The international trade at this time can best be understood as a complex network of interlocking circuits, each one controlled and exploited by a single political unit. The detailed study of the Old Assyrian circuit cannot be matched by similarly fine-grained investigations of, for instance, the trade of the cities in southern Mesopotamia (Leemans 1960, 1968), and it is entirely possible that substantially different patterns existed there. However, the rejection of Polanyi's specific interpretation of the Old Assyrian evidence must be seen within the framework of his inability of his theoretical orientation to provide any usable concepts that could incorporate and account for the Old Assyrian economic and social system. The vague and undeveloped term *trading peoples* is of no assistance. Polanyi's special emphasis on the redistributive aspects of Mesopotamian society obscures the vitally important role played by the private sector and by commercial accumulation. It is precisely the interplay of centralization and bureaucratic features on the one hand and decentralization and private economy on the other that is likely to provide us with a better understanding of long-term developmental patterns in Mesopotamian history.

## LATE HORIZON MESOAMERICA:
## THE EMBEDDED ECONOMY AND SOCIAL DYNAMICS

Polanyi's ideas have exerted a continuous if patchy influence on Meso-american studies since the publication of Chapman's justly celebrated ethno-historical study of Aztec–Maya trading in *Trade and Market* (Chapman 1957). Her work has subsequently been broadened in Berdan's substantivist analyses of the structure and functioning of the Aztec economy as a whole (Berdan 1977, 1978). In archaeology, important contributions addressed to the "port-of-trade" concept have been made by the Cozumel Project (Sabloff and Rathje 1975, Sabloff and Friedel 1975), and in Brown's model for the Teotihuacán–Kaminaljuyú relationship in an earlier period of Mesoamerican prehistory (Brown 1977). Yet the writings of the Cozumel team reveal a striking lack of real theoretical contact with Polanyi's "archaic economy" model. Their analytical categories are ahistorical. A critique of Polanyi should not lead us to "smudge over all historical differences and see bourgeois relations in all forms of society" (Marx 1973, 105). But a brief review of the data used to support the validity of Polanyi's generalizations for Mesoamerica does suggest problems here that are similar to those we encountered in the Mesopotamian case.

### Merchants and the Economic Role of the State

Chapman's model deals with a situation where professional merchants (*pochteca*) acted as agents of the Aztec ruler Ahuitzotl in acquiring goods from lowland producer zones outside the empire. Transactions took place in a series of small "ports of trade," which were densely packed in a large, politically neutralized region, a pattern that Polanyi himself recognized as somewhat unusual (Polanyi 1968). The *pochteca* were rewarded by gifts of precious things from the ruler. But the Sahagún text (Sahagún 1950–1969, IX, 9) makes it clear that the merchants also traded extensively on their own account in these centers, implying that mercantile arbitrage profit would at least supplement such revenues. Berdan has made a further observation on this point that might suggest qualification of Polanyi's contention that "during the pre-colonial era ports of trade not market places were the growing points of the world economy" (Polanyi 1968, 246). Archival sources indicate that cacao (a major money object) was acquired through private *marketplace* transactions by *pochteca* in the ports of trade (Berdan 1977, 97, see also Calnek 1978a, 104–106). Berdan also takes some cognizance of a detail in the Sahagún text of considerable potential significance.

The consignment of goods that Ahuitzotl handed over to the merchants of Tenochtitlán and Tlatelolco initially—1600 cotton capes (*quachtli*)—is not what is traded in the lowlands. The capes are taken to the marketplace of Tlatelolco where they are converted into feathered capes and other types of high-status apparel, following a ceremonial division preceded by gifts and orations "displaying rearing and upbringing" (Sahagún 1950–1969, IX, 8). The text then enumerates a long list of private goods of the merchants acquired for the expedition, aside from the items that are designated "the exclusive property of the ruler." These included both status goods and "things used by the common folk," something that may distinguish trading in this later period from that of the Teotihuacán horizon (see Brown 1977, 329). Berdan herself maintains that "personal transactions of the merchants in these extra-empire trading areas were essentially a by-product of the state-organised commercial relations" (1977, 98) on the grounds that access to this trade sphere was a monopoly granted by the Aztec state to merchants from only five of the Valley of Mexico city–states. These were drawn from the ranks of the wealthiest *pochteca*, who simultaneously occupied the highest rank positions within guildlike corporations into which the merchants of each city were organized. The status dimension of such trading, so important for Polanyi, is much in evidence in our text. But it seems to arise in the first instance within the guild structure, and it cannot be directly equated with ascriptive social status. The upper stratum of the *pochteca* rose in general social status within the imperial society, a process that Gledhill has argued elsewhere should be understood in terms of political conflict between rulers and the nobility (Gledhill in press). The Sahagún texts emphasize wealth acquisition as the goal of merchant activity, with much ideological stress on achievement through toil, hardship, and initiative. Rank order within merchant *calpultin* was correlated with wealth (Sahagún 1950–1969, IX, 12–14), though this does not establish the direction of the underlying relationship, and there is also considerable emphasis on matters of etiquette and "form" designed to support claims to social worth comparable to that of the nobility. One might say that the "principal merchants" were engaged in a kind of "potlatch"—a status-validating manipulation of wealth—among themselves and in the face of an ascriptive noble stratum reluctant to recognize their claims.

The *principales* therefore fail to fit neatly into Polanyi's conceptions of the possible status positions of traders in archaic societies, while at the same time diverging from the simple stereotype of a "businessman" in that their ultimate goal was a status position that could not be directly conferred by wealth. This view of the *pochteca* is, however, consistent with a model in which the corporate merchant organization already existed prior to the creation of a centralized Aztec empire, the latter intervening administratively simply to increase the degree of monopoly power in access of the lowland trade sphere, and politically, to permit merchants to rise in social status. As we have seen, the state's participation in the trading itself was in fact rather indirect, since the palace played no role in the mediating marketplace transactions in Tlatelolco. In effect, the ruler advanced "capital" to a merchant venture, which permitted him to realize probable tribute payments in liquid assets in the form of desired foreign commodities. The goods actually traded from the highlands at the ports of trade were products of the private artisan sector acquired by merchants on the market. The textual evidence is therefore most consistent with a model in which the state is an indirect participant in a trade system run and organized by independent merchant corporations. This immediately brings to mind the kind of situation suggested by Kraus for the Old Babylonian period in Mesopotamia. Indeed, the parallel can be pushed further in terms of the antagonistic relationships between "traditional" nobles and mercantile wealth. Our immediate problem is, however, that of the actual degree of administrative control over the economy that might have been exercised by the Aztec state. In the case of transactions in ports of trade—even if we accept the substantivist model of barter exchanges at fixed equivalencies—it is not easy to see how goods could have been transferred at the "strictly administrative level" in the sense that the Aztec state itself played a direct administrative role. Sahagún's informants themselves seem to stress the idea of an imposition of administrative and military controls on a preexisting trade system organized by the merchant "corporation," but it appears unlikely that these controls extended to the actual operations in foreign trade centers.

Even within the empire, market regulation was assigned to *pochteca*, and Sahagún's texts stress the independent nature of internal jurisdiction within the merchant community (Sahagún 1950–1969, IX, 23). Certainly, state administrative intervention in the functioning of the market system is widely attested to, including regulations that limited the sale of certain products to specific marketplaces (see, for example, Durán 1971, 277–278). Carrasco has proposed a distinction between *free* and *directed* markets in order to stress the role of central administrative mechanisms in the economic functioning of the market system (Carrasco 1978, 50–51). But, as noted above for Mesopotamia, administrative proclamations of prices may be of greater ideological than practical significance, and the substantivist writers themselves concede a degree of supply-and-demand price fluctuation in Mesoamerican markets (Berdan 1978, 79–80). Indeed, Berdan emphasizes that the market sphere does seem to emerge as the pivot of interaction for the Aztec economic system as a totality. It is taxation, the granting of monopoly privileges, and regulation of the flow of commodities within local and interregional exchange networks that emerge as the major facets of centralized economic administration in the Aztec system. Even this, however, encounters certain additional limitations in comparisons with Mesopotamia, perhaps reflecting the enhanced role of the marketplace in Mesoamerican economic integration. In particular, several different money objects coexisted, whose supply could not be effectively regulated by the state (Calnek 1978a, 111). *Quachtli* were probably the most significant of these, and are featured prominently in the tribute lists. But the state could not control *quachtli* production, nor that of cacao—the other main money object. This situation seems structural rather than contingent.

An emphasis on centralized political control over the economy links Polanyi's "archaic state" model with a wider stream of theory, posing the question of why precapitalist world empires do not evolve into modern capitalist formations. The work of Wallerstein (1974) draws on both Polanyi and Weber (see, for example, Weber 1951). Wittfogel (1935) proposed the "state-stronger-than-society" thesis, which recognized the significant development of private landed property, commercial and financial institutions, and price-making markets within "Oriental despotic regimes," but he insisted that the bureaucratic state would always check the private accumulation of wealth after a point and stifle nascent political opposition from private property interests. Wittfogel was, of course, partly reworking Marx's notion of an "Asiatic" mode of production in an ideologically restructured form (Bailey 1981). Carrasco (1978, 71) has attempted a synthesis of Marx and Polanyi for the Mesoamerican context, precisely to develop the thesis that both "feudal" and "Asiatic" systems are distinctive in that their economies are organized by and through political institutions rather than the market (see, however Hindess and Hirst 1975, Chapter 2). Carrasco thereby also recognizes that market elements may undergo significant development within "Asiatic regimes," but he points to society's foundation on relations of production secured through "political" relations of dominance. Although he discounts Wittfogel's emphasis on "despotism," he finds Polanyi's notion that the overall integration of the archaic economy is secured through politico–administrative mechanisms (redistribu-tion–centricity), a useful basis for distinguishing modern capitalist formations from their precursors once the substantivist category *forms of integration* is reorientated to production relations.

Carrasco's approach implies that macrosocial change is a product of trans-formation of production relations, but it takes us no further than this. As noted previously, Polanyi's writings contain at best a few undeveloped schematics for an account of the determinants of change in the institutionalization of the economic process. The Wittfogel thesis has a number of weaknesses, starting from its failure to explain how and why private proprietary relations and mercantile capital emerge and apparently expand within "Asiatic" formations, beyond positing this as a quasi-natural phenomenon in the manner of Adam Smith (see also Moulder 1977). But it does at least begin to pose the question of the dynamic relationships between the development of mercantile forms, political centralization, and transformation of production relations.

## Positive Analysis: The Market Problems

All analyses agree that precolonial Mesoamerica had a well-developed system of local, regional, and rural–urban integration through marketplaces. The system continues to operate in the ethnographic present in a few areas, though in an atrophied and structurally modified form, and the use of post-conquest data throughout this discussion must be premised on models of processes that occurred within the colonial formation (see also Gledhill in press).

In central Mexico, Michoacán, the valley of Oaxaca, and the western highlands of Guatemala, rural communities were integrated into the wider regional economy through the "solar system" type of marketplace network: Local periodic marketplaces were distributed around a major urban market center operating on a daily basis (see, for example, Beals 1971). Periodic markets lacked the range of goods available in the major centers, and they tended to specialize in certain local products—a phenomenon that should be seen as distinct from the state-regulated restriction of certain commodity markets to specific major centers referred to previously, which represents further central intervention on patterns of specialization established in conditions of greater political fragmentation by other mechanisms. We have particularly vivid descriptions of the great markets of the Aztec capital by Cortés (Zorita 1963, 157–159) and Diaz del Castillo (1960), supplemented by descriptions that embrace other Basin of Mexico centers and some periodic markets in smaller communities. As Calnek has pointed out, historical sources make it clear that the bulk of the basic foodstuffs consumed by the mass of the urban population of Tenochtitlán was imported and circulated through the market, rather than as redistributed tribute or rents, up to the conquest of Azcapotzalco. The establishment of Tenochtitlán's military hegemony over the basin did not significantly reduce the role of the marketplace provisioning (Calnek 1978a, 99–100). The notion of a "storage economy" would evidently be quite inappropriate here. This gives us a preliminary insight into the material–functional signficance of the marketplace system over a moderate timespan in which significant structural change in political–economic terms was occurring. But we must examine the organization and functioning of the system more closely to press the analysis of its social implications further.

In local markets, peasant producer–consumers confronted other peasant producer–consumers and itinerant petty traders. The general category *pochteca* embraces a range of different types of "professional" traders, from the elite enjoying access to foreign trade down to people trafficking in low-value goods in a local urban center–periodic market system. Cook (1976) has argued that Marx's notion of "petty" or "simple" commodity production–circulation best characterizes the activities of farmers, specialist craftsmen, and petty traders (often women) in the contemporary plaza system of Oaxaca, and at least descriptively, this conceptualization has some merit. Although transactions may be relatively "impersonal," "prices" exhibit short-run flexibility, and there exists a cultural notion of "profit" (*ganancia*). Surpluses above mundane consumption needs are invested in *fiestas* and other forms of social consumption primarily, not in the "processual expansion" of the petty "enterprise." Here we see why a naive "formalist" critique of Polanyi misses the point theoretically. Preconquest Mesoamerica is evidently not a "market-integrated" economy in Polanyi's sense, given the proportion of land and labor that remained locked away from the market. Commodity markets remained relatively regionalized. The mutual insulation of local networks created wide value differentials, though as we will see, the fact that mercantile agents integrated these local systems is highly significant. Furthermore, as substantivist theory presupposes, the marketplace as a site was as much a locus of social interaction as a facility for economic transactions (see, for example, Durán 1971, 274–277). But the obvious fact that ancient Mesoamerica is not a capitalist society (let alone an ideal type of nineteenth-century laissez faire capitalism) should not lead us to ignore the significant role played by mercantile elements and relations within this formation from the standpoint of its long-term developmental pattern.

Within the local network, whole villages might sometimes specialize productively, and households might be largely dependent on the marketplace for basic items of consumption and raw materials. Assessing the "solar system" as revealed archaeologically and by historical sources and ethnography, Sanders, Parsons, and Santley concluded that "most transactions were really not profit oriented, and so in this sense it was not a market economy." Instead, they suggested the marketplace network should be seen as "a special type of redistributive system," premised on unusually great local environmental diversity (Sanders et al. 1979, 404–405). Theoretically, this conclusion has drawbacks. It ignores the social implications of the fact that mercantile agents could move between local and regional markets and accumulate wealth by exploiting the differential values of individual goods at different points (see also Phillips and Rathje 1977). Certainly the petty trader was engaged in "trade for livelihood," so that trade specialization of this type would be an activity ultimately oriented to the acquisition of use values. But this would not be an adequate description of the activities of the wealthier *pochteca*. There are also theoretical deficiencies in presenting "peasants" as universally and "naturally" oriented to production for livelihood. In contemporary Mexico, there are clear constraints on the capacity of most *campesino* enterprises to engage in sustained accumulation, stemming from their mode of articulation into the wider society and that society's systems of resource appropriation (Bartra 1975, Marguis 1979). The rationality of economic activity cannot be divorced from its sociocultural context, and modern industrial capitalist enterprises are forced to accumulate for reasons specific to this mode of production. (For further discussion of this and the preceding points, see Gledhill 1981b.) But we cannot ignore the significance of the accumulation of wealth in precapitalist systems for the genesis of such social situations as debt slavery and transformations in appropriational relations within the "village community." We know, for example, that there was internal differentiation among households in Late Horizon corporate communities, including inequalities in the possession of usufruct rights to land that were permanent (Carrasco 1978, 37, Gledhill in press). Furthermore, Adams's observation that the Aztec state attempted to impose restrictions on the employment of extrafamily labor by commoners has clear implications in a system in which production for the market is of some structural importance (Adams 1979, 62). To describe the market system as a type of redistributive system obscures its role as a possible basis for private accumulation of wealth outside the state sectors of the economy and thereby part of the dynamic underlying its development and ramification—a part that cannot be ascribed to the state or to ecology.

Thus far we have ignored the urban community, except to note the role of the marketplace in the provisioning of the great cities of the basin. Late Horizon "towns" differ in the extent to which their populations were predominantly nonagricultural specialists (Sanders *et al.* 1979, 179), but this was clearly the case with Tenochtitlán. Sahagún distinguishes between "private" artisans that produced luxury goods and those that "pertained" to the ruler (Sahagún 1950–1969, 91–92). Calnek (1978a) has attempted to go beyond conventional emphasis on the production of sumptuary goods, and has provided a convincing account of the provision of nonagricultural products for mass consumption by small artisan workshops that realised their output on the urban marketplace, from where, as we have seen, they might be conveyed by merchants into long-distance trade alongside goods aimed at elite consumers. "Private-sector" urban workers received income from sale of products or as "wages" (*means to acquire subsistence goods from the market*), not rations, if they worked for an employer. Interestingly, some documented aspects of the preconquest urban economy survive to this day: Skilled artisans offer themselves for hire by the day in the central plaza of Mexico City, for example. We therefore have a quantitative predominance of the marketplace in everyday provisioning, together with a kind of "labor market," and the rulers of Mexico offered inducements to skilled craftsmen to settle in Tenochtitlán. Again, at the formal level, the bulk of production corresponds to the label *petty-commodity production*, a situation analogous to that in the Ottoman Empire, for example (Islamoğlu and Keyder 1977). As in other ancient civilizations, we may encounter some enterprises employing wage labor that resemble capitalist production forms. Here again, of course, we must beware of the error of using what Marx termed "simple abstractions" (Marx 1973, 100–107); the conditions for modern capitalist wage labor and industrial capitalist accumulation processes do not exist in these archaic contexts. We must also note that, like merchants, nonagricultural producers were organized in corporate bodies called *calpultin* (singular *calpulli*), orientated to protecting the position of their members economically (and derivatively from that, one suspects, quality standards) (Calnek 1978a, 103). If, then, the category *capital* is invoked in the analysis of the functioning and dynamic of the "private-sector" components of the Late Horizon socioeconomic totality, the only conceptualization that could be relevant is that of "merchant capital" and mercantile forms of accumulation (see, for example, Dobb 1963, Kay 1975).

We have now specified the nature of the market elements in the Aztec social formation. But our picture remains a synchronic "snapshot"; we have yet to undertake analysis of the dynamic articulation of these elements with the rest of the system. This alone will enable us to shift from description to a theory of the specific evolutionary dynamics of formations of this type. We therefore offer some working hypotheses leading in this direction, starting from the general observation that the debate about the dominance of "redistributive" forms in archaic states versus greater emphasis on the "market" distracts our attention from a potentially more illuminating line of enquiry: What is the significance of the coexistence of "state" and "private" sectors in specific kinds of articulations from the comparative and evolutionary perspectives?

## POSITIVE ANALYSIS: CONCLUSION—DYNAMICS OF CENTRALIZATION AND DECENTRALIZATION

We began by questioning the degree of centralized political control over the economy actually exercised by the Aztec state. At the level of production relations, the significance of "tributary" mechanisms in the extraction of economic surpluses for deployment by the center requires no further comment. But as Gledhill has argued elsewhere (Gledhill in press), we must recognize the emergence of an important division between the "state" and dominant class— the nobility—which was itself divided into factions whose interests might contradict each other and those of the rulers in political terms. The latter gained private sources of tributary revenue through their possession of "private lands" and titles to rents and services from dependent cultivators in the *mayeque* category (Katz 1966, Gibson 1964). To a considerable extent, the driving force beneath Late Horizon social change stemmed from contradictions at this level and their longer-term impact on interclass relations.

The developed state exercised regulation over the market system administratively and intervened indirectly in the conditions of production. But we must carefully examine the degree of control inherent in these regulatory interventions. After all, the state could not effectively control the supply of money. It did not exert complete control over the supply of raw materials. The tribute system, once imposed, did give it a direct form of appropriation in these spheres, but it could not meet its needs completely without operating through mercantile agents in other spheres of exchange. And provisioning the palace and administrative structure itself involved transactions with the market system, even if rents and tribute provided the primary revenues for this level of organization. Craft producers clearly acquired raw materials through marketplace transactions with merchants. The state taxed markets as a source of revenue and also sought to restructure the flows of commodities through the market network by administrative means. The granting of monopolies to certain categories of merchants and attempts to regulate the distribution of dependent labor in society (see Gledhill in press) are administrative actions clearly oriented toward controlling the distribution and accumulation of wealth in society, in the interests of strengthening the position of the state politically. Measures of economic regulation were supplemented by administrative, legal enactments in the so-called "aristocratic reaction" (see Calnek 1974). Power relations rather than morality therefore supply the key to understanding "economic policy" here. However, beyond the effects of the tributary system in re-organizing production and circulation patterns at the interlocal level, the degree of direct administrative organization of the economy does not seem great. The state did intervene directly at the level of production in the provinces by creating prebendal forms of landed benefices for its officials in which a separate functionary was assigned the administration of production (undertaken as corvée by free peasants) (Adams 1979). But although such measures were clearly designed to bureaucratize administration of the empire and limit the private power of the nobility, the extent to which the increasingly "orientalized" monarchic form of the late empire would have remained stable in the long term seems open to doubt. To examine this issue we must adopt a longer-run framework of analysis.

Analysis of settlement-pattern change in the Basin of Mexico from the Middle to Late Horizons (Parsons 1976, Sanders et al. 1979) reveals a long-term cycle of political centralization and decentralization in terms of the spatial range of political control. The regional dominance of the great Teotihuacán megalopolis is followed by political fragmentation in the basin during the eighth century A.D., with the progressive breakdown of the supraregional trade network centered on the Middle Horizon metropolis. In the basin, population nucleated into a series of discrete clusters focused on a few major population centers (Sanders et al. 1979, 133). This suggests the formation of city–state polities of the kind found in later periods. It is notable, however, that despite these indices of political fragmentation, stylistic regionalism in ceramics did not emerge, which offers us one of a number of indications that what collapsed was Teotihuacán's dominance over the larger trade network and not the network itself, which was being subjected rather to a process of restructuring. New supraregional centers were already developing outside the basin, culminating in the reestablishment of more extended territorial control in the period between A.D. 950 and 1150. Sanders and his colleagues hypothesized that recentraliza-tion involved the development of two systems—a northern one with Tula as its core and a southern one hegemonized by Cholula (1979, 149). As a con-sequence of this process of spatial core shift, population density in the southern basin declined significantly, and a virtual gap in occupation seemed to emerge in the central region, which is hard to see as an artifact of the survey methods used but is easy to interpret as a sociopolitical buffer zone. A city–state pattern returned after A.D. 1150, with population declining sharply in the north of the basin and with rebuilding in the center, though the Chalco–Xochimilco region was the area of greatest density. Short-lived conquest empires were formed by way of bilateral and multilateral alliances between city–states, but relatively effective control was not reestablished over the whole basin until the second half of the fifteenth century, which marks the beginning of Aztec dominance (Calnek 1978b).

The stabilization of an empire entails the development of new systems of political control that overcome the centrifugalism of city–state political economy. Calnek has postulated a process whereby the rulers of the center could subvert the loyalty of subordinate nobles in subject states and shift from a system of "indirect" rule to a more centralized and bureaucratized administrative system significantly reducing local autonomy in resource control (1978b, 467). While this tells us something about how empires are created, it does not explain why they are created. Mesoamerica offers us a particularly clear case of a system in which politico–military competition between polities and internal political conflict were tied to the acquisition of wealth and resources flowing through a large, intersocietal trade network in addition to the appropriation of agricultural supluses (Gledhill in press, Gledhill and Rowlands in press). While competition for land, water, and labor relates to essential prerequisities for local political hierarchization at the city–state level in the highlands, politico–administrative changes, coupled with controls over other economic sectors, provide the key to understanding the mechanisms underpinning the territorial extension of the political unit.

Discussion of the Late Horizon transition raises the question of processes of secular structural transformation that may have underpinned the cycle of centralization and decentralization revealed in the archaeological record. The latter indicates quite massive processes of demographic redistribution over time. On the basis of the historical sources, it is difficult to envisage the creation of the nobility's private lands and the *mayeque* stratum as a process associated primarily with the politically centralized phase of the Late Horizon. Furthermore, the state had an incentive to limit the formation of these private tributary domains as far as was consistent with other policy objectives and real power balances (Gledhill in press). Demographic upheavals, militarism, and recolonization do, however, provide a suitable context for these developments, when the maximal political unit was the city–state, and this hypothesis can be supported archaeologically if Sanders and his colleagues are correct to associate dispersed rural occupation forms with *mayeques* (Sanders et al. 1979, 178–179). This pattern begins to make its appearance before the formation of the Triple Alliance. In the long term, the creation of private tributary domains establishes a potential for "feudalizing" tendencies within the empire, if local potentates gain the capacity to defend their property rights without the support of a strongly centralized state. But we cannot explore the issue of the long-run stability of the system further without reexamining the question of the trade system and mercantile agencies.

More attention needs to be paid archaeologically to the functioning and organization of the market systems and long-distance trade within a developmental perspective. Many questions remain to be answered on the way in which Teotihuacán maintained some degree of supraregional dominance in organizational terms. At what date the ethnohistorically documented form of *pochteca* trading emerged is a subject of considerable debate, but we would doubt its direct applicability to Teotihuacán where specialist trading may have been more "embedded" in the political ranking system. Some analysts have seen *"pochteca* enterprise" as underpinning the opening up of trade with areas in northwestern Mexico and southwestern United States in the Toltec period (DiPeso 1974, Riley and Hendrick 1978, but see also Gledhill 1978). We have, however, noted the historical sources' insistent emphasis on a model in which politico–military control is imposed on a preexisting trade system organized by merchant corporate groups. Both the Mesopotamian and Mesoamerican cases suggest that independent mercantile organizations developed initially in peripheral regions and under relatively decentralized conditions. (In both cases, for example, "oligarchic" political forms seem to characterize the periphery.) For the Late Horizon transition, our discussion suggests the following model for further testing.

The merchant guilds were rather clearly dominated by groups that monopolized certain high-value branches of trade by virtue of superior assets and resources, probably in much the same way as the wholesale merchant houses of the colonial system (Parry 1966, 338–339), though noneconomic relations cemented ties between corporation members of different rank (Sahagún 1950–1969, IX, Garibary K. 1961). "Big-operator" trading seems to have been organized on the basis of kinship and perhaps contractual ties mediated by fictitious bonds linking big merchant families in different city–states, and the transfer of goods at "port-of-trade" centers may have been organized through similar, regularized and ritualized, channels. State patronage and the granting of benefices would have increased economic stratification among the *pochteca*, whose status promotion would serve the political ends of the rulers and was consciously seen in that way (Gledhill in press). The monopolies in foreign trade and similar internal controls imposed by the state may well have reflected a convergence of interests. If the corporation structure already functioned to regulate access to trade and to control transactions in certain commodities, the Aztec center may simply have been reinforcing existing de facto monopolies administratively. Where arbitrage provides a basis for mercantile accumulation and profit is generated ultimately at the expense of the direct producers, the survival of the system in the long term depends on the creation and preservation of insulations and restrictions on competition at some point or points in the network (Kay 1975).

Up to a point the state can foster the processes of mercantile accumulation, and participation in the trade system was clearly a signficant source of wealth conversion for the Aztec state that gave it advantages in its struggle to control the nobility. Tribute and trade were strategically interlinked, and it is not difficult to see why the tribute net was not extended to embrace the lowland production zones given the limits of the state's direct appropriational powers in relation to the costs of such a strategy. But the centralized state must also control private-sector accumulation of wealth by strata capable of exercising political power within the existing structure or of establishing an independent local power base. To the direct political motive for economic regulation we must also add the indirect concern of ensuring that the state can provision its own apparatuses effectively. If it cannot—under prevailing social and economic conditions—do this directly, it must attempt to intervene administratively in the functioning of the market system.

The significance of this line of interpretation can be gauged from the spatial structure of the Aztec center itself. Tlatelolco was a major market center, immediately adjacent to Tenochtitlán, which contained the more elaborate ceremonial precincts and palace–secular administrative structures. The two centers are conventionally treated as two autonomous city–states, with Tlatelolco's losing its political independence to Tenochtitlán. It is likely that Tlatelolco was an earlier settlement, but in most respects the two cities seem to have formed an integrated urban complex, a "dual city" whose spatial organization seems to reflect one processual model; the bureaucratic apparatus of the centralized state grafts itself onto the preexisting "world economy" of independent city–states, linked politically by warfare and alliances and also economically by a complex division of labor that is integrated by markets and mercantile trade.

The long-term survival of a centralized bureaucratic empire depends on the center's being able to extract and retain sufficient revenue from tribute and taxation. In Mesoamerica, the creation of office prebends from the "cargo" lands appropriated by the state in conquered territories did not immediately open the possibility that officeholders would appropriate these grants as private domain, though this did occur under postconquest conditions (Gibson 1964, Riley 1978). Nevertheless, private domains of other kinds could not be eliminated by the centralized empire, and they probably continued to multiply. It is true that a form of corporate peasant community continued to be the primary element in the rural social landscape of Mesoamerica in the Late Horizon, giving the formation a classically "Asiatic" stamp. Nor should we ignore the role of "peasant resistance" in various, not directly political, forms in shaping the development of this formation in conjunction with political conflicts at higher levels in the society (Gledhill in press). The extent to which commodity relations penetrated the rural production unit remained limited. But the clear evidence for the existence of economic forms of stratification in the countryside may in part reflect the development of mercantile relations, together with the mechanisms discussed previously that underlay the growing size of the *mayeque* stratum. Some of the wealthiest *pochteca* are recorded as holders of lands and tenants, alongside the ascriptive *pipiltin* stratum. As we have noted, the access of the wealthy to status and its prerequisites was politically mediated and still limited. But this kind of tendency, together with evidence for a marked and progressive deterioration in the position of the rural commoner population in the late Aztec period, indicates that both private and state action combined in the long run to promote significant and probably irreversible changes in agrarian structure. It does not therefore seem unreasonable to suggest that Mesoamerica was heading in the kind of direction presented by the Chinese case: a differentiated "ruling class" based on wealth as well as status, incorporating mercantile elements, and living from the rents of dependent tenant cultivators, with land and rent titles alienable within the "private sector" (Gledhill in press).

This does not imply that Mesoamerica was, or was tending toward a "feudal" system in the Western sense. From the comparative perspective, the significant questions relate to the specific factors and processes that generated the diverent developmental pathways that led to the formation of the "modern" type of bureaucratic nation–state in Europe, counterposed as a type to the centralized bureaucratic empires of other major civilizations. Within the latter type, we also require a theoretical basis for understanding the processes that underpin the continuity of those political–economic characteristics that Marx tried to define with his "Asiatic mode of production" construct despite considerable development of commercial institutions and private appropriation of land. These questions cannot be broached here, but it is worth noting them simply to indicate how far we have been forced to move in pursuing our analysis from the questions posed by Polanyi. We might merely add in conclusion that we have not really found that the Mesoamerican material supports an emphasis on the overwhelming developmental significance of political centricity per se, at least of the kind posited by Wittfogel. An "orientalizing" monarchic system was in the ascendant at the time of the conquest under Moctezuma Xocoyotzin, but the development of the "private sector" was far from being wholly eliminated. The scenario for revenue crisis based on key parts of the sustaining system of the center falling victim to local power holders who were exploiting local grievances is apparent, and the weaknesses of the empire's conrol over its peripheries were immediately manifest in the events leading up to the victory of Cortés. Both the Mesoamerican and Mesopotamian cases suggest that it may be more rewarding theoretically to focus on the processes that lead to cycles of recentralization after the "feudalizing" episodes to which all ancient empires are subject than to focus on essentially static questions that are concerned simply with the institutionalization of the economic process under phases of greater political centricity. A long-term perspective clearly suggests that ancient empires are more dynamic and complex in their evolutionary trajectories than is often supposed.

## REFERENCES

Adams, R. McC., 1966, *The Evolution of Urban Society: Early Mesopotamia and Pre-Hispanic Mexico,* Chicago Aldine.

Adams, R. McC., 1979, Late Prehispanic empires of the New World, in Larsen, M. T. (ed.), *Power and Propaganda: A Symposium on Ancient Empires, Mesopotamia* 7, Copenhagen, Akademisk Forlag, 59–73.

Bailey, A. M., 1981, The renewed discussions of the concept of the Asiatic mode of production, in Kahn, J., and Llobera, J. (eds.), *The Anthropology of Pre-Capitalist Societies,* London, Macmillan.

Bartra, R. (ed.), 1975, *Caciquismo y poder político en el México rural*, México, Siglo Veintuino Editores.

Beals, R. L., 1971, *The Peasant Marketing System of Oaxaca, Mexico*, Berkley, University of California Press.

Berdan, F. F., 1977, Distributive mechanisms in the Aztec economy, in Halperin, R., and Dow, J. (eds.), *Peasant Livelihood*, New York, St. Martin's Press, 99–101.

Berdan, F. F., 1978, Tres formas de intercambio en la economía azteca, in Carrasco, P., and Broda, J. (eds.), *Economía Política e Ideología en el México Prehispánico*, México, Editorial Nueva Imagen, 77–95.

Brown, K. L., 1977, The valley of Guatemala: a highland port of trade, in Sanders, W. J., and Michels, J. W. (eds.), *Teotihuacán and Kaminaljuyú: A study in Prehistoric Culture Contact*, Philadelphia, Pennsylvania State University Press, 205–395.

Butz, K., 1979, Ur in altbabylonischer Zeit als Wirtschaftsfaktor, in Lipiński, E. (ed.), *State and Temple Economy in the Ancient Near East 1–2*, Leuven, Departement Oriëntalistik, 257–409.

Calnek, E. E., 1974, The Sahagún texts as a source of sociological information, in Edmonson, M. S. (ed.), *Sixteenth Century Mexico: The Work of Sahagún*, Albuquerque, University of New Mexico Press, 189–204.

Calnek, E. E., 1978a, El sistema del mercado de Tenochtitlán, in Carrasco, P., and Broda, J. (eds.), *Economia Política e Ideología en el México Prehispánico*, México, Editorial Nueva Imagen, 97–114.

Calnek, E. E., 1978b, The city–state in the basin of Mexico: late pre-Hispanic period, in Schaedel, R., Hardoy, J., and Kinzer, N. (eds.), *Urbanisation in the Americas from Its Beginnings to the Present*, The Hague, Mouton, 463–470.

Carrasco, P., 1978, La economía del México prehispánico, in Carrasco, P., and Broda, J., (eds.), *Economía Política e Ideología en el México Prehispánico*, Mexico, Editorial Nuena Imagen, 15–76.

Chapman, A., 1957, Port of trade enclaves in Aztec and Mayan civilization, in Polanyi, K., Arensberg, C., and Pearson, H. W. (eds.), *Trade and Market in the Early Empires*, New York, The Free Press, 114–153.

Cook, S., 1976, The "market" as location and transaction: dimensions of marketing in a Zapotec stoneworking industry, in Cook, S., and Diskin, M. (eds.), *Markets in Oaxaca*, Austin, University of Texas Press, 139–168.

Dalton, G., and Bohannan, P. (eds.), 1962, *Markets in Africa*, Evanston, Ill., Northwestern University Press.

Diakonoff, I. M., 1971, On the structure of Old Babylonian society, in Klengel, H. (ed.), *Beiträge zur sozialen Struktur des alten Vorderasien*, Schriften zur Geschichte und Kultur des alten Orients 1, Berlin, Akademie Verlag, 15–31.

Diaz del Castillo, B., 1960, *Historia Verdadera de la Conquista de la Nueva España*, México, Editorial Porrúa.

DiPeso, C. C., 1974, *Casas Grandes: A Fallen Trading Center of the Gran Chichimeca*, Draggon and Flagstaff, Ariz., The Amerind Foundation and Northland Press.

Durán, D., 1971, *Book of the Gods and Rites and the Ancient Calendar*, edited and translated by Horcasitas, F., and Heyden, D., Norman, University of Oklahoma Press.

Dobb, M. 1963, *Studies in the Development of Capitalism*, London, Routledge and Kegan Paul.

Edzard, D. O., 1976, "Soziale Reformen" im Zweistromland, in Harmatta, J., and Komoróczy, G. (eds.), *Wirtschaft und Gesellschaft im alten Vorderasien*, Budapest, Akadémiai Kiadó, 145–156.

Falkenstein, A., 1954, La cité–temple sumériènne, *Journal of World History* 1, 784–814.

Farber, H., 1978, A price and wage study for northern Babylonia during the Old Babylonian period, *Journal of the Economic and Social History of the Orient* 21, 1–51.

Foster, B. A., 1977, Commercial activity in Sargonic Mesopotamia, *Iraq* 39, 31–43.

Garelli, P., 1977, Marchands et *tamkārū* assyriens en Cappadoce, *Iraq* 39, 99–107.

Garibay, K., A., 1961, *Vida económica de Tenochtitlán,* Textos de los Informantes Indigenas de Sahagún 3, México, Universidad Nacional Autónoma de México.

Gelb, I. J., 1979, Household and family in early Mesopotamia, in Lipiński, E. (ed.), *State and Temple Economy in the Ancient Near East* 1–2, Leuven, Department Oriëntalistik, 1–97.

Gibson, C., 1964, *The Aztecs under Spanish Rule: A History of the Indians of the Valley of Mexico 1519–1810, Stanford,* Stanford University Press.

Gledhill, J., 1978, Formative development in the North American Southwest, in Green, D., Hazelgrove, C., and Spriggs, M. (eds.), *Social Organisation and Settlement,* Oxford, British Archaeological Reports, 241–290.

Gledhill, J., 1981a, Time's arrow, *Critique of Anthropology* 16, 3–30.

Gledhill, J., 1981b, Towns, haciendas and yeomen: class relations and agrarian change in the Bajio region of Mexico, *Bulletin of Latin American Research,* I, 1, 63–80.

Gledhill, J., in press, The transformation of Asiatic formations, in Spriggs, M. (ed.), *Marxist Perspectives in Archaeology,* Cambridge, Cambridge University Press.

Gledhill, J., and Rowlands, M. J., in press, Materialism and socio-economic process in multilinear evolution, in Renfrew, C., and Shennan, S. (eds.), *Ranking, Resources and Exchange,* Cambridge, Cambridge University Press.

Hindess, B., and Hirst, P. Q., 1975, *Pre-Capitalist Modes of Production,* London, Routledge and Kegan Paul.

Humphreys, S. C., 1978, *Anthropology and the Greeks,* London, Routledge and Kegan Paul.

Islamoğlu, H., and Keyder, C., 1977, Agenda for Ottoman history, *Review* I, 1, 31–55.

Kay, G., 1975, *Development and Underdevelopment: A Marxist Analysis,* London, Macmillan.

Katz, F., 1966, *Situación social y económica de los aztecas durante los siglos XV y XVI* México, Universidad Nacional Autónoma de México, Instituto de Investigaciones Históricas.

Klengel, H., 1971, Soziale Aspekte der altbabylonischen Dienstmiete, in Klengel, H. (ed.), *Beiträge zur sozialen Struktur des alten Vorderasien,* Schriften zur Geschichte und Kultur des alten Orients 1, Berlin, Akademie Verlag 39–52.

Kraus, F. R., 1979, Der "Palast," Produzent und Unternehmer im Königreiche Babylon nach Hammurabi (ca. 1750–1600 v. Chr.), in Lipiński E. (ed.), *State and Temple Economy in the Ancient Near East* 1–2, Leuven, Department Orientalistik, 423–434.

Landsberger, B., 1925, *Assyrische Handelskolonien in Kleinasien aus dem dritten Jahrtausend, Der Alte Orient* 24/4, Leipzig, J. C. Hinrichs.

Larsen, M. T. 1967, *Old Assyrian Caravan Procedures,* Istanbul, Nederlands Historisch–Archaeologisch Instituut.

Larsen, M. T., 1976, *The Old Assyrian City–State and Its Colonies, Mesopotamia* 4, Copenhagen, Akademisk Forlag.

Larsen, M T., 1977, Partnerships in the Old Assyrian trade, *Iraq* 39, 119–145.

Larsen, M. T., 1979, The tradition of empire in Mesopotamia, in Larsen, M T., (ed.), *Power and Propaganda, a Symposium on Ancient Empires, Mesopotamia* 7, Copenhagen, Akademisk Forlag, 75–103.

Leemans, W. F., 1950, *The Old-Babylonian Merchant,* Leiden, E. J., Brill.

Leemans, W. F., 1960, *Foreign Trade in the Old-Babylonian Period,* Leiden, E. J. Brill.

Leemans, W. F., 1968, Old Babylonian letters and economic history, *Journal of the Economic and Social History of the Orient* 11, 171–226.

Leemans, W. F., 1977, The importance of trade, *Iraq* 39, 1–10.

Lipiński, E. (ed.), 1979, *State and Temple Economy in the Ancient Near East* 1–2, Leuven, Departement Oriëntalistik.

Liverani, M., 1978, Non-slave labour in Syria (Bronze Age), in *Seventh International Economic History Congress* 1978, Theme B4, Ancient History, 191–98.

Margulis, M., 1979, *Contradicciones en la estructura agraria y transferencias de valor,* México, El Colegio de México.

Marx, K., 1959, *Capital* 3, Moscow, Progress Publishers.

Marx, K., 1973, *Grundrisse*, Harmondsworth, Penguin Books.

Moulder, F. V., 1977, *Japan, China and the Modern World Economy*, Cambridge, Cambridge University Press.

Neumann, H., 1979, Handel und Händler in der Zeit der III. Dynastie von Ur, *Altorientalische Forschungen* 6, 15–67.

Oppenheim, A. L., 1964, *Ancient Mesopotamia: Portrait of a Dead Civilization*, Chicago, University of Chicago Press.

Oppenheim, A. L., 1969, Mesopotamia—and of many cities, in Lapidus, I. M. (ed.), *Middle Eastern Cities*, Berkeley, University of California Press, 3–18.

Polanyi, K., 1944, *The Great Transformation*, Boston, Beacon Press.

Polanyi, K., 1968, *Primitive, Archaic and Modern Economies: Essays of Karl Polanyi*, edited by George Dalton, Boston, Beacon Press.

Polanyi, K., 1977, *The Livelihood of Man*, New york, Academic Press.

Polanyi, K., Arensberg, C., and Pearson, H. W. (eds.), 1957, *Trade and Market in the Early Empires: Economies in History and Theory*, New York, The Free Press.

Powell, M. A. 1977, Sumerian merchants and the problem of profit, *Iraq* 39, 23–39.

Reade, J. E., 1973, Tell Taya (1972–1973): summary report, *Iraq* 35, 155–187.

Renger, J., 1979, Interaction of temple, palace, and private enterprise in the Old Babylonian economy, in Lipiński, E., (ed.), *State and Temple Economy in the Ancient Near East* 1–2, Leuven, Department Oriëntalistik, 249–256.

Riley, C. L., and Hendrick, B. C., (eds.) 1978, *Across the Chichimec Sea*, Carbondale, Southern Illinois University Press.

Riley, G. M., 1978, El prototipo de la hacienda en el centro de México: un caso del siglo XVI, in Florescano, E. (ed.), *Haciendas, Latifundios y Plantaciones en America Latina*, México, Siglo Veintiuno Editores, 49–70.

Röllig, W., 1976, Der altmesopotamische Markt, *Welt des Orients* 8, 286–295.

Sabloff, J. A., and Rathje, W. L., 1975, *A Study of Changing Pre-Columbian Commercial Systems*, Monographs of the Peabody Museum 3, Cambridge, Mass., Harvard University.

Sanders, W. T., Parsons, J. R., and Santley, R. S., 1979, *The Basin of Mexico*, New York, Academic Press.

Sahagún, B. de, 1950–1969, *Florentine Codex: General History of the Things of New Spain*, edited and translated by Anderson, J. O, and Dibble, C. E., Santa Fe, School of American Research and University of Utah.

Schneider, H. K., 1974, *Economic Man: The Anthropology of Economics*, New York, The Free Press.

Stone, E. C., 1977, Economic crisis and social upheaval in Old Babylonian Nippur, in Buccellati, G. (ed.), *Mountains and Lowlands: Essays in the Archaeology of Greater Mesopotamia*, Bibliotheca Mesopotamica 7, Malibu, Undena Press, 267–289.

Veenhof, K. R., 1972, *Aspects of Old Assyrian Trade and Its Terminology*, Leiden, E. J. Brill.

Wallerstein, I., 1974, *The Modern World System*, New York, Academic Press.

Weber, M., 1951, *The Religion of China*, edited by Gerth, H. H., New York, The Free Press.

Wheatley, P., 1971, *The Pivot of the Four Quarters*, Edinburgh, The University Press.

Wittfogel, K. A., 1935, The foundations and stages of Chinese economic history, *Zeitschrift für Sozialforschung* 4, 26–58.

Zaccagnini, C., 1977, The merchant at Nuzi, *Iraq* 39, 171–189.

Zorita, A. de, 1963, *Life and Labour in Ancient Mexico*, New Brunswick, N.J., Rutgers University Press.

# 14

# "Civilization," "Society," and "Anomaly" in Amazonia

*STEPHEN L. NUGENT*

The ethnography of lowland South American societies has been remarkably consistent in concentrating on the classic anthropological unit of analysis—the *tribe*. Although an increasingly elaborate theoretical apparatus has been brought to bear in recent work (C. Hugh-Jones 1979, S. Hugh-Jones 1979, Maybury-Lewis 1979), the basic concern has been to analyze the itnernal organization, leaving as unanswerable more general questions about the overall character of preconquest relations between what are now treated as discrete tribal units. Ethnographic particularism has not been complemented by parallel accounts of historical development in lowland South America, largely on the grounds that there is inadequate archaeological evidence (Basso 1973, vii, Sanders and Marino 1970, 50). The general account of such societies is presented in the form of taxonomies, frequently contradictory, that are based on linguistic or culture-type criteria (Dole *et al.* 1967, Steward 1946–1963).

The point I wish to make in this chapter is that the tendency to view the tribe as an adequate unit of analysis is mystifying, and that the grounds upon which archaeological and anthropological models have been treated as incommensurable—with the result that historical explanation in anthropology is suppressed—are insufficient.

The academic division of labor that has dictated that archeologists concentrate on South American "civilizations" and social anthropologists focus on "tribes" has led to the durable highlands–lowlands typology from which

**231**

THEORY AND EXPLANATION
IN ARCHAEOLOGY

a great number of contrasts are generated: centralized states–acephalous political groups, domestication–hunting and gathering, markets–nonmarkets, and so on (Sanders and Marino 1970, 45). If one looks at the basis upon which this dichotomous organization of archaeological and anthropological objects rests, it is possible to raise serious objections to a number of underlying common sense assumptions. These assumptions, which are the grounds upon which the highlands–lowlands distinction is perpetuated, include the depiction of lowland society as consisting of noncohesive social units with, at best, restricted trade relations (Radin 1969, 115), a homogeneous environment in which the even distribution of natural products discouraged trade (Willey 1962, 9), and a low population density and low absolute population resulting from the absence of agricultural–horticultural practices (Rosenblatt 1954, 103).

In the case of the first of these assumptions, work by Lathrap (1968, 25) has suggested that the fragmentary character of forest groups is perhaps attributable to their being "the degraded descendants of peoples who at one time maintained an advanced form of tropical forest culture" (cf. Ekholm and Friedman 1980). The implication of this hypothesis is quite clear: Anthropological practice that treats contemporary tribes as survivals of formations that antedated European colonization is ignoring the possibility that these tribes represent particular— and regressive—transformations within a much larger system. I shall return to Lathrap's argument, but for the moment it is sufficient to point out that the extensiveness of trade networks in preconquest Amazonia substantially undercuts the notion that the tribal object may be considered in terms of its internal dynamic alone.

The assumption of a homogeneous environment, with its implications for uniformity of access to natural products, is similarly problematic. If anything, the work of botanists and ecologists such as Richards (1952) and Goodland and Irwin (1975) suggests exactly the opposite: The distribution of plant and animal species is sporadic rather than even. Thus a local community's access to resources is certain to be limited. The natural setting, far from constraining the development of trade, would appear to provide the necessary conditions for flourishing trade (Lathrap 1973). Characterization of the lowland environment as homogeneous is only adequate when contrasted with the highlands.

The differences among estimates of preconquest aboriginal populations are large. Figures as low as 500,000 for Amazonia are frequently cited (Moran 1974, 137), yet recent work would suggest that a figure of at least 6,000,000 is more realistic (Denevan 1976, 232). The demographic implications of the highlands–lowlands typology and its attendant faults are well illustrated in Rosenblatt's arguments (1954). He argues that agricultural modes of existence imply large populations and the emergence of state formations. The formulation is innocuous enough, but the characterization of lowland societies that results is one in which hunting and gathering are predominant. It follows, according to Rosenblatt, that lack of agriculture in the lowlands leads to nomadism, low population density, and low absolute population. As Clastres (1977) has argued in criticizing Rosenblatt (1954) and using the Tupi–Guarani as his main example, the relative significance of agriculture was greater than that of either hunting or gathering. Population density was considerably higher than Rosenblatt's arguments would allow, and sedentary groups were by no means exceptional. In other words, the necessary conditions for the emergence of states—in Rosenblatt's argument—did exist in the lowlands; hence the attempt to account for their nonemergence on environmentally determinist grounds cannot hold.

I have discussed these three general assumptions not because they can be refuted easily but because they are more contentious than practical. They seem, particularly, to have had a profoundly regressive influence in shaping the character of subsequent research. This is most marked in ecologically oriented studies. Meggers (1971, 1977), for example, has offered a number of ecologically reductionist models of social adaptation that are more ethological than sociological in implication. Gross (1975) has similarly tried to argue that social evolution can be explained by reference to "natural scarcities"—in this case scarcities of animal proteins. This tendency to subsume lowland societies under nature is carried on in contemporary development literature concerning Amazonia (e.g., Goodland and Irwin 1975) where the issue seems to be one of "resource allocation," and in the policies of the Brazilian government toward the remaining aborigines—policies in which Indian societies are treated as virtual aspects of the Amazonian forest. If anthropologists and archaeologists have too readily assumed an uncritical and ahistorical position vis-à-vis preconquest Amazonian societies, historians have not changed matters. Even such authors as MacLachlan (1973)—whose analysis of Jesuit archives is one of the few serious considerations of official Indian policy in Amazonia during the early years of conquest—employ anthropological assumptions based on a characterization of scattered, fragmentary groups whose retrograde position is attributable to the paucity of material resources.

The limitations of current models purporting to offer explanations about the general features of social evolution in Amazonia have implications that go beyond consideration of the adequacy of scholarship within the scientific community. The functionalist emphasis typical of lowland ethnography is based on an ideal typification that at the very least is higly problematic. The results of the hegemony of this type of explanation when applied to contemporary non-Indian Amazonian societies are depressing. Accounts of contemporary peasantries that—if the word *Indian* were substituted for *peasant*— have a remarkably similar ethnographic format bear the same incorrect message: Scattered primitive hunters, gatherers, and horticulturalists are obliged by the vicissitudes of nature to disperse through the tropical forest and scratch a bare living. By considering the ways in which these idealized societies (precolonial aboriginal, postcolonial aboriginal, and peasant) were actually articulated in larger reproductive totalities, it is possible to call into question a number of common-sense assumptions and suggest that the distinction between highland and lowland societies obscures more than it reveals.

One way of considering in general terms the grounds upon which archaeological and anthropological models of lowland societies might be located conjointly is by looking at what each type of practice is trying to explain.

Archaeological explanation that depends on a data base that is comparable, for example, to that available for highland civilizations is frustrated in dealing with lowland sites (Sanders and Marino 1970, 50, 84, 89, Lathrap 1973, 176). The paucity of material evidence for tropical forest cultures is not, however, a realistic obstacle. It is simply a constraint on conventional archaeological practice. If one looks at Palmatary's work with the Tapajós collections (1960), for instance, it is quite clear that there is a lot of data—however poorly chronicled the information on the sites is and however limited are the prospects for further excavation. Nonetheless, what is known about the material recovered in Santarém is highly suggestive of hypotheses of the same order as that put forward by Lathrap concerning the extensiveness of precolonial trade networks (1968, 1973). The staple crop of the Tapajós was corn, not manioc; they used burial urns; there was extensive pottery manufacture and use of ceramic products not locally manufactured; and the use of nonpulverized sponges as clay-tempering elements indicates advanced pottery techniques (Palmatary 1960, 28). These bits of evidence alone are enough to suggest that the portrayal of preconquest societies in the region of lower Amazonia as nomadic hunters and gatherers is quite fallacious. Archaeological neglect of the region is a consequence of a general approach that requires that the "evidence" be of a highly restrictive type—that it be "evidence" that justifies the model employed.

Lowland ethnography has largely been concerned with salvage work: "Do" the ethnographies before the tribes disappear entirely. Accompanying this has been the effort at constructing taxonomies (e.g., Dole et al. 1973), again to organize what relatively little material—by comparison with Africa, for instance—was available. The taxonomic exercise took as granted a number of concepts that have tended to reify the notion of *tribe* as the unit of analysis for anthropology. The concept of "culture group," for example, at different times related to linguistic stocks or culture traits, steered research away from historical considerations. Early accounts of aboriginal societies have with few exceptions (e.g., MacLachlan 1973) been ignored, and accounts, for example, of large population densities have been casually dismissed (cf. Clastres 1977, Palmatary 1960). Heriarte's claims, for instance, that the Tapajós tribe that occupied the current site of Santarém do Pará could muster 60,000 warriors is invariably dismissed as unthinkable (cf. Nimuendajú 1949), Yet as Clastres (1977), Denevan (1976), and, by implication, Lathrap (1973) have tried to argue, there is no reason not to accept these figures as realistic—if not conservative. The main reason for ignoring such figures is that they call into question the ideal typification of the "Amazonia tribe." In the same way that "inadequate" data are disallowed by archaeologists on the grounds of being insufficient for supplying anything approaching a total picture of prehistoric societies, so have anthropologists rejected data that do not fit their models that are restricted to accounting for the internal dynamics of tribal social formations.

The appearance of *Dialectical Societies* (Maybury-Lewis 1979), a volume devoted to the Gê and Bororo of Central Brazil, a major ethnographic anomaly—rudimentary technology–elaborate social structure—has been seen by some to mark the coming of age of lowland ethnography (Rivière 1980). The grounds for this coming-of-age claim, however, are interesting in light of the tribal ideal type. The claim is not that there has been a reorientation of anthropolitical interests, only that the apparent anomalies of Gê social structure have been demystified by the volume's authors. That is, the anomalous features of Gê society are still firmly situated within a problematic in which the institutional focus is stressed. The coming of age of lowland ethnography is apparently a vindication of a traditional and eminently functionalist approach, but the major anomaly remains, and it is not the question, How do these societies function? Rather it is (given that they are defined as anomalous in relation to other tribes in the region), How did they come to differ so much from other tribes? While the work in *Dialectical Societies* (Maybury-Lewis 1979) is a significant comparative treatment of an interesting puzzle, it avoids locating the puzzle in a framework any larger than that that defines the narrowly ethnographic. Suggestions such as those of Zuidema (1962), Lévi-Strauss (1963), and Haeckel (1939) that the anomoly of Gê society may be traced to its involvement in a larger system are not seriously considered. The alternative explanation that the Gê anomaly is expressive of connections with the Inca civilization is one that by implication abolishes the notion of "tribe" as anything more than an artifact of anthropological discourse. And in *Dialectical Societies,* it receives the curt comment that "such learned speculations seem, to the writers of this volume, somewhat strained" (Maybury-Lewis 1979, 2). Gross (1979), whose own analysis of the anomaly is based on ecological teleology (Gross 1979, 330), is similarly brief in his treatment of the Gê–Inca connection: "But these explanations have not been supported with evidence, and fittingly, they have gained few adherents."

What is actually strained, however, is the notion that the boundaries of Gê society should be accepted as given by the ethnographers. To take an obvious problem: There is no neat fit between Gê language and Gê "social structure." Thus the Nambikwara and/or Bororo may or may not fit within the Gê "anomaly". Meggers's (1977, 298) analysis of linguistic distributions in relation to the periodic shrinking of the tropical forest has shown that there is no relation between culture-group areas and language (cf. Dole *et al.* 1973), nor is there any obvious connection between culture areas and refugia. It seems difficult in light of this to deal with the "Gê" as though the unit of analysis for explaining the anomalous features; that is, for arguing that the internal dynamic of the Gê bears only on the functioning of contemporary tribes.

There are two assumptions involved here that deserve attention, and these are common to both archaeological and social anthropological traditions of the region. One is that contemporary aboriginal societies are directly comparable to antecedent formations. Myers, for example, in writing about ceramic change in the upper Amazon says that "the Amazon Basin still contains large numbers of native peoples who are living in very much the same way that their ancestors lived thousands of years ago" (1976, 333). Hence, the argument seems to go, when one studies a contemporary Indian society, one is in effect studying a primordial one. There is no history.

The second assumption is that the relations among contemporary aboriginal societies are comparable to those that prevailed in prehistory. This assumption is not supported by evidence; it is sustained by lack of evidence to the contrary (cf. Sanders and Marino 1970, 50, 84, 89). Hence, we find today that aboriginal societies are fragmented, largely interior-dwelling, have low levels of technology, absence of state formation, and are to a great degree self-sufficent, reacting to territorial incursions with aggression. The common-sense assumption is that this is simply as far as they evolved (Lathrap 1968, 25).

The characterizations of preconquest and contemporary aboriginal societies most often presented in the literature are largely negative ones: By insisting on the putative backwardness of such societies, any question of historical process appears redundant. Because these societies didn't evolve—so the general argument goes—what has to be explained is how they functioned at all. Thus the overriding emphasis that appears in the work of Amazonianists, especially under the influence of Steward, is on *adaptation*. The environment is harsh, it is claimed, and it is only the mediation offered by culture that permitted the endurance of these aborigines. This early negative characterization predisposed analysis to be ahistorical and to focus on the institutional aspects to which functionalism has so assiduously applied itself.

Lathrap's discussion of the possible ways of dealing with problems raised in considering preconquest aboriginal societies in Amazonia is important in two respects: The conventional distinctions between the anthropological and archaeological objects are ignored giving rise to a view that stresses the possible historical relations between lowland and highland societies rather than succumbing to what is fundamentally a geographical distinction. Second, Lathrap's discussion is explicitly based on an hypothesis that can be examined without the usual constraint so often cited in the archaeological discussions of the lowlands—lack of an adequate database.

Lathrap's suggestion that contemporary tribes are best seen as "degraded descendants" of an advanced tropical forest culture is supported by the work of Denevan (1976) and Clastres (1977). Not only was there a higher absolute population than is frequently cited, but there were significant centers of population that were systematically linked through trade. Lathrap offers two models of outward migration that depend on rather different premises. In one of these, population pressure on the river plains forced groups into less-productive forest areas (1968, 28). The argument is not terribly rigorous, but it does offer a credible periodization and a rationale for plains occupation—namely, increased agricultural output in the service of expanding trade. The scarcity of soils sufficient to maintain large sedentary populations on the plains leads to the fragmentation of groups as they are pushed into the forest. This process might account for differentiation of tribes, on the one hand, and it might account for the predominance of the stereotypical contemporary tribe—interior hunter-gatherers relying on slash-and-burn horticulture. Since colonial penetration was along waterways, riverine-based tribes (i.e., the largest and most politically dominant) were the first to succumb. Those already occupying the relatively inaccessible forest endured. The latter, then, are the survivals of two processes: a phase of aboriginal conquest and a phase of colonial conquest.

With regard to the way in which different preconquest groups were integrated, Lathrap cites Sahlins's model of reciprocal trade networks in which groups occupying the middle positions are at an advantage because a given trade good is more likely to pass through the middle than at either end. Thus, groups at the ends are striving for a middle position by finding specialty goods available only from an outside neighbor, and not yet included in the system. As Sahlins (1972, 294) says, "Thus the system propogates itself at its extremities by a simple extension of reciprocity." The model is appropriate for Amazonia where river routes do constrain trade in a linear fashion. The eclecticism of artifact collections recovered in Santarém, for example, is reflective of Santarém's middle position on the Amazon River itself and of its being at the mouth of the Tapajós River, which extends far south into Mato Grosso. Lathrap cites trade networks with far fewer central positions that extended for distances of more than 1000 miles (1973, 172), particularly those analyzed by Roth (1924).

Perhaps the strongest part of Lathrap's argument concerns the specificity of trade goods—that is, food on the one hand and preciosities on the other. The existence of an apparatus whose function is the *provisioning* of trade expeditions permits a strong argument for the centrality of trade in systematic links between disparate groups. The critical argument here concerns the rationale for the production of bitter manioc. Manioc does not store well unless it is converted into flour. On the other hand, the tubers can remain in the ground for long periods (up to two years) before harvesting (i.e., there need not be a storage problem. In view of the great labor intensity involved in processing tubers into flour, it is difficult to explain why such processing of surplus manioc would occur, given local levels of consumption, except that increased production represents "an intensification of activity within these trade networks" (Lathrap 1973, 173). The widespread occurrence of griddles, whose only function is the preparation of manioc flour, leads Lathrap to argue that "manioc flour was providing the key commodity in trade networks at a very early time" (1973, 175).

Among other evidence for the extensiveness of regular trade networks are ceramic tempering materials in lower Amazonia that could only have come from outside the region since they are volcanic in origin; the distribution of piranha mandibles in preceramic decoration; habitual use of forest products (e.g., coca) in areas where these are not grown; and so on (Lathrap 1973, 176–181). The prominent position within the Inca tribute system of mature specimens of such lowland beasts as anaconda and crocodiles is something of particular interest inasmuch as Zuidema's analysis of the *ceque* system of Cuzco bears directly on certain "anomalous" features of the Gê.

From archaeological and anthropological points of view, a reconsideration of the basis upon which the separation of South American societies into highland and lowland entities came about seems not to be of interest. For archaeologists there is insufficient evidence to warrant a reconsideration. For anthropologists a reconsideration is too speculative, but what evidence there is for social systems that embrace both highlands and lowlands—however bedraggled it may at times appear—cannot be ignored simply because it does not fit the respective disciplinary limits on what can be accomodated within a model. The stereotype of Amazonian hunting, gathering, and swidden societies is a mystification. It is a mystification not only in terms of its being an inadequate example of precolonial social formations, but what is more important, it is inadequate as a starting point for an analysis of what underlies the typological separation of the problem into *highland civilizations* and *lowland societies*. It is important to emphasize the long-term effects of the domination of this view of precolonial South America because of its influence on analysis of contemporary non-Indian societies. In Brazil, for instance, the policies of the government toward Indians and peasantries have never been particularly enlightened. Current development policies in Amazonia treat the region as a natural preserve that is to be managed, as it were, by the patrimonial state. Indians are objects of nature in practice. Their destiny is either the reservation with its notoriously permeable boundaries or eradication—a process some would argue has virtually been effected. The position of the anthropological model is curious. History doesn't have to be written in order to lend scientific support to these development policies (cf. Davis 1977). The history has yet to be written. The civilization that gave birth to barbarism by discovering the savage has still not seen fit to locate the Amazonian savage in society rather than in nature.

The peasant in anthropological literature on Amazonia is structurally the same as the deceased Indian. The alleged backwardness of the peasant is seen as deriving from the peasant's reliance on indigenous economic forms (Alcarde 1962)—the economy of the tame wild man (*economía de bugre manso*). Just as the history of the aborigines has notable gaps, so does that of the modern Amazonian settler. Just as the savage is conventionally regarded as having been isolated from the more general tendencies of historical process in South America, so is the contemporary peasant treated as external to the development of the modern nation–state. These marginalizing developments cannot be wholly attributed to social-science practice, but the antihistorical and parcelized tendencies cannot be said to have ameliorated the situtation.

# REFERENCES

Alcarde, H. H., 1962, *O Caboclo "Indolente" e as Riquezas da Amazonia*, Belem.
Basso, E., 1973, *The Kalapalo Indians of Central Brazil*, New York, Holt, Rinehart & Winston.
Clastres, P., 1977, *Society against the State*, Oxford, Basil Blackwell.
Davis, S., 1977, *Victims of the Miracle*, Cambridge, Cambridge University Press.
Denevan, W. (ed.), 1976, *The Native Population of the Americas in 1492*, Madison, University of Wisconsin Press.
Dole, G. *et al.*, 1967, *Indians of Brazil in the 20th Century*, Washingon, D. C., Institute for Cross-Cultural Research.
Ekholm, K., and Friedman, J., 1980, Towards a global anthropology, in Blusse, L., Wesseling, H. L., Winius, G. D. (eds.), *History and Underdevelopment*, Leiden, Leiden Center for the History of European Expansion.
Goodland, R., and Irwin, H., 1975, *Amazon Jungle: Green Hell to Red Desert?*, Amsterdam and Oxford, Elsevier.
Gross, D., 1975, Protein capture and cultural development in the Amazon basin, *American Anthropologist* 77, 537–549.
Gross, D., 1979, Central Brazilian social organization, in Margolis, M., and Carter, W. (eds.), *Brazilian Anthropological Perspectives*, New York, Columbia University Press.
Haeckel, J., 1939, Zweiklassensystem, Männerhaus und Totemismus in Südamerika, *Zeitschrift für Ethnologie* 70, 426–454.
Hugh-Jones, C., 1979, *From the Milk River: Spatial and Temporal Processes in Northwest Amazonia*, Cambridge University Press.
Hugh-Jones, S., 1979, *The Palm and the Pleiades: Initiation and Cosmology in Northwest Amazonia*, Cambridge, Cambridge University Press.
Lathrap, D., 1969, The "hunting" economies of the tropical forest zone of South America: an attempt at historical perspective, in Lee, R., and Devore, I. (eds.), *Man the Hunter*, Chicago, Aldine.
Lathrap, D., 1973, The antiquity and importance of long-distance trade relationships in the moist tropics of pre-Columbian south America, *World Archaeology* 5, 2, 170–186.
Lévi-Strauss, C., 1963, The concept of archaism in anthropology, in *Structural Anthropology I*, London, Penguin Books.
MacLachlan, C., 1973, The Indian labor structure in the Portuguese Amazon, in Alden, D. (ed.), *The Colonial Roots of Modern Brazil*, Berkeley, Los Angeles, and London, University of California Press.
Maybury-Lewis, D. (ed.), 1979, *Dialectical Societies*, Cambridge, Mass., and London, Harvard University Press.
Meggers, B., 1971, *Amazonia: Man and Culture in a Counterfeit Paradise*, Chicago, Aldine.
Meggers, B., 1977, Vegetational fluctuation and prehistoric cultural adaptation in Amazonia: some tentative correlations, *World Archaeology* 8, 3, 287–303.
Moran, E., 1974, The adaptive system of the Amazonian *caboclo*, in Wagley, C. (ed.), *Man in the Amazon*, Gainesville, University Presses of Florida.
Myers, T., 1976, Isolation and ceramic change: a case from the Ucayali River, Peru, *World Archaeology* 7, 3, 333–351.
Nimuendajú, C., 1949, Os Tapajós, *Boletim do Museu Paraense Emilio Goeldi* 10, Belém.

Palmatary, H., 1960, The archaeology of the lower Tapajós, *Transactions of the American Philosophical Society* n. s., 50, 3.

Radin, P., 1969, *Indians of South America*, New York, Greenwood.

Richards, P., 1952, *The Tropical Rain Forest*, Cambridge, Cambridge University Press.

Rivière, P., 1980, Dialectical societies, *Man* 15, 3, 533–540.

Rosenblatt, A., 1954, *La Población Indígena y el Mestizaje en Amèrica*, Buenos Aires.

Roth, W., 1924, An introductory study of the arts, crafts, and customs of the Guiana indians, *Thirty-Eighth Annual Report of the Bureau of American Ethnology*, Washington, D.C.

Sahlins, M., 1972, *Stone-age Economics*, London, Tavistock.

Sanders, W., and Marino, J., 1970, *New World Prehistory*, Englewood Cliffs, N.J., Prentice-Hall.

Steward, J., (ed.), 1947–1963, *Handbook of South American Indians*, 7 volumes, Washington, D. C., Smithsonian Institution.

Willey, G., 1962, The early great styles and the rise of the pre-Columbian civilizations, *American Anthropologist*, 64, 1–14.

Zuidema, R., 1962, *The Ceque System of Cuzco: The Social Organization of the Capital of the Inca*, unpublished doctoral dissertation, University of Leiden.

# 15

# The Formation of Tribal Systems in Later European Prehistory: Northern Europe, 4000–500 B.C.

*KRISTIAN KRISTIANSEN*

## INTRODUCTION

The aim of this chapter[1] is twofold: (*a*) to model and explain long-term changes in Neolithic and Bronze Age tribal systems of northern Europe

[1] In recent years intensive research has drastically changed and added to our understanding of the Neolithic period in southern Scandinavia, and my explanation of the Neolithic production–reproduction cycle owes much to this research, part of which is not yet published. I want to thank the following persons for referring me to recent evidence, and for allowing me to cite papers not yet published: Poul Otto Nielsen, National Museum, First Department; Torsten Madsen, Institute of Prehistoric Archaeology, University of Århus; Niels Anderson, Prehistoric Museum, Moesgård, Århus; Henrik Tauber, National Museum, Eighth Department; Jørgen Troels-Smith, National Museum, Eighth Department, Bent Aaby, Geological Survey of Denmark, and Andrew Sherrat, Oxford University. For discussions and help on this chapter, I am grateful to my wife Lotte Hedeager. Figures 15.1, 15.4, 15.5, 15.6, 15.8, 15.9, 15.10 and 15.11 were drawn by Catherina Oxen.

It has not been possible to reference the vast literature on the Neolithic and the Bronze Age on which this chapter is based. I will therefore refer to a selection of recent Danish publications that cover the main topics. A reanalysis of stylistic groups in Neolithic TRB pottery has been carried out by Ebbesen (1975, 1978), Andersen and Madsen (1977), and Gebauer (1978). Flint axes have been classified by Nielsen (1977a, 1977b) and Højlund (1973–1974), settlements by Skaarup (1973) and Davidsen (1978), and causewayed camps in Andersen (1973–1974, in press). Megalithic ritual has been summarized in Daniel and Kjaerum (1973) and presented in detail by Strømberg (1971), with the most recent synthesis of premegalithic burial types in Madsen (1979). A classification of megaliths is found in Aner (1963). We are still lacking any up to date

THEORY AND EXPLANATION
IN ARCHAEOLOGY

(approximately 4000–500 B.C.) based on a regional sample (a vertical cut); and (b) to unfold and explain the dynamics of the larger tribal system based on the evidence of the Nordic Bronze Age (a horizontal cut).

Due to the scope of this venture and the limited space available, it is inevitable that I have to postulate certain premises. First, I propose that developments in the region chosen to exemplify long-term changes can be regarded as representative of main trends in the larger northern European area. Second, I propose that the Neolithic and the Bronze Age represent a long-term sequence of tribal systems that go through definite cycles and irreversible changes. Third, I propose that it is necessary therefore to establish a common frame of reference, theoretically and methodologically, in order to describe and explain their structural properties, their range of variation, and the structural changes they undergo.

As a starting point let us briefly recapitulate some trends in recent research.

Throughout the 1970s studies of Neolithic and Bronze Age social systems have significantly increased our knowledge of the relationship between settlement systems, economy, and social structure (e.g., Bradley 1972, 1977, Fleming 1971, Kristiansen 1978, 1980, Randsborg 1974, 1975, Renfrew 1973, Sherratt 1972, 1977, Welinder 1975, 1977). Such studies are, however, still rather few.[2] Widely separated in time and space, they represent a selection of static sequences between which one has to interpolate in order to reconstruct a coherent picture–and in terms of explanation this is often hampered by noncomparable methodological approaches and problems of representivity.

With respect to *theory*, the concept of tribal social organization in a prehistoric context needs elaboration badly. The traditional evolutionary framework of tribes and chiefdoms (e.g., Fried 1960, Sahlins 1968, Service 1962) seems too static and too general to account for the spatial diversity and the long-term changes of such systems in prehistory.

Another limiting factor is that much ethnographic evidence can hardly be regarded in isolation, but should rather be considered in the context of the

---

analysis of the Single Grave culture in Denmark in contrast to Sweden (Malmer 1962). Recent discussions have appeared in Lomborg (1975), Davidsen (1975), and Malmros (1979). Also the Pitted Ware culture was recently summarized in Nielsen (1979). The standard work on the Late Neolithic is still Lomborg (1973), with Jensen (1972) on settlements. With respect to the Bronze Age, see the bibliography in Kristiansen (1981), with the addition of recent research papers in Thrane (1980). Concerning vegetational development in southern Scandinavia, the standard summary is still Berglund (1969), with important additions in Andersen (1976), Göransson (1977), Welinder (1974), and Mikkelsen and Høeg (1979). Much work has been carried out in pollen analysis in recent years in all Scandinavian countries, but unfortunately most of the Danish research is still unpublished. In general the reader will find his or her own way to recent literature in *Nordic Archaeological Abstracts*.

[2]It should be added that much recent research is about to change this situation. This is reflected in Britain in several British Archaeological Reports publications (e.g., in Barret and Bradley 1980), in Scandinavia in a forthcoming volume, *Settlement, Economy and Ecology in Scandinavian Prehistory* (Kristiansen in press).

expanding world economy during the last few hundred years that both directly and indirectly may have influenced the present historical context of primitive social organization when viewed in an evolutionary perspective (Ekholm and Friedman 1980).

These limitations in the ethnographic evidence should not lead us to dismiss the significance of using general principles of social organization at various levels of complexity as an interpretative and explanatory framework from which more specific hypotheses may be deduced and tested. It should rather make us aware of the potential of the archaeological record for contributing to explaining processes of social evolution that demand both time depth and geographical scale—elements that can only be supplied by archaeology and history. Thus with respect to European prehistory, Andrew Sherratt's recent analysis of the technological, economic, and social changes that characterized the secondary products revolution is a major contribution toward understanding tribal transformations in Neolithic Europe (Sherratt 1981, also Fleming 1972). It may seem strange, then, that the rich European evidence has not invited more work along such general evolutionary lines. But the reason is probably that one is not only faced with an enormous amount of published evidence, but also with a theoretically very difficult and rather discouraging situation, when trying to explain what superficially may look like several thousand years of stagnation in traditional terms of social evolution. In comparison, the development of more complex societies in nontemperate habitats offers much more clear-cut examples of evolutionary trajectories, and most recent discussions have dealt with the explanation of such cases (e.g., Carneiro 1970, Flannery 1972, Friedman and Rowlands 1977, Sanders and Price 1968, Sanders and Webster 1978), not to mention the rich literature on the origins of the state.

In northern Europe, however, 3500 years of tribal life, from circa 4000–500 B.C., promises an opportunity to explore the structural diversity and possible long-term evolutionary trajectories of a tribal mode of production within a temperate habitat. The release of this potential, however, is not only a matter of empirical analysis. It demands the elaboration of theoretical concepts enabling us to frame and explain the evidence, a task to which we shall now turn (see Figure 15.1).

## THEORETICAL MODELS

### General Theory

Our general model will be based on the structural–Marxist notion of social reproduction, as presented by Friedman (1972–1979) and Friedman and Rowlands (1977) (see also recent discussions in *Critique of Anthropology* and in Ingold 1981). The model is defined by a set of functional categories and a set

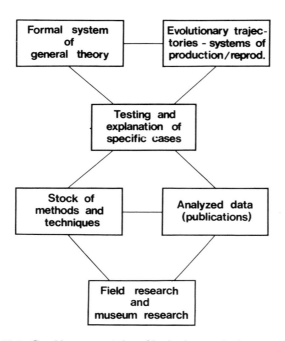

**Figure 15.1.** Graphic representation of basic elements in the research process.

of rules regarding their interrelations, which constitute a theoretical system that serves to frame and explain concrete forms of social reproduction. The structural categories are characterized by their relative autonomy, and they are linked by a variety of intra and intersystemic functions. The limits of functional compatibility within and between such structures defines the onset of contradictions.

These structural concepts are the basic theoretical tools. The object of analysis, however, is a social system, which comprises a set of productive relations that organize and dominate social reproduction. Dominant relations of production are those relations that take on these functions, whether kinship relations, religion, or any other set of institutional relations.

Working in the diverse direction, we find that the exploitation of the environment by a given social formation creates a hierarchy of constraints that determines the evolutionary potential of the system as a whole. This, however, should not lead us to postulate economic determinism, since it is the relations of production that dominate and hence determine the formation of such constraints and their impact on the course of development.

A transformation may occur when a given social system alters the economic conditions of production and thus imposes a new set of constraints on the system that are incompatible with the dominant social relations. Also, a positive altering of economic conditions and intensified production may lead to the evolution of new social formations.

The preceding implies that transformations can only be explained with reference to their previous forms. Social reproduction, however, is also a regional phenomenon distributed in space, thereby linking social units together in a larger system. Thus "the structures of the larger regional systems are determined by the dominant relations of production that make them up, e.g., the internal potential demands of local systems and the spatial distribution of constraints that determine the relative potential for development of the individual units with respect to one another. (Friedman and Rowlands 1977, 271). The crucial problem is: On what scale does evolution take place? This can only be answered by considering production and reproduction within the larger spatial framework on which it depends.

In the next section these general theoretical concepts will be applied to construct a more specific model of tribal production and reproduction.


## Specific Theory

The concept of a tribal mode of production, as applied in this chapter, is derived mainly from Sahlins (1972, 101–148) and Friedman (1975 and 1979). The basic premise is that the elementary properties of tribal production and reproduction generate a wider range of tribal variants, depending on a complex interplay between the spatial and temporal distribution of economic and ecological production. This implies that there exists a predictable and systemic relationship between spatial and temporal tribal variations as products of one or of several types of time–space cycles.

In the Friedman model, the basic production and exchange unit is the local lineage. Based on analysis of the articulation of marriage–exchange cycles and local production, it demonstrates how surplus is converted into higher status and utlimately into absolute rank through feasting and ritual (Friedman 1975, Figure 2). This analysis is then embedded in a larger time–space model of evolutionary and devolutionary cycles. The evolution–devolution cycle starts with the expansion of an "egalitarian" tribal system, which through intensified production creates extensive alliance networks. Wealth is channeled into a gradually evolving ranked system of conical clans (chiefdoms) and is sustained by ritual and chiefly mediations with the supernatural, displayed in the production and consumption of valuables. When territorial expansion can no longer take place, population increases and production is intensified, thus transforming the landscape and leading to degradation of the conditions of production. Population concentrates into larger units. Competition for rank is strongly itensified and individualized, but in the long run supralocal exchange and vertical relations gradually break down or are reduced in scale. The social

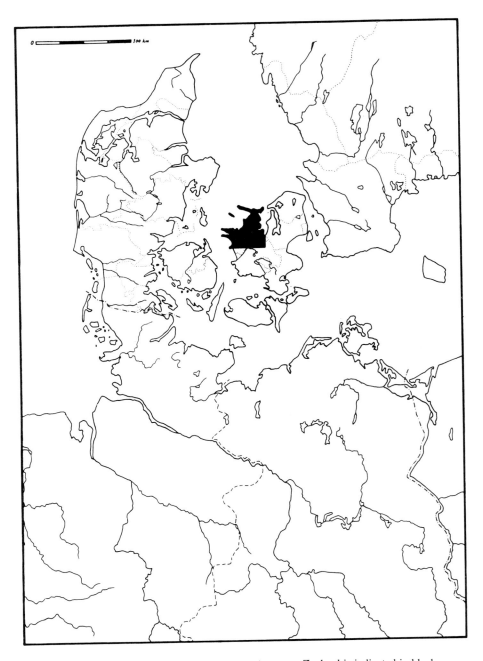

**Figure 15.2.** Map of northern Europe. Northwestern Zealand is indicated in black.

system returns to a more egalitarian level. Thus the cycle can also be described in terms of vertical and horizontal relations. The motor of the cycle is the articulation of exchange and production within an expansionist tribal economy that gradually changes the conditions of production. This imposes a new set of constraints on the social system that is gradually transformed as part of this process. A continuous contradiction between the dominant productive relations and the constraints they impose upon the productive forces determines the course of the cycle. A long-term cycle of several short-term cycles may then finally reach a point where conditions are sufficient for a transformation of the system as a whole to occur (Friedman 1975, 186, Figure 13).

The properties of the local production–exchange cycle referred to previously can never be demonstrated in the archaeological record. What can eventually be demonstrated are some of the material implications of the model on a larger time–space scale—that is, patterns of expansion–regression, settlement densities and systems of land use, degreee of and means of economic exploitation, and to some extent, systems of rank and ritual. The spatial and temporal variability of such variables may then serve as a preliminary test case for the more general aspects of the model.

Let us first turn to the temporal aspects of our model, exemplified by a long-term settlement sequence in the region of northwestern Zealand (Figure 15.2) from 4000–500 B.C.[3]

---

[3]Northwestern Zealand was intensively surveyed by field walking in the years 1948–1956 as part of a major research project carried out by the National Museum and published in 1959 (Mathiassen 1959). The aim was to achieve a representative record of all types of archaeological data in a typical East Danish environment. A similar project had earlier been carried out in a typical West Danish environment, and it was published in 1948 (Mathiassen 1948). In northwestern Zealand, approximately 2700 settlements, 3400 megalith barrows and burials, 240 hoards, and 10,000 single finds were recorded. The number of objects totaled 50,000.

The research area covers 1690 km$^2$, of late glacial moraine, mainly clay with scattered areas of more sandy clay. Clay dominated soils amount to 980 km,$^2$ sandy soils with some clay 435 km,$^2$ and moores (former lakes) more than 200 km.$^2$ The area is rather hilly and with its long coastline and inland lakes, it has attracted a dense settlement in all prehistoric periods.

A recent analysis of the impact of later surveys and excavations has confirmed that the main trends in the published data can be regarded as representative, with the exception of settlements in some areas (Thrane 1973). Neither this material nor that from Jutland has been utilized in any extensive settlement analysis, with the recent exception of Paludan-Müller (1978). With the aim of extracting some of the scientific potential of this vast amount of material, I began to computerize and analyze the raw data in 1979, primarily with the aim of testing the applicability of the land evaluations from 1688 and 1848 as a tool for settlement analysis within smaller regions compared to site catchment analysis of soil types.

In this chapter a few tentative, simple quantifications are presented, as the processing of data is not yet finished. It is presumed that the nature of the evidence is generally comparable from the EN to the LB, whereas the Iron Age marks a complete change in evidence. From EN to LB burials above the ground are common (megaliths–tumulis) in all periods, just as production of durable tools, weapons, and ornaments of flint and bronze, makes burials, hoards, and settlements easily recognizable and datable. I want to thank Bjarne Mortensen of the Niels Bohr Institute for carrying out the computer analyses.

## LONG-TERM CHANGES: NORTHWESTERN ZEALAND

Northwestern Zealand comprises most of the ecological and geographical variation found within the northern European lowland area, with the exception of the more sandy areas of northwestern Europe, to which I shall return later (see Figure 15.2). It can thus be regarded as a representative sample, both geographically and archaeologically.

The settlement history of the area is divided into five main chronological stages: Early Neolithic (EN), the period of thin-butted axes,[4] Middle Neolithic (MN) the period of thick-butted axes, Late Neolithic (LN), the dagger period, Early Bronze Age, and Late Bronze Age (EB and LB).

The Early Neolithic spans from 4100/4000—3500/3400 B.C. (in Mathiassens's terminology, from 3800/3200 B.C.), the Middle Neolithic from 3400–2400 B.C. (in Mathiassen's terminology from 3200–2400 B.C.), the Late Neolithic 2400–2300—1900 B.C., the Early Bronze Age 1900–1000 B.C. and the Late Bronze Age 1000–500 B.C. (for calibrated chronology, see in general Tauber 1972; Nielsen 1977a and Malmros and Tauber 1975).

### Settlement Structure and Subsistence Strategy

Overall changes in settlement patterns are demonstrated in Figure 15.3. The EN shows a rather dispersed pattern that can be regarded as an extension of the Late Mesolithic settlement base expanding from both the lakes in the interior and from the coastal areas (Paludan-Müller 1978). During the MN the interior was thinned out and some settlement concentrations occurred. Then in the LN the shift from inland to coast was completed, and settlement concentrations became a regular phenomenon—a tendency that continued during the Bronze Age (BA). During this period the interior was nearly empty, and settlement concentrations on the coast increased.

These trends in settlement patterns can be further illuminated by grouping the evidence as has been done in Figure 15.4 which shows degrees of settlement density (increasing from left to right) and numbers of geographical units (parishes) on the vertical axis. It demonstrates a gradual tendency toward settlement differentiation. The EN is characterized by gradual variations in degree of settlement density, which conforms well with a more dispersed settlement pattern, although it is rather dense. During the MN, several areas became less densely settled in the process of settlement displacement from the interior toward the coast, and settlement differentiation increased. This process finally achieved stability during the LN and the EB, and it was further differentiated in the LB.

---

[4]In Mathiassen's terminology, the EN (period of thin butted axes) composes what is today classified as EN BC to MN I, which dates from 3700–3200 B.C.

If we accept these gross tendencies as a starting point, several things can be predicted, among them increased exploitation of the environment within the more densely settled areas (and forest recovery in the less densely settled areas), changes in the organization of the economy in order to feed more people in smaller areas, and probably also changes in social organization.

Changes in subsistence strategy are demonstrated in Figure 15.5 and 15.6, using barrels of hard corn (htk) as indicators of the productive potential of a given area (parishes are used as areal units). The more hectares (ha) per barrel of hard corn, the less productive is a given area, and vice versa (for a general explanation of these concepts, see Kristiansen 1978, Note 9). Naturally this parameter can only indicate very general tendencies, and it is therefore most suitable for analyses and comparisons of larger areas (e.g., Randsborg 1974, Kristiansen 1978). In our small region, however, some general trends can be observed, which should then later be specified and tested by site catchment analysis.

Compared to the overall productive potential (PP) of northern Zealand, the Early Neolithic subsistence strategy seems to have been selective, the inhabitants preferring the most productive soil. Thus from EN A (4000 B.C.) to EN BC (3800–3200 B.C.), that is, after the first expansion period, the average PP in areas of continuous expansion (not settled in EN A, indicated by lack of point-butted axes) was slightly better than the region as a whole, a tendency that was accentuated from EN BC to MN. This seems to indicate that increased intensification took place in areas of high PP, while lesser productive soils already witnessed a gradual depopulation. From the LN and the EB, however, the PP was generally lower than the average of the region, whereas the range of soil quality increased. The tendency toward intensified settlement expansion within less productive areas continued during the LB.

Thus, the observed changes in settlement pattern and settlement structure were accompanied by a gradual change from heavier soils toward lighter ones. As we know that northwestern Zealand did not lack soils of high productive potential, the general change in subsistence strategy toward soils of less PP can only be explained by the operation of economic constraints. According to our model, we should expect these to be localized in changed conditions of production as reflected in the exploitation of the landscape and in patterns of land use.

## Ecology and Land Use

Vegetational changes in the exploitation of the landscape during the Neolithic are recorded in Figure 15.7. These general trends correspond with most pollen diagrams in southern Scandinavia (Berglund 1969, Andersen 1976). The initial phase of the Neolithic, the A phase (in the diagram, phase II), was characterized by "slash-and-burn" cultivation of small plots for cereal growing and pollarding

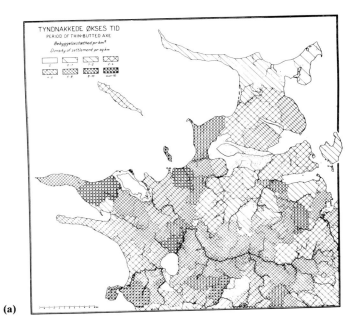

**(a)**

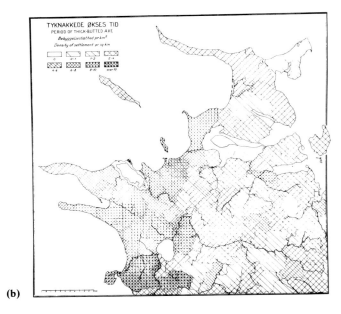

**(b)**

**Figure 15.3.** The prehistoric settlement of Northwestern Zealand, (*a*) Early Neolithic—period of thin-butted axe. (*b*) Middle Neolithic—period of thick-butted axe. (*c*) Late Neolithic—flint dagger period. (*d*) Bronze Age—early and late.

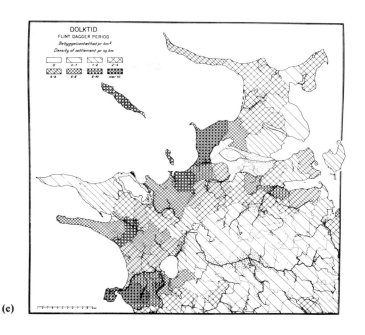

**(c)**

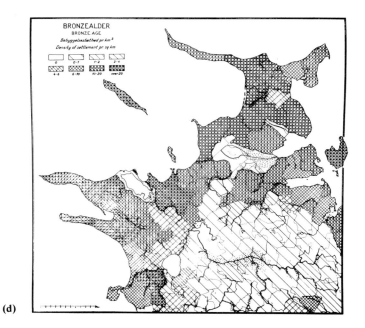

**(d)**

251

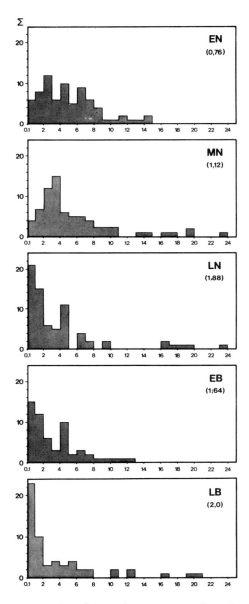

**Figure 15.4.** Graphic representation of the settlement structure in northwestern Zealand. (Based on Mathiassen 1959, Table VI.) Degree of settlement stratification is indicated by a numeric value dividing number of settlement units below density 4 with the number above. Number of settlement units (parishes) is on the vertical axis; degree of settlement density on the horizontal axis; and densities increasing from left to right.

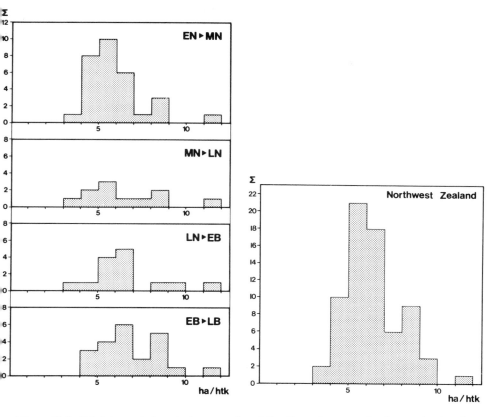

**Figure 15.5.** Subsistence strategy during expansion, defined by an increase of settlement density of more than .5, and from ENA to EN BC by lack of point-butted axes. Parishes are used as regional units; hectares per barrel of hard corn (ha/htk) as an indicator of productive potential. The representation of the whole region is shown at the right (N. W. Zealand).

of trees for leaf foddering of stalled cattle. The manipulation of the forest was modest. Not until the later Early Neolithic (EN BC) did a significant reduction of the forest (the "landnam") take place, with the aim of creating large areas of open land for open pastures and free-grazing cattle. An indication of this was the disappearance of ramson, which was much preferred by cattle, and the enormous increase of grasses and lanceolate plantain, while the high forest was correspondinly reduced (phase III). With degradation of the soil, a gradual displacement of settlement took place, which is reflected in the recovery of secondary oak mixed forest in the interior (this part of the diagram is from the

| Period transitition | Mean value | Standard deviation |
|---|---|---|
| EN A→EN BC | 6.67 | 1.94 |
| EN → MN | 6.43 | 1.65 |
| MN → LN | 7.00 | 2.32 |
| LN → EB | 7.07 | 2.05 |
| EB → LB | 7.45 | 1.56 |
| Northwest Zealand | 6.87 | 1.58 |

**Figure 15.6.** Subsistence strategy during expansion, represented by the numerical values of Figure 15.5.

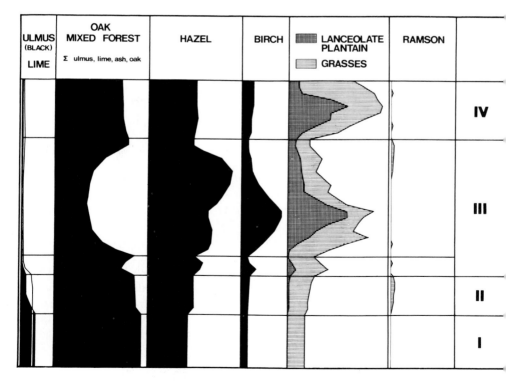

**Figure 15.7.** Pollen diagram, pieced together from diagrams from Aamosen and Sørbylille (Zealand) and Dyrholmen (East Jutland). (After Troels-Smith 1953, Figure 2.)

Aamosen Bog). A significant reduction of the forest and a corresponding expansion of open land with permanent pastures took place at the transition to the Late Neolithic in southern Scandinavia, while this had already occurred in Jutland with the appearance and expansion of the Single Grave culture or Battle Axe culture (phase IV in the diagram). During the Bronze Age the exploitation of the landscape steadily increased, especially during the Late Bronze Age. (This is not included in Figure 15.7.)

This picture of the vegetational development corresponds well with the observed changes in settlement structure and subsistence strategy (see Figures 15.4 and 15.5). It reflects the impact of different types of subsistence strategies on vegetation. The response of environmental constraints caused a gradual change from extensive to intensive "slash-and-burn," which was succeeded by an extensive "pastoral" economy and from small-scale land use toward large-scale land use. From a broad spectrum economy, based on an interaction between the production of the forest (leaf foddering, pigs, hunting) and the soil (cereal production and some grazing), a trend developed toward a narrow-spectrum economy based mainly on the production of the soil (stock-rearing and cereal production) and specialized exploitation of ecological niches, e.g., fishing.

The expansion of open land from the Early Neolithic to the Bronze Age can also be inferred archaeologically through the relative increase in settlement density (see Figures 15.3 and 15.4), and absolutely by calculating different open-land values for the recorded number of megaliths and tumuli, most of which have been registered in this area.[5] If we assume that each barrow (which in the Bronze Age utilized between 1 and 3 ha of grass turfs) would require a further 10–20 ha of permanent open land (fields, pastures) to preserve productivity, we arrive at the open-land figures in Figure 15.8. They demonstrate the economic and ecological differences between the EN and the BA and the corresponding changes in patterns of land use.

Thus the preference for light soils during the LN and the BA was not initially a result of blocked expansion on good soils and the budding-off of settlements on marginal lands. It reflects an economically determined preference for light soils whose more open forest was easy to transform into productive grassland (Kristiansen 1980). Gradually, however, the opposition between the open land of a dominant pastoral economy and the dense surrounding forest on the heavier soils would make its exploitation more and more difficult within the known range of the economy, thus creating a new set of constraints. This might explain the Late Bronze Age intensification on light soils, despite the availability of forested areas of higher PP.

---

[5]Naturally the present number of monuments is far below the original total. As both megaliths and tumulis normally cluster in smaller groups, these extra monuments would probably fall within the range of open land inferred in Figure 15.8. These figures, however, should be regarded as minimal ones.

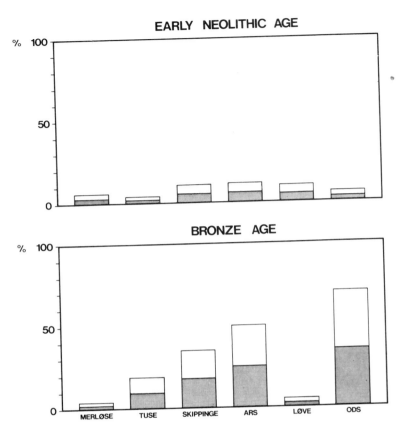

**Figure 15.8.** The supposed extent of permanent open land during the Early Neolithic and the Bronze Age in Northwestern Zealand calculated on the basis of open-land values per megalith–barrow of respectively 10 and 20 hectares. The regional units are the present districts.

When summarizing the evidence of this section it seems fairly safe to conclude that we are dealing with a long-term cycle of economic intensification within a tribal framework that led to a gradual transformation of both the economy and the ecology. I further suggest that these changes should be regarded as irreversible and that they by the end of the Bronze Age reached a point that did not allow the cycle to continue or to be repeated, resulting in a structural transformation of the tribal systems of northern Europe (Kristiansen 1978, 1980). Finally I suggest that this long-term cycle was made up by two rather distinct shorter cycles: the EN–MN cycle and the LN–BA cycle. In the following section a more detailed description of the cycles, based on recent research, will be presented in order to explain their dominant features and their internal dynamics.

## TRIBAL TRANSFORMATIONS: NORTHERN EUROPE

The relationship between production and reproduction determines to a large degree the potential for increased wealth accumulation and its transformation through alliances and feasting into status and increased hierarchization. The basic archaeological variables in the analysis of this process are the different stages in the exploitation of the landscape and their reflections in settlement patterns and in the display of wealth in ritual and burials. These variables link economic conditions of production with the organization of production and its investment in alliances, ritual, and rank. In what follows, these variables will therefore be considered in greater detail. The chronological and cultural succession described next is based on calibrated radiocarbon dates.

### 4100–3800 B.C. Early Neolithic A.

Agricultural colonization from a Mesolithic base was developed by small family groups practicing "slash-and-burn" cultivation on small plots for cereal growing and pollarding trees for leaf foddering of small numbers of fenced–stallfed cattle (Troels-Smith 1960). Local inland sites like St. Valby (Becker 1954) were based on cereal growing (wheat) in small cleared fields, probably by hoe cultivation. The dominant domestic animal was the pig, which foraged in the forest. Along coasts and lakes, seasonal hunting and fishing camps, like Muldbjerg in the Amosen Bog (Troels-Smith 1953), formed part of a mixed economy, based on exploiting a wide variety of resources, but mainly on the production of the natural environment (Mahler 1981).

The material culture was a continuation from the Mesolithic base, with simple pottery and thin-butted axes for clearing. Wooden bowls imply a tradition in elaborate woodcarving.

Exchange was regionally restricted, and burial and ritual reveals simple earth graves (Brinch Petersen 1974) with little ritual evidence, but some display of the use of status items like amber and the earliest battle axes. Small votive offerings of pottery containing food are found in bogs and lakes (Becker 1947).

### 3800–3400 B.C. Early Neolithic BC.

The rapid expansion and increase of population gradually led to an intensified exploitation of the environment. Large-scale forest clearings now took place (Iversen's so-called "landnam")(Iversen 1941, 1973). In opposition to the preceding slash-and-burn technique, which maintained a balance with the forest, the aim was now to create large and more permanent openings of the land, which was maintained by free-grazing cattle. Whether we should regard this landnam as the outcome of faster and more extensive slash-and-burn cultivation with cattle preventing the forest from regenerating, or, as definitely stated by Iversen and Troels-Smith, the result of a distinct new clearance strategy, is in my opinion still debatable.[6] According to Troels-Smith, it represents an agricultural economy distinctly different from the earlier long-house farmers of the Linear Pottery culture who practiced horticulture on small permanent fields and kept stall fed or fenced cattle (Troels-Smith 1980). But it quite evidently reflects a changed subsistence strategy that demanded the cooperation of several family groups (e.g., extended families). The opening of the forest was accompanied by technological, economic, and social changes. A more efficient agricultural practice, involving ard ploughing, was introduced, the number of cattle increased, and a general increase in productivity took place.

The settlement system stabilized and a complex territorial organization developed that was sustained by elaborate ritual and exchange. Impressive expressions of communal ritual are demonstrated in timber-constructed earthen long barrows from an early date, especially in Jutland, which were later succeeded by the earliest megaliths. Other ritual manifestations are found in the hoarding of large ceremonial axes, the sacrifice of cattle, etc., in bogs, which were accompanied by feasting. Also, the sphere of craft production witnessed a remarkable development. Flint mining gave rise to the increased production of long, polished flint axes that entered local, regional, and interregional exchange cycles. The latter also included amber and small numbers of imported copper axes from central Europe. A wide variety of fine decorated pottery was produced and consumed in rituals at megaliths. Also, elaborate battle axes and mace heads were employed in ritual and as status items for a small elite group. They were buried in earthen long barrows and in the earliest megaliths. These gradually developed from single chiefly burials of big-chiefs to local territorial cult places for ancestor worship and burial places of chiefly lineages that were descended from the ritual ancestors (the first "big-chiefs").

### 3400–3200 B.C. Transition between Early and Middle Neolithic

The transition from the Early Neolithic to the Middle Neolithic marks the continuation and culmination of processes begun in the preceding period. Over a few generations the construction of thousands of megaliths (in the latest phase they were virtual stone houses) took place, at the same time as impressive

---

[6]The "landnam" is very well documented since Iversen's pioneer work (1941), and it has been supported by experiment (Iversen 1973). It is not a synchronous phenomenon, but a clearance strategy that occurs repeatedly during several hundred years all over northern Europe—in some areas early, in others late. Evidence comparable to the Danish EN A— stallfed cattle and small permanent fields—has been very well documented in Switzerland (Troels–Smith 1981, Guyan 1981).

territorial causewayed camps (central places) for interclan activities were constructed. We are dealing here with a specific territorial pattern of chiefdom organization, which was paralleled in other areas of western Europe and which has been elegantly interpreted by Colin Renfrew (1973). In Denmark and southern Scandinavia the evidence displays basically the same features (Andersen in press, Löfeig 1980, Madsen in press, Persson 1979). At the local level megaliths served common functions as ritual central places for ancestor worship and burial places of chiefly lineages.[7] Wider interclan activities at a regional level, however, were carried out at central places—including feasting and ritual and probably marriage alliances between chiefly lineages, the planning of common agricultural activities, exchange and redistribution of food surpluses, and settlement of interclan hostilities, etc.

The "seasonal" function of communal and territorial central places conforms well with a dispersed settlement pattern of extended families in a forest environment who based their existence on intensive slash-and-burn agriculture. Small family groups lived in U-shaped huts, although the so-called long houses, now interpreted as barrows, has not been finally disposed of. Lakes, inland waters, and the sea served as communication lines and are reflected in the clustering of settlements close to main watercourses.

The economic basis of these territorial chiefdoms lay in the high productive potential of the former forest soils, which were exploited through intensive shifting cultivation on both forest and open land. Cereal samples reveal a very pure crop of wheat with a few weeds (Jørgensen 1977), indicating efficient cultivation and crop rotation with long periods of fallow, suitable for grazing cattle (Higham 1969). Annual weeds indicate repeated cultivation on the same fields over several years.

The regional diversity of basic and scarce resources—amber and flint—stimulated interregional and international exchange, channeling copper axes from central–eastern Europe and new religious ideas—megaliths—from western Europe back to Scandinavia.

The monopolization of valuable prestige items and the mobilization of surplus production for ritual and feasting was the basis of local alliance networks. At the top amber, copper, and battle axes circulated, while the polished thin-butted flint axe was the common medium of exchange. Thus in northern Zealand, the numerical relationship between battle axes, megaliths, and polished flint axes is 31:561:2439, indicating the exclusive nature of prestige items. The articulation of these factors at local and regional levels gave rise to the formation of the first chiefdoms in the prehistory of northern Europe in the late fourth millenium.

---

[7]The big dolmen and the passage graves should be regarded rather as the final deposition place of the bones of the deceased that had been through several ritual processes in wooden cult houses.

**3200–2800** B.C. **Middle Neolithic A.**
**2800–2300** B.C. **Middle Neolithic B.**

The 3200–2800 B.C. period witnessed the gradual disintegration of territorial chiefdoms, which is reflected in ritual, material culture, settlement patterns, and exchange systems. This chain of events was due to a complex interaction of ecological and economic factors that reached a threshold first of all within the settled areas of the TRB culture.

Within the economy, cattle held an increasingly dominant position, pig was reduced in number, while barley, less demanding with respect to soil, gradually replaced wheat (Madsen in press, Figure 18), apparently as an adapation to an open, degraded environment with increasing population and settlement clustering. This could be explained by a decline in cereal production, leading to a heavier stress on meat production and a gradually changed preference for light soils and open forest, which could be transformed easily to grassland. Areas that had been degraded from long cultivation were gradually left, and an increased exploitation of martime resources and hunting to balance diminishing agricultural yields is reflected in the appearance of a specialized tool kit of maritime hunters—the Pitted Ware culture—which originated in Norway and Sweden. Here the decline of agriculture production was much more significant, as is reflected in the pollen diagrams (Berglund 1969). Hunting replaced agriculture as the dominant subsistence strategy in marginal areas (e.g., Welinder 1975). This hunting–agricultural economy with a highly specialized and differentiated tool kit for both hunting and woodworking coexisted with the traditional agricultural communities for several centuries and was gradually acculturated during the 2800–2400 period (Welinder 1977–1978).

Thus it seems that overall agricultural production in Scandinavia declined during this period. At the local level this made the chiefly mobilization of surplus production for feasting and alliances more critical, as it demanded an increasing share of a decreasing production. These contradictions between the social and the economic systems probably triggered intensified production, e.g., shorter fallow periods, which resulted in the degradation of soil and imposed new constraints on the social system.

In the long run, competition for land and increased warfare would be a probable result of this development (Vayda 1961), leading to a reduction of intertribal alliances and exchange. Chiefly communal activities ceased. The final disintegration of the systems occurred when the contradictions between the economy and the social system led to a break up of the settlement pattern and of the territorial framework of chiefdom organization. This occurred in Jutland with the sudden, rapid expansion of small pastoral family groups of segmentary tribes—the Battle Axe culture—onto the light soils of central Jutland around 2800 B.C. In southern Scandinavia the settlement pattern largely remained intact, but the new ritual system and part of its social and economic basis was adopted.

In the archaeological record, the gradual disintegration of chiefdom organization is reflected by a decline in the building of megaliths, a gradual decrease of communal ritual and use of votive offerings, and a decline in the production of fine pottery for ritual and funerals that was replaced by simple domestic pottery. Small offerings of flint axes at megaliths replaced former ritual practices. Also causewayed camps disappeared, while at the same time settlements became larger. Interregional exchange ceased. This is reflected in regional cereamic groups and the fact that long-distance exchange of copper and amber came to an end at an early date. The crucial point was reached with the disintegration of the territorial organization of the settlement system in Jutland and the rapid expansion into a new environment around 2800 B.C. that released the potential of pastoral elements that had gradually developed during the 3200–2800 period. But it cannot be excluded that European migrations played a role, spreading the innovations of the secondary products revolution (Sherratt 1981, Figure 10.16, Stage II).

The Battle Axe culture, characterized by single burials of both men and women in small local lineage or family mounds made of grass and heath turf, reflects the reversion of a chiefly territorial clan organization into a segmentary organization suited to predatory expansion (Sahlins 1961).

The uncontrolled production of battle axes (each local lineage controlled by its own chief or big-man) reflects local competition and the lack of higher levels of social integration. Thus after the expansion stage, closed local exchange cycles developed, and these are reflected in the archaeological ceramics.

A massive, permanent opening of the landscape took place on the light soils of central Jutland and northwestern Europe, creating extensive permanent pastures dominated by heathland. Wheels and wagons were introduced for the first time, reflecting the communication potential of this new environment (Rostholm 1978, Sherratt 1981, Figure 10.9). The economy was probably based on cattle (meat and milk), sheep (wool production), ploughing, and some cereal growing (barley). The widely dispersed settlement pattern of small family groups clustered along ecological boundaries—e.g., heavy, hilly moraine and flat sandy soils—made possible the exploitation of both environments. But extensive sandy areas were also colonized. During the following 200–300 years, local cylces of expansion and regression, warfare and alliances, in a delicate environment with a local ecological threshold, kept the system in a state of evolutionary flux or equilibrium.

## 2300–1900 B.C. Late Neolithic;
## 1900–500 B.C. Bronze Age

The 2300–1800 B.C. period saw an enormous expansion of open land with the formation of permanent pastures throughout southern Scandinavia, which reflected a renewed spread of a pastoral economy that extended into marginal areas of former hunters and fishers in central Scandinavia. The change in settlement pattern and expansion onto light soils allowed increased surplus production for increased interregional exchange, and this was reflected in the spread of a new elaborate flint technology and the general use of flint daggers as prestige items. Interregional exchange of flint developed and by the end of the period bronze objects from Central Europe were entering the Scandinavian exchange systems.

With respect to ritual and social structure, individual burials in stone cists or small mounds predominated. The enormous production and ritual consumption–hoarding of daggers probably reflects a competitive big-man system of segmentary tribal groups without higher chiefly levels of integration since monopolization of production and prestige items could not take place. With the development of long-distance exchange in bronze, a new situation was established, in which articulation of exchange and local production could lead to monoplization of prestige items and increased hierarchization. During the Early Bronze Age this led to the formation of a theocratic chiefdom structure based on the principles of a prestige goods system, and characterized by elaborate communal ritual and feasting, the construction of thousands of impressive tumuli of local chiefly lineages, increased craft production for ritual purposes and controls over prestige items for the display of rank and wealth. In the Early Bronze Age this evolved into a complicated system of status distinctions. Local chiefdoms were distributed along regional alliance networks, as for example in northwestern Zealand, and these are reflected in the spatially hierarchical distribution of wealth and symbols of rank (Randsborg 1974, Levy 1979, Kristiansen 1981). Settlement hierarchies developed with central chiefly settlements controlling craft production, local exchange, and ritual. Chiefs sat on wooden stools, (preserved in oak coffins) and lived in large houses, some between 30–40m wide and 6–8 m wide. The culmination of this type of chiefdom organization was reached at 1500–1200 B.C. and 800–650 B.C.

With the advent of the Late Bronze Age at about 1000 B.C. changes in burial rites and in status display indicate a temporary crisis, in part due to decreasing supplies of metal (Kristiansen 1978). Agricultural production was intensified, and competition for alliance and exchange increased, resulting in more elaborate communal ritual and votive offerings of prestige items to reinforce chiefly organization and to maintain alliances and supplies of metal.The display of personal wealth in burials, however, was heavily reduced, and tumuli building came to an end. Increasing warfare and continuous ecological degradation led to settlement clustering, and this imposed new constraints on the economy.

Increasing contradictions between economic conditions of production and the reproduction of social organization caused a break up of the settlement system in the transition to the Iron Age. Settlements expanded into former unsettled areas of heavy soils (Kristiansen 1978, 1980), followed by the collapse of chiefly organization and of long-distance exchange. A more egalitarian social system developed, organized in autonomous local settlement units of fenced villages. Social and economic relations were based on the ownership of land divided into permanent fields. The elementary tribal structures of social reproduction no longer dominated the organization of production.

## REGIONAL AND LOCAL SYSTEMS

### Production–Reproduction Cycles

The long-term production–reproduction cycles described before are summarized in Figure 15.9. Naturally this figure represents an abstraction, summarizing the main trends. These are made up of numerous small local cycles whose dominant trends constitute a regional cycle. Several regional cycles may constitute dominant interregional or "global" cycles, as shown in Figure 15.9. This can be illustrated on a small scale (Figure 15.10), showing the articulation of local cycles in northwestern Zealand from the Early Neolithic to the Late

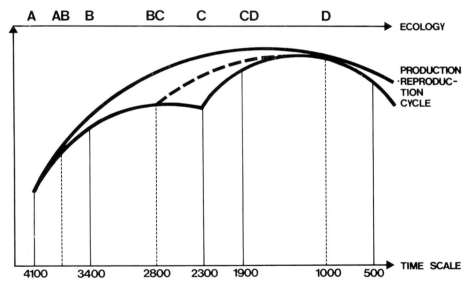

**Figure 15.9.** Production—reproduction cycle of northern Europe 4100–500 B.C.: (*a*) Slash-and-burn agriculture of small plots for cereal growing, hoe agriculture, and leaf foddering of stallfed cattle. (*b*) "Landnam" —opening of the forest. Free-grazing cattle and pastures, and agriculture. (*c*) Second landnam, in Jutland 2800 B.C., in southern Scandinavia 2400–1900 B.C. Significant reduction of forest and the formation of extensive permanent pastures and heath areas. Secondary-oak mixed forest and expansion of birch. (*d*) Intensified decimation of secondary forest, expansion of pastures. Third landnam in central and eastern Scandinavia.

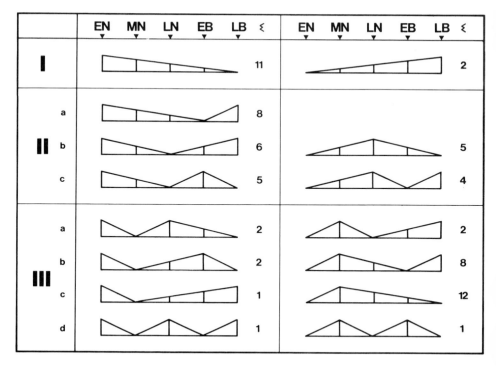

**Figure 15.10.** Local cycles of settlement increase–decrease in northwestern Zealand 4000–500 B.C. (Based on Mathiassen 1959, Table VII.) Parishes are used as areal units.

Bronze Age, indicating changes of settlement density but not their magnitude. The left and right sides are inversions of each other, and three main types of regression and expansion cycles have been classified.

It can be seen that the dominant trend of local cycles creates a regional cycle corresponding quite well to Figure 15.9. The Early Neolithic represents a climax period in the area (34 cases), just as settlement expansion from the EN to the MN is strong (34 cases). The MN displays a maximum in 23 cases. Intensification during the MN and expansion from the MN to the LN, however, is rare (11 and 6 cases), and the LN–EB represent peiods of stabilization with rather few maxima and few cases of increased settlement density from LN to EB. The LB, however, was a period of increased settlement density and internal expansion. Settlement density increases from EB to LB in 21 cases, and the LB displays a settlement maximum in 32 cases.

Thus, the cycle of northwestern Zealand corresponds to the main cycles in Figure 15.9 with the exception of an intensification in LB. It exemplifies the complicated spatial and temporal relations between production–reproduction cycles that led to the formation of dominant long-term cycles.

Returning once again to Figure 15.9, a few general points of explanation and clarification should be made. The gradual change in economy and ecology during the 4000–500 B.C. period displays a general evolutionary trend of economic intensification that created basic differences in the economic conditions of social organization. This implies that the territorial chiefdoms of the Early Neolithic period were basically different from the theocratic–prestige goods chiefdoms of the Bronze Age. The first type originated from a dispersed settlement pattern of extended families, who practiced slash-and-burn agriculture on good heavy soils in a forest environment. They were linked together in a territorial organization of local and regional central places, the ritual framework for the periodic execution of common economic tasks (e.g., cutting of forests, building of megaliths) and for the maintenance of interregional exchange. Members of a chiefly lineage were seen to be the descendants of founding ancestors who intervened on their behalf with the whole community. This chiefly control was simply an aspect of the ritualized extension of the communal lineage structure.

The theocratic chiefdoms of the Bronze Age, on the other hand, originated from a competitive segmentary tribal system of economically autonomous settlement units and lineages based on a pastoral economy in an open environment. Hierarchization was therefore triggered primarily by the monopolization of long-distance exchange networks that is reflected locally by clusterings of rich burials and settlements along important communications lines. However, population density and the distribution of wealth generally reflect the productive potential of larger areas (Randsborg 1974, Kristiansen 1978). Warfare was a prominent feature of this competitive and male-dominated system. An elaborate religious system, separated from the communal lineage structure, had evolved. Chiefly control was maintained partly by an increased monopoly of ritual functions as is reflected in rock carvings and bronze figurines. Priestly functions were therefore an extension and mystification of chiefly powers that were based, in reality, on the political monopolization of production, alliances, and long-distance exchange.

On an evolutionary scale of tribal variation, the two systems probably represent contrasting types of tribal hierarchies with many parallels in the ethnographic literature. With respect to the territorial clans of the EN, striking parallels are found in New Guinea, technologically, in terms of different stages of shifting cultivation and with respect to relations between ritual, local production, and the employment of axes and prestige items in alliance and local exchange (Clarke 1966, Højlund 1979, Bulmer 1960, Liep n.d.). On an evolutionary scale, New Guinea should probably be placed in the "decline" period of territorial chiefdoms, which is characterized by intensified shifting

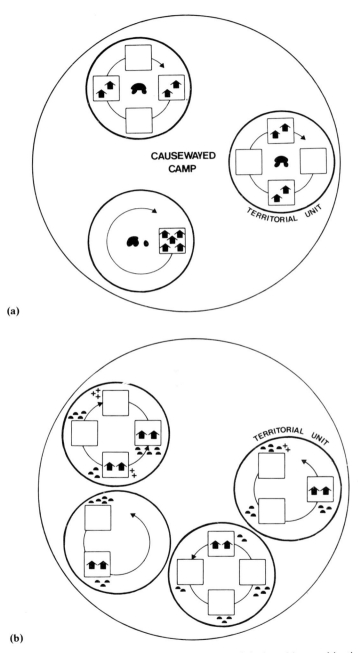

**Figure 15.11.** Settlement types: (*a*) The megalithic phase of slash-and-burn cultivation, megaliths and causewayed camps functioning as seasonal central places at local and regional levels, dispersed settlement in forest environment. (*b*) The late Neolithic phase of segmentary pastoral groups with a

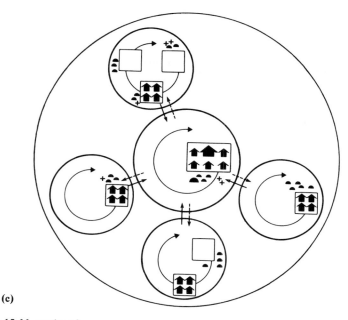

**(c)**

*Figure 15.11 continued.*
pastoral economy in an open environment. Barrows of local families and lineages close to settlement, dense settlement pattern with no central places. (*c*) The Bronze Age, showing a redistributive settlement system with a pastoral economy in an open environment, settlement hierarchization based on permanent settlements; ([*b*] and [*c*] after Thrane 1980); (*a*) to (*c*) presuppose a gradual cyclic movement of settlement sites within local territories.

cultivation, inflation of local exchange in axes, for example, and little or no chiefly monopolization of exchange.

The theocratic chiefdoms of the Bronze Age, based mainly on long-distance exchange, should be compared rather with Polynesian and Melanesian chiefdoms, where the monopolization of scarce valuables seems to have been of prime importance in opposition to ecological diversification, as was originally suggested (Brunton 1975, Earle 1977).

It may be suggested that these variants of a tribal hierarchy represent potentially different evolutioanry trajectories. In a temperate habitat, however, the successive transformation of the environment leads to a degradation in the economic conditions of production, which cannot be transcended by a tribal mode of production. Thus the development cycles summarized in Figure 15.9 seem to characterize a wider pattern to be found in temperate Europe (Sherratt 1981). In some areas the regional cycles were shorter, for example, in England (Bradley 1978); in other regions they were longer, for example, in southern Scandinavia, with the exception of Jutland, and were dependent on the overall productivity of the region and its articulation with other regional systems.

The very long period of decline and subsequent stagnation or flux between approximately 3200 and 1900 B.C. is another phenomenon that calls for explanation. It seems to reflect a period of change from approximately 2400 B.C. toward a pastoral economy on light soils in an open environment, which raised the overall productivity of the region. It corresponds with a similar trend in European prehistory (Sherratt 1981) that is characterized by closed regional systems that are linked together with the secondary spread and development of metallurgy toward the end of the period. This stresses the importance of interregional exchange and the monopolization of scarce and valuable resources as an important precondition of stratification. These three stages of tribal development, as reflected in settlement patterns, are summarized in Figure 15.11.

Although economic constraints imposed by the transformation of the environment quite evidently created barriers to the functioning of the social system, and thus seem to have determined both the decline of EN territorial chiefdoms and BA theocratic chiefdoms, it is worth reflecting on the fact that culmination periods in both cases correspond to periods of international exchange, making possible an increased monopolization of valuables. Also, in both cases the decline of chiefdom organization corresponds with a decline in long-distance exchange networks.[8] This places the problem of determining the causes of evolution and devolution in a  wider spatial context of interacting systems, which I shall try to exemplify very briefly in the final section (for a more extensive analysis, see Kristiansen 1978, 1981).

## Regional Dynamics: The Nordic Bronze Age

Figures 15.12a–d show the geographical expansion of the Nordic Bronze Age over 1000 years as reflected in the distribution of Nordic bronzes. Traditionally this expansion has been interpreted as a cultural and ethnic expansion. In the following paragraphs I shall try to explain these phenomena as reflections of variations in the consumption of prestige goods based on variations in exchange and local economic conditions of reproduction. Let us first consider exchange and consumption.

The eastward expansion of the Nordic BA, succeeded by retraction in western Scandinavia, can be closely linked to changes in the European–Scandinavian exchange networks in the Early Bronze Age and the Late Bronze Age (Figures 15.13 and 15.14).

---

[8]In the EN it should be noted that a corresponding decline seems to take place in the copper producing areas of eastern Europe (e.g., Vulpe 1976, Appendix 1).

The general eastward expansion of both consumption and exchange networks presented here can be exemplified in a local area in northwestern Jutland through an analysis of the circulation time of prestige goods.

Swords were classified according to degree of wear—that is, circulation time. If we apply this analysis in one of the central regions in northwestern Jutland we get the following picture (see Figure 15.15)—from period II to III a significant increase in heavily worn bronzes occurs, followed by a significant decrease in consumption in period IV. Prestige goods are now too few and rare to deposit in burials or hoards due to a lack of bronze. This development is accompanied by settlement concentrations, as seen in Figure 15.16.

The development in this local area, however, exemplifies the development of western Scandinavia from the Early to the Late Bronze Age, which reflects an economic–ecological crisis of the Bronze Age settlements on the light soils of northwestern Europe. Production for exchange to acquire bronze triggered ecological overexploitation, which resulted in a general economic crisis. The flow of bronze was reduced proprotionally, and a retreat from the most marginal land was followed by settlement concentrations. This is reflected in pollen diagrams that show the gradual expansion of heath areas.

In eastern Scandinavia, however, an opposite development took place. Settlements expanded into marginal lands, and for a period of some 100 years this led to new lines of exchange becoming established, constraining flows of goods and people, with the goods being displayed in extensive consumption. Only the central part of southern Scandinavia remained stable, in respect to economy, exchange, and consumption, due to the high productive potential of this area.

Thus the decline in western Scandinavia was counterbalanced by an economic expansion in the eastern region. Only the core area of southern Scandinavia–northern Germany was able to maintain its position throughout the period, partly because of its central position, but especially because of its high productive potential. The economic development of the Nordic Bronze Age was thus centered around a western axis in the Early Bronze Age and around an eastern axis in the Late Bronze Age. When viewed in this perspective we may regard these local economic cycles as part of the reproduction of the larger Scandinavian system. In terms of the productivity of the whole region, this probably remained stable throughout the whole period in question, but the reproductive process, responsible for regional expansions and regressions, exploited and exhausted different areas at different periods.

A balance between evolutionary–devolutionary processes could consequently be maintained throughout the Bronze Age. Gradually, however, contradictions built up both on local and regional levels, and these are reflected in increasing settlement concentrations, which were then dispersed at the transition to the Iron Age (Kristiansen 1978, 1980).

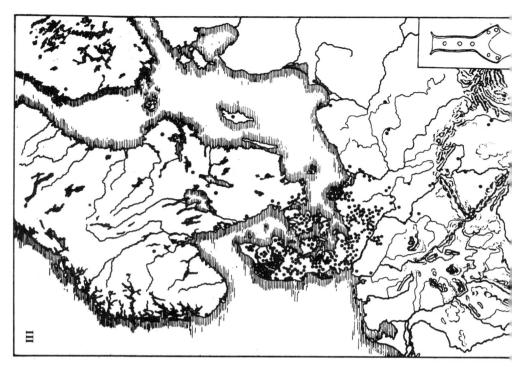

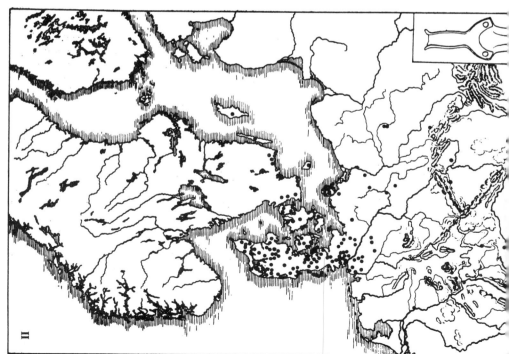

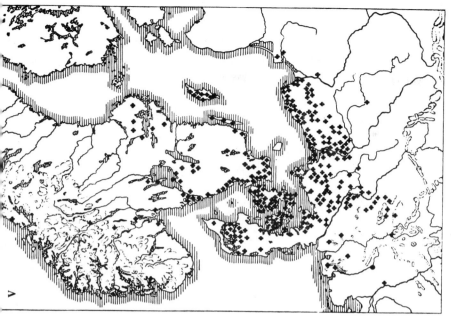

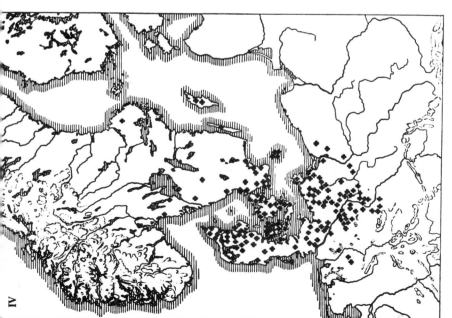

**Figure 15.12.** The expansion of the Nordic Bronze Age culture from periods II to V based on flange-hilted swords (Early Bronze Age) and Nordic hoards (Late Bronze Age). After Sprockhoff 1931, 1937.)

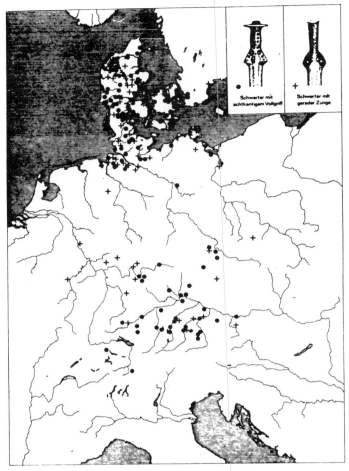

**Figure 15.13.** The distribution of imported swords or imitations of imports during period II of the early Bronze Age. (After Struwe 1971, Table 26.)

## CONCLUSION

It has been demonstrated that a specific theoretical model of cyclical tribal transformation can be applied to temperate Europe from 4000 to 500 B.C. Further, it has been shown that such long-term transformations can be explained as a function of the spatial and temporal distribution of production–

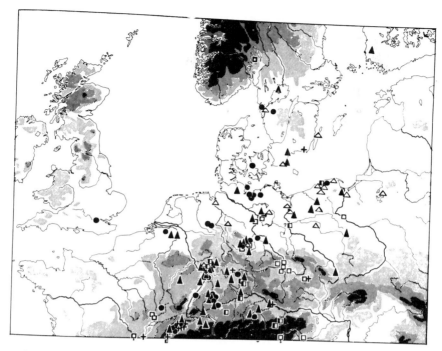

**Figure 15.14.** The distribution of imported swords or imitations of imports during period V of the Late Bronze Age. (After Thrane 1975, Figure 120.)

reproduction cycles whose articulation may define local, regional, or even "global" systems. A regional system may eventually be composed of several local cycles of expansion and regression, as is exemplified by the Nordic Bronze Age. The balance between these opposing processes of evolution and devolution determines the course of development within the larger system.

It was further suggested that developments in tribal hierarchization from 4000–500 B.C. were closely linked to such regional cycles—generating an Early Neolithic–Middle Neolithic cycle of territorial chiefdoms that were dependent upon slash-and-burn agriculture and a Late Neolithic–Bronze Age cycle of prestige good systems that were based on a pastoral economy. These two cycles of tribal transformations constitute a general evolutionary sequence of economic intensification and population increase, which at the transition to the Iron Age reached a point that would not allow the tribal cycle to continue or to be repeated.

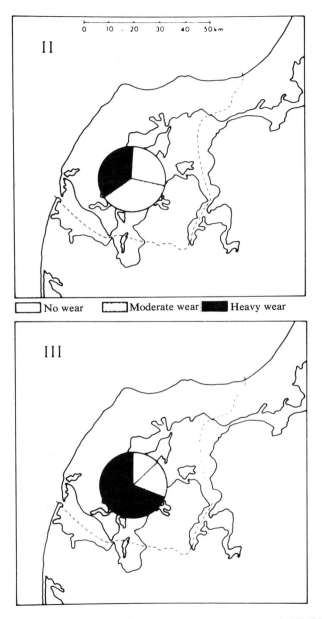

**Figure 15.15.** Variations in the degree of wear on full-hilted swords in period II (25 observations) and period III (26 observations) of the Early Bronze Age in the "Thy" region in northwestern Jutland. (After Kristiansen 1978.)

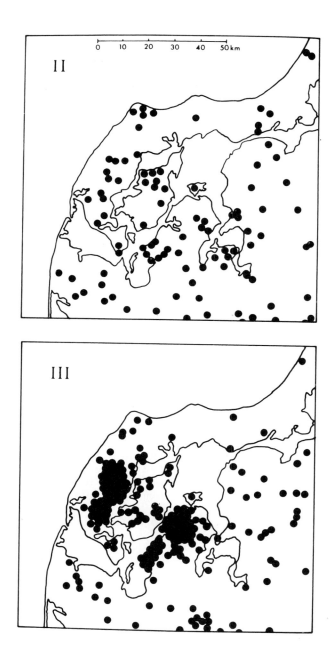

**Figure 15.16.** The distribution of burials in periods II and III of the Early Bronze Age in the "Thy" region in northeastern Jutland. (After Randsborg 1973–1974, Figures 1 and 2)

# REFERENCES

Andersen, S. Th., 1976, Local and regional vegetational development in eastern Denmark in the Holocene, Copenhagen, *D.G. U. Arbog*.

Andersen, N. H., 1973–1974, Sarup, et befaestet neolitisk anlaeg på Sydvestfyn (Sarup, a fortified neolithic site), *Kuml*, Aarhus, 109–120.

Andersen, N. H., in press, The funnel-necked beaker culture at Sarup and its bearing on the neolithic settlement of southwestern Fyn, Denmark, in Kristiansen, K. (ed.) *Settlement, Ecology and Economy in Scandinavian Prehistory and Early History*, Copenhagen, National Museum of Copenhagen.

Andersen, N.H. and Madsen, T., 1977, Skåle og baegre med storvinkelbånd fra yngre stenalder (Neolithic bowls and lugged beakers with chevron bands), *Kuml*, Aarhus, 131–160.

Aner, E., 1963, Die Stellung der Dolmen Schleswig-Holsteins in der nordischen Megalithkultur, *Offa* 20, Neumünster, 9–38.

Barrett, J. and Bradley, R (eds.), *The British Later Bronze Age*, Oxford, British Archaeological Reports, British Series 83.

Becker, C.J., 1947, Mosefundne lerkar fra yngre stenalder (Neolithic pottery in Danish bogs), *Aarbøger for nordisk Oldkyndighed og Historie*, Copenhagen.

Becker, C.J., 1954, Stenalderbebyggelsen ved St. Valby i Vestsjaellands amt. (The stone age settlement at St. Valby, West Zealand), *Aarbøger for nordisk Oldkyndighed og Historie*, Copenhagen.

Berglund, B., 1969, Vegetation and human influence in south Scandinavia during prehistoric time, *Oikos Supplementum* 12, Copenhagen.

Bradley, R., 1972, Prehistorians and pastoralists in Neolithic and Bronze Age England, *World Archaeology* 4, 192–204.

Bradley, R., 1977, Colonization and land use in the late Neolithic and Early Bronze Age, in Evans, J.G., Limbrey, S. and Cleere, H. (eds.) *The Effect of Man on Landscape: The Lowland Zone*, London, CBA Research Report 21, 95–103.

Bradley, R., 1978, *The Prehistoric Settlement of Britain*, London, Routledge Kegan Paul.

Brinch Petersen, E., 1974, Gravene ved Dragsholm. Fra jaeger til bonder for 6000 ar siden, *Nationalmuseets Arbejdsmark*, Copenhagen, 112–120.

Brunton, R., 1975, Why do the Trobriands have chiefs? *Man*, New Series 1, 544–558.

Bulmer, R.N.H., 1960, Political aspects of the Moka ceremonial exchange system among the Kayaka people of the western highlands of New Guinea, *Oceania* 3, 1–13.

Carneiro, R.L., 1970, A theory of the origin of the state, *Science* 169, 733–738.

Clarke, W.C., 1966, From extensive to intensive shifting cultivation: a succession from New Guinea, *Ethnology* 5, 4, 347–359.

Daniel, G. and Kjaerum, P. (eds.), *Megalithic Graves and Ritual* (Papers presented at the III Atlantic Colloquium, Moesgard, 1969). Jutland Archaeological Society Publications 11, Arhus.

Davidsen, K., 1975, Relativ kronologi i mellemneolitisk tid (Zur relativen Chronologie des Mittleneolithikums in Dänemark), *Aarbøger for nordisk Oldkyndighed og Historie*.

Davidsen, K., 1978, *The Final TRB Culture in Denmark—A Settlement Study*, Arkaeologiske Studier 5, Copenhagen.

Earle, T.K., 1977, A reappraisal of redistribution: complex Hawaiian chiefdoms, in Earle, T.K. and Ericson, J.E. (eds.), *Exchange Systems in Prehistory*, New York and London, Academic Press.

Ebbesen, K., 1975, *Die jüngere Trichterbecherkulture auf den dänischen Inseln*, Arkaeologiske Studier 2, Copenhagen.

Ebbesen, K., 1978, *Tragtbaegerkultur i Nordjylland* (Trichterbecherkultur in Nordjütland), Nordiske Fortidsminder Ser. B in quarto, Bd. 5, Copenhagen.

Eggers, H.J., 1951, *Der römische Import im freien Germanien*, Atlas der Urgeschichte, Hamburg.

Ekholm, K. and Friedman, J., 1980, Towards a global anthropology, in Blusse, L., Wesseling,

H.L. and Winius, G.D. (eds.) *History and Underdevelopment*, Leiden, Center for the history of European Expansion.

Flannery, K., 1972, The cultural evolution of civilizations, *Annual Review of Ecology and Systematics* 3, 399–425.

Fleming, A., 1971, Territorial patterns in Bronze Age Wessex, *Proceedings of the Prehistoric Society* 37 (i), 138–166.

Fleming, A., 1972, The genesis of pastoralism in European prehistory, *World Archaeology* 4, 179–191.

Fried, M.H., 1960, On the evolution of social stratification and the state, in Diamond, S., (ed.) *Culture in History*, New York, Columbia University Press, 713–731.

Friedman, J., 1979, *System, Structure and Contradiction in the Evolution of "Asiatic" Social Formations*, Copenhagen, National Museum of Denmark.

Friedman, J., 1975, Tribes, states and transformations, in Bloch, M. (ed.) *Marxist Analyses and Social Anthropology*, Association of Social Anthropologist Monograph Series 2, London, Malaby Press, 161–202.

Friedman, J. and Rowlands, M.J., 1977, Notes towards an epigenetic model of civilization, in Friedman, J. and Rowlands, M.J. (eds.), *The Evolution of Social Systems*, London, Duckworth, 201–276.

Gebauer, A.B., 1978, Mellemneolitisk tragtbaegerkultur i Sydvestjylland (The Middle Neolithic Funnel Beaker culture in southwest Jutland. An analysis of the pottery.) Kuml, Aarhus, 117–157.

Goransson, H., 1977, The Flandrian Vegetational History of Southern Ostergotland, University of Lund, Dept. of Quaternary Geology, Thesis 3.

Guyan, W. U., 1981, Zur viehhaltung im Steinzeitdorf Thayngen–Weier II, *Archaeologie der Schweiz*, 4, 3.

Higham, C.F.W., 1967, Stock rearing as a cultural factor in prehistoric Europe, *Proceedings of the Prehistoric Society* 33, 84–106.

Higham, C.F.W., 1969, The economic basis of the Danish Funnel-Necked Beaker (TRB) culture, *Acta Archaeologica* 40, Copenhagen, 200–209.

Hojlund, F., 1973–1974, Stridsøksekulturens flintøkser og mejsler (Axes and chisels of flint in the Battle-Axe culture), *Kuml*, Aarhus, 179–196.

Hojlund, F., 1979, Stenøkser i Ny Guineas højland (Stone axes in New Guinea highlands. The function of prestige symbols in the reproduction of a tribal society.), *Hikuin* 5, 31–49, Aarhus.

Ingold, T., 1981, The hunter and his spear: notes on the cultural mediation of social and ecological systems, in Sheridan, A. and Bailey, G. (eds.) *Economic Archaeology*, British Archaeological Reports, International Series 96, Oxford, 119–130.

Iversen, J., 1941, *Land Occupation in Denmark's Stage Age. A Pollen Analytical Study of the Influence of Farmer Culture on the Vegetational Development*, D.G.U. II, Ak, Nr. 66, Copenhagen.

Iversen, J., 1973, *The Development of Denmark's Nature since the Last Glacial*, D.G.U. V. Ak, Nr. 7, Copenhagen.

Jensen, J.A., 1972, Myrhøj, 3 hustomter med klokkebaegerkeramik (Myrhøj, three houses with Bell Beaker pottery), *Kuml*, Aarhus, 61–122.

Jorgensen, E., 1977, *Hagebrogård-Vroue-Koldkur. Neolitische Gräberfelder aus Nordwest-Jutland*, Arkaeologiske Studier, 4, Copenhagen.

Kristiansen, K., 1978, The consumption of wealth in Bronze Age Denmark. A study in the dynamics of economic processes in tribal societies, in Kristiansen, K. and Paludan-Müller, C. (eds.). *New Directions in Scandinavian Archaeology*, Studies in Scandinavian Prehistory and Early History, 1, Copenhagen, National Museum of Copenhagen, 158–190.

Kristiansen, K., 1980, Besiedlung, Wirtschaftsstrategie und Bodennützung in der Bronzezeit Dänemarks, *Praehistorische Zeitschrift* 55, 1, 1–37.

Kristiansen, K., 1981, Economic models for Bronze Age Scandinavia—towards an integrated approach, in Sheridan, A. and Bailey, G. (eds.) *Economic Archaeology*, British Archaeological Reports, International Series, 96, Oxford, 239–303.

Kristiansen, K. (ed.) in press, *Settlement, Ecology and Economy in Scandinavian Prehistory*, Studies in Scandinavian Prehistory and Early History, 5.

Løvy, J., 1979, Evidence of social stratification in Bronze Age Denmark, *Journal of Field Archaeology* 6.

Liep, J., n.d., Ranked exchange in Rossel Island, Exchange, production and social reproduction in Oceania, research seminar, Copenhagen, unpublished.

Löfvig, C., 1980, Megalitgravar och territoriell audeling på Västra Orust, Bohuslän, *Kontaktstencil* 17.

Lomborg, E., 1973, *Die Flintdolche Dänemarks*, Nordiske Fortidsminder Ser. B, in quarto, Bd.1, Copenhagen.

Lomborg, E., 1975, Klokkebaeger-og senere Beaker-indflydelse i Danmark (Einflüsse der Glockenbecher—und der späteren Beaker-Kulturen in Dänemark. Ein Beitrag zur Datierung der Einzelgrabkultur), *Aarbøger for nordisk Oldkundighed og Historie*, Copenhagen.

Madsen, T., 1979, Earthen long barrows and timber structures: aspects of the Early Neolithic mortunary practice in Denmark, *Proceedings of the Prehistoric Society*, 45, 301–320.

Madsen, T., in press, The settlement systems of the early agricultural societies in Eastern Jutland, Denmark. A regional study, in Kristiansen, K. (ed.) *Settlement, Ecology and Economy in Scandinavian Prehistory*, Studies in Scandinavian Prehistory and Early History, 5.

Mahler, D., 1981, Hunters storage—Farmers birth, *Kontakstencil* 19, Copenhagen.

Mahler, D., 1978, Den jyske enkeltgravskultur. Traek af de grundliggende dynamiske faktorer på basis af grave med rav, *Kontakstencil* 15, 15–45 Umeå.

Malmer, J.P. 1962, *Jungneolitischen Studien*, Acta Archeologia Lundensia, Ser. in 8°, No. 2.

Malmros, C., 1979, Den tidlige enkeltgravskultur og stridsøksekultur (The early Single Grave culture and Battle Axe culture), *Aarbøger for nordisk Oldkyndighed og Historie*.

Malmros, C., and Tauber H., 1975, Kulstof-14 dateringer af dansk enkeltgravskultur (Radiocarbon cates of the Danish Single Grave culture), *Aarbøger for nordisk Oldkyndighed og Historie*.

Mathiassen, T., 1948, *Studier over Vestjyllands Oldtidsbebyggelse*, Nationalmuseets Skrifter, Arkaeologisk-Historisk Ak.II, Copenhagen.

Mathiassen, T., 1959, *Nordvestsjaellands Oldtidsbebyggelse*, Nationalmuseets Skrifter, Arkaeologisk-Historisk Ak.VII, Copenhagen.

Mikkelsen, T. and Høeg, H.I., 1979, A reconsideration of Neolithic agriculture in eastern Norway, *Norwegian Archaeological Review*, 12, 1, Oslo, 33–47.

Nielsen, P.O., 1977a, De tyknakkede flintøksers kronologi (Zur Chronologie der dicknackigen Flintbeile), *Aarbøger for nordisk Oldkundighed og Historie*, Copenhagen.

Nielsen, P.O., 1977b, Die Flintbeile der frühen Trichterbecherkultur in Dänemark, *Acta Archaeologica*, 48, 61–138.

Nielsen, S., 1979, Den grubekeramiske kultur i Norden (The Pitted Ware culture in Scandinavia and some remarks about the tanged arrow heads from Hesselø), *Antikvariske Studier*, 3, Copenhagen.

Nordic Archaeological Abstracts (NAA), 1974–onwards, Viborg.

Paludan-Müller, C., 1978, High Atlantic food gathering in north-western Zealand, ecological conditions and spatial representation, in Kristiansen, K. and Paludan-Müller, C. (eds.) *New Directions in Scandinavian Archaeology*, Studies in Scandinavian Prehistory and Early History, 1, Copenhagen, National Museum of Copenhagen, 120–157.

Persson, P., 1979, Megalitgravarna och det neolitiska samhället Ett exempel från Västsrerige, *Kontaktstencil* 15, Umeå.

Randsborg, K., 1973–1974, Befolkning og social variation i aeldre bronzealders Danmark (Population and social variation in Early Bronze Age Denmark), *Kuml*, Aarhus, 197–208.

Randsborg, K., 1974, Social stratification in Early Bronze Age Denmark: a study in the regulation of cultural systems, *Praehistorische Zeitschrift*, 49, 38–61.

Randsborg, K., 1975, Social dimensions of Early Neolithic Denmark, *Proceedings of the Prehistoric Society*, 41, 105–118.

Renfrew, C., 1973, Monuments, mobilization and social organization in Neolithic Wessex, in Renfrew, C. (ed.), *The Explanation of Culture Change*, London, Duckworth, 539–558.

Rostholm, H., 1977, Neolitiske skivehjul fra Kideris og Bjerregårde i Midtjylland (Neolithic dish wheels from Kideris and Bjerregårde, Central Jutland) *Kuml*, Aarhus, 185–222.

Sahlins, M.D., 1961, The segmentary lineage: an organization of predatory expansion, *American Anthropologist*, 63, 322–345.

Sahlins, M.D., 1968, *Tribesmen*, New Jersey, Prentice Hall.

Sahlins, M.D., 1972, *Stone Age Economics*, London, Tavistock.

Sanders, W.T. and Price, B.J., 1968, *Mesoamerica: The Evolution of a Civilization*, New York, Random House.

Sanders, W.T., and Webster, D., 1978, Unilinealism, multilinealism and the evolution of complex societies, in Redman, C.R. (ed.), *Social Archaeology—Beyond Subsistence and Dating*, New York and London, Academic Press, 249–302.

Schiffer, M.B., 1976, *Behavioral Archaeology*, New York and London, Academic Press.

Schiffer, M.B., Sullivan, A.P. and Klinger,T.C., 1978, The design of archaeological surveys, *World Archaeology*, 10, 1–28.

Service, E.R., 1962, *Primitive Social Organization*, New York, Random House.

Shennan, S., 1975, The social organization at Brane, *Antiquity*, 49, 279–288.

Sherratt, A.G., 1972, Socio–economic and demographic models for the Neolithic and Bronze Age of Europe, in Clarke, D.L. (ed.), *Models in Archaeology*, London Methuen, 477–542.

Sherratt, A.G., 1977, Resources, technology and trade: an essay in early European metallurgy, in Sieveking, G., Longworth, I. and Wilson, K. (eds.) *Problems in Economic and Social Archaeology*, London, Duckworth, 557–581.

Sherratt, A.G., 1981, Plough and pastoralism: aspects of the secondary products revolution, in Hodder, I., Isaac, G., and Hammond, N. (eds.) *Pattern in the Past—Studies in Honour of David Clarke*, Cambridge, Cambridge University Press, 261–305.

Sherratt, A.G., in press, Mobile resources: settlement and exchange in early agricultural Europe.

Skaarup, J., 1973, *Hesselø–Sølager. Jagdstationen der südskandinavischen Trichterbecherkultur*. Arkeaologiske Studier, 1, Copenhagen.

Sprockhoff, E., 1931, *Die Germanischen Griffzungenschwerter*, Römisch-Germanische Forschungen, 5, Berlin.

Sprockhoff, E., 1937, *Jungbronzezeitliche Hortfunde Norddeutschlands (Periode IV)*, Römisch-Germanisches Zentralmuseum zu Mainz.

Strömberg, M., 1971, *Die Megalitgräber von Hegestad*, Acta Archeologia Lundensia, Series in 8° No. 9.

Struwe, K.W., 1971, *Die Bronzezeit, Periode I–III*, Neumünster, Karl Wachholtz.

Tauber, H., 1972, Radiocarbon chronology of the Danish Mesolithic and Neolithic, *Antiquity*, 46, 106–110.

Thrane, H., 1973, Bebyggelseshistorie—en arkeaologisk arbejdsopgave, *Fortid og Nutid Bd. XXV, Hf. 3/4*, Copenhagen.

Thrane, H., 1975, *Europeaiske forbindelser*, Nationalmuseets Skrifter, Arkeaologisk-historisk reakke 16, Copenhagen.

Thrane, H. (ed.), 1980, *Bronzealderbebyggelse i Norden. Beretning fra det andet nordiske symposium om bronzealderforskning, 1980*. Skrifter fra historisk institut, Odense universitet, nr. 28, Odense.

Troels-Smith, J., 1953, Ertebøllekultur-bondekultur. Resultater af de sidste 10 års undersøgelser i Åmosen (Ertebolle Culture-Farmer Culture. Results of the past ten years of excavation in Aamosen Bog, West Zealand), *Aarbøger for nordisk Oldkyndighed og Historie*, Copenhagen.

Troels-Smith, J., 1960, *Ivy, Mistletoe and Elm, Climate Indicators—Fodder Plants. A*

Contribution to the Interpretation of the Pollen Zone Border VII-VIII, D.G.U. IV. Ak. Bd. 4, Nr. 4.

Troels-Smith, 1981, Naturwissenschafliche Beiträge zur Pfahlbauforschung, *Archaeologie der Schweiz*, 4, 3.

Troels-Smith, in press, Vegetationshistoriske vidnesbyrd om skovrydninger, planteavl og husdyrehold i Europa, specielt Skandinavien.

Vayda, A. P., 1961, Expansion and warfare among swidden agriculturalists, in Vayda, A. P. (ed.), *Environment and Cultural Behavior*, New York, American Museum of Natural History, 202–220.

Vulpe, A., 1976, Zu den Anfängen der Kupfer- und Bronzemetallurgie in Rumänien, *Les Débuts de la Metallurgie*, Union Internationale des Sciences Préhistoriques et Protohistoriques, IX[e] Congrés, Nice, 134–175.

Welinder, S., 1974, *Kulturlandskapet i Mälaromradet*, University of Lund, Dept. of Quaternary Geology, Rep. 5.

Welinder, S., 1975, *Prehistoric Agriculture in Eastern Middle Sweden*, Acta Archeologia Lundensia, Ser. in 8° Minore, No. 7.

Welinder, S., 1977, *Ekonomiska Processer i Forhistorisk Expansion*, Acta Archeologia Lundensia, Ser. in 8° Minore, No. 7.

Welinder, S., 1977–1978, The acculturation of the Pitted Ware culture in eastern Sweden, *Medd. fran Lunds Universitats Historiska Museum, New Series*, 2.

# III

# MORPHOGENETIC CHANGE IN COMPLEX SOCIETIES

The primary requisite of an archaeological science, wholly congruent with that of all other scientific disciplines, is a general and abstract framework on which an ultimately exact theory can be constructed (cf. Darwin 1909, 508, Heisenberg 1958, 171). The social and biological sciences, in particular, require fundamental concepts for dealing with the temporal and spatial transformations of markedly complex dynamical systems (e.g., Lewontin 1969, Renfrew and Cooke 1979, Stebbins 1977, 251–252).

Just such an abstract framework is suggested in a highly general systems theoretic or *contextual* approach. As Rosen proposes and exemplifies (1979, 109, Chapter 17 this volume), systems must be embedded in a "context," a class of systems that behave in similar fashion. The context itself can then be utilized as a source of information concerning specific classes or instances of system organization and change. In all instances the development of this context necessarily implies the recognition of an analogy, isomorphism, or logical and functional homology between one particular phenomenon and another. That there exist isomorphisms, whether total or partial, established or conjectured, is neither accidental nor mysterious: Many systems manifest a fundamental similarity in structure and operation when considered in the abstract (the "biological analogy," so long the object of excessive anxiety on the part of many anthropologists and archaeologists, is nothing more—nor less—than a systemic homology). A detailed examination of one of the hydrocarbons, for example, reveals a striking similarity of the molecular system to the interactions that characterize cell-to-cell, tissue-to-tissue, and organ-to-organ relations. While behavior becomes increasingly complex as one moves to higher-order systems, a common core of relationships appears to be present at each phenomenal level (Berrien 1968, 6). Each level represents a distinct instance of a basic organization—a system, a complex of elements standing in interaction.

The recognition of these functional isomorphisms is basic, certainly, to any modeling relation, as noted by Rosen 1979, 109–110; (cf. Clarke 1968, 39, Renfrew 1979a, 16, 22–30, 1979b, 505). Models as heuristic devices facilitate the entire scientific process, from proposition formation, to research design, to test. As analytical tools, a model's validity is not at question, only its *utility*. Models are selective: Focusing only on those characteristics significant for the question under investigation, these selected features are combined into a unified conceptualization according to predetermined logical principles. In this way models can alert us to similarities existing among several seemingly dissimilar phenomena. It is precisely the utility of the systemic or contextual model that explains its explicit adoption and application in such a variety of scientific fields. A major advantage lies in its parsimony, its capacity for encompassing a wider variety of phenomena and established observations than is often true of theories limited to a particular discipline.

On the methodological level, the avoidance of duplication of effort in various disciplines is thus made possible by a single formal apparatus. Further, a general contextual or systemic approach has directed attention to gaps in more limited theoretical models, and pointed toward methods of filling them. In facilitating a useful transfer from one field of inquiry to another, it encourages the development of adequate theoretical models in disciplines that lack them. This is particularly relevant to a new and as yet underdeveloped science, such as archaeology, a discipline still variously defined and thus without a specified and unifying general theory. In pointing to a large number of cross-disciplinary regularities, the developing area of study is alerted to the significance of these aspects of regularity. And thus a set of observations at one level of system operation can be associated with findings at another, to support powerful critical generalizations. The history of major theoretical developments in the sciences provides innumerable examples of the utility of analogically based systemic models and the fruitfulness of this conceptual procedure. For example, Fourier's theory of heat conduction was constructed on the analogy of the known laws of the flow of liquids, and the kinetic theory of gases was modeled on the behavior of elastic particles, whose motions conform to the established laws of Newtonian mechanics (cf. Geller 1978, 176–77, 183, Spencer 1904, 433, Weisskopf 1977, 410).

For the archaeologist as well as the biologist, one context of fundamental importance for theoretical and analytical investigation is necessarily morphogenetic. All living, veridical systems, whether organisms or societies, are open systems organized on the exchange of matter and energy with their respective environments. Morphogenesis—the generation of this pattern and form and the dynamics of its spatial and temporal transformations in populations of interacting elements—is thus a process of great generality and, accordingly, of widespread interest in a large number of scientific fields. The chapters in this section of the volume reflect this interdisciplinary concern with morphogenetic problems, with contributions not only from archaeology (Johnson, Ransdborg, van der Leeuw, Renfrew, Segraves) but from biology (Rosen), physics and chemistry (Allen), mathematics (Zeeman, Rosen) and the computer sciences (Doran).

Essential to the comprehension of the most important contributions of the following chapters is the concept of the interrelationship or interaction of parts that defines a system. A system can be generally understood as a complex of interacting components, or more precisely, as a complex of elements or components directly or indirectly related in a "causal" network in such a manner that each component is related to at least some others in a more or less stable way within any given temporal space. The components may be relatively simple and stable, or complex and shifting. They may vary in only one or two properties, or take on a variety of different states. The relationships between them may be mutual or unidirectional, linear, nonlinear, or intermittent, and varying in degress of "causal" efficacy or priority. The particular kinds of more or less stable interrelationships of components that become established at any time constitute the particular structure of the system at that time, thus achieving a unity or whole with some degree of continuity and boundary.

As this broadened definition shows, organization or structure is the fundamental research cynosure in any systemic analysis. It is not the nature of the parts in and of themselves that are basic to the system, but the way in which they interrelate. And this, in turn, imparts to the components themselves their characteristic properties (cf. Darwin 1869, 93–94). In other words, it is the network of interaction between intercommunicating parts that specifies the state of the population. Thus the state of the population cannot, by definition, be determined by the simple specification of the state of its members (Rosen 1979, 104). As Hall and Fagan (1956, 28) have put it, "A scientist in his analysis, evaluation and synthesis of systems is not concerned primarily with the hardware that makes up a system, but with the concept of system as a whole; its internal relations, and its behavior in a given environment." Or, in Ashby's (1956, 1, 1968, 111) terms, *the nature of materiality is irrevelant*. It could be "angels" or "ectoplasm," he asserts, for as long as conditionality or constraints—and this, of course, assumes communication—operate between them, and they exhibit regularity in behavior, then organization or system is defined. In this focus on interrelationships we are less inhibited from engaging in a comparative study of systems of all kinds, regardless of their substantive nature, and can thus better come to apprehend their structural and processual similarities and distinctions.

Interaction fields of all sorts manifest a singular characteristic that bears directly on the general nature of the mechanisms that generate pattern and form. Within an interaction field, disequilibrium, which is a requisite for system change, is a chronic condition (Carlsson 1968, Hawley 1979, 25). In an unstable system, one or more of the stochastic fluctuations that are constantly testing and probing the open system may be amplified rather than moderated, and the amplification in turn of these nonlinear interactions may result in a new system trajectory. The related mathematical models of bifurcation theory (Nicolis and Prigogine 1977, Prigogine 1969) and catastrophe theory (Thom 1975, Zeeman 1977) have been proposed as descriptive of the nature of the very general mechanism underlying morphogenesis in complex, open systems. Elements of these two models are explicitly employed in an examination of certain of the general features of societal development and evolution in three of the chapters that follow (Allen, Zeeman, Segraves).

Each of the nine chapters in this final section of the volume are concerned with the development of an increasingly rigorous theoretical framework for archaeology. They also share a common interest in the morphogenetic problems posed by the evolution of complex human societies. In most other respects there is considerable variation in these contributions, which is, however, a reflection, for the most part, of both the highly general nature of the topic and the broad range of disciplines represented among the participants.

Drawing on some of the recent work in bifurcation theory, organizational sociology, and theoretical biology, the first chapter (16) outlines certain of the abstract features of macroevolution, considering the general organizational characteristics of increasing complexity on the one hand and its underlying mechanism on the other. This brief introductory piece is followed by Rosen's contribution (Chapter 17), which, through an examination of Thompson's "theory of transformations," indicates some of the basic principles that inform morphological studies of any kind. In particular, Rosen discusses how these fundamental principles bear on our understanding of the development and evolution of human societies.

Applying catastrophe theory to Bayesian decision theory, Zeeman (Chapter 18) compares decision-making with biological evolution in order to better understand societal evolution and the global and local minima it follows. Allen (Chapter 19) likewise examines the evolution of complex systems and the question of local or global potentials. Utilizing bifurcation theory's general concept of "order by fluctuation" or "self-organization," a model of the central aspects of urban and regional growth and evolution is formulated, and the complementary roles in morphogenesis of both determinism and stochasticity— the "chance" and "necessity" of Democritus (Monod 1970)—are discussed.

While exemplified and discussed in reductionist fashion, Allen's general model of the evolution of structure is, in fact, quite the opposite, That is to say, it is the network of interactions between intercommunicating parts (Allen's nonlinear kinetics) that specifies the state of the system. Doran's Chapter (20), however, is fundamentally and explicitly reductionistic, hypothesizing that a society can be explained by its individual or aggregate membership—that the state of the system can be determined by the specification of the (cognitive) state of its members. While Rosen (1979, 104), as mentioned before, and others (e.g., Krippendorff 1971) have found this definitionally or logically problematic, such a perspective remains popular among many social scientists. Doran's discussion of the possibilities for a computational model of the dynamics of society insofar as it "reflects and derives from the nature of the cognitive processing of its actors" is a notable example of the current diversity of perspectives on theory and explanation in sociology, anthropology, and archaeology.

Johnson (Chapter 21), within a highly limited range of variation, empirically demonstrates the correlation between scale and complexity that the opening chapter of this section has argued must theoretically exist. Scalar stress (information-processing constraints) is manifest even in some egalitarian groups, and can be mitigated, Johnson proposes, by an interesting variant of hierarchy formation that is sequential rather than simultaneous and based on an indirect measure of population size provided by basal units of organization such as the extended family.

Randsborg's contribution (Chapter 22) provides a personal and tentative consideration of a number of philosophical issues that are seen to bear on theory building in archaeology. Van der Leeuw (Chapter 23) examines in organized fashion and in some detail one of these issues—the philosophical problem of the interaction between the investigator's sets of ideas and the structure of "reality" inherent in the data. He is concerned to clarify the nature of the mutual influence of the one upon the other in order to better understand how such interactions between subject and object might affect the way in which archae-ologists describe the world and construct their explanations of it.

In the final Comment, Renfrew places the preceeding chapters and the contributions they have sought to make in critical perspective. Outlining the general history of theoretical advances in our understanding of the emergence and development of complex societies, the basic elements that may together form a new morphogenetic paradigm in archaeology are seen the more clearly.

While the fundamentals of such a general model for the discipline are introduced or considered in these chapters, the paradigm has yet to be rigorously constructed and the evolution of societal complexity explained, as Renfrew concludes. However, we may yet seek consolation in the fact that "an unresolved problem is the most likely initial disguise for a really important discovery" (Hutchinson 1980, vii).

—B. A. S.

# REFERENCES

Ashby, W. R., 1956, *An Introduction to Cybernetics*, London, Chapman and Hall and University Paperbacks.

Ashby, W. R., 1968, Principles of the self-organizing system, in Buckley, W. (ed.), *Modern Systems Research for the Behavioral Scientist: A Sourcebook*, Chicago, Aldine.

Berrien, F. K., 1968, *General and Social Systems*, New Brunswick, N. J., Rutgers University Press.

Carlsson, G., 1968, Change, growth, and irreversibility, *American Journal of Sociology* 73, 706–714.

Clarke, D. L., 1968, *Analytical Archaeology*, Lodnon, Methuen.

Darwin, C., 1869, *On the Origin of Species by Means of Natural Selection, or the preservation of favoured races in the struggle for life*, 5th edition, London, John Murray.

Darwin, C., 1909, *The Voyage of the Beagle*, New York, Collier and Son.

Geller, M. J., 1978, Large scale structure in the universe, *American Scientist* 66, 176–184.

Hall, A. D. and Fagan, R. E., 1956, Definition of system, *General Systems* 1, 18–28.

Hawley, A. H., 1979, Cumulative change in theory and history, in Hawley, A. H., (ed.), *Societal Growth: Processes and Implications*, New York, The Free Press & The American Sociological Association, 19–29.

Heisenberg, W., 1958, *Physics and Philosophy: The Revolution in Modern Science*, New York, Harper and Row.

Hutchinson, G. E., 1980, Forward, in Cohen, M. N., Malpass, R. S., and Klein, H. G. (eds.), *Biosocial Mechanisms of Population Regulation*, New Haven, Yale University Press, vii–viii.

Krippendorff, K., 1971, Communication and the genesis of structure, *General Systems* 16, 171–185.

Lewontin, R. C., 1969, The meaning of stability, *Brookhaven Symposium in Biology* 22, *Diversity and Stability in Ecological Systems*, Upton, N.Y., Biology Department, Brookhaven National Laboratory, 13–24.

Monod, J., 1970, *Le Hasard et la Necessite*, Paris, Editions du Seuil.

Nicolis, G., and Prigogine, I., 1977, *Self-organization in Non-equilibrium Systems: From Dissipative Structures to Order through Fluctuations*, New York, Wiley.

Prigogine, I., 1969, Structure, dissipation and life, in Marois, M. (ed.), *Theoretical Biology and Physics*, Amsterdam, North Holland, 23–52.

Renfrew, C., 1979a, Transformations, in Renfrew, C., and Cooke, K. L. (eds.), *Transformations: Mathematical Approaches to Culture Change*, New York, Academic Press, 3–44.

Renfrew, C., 1979b, Systems collapse as social transformation: catastrophy and anastrophy in early state societies, in Renfrew, C., and Cooke, K. L., (eds.), *Transformations: Mathematical Approaches to Culture Change*, New York, Academic Press, 481–506.

Renfrew, C., and Cooke, K. L., (eds.), 1979, *Transformations: Mathematical Approaches to Culture Change*, New York, Academic Press.

Rosen, R., 1979, Morphogenesis in biological and social systems, in Renfrew, C., and Cooke, K. L., (eds.), *Transformations: Mathematical Approaches to Culture Change*, New York, Academic Press, 91–111.

Spencer, H., 1904, *An Autobiography*, Vol. II, London, Williams and Norgate.

Stebbins, G. L., 1977, *Processes of Organic Evolution*, 3rd edition, Englewood Cliffs, N.J., Prentice–Hall.

Thom, R., 1975, *Structural Stability and Morphogenesis*, Reading, Mass., Benjamin.

Weisskopf, V. F., 1977, The frontiers and limits of science, *American Scientist* 65, 405–411.

Zeeman, E. C., 1977, *Catastrophe Theory: Selected Papers 1972–77*, Reading, Mass., Addison–Wesley.

# 16

## Central Elements in the Construction of a General Theory of the Evolution of Societal Complexity

*BARBARA ABBOTT SEGRAVES*

### INTRODUCTION

In the absence of the appropriate organizing principles and theories, "However important and numerous may be the facts collected, we are in possession of only erudition, and not science. To suppose otherwise is to mistake a quarry for an edifice [Comte 1974, 200]." Just as the knowledge and competence of an archaeologist would be seriously in question if he mistook the remnants of a mining operation for a discrete architectural feature, so the body of knowledge that comprises the discipline of archaeology is profoundly limited, and its value for understanding man's past just as seriously in question, in the absence of a generalizing framework or theoretical context.

This chapter suggests, in outline, the potential utility of one such theoretical synthesis in comprehending certain of the fundamental characteristics of societal complexity. Basic aspects of evolutionary theory, bifurcation theory, and organizational theory will be considered in a general systemic or "contextual" perspective (Rosen 1979, 109–110) for the light they can shed on the structure, operation, and transformation of complex societies. Specifically, the difficult problem of the generation of centralized system coordination and regulation will be addressed.

The approach taken here is heavily based on lines of thought developed in fields of inquiry other than that of archaeology. Such an approach is useful and

**287**

THEORY AND EXPLANATION
IN ARCHAEOLOGY

legitimate not only in a newly defined science but also in branches of science generally considered relatively well developed, as Einstein's and Infeld's (1938, 35–36, 270, 273) discussion of the history of physics so amply attests. The association of problems that have been substantially resolved with those yet to be answered can often alleviate our difficulties with the latter by suggesting new ideas and research directions. Scientific advances in the formation of new and successful theories have often been achieved by carrying out a consistent analogy that represents some essential, common trend or feature previously hidden beneath a surface of ultimately superficial differences. This points up an important aspect of the present approach, namely, its highly general nature. The essential trends or features that permit explanation and prediction exist and can be recognized only at the macroscopic level (Margalef 1968, 27, cf. Segraves 1974).

## DEFINITIONS

Before proceeding further, brief clarification of two concepts central to this exposition will be necessary, as their use in the literature reflects a general lack of consensus as to their meaning.

First, the term *complex* sometimes means or is often understood to mean "something too complicated to understand adequately" or even "something we have no means of (perhaps ever) understanding." While, of course, we do not yet understand complex systems fully, or perhaps even adequately in certain or even a great many cases, this is not to say that such a distinction (i.e., "simple" versus "complex") is not a valid and important one for many purposes. It is also empirically demonstrable. Biology, the discipline that has grappled with enormously complicated and difficult entities for some not inconsiderable length of time, provides for our use a very straightforward definition of complexity. It is understood to mean *differentiated* (which significantly presupposes the attainment or surpassing of a certain size threshold), an entity composed of many different parts (for example, a multicellular as opposed to a unicellular organism). Furthermore, this simple differentiation into distinct, numerous parts ultimately becomes the basis of a *specialization or variety of parts:*

| A ⟶ AAAAAA ⟶ AABBCCDD |
| :-: |

| (wholly simple entity) | (differentiated entity) | (specialized or heterogeneous entity) |

Second, *organization* (a term that will be used here interchangeably with "structure") is understood to be *the definitive societal variable*, the variable through which a population takes on its systemic aspect. Sociocultural organization is the outcome of a system of interaction, in which a number of people adjust their activities and ideas to each other. The result is *a structural arrangement* of activity and ideas, or energy and information flow. Significantly, this notion of organization is wholly congruent with the highly general model, discussed below, of nonlinear, self-organizing systems developed by Prigogine and his co-workers. In fact, while not its original intent, this recent work at the Free University in Brussels has served to help confirm the very general nature of this concept of organization. The structure or organization we call society or culture, therefore is something quite other than an aggregate of individuals. The properties of sociocultural systems reside not in individuals or their characteristics, but in *relations generated in interaction.* In other words, significant societal elements are the relationships between people or groups, defined by stabilized interaction, and societal phenomena are derivatives of these social, interactive networks, not of individual action. Likewise, the articulation of human populations with their environment, and hence the human adpative process, is a collective, organizational phenomenon.

## BASIC ASPECTS OF SOCIOCULTURAL OPERATION AND EVOLUTION:
*Nonlinear Dynamics and the Integrated Coordination of Complex Systems*

Ashby (1972, 80) properly has called attention to the fact that "modern science . . . is characterized by an uninhibited advance into the non-linear. It not merely studies systems with high internal interaction but also confidently tackles systems in which it is the interactions themselves that are of interest." And therefore, he continues, "It is now possible to treat biological systems [and particularly sociocultural systems, I must add] in all their complexity and richness." Perhaps the most significant advance into the realm of the nonlinear has been made in theoretical physics and physical chemistry (work on irreversible thermodynamics) in Brussels (Glansdorff and Prigogine 1971, Nicolis and Prigogine 1977, Prigogine, Allen, and Herman 1977, see also Allen Chapter 19 this volume). The implications of the dynamic and nonlinear nature of irreversible systems that this work has suggested are proving of profound importance to our comprehension of societal operation, development, and evolution.

The most general theoretical model developed within the context of the study of dynamic, nonlinear systems is that of *bifurcation theory.* Bifurcation theory has allowed marked progress in the comprehension of *transitions of state,* among other problems. It is therefore of central relevance to our understanding of societal transformations, for while societies can and do exhibit flux equilibria for periods of time, they can also make remarkably rapid transitions of state, which are similar to phase changes in chemical systems.

It is interesting also to make brief mention here of the general conclusions reached by a significant number of theoretical biologists and paleontologists at a recent conference on macroevolution held at Chicago's Field Museum, a conference felt by many to be potentially the most important on evolutionary change in more than 30 years. The emerging picture of evolutionary change would appear to be one of "punctuated equilibria," that is, of relatively long periods during which species remain essentially unchanged, punctuated by brief evolutionary events (e.g., the discrete branching of a new species from an established one) (Cracraft and Eldredge 1979, Eldredge and Gould 1972). Evidently a number of workers in physics, chemistry, and biology have come, independently, to significantly similar conclusions.

Allen (Chapter 19 this volume) examines certain dynamic aspects of the evolution of complex, urbanized societies in the new "paradigmatic" context of bifurcation theory. Therefore, I shall note only briefly the major features of this general model, preparatory to a discussion of its relevance to the present thesis.

Open systems characterized by nonlinear reactions exhibit spontaneous self-organization, a structuring maintained by the flow of matter and energy through the system. Nonlinear interactions of system elements involve positive and negative "feedback loops." A system maintained far from equilibrium will organize or reorganize only if there is an amplification (generated by a random or stochastic event, a "fluctuation") of these nonlinear interactions. This can result in an instability affecting the trajectory of the (original) system. In other words, the numerous and varied mutual interactions between system components lead to a complex nonlinear kinetic, and this can give rise to self-organization of the system as a whole through successive instabilities of the collective structure (cf. Burgess 1963). As Allen and colleagues (1979, xi) have stressed, this process is of "great generality"—and hence explanatory power—for our comprehension of the evolution of complex systems. And as noted earlier, it is this very generality that gives us confidence in its significance for those systems of particular interest to archaeologists.

In the process of sociocultural development and evolution, the patterned interactions by which a society is defined are congruent with the systemic intercommunication implicit in the nonlinearities of the dynamic self-organizing system. Within a cybernetic system characterized by multiple and recursive feedback channels, a process that creates differences or divisions will also ultimately give rise to mechanisms that link the divisions or bridge the differences, if the system is not only to persist but continue to develop. If a deviation from the average value of a major variable or system parameter occurs, the fluctuation can very possibly be suppressed, and the system will then return to its original path. However, the nonlinear reactions may well react positively to the initial perturbation and magnify or amplify its newly deviant value, causing the original fluctuation to become increasingly large and its system-wide effects more uniformly pervasive. The system, now highly unstable, can in this manner depart from the path or "trajectory" on which the system was initially defined. The system has become labile, what Prigogine has termed a "dissipative structure." After a length of time it may move toward another stable trajectory that will most probably result in a qualitative change in the average configuration of its subsystems or component parts. In other words, this process of "self-organization" can be a transformative, evolutionary process, resulting (over time) in substantial change in system structure or organization.

At a "bifurcation point," a point at which there might be more than one possible path or trajectory, stable to perturbation, which the system far from equilibrium could assume, the path traced by the system depends on the nature of the fluctuation that has occurred (Allen *et al.* 1978, 1–5, Prigogine, Allen, and Herman 1977, 38). This assertion is made with some confidence on the macroscopic, general evolutionary level for both biological and sociocultural systems.

In a context of the broad application to both biological and social systems of a dynamic model of the generation of order and its transformations made possible by this recent work on irreversible thermodynamics and bifurcation theory, certain significant or "baseline" features or variables (fluctuations) critical to systems with a high degree of internal differentiation, specialization, and interaction of parts may now be discussed—in particular the unitary coordination and integration on which the complex system, in significant measure, is defined.

A fluctuation of primary importance for biological and societal restructuring is that of (significant) change in spatial dimension or population size: For qualitative system change to occur, critical spatial dimensions must be exceeded. As system size, or number of population elements per unit area, increases beyond certain critical thresholds, structural differentiation and functional specialization increase. That is to say, structural differentiation and functional specialization are increasing functions of system size. Reminding the reader once again that we of course are speaking on the most highly general— and hence most powerfully subsumptive level, this is the basic process of growth and evolution common to all complex living systems (von Bertalanffy 1962, 16, Hall and Fagan 1956). The relationship is assumed to be curvilinear, certainly, rather than linear. We are reminded by Carneiro (1967) that in systems of a certain size—as the value of this quantitative demographic variable must define a requisite threshold—demands placed on society by external conditions or agencies (for example, requirements of subsistence and defense) ultimately will be responsible for generating or initiating new and increasingly complex structural features without the necessity for any further associated increase in population.

As the paleontological, archaeological, and historical records attest, biological and sociological evolution "were linked from the start to increasing complexity" (Prigogine, Allen, and Herman 1977, 5–6, 8, Jacob 1976, 310–311, Stebbins 1969, 29, 124–127). The organization of systems through progressive differentiation and increasing complexity, a shift in the direction of increasing division into subsystems or differentiation of functions, is a macroscopic system property amenable to measurement (on the most fundamental level, of course, in terms of decreasing entropy or increasing order) (Segraves 1977, 193–195.).

In other words, both in biological systems and in human societies, the path of "complexity" (as earlier defined), on the most abstract level, is the general trajectory or stable path necessarily followed by an initially unstable system characterized by significantly increased size. Population or system size has long been recognized as a critical threshold variable in biology (classically, e.g., Rensch 1959, 281ff, also Bonner 1974, 22–29, 258–259), as well as in sociology and anthropology. As Maurice Halbwachs noted (1960, 191): "Far from being the effect and the necessary consequence of other orders of social facts, it is population itself, its size and distribution, resulting from a spontaneous development, that most often makes these other facts possible" (cf. Duncan 1957, 366, Hawley 1979, 23, MacCannell 1968, Mayhew and James 1972, 757, Narroll 1956). Dumond (1965, 319–320) writes that "the relationship between the size of a population and the organization of that population is such that a drastic reduction of the population size undermines the existing social organization, in virtually all its aspects."

These similarities of evolutionary process that unify the living world, both biological and social, clearly reflect the fundamental nature of that process. The cell and the multicellular organism are made up of varying kinds of parts that are organized into a unity regulated and controlled by the interactions between them. Biological order is both architectural and functional, and at the cellular level and above, it manifests itself by "a series of structures and coupled functions of growing complexity and hierarchical character" (Prigogine, Allen, and Herman 1977, 18). The same is true in the sociocultural sphere. As I pointed out previously, in the realm of the biological, the evolutionary process moves in a direction opposite to that specified globally by the Second Law: i.e., in the "direction" of Schrödinger's (1967) "negative entropy." This is also the case in the evolution of culture or society. In the process of both biological and societal evolution we witness a progressive differentiation of structure and a corresponding specilization of function: " Wherever we look we discover evolutionary processes leading to diversification and increasing complexity" (Prigogine, Allen, and Herman 1977, 5–6, White 1957, 57–58).

Furthermore, this close relationship between population size and organizational complexity is in most instances a necessary and predictable system trajectory—in the highly generated, macrolevel sense, of course—for the only way in which a biological organism, population, or human society can accomodate continued growth or increase in mass, short of fissioning (impossible for most biological organisms, certainly, and problematic for sociocultural systems in an increasingly competitive social environment), is by periodically elaborating its structure or organization: by "developing" and "evolving," in other words (Bonner 1974, 24–25, 30, Carneiro 1969, 1021, Futuyma 1979, 48–49). While there are many ways an organism can multiply exchanges with its environment (the specialized organelles of protozoa show a surprising degree of complexity, for example), "There is a limit to the number and size of structures compatible with reproduction. Beyond a certain threshold, to increase the number of cells and differentiate them becomes a way of economizing . . . as long as activities are coordinated [Jacob 1976, 312]." In fact, sociocultural evolution on the most general level can be characterized as the struggle to elaborate societal organization in proportion to the imperatives of an increasing population (Carneiro 1967, 241, note 8, White 1975, 20, 57–58).

Thus with an increase in magnitude of the result (the multiplication of individual organisms and groups), there is a progressive differentiation of structure and specialization of function (an increase in the number of *kinds* of parts that compose the evolving system). How is this expanding and increasingly differentiated or complex system integrated? How are these various and proliferating parts coordinated, in order that a coherent, patterned interaction among them is effected?

This is a very important question, for if a *system* is to be defined, and if it is to persist and to evolve in the thermodynamically irreversible evolutionary direction of increasing order and complexity, its parts much cohere in a structured network of interrelationship and interdependence. Parts must be subordinated to the whole; the parts must be related to each other, and the role of each regulated. Finally, a centralized coordination of structure and the specialization of function, which *require* ways and means to coordinate, regulate, and control the increasingly complex system, is achieved. And therefore, increasing system size, accompanied by an increasing number and variety of elements and components, gives rise to new organizational mechanisms to integrate the ever-increasing organic or social aggregate: Means of integration, regulation, and control are developed. Growth has provided the impetus for such development to occur. The pressure brought about by a quantitative increase of like units leads inevitably to a critical point or "threshold" at which the system, as noted previously, must collapse, fission, or reach a new organizational level by undergoing a qualitative transformation. "If it is to continue to accommodate and integrate its increasing units successfully, the system must elaborate its structure. It must develop [Carneiro 1967, 240, cf. White 1975, 21, 90]."

Functional specialization of units and an increasingly centralized integration of the system as a whole is the general response of a biological or social system to the stress occasioned within it by the multiplication of its units.

> For an organism to differentiate, for it to become more independent and to extend its exchanges with the outside world, there must be a development not only of the structures which link the organism to its environment, but also of the interactions which coordinate its constituents. At the macroscopic level, therefore, evolution depends on setting up new systems of communication, just as much within the organism as between the organism and its surroundings [Jacob 1976, 308].

The unitary, centralized coordination of functionally specialized parts constitutes, as a highly general case, the new system trajectory—stable to the equilibrium–destroying fluctuations generated by the proliferation of system parts.

Both the phenomenon of structural differentiation and that of a centralized coordination can readily be documented for biological and sociocultural systems. For example, social stratification is an important type of structural differentiation (Segraves 1977, 193–194). Prior to the Neolithic period, small and mobile groups often could fission relatively readily and establish themselves in new and less circumscribed areas. But with the relatively rapid expansion of settled communities based on plant cultivation and animal husbandry, fissioning was no longer a viable means of assuring access to sufficient resources, that is to say, access to a sufficient energy supply. And thus as human societies grew in size, they became increasingly stratified, for social ranking or stratification effectively regulated population vis-à-vis the available natural resources or major factors of production—land, labor, capital. That this establishment of what is purely and simply a dominance hierarchy functions as a mechanism for the regulation of the size of the population has been demonstrated by extensive research on the biological and the societal level of organization. It is well established that an unequivocal "pecking order" in animals emerges under signficantly constricted or circumscribed conditions (Schjelderup-Ebbe 1921). *Lepomis cyanellus,* the green sunfish, is an excellent case in point. In growing populations in (finite) aquaria, territories will be established by the males, the dominants rapidly obtaining the more choice territories. The lowest-ranking males are left with the poorer territories, or no territory at all (Greenburg 1947). In human societies, status differentiation is vividly documented for periods as early as the initial years of the Bronze Age in Denmark, where archaeologists have recorded a strong, positive correlation between size and density of settlement and (male) degree of social stratification (Randsborg 1975, 159, Figure 11). A recent mathematical model in sociology (Mayhew and Schollaert 1980) has shown that in an open distribution system—which takes into account the whole range of society from those of lowest status on—by chance alone, an increase in population size creates an increasing concentration of social inequality, ultimately pressing the system toward the maximum possible inequality.

It should be noted here that no knowledge of individual characteristics is necessary to a highly parsimonious and adequate explanation of social inequality (inequality in the amount of any social resource, be it power, prestige, or wealth, for example) as it occurs in any human group. Social inequality here is a societal variable, an organizational or structural characteristic of an evolving, self-organizing system. The general significance of this will be further clarified and discussed below.

On the most general level, political centralization is, like social stratification, a positive function of system size. Increasing system coordination, centrally integrated by a "decider" component (Miller 1965), is exemplified in the biological organism by the development of a central nervous system (CNS) and brain. For our purposes, political centralization, or the evolution in societies of a unitary coordinating and integrative component, is the major focus of concern. Paraphrasing Montesquieu (1978, 199), the nature of the system changes to the extent that the system constricts or extends its limits (see also Durkheim 1933, 223, Spencer 1967, 79, 162). As Hall and Fagan (1956, 86) have noted, as a system evolves in size and complexity, a progressive centralization occurs, and one part of the system emerges as a "central and controlling" agency (Miller's "decider" component).

Clearly, the sociocultural system constitutes a primary example of a "dissipative structure" in the terms of Prigogine, Allen, and Herman (1977, 2, 36). The spontaneous formation of a "new" coherent organization, a centrally coordinated organization, is attendant upon the instability generated by a sizeable, differentiated, and internally specialized system (in the absence of an adequate means of integrated functioning). The new structure or "stable trajectory" is a subset of the (more general) self-organizing system: It is a self-*regulating* system. The self-regulating system, characterized by a controlling component that coordinates in unitary fashion the direction or activity of the system, as a whole, is also a self-organizing system, in that its structure emerges out of a set of laws of nonlinear interaction as defined within bifurcation theory.

However, a highly general or "simple" self-organizing system—in which the numerous (otherwise) independent elements interact and do create some degree of organization, but no one of them controls the system—is not, as defined, a self-regulating system. This most basic level of interaction characteristic of the self-organizing system is exemplified by the small, acephalous groups anthropologists call "band-level" societies, egalitarian groups differentiated essentially only along the biological lines of age and sex. The transformative change or evolution in the organizational morphology of human societies from the Upper Paleolithic to the present documents the stepwise emergence and consolidation of increasingly complex self-regulating systems.

The proliferation and ramification of differentiated structures and specialized functions is necessarily accompanied by ever-increasing political centralization, control functions that determine guidelines under which these myriad system parts are efficiently organized and these various specialized functions are carried out and integrated, one with another. From "tribes" to "chiefdoms" to "the state," an ever-increasing degree of centralized coordination and control is evidenced. This trend is marked concretely by increasingly powerful leadership roles accompanied by increasingly numerous and ramiform levels of a generalized administrative and control hierarchy. This trend has been observed in band-level hunting and gathering groups that exceed a critical size. Larger and less mobile groups will tend ultimately to evolve in the general direction of a unitary, centralized coordination of group structure and operation (e.g., Lee 1972, 183). Further increases of political centralization and development are documented on the level of chiefdoms. It has been noted in these groups that the more centralized the control of the units of production, the more effective the means of societal collaboration in the economic and political spheres, and, indeed, on all societal fronts (Sahlins 1963, 300). Jacoby (1969) has examined the ultimate culmination of this trend toward bureaucratization and centralization of control in all aspects of life in highly complex state-level societies. This is a predictable outcome, for as system size increases, the rate of interaction among system parts increases, and the system becomes significantly more fragile to the commonly occurring stochastic perturbations or fluctuations that beset any system that depends for its existence and continued viability upon exchanges of matter, energy, and information with its environment (an "open" system).

A large system is inherently more "point vulnerable," having more points of articulation, both internally and externally, with its (social and biophysical) environment. It therefore has more points at which partial or complete disarticulation can occur (Mayhew 1980, 343–344, Figure 4, Segraves 1977, 194–195). A unitary control structure, the form of control structure characterized by a minority elite, minimizes the problem of point vulnerability in human societies (Mayhew 1973), just as do the CNS and the brain in biological organisms. In other words, a pressure to minimize this system vulnerability generates an oligarchy, a political structure in which a minority of the population governs or controls the system as a whole (Michels 1910, Pareto 1916). The relative size of this ruling elite or administrative component is thus a decreasing function of the size of the system it governs (Mosca 1896).

In both biological and sociocultural systems the form of system-wide administrative control or integration is hierarchical (Bowler 1980). This is not surprising, as the increase in complexity of a unitary regulatory mechanism is positively associated with stepwise increments in the efficiency with which this regulation or control is effected. Vertical and (immediately subsequent) horizontal specialization of such a regulatory mechanism results in an absolute decrease in the amount of time and energy expended in the integration of an increasing number of system parts and subparts. As suggested earlier, these step functions would seem to be of considerable significance for the study of the evolution of complex sociocultural systems, as they appear to indicate clear points of qualitative evolutionary change.

While it has been argued here that a complex system is necessarily a well-coordinated, centralized system, it is of course the case that some complex systems are less highly centralized or smoothly and efficiently coordinated than others. In part, this is a function of the expectation that, unit for unit, a society's structural complexity will increase more slowly than its population size or its spatial dimensions (Carneiro 1967, 240). In nature, there is rarely an absolute fit between size and organizational development. While villages, cities, provinces, and regions are all ultimately under the central administration of the more inclusive system (the society or integral region), the generation of increasingly numerous and ramified levels of hierarchy in large and highly differentiated systems means that urban centers and their regions must, and will, be delegated certain coordination and control functions by the central governing body of the wider state. And just as states or empires can be less tightly or more tighly coordinated, so some urban centers will be subject to a control more or less pervasive by their effective region or nation–state. There will be variable degrees of system integration, although the immediate (local) controlling agency, it should be supposed, is operating in just such a control capacity as a responsive extension of the central government.

In summary, if a complex system is to persist effectively, it must (in all system-critical respects) subordinate its parts to the whole, ensuring the coherence of these parts as hierarchical units in a network of interdependent interrelationships. Considering the marked heterogeneity of such a great many parts, there is, speaking on the most general level, only one basic organizational form that can be certain to ensure such an outcome. A control must be exercised over the system as a whole, coordinating its parts and regulating the role and activity of each. This is an organizational principle of near-uniform generality in the living world. It is clearly exemplified in complex biological and social systems, from multicellular organisms to the early states and classical empires. The behavior of a large and complex system, its efficiency, temporal persistence, competitive success, and probability of spatial expansion, are functions of the effectiveness of its centralized coordination and the integration of its multitude of varying parts.

One important implication for archaeologists (as for social scientists generally) of the abstract organizational nature of the constraints on system operation and evolution discussed here cannot go entirely unmentioned: Briefly, explanation and prediction of societal structure, operation, and transformation do not require the introduction of the individual (or his characteristics, such as "preferences" or "values") as relevant variables (q.e.d. Krippendorff 1971). Individual behavior or cognition is, quite simply, irrelevant to a rigorous comprehension of societal statics and dynamics. It is the general societal variables with which we must be concerned in our formulation of social theory, variables of social differentiation, such as stratification, the emergence and development of hierarchy, and political centralization. People's "beliefs" and even their value systems as a whole will ultimately change as the mutual and reinforcing feedback between population size and technological and economic organization presses the system in a new direction (cf. Allen Chapter 19 this volume). Ultimately, the ideological component of the system and people's values, beliefs, "choices," and so-called moral "imperatives" will come to conform in general fashion to the material organization that results from these structural shifts and the attainment of new dynamically steady states. It is society that is the principal, subsumptive, and definitive prior constraint. Without society, man is not man as we know him, but simply a rather highly developed biological organism.

## CONCLUDING REMARKS

It is assumed here that a general contextual or system perspective must inform our study and research, whether theoretical or empirical, analytical or applied. And because systems by definition are organized and coherently integrated entities rather than fortuitous aggregations of components, certain critical threshold values, and nonrandom and relatively regular nonlinear associations between certain system variables, generate a number of important general expectations of system operation, development, and transformation. As the combined experience of theoretical biology, paleontology, organizational sociology, and evolutionary anthropology and archaeology is witness to their broad spatio-temporal reality, it should be useful to take these relationships more explicitly into account in our research design and analysis, and perhaps particularly with respect to the concrete applications of general theory to the structure and functioning of the real world. To paraphrase Hutchinson (1978, 108): "It is quite likely that as the history of [archaeology] is better understood, it will appear that most [archaeological] discoveries consist in the recognition of significance rather than in the discovery of facts."

## REFERENCES

Allen, P. M., Denenbourg, J. L., Sanglier, M., Boon, F., and de Palma, A., 1978, *The Dynamics of Urban Evolution. Vol. I: Inter-urban Evolution*, Report No. DOT/TSC-RSPA-78-20, I, prepared for the U.S. Department of Transportation, Transportation Systems Center, Cambridge, Mass.

Bertalanffy, L. von, 1962, General systems theory—a critical review, *General Systems* 7, 1–20.

Bonner, J. T., 1974, *On Development: The Biology of Form*, Cambridge, Mass., Harvard University Press.

Bowler, T. D., 1980, Civilizations as systems, *Proceedings of the 25th Annual North American Meeting of the Society for General Systems Research with the AAAS*, Louisville, Society for General Systems Research, 509–517.

Burgess, J. M., 1963, On the emergence of patterns of order, *Bulletin of the American Mathematical Society* 69, 1–25.

Carneiro, R. L., 1967, On the relationship between size of population and complexity of social organization, *Southwestern Journal of Anthropology* 23, 234–243.

Carneiro, R. L., 1969, The measurement of cultural development in the ancient Near East and in Anglo–Saxon England, *Transactions of the New York Academy of Sciences*, Series II, 31(8), 1013–1023.

Comte, A., 1974, *The Positive Philosophy* (reprint of the 1855 translation by H. Martineau), New York, AMS Press.

Cracraft, J., and Eldredge, N., 1979, *Phylogenetic Analysis and Paleontology*, New York, Columbia University Press.

Dumond, D. E., 1965, Population growth and cultural change, *Southwestern Journal of Anthropology* 21, 302–324.

Duncan, O. D., 1957, Population distribution and community structure, in *Cold Spring Harbor Symposia on Quantitative Biology 22, Population Studies: Animal Ecology and Demography*, 357–371.

Durkheim, E., 1933, *The Division of Labor in Society*, New York, The Free Press.

Einstein, A., and Infeld, L., 1938, *The Evolution of Physics: From Early Concepts to Relativity*, New York, Simon and Schuster.

Eldredge, N., and Gould, S. J., 1972, Punctuated equilibrium: an alternative to phyletic gradualism, in Schopf, T. J. M. (ed.), *Models in Paleobiology*, San Francisco, Freeman, Cooper and Co., 82–115.

Futuyma, D. J., 1979, *Evolutionary Biology*, Sunderland, Mass., Sinauer Associates.

Glansdorff, P., and Prigogine, I., 1971, *Thermodynamics of Structure: Stability and Fluctuations*, New York, Wiley.

Greenburg, B., 1947, Some relations between territory, social hierarchy and leadership in the green sunfish (*Lepomis cyanellus*), *Physiological Zoology* 20, 267–299.

Halbwachs, M., 1960, *Population and Society: Introduction to Social Morphology*, trans. by O. D. Duncan and H. W. Pfantz, New York, The Free Press.

Hall, A. D., and Fagan, R. E., 1956, Definition of system, *General System* 1, 18–28.

Hawley, A. H., 1979, Cumulative change in theory and history, in Hawley, A. H. (ed.), *Societal Growth: Processes and Implications*, New York, The Free Press and the American Sociological Association, 19–29.

Hutchinson, G. E., 1978, *An Introduction to Population Ecology*, New Haven, Yale University Press.

Jacob, F., 1976, *The Logic of Life: A History of Heredity*, trans. by B. E. Spillman, New York, Vintage Books.

Jacoby, H., 1969, *Die Buerokratisierung der Welt*, Berlin, Hermann Luchterhand Verlag.

Krippendorff, K., 1971, Communication and the genesis of structure, *General Systems* 16, 171–185.

Lee, R. B., 1972, Work, effort, group structure and land-use in contemporary hunter–gatherers, in Ucko, P. J., Tringham, R., and Dimbleby, G. W., (eds.), *Man, Settlement and Urbanism*, London, Duckworth, 177–185.

MacCannell, E. D., 1968, Structural differentiation and rigidity in forty-eight states of the United States of America, Cornell University, unpublished doctoral dissertation.

Margalef, R., 1968, *Perspectives in Ecological Theory*, Chicago, University of Chicago Press.

Mayhew, B., 1973, System size and ruling elites, *American Sociological Review* 38, 468–475.

Mayhew, B., 1980, Structuralism versus Individualism: Part I, *Social Forces* 59(2), 335–375.

Mayhew, B., and James, T. F., 1972, System size and structural differentiation in military organizations: testing a harmonic series model of the division of labor, *American Journal of Sociology* 77, 750–765.

Mayhew, B., and Schollaert, P. T., 1980, The concentration of wealth: a sociological model, *Sociological Focus* 13, 1–35.

Michels, R., 1910, La democrazia e la legge ferrea dell'oligarchia, *Rassegna Contemporanea 3*, 259–283.

Miller, J.G., 1965, Living systems: basic concepts, *Behavioral Science* 10, 193–237.

Montesquieu, C. L. de S., 1748, *De l'Esprit des Loix*, I, Geneva, Barrillot et Fils.

Mosca, G., 1896, *Elementi di Scienza Politica*, Rome, Fratelli Bocca.

Narroll, R. S., 1956, A preliminary index of social development, *American Anthropologist* 57, 687–715.

Nicolis, G., and Prigogine, I., 1977, *Self-Organization in Non-Equilibrium Systems: From Dissipative Structures to Order through Fluctuations*, New York, Wiley.

Pareto, V., 1916, *Tratto di Sociologia Generale*, 2 vols., Firenze, Barbera.

Prigogine, I., Allen, P.M. and Herman, R., 1977, Long term trends and the evolution of complexity, in Laszlo, E., and Bierman, J. (eds.), *Goals in a Global Community: A Report to the Club of Rome, Vol I: Studies on the Conceptual Foundations*, New York, Pergamon Press, 1–63.

Randsborg, K., 1975, Population and social variation in Early Bronze Age Denmark: a systemic approach, in Polgar, S. (ed.), *Population, Ecology and Social Evolution*, The Hague, Mouton, 139–166.

Rensch, B., 1959, *Evolution above the Species Level*, New York, Columbia University Press.

Rosen, R., 1979, Morphogenesis in biological and social systems, in Renfrew, C., and Cooke, K.L. (eds.), *Transformations: Mathematical Approaches to Culture Change*, New York, Academic Press, 91–111.

Sahlins, M. D., 1963, Poor man, rich man, big-man, chief: political types in Melanesia and Polynesia, *Comparative Studies in Society and History*, 5, 285–303.

Schjelderup-Ebbe, T., 1921, *Beitraege zur Sozial- und Individualpsychologie bei Gallus domesticus*, Greifswald, published by the author.

Schrödinger, E., 1967, *What is Life? The Physical Aspect of the Living Cell*, Cambridge, Cambridge University Press.

Segraves, B. A., 1974, Ecological generalization and structural transformation of sociocultural systems, *American Anthropologist* 76, 530–552.

Segraves, B. A., 1977, The Malthusian proposition and nutritional stress: differing implications for man and for society, in Greene, L.S. (ed.), *Malnutrition, Behavior and Social Organization*, New York, Academic Press, 173–218.

Spencer, H., 1967, *The Evolution of Society: Selections from Herbert Spencer's Principles of Sociology*, edited by R. L. Carneiro, Chicago, Aldine.

Stebbins, G. L., 1969, *The Basis of Progressive Evolution*, Chapel Hill, University of North Carolina Press.

White, L. A., 1975, *The Concept of Cultural Systems: A Key to Understanding Tribes and Nations*, New York, Columbia University Press.

# 17

## On a Theory of Transformations
## for Cultural Systems
*ROBERT ROSEN*

## INTRODUCTION

Morphogenesis is the study of the mechanisms that generate pattern and form. Morphogenetic problems are thus central to every scientific discipline. Until rather recently, each discipline dealt with the morphogenetic problems it faced entirely within its own intradisciplinary context. Lately, however, it has become clear that the basic features of morphogenesis are of a more universal currency, and that when these features are articulated and clarifed, *intra*disciplinary morphogenetic problems may be viewed in a more profound *inter*disciplinary light. The purpose of the present chapter is to sketch some of these universal features of morphogenesis, to indicate some of their implications, and to suggest how they may bear on the human sciences.

One of the first articulate advocates of a universal approach to morphogenesis was the British naturalist D'Arcy Wentworth Thompson. In his classic book *On Growth and Form*, which first appeared in 1917, he developed this thesis in two ways. On the one hand, he argued at great length that the same forces that give shape to inanimate objects also manifest themselves in the biosphere. Thus a large part of the book was devoted to analyses of specific kinds of form-determining forces, such as cohesion and surface tension. In the remainder of the book, however, Thompson sought to develop the general principles governing the interrelationships between magnitudes that characterize form. The point of

**301**

THEORY AND EXPLANATION
IN ARCHAEOLOGY

departure here was the basic laws of scaling and similitude. These were already known to the Greeks, and their systematic study in modern times originated with no less a person than Galileo. From our present perspective, I would venture to suggest that the study of similarity has, in its most general context, become the most potent and fertile force in modern science.

In the final chapter of his book, D'Arcy Thompson proposed that considerations of similitude could provide an analytic tool for understanding the dynamics of successions of forms in biology, both in their developmental and their evolutionary context. His formulation of these ideas has become known as the "theory of transformations," and may be paraphrased as: *closely related forms are similar.* This assertion is far from trivial or tautological in biology, for it relates two disparate functional realms. "Closely related" is a concept pertaining to *genotype*, while "similarity" pertains to *phenotype.*

It might be thought that Thompson's theory of transformations has no content outside biology, for only in biology do the concepts of genotype and phenotype appear meaningful. Thus in particular, we might suppose that Thompson's ideas could have no bearing on successions of form in inanimate nature, nor in the human sciences. It will be shown, however, that this is not so—that Thompson's ideas have a far more universal currency than commonly assumed, and have implications of the most profound sort for any kind of morphogenetic processes. In the course of justifying this last assertion, we will incidentally show that the basic concepts of phenotype and genotype themselves have a universal significance. This fact alone turns out to be basic for establishing fruitful homologies between apparently disparate scientific realms. The remainder of our discussion is intended to suggest how these assertions may be justified, and to indicate how they may be applied.

## SOME GENERALITIES: GENOTYPE, PHENOTYPE, AND ENVIRONMENT

The external world presents us with a spectrum of percepts, which it is the task of the mind to organize in some coherent fashion. The basic act of organization is the segregation of certain of these percepts into a common category. Such a common category of distinguished percepts is, broadly, what we call a "system." Those percepts assigned to a particular system may variously be called its attributes, or modalities, or observables. All those percepts not assigned to a system thereby fall into the complementary category, that of "environment." The boundary separating system from environment is to a large extent subjective, in that it may be drawn in an arbitrary way, but the drawing of such boundaries is the first essential act of the mind in organizing the percepts impinging upon it.

Once a class of percepts is segregated together to constitute a system, a mind must perform a second act of classification. Namely, we recognize that certain system modalities or observables can change their values from moment to moment, without our perceiving that an essential change has occurred in the *identity* of the system. The identity of the solar system, e.g., is unaffected by the fact that the constituent planets constantly change their positions in the sky. The identity of an organism is conserved despite the often dramatic changes that occur during its development, etc. Those percepts that can change their values without affecting the identity of a system may generally be called its "variables of state," and the totality of different values that these state variables may assume defines for us the totality of different "states" in which our system may be found.

The remaining system percepts, by definition, must be those that confer specific identity on our system. Their values must be conserved, regardless of whatever changes of state are occurring in the system. They thus define for us the "species" of system with which we are dealing. The totality of different values that these percepts can assume thus comprises the totality of different system species that can exist. Borrowing a pregnant term from biology, percepts in this category will be called "genotypic." If we adopt this terminology, it is therefore natural to call the class of particular states in which a given species of system may be found the class of possible "phenotypes" for that system.

Let us visualize this situation pictorially. Let us think of the totality of values that may be assigned to the genotypic percepts as constituting a space $A$. To each element $a$ of $A$ (i.e., to each species of system) there is a corresponding space $X_a$ comprising the states or phenotypes in which that system may be found. The resulting picture may be visualized as in Figure 17.1.

Let us note explicitly that, just as was the case in distinguishing system from environment, the boundary we draw between those percepts we assign to genotype and phenotype are to some extent subjective and arbitrary. Nevertheless, just as before, the boundary *must* be drawn somewhere, or else our perceptual world degenerates into chaos.

We wish to stress the fact that the segregation of system observables into the categories of phenotype and genotype is as fundamental as the prior segregation of percepts into the categories of system and environment. Thus, the concepts of genotype and phenotype are meaningful and basic to the definition of *any* system, and are not restricted to those systems of biological origin. These facts alone have many important consequences, which, however, we shall not pause to discuss here.

There is one final basic feature of system perception that must be mentioned. Namely, underlying our very definition of a class of percepts as a system is the intuition that these percepts do not change independently and arbitrarily. This means that the various behaviors that a system can exhibit must obey definite rules or laws, which serve to *link* the values of system observables. Such rules or laws will generally be called "equations of state" for the system.

In general, then, we would expect that any system behavior is described by a corresponding equation of state, linking together observables pertaining to each of the three categories we have isolated above. That is, any system behavior is

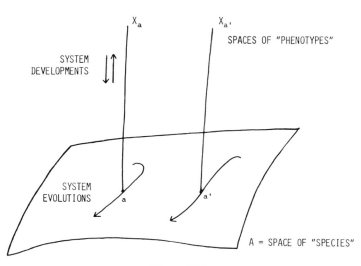

**Figure 17.1.**

described by relations linking together genotypic, phenotypic, and environmental qualities. Such a relation may be written schematically in the form

$$\Phi(a, x, e) = 0,$$

where $a$ is an element of the space $A$ of species, $x$ is an element of the corresponding space $X_a$ of system phenotypes, and $e$ is an element of some appropriate environment space $E$.

Certain of the phenotypic observables appearing in such an equation of state may represent the rates of change or velocities with which other phenotypic observables are changing in time. Equations of state that relate such velocities to other magnitudes are generally called "dynamical laws" or "rate equations" for the system. They provide the vehicles through which temporal predictions about our system may be made. Further, if we let time become infinite in such a rate law, it often happens that time disappears from the relation. The resulting time-independent law then characterizes those states or phenotypes pertaining to *steady-state* or *system equilibrium*.

An equation of state in which only phenotype is changing describes what we shall call a "development" of the system. A system development is thus visualized as some curve or trajectory in a fixed space $X_a$ of phenotypes. On the other hand, a situation in which the genotypic qualities are themselves changing will be called a system "evolution." Thus, a system evolution is visualized as a curve or trajectory in the space $A$ of species. These concepts are schematically indicated in Figure 17.1. The distinction between *intraspecific* change, or development, and *interspecific* change, or evolution, is a fundamental one. It must not be (though it generally has been) ignored.

## SIMILARITY

In the present section, we shall sketch the final basic idea needed to properly formulate D'Arcy Thompson's assertion that "closely related forms are similar." What follows is not intended to be a rigorous or fully general exposition of the concept of similarity. It is meant to indicate the flavor of the basic ideas and to illustrate the conclusions to be drawn subsequently.

Let $X$ be any collection of things. A relation of *similarity* among the elements of $X$ may be most simply established by the positing of numerical criteria $r_1, \ldots, r_k$ that may assume definite numerical values on the elements of $X$. We then define two elements, $x, x'$ of $X$ to be *similar* if and only if $r_i(x) = r_i(x')$ for each $i = 1, \ldots, k$. That is, $x$ and $x'$ are similar if our numerical criteria cannot distinguish between them. The similarity relation thus imposed is clearly one of equivalence. Under it, the set $X$ falls apart into disjoint equivalence classes, each of which consists of all the elements of $X$ that are similar to any given one of them.

Given a similarity relation defined in this way, there is an associated set of *similarity transformations* of the set $X$. A similarity transformation is a 1–1 correspondence, or permutation, of the elements of $X$, with the property that

$$r_i(Tx) = r_i(x), \qquad i = 1, \ldots, k.$$

The totality of similarity transformations of $X$ comprises a set $G$. In fact $G$ is mathematically a group under the operation of composition of mappings. Then it is easy to show that two elements $x, x'$ of $X$ are similar if and only if there is a similarity transformation $T$ in $G$ such that $x' = Tx$. Thus, the equivalence class of any element $x$ of $X$ (i.e., the set of all $x'$ similar to $x$) consists of the set of images of $x$ under all the similarity transformations in $G$.

Conversely, we may define a similarity relation on $X$ by *positing* by fiat that a particular group $G$ of permutations of $X$ shall be the similarity transformations. Thus, two elements $x, x'$ of $X$ are similar if and only if $x' = Tx$ for some $T$ in $G$. A numerical criterion $r$ on $X$ is called an *invariant* of the similarity relation if it cannot distinguish between similar elements; i.e., if $r(Tx) = r(x)$ for every $x$ in $X$ and every $T$ in $G$. It follows that, if $r(x) \neq r(x')$, then $x$ and $x'$ cannot be similar. However, if $r(x) = r(x')$, we cannot conclude that $x$ and $x'$ actually are similar. A *complete set* of such invariants is a of family criteria $r_1, \ldots, r_k$ (we will suppose $k$ is finite) such that $x, x'$ are similar if and only if $r_i(x) = r_i(x')$ for each $i = 1, \ldots, k$.

Thus in general a similarity relation on any collection of things $X$ can be defined *either* by positing a set $r_i$ of numerical criteria, *or else* by mandating that a preassigned group of permutations of $X$ shall constitute the similarity transformations.

Now let us imagine that the set $X$, and a set of similarity criteria $r_1, \ldots, r_k$ are given. We are going to introduce a set of *co-ordinates* into $X$ in the following way: We can characterize the equivalence class to which a given element $x$ in $X$

belongs by a *k–tuple* of numbers $(u_1, \ldots, u_k)$, where $u_i = r_i(x)$, $i = 1, \ldots, k$. We shall suppose further that we can locate the elements $x$ within its equivalence class with another $m$–tuple of numbers $(v_1, \ldots, v_m)$. Thus, the specific element $x$ in $X$ can be located exactly by a set of $m + k$ numbers:

$$x \to (u_1, \ldots, u_k, v_1, \ldots, v_m)$$

where the first $k$ numbers specify the equivalence class to which $x$ belongs, and the last $m$ numbers specify $x$ within its equivalence class.

This choice of co-ordinates partitions $X$ in a way reminiscent of that shown in Figure 17.1 above. Namely, we can regard the co-ordinates $u_1, \ldots, u_k$ as comprising a set $U$. To each element of $U$, there is an associated set $V_u$, consisting of all elements of $X$ lying in the equivalence class defined by $u$. Thus, we have the situation diagrammed in Figure 17.2.

The point of this co-ordinatization is the following: Under it, a similarity transformation $T$ on $X$ takes a particularly simple form. By definition, such a transformation must be the identity on $U$, whereas it can be an arbitrary permutation on each of the sets $V_u$. More formally, in this co-ordinatization, a similarity transformation must satisfy

$$T(u_1, \ldots, u_k, v_1, \ldots, v_m) = (u_1, \ldots, u_k, \bar{T}(v_1, \ldots, v_m))$$

where $\bar{T}$ is an arbitrary permutation.

Next, let us suppose that we have at our disposal some other, independent means for introducing co-ordinates into $X$. That is, suppose that we can locate an element of $x$ as an ordered $n$–tuple of numbers:

$$x \to (x_1, \ldots, x_n).$$

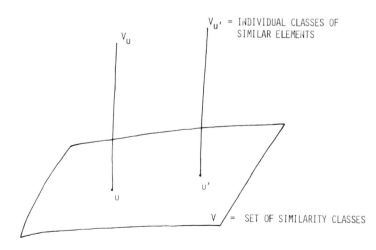

Figure 17.2.

There must then be a relation, or co-ordinate transformation, by means of which we can translate between the two co-ordinate representations imposed on the same set $X$. Such a co-ordinate transformation can be expressed in the form

$$\begin{cases} u_i = u_i(x_1, \ldots, x_n) \; i = 1, \ldots, k; \\ v_i = v_i(x_1, \ldots, x_n) \; i = 1, \ldots, m. \end{cases}$$

Let us eliminate the $k$ numbers $u_i$ from among these relations, by expressing them in terms of the $v$'s and the $x$'s. When we do this, we obtain yet a third co-ordinatization of $X$, of the form

$$x \rightarrow (v_1, \ldots, v_m, \; \xi_1, \ldots, \xi_{n-k}).$$

Here the values of the new co-ordinates $\xi_i$ depend on the $x$'s and the $v$'s. For this reason, the co-ordinates $\xi_i$ will be called "derived" quantities. The original co-ordinates $v_i$, which are unaffected by the transformation we have made, will be called "fundamental."

Now let us see what a similarity transformation $T$ looks like in this final set of co-ordinates. We recall that a similarity transformation could be *arbitrary* on what we are now calling the fundamental quantities. However, on the derived quantities, $T$ is strongly constrained by the condition that it must be the identity on the set $U$. To see more explicitly what is happening, let us visualize the situation analogously to our diagrams of Figures 17.1 and 17.2:

In this figure, we have decomposed our original space $X$ into a manifold $V$ or fundamental quantities, and to each element $v$ in $V$, an associated set $X_v$ of derived quantities, co-ordinatized by $\xi_1, \ldots, \xi_{n-k}$. In these co-ordinates, a similarity transformation is *arbitrary* on the set $V$ of fundamental quantities,

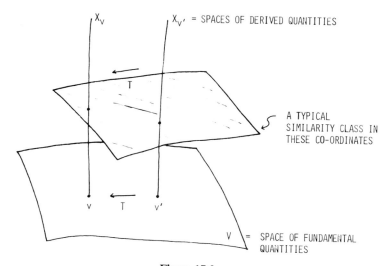

Figure 17.3.

i.e., given two elements $v$, $v'$ in $V$, there is a similarity transformation such that $v' = Tv$. Furthermore, $T$ induces a highly restricted correspondence between $X = X_v$ and $X_{v'} = X_{T(v)}$. It is these restricted correspondences between spaces of derived quantities that are usually called "similarities" in the literature.

The essence of the preceding discussion is the following: *Given a similarity relation imposed on a class of systems, we can classify all system observables relative to that similarity relation into two classes—those observables that are* fundamental, *and those that are* derived. *The fundamental observables are those that can transform* arbitrarily *under a similarity relation. The derived quantities are those that cannot. This distinction between fundamental and derived quantities is the final thread we need. Now we can begin to make the tapestry.*


## THE THEORY OF TRANSFORMATION

We now return to a consideration of D'Arcy Thompson's assertion that "closely related organisms are similar."

The crux of our discussion involves the juxtaposition of the different ways of classifying system observables that we developed in the preceding two sections. In the first of these, we classified observables as genotypic, phenotypic, or environmental. Under this classification, then, we may say that two systems are *closely related* if their genotypic observables assume values that are numerically close, i.e., if their genotypes lie in the same small neighborhood in the genotype space $A$ sketched in Figure 17.1.

On the other hand, in the last section, we classified observables as fundamental or derived with respect to a similarity relation. We saw that if we impose a concept of similarity, certain observables (the fundamental ones) transform arbitrarily under similarity transformations, while others (the derived ones) do not.

From these facts, we can immediately conclude that ($a$) the D'Arcy Thompson assertion is, in fact, meaningful universally, since the phenotype–genotype distinction is itself universal; ($b$) the assertion *must* be false if there are genotypic quantities that are not fundamental; and ($c$) the assertion is unrestrictedly true if every genomic quantity is also fundamental.

Let us enlarge a bit on these conclusions. We begin by restating the situation described at the end of the preceding section. We saw that any system state could be represented as an ordered pair of the form $(\mathbf{v}, \xi)$ where $\mathbf{v}$ is a vector of fundamental quantities, and $\xi$ in $X_v$ is a vector of derived quantities. A similarity transformation applied to such a pair $(\mathbf{v}, \xi)$ gives us a new pair $(\mathbf{v}', \boldsymbol{\xi}') = (v', \overline{T}\xi)$, where $\overline{T}\xi$ is in $X_{v'}$. Under these circumstances, we say that $\xi$ in $T_v$ and $\xi'$ in $T_{v'}$ are *corresponding states*.

If now every genomic quantity is fundamental, then every genomic quantity is a component of the fundamental vectors **v**. An arbitrary change or "mutation" in the value of such a genomic quantity results in the replacement of a given vector **v** by some new vector **v'**. But there is also a similarity transformation $T$ whose restriction to **V** also satisfies $Tv = v'$. For any derived vector in $X_v$, this transformation determines a corresponding vector $\xi' = \bar{T}\xi$ in $X_{v'}$; the difference between $\xi$ and $\xi'$ represents the phenotypic effect of the "mutation." Further, by definition, $\xi$ and $\xi'$ differ by a similarity. This is an abstract version of the familiar "law of corresponding states" in physics and of the various principles of similitude in engineering. In such a situation, if we know a system state $(v, \xi)$, then we can *infer* the properties of any corresponding state, through an application of the appropriate similarity transformation.

This is the basic principle behind such diverse activities as the employment of "scale models" in engineering, and the extrapolation of physiological, medical, and pharmacological properties from rats to man. As we have seen, it depends on an assumption of the unrestricted validity of D'Arcy Thompson's hypothesis, and hence on the condition that all genotypic quantities are also fundamental.

Now let us suppose that there is a genotypic quantity that is not fundamental. Such a quantity must then constitute a component of the derived vectors $\xi$. A "mutation" in such a quantity will then leave every vector **v** of fundamental quantities *unaffected* (i.e., will give rise to the identity transformation on **V**), but it will induce a mapping $\xi \to \xi'$ on the $X_v$. In general, such a mapping can not arise from a similarity transformation, and hence the original and "mutated" phenotypes must be *dissimilar*. Thus, the D'Arcy Thompson hypothesis necessarily fails in this case.

When an unmutated and mutated genotypic quantity give rise, respectively, to fundamentally dissimilar phenotypes, we may speak of an "emergence" or an "emergent evolution." In such a case, the properties of the new phenotype cannot be predicted by applying a similarity transformation to the original one. Any measure of the deviation between the actual new phenotype and that predicted from similarity considerations will measure the extent of the emergence. Any such measure can be thought of as a "new variable of state" for the mutated phenotype. For this reason, emergent phenomena generally seem to be accompanied by a corresponding "increase in complexity." A corollary of this viewpoint is that the intuitive concept of "evolutionary levels" becomes concretely realized in terms of successive changes in the nonfundamental genotypic quantities, and hence by the projection of an evolutionary trajectory onto the subspace spanned by these qualities. These successive changes can be interpreted as forming a hierarchy in the usual way.

Another corollary is that the capacity of a given system for emergent evolution depends on the criteria for similarity that we initially impose on the system. This is because the classification of system qualities as fundamental or derived depends entirely on these similarity criteria, and hence so too does the existence of the nonfundamental genotypic qualities on which emergent evolution depends. In mathematical terms, the determining feature is the size of the group of similarity transformations. Roughly, if this group is small, emergence is generic. If the group is large, emergence will be rare.

There are many other interesting conclusions that may be drawn from the scheme we have sketched here, but that we cannot develop further in this short space. For instance, the well-known biological phenomenon of pleiotropy (the extent to which a single genotypic quality influences a spectrum of phenotypic qualities) and the dual phenomenon of polygeny (the extent to which a single phenotypic quality is influenced by a spectrum of distinct genotypic qualities) has many interesting ramifications. We shall content ourselves with pointing out a few properties of developmental phenomena, which we have relatively ignored so far, and which in biology represent the main thrust of morphogenetic studies.

Developmental phenomena are governed by dynamical laws imposed on sets $X_a$ of phenotypes. We can think of comparing the dynamics of development of a species $a$ to that of a different species $a'$. In particular, we can ask whether the developmental trajectories of the first species can be transformed into those of the second by means of similarity transformation $T$. If this is the case, then we automatically obtain a transformation relating the *rates* at which developmental processes occur in the two species and hence of the time scales governing these developments. This is often paraphrased in biology by the assertion that developing species are in corresponding states at corresponding instants, and it shows that time must be scaled (i.e., is subject to consideration of similarity) in the same way that all other system qualities are.

A second idea that may be explored in this context is that of *recapitulation*. In biology, recapitulation asserts a relation between a *developmental* trajectory in a space $X_a$ and the *evolutionary* trajectory in $A$ through which the species $a$ was generated. The hypothesis of recapitulation is schematically indicated in Figure 17.4.

Briefly, in recapitulation, the developmental process of a species $a$, which evolved along a trajectory in $A$ passing successively through species $a'$, $a''$, $a'''$, etc., passes through the same forms on its developmental trajectory $X_a$. Or, still more briefly, ontogeny recapitulates phylogeny. Such a relation between evolution and development is probably not true in the simple-minded form we have stated, but some related principle may be of general validity. It would clearly be of great importance to formulate such a principle correctly.

## SOME IMPLICATIONS FOR CULTURAL MORPHOGENESIS

The considerations developed in the preceding sections are completely general. They pertain in a basic way to the study of any class of systems that can evolve and develop. In order to apply them systematically, we must make a

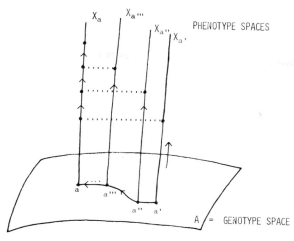

**Figure 17.4.**

number of initial classifications or choices. How we make these choices determines the character of our science.

As we have seen the nature of these classifications is imposed on us by the manner in which the mind organizes percepts. Our only option here is to make these classifications explicit, or leave them tacit. In the latter case, since different observers organize percepts in different ways, the result will be endless and furitless controversy. A viable morphogenetic science begins only when our classifications are made explicit.

To begin, we must decide which system qualities pertain to system identity, and which pertain to system phenotype or state. On this choice depends the very manner in which we discriminate between one system and another, as well as the crucial distinction between system development and system evolution. Having made this decision, we must then decide on how similarity between different systems is to be recognized. From this choice follows the classification of system qualities as fundamental or derived. This distinction is central to the study of succession of form, to the notion of emergent novelty, and to the systematic generation of hierarchies of organization in the course of morphogenesis.

In anthropological, sociological, and archaeological studies, the basic systems of interest are cultures of societies. The primary goal is to understand the manner in which they evolve and develop. In such a context, our first choice must be to characterize those qualities that convey essential identity to a culture (i.e., its genotype) and whose specific values distinguish one species of culture from another. The remaining qualities are then phenotypic, and may vary without affecting the basic identity of the culture. As usual, changes in the former qualities are the hallmark of culture evolution. Changes in the latter qualities characterize cultural development.

Our next choice is to specify the circumstances under which we will characterize cultures as similar or dissimilar. As we have seen, this will define for us a class of similarity transformations, with respect to which a particular system quality is either fundamental or derived. From this will follow, among other things, the laws of scale governing evolution within similarity classes and the character of emergent evolution that occurs when we pass from one such class to another.

One important benefit of organizing morphogenic studies in this manner is that morphogenetic processes occurring in different realms immediately become comparable. Thus, for example, the morphogenetic processes occurring in biology may be compared with those studied in anthropology and archaeology. The results of such comparisons should be exceedingly fruitful for both disciplines.

Let us consider one example. Biological evolution is governed by principles of natural selection, which may roughly be formulated in the following way: Under a given set of environmental circumstances there is some optimal or "fittest" phenotype. Similarity criteria should be chosen in such a way that similar phenotypes have the same fitness. The role of natural selection is to impose a kind of dynamics on the space of genotypes having the following property: When an arbitrary genotype is placed into a given environment, the trajectory it determines will coverge to that genotype producing the optimal phenotype in the given environment. Thus, selection is a device for allowing phenotypes to act on genotypes.

Something analogous must happen in the evolution of cultural systems. The specific *mechanism* by which phenotype acts on genotype in cultural evolution is, of course, different from that occurring in biology, since there is no direct analog to biological hereditary mechanisms in cultural systems. Indeed, we might suppose that the nature of the action of phenotype on genotype that drives cultural evolution is more like what in biology is called Lamarckian, i.e., that cultural evolution is like the biology of Lamarckian organisms. In such a situation, the selection criteria driving the evolution are internalized, instead of being imposed from without as in the Darwinian case.

On the other hand, cultural *development* may be much more contingent on environmental factors than is biological development. In the biological realm, the environmental features governing developmental (and physiological) processes have been internalized, perhaps to a far greater extent than is the case in cultural systems, and hence these processes appear to be self-organizing and relatively independent of environment. Perhaps we may argue that the distinction between cultures and organisms is essentially this: that human systems have internalized their selection mechanisms while organisms have internalized developmental and physiological ones.

Any further pursuit of these ideas in the realm of cultural dynamics will have to await someone more knowledgeable than the present author. However, we hope to have at least indicated some of the basic principles underlying morphological studies of any kind and to have convinced the reader that their systematic pursuit is of importance.

# 18

## Decision Making and Evolution

*E. C. ZEEMAN*

## INTRODUCTION

We shall compare decision making with biological evolution and discuss some of the similarities and differences between them. The aim is to shed light on social evolution, because the structure of society is sometimes changed by decision makers but at other times it seems to adapt to socioeconomic pressures in a manner more similar to the way a biological species evolves.

The discussion is based on the application of catastrophe theory (Thom 1972, Zeeman 1977) to Bayesian decision theory (Smith, Harrison, and Zeeman 1981). Bayesian theory is one of the standard planning tools used in industry and government. The decision $x$ lies in some space $X$ of possible decisions. The choice of decision is based on two things: first, information or beliefs about the future, and second, the utilities or preferences of the decision maker. I will explain in the next section how the information and utilities can be expressed mathematically as functions and integrated together to give a risk function $R$ on the decision space $X$. The decision maker then chooses the minimum of $R$, in other words selects the decision $x$ that minimizes the risk $R(x)$. This is called the *Bayes decision* (see Figure 18.1).

Meanwhile, in biological evolution the space $X$ represents the possible mutations of a species. The function $R$ represents unfitness, and is based on the likelihood of the future environment and the adaptability of possible mutants

**315**

THEORY AND EXPLANATION
IN ARCHAEOLOGY

to that environment. Darwinian natural selection then causes the species to evolve to a local minimum of $R$, representing minimal unfitness or, in other words, maximal fitness.

The similarity between the two processes is that they both select a minimum of $R$; the difference between them is that in the first case the minimum is *global*, whereas in the second case it is only *local*. The reason that the minimum is global in the first case is that the decision maker has access to the risk function defined over the whole of the decision space and can therefore select the global (or absolute) minimum. By contrast, in the second case mutation is only local, and if a species is already at a local minimum then natural selection will act against mutants to keep it there. If there is another lower minimum, the species will be denied access to it, even though it offers a better chance of survival. In this sense biological evolution appears to act blindly, because it cannot see the valley over the next hill.

It is a pertinent question to ask whether the evolution of human society can act equally blindly. For it is a familiar paradox to see society drifting toward some impending catastrophe or other, with the individuals in that society aware, yet apparently powerless to prevent it. By the word *catastrophe* in this context we mean some discontinuity in the structure of society brought about by gradually changing circumstances. At first sight it is not clear why gradually changing circumstances should produce a discontinuous effect—indeed it violates the intuition, since continuous causes normally produce continuous effects. However, there has been a considerable advance in the mathematical understanding of such phenomena during the last decade, and the method of modeling them is called *catastrophe theory*. The originator of the theory, René Thom (1972), chose the name to emphasize the unexpectedness of the discontinuities. Assuming very general hypotheses, there are theorems classifying the types of discontinuity that can occur, and if a phenomenon satisfies these hypotheses, then it can be modeled by one or another of a few standard geometric shapes. Although the proofs of the theorems are difficult for the nonspecialist, some of the geometric shapes are easy to visualize, as will be shown.

Let us return to the decision maker and ask what governs changes of decision. As time progresses, both the information and the utilities may be gradually changing, and consequently the risk function $R$ will be gradually changing. Assuming that the decision maker abides by the rule of minimizing the risk, then this in turn will cause the decision $x$ to vary in $X$. For most of the time this variation will be continuous, but at certain moments there may be abrupt switches of decision. For example, suppose a decision maker is holding the decision $x_0$ at the global minimum of $R$ and observes that the risk at another local minimum of $R$ at a distant decision point $x_1$ is gradually falling relative to the risk at $x_0$. Then as soon as $R(x_1)$ falls below $R(x_0)$ the decision maker will switch from $x_0$ to $x_1$ in order to abide by the rule of always minimizing the risk. This is illustrated in Figure 18.1 (a). Here the decision space $X$ is represented by the horizontal axis, and the risk $R$ by the vertical axis. The gradually changing risk function is illustrated by the sequence of seven graphs, labeled 1, 2, ..., 7. Notice that the way we have drawn the graphs the risk is in fact steadily rising everywhere, including at $x_0$ and at $x_1$, but nevertheless $R(x_1)$ is falling *relative* to $R(x_0)$. The switch from $x_0$ to $x_1$ takes place at the time of graph number 4. In the language of catastrophe theory, the *decision switch* takes place at the *Maxwell point* 4, where the two minima are at the same level, and the *decision path* is said to obey the *Maxwell convention* (Thom 1972, Zeeman 1977).

The reader may protest that these graphs, which we have drawn to illustrate the point, are perhaps somewhat artificial; in fact the opposite is the case, because such graphs arise naturally from integrating together typical hypotheses about information and utilities, as we shall see in Example 2 and Figure 18.8.

In practice the decision maker may delay making the switch due to investment in the previous decision: For example, an industry may delay changing production due to investment in a plant, or a government may delay changing policy due to investment in credibility. This type of delay can be incorporated into the risk function, or specified in terms of thresholds that the excess risk must reach before the switch is made. However, for simplicity we shall ignore such thresholds in this chapter, because we want to contrast decision switches with the more fundamental type of delay that occurs in evolution.

Figure 18.1 (b) illustrates the analogous situation in biological evolution. Here the seven graphs represent a gradually changing unfitness function, caused, for example, by a gradually changing environment. The species starts at the local minimum at $x_0$ and will be held there by natural selection as long as that minimum exists. The resulting behavior is different from that of the decision maker because, for instance, by the time of graph number 5 the species will still be held at $x_0$, in spite of the fact that the minimum at $x_1$ is already lower. Therefore the switch will be delayed until graph number 6, where the minimum at $x_0$ coalesces with the maximum and disappears. The disappearance of the minimum causes a breakdown in the stability of the species, because now any mutation toward $x_1$ will be fitter, and so natural selection will automatically cause the species to evolve rapidly in that direction until it reaches $x_1$. Of course the evolution $x_0 \rightarrow x_1$ may in fact take many generations, but it is still "rapid" when compared with the evolutionary time scale, and it is liable to produce a discontinuity in the fossil record. Such a discontinuity is sometimes called a quantum evolution (Dodson 1972). In the language of catastrophe theory, the *evolution switch* takes place at the *bifurcation point* 6, where the maximum and minimum coalesce and the *evolution path* is said to obey the *delay convention* (Thom 1972, Zeeman 1977).

It is somewhat surprising to find that the same underlying mechanism of natural selection is responsible for two such manifestly different types of evolution as gradual adaptation and sudden switches. Indeed some present-day biologists, when they find that the fossil record consists of periods of relative

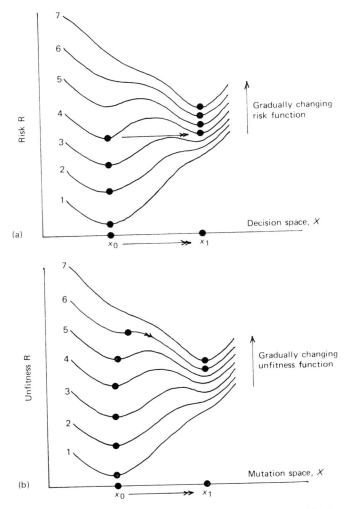

**Figure 18.1**(a) Graphs 1–7 show a gradually changing risk function. The resulting Bayes decisions are shown by dots. The decision switch $x_0 \rightarrow x_1$ occurs at graph number 4, where the two minima are at the same level. (b) Graphs 1–7 show a gradually changing unfitness function. The resulting evolution path is shown by dots. The evolution switch $x_0 \rightarrow x_1$ occurs at graph number 6, where the minimum at $x_0$ coalesces with the maximum and disappears.

constancy separated by discontinuities, mistakenly conclude that Darwin must have been wrong. On the contrary, the geometry of Figure 18.1 (b) shows that when Darwin's original concept of natural selection is applied rigorously, it predicts precisely that type of fossil record. When a fossil species terminates, indicating that the species became extinct, it does not necessarily mean that that evolutionary line died out, because it may have survived by means of an evolution switch into what appears to be a different species. Birds may be the surving dinosaurs.

SUMMARIZING:

Gradually changing risk →
$\left\{\begin{array}{l}\text{Gradual adjustment of decision, most} \\ \text{of the time} \\ \\ \text{Sudden switches of decision, sometimes}\end{array}\right.$

Gradually changing unfitness →
$\left\{\begin{array}{l}\text{Gradual evolution, most of the time} \\ \\ \text{Sudden switches of evolution,} \\ \text{sometimes}\end{array}\right.$

The comparison between the decision path and the evolution path is shown in Figure 18.2. Here the horizontal axis represents a one-dimensional parameter space $C$ parametrizing the gradually changing risk and unfitness functions pictured in Figure 18.1. The vertical axis represents the decision space or mutation space $X$. The curve $S$ represents the set of critical points of the risk and

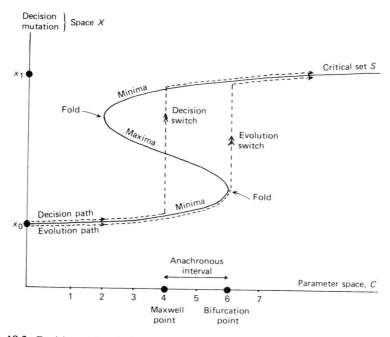

**Figure 18.2.** Decision and evolution paths due to a gradually increasing parameter. The decision path switches at the Maxwell point 4. The evolution path delays during the anachronous interval 46 and switches at the bifurcation point 6.

unfitness functions, the upper and lower branches representing minima, and the middle folded-over piece representing maxima. For example, over the parameter point 1 there is a single point on $S$ corresponding to the single minimum at $x_0$ of graph number 1 in Figure 18.1. Meanwhile over the parameter point 3 there are three points on $S$, the upper and lower points representing the two minima of graph number 3 in Figure 18.1, and the middle point representing the maximum between.

The reader may wonder why I have drawn $X$ horizontally in one picture and vertically in the other. There are good reasons: In Figure 18.1 it is natural to draw $X$ horizontally because the risk $R$ is a function of $X$. In Figure 18.2, on the other hand, we want to think of $C$ as the *cause* and $X$ as the *effect*, and so it is natural to draw $C$ horizontally and $X$ vertically. The curve $S$ is then the graph of cause and effect, but what is unusual about this graph is that it is folded over, and it is this quality that is essentially responsible for the switches.

If the parameter is gradually increased then the decision and the evolution follow slightly different paths as shown by the dotted lines. Both start on the lower branch of $S$ and then switch to the upper branch, but the decision switch occurs at the Maxwell point 4 while the evolution switch delays until the bifurcation point 6. We call the interval between the two switches the *anachronous interval*, because it is this interval that characterizes the difference between the two paths.

Let us examine in more detail the mechanisms that must underlie the two processes. In each case there is a *local mechanism*, and in the decision case there must also be a *global mechanism*. A local mechanism always acts by moving $x$ in a direction that will locally reduce $R$. Therefore it is responsible for *stability*, because it will hold $x$ stably at a local minimum, and if that local minimum moves, it will move $x$ along with the local minimum. If the local minimum disappears at a bifurcation point, then the local mechanism will cause an evolution switch. Therefore a local mechanism is always responsible for both stability and evolution switches. After an evolution switch, the local mechanism will hold $x$ stably in the new minimum, and even if the parameter is moved back across the bifurcation point where the switch occurred, it will still hold $x$ stably in the new minimum. For instance in Figure 18.2 the parameter has to be moved right back to point 2 before the reverse evolution switch will occur at the other fold point. The difference between the two bifurcation points 2 and 6, where the opposite evolution switches take place, is called *hysteresis,* and this is a characteristic feature of local mechanisms. In the evolution case the local mechanism is natural selection, and this is the only mechanism.

By contrast, in the decision case there is both a local mechanism and a global mechanism. The local mechanism is the procedure whereby a decision maker continually explores local variations of his current decision and continually adjusts it to keep the risk at the local minimum. For example, most financial policies operate on this principle, by making incremental adjustments on the previous budget. Meanwhile the global mechanism is a much more complicated affair because it involves three ingredients: First, it involves globally exploring the risk function in order to find the global minimum. Second, it involves overriding the local mechanism at the Maxwell point in order to break the stability of the old decision and make the switch to the new decision. Third, it involves reinforcing the stability of the new decision in order to prevent a reverse switch back again and to allow time for the temporarily overridden local mechanism to reestablish itself as the natural stabilizing force at the new decision. If there is a global mechanism, the decision switch always preempts the evolution switch that would have occurred had there been no global mechanism, as can be seen from Figure 18.2. In contrast to the hysteresis at an evolution switch, there is no hysteresis at a decision switch, because if the parameter is moved back again then the reverse switch occurs at the same Maxwell point. Therefore, after a decision switch the new decision is vulnerable to reversal, especially if there is any stochastic noise in the parameter, which explains why the third ingredient of the global mechanism is necessary. The capacity to perform these three ingredients demands intelligence, and this is of course the main difference between decision making and biological evolution.

Let us now apply these ideas to *social* evolution. It is tempting to speculate (Renfrew 1978, 1979) that certain discontinuities in the archaeological record may have been caused by switches in social evolution, just as certain discontinuities in the fossil record may have been caused by switches in biological evolution. In this case, $X$ would be a multidimensional space representing possible structures of society, and $R$ an unfitness function that was gradually changing due to variations in population, environment, resources, technology, culture, etc. The local mechanism would be socioeconomic pressure, and this would continually adapt the structure of society to the changing conditions, just as natural selection continually adapts a biological species. An evolution switch in the structure of society would be triggered by the breakdown of the stability of an existing structure, and then the very same local mechanism of socioeconomic pressure would cause a rapid evolution to a different structure.

As yet we have not introduced intelligence, nor a global mechanism, which is the essential difference between social and biological evolution. In the social case individuals can foresee an approaching catastrophic switch, especially during the anachronous interval, during which the old structure of society is still stable and the new structure is both potentially stable and fitter. Consequently society tends to appoint decision makers who can preempt the evolution switch by means of a decision switch. Instead of having to suffer the instability that must necessarily follow the breakdown of the old structure, they can utilize the remaining stability of the old structure during the anachronous interval to usher in the new structure before the stability of the old structure has broken down.

The three ingredients that the decision makers need to establish a global mechanism are as follows. First they must collect information about alternative structures of society, decide utilities, and choose the structure that maximizes fitness (or minimizes risk). Second, they must override the local socioeconomic pressure in order to make the switch. Third, they must reinforce the stability of the new structure in order to allow time for socioeconomic pressure to reestablish itself there as the natural stabilizing force. In other words they must introduce the three familiar branches of government—the executive, the legislature, and the judiciary. In primitive societies it was often found efficient to embody all three branches in a single decision maker, such as a king or chieftain. However, as society became more complex more decision makers were needed, leading to democratization and the separation of the three branches of government.

In some societies the rulers have identified themselves too strongly with the local mechanism maintaining an existing structure and have failed to perceive the increasing unfitness of that structure, particularly if it involved too great an imbalance in the distribution of resources. As a result, society has tended to throw up other decision makers in the form of revolutionaries. The revolution is then the switch, and the three ingredients of the global mechanism that the revolutionaries need are to plan, execute, and consolidate the revolution. Since it usually takes some time for the socioeconomic pressure to reestablish itself again as the stabilizing force after a revolution, successful revolutionaries are aware of their vulnerability to the reverse switchback, and so as part of the third ingredient of consolidation they tend to be particularly severe toward counter-revolutionaries.

Some historians suggest that on the whole man's social structures are surprisingly ephemeral and short-lived, but here they may be making the same mistake as the biologists. For we should expect gradual changes of population, resources, and culture to produce periods of continuity separated by discontinuities in the historical record, analogous to those in the fossil and archaeological records. And just an an evolutionary line may survive through many switches of species, so a society may survive through many switches of structure.

So must for generalities: I shall now give the mathematics and then a number of examples. I begin by describing the general Bayesian model for decision theory. When parameters are introduced, the Bayesian model falls naturally into the mathematical domain of catastrophe theory, where there are theorems classifying the geometric shapes of decision sets. The main purpose of the examples is to demonstrate the potential of this method of modeling. A secondary purpose is to treat each example as a speculative model in its own right. However, to do each example justice would require considerably more detail in defining terms, presenting supporting evidence, specifying methods of measurement, and collecting and fitting data, than would be possible within the scope of this chapter.

Examples 1 and 2 are meant to illustrate the mathematics and show how quite simple assumptions can lead into the subleties of the cusp catastrophe. They concern predictions in the case of a one-dimensional spectrum of choice. For example, an investor might be trying to predict the price of a particular stock on the stock market in the face of ambiguous information. A government might be trying to predict its budget or a primitive society the best allocation of its resources. In each case the information is presented to the decision maker in the form of a probability distribution with a single peak, but if the distribution is skew, then the information will be ambiguous in the sense that the decision maker will not know whether to follow the mean or the mode. The ambiguity is resolved by a suitable choice of utilities, and the model gives rise to a cusp catastrophe that reveals the divisions and switches among the decision makers.

Example 3 is a more abstract model concerning the evolution of bird's beaks. Changes in the food supply cause evolution switches between specialist beaks filling ecological niches and general-purpose beaks that are suitable for a variety of foods.

Example 4 is an analogous model concerning the evolution of roles within a society, with changes in the resources and technology causing the evolution of specialist roles filling sociological niches and general purpose roles that are suitable for a variety of activities. The paradox here is that individuals can decide to switch to fitter roles, but the roles themselves tend to evolve blindly like the bird's beaks. Thus social evolution can simultaneously reflect aspects of both decision making and biological evolution.

Example 5 is an analogous model concerning the evolution of the structure of society. The main difference here is the existence of a global mechanism that eliminates anachronous structures, whereas in the previous example the harmless anachronous roles were allowed to survive.

Example 6 is a more specific version of the last example, concerning the policies put forward by political parties at elections, and discussing the splits that can occur between specialist policies and more general platforms aimed at broader constituencies.

Example 7 describes the confusion between two decision makers with different utilities and hence different risk functions, as exemplified by the misunderstandings that can arise between doctor and patient. In particular, the model sheds light on the delays that sometimes occur before a patient will admit he or she is ill or admit that he or she is better again. Further examples can be found in Harrison and Smith (1979) and Zeeman (1980).

## BAYESIAN THEORY

In the next two sections I describe the general mathematical model, and in Examples 1 and 2 I give simple illustrations of the mathematics. The reader may find it helpful to read the examples alongside the general model. The model will apply to both decision making and evolution, but for simplicity I phrase it mainly in terms of decision theory (Smith, Harrison, and Zeeman 1981).

Let $R$ denote the real numbers (the heavy type distinguishes $R$ from the risk function $R$), and let $R^n$ *denote* $n$-dimensional space. The data in a Bayesian model consist of four things: $X = $ decision space; $Y = $ future space; $P = $ probability distribution; and $L = $ loss function. From this data we shall construct the following: $R = $ risk function.

The *decision space* $X$ is the set of possible decisions $x$. In some examples we shall have a single spectrum of decisions, $X = R$. In other examples the decisions may depend on $n$ variables, so that $X$ will be an open subset of $R^n$. Indeed in some applications it is necessary to have $n$ large in order to represent all the multiple relevant interacting factors involved, but then the mathematical theorems will allow us to leave most of these variables implicit, as is explained below.

The *future space* $Y$ is a set of future possibilities $y$. These possibilities may refer to some specific time in the future, or they may represent future developments over a specified period. In some examples there will be a single spectrum of possibilities $Y = R$, but in other examples $Y$ may be multidimensional, or more complicated. The only mathematical requirement on $Y$ is that it should have a measure, so that we can integrate over it to cover all possibilities. The particular measure on $Y$ is unimportant because the risk function turns out to be independent of the measure. This is useful because different decision makers can then use different measures, but they will arrive at the same decision, provided they have the same information and utilities. If the decision is merely a prediction of the future then we shall have $X = Y$. On the other hand, $Y$ may be much more complicated than $X$, because the future may hold many more possibilities than there are options open to the decision maker. Indeed the very purpose of Bayesian decision theory is to enable the decision maker to allow for the complexity of the future.

The *information* about the future, or the decision maker's belief about the future, is contained in the probability distribution $P:X \times Y \to R$. Here $P(x, y)$ is the probability that if the decision $x$ is made then the future $y$ will occur. More precisely, if $dy$ is a measure-element of $Y$ at $y$, then $P(x, y)dy$ is the probability that the future will lie in $dy$. Therefore, for each $x$ in $X$,

$$\int_Y P(x, y)dy = 1.$$

If the decision has no effect upon the future, then $P$ will be independent of $x$, $P(x, y) = P(y)$.

The *utilities* or preferences of the decision maker are contained in the *loss function* $L:X \times Y \to R$. Here $L(x, y)$ is defined to be the loss that the decision maker will incur if decision $x$ is made and then the future $y$ subsequently happens.

Having been given the data we can now define the *risk function* $R:X \to R$, as follows:

$$R(x) = \int_Y L(x, y)P(x, y)dy.$$

In other words the risk function is the expected loss: The decision maker weights each future probability-element $P(x,y)dy$ by the appropriate loss $L(x,y)$ and then integrates over $Y$ to cover all possibilities in order to obtain the expected loss for that decision. We assume that the resulting function $R$ depends smoothly on $x$ (see the Appendix).

Call $x$ a *critical point* of $R$ if the gradient $\nabla R$ of $R$ vanishes at $x$. Generically the critical points of $R$ will be minima, maxima, and saddles (if $n > 1$). However nongeneric critical points may occur generically in a parametrized family of $R$'s, as for example the point where the maximum and minimum have coalesced on graph number 6 in Figure 18.1 (b). Such points are fundamental in catastrophe theory because they are responsible for the evolution switches. Let $S =$ the set of critical points, given by $\nabla R = 0$; $E =$ the subset of minima; and $D =$ the subset of absolute minima. Then $D \subset E \subset S \subset X$, and generically $D$ will contain exactly one point that is the *Bayes decision* minimizing the risk. However, it may occur generically in a parametrized family of $R$'s that some $D$'s will contain more than one point, as for example in graph number 4 in Figure 18.1 (a) where both minima are the same level. Such points are also fundamental in catastrophe theory because they are responsible for the decision switches.


## CATASTROPHE THEORY

We now formally introduce the parameters. Let $C$ be a *parameter space* governing $P$ and $L$. For example if $P$ and $L$ depend upon $k$ continuous parameters, then $C$ will be an open subset of $\mathrm{R}^k$. Usually $k$ is small because we are interested in what happens to the decision when we change only a few parameters.

For each point $c$ in $C$, we are given a probability distribution $P_c$ and a loss function $L_c$, from which we can calculate the risk function $R_c$, and hence deduce the critical points $S_c$, minima $E_c$, and absolute minima $D_c$. Now let $c$ vary in $C$ and define the

*critical set* $S = \{(c, x); S_c \text{ contains } x\} =$ all critical points,
*evolution set* $E = \{(c, x); E_c \text{ contains } x\} =$ all minima,
*decision set* $D = \{(c, x); D_{c_1} \text{ contains } x\} =$ all absolute minima.

Then

$$D \subset E \subset S \subset C \times X.$$

If $L$ is generic for $P$ (see the Appendix for a precise definition) then $S$ turns out to be a smooth $k$-dimensional submanifold of $C \times X$, the same dimension as $C$, and independent of the dimension of $X$. Furthermore $E$ and $D$ are submanifolds of $S$ of the same dimension. The significance of $E$ and $D$ are that evolution paths lie in $E$ and decision paths lie in $D$, and the respective switches occur whenever the paths cross the boundaries of these submanifolds.

For example in Figure 18.2, $C \times X$ is two-dimensional, and the critical set $S$ is the one-dimensional S-shaped curve. The evolution set $E$ consists of the upper and lower branches of $S$, and is obtained from $S$ by removing the folded-over middle piece. The decision set $D$ is obtained by further removing the two short pieces of $E$ not in the decision path. In other words $D$ is the intersection of $E$ with the dotted decision path. In Figure 18.10, $C \times X$ is three-dimensional and $S$ is the two-dimentional folded surface. $E$ is obtained from $S$ by cutting along the fold curve and removing the folded-over middle piece. $D$ is obtained by cutting along the dotted line and further removing the two pieces in between the dotted line and the fold curve.

Let $\chi$ denote the map projecting $S$ onto $C$, which is called the *catastrophe map* because it is mathematically important. Let $\partial E$, $\partial D$ denote the boundaries of $E$, $D$ and define their projections in $C$ to be the

$$\begin{aligned} \textit{bifurcation set } B &= \chi(\partial E), \\ \textit{Maxwell set } M &= \chi(\partial D). \end{aligned}$$

The significance of $B$ and $M$ is that evolution switches occur at bifurcation points in $B$, and decision switches occur at Maxwell points in $M$. For example, in Figure 18.2 $\partial E$ consists of the two fold points of $S$, and the bifurcation set $B$ consists of the two points 2 and 6 beneath them on the $X$ axis. Meanwhile $\partial D$ consists of the two ends of the decision switch, and the Maxwell set $M$ is the single point 4 beneath them. In Figure 18.10 $\partial E$ is the fold curve, and the bifurcation set $B$ is the cusp beneath it; $\partial D$ is the dotted line on $S$, and the Maxwell set $M$ is the dotted line beneath it inside the cusp.

One of our main objectives is to understand what types of decision and evolution paths are possible when the parameters are varied, in order to fully comprehend the relationship between gradual changes and sudden switches. This is where catastrophe theory comes to our assistance because its theorems classify the possible shapes of $S$. More precisely they classify the singularities of the catastrophe map $\chi:S \to C$.

What is a singularity? A point of $S$ is defined to be a *singularity* of $\chi$ if it has a vertical tangent.[1] For example in Figure 18.2 the singularities are the two fold points. In Figure 18.10 the singularities are the points along the fold curve, and the point vertically above the cusp point. In general, the set of singularities contains $\partial E$ and other points (but the other points, such as those bounding the set of maxima, are less important because they do not represent evolution switches if $n > 2$).

Most points of $S$ are nonsingular, and a characteristic property of a nonsingular point is that it has a neighborhood in $S$ that is mapped by $\chi$ into $C$ in

---

[1]Here *vertical* means parallel to $X$. This definition is equivalent to the usual mathematical definition that the derivative of $\chi$ drops rank.

a one-to-one manner. Consequently local variations of the parameters at a nonsingular point can only cause local variations of evolution, and so the evolutionary state is stable. By contrast, a singularity has no such neighborhood, and so a small variation of the parameters is liable to cause an evolution switch. If there were no singularities, then there could be no evolution switches. Nor could there be any decision switches if $S$ were connected, because then $\chi$ would have to map $S$ onto $C$ in a one-to-one manner. Therefore it is the singularities of $\chi$ that are ultimately responsible for both types of switch, and that is why we need to classify them.

If $C$ is one-dimensional, that is to say there is only one parameter, then there is only one type of singularity, namely the *fold*, which is illustrated in Figure 18.2. If $C$ is two-dimensional, that is to say there are two parameters, then a new type of singularity appears, namely the *cusp* illustrated in Figure 18.10. If $C$ is three-dimensional, then three more types appear, if $C$ is four-dimensional two more types appear, and so on.

Thom calls the structure of $S$ surrounding one of these singularities an *elementary catastrophe*, and descriptions of the elementary catastrophes together with a proof of the classification theorems can be found in Thom (1972) and Zeeman (1977). In the Appendix to this chapter we give a precise definition of genericity of $L$ sufficient for the theorems to hold. A fundamental property of elementary catastrophes is their stability under perturbations of $P$ and $L$.

Of the elementary catastrophes the *fold* is important because it models the evolution switch. The *cusp* is important because, as we shall see later in Example 2, it models conflicting decisions. When $C$ is four-dimensional, one of the elementary catastrophes is called the *butterfly*, and this is important because it can be used to model the emergence of compromise decision (Isnard and Zeeman 1975). When $C$ is five-dimensional there is another catastrophe called $E_6$ that is being increasingly used to model various forms of psychological decision making and psychotherapy (Zeeman 1977, Callahan 1981). When $C$ is eight-dimensional there is an important catastrophe called the *double cusp*, which already has several applications in physics and can also be used to model the interference between two conflicts (Zeeman 1977).

One of the advantages of concentrating on $S$ rather than $X$ is that it enables us to reduce the number of variables and make the model quantitative. For example suppose $N = 1000$ and $k = 2$, in other words there are 1000 relevant interacting factors involved in the decision, and we are interested in the effect of two particular parameters. Then $C \times X$ will be 1002-dimensional, but the theorems reassure us that $S$ is nonetheless a smooth two-dimensional surface lying inside this 1002–dimensional space. Therefore it is possible to represent $S$ as an ordinary two-dimensional surface in three dimensions lying over the horizontal plane $C$, with the vertical axis being a suitably chosen $X$ variable. In other words, to describe $S$ quantitatively it suffices to measure only one of the 1000 $X$ variables explicitly and leave the other 999 implicit. Moreover, the theorems tell us that the most complicated shape that $S$ can have locally is the cusp catastrophe shown in Figure 18.10. Globally there may be several cusps and folds, as for instance in Figure 18.11.

A *local mechanism* can be represented mathematically by a differential equation on $X$ parametrized by $C$ that reduces $R$, in other words, such that $\dot{R} < 0$ whenever $\nabla R \neq 0$, and $\dot{R} = 0$ whenever $\nabla R = 0$ (where the dot denotes the rate of change). For example, the gradient differential equation $\dot{x} = -\nabla R$ is of this type. Such a differential equation will cause $x$ to seek $E$, to stay on $E$ if the parameters are changed, and to switch to other parts of $E$ if $\partial E$ is crossed. Thus the differential equation provides both the stability and the evolution switches of a local mechanism.

Note that the differential equation itself is defined on the 1002-dimensional space $C \times X$, and must therefore usually remain implicit, but the resulting evolution paths can be represented explicitly on $E$ in the three-dimensional picture. Similarly, if there is an implicit global mechanism in addition to the implicit local mechanism, the resulting decision paths can be represented explicitly on $D$ in the three-dimensional picture.

In summary, in effect the general mathematical model has three levels of complexity. First, the possibilities $Y$ of the future may be very complicated. Second, the possible decisions $X$ are usually simpler than $Y$, but may still be highly multidimensional. Third, when we get down to the decision set $D$, this can sometimes be measured because it is low-dimensional, but may be subtle because of the switches. However, the switches are determined by the singularities, and they are classified by the theorems.

## Example 1 : Predicting the Price of Stock

For the first example I choose something that is easy to understand and easy to calculate. Consider the problem of whether to buy or sell a particular stock on the stock market. Let $x$ denote today's prediction of tomorrow's price, and let $y$ denote tomorrow's price. In other words, the decision $x$ is a prediction of the future $y$. Since $x, y$ are both numbers, we have $X = Y = \mathbb{R}$.

The reader may well ask what has this to do with archaeology? In fact the same model can be applied to any situation where a decision maker is trying to predict something that can be measured. For instance, an archaeologist might be trying to predict next year's budget, or a government might be trying to predict the rate of inflation or the future food supply. And of course these are not only current problems, but must also have preoccupied the rulers of primitive tribes and ancient civilizations, who must have been faced from time to time with famines, or increasing populations and dwindling resources, and decisions about whether to hunt or to cultivate or to emigrate.

So let us return to the stock market in order to fix our minds. Suppose that the information about the future is given by the probability distribution $P$ shown in Figure 18.3. Being only a small investor we assume that our decision $x$ has no effect on the future $y$, and so $P$ is only a function of $y$ and independent of $x$:

$$P(x, y) = P(y) = \text{probability that tomorrow's price is } y.$$

We have deliberately chosen a skew distribution so that the mode $m$ is different from the mean $\mu$. This makes the information ambiguous, because it is not clear whether we ought to follow the mode or the mean. The mode is the most likely price tomorrow, and the mean is the expected price tomorrow. If today's, price happens to lie between them, then following the mode would suggest selling stock because the most likely price tomorrow will be lower than today's, whereas following the mean would suggest buying because the expected price tomorrow will be higher. Statistics emphasizes the importance of the mean, but stockbrokers, who are generally richer than statisticians, tend to follow the mode, so whom should we follow? The ambiguity and indecision are resolved by choosing a loss function $L$.

The simplest loss function is the parabola $L(x, y) = (x - y)^2$ (see Figure 18.4). If the prediction is correct, $x = y$, then there is no loss. If not, then $x - y$ is the error of prediction, and the parabola can be regarded as a translation into mathematics of the qualitative statement "*The greater the error the greater the loss.*" Using this loss function we can now calculate the risk function, which is shown in Figure 18.5.

*Lemma.* The risk function is a parabola with minimum at the mean $\mu$. Hence the Bayes decision is the mean.

Proof: The risk $R(x) = \int L(x, y)P(y)dy = \int (x - y)^2 P(y)dy.$

The variance of $P$, $\qquad V = \int (\mu - y)^2 P(y)dy.$

Therefore $R(x) - V = (x^2 - \mu^2)\int P(y)dy - 2(x - \mu)\int yP(y)dy$

$$= (x^2 - \mu^2) - 2(x - \mu)\mu$$

$$= (x - \mu)^2.$$

Therefore $R(x) = V + (x - \mu)^2$, as required.

It is a confusing coincidence that a parabolic loss function should give rise to a parabolic risk function, because generally the two functions are quite different from one another as in our next example. The parabolic loss function can be criticized on the grounds that it is unreasonable for the loss to tend to infinity as the error increases. More commonly the decision maker has an upper bound to his losses because he cannot lose more than he possesses. Therefore it is more reasonable to assume a fixed loss for sufficiently large error, and so I have incorporated this assumption into the next example.

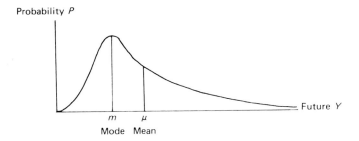

Mode   Mean

**Figure 18.3.** Skew probability distribution.

## Example 2 : Ambiguity and Caution

Example 1 is modified by replacing the parabolic loss function of Figure 18.4 with the two-step loss function shown in Figure 18.6. As before $L$ depends on the error but this time it is given by the formula

$$
L = \begin{cases}
0, & 0 \le |x - y| \le a \\
1 - \alpha, & a < |x - y| \le b \\
1, & |x - y| > b
\end{cases}
$$

where $a$, $b$, $\alpha$ are constants, $a$ small, $b$ large, and $0 \le \alpha \le 1$. Although $L$ is discontinuous at $\pm a$, $\pm b$ it is nevertheless generic for the probability distribution $P$ shown in Figure 18.3, according to the definition in the Appendix.

The two-step loss function can be regarded as a translation into mathematics of the qualitative statement "*Spot on you win; way out you lose.*" For suppose $L^*$ is the loss function in which the decision maker makes a fixed profit $p$ (in other words a negative loss $-p$) if the error is sufficiently small $|x - y| \le a$, and makes a fixed loss $q$ if it is sufficiently large $|x - y| > b$, and otherwise breaks even. Then we can normalize $L^*$ by defining

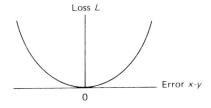

**Figure 18.4.** Parabolic loss function.

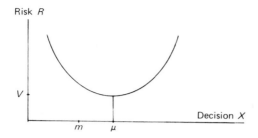

**Figure 18.5.** Parabolic risk function.

$$L = \frac{p + L^*}{p + q}, \qquad \alpha = \frac{q}{p + q},$$

and this gives the two-step loss function $L$ above, shown in Figure 18.6. Such a normalization is admissible because affine changes of $L$ (that is adding and multiplying by constants) induce the same affine changes in $R$, and so do not alter the critical points of $R$ nor the Bayes decision.

If $\alpha = 0$ the decision maker is only concerned with his profits, and therefore will behave like a *speculator*, being primarily interested in increasing his capital by speculating with those stocks giving the greatest return. On the other hand, if $\alpha = 1$ the decision maker is only concerned with his losses, and therefore will behave like an *investor* who is primarily interested in conserving his capital by investing in securities. Therefore we can interpret the parameter $\alpha$ as a measure of the *caution* of the decision maker, varying from speculator to investor as the caution increases.

The risk function $R$ can now be computed as follows. Regard $L$ as the

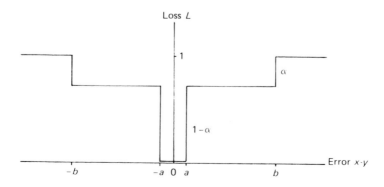

**Figure 18.6.** Two-step loss function.

constant function, with value 1, minus two rectangles, the first of width $2a$ and height $1 - \alpha$, and the second of width $2b$ and height $\alpha$. Therefore

$$R(x) = \int L(x, y)P(y)dy = 1 - (1 - \alpha)A(x) - \alpha B(x),$$

where

$$A(x) = \int_{|x - y| \le a} P(y)dy = \int_{x - a}^{x + a} P(y)dy$$

$$B(x) = \int_{|x - y| \le b} P(y)dy = \int_{x - b}^{x + b} P(y)dy.$$

The critical points of $A$ are given by

$$\frac{dA}{dx} = P(x + a) - P(x - a) = 0.$$

Therefore $A$ has a unique maximum at $m'$ say, where $m'$ is the midpoint of the unique horizontal chord of $P$ of length $2a$. Since $a$ is small, $m'$ is near the mode $m$ of $P$. Similarly $B$ has a unique maximum at $\mu'$ say, where $\mu'$ is the midpoint of the chord of length $2b$. If $b$ is of the order of about twice the standard deviation of $P$ then it can be seen from Figure 18.3 that $\mu'$ is near the mean $\mu$ of $P$, as shown in Figure 18.7. Therefore if $\alpha = 0$ then $R$ has a unique minimum at $m'$, and if $\alpha = 1$ then $R$ has a unique minimum at $\mu'$. If $0 < \alpha < 1$ then $R$ is a linear combination of $A$ and $B$, and so it is either unimodal, with a unique minimum in between $m'$ and $\mu'$, or else bimodal with two minima, one near the mode and the other near the mean, as shown in Figure 18.8. It is surprising at first sight that a bimodal $R$ can arise from a unimodal $P$ and unimodal $L$, but the way we have computed $R$ explains how this phenomenon arises, and shows it to be stable under small perturbations of $P$ and $L$. As the parameter $\alpha$ varies from 0 to 1 the decreasing family of loss functions give rise to a smoothly decreasing family of smooth risk functions, as shown in Figure 18.8 (compare Figure 18.1).

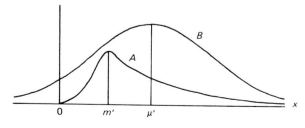

**Figure 18.7.** The functions $A$ and $B$.

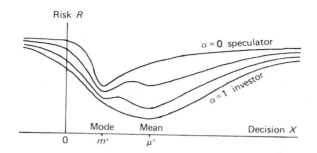

**Figure 18.8.** The family of risk functions.

Therefore the speculators ($\alpha = 0$) will follow the mode and the investors ($\alpha = 1$) will follow the mean. If a decision maker is gradually becoming more cautious ($\alpha$ increasing), then he will suddenly switch from mode to mean at the Maxwell point when the two minima are level. Conversely, if he is gradually becoming more adventurous ($\alpha$ decreasing) he will make the reverse switch at the same point. The bimodality of $R$ resolves the original dilemma posed by the ambiguity of the information $P$ as to whether to follow the mode or the mean, and shows how it depends upon the choice of loss function.

We now introduce a second parameter $\beta$ that measures the *ambiguity* of the information, or in other words the skewness of $P$. Define

$$\beta = \mu - m = \text{mean minus mode.}$$

A symmetrical distribution like the normal distribution would have $\beta = 0$. If $\beta > 0$, then $P$ is skewed to the right as in Figure 18.3, and if $\beta < 0$, then $P$ is skewed to the left.

Suppose we are given a one-parameter family of distributions all skewed to the right as in Figure 18.3 and parametrized by their skewness $\beta$. Then our parameter space $C$ will now be two-dimensional with coordinates $\alpha$ measuring the caution of the decision maker and $\beta$ measuring the ambiguity of information. In order to find the critical set $S$ we must investigate the modality of $R_c$ for each parameter point $c = (\alpha, \beta)$. Given $\beta$, let $A_\beta$, $B_\beta$ denote the corresponding functions of Figure 18.7, let $m_\beta$, $\mu_\beta$ denote their maxima, and let $S_\beta$ denote the resulting section of $S$ over the interval $0 \leq \alpha \leq 1$.

If $\beta$ is small then $m_\beta, \mu_\beta$ will be too close together for there to be any points of inflexion of $A_\beta$, $B_\beta$ between them, and this condition is sufficient to ensure that $(1 - \alpha)A_\beta + \alpha B_\beta$ has a unique maximum, for all $\alpha$, $0 \leq \alpha \leq 1$ (Smith 1977). Therefore $R_c$ has a unique minimum for all $\alpha$, and so $S_\beta$ is single-valued over $\alpha$, as in Figure 18.9 (a).

If $\beta$ is large, then $R_c$ will be bimodal for some value of $\alpha$, $0 < \alpha < 1$, as in Figure 18.8, and therefore $S_\beta$ will be folded over as in Figure 18.9 (b) (compare Figure 18.2). Since these are the only two types of section, there must exist a critical value $\beta_0$ such that if $\beta < \beta_0$ then $S_\beta$ is as in the case (a) and if $\beta > \beta_0$

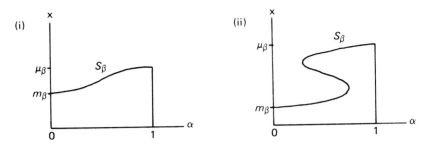

**Figure 18.9.** Sections of $S_\beta$ for (a) small $\beta$ and (b) large $\beta$.

then $S_\beta$ is as in case (b). Then it is a theorem (Zeeman 1977) that the sections can be assembled into a surface $S$, as shown in Figure 18.10. This is called a *cusp catastrophe* because its bifurcation set is a cusp, and it is the unique elementary catastrophe for a two-dimensional parameter space. Furthermore it is stable, and so its qualitative properties are preserved under perturbations of $P$ and $L$. Figure 18.10 provides a synthesis of these qualitative properties, as follows.

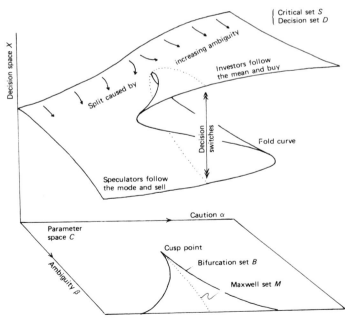

**Figure 18.10.** The predicted price of stock is a cusp catastrophe with the caution of the decision maker as normal factor and the ambiguity of information as splitting factor. The continuous spectrum of decision makers is split into buyers and sellers by increasing ambiguity of information. Individuals switch decision if their level of caution crosses the Maxwell set.

The decision set $D$ is bounded by the dotted line on $S$ vertically above the Maxwell set $M$, which is the dotted line inside the cusp in $C$. Since the decision $x$ is correlated with the caution $\alpha$ we call $\alpha$ a *normal factor*. Since increasing ambiguity $\beta$ has the effect of splitting $D$ apart we call $\beta$ a *splitting factor*. The $\beta$ coordinate of the cusp point is the critical value $\beta_0$ separating the two types of section $S_\beta$ shown in Figure 18.9. Therefore if $\beta < \beta_0$ the decision makers of varying levels of caution $\alpha$ will be spread continously along the section $S_\beta$, and so their predictions $x$ of tomorrow's price of the stock will form a continuous spectrum. If, however, the ambiguity $\beta$ is increased beyond the threshold $\beta_0$ then they will be split into two groups (as indicated by the arrows on $S$ in Figure 18.10), with the speculators following the mode and the investors following the mean. Therefore if today's price of the stock happens to lie between the mode and mean, the speculators will begin to sell and the investors will begin to buy (which is very convenient to both parties).

If the decision maker's path in the parameter space happens to cross the Maxwell set, for instance if he changes his level of caution while believing the information to be ambiguous, then this will cause him to suddenly switch his decision from buying to selling, or vice versa.

When $\beta > \beta_0$ what is surprising is that *all* the decision makers are split, including those of moderate caution. Although some people are predicting that tomorrow's price will be higher than today's, and others are predicting that it will be lower, no one is actually predicting that it will be the same, or anywhere near the same. The switch from one group to the other jumps right over this possibility. This phenomenon is called *inaccessibility*, and is a characteristic feature of the cusp catastrophe (Zeeman 1977). It is particularly useful in modeling polarized situations, where a population may initially exhibit a continuous spectrum opinion over some issue, but if that issue increases in urgency beyond some threshold then the population may find itself split into taking sides, with a sharp division of opinion between the two sides, the intermediate ground being inaccessible (Isnard and Zeeman 1975).

If the information is skewed the other way, $\beta < 0$, implying $\mu < m$, then another symmetrically placed cusp appears, with the orientations reversed as in Figure 18.11. As the market oscillates back and forth, first skewed one way and then the other, the speculators and investors interchange their roles of buying and selling to each other. Michael Thompson (1981) has used this geometry to analyze structures of society.

## Example 3 : The Evolution of Bird's Beaks

We apply a generalization of Example 2 to the evolution of bird's beaks. Consider how the shape of a beak is affected by the variety of food available and the suitability of that beak for the various types of food. Let $X$ describe the possible shapes of beak. For example, if we use $n$ variables to measure the

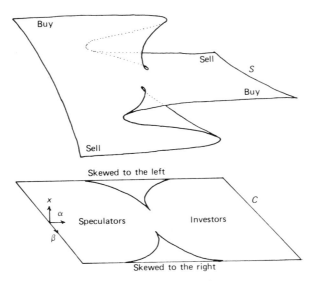

**Figure 18.11.** Skewing either way gives two cusps.

shape of a beak, and represent these measurements by a point $x$ in $R^n$, then $X$ will be a subset of $R^n$. Let $Y$ denote the set of available foods, and let $P$ be a probability distribution on $Y$ representing the probable availability of each food in the given environment. Let the function $L(x, y)$ represent the inefficiency of beak $x$ for food $y$. For instance we might invent some scale running from perfectly efficient at $L = 0$ to useless at $L = 1$. Then $R(x) = \int L(x, y)P(y)dy$ will measure the unfitness of beak $x$ for that environment. Natural selection will be the local mechanism that evolves the beak to a local minimum of $R$.

If there is a dominant food supply $y_0$ then the integral will be dominated by $L(x, y_0)P(y_0)$, and so $R$ will be minimized by evolving a specialist beak $x_0$ with the minimum inefficiency $L(x_0, y_0)$ (or maximum efficiency) for eating food $y_0$. In other words, the beak $x_0$ is specialized to fill the ecological niche $y_0$. However, the very success of a species in filling an ecological niche will tend to increase the number of individuals competing for that niche, and hence reduce the food available to each individual. This in turn may produce a selection in favor of some form of population control, for example, the development of a territorial instinct, which will maintain $P(y_0)$ at a sufficiently high individual level. Otherwise, the expanding population may have an effect similar to the skewing of $P$, by increasing the relative importance of other food supplies. Consequently, a bimodality may appear in $R$, as in Example 2, between the specialist beak $x_0$ filling the niche $y_0$ (corresponding to the speculator) and a general purpose beak $x_1$ adapted to eating a wide variety of foods (corresponding to the investor). Therefore the gradually increasing skewness of the food supply caused by the success of a species may in turn cause a bifurcation of the species into the gradual divergent evolution of two different types of beak, one a specialist and the other a generalist.

Figure 18.12 shows a cusp catastrophe that synthesizes the preceding discussion. We have assumed a two-dimensional parameter space $C$, with the normal factor $\alpha$ representing the scarcity of food, and the splitting factor $\beta$ representing the size of population. Unlike Figure 18.10, the vertical axis is not $X$ because $X$ is multidimensional. However, we know that the critical set $S$ is a two-dimensional surface, and if it contains a cusp then any measurement $\bar{x}$ of the beak that distinguishes between specialist and generalist will suffice for a vertical coordinate if we want to plot that cusp catastrophe as a surface in three dimensions, as in Figure 18.12.

We now consider the evolution switches. Suppose a specialist beak $x_0$ is filling the niche $y_0$, which is disappearing due to gradually increasing scarcity, caused perhaps by increasing competition from other species. When the parameter crosses the right side of the cusp then the local minimum of $R$ at $x_0$ will disappear [as in Figure 18.1(b)] and then natural selection will cause an evolution switch to the general-purpose beak. Conversely a gradual growth in a dominant food supply may cause the parameter to cross the left side of the cusp and induce the reverse switch from the general-purpose beak to a specialist beak. Normally abundance encourages specialists, and scarcity encourages generalists. For instance, the abundance of plant life has encouraged many striking examples of specialists in the insect world, adapted to one type of food only.

Before we leave this example, notice the difference between Figure 18.12 and Figure 18.10. In Figure 18.12 the evolution switches take place at the fold curve over the bifurcation set $B$, with a hysteresis in between them. After an evolution switch the new species is stable, and it remains stable even if the

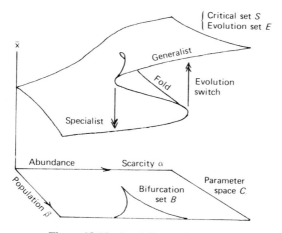

**Figure 18.12.** Specialists and generalists.

parameter is moved back again across the bifurcation set where the switch occurred. Therefore both types of beak can coexist stably together over the same parameter point in the interior of $B$. By contrast, in Figure 18.10 the decision switches take place over the Maxwell set $M$. There is no hysteresis, and therefore two decision makers cannot hold opposite decisions over the same parameter point. After a decision switch, the new decision is vulnerable to reversal if the parameter is moved back again across the Maxwell set, unless its stability is reinforced by the third ingredient of the global mechanism.

### Example 4 : The Evolution of Roles in Society

The last example of biological evolution suggests a model for the social evolution of roles in society.

Let $X$ be a space describing the roles. For example, if we were studying prehistoric hunter–gatherer roles (Reynolds and Zeigler 1979), we might take $X = \mathbb{R}^2$, with the first variable measuring the proportion of time spent in hunting and the second measuring that spent in gathering. If we were studying the present-day roles of men and women we might take $X = \mathbb{R}^2$ to measure the time spent in jobs and careers compared with that spent in domestic work. If we were interested in a more complicated combination of roles· we could take $X$ multidimensional.

Let $Y$ describe the possible future structures of society, including the size of population, the resources and technology, etc., and let $P$ be the probability of such structures. Let $L(x, y)$ represent the unsuitability of role $x$ for society $y$. For instance, we might invent some scale running from perfectly suited at $L = 0$ to totally unsuitable at $L = 1$. Alternatively, we might use $L$ to measure the rewards offered to role $x$ by society $y$. Then $R(x)$ will represent the unfitness of role $x$ for the future society.

For example, in a hunter–gatherer study it could be that most of the individuals in the society did both jobs, and so the existing role would be presented by a single minimum of $R$ near the point $(h, 1 - h)$, where $h$ is the average proportion of time spent in hunting. However if the parameters of society changed, for instance if there were an increase in population or technology, then $R$ might develop two minima, which would then drift toward the points $(1, 0)$ and $(0, 1)$. In other words a division of labor would occur. The individuals, particularly those growing up, would perceive that in the future it would probably be more rewarding to become either a specialist hunter or a specialist gatherer. In some societies the specialist roles became sex-linked.

An interesting point to notice is that although society may be changing gradually, or the population growing slowly, the resulting division of labor and separation of roles may occur suddenly. For instance, in Figure 18.12 it occurs at the threshold represented by the cusp point. Figure 18.12 also suggests that long periods of abundance, perhaps stimulated by new technology, may encourage the evolution of specialists to fill sociological niches and therefore favor the division of labor. Conversely, long periods of scarcity may have the opposite effect, encouraging the evolution of generalists and favoring self-sufficiency. Even today, during periods of prosperity specialists tend to thrive, but during recessions the adaptable survive better.

In a more general model the various local minima of $R$ represent a variety of well-defined roles or sociological niches that a young person can aim for. Here the roles are in fact perceptions in the eyes of society, and the local mechanism that keeps a role at a minimum of $R$ is natural selection, just as in biological evolution. If a gradual change in society causes a local minimum of $R$ to move gradually, then society will perceive that a slight change in the role would make it fitter, and so the role will change accordingly. The role will respond continuously at the same time as keeping its name.

Meanwhile there is no global mechanism because different roles can coexist. The fact that the local minimum representing role $B$ might be dropping until it is lower than that representing role $A$ does not mean that role $A$ will switch into role $B$. On the contrary, it is the *individual* who can decide to switch from $A$ to $B$, while both *roles* continue to exist.

As well as the creation of roles we also observe their disappearance. The butcher and baker continue to thrive, but the candlestick-maker has been replaced by craftsmen, electricians, and manufacturers. This disappearance of roles gives a nice illustration of the difference between decision making and evolution. For individuals can decide to switch to a more rewarding role as soon as it becomes fitter, but the old role may survive in a anachronous form as long as the local minimum of $R$ continues to exist. If the minimum ceases to exist (as in Figures 18.1 and 18.2), then the role will suddenly disappear. Thus society tends to be littered with dying anachronous roles existing alongside the living roles (where living means occupied by living individuals).

Of course different individuals will have different preferences. So far we have only considered a single loss function $L$ representing the rewards offered by society as a whole, but each individual will have personal skills and preferences, and therefore will have a separate $L$ for his or her own role. Consequently, a role that appears anachronous to society could appear fit to a particular individual and could even provide an unoccupied sociological niche. Thus society tends to be enriched by a few individuals keeping the anachronous roles alive. For instance, the hunter's role was probably jealously guarded by a few eccentrics long after their society had turned to agriculture, and no doubt the cherished weapons of those eccentrics were buried affectionately alongside them, providing the unsuspecting archaeologist with some anachronous data. Instances of anachronous roles can be observed amongst academics today, e.g., the old-fashioned archaeologist who refuses to believe in carbon dating.

In summary, the purpose of this example was to show how aspects of both decision making and biological evolution can appear in the same model of social evolution. Individuals can decide what role to adopt with their eyes open, but the roles themselves evolve blindly by natural selection, as in biological evolution.

## Example 5 : The Evolution of Society

This example suggests the underlying data for the social evolution described in the Introduction.

Let $X$ denote the possible social structures of a society. Let $Y$ denote the possible future resources of the society, including not only the positive resources such as food, labor, energy, raw materials, technology, etc., but also the negative resources such as mouths to feed, bodies to house, territories to defend, and so forth. Given structure $x$, let $P(x, y)$ denote the probability of resources $y$. Here $P(x, y)$ may depend strongly on $x$, as illustrated by the different standards of living achieved by countries with comparable potential resources but different social structures in the world today.

Given resources $y$, let $L(x,y)$ measure the intolerance of society towards structure $x$. We invent some scale running from desirable at $L = 0$ to intolerable at $L = 1$. For example, if resources are scarce then society may not tolerate too great an imbalance in their distribution. If, however, there is a likely improvement of resources in the future, then society may be prepared to tighten its belt and accept the loss of a certain amount of individual freedom for a while in order to serve the needs of production. As resources improve, society may no longer tolerate such loss, and may demand less authoritarian a structure. And so on. Obviously $L$ will depend on cultural parameters as well as the economic variables represented by $y$.

Then $R(x) = \int L(x,v)P(x,y)dy$ will measure the unfitness of structure $x$. As the resources $P$ change, and as the cultural concept $L$ of what is tolerable changes, so the unfitness $R$ will change. The local mechanism keeping the structure at a local minimum of $R$ is socioeconomic pressure, and the global mechanism for switching it to the fittest structure at the global minimum of $R$ is government or revolution, as explained in the Introduction.

The main difference between this example and the last is the presence of the global mechanism, which eliminates the anachronous structures. In the last example the anachronous roles were harmless, because individuals could decide to switch out of them, and so society did not bother to invent a global mechanism to eliminate them. By contrast, individuals cannot escape an anachronous structure, and so they combine to devise a global mechanism to eliminate it.

## Example 6: Political Parties

This example is a simpler version of the last, relating it to current politics. One of the problems facing a political party at the approach of an election is the decision as to what policy or what electoral image to present to the electorate. Suppose for the sake of simplicity that this decision can be represented by a point on the traditional political spectrum running from the Left to the Right. Take this spectrum to be the decision space $X$. The model also holds equally well for more complicated spaces of ideologies (Zeeman 1979).

Let $Y$ represent the different types of voters in the electorate. $Y$ may contain recognizably different components, and each component may contain a spectrum of types or be multidimensional. Let $P(y)$ measure the electoral strength of type $y$. Let $L(x, y)$ measure the lack of appeal of policy $x$ to voter of type $y$. The $R(x)$ will measure the electoral weakness of policy $x$, and the local minima of $R$ will represent electorally the strongest policies. The local mechanism is cooperation and realism, for politicians with similar ideologies will tend to cooperate together to present a common policy, and that policy will tend to be drawn to the nearest local minimum of $R$ by the realism of having to appeal to the electorate. Meanwhile the global mechanism is the election and the constitution, for the election will select the lowest minimum, and the constitution will maintain that policy in power for a specified period.

The establishment of a particular social class, or the persistence of a particular economic problem, may cause the growth of an electorally strong component of $Y$, thus providing an electoral niche and stimulating the evolution of a political party and specialist policy to fill that niche. Conversely, the blurring of class differences may tend to skew $P$, and may cause the evolution of more generalist policies toward the center. The onset of short-term economic problems may have a similar effect and cause a party to be split between a specialist policy and a generalist policy. In other words if $P_0$ represents the party membership, then $R_0(x) = \int L(x,y)P_0(y)dy$ will be bimodal, with its two local minima representing the two policies. This can be represented by Figure 18.12, with the normal factor $\alpha$ representing the proportion of party membership outside the original traditional constituency, and the splitting factor $\beta$ representing the onset of economic problems. Figure 18.13 illustrates various time paths in the parameter space.

Path 1 represents a gradual broadening of party membership followed by a gradual onset of economic problems, resulting in the gradual evolution from a specialist policy to a generalist policy. Path 2 represents a similar change, except that the events happen in the opposite order, so that the path crosses both sides of the cusp $B$ as well as the Maxwell set $M$. For simplicity of exposition suppose we are discussing a party of the Left, so that initially $R_0$ has a unique minimum to the left of $X$. When path 2 crosses the left side of the cusp, another local minimum is created near the center of $X$, and a right wing of the party is formed in support of the corresponding alternative policy. When the Maxwell set $M$ is crossed, the right wing achieves a majority in the party. There is then a conflict between local and global mechanisms, because the local mechanism tends to split the party, attracting each wing to its local minimum. Meanwhile the global mechanism is the party voting procedure and constitution, and if this

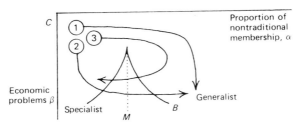

**Figure 18.13.** Time paths in the parameter space.

is strong enough it will unify the party at the lower minimum. Therefore it will cause a policy switch from left to center as the path crosses $M$. The old left policy will be retained as a possible alternative during the anachronous period, but will disappear when the path crosses the right side of $B$. Path 3 represents the opposite route: The onset of economic problems is followed by an increase of traditional membership, or equivalently a decrease in the nontraditional membership (attracted away, perhaps, to other parties). The result is the formation of a left wing as the path enters the cusp, a switch back to a traditional left-wing policy as the path crosses $M$, and the disappearance of the alternative center policy as it leaves the cusp.

## Example 7: Doctors and Patients

In this last example we study the confusions that can arise when two decision makers use different loss functions and hence arrive at different risk functions. Call a decision maker *limited* if he or she only has local information and local utilities, so that a local minimum appears global. Call a decision maker *timid* if he only has a local mechanism, and no global mechanism. Both limited and timid decision makers will stay in a local minimum until it disappears, and so will appear to act blindly—like evolution—during an anachronous interval.

One can imagine many examples. For instance, without modern scientific tools some archaeological speculations were necessarily limited. To a government an electorate may appear limited in its lack of understanding of the need for unpopular measures. Conversely, to an electorate a government may appear timid in its reluctance to switch decisions. To illustrate the subtleties of the point we choose a domestic example of misunderstandings between a doctor and his patient.

There is often a delay, during which the symptoms of an illness are increasing before a person will acknowledge that he is ill, and likewise a delay before he acknowledges he is well again. The doctor has two problems: First, he may be curious to know what prompted the patient to decide that he was ill and what triggered the decision to come to the doctor for advice. Second, he may be frustrated when the recovering patient stubbornly persists in behaving as if he were still ill, when it would be to his advantage to behave as if he were well again. We apply the model to elucidate these problems.

Let $X$ represent the possible treatments. For instance, if we measure the time spent on various strategies such as going to bed, visiting the doctor, going to the hospital, etc., then the treatment will be represented by a point $x$ in $\mathbb{R}^n$. In particular, there is a point $x_0$ representing no treatment, i.e., normal life. Let $y$ represent the possible symptoms of the illness. For instance, if we measure the intensity of each $q$ different symptoms, each on some scale, then all the symptoms will be represented by a single point $y$ in $\mathbb{R}^q$. Let $P(x,y)$ denote the probability of having symptoms $y$ in the future as a result of treatment $x$ today. Let

$$L_0(x) = \text{the cost to the patient of treatment } x;$$

$$L_1(y) = \text{the cost to the patient of symptoms } y.$$

We assume that the costs include not only financial costs, but also penalties for time lost, inconvenience, physical and psychological handicaps, etc., and that they can be measured compatibly so as to be added together to give a total cost $L(x,y) = L_0(x) + L_1(y)$. Consequently there are three risk functions:

$$R_0(x) = \int L_0(x)P(x,y)dy = L_0(x) = \text{cost of treatment } x,$$

$$R_1(x) = \int L_1(y)P(x,y)dy = \text{medical risk of treatment } x,$$

$$R(x) = \int L(x,y)P(x,y)dy = R_0(x) + R_1(x) = L_0(x) + R_1(x)$$
$$= \text{total risk of treatment } x.$$

We assume $L_0$ has a minimum at no treatment $x_0$, that is to say normal life. Suppose that $x_1$ represents the appropriate treatment for the illness, so that $R_1$ has a minimum at $x_1$. For instance in Figure 18.14 the point $x_1$ represents going to the hospital. Initially, before the patient becomes ill, the probability of no symptoms is 1, and the cost of no symptoms is 0, and so $R_1 = 0$. Therefore $R = R_0 = L_0$, with minimum at $x_0$, so the patient leads a normal life. Then as the symptoms appear, $R_1$ increases, causing $R$ to follow an increasing sequence of graphs as in Figure 18.1 (remembering of course that $X$ may be $n$-dimensional, whereas in Figures 18.1 and 18.14 it is drawn as only one-dimensional). The patient will decide to switch to treatment $x_1$ at the Maxwell point [graph number 4 in Figure 18.1(a)]. The timid patient will delay until the bifurcation point [graph number 6 in Figure 18.1(b)], although during the anachronous interval it would have been better for him to have sought treatment.

Let us look at the doctor's first problem—his curiosity as to what prompted the switch. From the medical point of view of treating this type of illness, as opposed to treating this particular patient, the doctor will be looking at the risk function $R_1$, with a unique minimum at $x_1$. Until he begins to treat this parti-

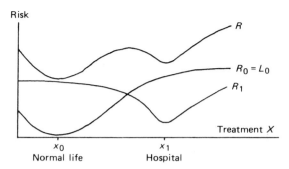

**Figure 18.14.** Three risk functions, $R = R_0 + R_1$.

cular patient he cannot know $R_0$, which is the cost to this patient of the treatment in terms of disruption to normal life, and so he must either ignore $R_0$, or include an estimated value for the hypothetical general patient. If he ignores $R_0$, then $R_1$ can only give him information on the best treatment $x_1$, and cannot give him any information about either of the switch points 4 or 6. Therefore, there can be no general answer as to what triggers the switch. Moreover from the point of view of $R_1$, even the intelligent decision switch 4 may appear as timid, while from the point of view of $R$ prior to the decision switch the medical assessment $R_1$ must appear limited. Therefore, initially the patient may appear timed to the doctor, and the doctor may appear limited to the patient, because they are necessarily using different loss functions and therefore different risk functions.

We now turn to the doctor's second problem of frustration at the stubbornness of the recovering patient who persists in behaving as though he or she were still ill. The situation is represented by the graph of Figure 18.1 played in the reverse order 7, 6, . . . , 1. Since the doctor is by now treating the individual patient rather than thinking in terms of the general patient, he will have abandoned $R_1$ in favor of $R$, and be expecting the patient to make the decision switch back to normal life at the Maxwell point 4. However, by this time, the patient may have become an expert on his own illness. He may have become so accustomed to paying the fixed penalty $L_0(x_1)$, that he now discounts it by adopting the limited medical point of view of minimizing $R_1$ at $x_1$. Thus he is lead into persisting in the local minimum $x_1$ during the anachronous interval from 4 to 2 to the doctor's frustration. This time it is the patient who is limited, although to the doctor he again appears timid.

## APPENDIX

Here is a definition of genericity sufficient for the classification theorems to hold. *Smooth* means that all partial derivatives exist to all orders. Let $X \subset \mathbb{R}^n$.

Let $E$ be the ring of germs of smooth functions $\mathbb{R}^n, 0 \to \mathbb{R}$ stratified by the orbits of the group of germs of smooth diffeomorphisms $\mathbb{R}^n, 0 \to \mathbb{R}^n, 0$ acting on the right. Given $P{:}C \times X \times Y \to \mathbb{R}$ such that $\int P_c(x,y)dy = 1$, for all $c \in C,\ x \in X$, and given $L{:}C \times X \times Y \to \mathbb{R}$, define $R{:}C \times X \to \mathbb{R}$ by $R_c(x) = \int L_c(x,y)P_c(x,y)dy$. Call $L$ *generic for* $P$ if $R$ is smooth and the map $R^+{:}C \times X \to E$ given by $R_c^+(x)(x') = R_c(x + x') - R_c(x)$ is transverse to the stratification. Suppose dimension $C \le 5$.

*THEOREM 1. If* L *is generic for* P *then* L' *is generic for* P', *for sufficiently small perturbations* L', P' *of* L, P. *If* L *is not generic for* P *then there exist arbitrarily small perturbations* L' *of* L *that are generic for* P.

In other words genericity is open dense. Therefore we are justified in using generic models.

*THEOREM 2. If* L *is generic for* P *then the resulting map* $\chi{:}S \to C$ *is stable under sufficiently small perturbations of* L *and* P, *and all its singularities are elementary catastrophes.*

Therefore we are justified in using elementary catastrophes as models.

For proofs, see Zeeman (1977), together with the observation that any required perturbation $R'$ of $R$ can be obtained by choosing $L' = L - R + R'$.

## ACKNOWLEDGMENTS

I am indebted for discussions to Maurice Dodson, Dermott Greene, Jeff Harrison, Colin Renfrew, Jim Smith, and Michael Thompson.

## REFERENCES

Callahan, J., 1981, Bifurcation geometry of $E_6$, *Mathematical Modelling* 1, 283–309.

Callahan, J., 1982, A geometric model of anorexia and its treatment, *Behavioral Science*.

Dodson, M., 1975, Quantum evolution and the fold catastrophe, *Evolutionary Theory* 1, 107–118.

Harrison, P. J., and Smith, J. Q., 1979, Discontinuity, decision and conflict, in Bernado, J. M., DeGroot, M. H., Lindley, D. V., and Smith, A. F. M. (eds.), *Bayesian Statistics*, Proceedings First International Meeting, Valencia University Press, Spain.

Isnard, C. A., and Zeeman, E. C., 1976, Some models from catastrophe theory in the social sciences, in Collins, L. (ed.), *The Use of Models in the Social Sciences*, London, Tavistock Publications, 44–100.

Renfrew, C., 1978, The anatomy of innovation, *British Archaeological Reports International Series (Supplement)* 47, 89–117.

Renfrew, C., 1979, Systems collapse as social transformation: catastrophe and anastrophe in early state societies, in Renfrew, C., and Cooke, K. L. (eds.) *Transformations: Mathematical Approaches to Culture Change*, New York, Academic Press, 481–506.

Reynolds, R. G. D., and Zeigler, B. P., 1979, A formal mathematical model for the operation of consensus-based hunting–gathering bands, in Renfrew, C., and Cooke, K. L. (eds.), *Transformations: Mathematical Approaches to Culture Change*, New York, Academic Press, 405–418.

Smith, J. Q., 1977, *Problems in Bayesian Statistics Relating to Discontinuous Phenomena, Catastrophe Theory and Forecasting*, Doctoral dissertation, Warwick University.

Smith, J. Q., Harrison, P. J., and Zeeman, E. C., 1981, The analysis of some discontinuous decision processes, *European Journal of Operational Research*, 7, 30–43.

Thom, R., 1972, *Structural Stability and Morphogenesis*, English translation D. H. Fowler, 1975, New York, Benjamin.

Thompson, M., 1981, A three-dimensional model, in Douglas, M., and Ostrander, D. (eds.), *Essays in the Sociology of Perception*, London, Routledge and Kegan Paul.

Zeeman, E. C., 1977, *Catastrophe Theory: Selected Papers 1972–1977*, Reading, Mass., Addison–Wesley.

Zeeman, E. C., 1979, A geometrical model of ideologies, in Renfrew, C., and Cooke, K. L. (eds.), *Transformations: Mathematical Approaches to Culture Change*. New York, Academic Press, 463–479.

Zeeman, E. C., 1980, Catastrophe models in administration, *Association for Institutional Research, Annual Forum Proceedings* 3, 9–24.

# 19

## The Genesis of Structure in Social Systems: The Paradigm of Self-Organization

*P. M. ALLEN*

A central question that has long been a subject of contention among historians concerns the nature of the historical process. Is it characterized by the conflict of great forces, moving inexorably toward their "natural" conclusions, uplifting some parts of humanity and crushing others, or is it rather the tale of great men, whose initiatives and decisions have written history, reversing desperate situations and opening new paths and horizons?

In other words, is the future already contained in the present, or is it, on the contrary, for us to create? Is free will a fiction or a fact?

Such questions underlie all attempts at "modeling" the behavior of a system, and of course in "planning" and "predicting" its evolution, and our first reaction may be to say that the "understanding" of the evolution of some past or present society demands precisely the capacity of a model to reproduce the subsequent behavior of the system. Such an attitude would indeed imply a belief in determinism, in the future being already contained in the present and the present in the past. On the other hand, is the only possible alternative to this an understanding of history obtained simply from the cataloging of the succession of events and decisions, of successes and failures, of whims and fantasies, of the many different actors of the systems?

If we ask what light the paradigms of natural science can throw on this issue, then we see that they offer either the total determinism of a dynamic trajectory, or the "equifinality" of an approach to an equilibrium state. Such a movement

**347**

THEORY AND EXPLANATION
IN ARCHAEOLOGY

to equilibrium would be accompanied by the elimination of any nonuniformities and the destruction of order existing initially in the system. This latter perspective is of course quite at odds with the evolution of human societies where organization and hierarchy can be created, where diversity and specialization may increase, and where successive civilizations can show their particular genius in exploring new and original forms and dimensions.

Neither the paradigm of equilibrium physics nor that of the deterministic, timeless trajectories of the stellar bodies can describe the burgeoning activities of living systems. Recently, however, progress in the natural sciences has led to a new and fascinating paradigm of potentially great importance for our understanding of social systems—that of self-organization.

In order to understand this term we must briefly examine the essence of mathematical modeling. This consists in the representation of some complex, multiple interacting system by a "reduced description" where "superfluous" details and particularities are passed over and only the "essential" remains. Briefly, then, we search for something that is easy enough to work with, but that nevertheless captures and governs what we consider to be the important features of the system. Thus a mathematical model always entails the passage from the "complete" to a "reduced" description, by invoking some average or typical behavior, whether it is of molecules undergoing on average a certain number of collisions per unit time, a blue-collar population making trips at a certain rate, or the different "levels" and "roles" of a society behaving in certain ways.

When is the passage from the complete to the reduced deterministic description adequate? The answer is that it is valid, providing that the average behavior invoked is indeed a good representation of reality. In other words, when the variance or deviation from the mean is small. We have habitually simply supposed that providing we have a sufficiently large number of individuals, then this variance will be small. However, such a hypothesis is based on the assumption that we have a Poisson or Gaussian distribution for the probability of a given behavior. What the paradigm of self-organizing systems is concerned with is this: For systems open to flows of energy and/or matter, nonlinear interactions can occur and these can lead to distributions of probability, which, far from being Poissonian (sharp and singly humped), can become bi-, tri-, or polymodal, giving rise to large variances and causing the breakdown of the reduced description. Such moments are associated with bifurcations in the solutions of the reduced description. Let us briefly describe some bifurcations and give some examples of self-organization in physical systems.

As we shall see, the evolution associated with open, nonlinear systems in which bifurcations occur offers us a new paradigm in which the history and evolution of a system is neither totally deterministic, nor entirely chaotic or "free." It is a mixture of both: Sometimes its trajectory is very stable, and its history is "inexorable," while at other times several possible paths may be open, and it is the individuals in the systems who will decide the future.

Consider the modeling of the change of a population $X$, which inhabits a region with limited resources and is hunted and killed by a predator population $Y$, the change resulting from the net effect per unit time of births and deaths. Next to the real system, the most basic description is one in which sub-populations of the whole systems (predator:prey, for example; but we could also separate age groups, sexes etc.) are assigned probabilities of birth or death per individual that depend on the particular state of the system (i.e., how many preys or predators are present, etc.). This hypothesis allows us to construct the so-called "master equation" that determines how any particular probability distribution of $X$ and $Y$ will evolve. By considering the probable gains and losses of each "slice" of probability resulting from the birth and death processes, it determines both the movement and the change of shape of the distribution over time. For example, historical determinism means that starting from some initial sharply peaked distribution, the master equation maintains the sharpness, and after even a long period has merely traced out a trajectory of $X$ and $Y$, while remaining sharply and singly humped. The opposite notion of complete in-determinism and "free will," however, would correspond to an initially sharp distribution spreading and flattening in time until finally all values of $X$ and $Y$ were equally attainable.

In reality, life is more interesting than either of these extremes, and in general, as we shall see, the master equation tells us that various futures are possible, and some are more probable than others.

While the master equation is a very complete description of the system, it is also very difficult to solve and often corresponds to a greater level of detail than may interest us. We may merely be interested in what the evolution of the system will be on average, and it is this averaging of the master equation that leads directly to the kinetic equations that we are used to seeing in population dynamics, geography, ecology, and so forth. This average level of description is the level at which most models function; obviously it contains much less information than the whole probability distribution, but clearly will only have an unambiguous meaning provided that the probability distribution in fact remains sharply and singly humped. In other words, if the master equation leads to a clean deterministic trajectory, then the "average" description will be both legitimate and meaningful. However, if the master equation leads to a dis-tribution that ceases to be sharply humped around a single value for each variable, then the "average" behavior of the variables is no longer related to what we shall actually observe for any particular case: The passage to the reduced description is compromised, along with its associated determinism.

At the level of the kinetic equations (the model, the average description), such an occurrence is marked by a bifurcation of the solution to these equations, that is, the appearance of a choice of possible paths for the system that may either diverge smoothly from the existing one, or may correspond to a "sudden" jump to some new regime. However, the information about how and at what moment this jump may occur is not contained in the reduced description, which can simply tell us that several solutions are possible, some of which are stable. In order to see the importance of these ideas to the understanding of structure and organization, and indeed of "systems," let us briefly describe some of the phenomena concerning "dissipative structures" from which these concepts were derived.

Chemical kinetics was a long-established subject concerning which, it seemed, there remained very little interesting work to be done, where almost everything was clear and well understood, a fitting tribute to the power of the reductionist, analytic, "hard" scientific method. So it seemed. However, when nonlinear chemical schemes were studied (for example, ones where the density of a component feeds back on its own rate of production), it was found that such systems, when maintained out of thermodynamic equilibrium, gave rise to new and surprising phenomena. They could spontaneously produce patterns of moving waves of concentration, or they could change color in a regular oscillation—a chemical clock—or adopt different stationary patterns. Suddenly, some reports of chemical experiments showing oscillations and patterns that had hitherto been partially dismissed (not to say "explained") as being anomalous were brought into the limelight, and now, just a few years later, whole conferences are devoted to this subject.

For example, the reaction scheme,

$$
\begin{aligned}
A &\rightarrow X \\
B + X &\rightarrow Y + D \\
2X + Y &\rightarrow 3X \\
X &\rightarrow E,
\end{aligned}
$$

with kinetic equation (model),

$$
\frac{\partial X}{\partial t} = A - (B + 1)X + X^2Y - \nabla^2 X
$$

$$
\frac{\partial Y}{\partial t} = BX - X^2Y - \nabla^2 Y
$$

where $X$ produces $Y$, which in turn produces $X$, has been intensively studied by the "Brussels School" (it is even known as the Brusselator), and various different types of self-organizations have been found. By regulating the flows of the initial and final products, $A$, $B$, $D$, and $E$, one can move away from equilibrium and, at a certain critical distance, an instability occurs. This threshold marks the point at which the least fluctuation can cause the system to leave its uniform stationary state.

When this occurs, a fluctuation is amplified and drives the system to some state characterized by the coherent behavior of an incredible number of molecules, forming perhaps a moving zone of high concentration of components—a chemical wave—wherein the chemical reactions maintain the spatial organization.

These are "dissipative structures," new, organized states of matter, some examples of which are shown in Figures 19.1 and 19.2. They correspond to organizations of the system that exceed by many magnitudes the scale of the interactions between the individual elements, in this case molecular forces, in fact over lengths related to the nonlinearities and the diffusive forces in the system. All that is required by a structure to "explain" its persistence, once it has arisen stochastically from an instability, is that it be stable.

This description contains both deterministic mechanisms (the chemical equations) and stochastic, random effects (the fluctuations), and it is these latter that are of particular importance when the system is near points at which an organization may change. These points are called "bifurcation points."

Complex systems can, of course, have a whole series of bifurcation points, as, for example, is shown in Figure 19.3, where the diagram of possible solutions is drawn as a function of some parameter $P$ involved in the interactions.

Between two bifurcation points, the system follows deterministic laws (such as those of chemical kinetics). But near the point of bifurcation, it is the fluctuations that play an essential role in determining the branch that the system chooses. Such a point of view introduces the concept of "history" into the explanation of the state of the systems. For example, in Figure 19.3, the "explanation" of the fact that the system is organized according to the solution $C$ necessarily refers to the passage through the structures $B$ and $A$. No "explanation" can ever deduce the unique necessity of finding the system in state $C$ for the particular value of the parameter $P$.

Near a bifurcation point the nonlinearities of the interactions can cause the form of the probability distribution to become bi-, tri-, or polymodal. Thus, the first moment or average description is hopelessly inadequate to describe what the system will now do, and, in fact, what occurs is that the system may jump to one or another of the humps. It is important to note the "danger" of interpreting the behavior of a system as being governed by a potential function. For example, one could, retrospectively, construct a "potential" that behaved as

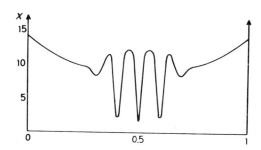

**Figure 19.1.** Here we see the density profile of the component $X$ across the vessel, when the initial component $A$ is supposed to diffuse in from either side. A dissipative structure forms, having its own length scale.

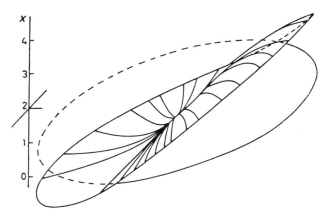

**Figure 19.2.** This illustrates the density of component $X$ in a circular dish, as a dissipative structure consisting of a spiral wave evolves in the system.

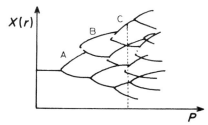

**Figure 19.3.** A bifurcation diagram showing the possible solutions as a function of parameter $P$ involved in the interaction.

some inverse probability function, but in general such a construction serves no purpose. First, for more than one variable it is, in general, impossible to construct such a function, meaning that the class of nonlinear dynamical systems contains as a small subset those derived from a potential function. Second, we must recall that the differential equations of our "model" are in fact only the first-moment approximations to the master equation, and that it is this latter equation that really governs the system. Thus, even for a one-variable problem, where it is possible to integrate the right-hand side of the differential equation in order to obtain a potential function, there is no guarantee that this *in fact* will imitate correctly the true shape of the probability distribution. For example, it is true that we can integrate the logistic equation $(dx/dt) = ax - bx^2$ to give a "potential," $V_x = (ax/2)^2 - (bx/3)^3$, but in reality, we could have different stochastic dynamics underlying the first-moment approximation. For example, the presence of terms where there is a chance of $X$ increasing or decreasing:

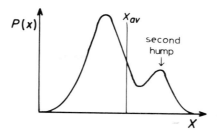

**Figure 19.4.** Appearance of a second hump due to nonlinear interactions.

$$X \to X + 1 \text{ with probability } \frac{AX^2}{2}$$

and

$$X \to X - 1 \text{ with probability } \frac{AX^2}{2}$$

does not change the "average" equation, but does change the "shape" of the probability distribution $P(X, t)$, and hence the "potentials" obtained by in-

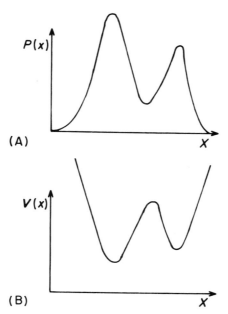

**Figure 19.5.** (*a*) Double-humped probability distribution; (*b*) potential well designed to "mimic" (*a*).

tegrating the first-moment equation would mimic incorrectly the behavior of the system when perturbed from its stationary state. In a word, then, the clean, closed, geometrical world of potentials and catastrophe theory is, in general, not relevant to the real, somewhat messy, but much more interesting world of complex systems evolving through successive structural instabilities.

Summarizing the main points concerning the paradigm of self-organization, we find three central issues:

1. The evolution of a complex system involves both determinism and chance. Far from a bifurcation the "reduced" description (the model, the equations) is valid and *determines* the evolution. Near a bifurcation the "reduced description" is ambiguous and inadequate. Chance is important, and the system is open to the "richness" of its interior. It has some autonomy.

2. The "explanation" of a particular structure and functioning is partly historical. The structure must be "compatible" with the model, but is not a *necessary consequence* of it. There is, in general, no global potential, and the system is not going anywhere in particular. The only "explanation" required for a structure to persist is that it be stable. An organization does not have to work "well" in order to survive. It just has to resist sufficiently the forces that menace it.

3. The stability of a system is being "probed" constantly by fluctuations of different types: (*a*) fluctuations of the variables; (*b*) fluctuations of the parameters; and (*c*) innovations–mutations.

Any particular state of organization results from a dynamic dialogue between the physical, social, and economic laws of the moment, and a particular succession of historical accidents of the preceding three types, whose action has marked the evolution of the system. The future will also be marked by "historical accidents" to come.

This type of evolution has been called "order by fluctuation" (Nicolis and Prigogine 1977), and we see that this extension of the physical sciences offers us a paradigm that is potentially of great importance for the biological and social sciences (Prigogine, Allen, and Herman 1977). There is already an extensive literature concerning different applications of these new ideas in various domains: This is exemplified in the study of oscillatory biological phenomena (Goldbeter and Caplan 1976, Goldbeter and Nicolis 1976), for example, and in the problem of "morphogenesis" in the early states of embryo development (Erneux and Hiernaux 1979). Also models treating the problem of cancerous growth as one resulting from an instability of the immune system have been made and explored in both steady and "noisy" environments (Lefever and Horsthemke 1979). Other studies have been undertaken that explore the role of these new ideas in our understanding of the "order" that reigns within animal populations and, in particular, in colonies of social insects (Deneubourg and Allen 1976, Deneubourg 1976). We shall not go further into such questions here, but shall move on to discuss the impact of these new ideas on our understanding of human social systems.

## SELF-ORGANIZATION OF HUMAN SETTLEMENTS

Having discussed the evolutionary paradigm offered by "dissipative structures" in the realms of chemistry, biology, and ecology, we now turn to a brief description of some recent applications to urban systems. The chief characteristic of such systems is that they are made up of a multitude of "actors" of different types, each having its own particular criteria and values, as well as different opportunities and power in the systems.

The next step is to attempt to construct the interaction mechanisms of these actors, which in principle requires a knowledge of their values and preferences, and, of course, how these values conflict and reinforce each other as the system evolves.

How can several different criteria be "combined" in order to give a measure of the probability of a particular decision (Roubens 1980)? The basic idea accepted by multicriteria analysts is that we may suppose that a given actor is at least conscious of some major criteria, in each of which he can define a direction of preference. In addition, he can assign some measure of their relative importance, even if it is very vague. Clearly, the idea of a "payoff" that will occur in the future following an action involves the actor's capacity to believe that he or she can predict the future over such a time. Thus it depends on the confidence he or she has in the model he or she is using. This is yet another aspect of "learning", which, as we shall see, permeates the discussion of the modeling of human systems.

Another vitally important factor that must be included in any modeling of decisions is the fact that we usually have nonlinear responses to given changes in stimuli. In general, then, the problem of assigning a number to a given value of a criterion (e.g., price), such that it measures our "reaction" and "sensitivity" to that reading, comes down to some nonlinear projection. However, such an approach will also open the door to the consideration of qualitative factors, for in reality there is no difference between the input of a "quantity" to which we have a nonlinear sensitivity and a "quality" that, although the input is not strictly a number, nevertheless may have a number assigned to it.

The observed behavior of individuals results from the "dialogue" between the choices available to them, and their needs and constraints. Adversity can be either a spur to the search for a new, more acceptable solution, leading through instability to some new qualitative feature, or it may lead to the rejection of all the choices available, and to the destruction of the system offering them.

Returning to the problem of building our model, how, we may ask, can the existence of uncertainty and lack of information concerning the payoffs associated with choices be allowed for in the structure of the model? This can be handled quite simply in the following way. As we mentioned before, it is reasonable to suppose that the probability of making a particular choice is inversely proportional to its "distance," in the value space of the decider, from the origin that represents the most favorable or preferable value imaginable in each dimension separately.

Suppose now, however, we wish to consider a situation in which there was no information concerning these "distances." If this were so, then clearly, if there are two choices, they have an even chance of being selected. On the other hand, if there is absolute and certain knowledge that one of the choices is better than the other, then we may suppose that there is a probability of 1 that it will be adopted. An expression that fulfills these requirements is as follows.

Probability of choice $i$ among all those possible $j$

$$P(I) = \frac{A_i}{\sum_j A_j} = \frac{(1/d_i)^I}{\sum_j (1/d_j)^I}$$

where $I$ is a measure of the amount of information the individual has to make his decision, $A_i$ is the perceived "attractivity."

When $I \to 0$ we have equiprobability for all the choices possible, but when $I \to \infty$ then we have probability 1 for the choice corresponding to the shortest "distance." Of course, we could also take each axis separately and look at the uncertainty in that, since some facts may be known precisely and others extremely vaguely. However, this would make our calculations very much more complicated in the modeling that we shall present here, and so while noting that that is the correct procedure, we shall not pursue it further.

The main feature of the approach we are attempting to build here is that each type of actor, according to his or her means and his or her role, etc., will have a different value space. It may be simply a matter of degree, or it may also be that he or she has a quite different set of values, probably related to a different "role" in society. We have a characteristic and bounded rationality for each type of actor.

So far we have been discussing decision-making behavior without taking into account the fact that the system may be evolving.

In a dynamic system the payoffs that characterize each choice will change in time, as will the "choices" open to individuals, and this evolution will be predicted by the decision-maker according to the "model" he or she is either implicitly or explicitly using. It is somewhat disquieting to realize that the models we are going to build will contain the behavior of actors, which will in turn depend on the models available to them. This is an important point because it may influence the confidence that any forecast may be accorded, and in that case the behavior of actors may be more dominated by "satisficing" than "optimising." I shall return to this point later because it may be of importance in discussing the use to which modeling should be put—that of predicting the future evolution and of making the "best" decision, or rather of exploring the "dangers" and "uncertainties" of the future and attempting to evaluate acceptable and robust decisions.

In an evolving system, then, each actor will attempt to estimate the payoffs associated with a given choice, not only instantaneously, but also over future times, and according to the importance or "weighting" that he or she accords to future times, he or she will decide which choice he or she prefers.

Let us now suppose that the probability of making a particular decision $i$, from $\Sigma_j j$, per unit time is proportional to the relative attractivity. From this it is now possible to construct kinetic equations governing the evolution of the numbers of individuals adopting each choice. What is of vital importance, however, is that as a given option is adopted, so the payoff (costs, prestige, comfort, etc.) will change, and the choice pattern of the population will reflect this, as choices get nearer or farther along the different dimensions of various value systems of the actors.

Consider a homogeneous population $x$ faced with several possible choices. Then, we may write down that for any particular consumption pattern (i.e., number of clients, $s_1, s_2 \ldots , s$) we will have the $i$th choice,

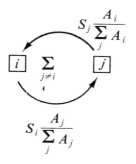

Then, if $x = \displaystyle\sum_j S_j$

$$\frac{dS_i}{dt} = aS_i\left( \sum_{j\neq i} S_j \frac{A_i}{\sum_j A_j} - S_i \sum_{j\neq i} \frac{A_j}{\sum_j A_j} \right) \qquad (1)$$

$$\frac{dS_i}{dt} = aS_i\left( x\frac{A_i}{\sum_j A_j} - S_i \right) \qquad (2)$$

and for several populations, $x_j$, each with its own view of the relative attractiveness of the choices, $A_{ij}$, we have,

$$\frac{dS_i}{dt} = aS_i\left( \sum_j X_j \frac{A_{ij}}{\sum_{i'} A_{i'j}} - S_i \right) \qquad (3)$$

where the attractivity $A_{ij}$ of the $i$th choice, viewed by the population type $j$, is thus some inverse of the "distance" from the origin of $i$ in the value space of the type $j$, raised to a power $I$, as explained earlier, related to the information available in the system.

In the first example that we briefly describe here, we have studied the dynamic evolution of the urban centers growing and declining within an urban region. Using the equations of type (3), we have developed a model of the competition between economic functions and services situated in different urban centers, and their changing capacity of employment that in turn acts on the migration pattern of the population. The model is based on some of the concepts underlying central place theory (Berry 1967, Christaller 1933, Lösch 1954), but, of course, in terms of a dynamic and not a static representation of these concepts.

The equations that we have used express the interaction of the distribution of employment opportunities with that of the population. Individuals "react to" or are "attracted by" employment opportunities, and the latter are changed by the movement of population. The dynamic interaction scheme is shown in Figure 19.6. The installation of an exporting activity at a given point will result in an increase in the domestic sector of the town's economy as the population at this point increases. This augmentation in the demand for local goods and services results in an increased employment capacity in the domestic sector, which in turn causes a further increase in local population, and so on, increasing local demand and local population until a new steady state is attained, marked by a total increase in population that is considerably greater than that initially introduced directly by the implantation of the export activity. This amplifying mechanism is called the "urban multiplier," and it appears quite naturally in the dynamic scheme. The second mechanism present in the model is that as the system develops and populations grow as a result of the implantation of various functions, so new market thresholds are exceeded at these points, with the result that still more activities may appear at points where several are already concentrated. These will add to the export sector as well as to the domestic, broadening the base and diversifying the urban economy. We again notice the fundamental irreversibility of the system, where some initial implantation in the basic sector can lead to the growth of a diversified, thriving urban concentration that will not necessarily collapse if at some later time this initial investment should be withdrawn.

In Figure 19.7 we show the emergence of structure in a typical simulation based on the interaction scheme of Figure 19.6. It represents a running dialogue between the deterministic "rationality" of the interaction scheme 6 and the effect of random implantations and initiatives. As the simulation progresses, so

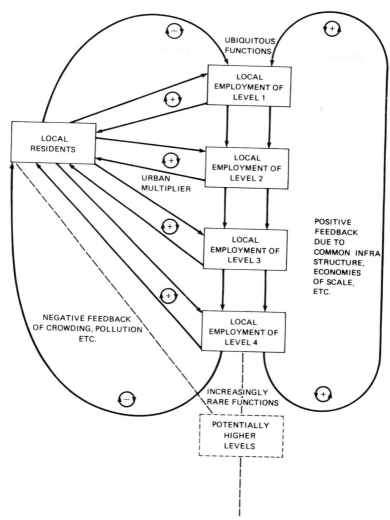

**Figure 19.6.** This is the interaction scheme underlying the model of regional evolution, as different localities that receive economic activities grow under the influence of the "positive feedback" (the urban multiplier, effects of common infrastructure etc.), but also compete with each other for markets, and for space within each center. (Allen and Sanglier 1979, Allen, Deneubourg, Sanglier, Boon, and De Palma 1978, 1979).

gradually the urban structure becomes fixed and stable. Initially, starting from complete homogeneity, many futures are possible, but as time goes on, we move along particular branches of the tree of possibilities (Figure 19.3), and some of the other branches become virtually inaccessible. In any particular case, in reality, the geographic details of the terrain, the direction of other

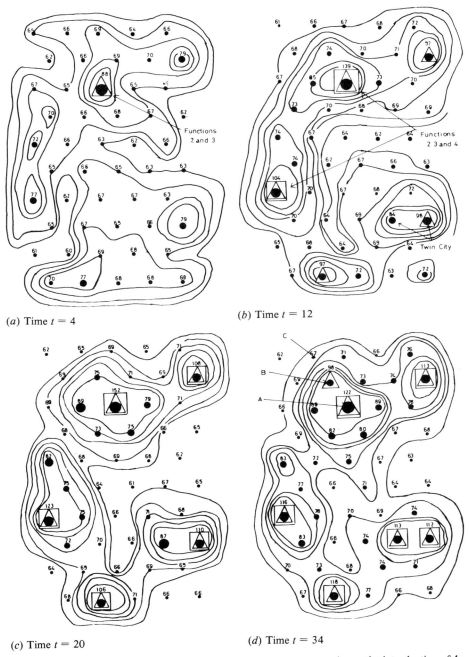

(a) Time $t = 4$

(b) Time $t = 12$

(c) Time $t = 20$

(d) Time $t = 34$

**Figure 19.7.** Here we see the gradual emergence of urban structure owing to the introduction of 4 levels of economic activity at different points in the system. Initially the region is perfectly homogeneous, and low-level economic functions appear at entirely random locations. The populations at each point are fluctuated randomly by some 4% and higher levels of economic function are introduced when a threshold of population is exeeded at a given point.

settlements, etc. will make certain future evolutions, certain parts of the tree, more and less probable. However, this does not eliminate the branching nature of the evolutionary possibilities.

In Figure 19.8 we see the evolution over time of the points A, B, and C indicated in Figure 19.7. These show an evolution over time that is entirely typical of the urban centers throughout the region: First we have central-core growth, then residential sprawl, followed by economic decentralization and central-core decay and subsequently interurban growth. These different phases of urban evolution result quite naturally from the simple scheme 7 for other simulations that differ in the details of their particular histories, but also show the same trends. A different history of fluctuations leads, of course, to a different distribution of urban centers, although the same phases of growth are present, and the number of larger centers that emerge is roughly maintained. However, these different structures are nevertheless characterized by different average distances for consumers to obtain goods and services and to go to work, and hence by different travel costs and energy consumption.

The particular structure that evolves may be stable to small fluctuations in its structure, and reflects both the values of the parameters involved in the interactions (e.g., productivity, local resources, transport costs, etc.) as well as the particularities of its history. Clearly, the model can be used to explore the probable effects of different decisions that may change the values of these parameters, or may be specific perturbations of the variables, on the modified evolution of the whole system, including the possibility of "unexpected" structural changes. The word "unexpected" is used because until now models

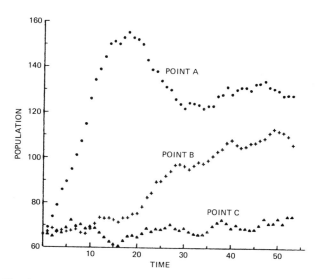

**Figure 19.8.** The time evolution of the points A, B, and C that are indicated in Figure 19.7d.

have been unable to handle problems involving structural change, particularly a symmetry-breaking "creation" of some new element, with the result that decisions made by planning authorities, and local and national agencies, have often had, in fact, the opposite result to that desired. For example, a decision to reduce transportion costs for commuters and shoppers may indeed result in improved access initially, but the repercussions are carried through the various links of the system, and the increased range of economic competition may lead to the elimination of some local centers of employment and services, and to decreased access and higher costs for commuters and shoppers in the long run. Thus the payoffs that result from different decisions can be explored, not only for those immediately concerned and in the short term, but also for the long-term global effects on the changed evolution of the whole.

Another experiment we have performed is to examine the effects of lifting a trade barrier separating two regions. This is, of course, only the first, very simple analysis of the very complex effects resulting from the economic fusion of the two hitherto separate markets, which could differ in the number and types of products offered. Here, we have simply examined the influence of the timing of such a fusion for two regions having the same economic functions. In Figure 19.9 we show the different stable structures that emerge as a result of either uniting the two regions immediately, or uniting them at a later stage of their separate development. Once again, we see that the "timing" of the dynamics matters, and from calculations of the transportation costs involved in each structure we see that "evolution" is, in general, not optimizing anything in particular, and that different solutions involve higher or lower costs for different functions.

The point of principal concern here is that our analysis shows us that for the same population, having the same "value system," for the same technology and the same products, the flow of goods in a given market can be both qualitatively and quantitatively different depending only on the "history" of the system. Thus, the fundamental diagram of "supply" and "demand" (Figure 19.10) is misleading, because it can only be constructed in retrospect. It refers to a particular outcome, and the intersection could have been elsewhere. The model shows us that the "free market" is not equally open to all agents, since the possibility of successful implantation on an existing market depends on the size of initial investment that can be made.

We see also that under some slow change in the parameters of the system (e.g., market size, economies of scale, current interest rates) a relatively sudden reorganization of the pattern of the consumption could occur when the previous one becomes unstable. In such changes, relatively small differences of possibly random origin or new initiatives (fluctuations) would prove decisive in the forging of a new structure. Our image of such a system, therefore, is that of a dynamic "game" with a varying number of players and stakes, where periods of "adaptive" jockeying are separated by successive "crises" or periods of major reorganization (Day 1980).

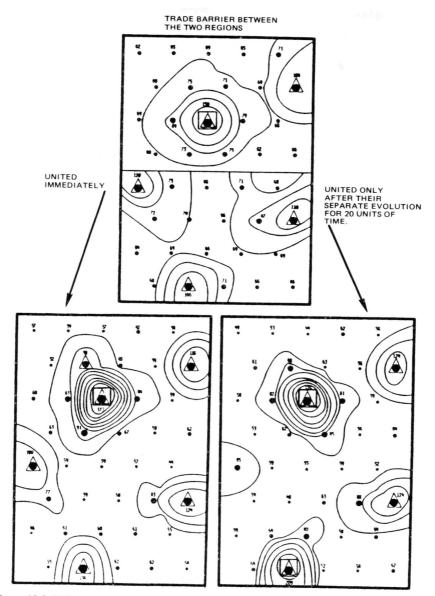

**Figure 19.9** Different stable urban structures resulting from the same initial condition. For (b) the frontier was removed at the initial moment, while for (c) it was only lifted after 20 units of time during which the two regions evolve separately. Thus a "market equilibrium" depends both quantitatively and qualitatively on the "timing" of the particular interactions and is not determined uniquely by the initial condition and the criteria of the actors.

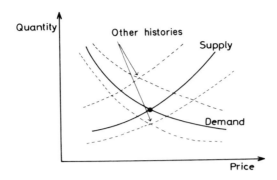

**Figure 19.10.** Alternative "histories" of supply and demand.

If we consider the long-term evolution of our system, then certainly the effects of "innovations" will be of great importance. In general, these innovations will occur in some sense around existing dimensions and structures, causing the system and the "values" of the population to evolve in new directions, so that societies with different histories will exhibit not only different socioeconomic patterns but also in the long run, different "value systems." For example, in Western society the automobile was considered simply as an amusing luxury only some 40 or 50 years ago; but the evolution of the system as a whole has led to its being viewed now as a basic necessity for millions. Similarly, it seems clear from this point of view that the impact of one society on another is a complex and dangerous phenomenon, involving a clash of values that the market does not necessarily "translate" in a neutral manner. Of course, it remains true that the "market" system nevertheless does involve an exploration of the potential demand among the population for different goods (although it may be imperfect), while this is not necessarily the case for a "planned economy." For such a complex system as this there is probably no simple answer to the problem of how a society should best be run, but then why should there be?

## THE EVOLUTION OF URBAN CENTERS

Having shown how the spatial organization of a region does not result uniquely and necessarily from the "economic and social laws" enshrined in the equations, but also represents a "memory" of particular specific deviations from average behavior, let us now turn instead to the question of the evolution of urban structure within a city (Allen, Boon, and Sanglier 1980).

In agreement with much previous work, particularly, for example, the philosophy of a "Lowry" type of model, first we consider the basic sector of employment for the city, and in particular, two radically different components of this employment sector—the industrial base and business and financial employment. Next we consider the service employment generated by the population of the city and by the basic sectors, supposing two levels—a short-range set of functions and a long-range set. The residents of the city, depending on their type of employment etc., will exhibit a range of socioeconomic behavior, and for this we have supposed two populations corresponding essentially to blue- and white-collar workers.

The next phase of the modeling is an attempt to construct the interaction mechanisms of these variables, which requires, as we have discussed, knowledge of the values and preferences of the different types of actors represented by the variables and, of course, how these values conflict and reinforce each other as the system evolves. In Figure 19.11 we show the basic interaction scheme for six variables whose mutual interaction leads, it is supposed, to many of the important features of spatial structure. These variables reflect the decisions, particularly locational ones, of six basic types of actors.

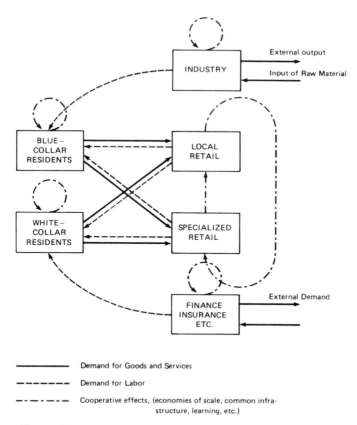

**Figure 19.11.** The interaction scheme of our simple city system.

We then construct the kinetic equations as in the previous section, expressing the evolution of each variable in each locality. As an example, let us write explicitly,

$$\frac{dx_i^k}{dt} = a x_i^k \left( \sum_j J_j^k \frac{A_{i'j}}{\sum_{i'} A_{i'j}} - x_i^k \right) , \tag{4}$$

which expresses how the number of residents $x_{i,k}$ of socioeconomic group $k$, at the point $i$, change in the time by the residential decisions of the sum of all those employed in the different possible sectors $J_j^k$, whose jobs are located at $j$. Thus, $A_{ij}^k$ is the attractivity of residence at $i$ as viewed by someone of socioeconomic group $k$, employed in sector $m$ at the point $j$.

$$A_{ij}^k = \frac{\overset{\text{cooperativity}}{v^k (1 + \sigma^k x_i^k}) \, \overset{\text{distance}}{e^{-b^k \Delta_{ik}}}}{(v^k + \sum_k x_i^k + \sum_L J_i^L)} \longleftarrow \text{crowding} \tag{5}$$

where $v^k$, $\sigma^k$, $b^k$ are characteristic constants. These include the considerations of cost and time in travel to work, the price of land, pollution, noise levels, etc., as well as the character of the neighborhood.

We have written down similar equations for the other actors, which briefly express, for example, the need for industrial employment to be located at a point with good access to the outside, and for a large area of jobs, as well as some 85% of their work force being taken to be in the lower socioeconomic group. We have also added the fact that the interdependence of many industrial activities leads to a preference for locations adjacent to established industrial locations. This term also covers many subtle effects of the infrastructure that grows around existing situations. The main effects are all noted on the interaction scheme of Figure 19.11.

Here we shall briefly describe some of the simulations that we have made using this simple model. In the first case, we have looked at the evolution of a center, which initially is only a small town, but throughout the simulation, due to population growth and expanding external demand from the industrial and financial sectors, the town grows, spreading and sprawling in space as it does so, and also developing an internal structure.

The initial condition of the simulation is shown in Figure 19.12. After 10 units of time, the situation has evolved to that shown in Figure 19.13, where already an internal structure has appeared. Industrial, commercial, and financial employment are all still located at the center, but now we observe residential decentralization, particularly on the part of the upper socioeconomic group. The center is very densely occupied and is strongly "blue collar."

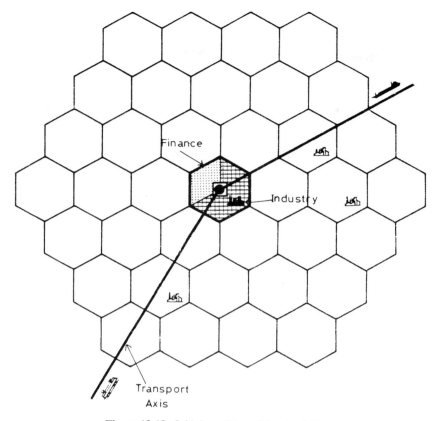

**Figure 19.12.** Initial condition of the simulation.

As the simulation proceeds, however, at around 15 units of time this urban structure becomes unstable. It is not a question of simply growing or shrinking; what is at issue is the qualitative nature of the structure. At this point in time, the very dense occupation of the center is beginning to make industrial managers think about some new behavior. For some of them the cost of continuing to operate in the center is making them contemplate the abandonment of the infrastructure and mutual dependencies that have grown up with time. At this point, as for a dissipative structure, it is the fluctuations that are going to be vital in deciding how the structure will evolve. At some point there is an initiative, when some "brave" (if it works out; "stupid" if it doesn't) individual decides to take his or her chances and to try to relocate at some point in the periphery. Where, exactly, will depend on his or her particular perceived needs and opportunities. However, what is important is that whereas before this time such an initiative would have been "punished" by being less competitive, now,

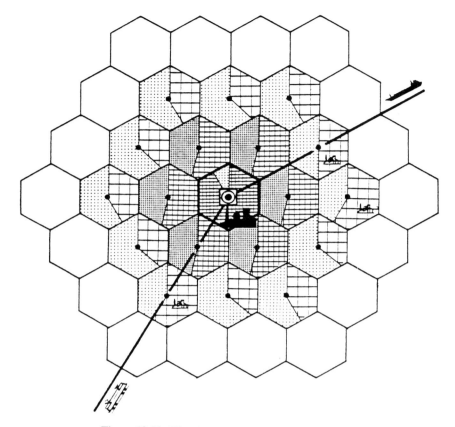

**Figure 19.13.** The simulation after 10 units of time.

around $t = 15$, the opposite is true. Once the nucleus is started and, of course, its own infrastructure begins to be installed, so almost all the industrial activities decentralize and establish themselves in this new position in the periphery.

At this point, many different initiatives could succeed in carrying the system off to some particular new state of organization. However, those that succeed with the least effort are the industrial nuclei in the periphery, lying along the communication axis.

From this point on, however, the locational decisions of the blue-collar workers are particularly affected by the fact that their value systems are now based on the fact that industrial employment has relocated in the southwestern corner of the city. Thus, the spatial distribution of blue-collar residents in the city starts to change, having in a sense a new focus. This in turn acts on the locational choices of the white-collar workers, who find space easily in the regions of the city less favored by the "blue collars," and whose spatial

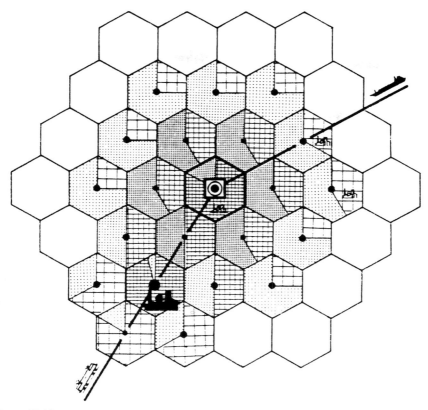

**Figure 19.14.** By time $t = 40$, the urban structure has changed qualitatively from that of Figure 19.13. It has developed a second focus and has structured functionally. That is, one center is essentially an industrial satellite, while the traditional center has become largely a central business district and the important shopping center. Also note that in the traditional center, retail employment has moved outward to the second ring (suburan shopping centers), while retail employment is still centralized in the industrial center.

distribution adjusts accordingly. Changes in the distribution of local service employment also then occur, and the whole structure evolves to the pattern shown in Figure 19.14 by time $t = 40$. Here, we see that we have actually displaced the center of gravity of the urban center, and have an urban structure that resembles two overlapping urban centers of different character. In the southwest we have a predominantly working-class, industrial-satellite area, while the original city center is a central business district and important shopping and commercial area with predominantly white-collar suburbs stretching away from it on three sides. In this part of the city, it is the second ring that has attracted the local shopping centers, while in the industrial satellite, it is the heavily populated, industrial district itself that has become an important shopping center. From our simulation we can calculate traffic patterns, travel distances, and energy costs, and we find a complicated behavior for these.

This shows us the dangers involved in global modeling, for on that scale what we see is an apparently inexplicable change in behavior, in which the distance traveled per person, and the average energy consumption per person, stops rising and even decreases. Only a model that can describe the internal restructuring of the city could have predicted such a change, and linear systems theory, and input–output flow models would have to be recalibrated at this point. In other words, relationships between global variables of complex systems nearly always involve nonlinearity, and a systems analysis that assumes linearity will only be reasonable in the short term, or in the neighborhood of the calibration.

## CONCLUSIONS

One of the most important points that arises from the discussion and simulations concerns the level of explanation that is aimed at by a model. If we approach a complex system with a desire to model it so that we may understand its evolution, then clearly we must first set up what we consider to be the "structure" of the system. However, if this structure simply reflects the "structure–function" present in the system at the initial moment, and we then calibrate the "model" on this initial state, then any "prediction" that the model makes assumes that the function and structure do not change. This may be quite wrong. Our point of view, derived from the concepts underlying dissipative structure, is that the initial structure–function of the system (pattern of consumption, or where different populations and jobs are located and the traffic flows between them) is itself the result of an evolutionary process that, after a particular history involving both macroscopic and microscopic factors, was established in the system. Because of the existence of multiple solutions, the dynamic equations of the macroscopic variables (the "model") are ambiguous and could have given rise to "other" structures if the particular history had been different. Thus, if we admit that the particular initial structure–function of the system with which we start is a "special case," and that microfactors outside the model led to its establishment, then we must also admit that this will be true of the future evolution. In other words, the future will also have its "historical accidents" when we look back on it. Archaeologists should be aware then, that any model based on infrastructural constraints of a given society will not, in general, be sufficient to explain its subsequent evolution. However, it will be a necessary part of that explanation.

Therefore, in order to build models that can cope with such problems, we must look for the underlying interaction processes that can give rise to the many different structure–functions that are observed for different circumstances and histories. The basis of such a search must be human behavior, outside of explicit statements about space. Thus, the "structure" of the model should not explicitly contain spatial structure, but this should result from interactions of the humans in the system as they make "choices" according to their value systems and constraints, choices that arise because of particular initiatives by other actors in the system following the same program but viewed from a different place and role in society. A part of these choices is indeed that relating to the evolution of the numbers of individuals in each role, and the invention of new roles.

If we look at the interaction diagram for the intraurban system, then we see that this type of approach is indeed initially nonspatial. Thus the interaction scheme could perfectly well exist with identical values of variables at each point of the system. It is, potentially, totally symmetrical. However, because fluctuations, both in the "real world" and in the "mental maps" of individuals, explore possibilities outside the reduced description of the world that is a model, this symmetry can be broken and, having been broken, can be amplified if some actors perceive an advantage in the new behavior and have the "power" necessary to adopt it. Thus evolution is always characterized by events in which "abnormal behavior" becomes "normal behavior," when "informal structure" becomes "formal." Small fluctuations are amplified by the advantages perceived by at least some of the actors. Even if such advantages correspond to disadvantages for other actors, then it would depend on the "power" or "leverage" of the opposing groups as to whether or not the changes would take place.

Clearly, decision is related to perception, and by manipulating information one can change the evolution of the system. Both direct advertising and propaganda, as well as social pressure in the form of fads and fashions, can create desires and frustrations that may mark the system permanently. Values, it seems, are not the simple, self-evident certainties that we may have believed. Even such "sure-fire" values as maternal love have recently been shown to be subtle and changing. What one must face is that almost all our everyday actions are not the expression of an absolute rationality, but the result of a dynamic dialogue between "system" and "values," between "supply" and "demand," during which bifurcations occur. Their rationality is simply conferred on them by the society in which they are thought "normal," where they have evolved, and they can, and will, change. The problem of policymaking in a world with changing values is indeed a fundamental one. If we are ever to be able to understand such an evolution, then our models must not simply say: The system is organized like this. They must also examine the question, why is it like this? The reply necessarily will involve an understanding of the reasons for its stability, and this in turn will allow an appreciation of its potential instability, and of the new dimensions and levels of organization that will be created (Jantsch 1980).

Summarizing the main points made previously, we have examined the behavioral basis of our models and shown how a multiple criteria (both quantitative and qualitative) can be inserted in the equations. An important general point that arises is that a structural reorganization of, say, the urban space leads to a corresponding reorganization of the mental maps and values of the various actors. The symmetry-breaking properties of nonlinear systems lead to a corresponding expansion of the dimensions of the actors' value space. For example, in the case of an initially circular city, the variables and parameters of decisional criteria can all be expressed in terms of the scalar distance from the center. Once the circular symmetry is broken, however, the value space expands to include all the angle-dependent possibilities. Similarly, when all cars were black, the question of value attached to color was of no importance. Once the symmetry was broken, however, and cars of other colors appeared, a new dimension was created in the value space of buyers and finally could become an important factor in sales.

The important point is that fluctuations around "normal" behavior in the real world, and fluctuations in the mental models of actors, both explore situations that are "richer" than the reduced description of the world that is given by the model. These explorations can be amplified by the nonlinearities in the system and lead to a structural evolution of it. What we add to Herbert Simon's concept of the bounded rationality of the actors in a system are the additional bounds that are always introduced by a model. The bounded rationality of the "modeler" means that he or she is obliged to look for a simplified description, he or she is incapable of "knowing" what it is like to "be" each and every individual in the system.

It is this bounded rationality of the modeler, together with that of the actors, which renders the predictions of the model probabilistic. Using hindsight, deterministic causes can always be assigned to what happened, but in speaking of the future or subsequent evolution of a system, chance and randomness will play a role. If a particular change in society could be repeated under identical experimental conditions an infinite number of times, then it is true that precise probabilistic statements could be made. But in any real situation these conditions are not met, and we are forced to admit that near a "pitchfork" bifurcation, for example, although some weak "cause" will, in fact, "choose" a branch, we cannot know in advance which weak force will win, and what its direction will be at the critical time. Near bifurcations what really occurs is that the "major" forces present reach some impasse where they balance each other out. At such a time the system becomes sensitive to "weak forces" and "imperfections" and to the hitherto unimportant explorations around the "normal," and instability occurs, possibly sweeping the system off to some new level of complexity.

Complexification feeds on itself because it creates new situations and dimensions, which widen the experience of people and create new tastes and qualities, leading to new behaviors and to further complexification and to the creation and destruction of patterns and organizations. Only a much more profound understanding of such self-organization, whose complex nature is merely glimpsed in the above, can help us steer a course in such an unfolding universe of self-discovery.

## ACKNOWLEDGMENTS

The author wishes to thank Professor I. Prigogine, whose ideas have inspired this approach, for his constant interest and invaluable comments. The dynamic model of a simple market system was developed in collaboration with Dr. R. Frere and Dr. M. Fisher-Sanglier. The urban modeling was performed with the help of Mme. F. Boon and Dr. M. Fisher-Sanglier, and owes much also to discussions with and help and support from R. Crosby and David Kahn from the U.S. Department of Transportation during the completion of contracts TSC–1185, 1460, and 1640. This work was supported by the Actions de Recherche Concertées of the Belgian Government, 76/81 II.3. The author is also grateful to P. Kinet for drawing the figures.

## REFERENCES

Allen, P. M., and Sanglier, M., 1979 A dynamic model of a central place system, *Geographical Analysis*, 11, No. 3.

Allen, P. M., Boon, F., and Sanglier, M., 1980, Dynamic models of urban systems, (Report to the Department of Transportation of the U.S.A., under contract TSC-1640. See also contracts TSC-1185, and 1460.)

Berry, B. J. L., 1967, *Geography of Market Centres and Retail Distribution*, Englewood Cliffs, New Jersey, Prentice-Hall.

Christaller, W., 1933, *Die Zentralen Orte in Suddeutschland*, Jena, Gustav Fischer, translation, C. Baskin, Bureau of Population and Urban Research, University of Virginia, 1954.

Day, R., 1980, Adaptive economics. (Paper presented at the Third Annual Urban and Regional Systems Workshop, Milwaukee, Wisconsin.)

Deneubourg, J. L., 1977, Application de l'Ordre par Fluctuation à le Description de Certaines Etapes de la Construction du Nid chez les Termites, *Insectes Sociaux*, 24, No. 2.

Deneubourg, J. L., and Allen, P. M., 1976, Un Modèle Théorique de la Division du Travail dans les Colonies d'Insectes, *Bull. Class. Sci. Acad. Roy. Bel*, LXII, 5, No. 6.

Erneux, T., and Hiernaux, J., 1979, Chemical patterns in circular morphogenetic fields, *Bull. Math. Biol.*, 41

Glansdorff, P., and Prigogine, I., 1971, *Structure, Stability and Fluctuations*, London, Wiley Interscience.

Goldbeter, A., and Caplan, S. R., 1976, Oscillatory enzymes, *Annual Review of Biophysics and Bioengineering*, G.

Goldbeter, A., and Nicolis G., 1976, An allosteric enzyme model with positive feedback applied to glycolytic oscillations, *Progress in Theoretical Biology*, 4.

Isard, W., 1956, *Location and the Space Economy*, Wiley, N.Y.

Jantsch, E., 1980, *The Self-Organizing Universe*, New York, Pergamon Press.

Lefever, R., and Garay, T., 1977, A mathematical model of the immune surveillance against cancer, *Theoretical Immunology*.

Lefever, R., and Horstemke, W., 1979, Bistability in fluctuating environments, *Bull. Math. Biol.*, 47.

Lösch, A. 1954, *Economics of Location*, translation by W. Woglan and W. Stolper, New Haven, Yale University Press.

Lowry, I. S., 1964, Model of Metropolis, Santa Monica, RM–4035–RC, Rand Corporation.

Nicolis, G., and Prigogine, I., 1977, *Self-organization in Non-equilibrium Systems,* New York, Wiley Interscience.

Prigogine, I., Allen, P. M., and Herman, R., 1977, The evolution of complexity and the laws of nature, in *Goals for a Global Community,* New York, Pergamon Press.

Roubens, M., 1980, Analyse et agrégation des préférences : modélisation, adjustment et résumé des données rationnelles, Tutorial Paper II, *Revue Belge de Statistique, d'Informatique et de Recherche Opéationnelle*, 20, No. 2, 36–67.

Wilson, A. G., 1974, *Urban and Regional Models in Geography and Planning,* London and New York, Wiley Interscience.

# 20

# A Computational Model of Sociocultural Systems and Their Dynamics

*JAMES DORAN*

*Civilisation is hooped together, brought*
*Under a rule, under the semblance of peace*
*By manifold illusion . . .*
*—W. B. Yeats*

## INTRODUCTION

In this chapter I shall propose and discuss a model that seems to offer a useful approach to the study of the dynamics of a sociocultural system in its environment. The model is computational: That is, its design is based on existing digital computer studies and recognizes the requirement that an implementation on a digital computer should be possible within the foreseeable future. Although no actual program has yet been written, the use of a computational model opens the prospects of a detailed and rigorous examination of the model's behavior.

An important feature of the model is the prominence it gives to the relationship between the behavior of a sociocultural system and the cognition that takes place within it. This stress reflects both certain existing theoretical insights into sociocultural phenomena and the rapid development of computational models of cognition grounded in advances in the design of high-level programing languages. It is a major assumption of the research presented in this chapter that the time has come to begin to put these two domains of inquiry together.

THEORY AND EXPLANATION
IN ARCHAEOLOGY

## STUDIES OF SOCIOCULTURAL SYSTEMS

Fortunately there is no need to survey here the vast literature devoted to sociocultural systems, and indeed I am not competent to do so. However, it is important to point to those recurring hypotheses and insights in the literature that have substantially determined the structure of the model to be proposed.

It is an established notion that a society progesses through successive stages. The most often considered sequence of stages is, of course, that proposed by Service (1962):

$$\text{Band} \rightarrow \text{Tribe} \rightarrow \text{Chiefdom} \rightarrow \text{State}$$

It is not necessary to accept this particular sequence as valid (and it has been much disputed and modified), or even necessary to accept the notion that there are indeed discernable stages of development, to accept that there is progression and a pattern of structural variation. The study by Sanders and Webster (1978), in which they propose multilineal development and seek systematically to relate structural transitions to environmental conditons, encourages the consideration of models of sociocultural development that embody substantial complexity.

The idea that a sociocultural system is indeed a system—and therefore appropriately discussed in terms of subsystems, information flow, hierarchy of control, feedback, and the like—has been widely explored, though rarely with much precision. The study by Flannery (1972) has been influential. He attempted to relate particular mechanisms of change to an essentially stable sociocultural structure. Interestingly, although these mechanisms were not elaborated in any very rigorous way, Flannery did present his work as ultimately aimed at computer simulation. The notion of sociocultural system as some kind of information processor and decision maker is often discussed, though again rarely with much precise detail. Isbell and Schreiber (1978), for example, conceptualize the state as "an integrative mechanism for gathering and processing information and for deliberating decisions" and seek to identify archaeological criteria for the existence of such processes in the context of the indigenous cultures of the central Andes. This is a thought-provoking example of a study relating high-level sociocultural structure to the archaeological record.

Yet while adopting an essentially systemic approach, Rappaport (1971) and Flannery (1972) stress the importance of social belief systems and the important part they play in the stabilization of society. Rappaport uses the term *cognized model* to designate the world representation and beliefs of an individual, and he examines their importance. In particular he explores the function of ritual and of sacred belief. A similar emphasis can be found in Service (1975) but without the systemic flavor. Considering the origins of chiefdoms, he comments that: "One of the most powerful of the new politically integrative ingredients is ideological: The hierarchy of the authority system has become supernaturally sanctioned in mythology . . . supernatural beings support the extant structure". An important discussion of the function of religious belief in primitive society from a Marxist standpoint is provided by Godelier. His remark (1977, 7) that "in religious representations imaginery causes are substituted for real causes" is characteristic of these discussions and closely relevant here.

There are two important computer studies that are useful to keep in mind. Hosler, Sabloff, and Runge (1977) have published a computer simulation study of the Classic Maya collapse using "systems-dynamics" techniques and incorporating ideas from current theories of the collapse. They demonstrate that their model, if suitably parameterized, can be persuaded to reproduce the main lines of the collapse itself. Cooke and Renfrew (1979) have also implemented a model based on systems concepts. Their study is aimed, however, at explanation of the characteristic form of long-term sociocultural change rather than the simulation of any particular system or event. They find this a task of considerable difficulty and hence feel that "lengthy discussions of input (or output) data can usefully be deferred until the range of behavior of the model . . . has been examined and found plausible [Cooke and Renfrew 1979, 347]."

Both these computer studies use a model formulated as a set of mathematical equations. In both cases the behavioral implications of the equation model are obtained by executing a computer program that embodies them. It is important to recognize that while this conforms to the classic and often highly effective approach to mathematical modeling, it does not fully exploit the modeling capabilities of programed digital computers. That these models contribute nothing to the understanding of the mechanisms of belief or meaning in sociocultural systems is predictable from their form.

## TWO KINDS OF SIMULATION MODEL

A distinction should be made between mathematical equation models, whose behavior is specified by writing down a set of mathematical equations of some reasonably conventional variety, and a computational model whose behavior is directly specified within the much more flexible control and data structures of a high-level computer programing language. Of course, it is by no means entirely a disadvantage of conventional mathematical formulations that they are limited in their ability to capture behavior. Restricting the range of possible models makes formal analysis much more tractable. Nevertheless, it is the major advantage of computational models that they can encompass much wider behaviors even if those behaviors can only fully be examined operationally—by running programs on computers.

One important class of computational models is that of event-based queuing models. These are much used in operations research studies and have found some application in archaeological work. However, they presuppose an ability to characterize the situation being studied in terms of a limited number of discrete events. This is not often natural, and it does not seem so for sociocultural systems.

Much more directly relevant are the computational models commonly used to study cognitive processes (for example, visual information processing, natural language understanding, cognitive maps). The very substantial amount of past and present research in this area means that considerable experience of such models and their use has been acquired. Much of this experience has been embedded in specialized computer-programing languages. As understanding of the form and value of computationally based models of cognition develops, the impact upon cognitive psychology (Pylyshyn 1980) and upon philosophy (especially philosophy of mind and theories of explanation) is growing rapidly (Haugeland 1978).

## HYPOTHESES EMBODIED IN THE MODEL

The four following major hypotheses are embodied in the model to be presented. I shall state each, together with a brief comment on its meaning and significance.

HYPOTHESES 1. *The structure of a sociocultural system reflects an inherent goal, which is the optimal exploitation of its environment.*

COMMENT: *This is a commonplace suggestion. Note that the environment should be taken to include both the natural environment and other competing sociocultural systems, and that, in this context, exploitation can be simplified to the acquisition of resources that provide energy.*

HYPOTHESIS 2. *The goal of the sociocultural system derives from the goals of its component actors. The system's structure therefore reflects the need to satisfy the actors' individual goals in spite of their spatial distribution.*

COMMENT: *This implies a degree of reductionism. The behavior of the system as a whole is to be derived from that of its component parts, commonly regarded as at a different theoretical level. The concept of an actor will be elaborated shortly—it corresponds to some category of component of the system that may be conceived as acting (e.g., class, nuclear family, individual person).*

HYPOTHESIS 3. *The structure of the system also reflects and derives from the nature of the cognitive processing of its actors: notably mechanisms of (social) perception, goal achieving, and knowledge manipulation.*

COMMENT: *This takes the reduction a step further. Note that it is the form (and limitations—next hypothesis) of the processual structure attributed to the actors that is at issue, not the content of their cognition.*

HYPOTHESIS 4. *The need for cognitive economy is a major determinant of an actor's cognition.*

COMMENT: *By cognitive economy I mean the necessity for any actor to achieve effective cognition within a limited cognitive capability—limited in speed and effective capacity. Strategies for cognitive economy (for example, adapting the solution to a prior problem rather than solving a new problem from the beginning) typically imply inaccuracy and may lead to major distortion. There is much evidence for the validity of this hypothesis from cognitive science.*

There are, of course, many ways in which these hypotheses might be subjected to test. The strategy adopted here is to embed them in a computational model, and to try to show that the behavior of the model is then sufficiently akin to that of actual sociocultural systems (insofar as we know how to describe their behavior) to give us confidence in their validity.

## COMPUTATIONAL BACKGROUND

There are a number of important computational ideas and mechanisms that underpin the structure of the model.

Fundamental is the notion of a computational process. A process is an ongoing activity—a computational process may be identified with the execution of a conventional program (in FORTRAN, say). A computation does not necessarily involve numbers or arithmetic; those at issue here are much more concerned with abstract symbol manipulation.

We need the concept of a set of processes that run concurrently, which in some suitable way exchange information ("pass messages") and which thus collectively effect some required computation. The specification and powers of such sets of "communicating sequential processes" (Hoare 1978) have become much better understood in recent years, partly due to greatly increased availability and use of distributed computing systems.

Discovering ways in which a system of concurrent communicating processes can engage in heuristic human-like problem-solving is an important current research topic (for example Smith 1979). This work is closely relevant to the study of the capabilities of sociocultural systems, as I shall explain shortly.

Recent years have seen many computational studies of processes designed to generate and to execute plans in particular task domains. Sacerdoti (1979) provides an overview of this work. A typical planner, given a goal to achieve in its domain, uses its knowledge of the domain to generate by successive elaboration (and reelaboration where needed) a detailed plan of action to achieve the goal. Plan execution implies carrying out and monitoring the plan as generated, possibly with replanning if things do not work out as expected.

Important for what follows is the notion of a plan schema—a plan structure that has been abstracted away from the context in which it was created and that is therefore applicable to a range of situations (Fikes, Hart, and Nilsson 1972, Schmidt, Sridharan and Goodson 1978, Schank and Abelson 1977). If a plan schema is available for a particular task then it can merely be matched to the task (instantiated) and no new effort of plan generation is needed.

Distributed processing implies a focus upon communication. When the communication is between processes that are generating and executing plans, then communication is a matter of communication acts, a concept that generalizes the natural-language concept of a speech act (Grosz 1979). Further, it becomes natural to study interaction and cooperation between planners (in this sense), and there is current and promising research in this area (see for example Konolige and Nilsson 1980, Levin and Moore 1977).

I have already stressed the importance of cognitive economy. Although rarely addressed in its own right (but see Lenat, Hayes-Roth, and Klahr 1979), this concept is repeatedly encountered in computational studies of cognition. Consider the reasons of the use of plan schemata. It is a natural extension of the concept of computational efficiency, ubiquitous in computing work.

## THE MODEL

The model now to be described is aimed not at the study of any particular sociocultural system, but at the common properties of all such systems. Naturally, it addresses only a subset of the features of sociocultural systems though this subset is, I believe, a fundamental one.

The model (see Figure 20.1) may conveniently be described in four stages:

1. There is a set of communicating concurrent processes. Of these one corresponds to the ENVIRONMENT of a sociocultural system and the remainder compose a set of ACTORS corresponding to the system itself (note that the term *actor* is being used both for a component of an actual sociocultural system, and also for a particular kind of process in the model). Collectively, this set of actors will be referred to as the multiactor system. Notice that actors neither come into being nor disappear, and that therefore the total number of actors in the system (say of the order of 100) is fixed.

2. The communication structure between actors and the environment reflects the structure of action, perception, and interactor communication. Any actor can act upon (send messages to) and perceive (receive messages from) the environment, but only subject to constraints reflecting spatial location. Any actor can communicate (exchange messages) with only a small subset of others; this restriction also reflects the realities of spatial location.

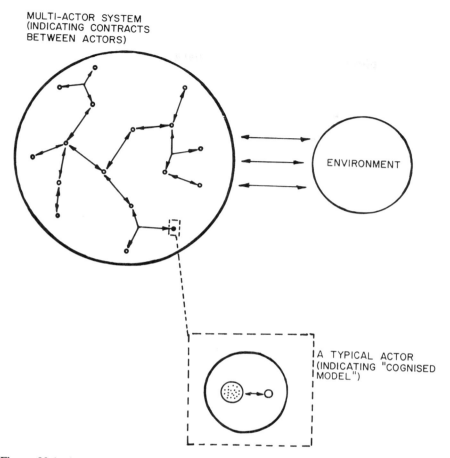

**Figure 20.1.** A sketch illustrating the model of a sociocultural system and its environment presented in the text. A set of concurrent actors, the multiactor system, is structured by a pattern of contracts that effects exploitation of the environment. Each actor has its own simplified and typically distorted representation ("cognized model") of the multiactor system and environment, and this representation determines its individual contract participation.

3. The environment is exploitable. A suitable space–time pattern of actions upon it (that is, messages to it) achieves desirable responses (that is, cause messages to be sent from the environment to one or more actors signifying their acquisition of energy resources). Further, the environment's response is benevolently structured. By this I mean that steadily enlarged resource acquisition from the environment can be achieved by successive small increases in the complexity of the pattern of action upon it (normally involving an increase in complexity of the pattern—compare the notion of a "cognitively friendly world" in Sloman and Owen [1980]).

4. Each actor has the inherent goal of acquiring energy resources and each is structured as three concurrent subprocesses:

(a) *A subprocess that administers a "knowledge base" of process and plan schemata.* A process schema is an abstracted representation of a process observable in the actor's environment. A schema may refer to the typical behavior of a part of the multiactor's environment or to another actor or to a group of actors perceived as a single process. A process schema may also have no actual referent at all in the structure of the model. Process schemata embody the actor's knowledge of the behavior of (its) world. As described earlier, a plan schema is an abstracted representation of a possible piece of behavior by the actor (built of actions and their corresponding subgoals) keyed to the achievement of some goal. A multiactor plan schema is a similar structure but involving interaction with one or more other actors, and therefore involving communication acts. Multiactor plan schemata embody the actor's knowledge of how to cooperate with other actors to particular ends. This knowledge base of schemata corresponds to the actor's "cognized model," in Rappaport's terminology. It is continuously updated (by observing the consequences of action including perceptual acts) but is always liable to be a grossly simplified and distorted representation of the actors actual context (in the model).

(b) *A subprocess that starts from the actor's main goal (energy resource acquisition) and generates alternative plans of action to achieve it.* These will involve subgoals and corresponding subplans, and wherever economical the instantiation of appropriate schemata from the knowledge base. Since the main goal is recurring, the plans are likely to involve recurring patterns of behavior and to be used repeatedly. And, of course, they will commonly involve some form of interaction with other actors. Decision making is inherent. Apart from the decisions involved in plan elaboration, the choice between alternative plans of action involves an assessment of the likely outcome of each. Those promising to be most effective in resource acquisition are adopted for execution.

(c) *A subprocess that monitors the execution of plans, arranging for replanning if difficulties are encountered.* In general, several plans may be executed concurrently involving decisions as to priority.

Observe that these three subprocesses must exchange information and cooperate to give rise to the typical behavior of an actor: goal-achieving behavior based upon past experience of action and its outcome.

To elaborate an actual computer program from this model, even in the simplest of the many detailed forms it might take, would be a major undertaking addressing a number of research issues that we currently only partly understand.

However, the structure of the model has been sufficiently specified here to permit meaningful discussion of its behavior and properties.

## THE BEHAVIOR OF THE MULTIACTOR SYSTEM

It is apparent that the behavior of the model, when set in motion, will be of considerable complexity. The immediate aim, therefore, is to identify recurring patterns of behavior and to assess their implications. A number of important observations follow:

OBSERVATION 1. *Since cooperation between two or more actors will allow more effective exploitation of their (local) environment, and since one actor has the power internally to represent the behavior of another and to plan in terms of it, then cooperation will commonly occur. Notice that I am using the term* cooperation *in a very broad sense to encompass any form of mutually coordinated behavior where the balance between the actors may be anywhere from parity to total domination. The important thing is that each actor sees the cooperation as temporarily beneficial (or the least unpleasant of the available alternatives).*

OBSERVATION 2. *On occasions where cooperation persists (as it surely often will), it will give rise to corresponding multiactor plan schemata in the two (or more) actors concerned. These schemata, although abstracted from some of the incidentals of actual behavior, will normally be specialized to the form of cooperation at issue and its particular context. They will make it likely that this kind of cooperation will be repeated in similar contexts, possibly involving new actors who will, in turn develop relevant schemata. I shall call a recurring piece of behavior, standardized by schemata in the actors participating in it, a* CONTRACT. *Particular actors will become equipped to play particular specialized roles in particular contracts. (Note that it is consistent with this usage to say that an actor has a contract with the environment, meaning that the author has a particular recurring pattern of interaction with the environment based upon a plan schema involving no other actors.)*

OBSERVATION 3. *Cooperation can also develop between two or more already cooperating sets of actors. For example, where two actors respectively control (that is, select goals to be pursued and allocate subgoals to) sets of subordinate actors, then cooperation between these two "leaders" will be, in effect, cooperation between their "followings." However, there is a more fundamental force for aggregation. In many situations an actor will internally represent a cooperating set of actors by a single process schema and use this internalized "compound" actor in instantiations of plan schemata, perhaps treating it as*

*an agent. (Consider: "I'll get the administrative people to do it".) Clearly these*
*mechanisms of aggregation will have a cumulative effect.*

Taken together, these observations imply the following developmental path
for the multiactor system. By a process of cooperation and successive
aggregation, accompanied by the formation of plan schemata in the actors and
consequent stabilization, a PATTERN OF CONTRACTS is established that structures
the multiactor system as an effective exploiter of its environment. That
the contract pattern will be effective (to at least a modest degree) follows from
the way in which it is formed—each instance of cooperation must itself prove
effective or it would not survive. The form taken by a multiactor system with a
developed contract pattern is strongly reminiscent of the distributed problem-
solving systems modeled on a computer by Smith (1979) and others.

This analysis may seem to imply the development of a structure in which
there is one actor who knows and controls all. However this is not so. All actors
will be involved in contracts, and it is the pattern of contracts that is effective.
Effectiveness may be neither intended by the actors nor even represented in
their cognized models. In fact it is entirely consistent with actors' cognitive
mechanisms that a multitude of PSEUDOCONTRACTS will develop. By this
I mean that actors will relate repeatedly to processes that exist only as process
schemata in the actors' cognized models, with no reality—not even the reality of
a set of cooperating actors—in the multiactor system or environment.

## STABILITY AND CHANGE

The developmental path assigned to the model begs an awkward question.
Why does the multiactor system not lock into some suboptimal contract
pattern and stick there? A major consequence of the actors' need for cognitive
economy is that they will strongly tend to instantiate plan schemata already in
their repertoire rather than develop new plan structures. Suboptimal contract
patterns therefore seem likely to be the exception rather than the rule.

And indeed it is clear that actual sociocultural systems do commonly stick for
very long periods with suboptimal contract patterns, perhaps then to change
them relatively rapidly. In fact, the question that must be asked is: How is it that
suboptimal contract patterns are ever superseded? The question is all the more
pressing because, as stressed earlier, actors' cognized models will more often
than not involve major distortions of reality (that is, the reality of the model's
current structure), and these distortions will presumably constitute a major
hinderance to the system's manipulation of its environment.

The following scenario seems a plausible answer to this question:

1.  Changes in the environment (which is, of course, dynamic in its own right)
    render the system's existing contract pattern substantially less effective as
    a solver of resource extraction problems.

2. In consequence, many actors in the system discover that their existing contracts no longer satisfy expectation (resource acquisition) and therefore withdraw from them and seek to negotiate new agreements, which, in the actors' limited view, appear likely to prove more rewarding.
3. There is therefore a period of flux, the ultimate outcome of which will be a new pattern of cooperation. This may or may not be more successful than that that it replaces—if not, it will in turn be replaced, unless the actors have exhausted plausible alternatives.
4. New plan schemata will not be established immediately. Until they are, the system will easily revert to the preexisting contract pattern, particularly if the environment should itself revert.

This scenario identifies environmental change as the initial trigger of structural change. However, any internal mechanism, which has the effect that actors judge alternative behavioral strategies to be more rewarding than existing ones, will provoke a similar crisis. Although such mechanisms are not apparent in this model, it is not difficult to begin to see how it might be extended to incorporate them (involving, for example, changes in population distribution or the cognitive impact of another more highly structured system).

## VALIDATION OF THE MODEL

To validate the model requires a comparison of its behavior with that typical of actual sociocultural systems. Unfortunately, even were the model already in the form of a working program, so that the behavior of its multiactor system could be exhaustively established, there would still be a substantial problem in making the actual comparison. The difficulty is that we simply do not know what is important in the behavior of sociocultural systems. When does a divergence between the model and reality matter, and when does it not? This is much more than merely a matter of devising a statistical test of significance. It depends upon our interpretation of sociocultural phenomena and therefore to some extent on the long-term outcome of this kind of research.

Common sense suggests that, initially at least, we require that a model reproduce the more obvious macrobehavior. In the same spirit it seems reasonable to ask that some of the more prominent features of sociocultural systems should appear in the model and in a way that sheds light on their function in the whole.

I have already suggested that the model presented would display the "stop–go" development so often attributed to sociocultural systems, and that this development would be from the simple and inefficient to the complex and efficient, where efficiency refers to success in exploiting the environment.

However, more can be claimed. Thus the progression from *segmental society* to *state* is a shift away from a social structure based primarily on kinship relationships toward one structured much more "artificially" and with a diversity of specializations. This can be related to the model by identifying kinship relationships with relatively simple plan schemata loaded into actors as part of the initial setting up of the model prior to letting it run. The development of these plan schemata, and their ultimate replacement by others more appropriate to the problem-solving needs of the multiactor system, is then an integral part of the multiactor systems' behavior. Similarly, the development of specific roles (for example that of chief) can be explained as a two-stage process:

1. An actor functions as a leader in crisis circumstances because that is, or seems, effective, and is therefore at least temporarily acceptable to other actors.
2. If (and only if) schemata become established based upon the "crisis" organization, then these will necessarily involve a role "chief"—that is, a typical actor will possess a process schema expressing "chiefly" behavior and plan schemata involving another actor identifiable as a "chief."

The mechanism of redistribution, argued by Service (1975) to be central to the functioning of chiefdoms—but given much less importance by, for example, Peebles and Kus (1977)—is naturally compared with the requirements in the model that all the individual resource needs of the set of actors should be satisfied. In the developmental progression of the model, any stage of development comparable in structure to a chiefdom, involving centralized and relatively efficient decision making, would naturally involve actions directed to the collection and redistribution of resources.

As stressed earlier, the cognitive mechanisms incorporated in the model will be error-prone. They will therefore recognize and work with roles and attributed behavior that do not conform to what is actually there in the multiactor system and its environment—in particular, pseudocontracts will proliferate. That some of these distortions will be both inherently self-consistent and of such a nature as to stabilize the existing contract pattern against crisis change is plausible, and in line with the assessment of the role of sacred belief systems formulated by Rappaport (1971), Service (1975), and others. The model suggests that such "ideological" distortions are habitual and functional side effects of basic cognitive mechanisms rather than, say, the construct of some social component.

It is not clear how far the phenomenon of sociocultural collapse (see for example Renfrew 1979) can be reflected by this model. A crisis of the type sketched in the preceding section includes disintegration of a substantial part of a contract pattern. For this to be manifest as a collapse requires that the replacement pattern be a great deal less structured than that lost. One may speculate that a contract pattern that is effective, but sustained by some distorted belief system rather than knowledge of (the model's) reality, might prove fragile in the face of environmental change.

## CONCLUDING REMARKS

The model that has been proposed is of great potential complexity. Much remains to be done even to complete its specification in consistent detail. Nevertheless, it is reasonable to make a number of claims for it.

First, it is a natural extension of previous work, notably that of Flannery (1972), and goes some way toward integrating a number of different strands of thought including the insights of Rappaport (1971) and Service (1975) into the functional significance of the sacred in sociocultural systems.

This would be of little significance were the model merely descriptive, a throwing together of fragmentary descriptions of various aspects of actual sociocultural systems. What makes the model more than this is that it is computationally based. Its various mechanisms are all to be found working in existing computer programs, if sometimes only in very limited form.

The final claim, therefore, is that models, such as that presented here, are capable of offering a new perspective on sociocultural change, including sociocultural collapse, which is interesting and possibly powerful.

## ACKNOWLEDGMENTS

I am grateful to a number of people who commented helpfully on an earlier version of this chapter. They include Bruce Anderson, Lew Binford, John Evans, Pat Galloway, Colin Renfrew, Tony Rhodes, and Yorick Wilks.

## REFERENCES

Cooke, K. L., and Renfrew, C., 1979, An experiment on the simulation of culture changes, in Renfrew, C., and Cooke, K. L. (eds.), *Transformations: Mathematical Approaches to Culture Change*, New York, Academic Press, 327–348.

Fikes, R. E., Hart, P. E., and Nilsson, N. J., 1972, Learning and executing generalised robot plans, *Artificial Intelligence* 3, 251–288.

Flannery, K. V., 1972, The cultural evolution of civilizations, *Annual Review of Ecology and Systematics* 3, 399–426.

Godelier, M., 1977, Economy and religion: an evolutionary optical illusion, in Friedman, J., and Rowlands, M. J. (eds.), *The Evolution of Social Systems*, London Duckworth, 3–11.

Grosz, B. J., 1979, Utterance and objective: issues in natural language communication, in *Proceedings of the Sixth International Joint Conference on Artificial Intelligence*, Tokyo, 1067–1076.

Haugeland, J., 1978, The nature and plausibility of cognitivism, *Behavioral and Brain Sciences* 1, 215–260.

Hoare, C. A. R., 1978, Communicating sequential processes, *Communications of the Association for Computing Machinery* 21, 667–677.

Hosler, D., Sabloff, J. A., and Runge, D., 1977, Situation model development: a case study of the

Classic Maya collapse, in Hammond, N. (ed.) *Social Processes in Maya Prehistory*, London and New York, Academic Press, 553–590.

Isbell, W. H., and Schreiber, K. J., 1978, Was Huari a state?, *American Antiquity* 43(3), 372–389.

Konolige, K., and Nilsson, N. J., 1980, Multiple-agent planning systems, in *Proceedings of the First Conference of the American Association for Artificial Intelligence*, 138–142.

Lenat, D. B., Hayes-Roth, F., and Klahr, P., 1979, Cognitive economy, in *Proceedings of the Sixth International Joint Conference on Artificial Intelligence*, Tokyo, 531–536.

Levin, J. A., and Moore, J. A., 1977, Dialogue-games: metacommunication structures for natural language interaction, *Cognitive Science* 1, 395–420.

Peebles, C. S., and Kus, S. M., 1977, Some archaeological correlates of ranked societies, *American Antiquity* 42(3), 421–448.

Pylyshyn, Z., 1980, Computation and cognition: issues in the foundation of cognitive science, *Behavioral and Brain Sciences* 3, 111–169.

Rappaport, R. A., 1971, The sacred in human evolution, *Annual Review of Ecology and Systematics* 2, 23–44.

Renfrew, C. A., 1979, Systems collapse as social transformation, in Renfrew C., and Cooke, K. L. (eds.), *Transformations: Mathematical Approaches to Culture Change*, New York, Academic Press, 481–506.

Sacerdoti, E., 1979, Problem solving tactics, in *Proceedings of the Sixth International Joint Conference on Artificial Intelligence*, Tokyo, 1077–1085.

Sanders, W. T., and Webster, D., 1978, Unilinealism, multilinealism, and the evolution of complex societies, in Redman, C. L., and others (eds.), *Social Archaeology: Beyond Subsistence and Dating*, New York, Academic Press, 249–302.

Schank, R. C., and Abelson, R. P., 1977, *Scripts, Plans, Goals, and Understanding*, Lawrence Erlbaum.

Schmidt, C. F., Sridharan, N. S., and Goodson, J. L., 1978, The plan recognition problem, *Artificial Intelligence* 11, 45–83.

Service, E. R., 1962, *Primitive Social Organization: An Evolutionary Perspective*, New York, Random House.

Service, E. R., 1975, *Origins of the State and Civilization*, New York, Norton.

Sloman, A., and Owen, D., 1980, Why visual systems process sketches, *Proceedings of the AISB Conference on Artificial Intelligence*, Amsterdam.

Smith, R. G., 1979, A framework for distributed problem solving, in *Proceedings of the Sixth International Joint Conference on Artificial Intelligence*, Tokyo, 836–841.

# 21

## Organizational Structure and Scalar Stress

*GREGORY A. JOHNSON*

## INTRODUCTION

It is a common observation in anthropology that larger societies tend to be more complex than smaller ones, and both size and complexity are normally considered to be major axes of variability in social evolution. Indeed, various measures of social-system size and organizational complexity are highly correlated. Naroll (1956), for example, reports strong positive relationships between the population size of the largest settlement in a society ($N = 25$) and both degree of craft specialization and a measure of organizational ramification. Carneiro (1967) notes a similar relationship between population size and organizational complexity in a sample of 46 single-community cases, while Ember (1963) reports strong relationships between the number of types of political officials (both formal and informal) in a society ($N = 24$) and both population of the largest community and population of the largest territorial unit on behalf of which government activities are initiated. The relationships reported in these studies are linear in logarithmic transformation.

Figure 21.1 uses Ember's data to illustrate the relationship between types of political officials and population sizes of the largest organizational (territorial) unit. Twenty-three of Ember's 24 cases are used here, giving a correlation between the variables examined of .828. One case (Thai: types of political officials = 100+, largest organizational unit = 20 million) was deleted as an

**389**

THEORY AND EXPLANATION
IN ARCHAEOLOGY

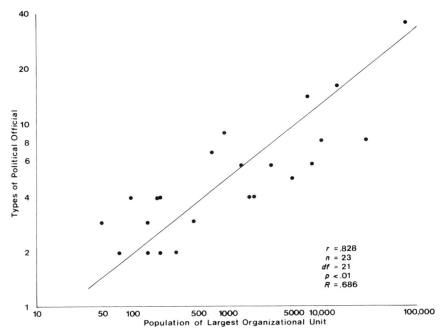

**Figure 21.1.** Societal scale and political complexity.

extreme value outlyer. If it were included in the analysis, the correlation would be increased to .905.

In any case, the relationship between system scale and organization evidenced in these studies is striking. As Carneiro (1967, 239) has put the matter: " . . . if a society does increase significantly in size, and if at the same time it remains unified and integrated, it must elaborate its organization."

A common reaction to this scale–complexity relationship has been to account for increasing complexity of social organization through population growth. Population–resource imbalance (population pressure) is often evoked as the source of stress to which organizational change is a response (Carneiro 1970, M. N. Cohen 1977, Harner 1970, Sanders, Parsons, and Santley 1979, Smith and Young 1972). Although subsistence stress may well have been a critical factor in particular cases, it is unlikely to have been a universal source of stress leading to increasing social complexity (Cowgill 1975, Hassan 1979).

Hassan (1975, 38), for example, makes an important distinction between hunter–gatherer population density and hunter–gatherer group size that is too often ignored. He notes that, in general, there is much less variability in group size than in environmental conditions. This would suggest that the linkage between resource availability and hunter–gatherer organization is looser than has often been assumed.

The difficulty of relating complexity of organization to population size through subsistence stress does not, however, eliminate the problem of accounting for the relationship between population size and organizational complexity that has been demonstrated so often. Perhaps one problem is that the relationship between population size and complexity is itself fairly loose, and it is most evident only when systems that differ considerably in size are compared.

Ember's (1963) data (illustrated in Figure 21.1) are instructive on this point. Examination of this plot of types of political officials on population of largest organizational unit suggests the presence of a differentiated cluster of data points at population size 50–500. Within this range, there is no correlation between population and number of political officials ($r = -.019$). Even in a second possible cluster of points incorporating a much greater population range (700–30,000), the correlation between size and complexity is only .431 ($p > 0.5$). If these two ranges are combined, however, the size–complexity correlation is raised to .781 ($N = 22$, $p < .01$, $R$ or $r^2 = .610$).

Table 21.1 summarizes these data on the effect of expanding the population-size range considered on the size–complexity correlation. This table incorporates data on Thailand originally considered by Ember, but deleted in Figure 21.1. Few would dispute the evolutionary importance of the relationship between social-system population size and social-system complexity, and it is tempting to argue simply that population growth generates complexity. Unfortunately, scale–complexity relationships are apparently more complicated than this.

The problem is that a very strong scale–complexity relationship is observable only when a very large range of system scale is examined. The relationship is weaker, if extant at all, when narrower ranges of variability are considered. This suggests that while there is an underlying process that governs the scale–complexity relationship, this process is subject to significant "local" variation.

I will try to deal with some of this local variation by suggesting that while scale is a critical factor in social change, population is not necessarily the best

**TABLE 21.1**
**Effects of Population Range on Population–Complexity Correlations[a] (Variables in Logarithmic Transformation)**

| Population range | N | r | R |
|---|---|---|---|
| 50–500 | 10 | −.019 | .000 |
| 50–1000 | 12 | .612 | .375 |
| 50–5000 | 17 | .626 | .392 |
| 50–10,000 | 20 | .738 | .545 |
| 50–75,000 | 23 | .828 | .686 |
| 50–20,000,000 | 24 | .905 | .819 |

[a]Data are from Ember 1963.

measure of scale. Many other measures of scale are possible, and I will focus here on what might be called "organizational scale."

The term *organization* has appeared several times in this chapter, and anthropologists are increasingly looking at societies as kinds of organizations (Claessen 1978, Flannery 1972, Johnson 1978, Peebles and Kus 1977, Service 1975, Synenki and Braun 1980, Wright 1977).

Viewing social systems as organizations has the salubrious effect of making a large body of literature outside anthropology relevant to the problems at hand. Varieties of organizations have been studied by sociologists, social psychologists, administrative scientists, and others. I will try to suggest that the insight gained by these studies may be very helpful in the investigation of ethnographic and archaeological cases of organizational change.

## SMALL-GROUP STUDIES

Although organizations of very different sizes have been studied, it might be well to consider very small and simple groups first. Study of such minimal social organizations is the province of "small-group dynamics."

These organizations are composed of a very limited number of people and the groups of interest here are "task-oriented" (Mayhew and Levinger 1976, 1023). A variety of experimental studies have been undertaken in which group size ranges from about 2 to 20 or so, and group tasks involve problem solution (decision making). Two questions about such groups are of interest here. What are the effects of group size (number of individuals) on group performance, and what is the relationship between group size and group organization?

Figure 21.2 illustrates the results of a series of such studies (Cummings, Huber, and Arendt 1974) relative to a plot of group size against the number of possible pairs of individuals within groups of different sizes. The idea here is that potential exchange of information in group decision making should be a function of maximum potential group interaction, and maximum interaction is defined as a situation in which each group member interacts with every other group member on a one-to-one basis. The number of potential pair relationships within a group is thus taken as an index of potential information exchange.

Note that the number of pair relationships, $(n^2 - n)/2$ where $n =$ group size, is nonlinearly related to group size (Dubin 1959). Increase in group size thus generates a disproportionately greater increase in potential information exchange. This power relationship between group size and number of group-member pairs is approximately linear in logarithmic transformation.

The data in Figure 21.2 suggest that there is some kind of organizational threshold (indicated by a dashed line) in groups of approximately six individuals. Note that:

1. The development of within-group leadership (hierarchical organization) appears to be most common in groups of six individuals.

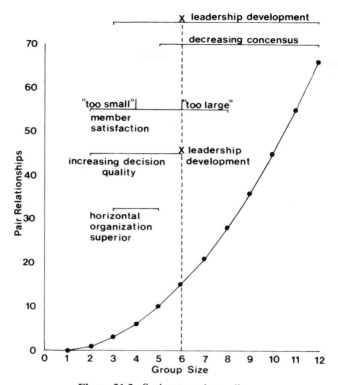

**Figure 21.2.** Scalar stress in small groups.

2. Horizontally organized (nonhierarchical) groups of greater than six members appear to be under some kind of stress as evidenced by decreasing concensus in decision making and decreasing member satisfaction with group performance.

3. In groups of less than six members, not only does decision quality increase with group size, but horizontally organized groups may exhibit superior performance in comparison to hierarchically organized ones. (See also Bridges, Doyle and Mahan 1968).

Increased interaction apparently facilitates problem solution, at least up to a point. Hierarchical organization at group sizes 5 and less would effectively decrease potential interaction.

If hierarchy development is related to some kind of scalar stress, why should it occur at around group size 6? Unfortunately this question is much more easily asked than answered.

One direction of inquiry involves examination of the capacity of an individual to monitor and process information. People do have a finite capacity for this activity, and experimental studies of both individuals and small groups reveal a general pattern of performance in which performance increases with demand to a level constrained by capacity, and then declines as capacity is exceeded and decision errors increase. The resulting performance curve has an "inverted-U" shape (Meier 1972). Miller (1956, 86) suggests that people have a span of absolute judgment of unidimensional stimuli that is limited by the amount of information (in bits) that must be processed, and a span of immediate memory limited by the number of items (information chunks) that can be simultaneously retained. Both spans are fairly narrow, and average about 7.

It is possible then, that the "scalar" stress evident in the small-group studies discussed earlier may be identifiable as "communications" stress occasioned by information-processing workloads exceeding individual capacities. Certainly, communications stress has been shown to produce various physiological changes, anxiety, and performance reduction in individuals (Meier 1972, 298) that would be consistent with the decreasing concensus and member satisfaction observed in small groups of greater than 6 members.

Figure 21.3 illustrates possible relationships among group size, communications load, and decision performance that might be expected if individual information-processing capacity is a limiting factor on nonhierarchical task-group size. Again, the number of pair relationships within groups of different sizes is used as an index of communications load. An approximate information-processing capacity (indicated by a dashed line) is set as equal to the communications load generated in a group of 6 members [load $= (6^2 - 6)/2 = 15$]. Below capacity, decision performance is here calculated as communications load as a proportion of capacity (e.g., when group size $= 4$, communications load $= 6$, and performance $=$ load/capacity $= 6/15 = .40$). At and above capacity, performance is calculated as capacity as a proportion of communications load (e.g., when group size $= 10$, load $= 45$, and performance $=$ capacity/load $= 15/45 = .33$). The resulting performance curve, if "rounded out" to some extent, approximates the "inverted-U" performance curves obtained from experimental studies on individuals and small groups.

Performance can be expected to increase with information-processing demand until approximate capacity is reached. It does not completely collapse after capacity has been exceeded, but degrades. The point at which some kind of organizational change is to be expected in response to stress is thus dependent not only on group size, but on "acceptable" performance levels. Acceptable decision quality can be expected to vary from one task situation to the next, and thus maximal possible group size may be expected to vary accordingly. Operation of this source of variability would give the performance curve illustrated in Figure 21.3 more of an inverted-U shape.

There appear, then, to be rather severe limits on the maximum size of task-oriented groups that are organized horizontally (nonhierarchically), and these limits may be related to individual information-processing capacity. A wide variety of studies suggests that an effective limit on group size is somewhere around six group members. This apparent constraint on operational task-group

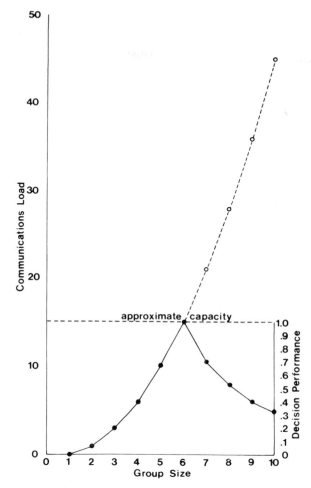

**Figure 21.3.** Scalar-Communications stress and decision performance.

size poses a theoretical problem when more traditional anthropological data are considered.

Human groups with little or no evidence of internal hierarchy are very common in the ethnographic and archaeological record. Not only are they common, but group sizes among egalitarian hunters and gatherers, for example, obviously far exceed the figure of six group members discussed here. A portion of this variability may be due to the fact that such groups are not in continual "face-to-face" interaction that is characteristic of the small-group studies discussed earlier. Group decision making in such societies is, however, based on consensus (Reynolds and Zeigler 1979), and achieving consensus requires such face-to-face interaction. Given the evidence discussed here on small-group dynamics, such egalitarian societies must have some mechanism to overcome the scalar-communications stress problem that does not involve what we would normally recognize as hierarchical organization.

## SEQUENTIAL HIERARCHIES: AN EGALITARIAN ALTERNATIVE

I attempted to show in a previous publication (Johnson 1978) how increase in the number of information sources contained within an integrated system increases the probability of either system collapse or the development of hierarchical organization. These "information sources" were defined on a very general level as minimal relevant organizational units that might be territorial, population, residence, activity units, etc.

The structures developed in that model might be termed "simultaneous" hierarchies. These are hierarchies of the familiar sort in which system integration is achieved through the exercise of control and regulatory functions by a relatively small proportion of the population. Such functions may be exercised simultaneously at a number of hierarchically structured levels of control. As such, the entire control hierarchy "exists" at any given time.

System disruption or simultaneous hierarchy development may not, however, be the only alternatives available to deal with scalar-communications stress. If a problem is being generated by the presence of too many units in the system, it might be possible to make the operational size of these units (kinship groups, residence units, etc.) larger, and thus the number of units in the system smaller. Perhaps some illustrative ethnographic material would be useful here.

### Ethnographic Cases

Two kinds of data are required for looking at egalitarian groups in terms of scaler stress:

1. Data on group organization involving kinds of social groups present and their sizes are required.
2. If an increase in operational unit size is to be analyzed in relation to scalar stress, data on scalar stress at different group sizes are also required. (The latter are, unfortunately, very difficult to find.)

The !Kung San, or žu/õasi as they call themselves, (Wilmsen 1980) of southern Africa are at least one group for whom both organization and stress data are available. Several different potential organizational units can be defined for the !Kung (Yellen 1977). All of these units can be observed "on the ground" in !Kung camps.

Large dry-season camps exhibit extended families made up of nuclear

**TABLE 21.2**
**!Kung Groups and Organizational Units**

| Group | Organizational units | Units per group Range | Mean |
|-------|---------------------|-------|------|
| Dobe: Dry-season camps, $N = 2$ | Extended families | 3–4 | 3.50 |
| (Yellen 1977, 70–71) | Nuclear families | 9–12 | 10.50 |
| | Social units | 12–15 | 13.50 |
| | Adults | 22–28 | 25.00 |
| | Population | 35–45 | 40.00 |
| Extended families, $N = 7$ | Nuclear families | 1–5 | 3.00 |
| (Yellen 1977, 70–71) | Social units | 1–7 | 3.86 |
| | Adults | 2–12 | 7.14 |
| | Population | 2–22 | 11.43 |
| Rainy-season camps,[a] $N = 24$ | Nuclear families | 2–6 | 3.08 |
| (Yellen 1977, 147–236) | Social units | 2–8 | 3.08 |
| | Adults | 3–15 | 7.13 |
| | Population | 7–24 | 14.83 |
| Nuclear families, $N = 21$ | Adults | 2–3 | 2.10 |
| (Yellen 1977, 70–71) | Population | 3–6 | 3.43 |
| Social units, $N = 27$ | Adults | 1–3 | 1.86 |
| (Yellen 1977, 70–71) | Population | 1–6 | 2.96 |

[a]Some camps had more than one occupation. These figures are based on individual occupations.

families, or social units, that in turn consist of individuals. (A "social unit" can be either a nuclear family or an individual occupying a separate hut.) Small rainy-season camps are made up of nuclear families, or social units, and their constituent individuals. Table 21.2 presents data on the sizes of these various organizational units derived from Yellen (1977).

Note that data reported from the large dry-season camp at Dobe represent upper-limit figures as, "Any !Kung with a hut at the camp was included, whether he was present most of the time or not. [Yellen 1977, 69]." Camp size

**TABLE 21.3**
**!Kung Group Organization (Basal Units)**

| Group | Basal unit | Units per group Range | Mean | Mean group population |
|-------|-----------|-------|------|----------------------|
| Dry-season camp | Extended family | 3–4 | 3.50 | 40.00 |
| Rainy-season camp | Nuclear family | 2–6 | 3.08 | 14.83 |
| Extended family | Nuclear family | 1–5 | 3.00 | 11.43 |
| Nuclear family | Adult | 2–3 | 2.10 | 3.43 |
| Social unit | Adult | 1–3 | 1.86 | 2.96 |

can vary considerably over time. Lee (1969, 66), for example, provides data on the number of people present at Dobe over a 28-day period from July 6 to August 4, 1964. While the average camp size was 30.9 people, the range over the 28 days was 22–40 (SD = 5.4).

Table 21.3 presents possible !Kung organization in simplified form. Social groups are viewed here as being composed of "basal units." As children contribute little to food supplies (Lee 1979, 67), adults are considered to be the basal units of nuclear families and social units. Nuclear families are the basal units of both rainy-season camps and extended families, while extended families are the basal units of large dry-season camps.

Note that although the mean population of social groups increases from the social unit to the dry-season camp (2.96–40.00), the mean number of basal units per larger social group is fairly constant at around 3 (mean = 2.71, range = 1.86–3.50). Note also that the range (1–6) of basal units that constitute a larger social group is very restricted and does not exceed 6.

I suggest that these data are consistent with those discussed earlier on small-group dynamics. Larger numbers of people can be accommodated with a horizontally organized social group by expanding the size of the basal units of which the group is composed. In the case of the !Kung, extended families appear in large dry-season camps where their constituent nuclear families occupy huts adjacent to one another.

The proposition that expanded basal unit size is a mechanism allowing larger !Kung aggregations can be partially evaluated with available data on serious disputes in !Kung camps. These disputes appear to reflect problems in the organization of the economic system, in that they most commonly involve "Accusations of improper meat distribution, improper gift exchange (hxaro), laziness, and stinginess... [Lee 1979, 372]." I suggest that these disputes minimally represent failures to reach consensus, which in a consensus-based decision-making system reflect degraded decision performance.

Quality of decision performance should be inversely related to scalar-communications stress (among other things), and !Kung dispute frequency is apparently scale dependent. Lee (1979, 366) reports that while at camps like Dobe and Mahopa (population 40–60) serious disputes occur at a rate of only three or four a year, dispute frequency is about one every two weeks at a much larger camp like /Xai/xai (population 100–150).

Consider the following propositions:

1. If dispute frequency among the !Kung is the product of scalar stress, then some measure of group size should predict dispute frequency.
2. If extended families are operationally the basal units of organization in large camps, then number of extended families should predict dispute frequency more accurately than other possible group-size measures such as gross population, etc. Data allowing evaluation of these propositions is presented in Table 21.4.

**TABLE 21.4**
**Estimating Scalar Stress in !Kung Camps**

| Camp: /Xai/xai | Population = 100 | | Population = 150 | |
|---|---|---|---|---|
| | Unit frequency | Scalar stress | Unit frequency | Scalar stress |
| Basal units | | | | |
| Extended families | 8.7 | 33.5 | 13.1 | 79.2 |
| Nuclear families | 29.2 | 411.7 | 43.7 | 933.0 |
| Social units | 33.8 | 554.3 | 50.7 | 1259.9 |
| Adults (.63) | 63.0 | 1953.0 | 94.5 | 4417.9 |
| Adults (.71) | 71.0 | 2485.0 | 106.5 | 5617.9 |
| Population | 100.0 | 4950.0 | 150.0 | 11,175.0 |

| Camps: Dobe and Mahopa | Population = 40 | | Population = 60 | |
|---|---|---|---|---|
| | Unit frequency | Scalar stress | Unit frequency | Scalar stress |
| Basal units | | | | |
| Extended families | 3.5 | 4.4 | 5.2 | 10.9 |
| Nuclear families | 11.7 | 62.6 | 17.4 | 142.7 |
| Social units | 13.5 | 84.4 | 20.3 | 195.9 |
| Adults (.63) | 25.2 | 304.9 | 37.8 | 695.5 |
| Adults (.71) | 28.4 | 389.1 | 42.6 | 886.1 |
| Population | 40.0 | 780.0 | 60.0 | 1770.0 |

The goal here is not to predict absolute dispute frequency, but relative frequency by camp size. Six possible measures of camp size are used: number of extended families, nuclear families, social units, adults (two estimates), and population. Two estimates of the number of adults are used, because while Lee (1979, 46) notes that children constitute some 29% of the population in the Dobe area (adults = 71%), Yellen's data indicate a figure closer to 37% (adults = 63%).

Smaller and larger estimates of scalar stress are made because Lee gives his camp-size data relative to disputes in ranges (Dobe and Mahopa 40–60 people, /Xai/xai 100–150 people). The number of different possible organizational units (extended families, nuclear families, etc.) likely to be present in camps of these sizes was calculated from the mean units-per-group data in Table 21.3. Given, for example, a camp-population size of 100 and an average extended family size of 11.43, that camp is estimated to contain 8.7 extended families. Similarly, one would expect 13.1 extended families in a camp of 150 people.

These smaller and larger frequency estimates were then converted into scalar-stress indices using the formula $(n^2 - n)/2$ where $n =$ the basal-unit frequency estimate. For example, an estimate of 8.7 extended families in a camp of 100 people would be associated with a scalar-stress index of 33.5. The formula used here is the same as that for number of "pair relationships" or "communications stress" used previously in Figures 21.2 and 21.3.

Finally, these calculations were made separately for the population ranges reported at Dobe and Mahopa, and /Xai/xai. The result is a series of scalar-stress indices based on different basal-unit scale measures for the two relevant population ranges.

Table 21.5 uses these indices and the dispute data to evaluate the propositions stated earlier. When standardized to yearly estimates, Lee's dispute data can be expressed as a ratio range of 1 dispute per year of occupation at a smaller camp (Dobe or Mahopa) to 6.50–8.67 disputes per year at a larger camp (/Xai/xai). An average figure would be 1 dispute at a smaller camp to 7.59 disputes at a larger one.

The scalar-stress indices over six scale measures for the smaller and larger camp population ranges cited by Lee were then used to calculate expected dispute ratios between smaller and larger camp sizes. Calculation of expected dispute ratios can be illustrated with the following example.

Note from Table 21.4 that the smaller population size of a larger camp (/Xai/xai) is 100. A camp of 100 individuals is expected to contain (on the average) 8.7 extended families. The scalar-stress index associated with 8.7 extended families is 33.5. Similarly, the smaller population size of a smaller camp (Dobe or Mahopa) is 40. A camp of 40 is expected to contain approximately 3.5 extended families, and the scalar-stress index associated with this figure is 4.4. The expected dispute ratio between the smaller and larger

TABLE 21.5
**!Kung Camps: Observed and Expected Ratios of Serious Disputes**

|  | Smaller estimate[a] | Larger estimate[b] | Average estimate |
|---|---|---|---|
| Observed disputes | 1:8.67 | 1:6.50 | 1:7.59 |
|  | Smaller estimate[c] | Larger estimate[d] | Average estimate |
| Expected disputes |  |  |  |
| Basal units |  |  |  |
| Extended families | 1:7.61 | 1:7.27 | 1:7.44 |
| Nuclear families | 1:6.58 | 1:6.54 | 1:6.56 |
| Social units | 1:6.57 | 1:6.43 | 1:6.50 |
| Adults (.61) | 1:6.41 | 1:6.35 | 1:6.38 |
| Adults (.71) | 1:6.39 | 1:6.34 | 1:6.37 |
| Population | 1:6.35 | 1:6.31 | 1:6.33 |

NOTES:
[a]Assumes three disputes per year at Dobe or Mahopa.
[b]Assumes four disputes per year at Dobe or Mahopa.
[c]Based on lower end of camp size ranges.
[d]Based on upper end of camp size ranges.

camp sizes is taken as the ratio of their associated scalar-stress indices— 4.4:33.5 or 1:7.61.

This process is then repeated for the larger population-size figures of both the smaller and larger camps. For a larger camp, population = 150, expected extended families = 13.1, and associated scalar stress = 79.2. For a smaller camp, population = 60, expected extended families = 5.2, and associated scalar stress = 10.9. The expected dispute ratio is then 10.9:79.2 or 1:7.27.

Now we have two expected dispute ratios based on the number of extended families as a scale measure. The first ratio (1:7.61) was calculated from the smaller population figures of 100 and 40. The second ratio (1:7.27) was calculated from the larger population figures of 150 and 60. The final expected dispute ratio is taken as the average of the smaller and larger estimates. In this case, it is the average of 1:7.61 and 1:7.27, and thus = 1:7.44. These ratios appear in Table 21.5 along with those based on the remaining five possible scale measures.

Note again that the average expected dispute ratio based on extended families is 1:7.44, reasonably close to the average observed figure of 1:7.59. Note also that the other possible scale measures are consistently poorer estimators of disputes, and that the poorest of these is group population. (The error associated with the extended-family-based estimate is 2%, while that associated with the estimate based on gross population is 17%.)

The primary results of this analysis are that first, the number of extended families is the best (and quite accurate) predictor of relative dispute frequency. Second, an exponential function of this scale measure is required for accurate prediction. (Recall that it was scalar-stress indices that were used to calculate expected dispute ratios. Untransformed frequency estimates yield quite different results. The predicted average dispute ratio based on simple extended-family frequency would be 1:2.50, the same figure as that based on untransformed population size. The error associated with these estimates would be 67%.)

I would draw three conclusions from these results. First, dispute frequency is a function of scalar–communications stress. Second, this stress is an exponential function of organizational scale. Third, organizational scale is best measured in terms of number of basal organizational units, which may or may not be equivalent to the number of individuals. These conclusions have implications for the organization of smaller !Kung aggregates.

If the dispute frequency at /Xai/xai, where the extended family is apparently the basal organizational unit, is taken as indicative of "high stress," at what point would similar stress levels be reached under other organizational modes (such as the adult or the nuclear family) as the basal organizational unit? This question is investigated in Figure 21.4, where three scalar-stress curves are given, based on number of adults, nuclear families, and extended families.

These curves were constructed using the mean nuclear- and extended-family sizes from Table 21.3, and considering adults to constitute 71% of the

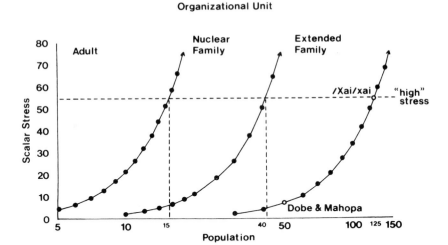

**Figure 21.4.** Scalar stress and !Kung organization.

population (Lee 1979, 46). The number of adults, nuclear and extended families expected in populations of different sizes were transformed into scalar-stress indices following the procedure discussed earlier, and then plotted against population size. The positions of /Xai/xai and Dobe and Mahopa on the extended-family scalar-stress curve are indicated by open circles.

Note that the "high-stress" line at /Xai/xai (average size 125 people, extended families = 10.9, scalar stress = 54.) intersects the nuclear-family scalar-stress curve at just over population size 40. This would suggest that an organizational transition from nuclear to extended families could be expected at about this population size. Yellen's data (Table 21.2) shows extended families at camp population size 35–45.

The same "high-stress" line intersects that adult stress curve in Figure 21.4 at just over 15 people, suggesting that nuclear families should be the basic organizational unit for groups of approximately this size. Recall that nuclear families are the basal units of rainy-season camps and that these camps have an average size of 14.83 people.

Groups of adults in rainy-season camps would appear to be under similar constraints as groups of nuclear families in dry-season camps. In the former case, groups of adults are combined into nuclear families. In the latter case, groups of nuclear families are combined into extended families.

The available data, even if limited, suggest that !Kung organization incorporates an operational hierarchy. This is apparently not the kind of simultaneous hierarchy with which we are so familiar, but something that might be called "sequential" hierarchy.

Introduction of new terms such as this normally should be avoided, but it seems necessary in this case. The problem is one of describing the hierarchical organization of a nonhierarchically organized group. Evidently something in our anthropological concept of hierarchy is lacking.

I mentioned before that normal (what I have called "simultaneous") hierarchies imply the exercise of integrative and control functions by a minority over the majority of a population. It does not seem useful to describe the consensus-based !Kung in these terms. I find it difficult, however, to characterize sequential hierarchy. While the "hierarchic" organization of the !Kung seems reasonably clear in light of the material presented previously, I do not know how it works.

One possibility may involve sequential decision making. If consensus were achieved first within nuclear families, then within extended families, a group decision would only require concensus among extended families. Discussion at the extended-family level, however, might often require a new concensus to be reached at lower levels, and the whole process is likely to be often lengthy. Sequential achievement of concensus should imply sequential suppression of disputes, and one might expect dispute frequency to be directly related to kinship distance (Sahlins 1972, 196).

Such sequential decision making might be observed in the field simply in terms of individual interaction rates that are inversely related to kinship distance. In this case, operational-unit boundaries would also function as information filters reducing what would otherwise be a very high-stress communications load on individuals.

If the specific mechanism(s) of sequential hierarchy is unclear, so are the limits of its ability to integrate increasingly larger social groups. While groups of 125 !Kung are under high scalar stress given !Kung organization, group size in egalitarian societies may be considerably higher. What if, for example, larger social aggregates such as clans were basic operational units?

Table 21.6 presents data on clan organization in highland New Guinea derived from Brown and Podolefsky (1976). While New Guinea groups are egalitarian in social organization, they do incorporate so-called "big-men" who exercise hierarchically differentiated integrative and control functions. Leadership in big-man societies is, however, typically a temporary affair (Sahlins 1963) and does not represent a well-established simultaneous hierarchy.

Note in Table 21.6 that while size of the local exogamous clan and size of the largest political unit of which they are a part show a great deal of variation, the mean number of such clans per political unit has very little variability. The range in these data is from 1.24 to 7.50 exogamous clans per largest political unit, with a mean of 4.22. Operational clan groups in New Guinea would thus seem to be under very similar scalar constraints as !Kung extended-family aggregations. These scalar constraints are not in terms of population, but in terms of number of operational units per larger aggregation.

Given the presence of emergent simultaneous hierarchy in New Guinea

TABLE 21.6
Clan Organization in Highland New Guinea[a]

| Group | Mean population of local exogamous clan | Mean population of largest political unit | Mean number of clans per unit |
|---|---|---|---|
| Gahuku Gama | 100 | 750 | 7.50 |
| Mae Enga | 350 | 2290 | 6.54 |
| Maring | 40 | 200 | 5.00 |
| South Fore | 39 | 180 | 4.62 |
| Siane | 200 | 840 | 4.20 |
| Kyaka Enga | 200 | 800 | 4.00 |
| Bena Bena | 188 | 750 | 3.99 |
| Raiapu Enga | 270 | 1072 | 3.97 |
| Chimbu | 650 | 2400 | 3.69 |
| Kapauku | 200 | 600 | 3.00 |
| Mt. Hagan | 280 | 820 | 2.93 |
| Kakoli | 383 | 474 | 1.24 |
| N = 12 | | | |
| X̄ | 242 | 875 | 4.22 |
| S.D. | 168 | 751 | 1.63 |
| Range | 39–650 | 180–2400 | 1.24–7.50 |

[a]Data from Brown and Podolefsky (1976, 218).

represented by big-men, these data may represent the upper range of sequential hierarchy for sedentary groups. Certainly these New Guinea groups are under considerable stress, for, as Brown (1978) notes, the area is characterized by high levels of warfare, and larger tribal or alliance groups are highly unstable.

Increase in sequential hierarchy implies increasing difficulty in the decision process as consensus must be reached at a greater number of operational levels. The complexity of the decision process is related, however, to additional factors beyond organizational scale. One might expect, for example, that decision complexity in the realm of subsistence organization is inversely related to resource predictability. If this is the case, one might further expect that the integrative potential of sequential hierarchy is directly related to resource predictability (other things being equal). Other things are very seldom equal, however, and determinations of the local constraints on potential sequential hierarchy is likely to be a very complex affair.

These problems aside, elaboration of essentially horizontal social organization in sequential hierarchies decreases the complexity of regulating social relationships—a nice example of Ashby's (1968, 135) "law of requisite variety." Given that groups of 6 and more individuals are under increasing scalar stress, and if approximately 25 and 500 represent minimum equilibrium group sizes for hunters and gatherers under specifiable demographic conditions (Wobst 1974), it would appear that sequential hierarchies should be a basic feature of egalitarian societies.

## Ritual and Sequential Hierarchies

Elaboration of sequential hierarchy is unlikely to be the only social mechanism allowing large aggregations among egalitarian groups. Ceremony, ritual, or what might be called "generalized feather-waving" is probably another. Scale-dependent ceremonial activity is commonly reported for egalitarian groups (Lee 1979, Gross 1979, Bohannan 1967).

Gross (1979) presents a particularly interesting case from Brazil. Many central Brazilian groups are something of an anthropological problem in that, while politically egalitarian, they exhibit very large aggregations and very complex social and ritual organizations. These groups are fragmented into small, nomadic foraging units for most of the year, but aggregate into villages of up to 1400 people for the horticultural rainy season. The extended family is the smallest nondivisible economic unit, and social organization involves varied mixes of age sets, formal friendships, nondescent "moieties", men's societies, etc. Sequential hierarchy would appear to be the order of the day during these annual agglomerations.

Ceremonial activity is particularly intense in these rainy-season villages. "Several authors report that no sooner has one ceremonial been staged than preparations for another begin, although there apparently is no fixed annual cycle of ceremonials for most groups [Gross 1979, 328]." Both ceremony and elaboration of social organization are scale dependent, in that " . . . little of the social elaborateness reported for village aggregates is present in the small foraging units, and ceremonialism appears to atrophy in villages which become seriously depopulated [Gross 1979, 330]." Gross (1979, 334) argues that both social and ceremonial organization serve integrative functions that allow maintenance of large-group size for the horticultural period of the annual subsistence cycle.

There are a variety of ways in which ceremony might reduce scalar stress. Ceremonial activity typically involves a great deal of stylistic variability in dress, ritual paraphernalia, etc., and the importance of style as an information-transfer device has been emphasized by Wobst (1977) and Conkey (1978). Passive stylistic signaling of individual subgroup affiliation, etc., may reduce the active communications load associated with larger aggregations. Participation in ceremony that prescribes patterns of behavior and interaction may reduce required integrative decision making, and ceremony may provide a social context for organizations that have nonceremonial integrative functions (see Plog 1978, 360, on the latter possibility.) Indeed, general arguments for ritual regulation of important aspects of subsistence and social systems are well known (Rappaport 1968, 1971).

"Feather-waving" may operate in such a manner as to simply reduce the operational size of the social group and thus reduce scalar stress as well. Lee (1979) notes, for example, that traditional !Kung aggregations were a time for curing (and other) ceremonies. The more people participating in such ceremonies, the more efficacious they were thought to be. One result of such ceremonies was to put the burden of food acquisition on a smaller group of people than would otherwise be the case. Operational group size for coordination of the subsistence system was thus reduced.

This is not the place to get deeply involved in the complex topic of ritual and ritual functions. I think that it is important to note, however, that ritual is often scale dependent, and I suspect that it may often serve to reduce the kind of scalar–communications stress discussed in this chapter. It may be tempting to interpret archaeological evidence of increasing ritual behavior as evidence of particularly "successful" system operation. Upper Paleolithic art in Europe or the Neolithic "shrines" of Catal Hüyük in Turkey (Mellaart 1967) generally have been viewed in this manner. Intensification of ritual, however, may signal a system in trouble rather than one doing particularly well. Conversely, absence of elaborate ritual need not be taken as evidence of a benighted population so occupied with a struggle for subsistence that they have no time for more "intellectual" affairs. (Consider the earlier European Mesolithic, for example.)

Although ritual often appears to be scale dependent, scalar thresholds vary. Other things being equal, I would expect scalar stress to be reflected in ceremonial elaboration at smaller population sizes among groups with smaller basal-unit sizes than for those with larger basal-unit sizes. This, simply, is because a system with a larger basal-unit size can incorporate more people than a system with a smaller basal-unit size at an equivalent scalar-stress level. This appears to be the case in comparing the !Kung with the central Brazilian groups discussed by Gross, and similar patterning should be evidenced archaeologically.

European Bandkeramik settlements, for example, contain little if any artifactual evidence for ceremonial activity. Bylany in Czechoslovakia is one of the better known such settlements, and Soudský and Pavlů (1972, 322) present data on seven occupational phases at the site, suggesting the presence of an average of 16.7 nuclear families grouped into 7.3 extended families per phase (range = 6–9). Many southeastern European neolithic villages are estimated to have had similar population sizes, but nuclear-family residence units. These settlements are also famous for their figurines and other "elaborate" artifacts suggesting intensive ceremonial activity (Milisauskas 1979, Tringham 1971).

## Accounting for Organizational Units and Organizational Growth

Egalitarian-group size appears to be constrained by the degree to which sequential hierarchy, and possibly ritual, can mitigate scalar stress. (There are, of course, other constraints on size.) There is, however, considerable variability in degree of sequential hierarchy among egalitarian groups and associated variability in group size. Predicting stress points at which either fission or simultaneous hierarchy development is likely to occur requires knowledge of underlying group organization. Simple knowledge of group-population size is unlikely to be very useful in predicting stress points, because of the organizational reasons discussed earlier.

Accounting for egalitarian group population size will thus, in part, require accounting for group organization. It seems very unlikely to me that organization is simply a response to scalar stress. We need to know more about the nonscalar determinants of organizational unit size. Pasternak, Ember, and Ember (1976) have suggested, for example, that the presence of extended-family households may be related to activity-scheduling difficulties encountered at a smaller residence unit size. Netting (1974, 29–30) reviews similar studies suggesting that residence unit size is related to labor requirements and form of land tenure. Thus while some aspects of social organization, ritual, etc., may be identified as direct responses to scalar stress, others may have developed through different processes but have implications for response to stress.

An equally important problem involves accounting for the system growth that generates scalar stress. It is important, perhaps even vital, to recognize that there is a substantial difference between organizational growth and population growth. Population on the Susiana Plain of southwestern Iran increased an estimated 33% during the immediate period of state formation in the area. Administered population, on the other hand, increased an estimated 118% during the same period (Johnson in press).

When hunters and gatherers aggregate into large camps, organizational growth has occurred while population growth has not. I suspect that many cases of colonial intervention in indigenous societies have generated simultaneous population decrease and organizational growth though forced sedentarization or aggregation.

Expansion of organizational and/or population size probably often is related to demand for labor (White 1973). As R. Cohen (1978, 42) notes, "Sedentarization is associated with an increased demand for persons among kin groups, settlements and domestic units." In is phrase, "person acquisition" becomes increasingly important (see also Bargatzky 1981). Whether or not organizational growth involves population growth, sequential hierarchy has a limited ability to deal with scalar stress, and either group fission or development of simultaneous hierarchy is expected.

## SIMULTANEOUS HIERARCHIES: THE NONEGALITARIAN IMPERATIVE

Although the integrative functions of simultaneous hierarchy are clear, the mechanisms of hierarchy development are not. Mayhew and Levinger (1976) have formulated a model for the development of a differentiated power structure (differential control by individuals) in small, face-to-face groups. The model is based on individual information-processing constraints, and suggests that even in the context of random interaction, the probability of differential domination of interaction increases as a function of group size. Most probable constraint values suggest development of differential control at around group size 7 (Mayhew and Levinger 1976, 1030).

I view their approach as complementary to the persepective presented here. I would suggest that either sequential or simultaneous hierarchy development (or system collapse) are responses to scalar communications stress and degrading decision performance with increasing organizational scale. Mayhew and Levinger would see what I have termed simultaneous hierarchy development as a probabilistic function of increasing group size. Both processes are scale dependent and could operate simultaneously.

Within the limits imposed by the regulatory potential of essentially egalitarian sequential hierarchies, simultaneous hierarchy or group fission is clearly the price of increasing organizational scale. Given the variability in sequencial hierarchies in the ethnographic record, and the very small organizational scale at which either communications stress or the Mayhew–Levinger model operates, we should have evidence of simultaneous hierarchy development at relatively small group sizes—this aside from the evidence on small-group dynamics discussed earlier.

It is now commonplace to suggest that many groups of egalitarian hunters and gatherers were not so egalitarian after all. Differentiated leadership and ascribed-status hierarchies have now been suggested for any number of cases such as the Natufian (G. A. Wright 1978), prehistoric Great Basin (Bettinger 1978), prehistoric central California (King 1978), and perhaps groups of the later northern European Mesolithic (Price 1980).

While these and other cases of simultaneous hierarchy development are being increasingly recognized, it is also apparent that group fission has been a much more common response to scalar stress. R. Cohen (1978, 53) notes that fissioning is characteristic not only of egalitarian groups, but of prestate polities in general. Suppression of fissioning is most often accounted for by some kind of social or environmental circumscription following Carneiro's (1970, 1978) position on the matter. Groups do not fission because the fission products have no place to go.

Scalar increase, however, may have advantages as well as disadvantages. Yellen (1977, 69) notes a positive correlation between !Kung camp size and duration of occupation. He attributes this to advantages of scale. Larger groups can commit more personnel to activities having a low probability of return but potentially high yield, such as hunting. Greater group size in the context of dispersed activities generates increased acquisition of information on resource availability.

There are informational economies of scale, but these are difficult for nonhierarchically organized groups to exploit. Indeed, limitations on nonhierarchal information processing have been suggested recently as effective contraints on the number of hunter–gatherer groups that can exploit a given area (Moore in press), or the size of a region maximally exploitable by a given group (Reynolds and Zeigler 1979). Informational as well as economic advantages of scale (Johnson 1977, 489) suggest that simultaneous hierarchies may well develop as a response to scalar stress, in the absence of fission-inhibiting group circumscription.

## Simultaneous Hierarchy and Social-Status Differentiation

I have suggested elsewhere (Johnson 1978) that status ascription and social ranking may be associated with the development of group control-hierarchies. Two operational problems of hierarchical control were identified: decision implementation and decision making. Given the observation that social-status differences are often used to structure or supplement differential influence in hierarchical organizations (Sutherland 1975, 290, Udy 1970, 48), I suggested that the association of leadership functions with high status would facilitate implementation of leader decisions. Status ascription through inheritance would similarly resolve problems of leadership recruitment, training, and continuity that would otherwise inhibit effective decision making in the long term.

The association of status differentials with differential access to resources, which is characteristic of many systems, is a different problem. It seems reasonable to suggest that some degree of control of resources (land, labor, production, etc.) is required for coordination and regulation of their utilization. To the extent (usually considerable) that hierarchical organizatons are engaged in such integrative activity, there should be a positive relationship between position in such a hierarchy and resource access. Higher positions should be associated with greater access to resources than lower positions. If social status is also associated with relative hierarchical position, then status and resource access should covary. The suggestion here is that integrative function, social status, and access to resources may be functionally related to one another. These relationships can, however, be expected to be complicated in complex societies characterized by multiple and overlapping integrative hierarchies.

I might note that this suggestion is very different from that of Davis and Moore (1945) that has generated so much debate in sociology. (See Abrahamson 1973, Broom and Cushing 1977 for recent discussion). They suggested that social and economic stratification systems represent a differential system of rewards to ensure performance of functions of differential importance. The suggestion here is that differential access to resources is a structural consequence of a hierarchically ordered integrative-control system. (This does not, by the way, imply the absence of other mechanisms of socioeconomic differentiation.)

A detailed argument for the functional relationship of hierarchical position, status, and wealth would not, of course, necessarily account for the initial development of these differentials. Mayhew and Schollaert (1980) have developed a model for the development of inequality in status characteristics (wealth, power, prestige, etc.) that generates inequality as the result of a scale-dependent random process. Application of their perspective would require only that the limits of sequential hierarchy had been reached for a given system, and that group fission had been inhibited either by circumscription or by economies of scale.

Whatever the specific processes generating functional, social, and economic hierarchies in particular cases, the resulting organizations are far more similar to those studied by sociologists than are the simple, relatively egalitarian systems discussed thus far. Anthropological study of these more complex systems could well benefit from many of the concepts used in the investigation of variability in complex organizations. *Span of control* is one such basic concept.

## Span of Control

Span of control refers to the number of individuals or organizational units directly subordinate to a given individual or organizational unit within a hierarchical structure. Span is said to range from narrow, with few subordinates, to wide, with many. Studies of a wide variety of organizations have produced the empirical generalization that the range of variation in observed span of control is narrow, and that an optimum span may be somewhere around the interesting figure of 6 (Urwick 1956, 41).

To cite a few examples, Pugh *et al.* (1968, 104) report an average span for chief executives of 52 organizations in the area of Birmingham, England, to be 6.08 (range = 2–14, S.D. = 3.08). These organizations ranged in number of employees from 251 to 16,500, and were very diverse. "They include firms making motor cars and chocolate bars, municipal departments repairing roads and teaching arithmatic, large retail stores, small insurance companies and so on" (Pugh *et al.* 1968, 67)

Klatzky (1970, 433) reports, in a study of 53 state and territorial employment agencies in the United States, that the average number of major subdivisions per agency is 6.6 (range 2–13, S.D. 2.5). These agencies varied in number of employees from 50 to 9078 (mean = 1194.7, S.D. = 1675).

Jones (1966, 65) provides data on local communities controlled by subchiefs in the state organization of Basutoland in 1938. Local communities averaged about 183 tax-paying males (range = about 88–253, S.D. = about 46.7), and subchiefs had an average span of control of 5.13 ($N = 8$, range = 2–11, S.D. = 2.75).

Skinner (1977, 305) reports that the average span of control for prefectural level units of the field administration of Late Imperial China was between 5 and 6, with a range of 1 to 24. This large range is interesting, and I will return to it later.

Carzo and Yanouzas (1969) report an experimental study that bears directly on this question. They compared decision performance in two types of organizations, each with 15 members. The first type had a single executive with a span of control of 14. The second type of organization was structured in four levels, with a span of 2 for each but the lowest level. Not surprisingly, the organization with the span of 2 showed significantly higher performance levels than that with a span of 14.

It appears, then, that these complex organizations may be under very similar structural constraints as the egalitarian societies discussed earlier in this chapter. Table 21.7 reviews data presented earlier on !Kung rainy-season camps, highland New Guinea tribal or alliance groups, Basutoland subchief territories, and Klatzky's data on employment agencies. Taken as a group of 97 organizations, organizational population ranges from 7 to 9078. Organizational unit (nuclear family, local exogamous clan, local community, major subdivision) population ranges from 3 to about 698. Horizontal span shows much less variability, from 2 to 13 with means from 3.08–6.60. These figures

**TABLE 21.7**

**Horizontal Spans of Organizations**

| | Organization population | Basal unit population | Horizontal span |
|---|---|---|---|
| ID | !Kung rainy season camp (N = 24) | Nuclear family | |
| Range | 7–24 | 3–6 | 2–6 |
| Mean | 14.83 | 3.43 | 3.08 |
| S.D. | 5.16 | 1.36 | 1.35 |
| ID | New Guinea tribe or alliance (N = 12) | Local exogamous clan | |
| Range | 180–2400 | 39–650 | 1.24–7.50 |
| Mean | 875 | 242 | 4.22 |
| S.D. | 751 | 168 | 1.63 |
| ID | Basutoland[a] subchief territory (N = 8) | Local community | |
| Range | 352–2011 | ca. 88–253 | 2–11 |
| Mean | 951.3 | ca. 183.0 | 5.13 |
| S.D. | 581.5 | ca. 46.7 | 2.75 |
| ID | Employment agency (N = 53) | Major subdivision | |
| Range | 50–9078 | ca. 25–698 | 2–13 |
| Mean | 1194.7 | ca. 181 | 6.60 |
| S.D. | 1675.7 | ? | 2.50 |

[a]Population figures = tax-paying males.

are remarkably similar, and are consistent with the experimental results on small-group decision making discussed earlier.

Constraint on span of control has some interesting implications for degree of control in simple hierarchies. Recall that egalitarian organizations incorporating six or more basal units are under increasing scalar stress. Development of simultaneous hierarchy with a single vertical control-unit (chief, etc.) would imply that this single unit would have a span of control of 6+. Such a span could itself be a source of scalar stress on the control unit, and I would expect horizontal differentiation of this unit (multiple chiefs) along territorial or activity lines. Territorial differentiation might simply be reflected in a mosaic of relatively small and "autonomous" groups, each with a single integrative and control unit (see also Johnson 1978, 94).

The high probability of differentiated highest-order control in simple hierarchies suggests that the degree of control exercised by any given unit is structurally limited. Differentiation of second and subsequent levels of hierarchy, however, should allow concentration of power not possible in simpler systems. As Wirsing (1973) has shown with ethnographic data, there is a positive relationship between levels of hierarchy in a society and degree of power exercised by its control mechanism.

## Variability in Span of Control

Skinner's (1977) data on span of control for prefectual-level units of Late Imperial China indicate an average span of between 5 and 6, but a wide range of variation from 1 to 24. He notes that wide spans were found in regional core areas where formal administration was concerned almost exclusively with tax collection. Other regulatory functions were exercised through political mechanisms outside the structure of formal field administration (Skinner 1977, 336). Narrow spans were associated with regional peripheries where, along with tax collection, a high degree of social control was required in areas of potential military disruptions (Skinner 1977, 321). Span of control was thus inversely related to the variety of activities for which the field administration was responsible.

This pattern of variability in span of control agrees well with results obtained on other types of organizations in which span width is inversely related to task complexity or scope of unit responsibilities (Blau 1968, 460). Unusually wide spans were possible in regional core areas of China because of the operation of an dual hierarchy, allowing reduction in the scope of responsibilities of the formal adminsitrative system.

Span of control may also vary with degree of control exercised by an organization on its component parts. Variability of this sort should be particularly common in cases of developing complex societies of interest to anthropologists. We might well expect to see a decrease in span of control within such societies as the degree of control exercised by administrative elites increases (see Johnson in press for an archaeological example).

Span of control must be maintained within relatively narrow limits if a relatively high degree of control is to be maintained. System growth, then, should often generate an increase in the hierarchical complexity of system organization. It should be no surprise, therefore, that those who study modern organizations have been interested in the relationship of organizational scale and complexity.

## Size and Structure

The literature on organization contains a very wide variety of studies of the relationship between organizational size and various measures of organizational complexity (see Scott 1975 for a review). Although results of specific studies are highly variable (probably because organizational population is the most common measure of size), Blau (1970, 201) concludes that "(1) increasing organizational size generates differentiation along various lines at decelerating rates; and (2) differentiation enlarges the administrative component in organizations to effect coordination."

One implication of these empirical generalizations is that while the absolute number of administrative personnel increases with organizational size, their relative number generally declines (see also Campbell and Akers 1970). This phenomenon may also characterize nonmodern systems.

Although data of this sort are difficult to obtain from the ethnographic literature, Ember's (1963) material discussed earlier may provide a reasonable approximation of size-controlling component relationships. Recall that Ember provided data on system size (largest political unit) and the number of types of political officials for 24 societies. These data can be used here if we assume that the number of types of political officials is proportional to the number of political officials.

As in Figure 21.1, Figure 21.5 presents 23 of Ember's 24 cases. If types of political officials are transformed into types of officials per 1000 population of the largest political unit, there is a very clear inverse relationship between officials per 1000 and the largest organizational unit size ($r = -0.962$, $R = .925$). (Addition of Ember's twenty-fourth case, Thai, increases this correlation to $-.980$.)

These data contain what would appear to be a basic contradiction. If scalar stress increases as a function of size, how can an increment in the apparent response to stress decrease with increments in size? The size of basal organizational units must be increasing, while the size of the system itself is increasing. One would expect the basal units in Ember's data to increase, for example, from the nuclear family to the extended family to the household cluster, clan, village cluster, etc. This unit-size increase with system scale

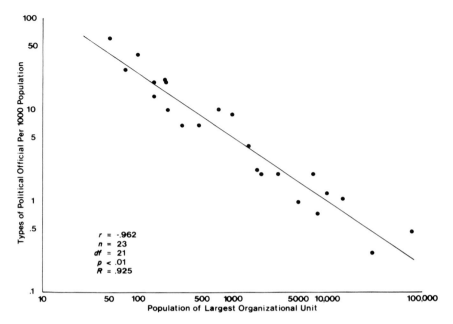

**Figure 21.5.** Societal size and relative size of controlling component.

occurs in modern organizations (Blau 1970, 207), and suggests that sequential hierarchies may not lose their importance with the development of simultaneous hierarchies.

I suggested earlier that access to resources may be associated with individual position in a control hierarchy. If the relative size of the controlling component of an organization is inversely related to system size, then increasingly fewer people (proportionally) will have access to increasingly greater resources (absolutely). Effective stratification should become increasingly pronounced. As Sahlins (1958, 249) notes in his study of social stratification in Polynesia, "It was suggested, therefore, that stratification is directly related to productivity, [and] productivity was *measured by the number of people embraced in the largest redistributive network* of food and how frequently this overall network was utilized [emphasis added]."

## Organizational Limits to Growth?

Are there inherent organizational limits to growth? This is one of those questions to which the answer is both "yes" and, perhaps, "no." Carneiro (1978) looks at the decrease in the number of autonomous political units in the world over time, and the resulting curve is exponential. I suspect that this pattern is probably attributable to the observation that linear increase in levels of system hierarchy generates an exponential increase in potential system size that is constrained by span of control and population size of basal organizational units. The population potentially integrated in a hierarchical system is roughly given by the expression $S(C)^L$, where $S$ = basal unit size, $C$ = average span of control, and $L$ = number of levels of control.

I mentioned earlier that increasing hierarchical complexity of control appears to be associated with both increasing degree of control and proportionally increasing elite access to resources. These, in combination with exponential increase in potential system size, should help to account for the rapid expansion of many early complex societies. Yet each increase in levels of hierarchy, basal unit size, etc., also represents a stress point that may inhibit further development.

Organizational limits to growth may be observed spatially, beyond simple limits to space (circumscription). Renfrew (1975, 14), for example, describes a frequently observed "early state module" consisting of a central place and associated hinterland. These units avered about 1500 km$^2$ in size and often are spaced such that adjacent central places are about 40 km apart. The spatial organization of the Susiana Plain of Iran during the period of early state formation (Johnson in press) appears to conform to Renfrew's observations. Administrative control was limited to a radius of about 20 km (a one day round-trip distance) from a given high-order center.

This "spatial" limit apparently represented an organizational constraint related to the ability of administrative elites in early complex societies to control rural populations. Such societies are increasingly recognized to have operated with a combination of coersion and consensus (Claessen and Skalnik 1978, 640, Goldelier 1978, 767–768, Service 1975, 266), and this 20-km radius of adminstrative influence was probably related to movement costs of rural participation in center economies (Johnson in press).

This organizational problem could be resolved through development of an additional level of hierarchy such that subordinate centers could be spaced at less than one-day round-trip intervals across the landscape (see Johnson 1975 for an example). This solution need not be achieved, however, and an early state system may collapse, as it did in the Susiana case mentioned before.

Other limits to growth may be more technological than strictly organizational. One interesting example has been raised by Williamson (1967). He developed a model of "control loss" in which potential control decreases with increase in the number of organizational levels due to loss and distortion of information in transmission from level to level (see also Athanassiades 1973). Potential countermeasures, "anti-distortion control devices" (Williamson 1967, 127), prominently include technical improvements in data processing. Were some cases of the development of writing systems in part a response to problems of control loss in increasingly hierarchically organized systems? The answer is unclear, but the development of writing systems is increasingly being viewed in terms of the development of information storage, retrieval, and transfer technology in the context of developing hierarchical organizations (Green in press, Schmandt-Besserat 1980).

There are limits to growth. Limits may, however, be overcome, at least within the organizational range considered here. These limits represent stress points in organizational development, and increasing our understanding of response to stress will require increasing examination of processes of system collapse as well as those of development (see Yoffee 1979).

### Variance and Mean in Organizational Change

Understanding organizational structure and change will require accounting for both the variances and means of critical organizational variables. As I noted earlier, there is considerable variability in the system population size at which simultaneous hierarchies appear in social groups. I suggested that this variability was related to the extent to which sequential hierarchy is, and can be, a response to scalar–communications stress. Comparable variability is common in modern organizations (Reimann 1973) in which alternative structural arrangements are possible to resolve the same underlying problems. In general, trajectories of organizational development will depend in part on response sequence, i.e., the temporal order in which sequential and/or simultaneous hierarchy development or elaboration occurs.

Whatever the response sequence, we can probably expect organizational change under scalar stress to be more discontinuous than continuous. Stress may build slowly, but its resolution in either collapse or development is likely to be much more rapid (see also Flannery 1972, Johnson 1978). Indeed, discontinuous change is increasingly a critical element in theories of change in complex systems (Allen in press, Zeeman 1977).

While there is considerable variability in organizational development, mean values of critical variables such as span of control seem to be heavily constrained. The possible linkage of span of control to underlying human information-processing capacities may contribute to an explanation for this important mean value of organizational structure (see also Mayhew and Levinger 1976, 1038).

## CONCLUSIONS

I have essentially argued here for a uniformitarian approach to the study of organizational structure and change. The justification for this approach is that all organizations appear to face certain similar problems, and scalar–communications stress has been emphasized in this chapter as one such important problem. Accounting for change may, however, require a more uniformitarian approach than the one taken here. Hierarchies are not the special province of human organizations, but of structure complex systems in general. They are pervasive in organizations of atoms, molecules, cells, and so on. Hierarchies are so pervasive that understanding why they should exist is not as simple a matter as it might seem (Pattee 1973, 101).

Origin problems aside, studies of the general properties of hierarchical organizations should be of some interest to anthropology and archaeology. Simon (1973, 7) remarks, for example, that degree of hierarchy can be readily related to the rate of system evolution.

Potential system size, degree of control, degree of status differentiation or stratification, degree of elite access to resources, and even rate of system evolution may all be related to general properties of hierarchies. I always wondered why so many things happened so quickly after the Neolithic.


## ACKNOWLEDGMENTS

An earlier version of this chapter was presented in a symposium on Morphogenetic Approaches to Sociocultural Change in Complex Societies at the Second Annual Theoretical Archaeology Group Conference in Southampton, December 1980. In addition to the other members of that symposium, I would like to thank Lewis R. Binford, Henri J. M. Claessen, Carol Kramer, Thomas McGovern, and John D. Speth for their helpful comments. Remaining sins of omission and commission are mine. I would also like to express my appreciation for support from the Alexander von Humboldt–Stiftung and the Institut für Vorderasiatische Altertumskunde, Freie Universität Berlin, during the academic year 1980–1981.

## REFERENCES

Abrahamson M., 1973, Functionalism and the functional theory of stratification: an empirical assessment, *American Journal of Sociology* 78, 1236–1246.

Allen P. M., in press, The evolutionary paradigm of dissipative structures, in Jantsch, E. (ed.), *The Evolutionary Vision,* American Association for the Advancement of Science.

Ashby, R. W., 1968, Variety, constraint, and the law of requisite variety, in Buckley, W. (ed.), *Modern Systems Research for the Behavioral Scientist,* Chicago, Aldine, 129–136.

Athanassiades, J. C., 1973, The distortion of upward communication in hierarchical organizations, *Academy of Management Journal* 16, 207–226.

Bargatzky, T., 1981, Person acquisition, energy, and the evolution of the early state. (Paper prepared for a symposium on the evolution of political organization, I.U.A.E.S. Intercongress, Amsterdam.)

Bettinger, R. L., 1978, Alternative adaptive strategies in the prehistoric Great Basin, *Journal of Anthropological Research* 34, 27–46.

Blau, P. M., 1968, The hierarchy of authority in organizations, *American Journal of Sociology* 37, 453–467.

Blau, P. M., 1970, A formal theory of differentiation in organizations, *American Sociological Review* 35, 201–218.

Bohannan, P., 1967, Homicide among the Tiv of central Nigeria, in Bohannan, P. (ed.), *African Homicide and Suicide,* New York, Atheneum, 30–64.

Broom, L., and Cushing, R. G., 1977, A modest test of an immodest theory: the functional theory of stratification, *American Sociological review* 42, 157–169.

Brown, P., 1978, New Guinea: ecology, society, and culture, *Annual Review of Anthropology* 7, 263–291.

Brown, P., and Podolesfsky, A., 1976, Population density, agricultural intensity, land tenure, and group size in the New Guinea highlands, *Ethnology* 15, 211–238.

Bridges, E. M., Doyle, W. J., and Mahan, D. J., 1968, Effects of hierarchical differentiation on group productivity, efficiency, and risk taking, *Administrative Science Quarterly* 13, 305–319.

Campbell, F., and Akers, R. L., 1970, Organizational size, complexity, and the administrative component in occupational associations, *The Sociological Quarterly* 11, 435–451.

Carneiro, R. L., 1967, On the relationship between size of population and complexity of social organization, *Southwestern Journal of Anthropology* 23, 234–243.

Carneiro, R. L., 1970, A theory of the origin of the state, *Science* 169, 733–738.

Carneiro, R. L., 1978, Political expansion as an expression of the principle of competitive exclusion in Cohen, R., and Service, E. R. (eds.), *Origins of the State: The Anthropology of Political Evolution,* Philadelphia, ISHI, 205–223.

Carzo, Jr., R., and Yanouzas, J. N., 1969, Effects of flat and tall organization structure, *Administrative Science Quarterly* 14, 178–191.

Claessen, H. J. M., 1978, The early state: a structural approach, in Claessen, H. J. M., and Skalnik, P. (eds.), *The Early State,* The Hague, Mouton, 533–596.

Claessen, H. J. M., and Skalnik, P. 1978, The early state: models and reality, in Claessen, H. J. M., and Skalnik, P. (eds.), *The Early State,* The Hague, Mouton, 638–650.

Cohen, M. N., 1977, *The Food Crisis in Prehistory: Overpopulation and the Origins of Agriculture,* New Haven, Yale University Press.

Cohen, R., 1978, State origins: a reappraisal, in Claessen, H. J. M., and Skalnik, P. (eds.), *The Early State,* The Hague, Mouton, 31–75.

Conkey, M. W., 1978, Style and information in cultural evolution: toward a predictive model for the Paleolithic, in Redman, C. L., *et al.* (eds.), *Social Archeology: Beyond Subsistence and Dating,* New York, Academic Press, 61–85.

Cogwill, G. L., 1975, On causes and consequences of ancient and modern population changes, *American Anthropologist* 77, 505–525.

Cummings, L. L., Huber, G. P., and Arendt, E., 1974, Effects of size and spatial arrangements on group decision making, *Academy of Management Journal* 17, 460–475.

Davis, K., and Moore, W. E., 1945, Some principles of stratification, *American Sociological Review* 10, 242–249.

Dubin, R., 1959, Stability of human organizations, in Haine, M., (ed.), *Modern Organization Theory,* New York, Wiley, 218–253.

Ember, M., 1963, The relationship between economic and political development in nonindustrial societies, *Ethnology* 2, 228–248.

Godelier, M., 1978, Infrastructures, societies and history, *Current Anthropology* 19, 763–771.

Green, M. W., in press, The construction and implementation of the cuneiform writing system, *Visible Language* 15.

Gross, D. R., 1979, A new approach to central Brazilian social organization, in Margolis, M. L., and Carter, W. E. (eds.), *Brazil: Anthropological Perspectives: Essays in Honor of Charles Wagley,* New York, Columbia University Press, 321–343.

Harner, M. J., 1970, Population pressure and the social evolution of agriculturalists, *Southwestern Journal of Anthropology* 26, 67–86.

Hassan, F. A., 1975, Determination of the size, density, and growth rate of hunting–gathering populations, in Polgar, S., (ed.), *Population, Ecology, and Social Evolution,* The Hague, Mouton, 27–52.

Hassan, F. A., 1979, Demography and archaeology, *Annual Review of Anthropology* 8, 137–160.

Johnson, G. A., 1975, Locational analysis and the investigation of Uruk local exchange systems, in Sabloff, J. A., and Lamberg-Karlovsky, C. C. (eds.), *Ancient Civilization and Trade,* Albuquerque, University of New Mexico Press, 285–339.

Johnson, G. A., 1977, Aspects of regional analysis in archaeology, *Annual Review of Anthropology* 6, 479–508.

Johnson, G. A., 1978, Information sources and the development of decision-making organizations, in Redman, C. L., *et al.* (eds.), *Social Archeology: Beyond Subsistence and Dating,* New York, Academic Press, 87–112.

Johnson, G. A., in press, The changing organization of Uruk administration on the Susiana Plain, in Hole, F. (ed.), *Archaeological Perspectives on Iran: From Prehistory to the Islamic Conquest,* Albuquerque, University of New Mexico Press.

Jones, G. I., 1966, Chiefly succession in Basutoland, in Goody, J. (ed.), *Succession to High Office,* Cambridge, Cambridge University Press, 57–81.

King, T. F., 1978, Don't that beat the band? nonegalitarian political organization in prehistoric central California, in Redman, C. L. *et al.* (eds.), *Social Archeology: Beyond Subsistence and Dating,* New York, Academic Press, 225–248.

Klatzky, S. R., 1970, Relationship of organizational size to complexity and coordination, *Administrative Science Quarterly* 15, 428–438.

Lee, R. B., 1969, !Kung bushman subsistence: an input–output analysis, in Vayda, A. P., (ed.), *Environment and Cultural Behavior: Ecological Studies in Cultural Anthropology,* Austin, University of Texas Press, 47–79.

Lee, R. B., 1979, *The !Kung San: Men, Women, and Work in a Foraging Society,* Cambridge, Cambridge University Press.

Mayhew, B. H., and Levinger, R. L., 1976, On the emergence of oligarchy in human interaction, *American Journal of Sociology* 81, 1017–1049.

Mayhew, B. H., and Schollaert, P. T., 1980, The concentration of wealth: a sociological model, *Sociological Forces* 13, 1–35.

Meier, R. L., 1972, Communications stress, *Annual Review of Ecology and Systematics* 3, 289–314.

Mellaart, J., 1967, *Çatal Hüyük: A Neolithic town in Anatolia,* London, Thames and Hudson.

Milisauskas, S. 1979, *European Prehistory,* New York, Academic Press.

Miller, G. A., 1956, The magical number seven, plus or minus two: some limits on our capacity for processing information, *Psychological Review* 63, 81–97.

Moore, J. A., in press, The effects of information networks in hunter–gatherer societies, in Winterhalder, B. and Smith, E. A. (eds.), *Hunter–Gatherer Foraging Strategies: Ethnographic and Archaeological Analysis,* Chicago, University of Chicago Press.

Naroll, R., 1956, A preliminary index of social development, *American Anthropologist* 58, 687–715.

Netting, R. McC., 1974, Agrarian ecology, *Annual Review of Anthropology,* 3, 21–56.

Pasternak, B., Ember, C., and Ember, M., 1976, On the conditions favoring extended family households, *Journal of Anthropological Research* 32, 109–123.

Pattee, H. H., 1973, The physical basis and origin of hierarchical control, in Pattee, H. H. (ed.), *Hierarchy Theory: The Challenge of Complex Systems,* New York, George Braziller, 73–108.

Peebles, C. S., and Kus, S. M., 1977, Some archaeological correlates of rank societies, *American Antiquity* 42, 421–448.

Plog, F., 1978, The Kerensan bridge: an ecological and archaeological account, in Redman, C. L., *et al.* (eds.), *Social Archeology: Beyond Subsistence and Dating,* New York, Academic Press, 349–372.

Price, T. D., 1980, The archaeology of hunter–gatherers: sedentism, population, and complexity. (Paper presented to a symposium on approaches to complexity, Instituut voor Prae- en Protohistorie, Amsterdam.)

Pugh, D. S., Hickson, J. J., Hinings, C. R., and Turner, C., 1968, Dimensions of organization structure, *Administrative Science Quarterly* 13, 65–105.

Rappaport, R. A., 1968, *Pigs for the Ancestors,* New Haven, Yale University Press.

Rappaport, R. A., 1971, Ritual, sanctity, and cybernetics, *American Anthropologist* 73, 59–76.

Reimann, B. C., 1973, On the dimensions of bureaucratic structure: an empirical reappraisal, *Administrative Science Quarterly* 18, 462–476.

Renfrew, C., 1975, Trade as action at a distance: questions of interaction and communication, in Sabloff, J. A., and Lamberg-Karlovsky, C. C., (eds.), *Ancient Civilization and Trade*, Albuquerque, University of New Mexico Press, 3–59.

Reynolds, R. G. D., and Zeigler, B. P., 1979, A formal mathematical model for the operation of concensus-based hunting–gathering bands, in Renfrew, C., and Cooke, K. L., (eds.), *Transformations: Mathematical Approaches to Culture Change*, New York, Academic Press, 405–417.

Sanders, W. T., Parsons, J. R., and Santley, R. S., 1979, *The Basin of Mexico: Ecological Processes in the Evolution of a Civilization*, New York, Academic Press.

Sahlins, M. D., 1958, *Social Stratification in Polynesia*, Seattle, University of Washington Press.

Sahlins, M. D., 1963, Poor man, rich man, big-man, chief: political types in Melanesia and Polynesia, *Comparative Studies in Society and History* 5, 285–303.

Sahlins, M. D., 1972, *Stone Age Economics*, New York, Aldine–Atherton.

Schmandt-Besserat, D., 1980, The envelopes that bear the first writing, *Technology and Culture* 21, 357–385.

Scott, R. W., 1975, Organizational structure, *Annual Review of Sociology* 1, 1–20.

Service, E. R., 1975, *Origins of the State and Civilization*, New York, Norton.

Simon, H. A., 1973, The organization of complex systems, in Pattee, H. H. (ed.), *Hierarchy Theory: The Challenge of Complex Systems*, New York, George Braziller, 3–27.

Skinner, G. W., 1977, Cities and the hierarchy of local systems, in Skinner, G. W. (ed.), *The City in Late Imperial China*, Stanford, Stanford University Press, 276–351.

Smith, P. E. L., and Young, Jr., T. C., 1972, The evolution of early agriculture and culture in greater Mesopotamia: a trial model, in Spooner, B. (ed.), *Population Growth: Anthropological Implictions*, Cambridge, Mass., MIT Press, 1–59.

Soudský, B., and Pavlů, I., 1972, The linear culture settlement patterns of central Europe, in Ucko, P. J., Tringham, R., and Dimbleby, G. W. (eds.), *Man, Settlement and Urbanism*, London, Duckworth, 317–328.

Sutherland, J. W., 1975, *Systems: Analysis, Administration and Architecture*, New York, Van Nostrand–Reinhold.

Synenki, A. T., and Braun, D. P., 1980, Organizational theory and social inference. (Paper presented in the symposium, Regional Social Networks: Measurement, Theory and Examples, Forty-fifth Annual Meeting, Society for American Archaeology, Philadelphia, (cited by permission of the authors).

Tringham, R., 1971, *Hunters, Fishers and Farmers of Eastern Europe 6000–3000 B.C.*, London, Hutchinson & Co.

Udy, Jr. S. H., 1970, *Work in Traditional and Modern Society*, Englewood Cliffs, N.J., Prentice-Hall.

Urwick, L. F., 1956, The manager's span of control, *Harvard Business Review* 34, 39–47.

White, B., 1973, Demand for labor and population growth in colonial Java, *Human Ecology* 1, 217–236.

Williamson, O. E., 1967, Hierarchical control and optimum firm size, *The Journal of Political Economy* 75, 123–138.

Wilmsen, E. N., 1980, Exchange, interaction and settlement in northwestern Botswana: past and present perspectives, *Working Papers No. 39, African Studies Center*, Boston University.

Wirsing, R., 1973, Political power and information: a cross-cultural study, *American Anthropologist* 75, 153–170.

Wobst, H. M., 1974, Boundary conditions for Paleolithic social systems: a simulation approach, *American Antiquity* 39, 147–178.

Wobst, H. M., 1977, Stylistic behavior and information exange, in Cleland, C. E. (ed.), Papers for the Director: Research Essays in Honor of James B. Griffin, *Anthropological Papers, Museum of Anthropology, University of Michigan* 61, Ann Arbor, 317–342.

Wright, G. A., 1978, Social differentiation in the early Natufian, in Redman, C. L., *et al.* (eds.), *Social Archeology: Beyond Subsistence and Dating,* New York, Academic Press, 201–223.

Wright, H. T., 1977, Recent research on the origin of the state, *Annual Review of Anthropology* 6, 379–397.

Yellen, J. E., 1977, *Archaeological Approaches to the Present: Models for Reconstructing the Past,* New York, Academic Press.

Yoffee, N., 1979, The decline and rise of Mesopotamia civilization: an ethnoarchaeological approach, *American Antiquity* 44, 5–35.

Zeeman, E. C., 1977, *Catastrophy Theory: Selected Papers 1972–1977,* Reading, Mass., Benjamin.

# 22

## Theoretical Approaches to Social Change: An Archaeological Viewpoint

*KLAVS RANDSBORG*

## USES OF THEORY

Over the last 10 to 15 years archaeology has experienced a marked growth in new concepts, theories, and methods pertaining to the dynamics of past societies. Archaeological data have been searched for patterns that might reflect specific operations of ancient social systems, and the social anthropological literature, in particular, has been scanned for data on actual behavioral patterns. This development has led to a branching of archaeological research in two directions. On the one hand, detailed information has been collected on possible material correlates of the actions of social systems. The research problems here are related to the uncertainty of the use of analogy and, on the whole, to the difficulties of detecting generalities about human behavior outside the realm of biology. On the other hand, the study of the archaeological record has concentrated on those aspects that are thought to bear on the crucial variables of social systems. The research problems here are connected with the changing quality of archeological data in terms of preservation and recovery and, especially, with the methodological problems of determining precise relationships between a specific data set and the phenomena responsible for it. And so, the focus of modern archaeology is ultimately linked with our view of the functioning of human societies and of their similarities and dissimilarities.

This situation has also created some frustrations. It has proved difficult to

THEORY AND EXPLANATION
IN ARCHAEOLOGY

establish common lines of research and, especially, to establish general patterns of human behavior. The scapegoats are the archaeological record and cultural diversity. While the record is often considered too fragmentary and culturally too diverse for actual studies of society, cultural diversity has in itself been considered an explanation of social behavior. This is to ignore the problems of adaptation, and to turn cultural traditions into generalities of society that they by definition are not. Actually, the so-called new archaeology set out to transcend the limits of cultures and to understand traditions in terms of the factors operating to condition, maintain, and change them.

When a subject is undergoing rapid change in concepts, theories, and methods, a few empirical results may be widely responsible for sustaining and directing the change. This underscores how dependent the society of scientists is on the general level and character of its field. In fact, archaeology, lacking a coherent methodological structure and a set of generalities, is to a large extent an open field for hypotheses that are difficult to falsify. When evaluation is such a tremendous task and problem, it is important to maintain a detailed knowledge of the context of the research. We may see this as a stream of consciousness reaching from data and data control over questions of scientific reasoning to the specific and the general milieus of the scientist, including the historical ramifications of all this. The present situation is somewhat schizophrenic. The new archaeology is urging a search for unification, but the research pertaining to this is going ahead with very few hardy demonstrations that the archaeological record and the social phenomena that produced it in fact are unitifed. It is impossible to do any kind of archaeological research outside of theoretical frameworks, but the uncertainty of the present situation calls for constant scepticism and relativism in actual work. This all means that very many new techniques, methodologies, or theories relating to human behavior must be scrutinized. We may, in this situation, see dimly three different archaeological personalities pertaining to three different strategies of research. This division is, however, crosscut by other dimensions, some of which are linked to different traditions of learning in, for instance, the United States, England, or in northwestern Europe. The first type of "modern" archaeologist is, in particular, interested in the classifications of social anthropology, and he or she tries to apply these to his or her data. The second type is more analytical, concentrating on problems in the data. The third type of new archaeologist is the creator of concepts and methodologies pertaining to "real-world" phenomena of a truly general, although often very abstract, nature, in principle linked with detailed data control.

It is evident that the situation is complex, often confusing, and holds little prospect for consensus despite a shared idea about the importance of the study of societies and functioning human systems from the "dead" archaeological record. It does seem of value, however, to consider the nature and the use of theory in archaeology. It should be stressed that theories are abstract, "man made," created, changed, and especially used only under a series of circumscribed conditions. The theories from which certain regularities are derived must not be considered as reified by the establishment of a test case for their implications, in particular because deductive testing can, if anything, only disprove, not prove a case. In the present state of affairs it seems safer to proceed inductively using the various theories as indicators of possible further directions of research and to form approaches rather than dogmatic, static frameworks into which "the data will organize themselves." (Often an interest in theory has turned into tutelage.) On the other hand, there is also a great danger inherent in the "liberal" attitude since an important aspect of the use of theories in archaeology is how to evaluate them, and to that end only strictness will do.

In the current period where ambiguity prevails, either due to the character of the data or the weakness of present theoretical approaches, it is crucial to establish systems of evaluation for the various theories that is, in fact, the same as to state the limitations of any given theory. This is usually not included in the work of modern archaeology, making it quite vulnerable with its presentations of new theories plus test cases without a methodology for evaluation. It should be added that such methodology ought not to be considered a step in the direction of finding one and only "truth," but as presenting a picture of the strength of various propositions that can only be measured fully in relation to the wider environment of the researcher. It is, as indicated before, important to encompass the full medium of investigation—the scientist, his instruments (including hypotheses), and his data—in the process of research.

With respect to the last point, another question of theory building must be considered, namely to what extent "the world" is a functioning, intelligible whole about which we can learn more and more. Such a view resembles the classic Western idealist perspective where the data eventually "speak for themselves." In day-to-day situations the world is made intelligible by the repetition of signals we have perceived through time and that we call our experience. Archaeological data do not differ ontologically from other components of the world. Working as an archaeologist is as real as reading a timetable or weeding the garden. The work a scientist is carrying out is also conditioned by experiences and training, and the archaeological data, contemporary in nature, can never be studied or made to convey anything about the past without taking into consideration the researcher and the process of the research. The logics applied to scientific work and thinking, or rather to the presentations of such, are only a necessary condition of scientific procedure, not a proof of such. The standardization required by research for the sake of compatibility is also a problem of procedure. Therefore, in spite of the coherence and causality in the world, as we experience it in daily situations, including the routines of archaeology, there remains a question: To what extent are the structures we do see the repeated signals of our experiences, created by ourselves in a need for order, or in a need for a specific kind of order, for instance, when adhering to a theory without being able to state its limitations?

## EXAMPLES

If, in spite of these cautionary remarks, we accept the possibility of perceiving organization, archaeological experiences have made it clear that some of this pertains to wider ranges in time, space, and function than others. Seemingly, two major forms of order and theories pertaining to such have a rather general nature. The first one is related to biological functions of the human body. In other words, to what has to do with diet, clothing, etc. Also, subsistence economies seem to be relatively easy to handle archaeologically, as the relevant material rarely has a ritual phenotype, unlike, for example, burials. (Probably burials also relate quite directly to the social dimensions of society, but they are difficult to understand due to their cultural "coding.") The other general area is the very abstract: Theories that, like information or catastrophe theory, for instance, are applicable to very many single cases (Renfrew and Cooke 1979). These theories are relatively easy to understand, at least in principle, and since the mathematical equations upon which they are based do not in and of themselves have any cultural or social implications—in that sense they resemble so-called "laws of nature"—it is evident that they are hypothetical in character and exist only within certain rather narrow limits of application. They serve, in other words, as guidelines for our thoughts but have no *necessary* "real-world" connotations as such. The major problem when using such theories or models is actually one of measurement, due to the character of the archaeological data. The data are fragmentary and very difficult to evaluate and reconstruct. It is often difficult to reach the level of analysis where material remains, while decayed and disturbed, are still sampled adequately enough for a study of a totality of a kind, despite their partial nature. In many cases spatial sampling only represents a futile attempt at reconstructing the full trace pattern of settlement or, in other words, an archaeological moon landscape. This means that temporal changes are often the only ones that can be relied upon, and even so, the requirements of the previously mentioned highly abstract models unfortunately can rarely be met in practice.

In some cases, however, it has been possible to apply the models of these abstract theories to several sets of data, often data for which we otherwise would have difficulties in establishing common cultural or social–behavioral norms. For instance, the model of settlement rank-size distribution, where log-normal is the supposed ideal pattern of size relationships between the major centers and an indication of a high degree of integration of society, has already been used in the archaeology of early Mesopotamia (Johnson in press), but is equally applicable, for instance, to the towns of the early Middle Ages in Denmark (Figure 22.1) or to the modern United States. Here, on an abstract level above the specifications of history, we encounter some of the phenomena that natural scientists are familiar with. In addition, the formal and very general character of the model, based on theories of social integration, makes it useful also for other studies of differentiation and integration, or processes of growth. Examples are

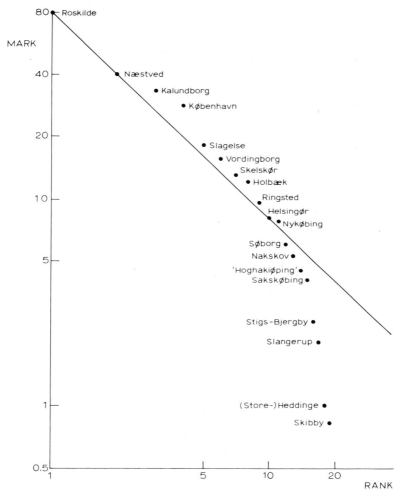

**Figure 22.1.** Rank–size distribution of medieval "towns" (by A.D. 1231) in Denmark (Zealand area). The "size" estimates are based on royal taxation (in mark silver). (Cf. Aakjaer 1926–1943, fol. 54v.)

certain functions of towns, such as minting, rank of individual personalities in society, or patterns of exploitation of the various, more or less common, resources in a given environment.

Other attempts at establishing "generalities," whether real-world phenomena or guidelines for research, have proved less successful. Classifications are especially problematic, as the case of the "port-of-trade" concept from economic history–social anthropology–archaeology. Rather than characterizing a fixed type of settlement, reappearing in a number of historical situations, this may be seen as an element of the function of a number of ports and towns dealing with "trade," being present to quite a varying degree from one site to the next.

In the case of "chiefdoms," a popular concept in the history of "social archaeology," we also have problems in actually identifying this class of human society on the basis of its key features. Originally the term was borrowed from the evolutionary-anthropological literature. A central institution in chiefdoms was seen as the redistribution of essential goods, especially subsistence surplus, by the chiefs. In the ancient Germanic societies, for example, that undoubtedly were chiefdoms in the sense of being stratified societies, redistribution of this kind played only a minor rôle, if any, according to the copious written historic evidence. The problem here is perhaps that the empirical data on which the mentioned generalization or concept was based are tropical societies with so-called elementary kinship structures and not the "Germanic," open society in which the kin groups do not correspond to the political units. It is interesting that the current concept of chiefdoms, with certain aspects that are not altogether of a general nature, has been heuristically sound and has led archaeologists in the "Germanic" areas of Europe, as one example, to ask questions about society that may never have been asked otherwise.

The same reservations can be stated in connection with the more complex societies where definitions based on the "core" areas of state formation, such as Mesopotamia, have been of only limited value when applied to other cases. The basic problem has been that similarity and order are found where they were never manifest or, rather, where they had other forms. What, as seen from the viewpoint of social or archaeological anthropology, may look like theories of social forms applicable to all similar cases, may from the point of view of other traditions of research look like generalizations based on a few special examples. In every case it is important that the propositions take a form that is testable.

Other recent theoretical approaches have been less concerned with classes of social phenomena or classes of societies than with social dynamics. One trend sees a search for "prime movers," like environmental change and population growth; other approaches have been more sophisticated, in fact looking for "behavioral laws" of social and cultural change, although with not too much success, at least until recently. What has been obtained is a scanning of data and problems with new concepts and new ideas about relationships in mind. In this way a link is formed to the previously mentioned highly abstract theories, among them catastrophe theory, that, unlike other ideas applied in archaeology, deal with short-term changes—an area that the subject normally is conceived of as not being able to command. The agreement is that short-term changes require a detailed scale of measurement, a case actually not proven. In fact, such perspectives are especially important for the understanding of change in complex social systems, where the direction of change may be guided by analogy, in fact copying and relating to achievements in other, often similar societies. This example should also underscore the need for further studies of communication and interaction, in short, of the sector of information processing, storage, and distribution in society. This is an area where studies of historically known cases may turn out to be very fruitful, since "prehistoric" archaeology, in the literal sense of the term and under the present theoretical achievements, has had difficulties in dealing with those parts of society that are outside the sphere of economy and the social structures immediately referring to this sphere. A case relating to the study of "information" flows is found in the different rates and, especially, the kinds of changes that are taking place across social and cultural boundaries, as between the Roman Empire and the less-complex societies of "Free Germany." Such relations are at present poorly understood and the models of trade too incomplete to account for them. For instance, the changes in settlement system and economy of the later Roman Empire in northwestern Europe are not without parallels in Free Germany in spite of the different social milieus. There development was toward a more balanced and integrated landed economy and, on both sides of the Limes, a movement away from simpler systems of exploitation—in fact, of overexploitation. This formed the basis for the establishment of complex "states" or "statelike" societies in northern Europe, which was always beyond the Roman Empire.

## A SUMMARY IN METAPHOR

We may at this point summarize the above by using a metaphor. If we compare social and cultural behavior and their expressions in toto to a railroad system, we may see the trains as cultural milieus, comparable to archaeological cultures, traditions, or even to societies in their historically specific forms. The rails resemble a mechanical principle or even a "law," determining the extension and the possibilities of the ride, but not sensu stricto when a train, nor what train, will be passing where. The "when's" and "where's," the behavior of the systems, are in the main determined by the timetable. We should not carry this analogy too far, but the capacity of the rail system, for instance, is not unimportant nor are the passengers on the trains or the passing landscapes outside. The problems of describing and understanding this system lie not so much in the trains themselves or even in the course and character of the rail system—if that is included—but in the timetable, the behavioral component. In archaeology the search for order in this area has not gone very far. Often the simple notion that the trains actually ran is about all that has been stated. A few cases have been exented to include comparisons with other rail systems, as in evolutionary models. Ultimate order and theories attaining to such seem to be frustrated by a "malign being," perhaps in our data, perhaps in the way we study data, perhaps in ourselves. What can be done in the present situation is the establishing of relationships: comparisons of types of trains, their possible junction, the transfers, the purposes of the rides, and even the routes. It is important to model this, but it is equally important to state the limitations of any theory, preventing a belief in preconceived behavioral "laws" that may turn out to be ossified theories. The only area where we may deal with relations resembling natural laws is that of the rails, the "mechanical" area, where nothing is said about specific historical situations.

It is well know that the historical and social sciences in particular have been and are conditioned by "community rules" among the scientists to a large extent. All sciences are, but in these "soft" studies testability of propositions often has not been given a rigorous form—in part due to the fragmentary, i.e., "preliminary," form of the data, in part due to the problems of isolating single social variables for study in the complex data sets. This so far has made it difficult to work with most of the current "ahistoric" and "acultural" models and theories, and hardy or "robust" arguments about past societies have rarely been found. The more durable a theory, the more abstract it has turned out to be and the less it states about the historical phenotypes of society and culture. This is, perhaps, the core of the problem of a unified science: the wider the perspective, the less the content. Without the web of transforming, or middle range, theories, pertaining ultimately to relationships, dynamics, and structural changes, archaeological research would in its present stage not be a satisfactory enterprise for scientific curiousity.

## ACKNOWLEDGMENTS

I should like to thank students and colleagues, among them Dr. Albertus Voorrips, at the Institute of Pre- and Protohistory (IPP), University of Amsterdam, for useful discussions on the present topics.

## REFERENCES

Aakjaer, S., 1926–1943, *Kong Valdemars Jordebog* I–III, København (Copenhagen), no publisher.

Johnson, G. A., in press, Rank-size convexity and system integration: a view from archaeology, *Economic Geography*.

Renfrew, A. C., and Cooke, K. L., (eds.), 1979, *Transformations: Mathematical Approaches to Culture Change*, New York, Academic Press.

# 23

## How Objective Can We Become? Some Reflections on the Nature of the Relationship between the Archaeologist, His Data, and His Interpretations

*S.E. VAN DER LEEUW*

## INTRODUCTION

This chapter argues that our present models for the study of morphogenesis are inadequate. It first examines the context in which archaeology studies the phenomenon, and notes the absence of an adequate awareness of the various subject–object relationships between archaeologists, the material culture they study, and the humans who have left these material remains. Next, it examines the consequences of various such subject–object relationships, and attempts to trace the nature of developments in archaeology from this point of view. It points to the fact that "objectivity" is a profitable kind of subject–object relationship as long as one is studying concrete objects and phenomena, but that it is inadequate when one is concerned with the context in which humans operate. In order to reconstruct the cultural context of humans, we must avail ourselves of a model of the nature of human perception.

In the second part of this chapter, the use of such a model of human perception is attempted in order to construct a model of human institutions as flow or "dissipative" structures.

THEORY AND EXPLANATION
IN ARCHAEOLOGY

# PART I: AN ANALYSIS OF CERTAIN PROBLEMS

## Preamble

In looking at morphogenesis from an archaeological perspective, it might be useful to remind ourselves of some essential differences between archaeology and some other disciplines.

A *first* contrast to be stressed is that between historical and nonhistorical sciences. Here, the main point is the clear way in which the temporal and spatial dimensions are twice involved in historical studies, and but once in the nonhistorical disciplines. In the historical fields, we distinguish (*a*) the point in space and time that is studied; and (*b*) the point in space and time at which the study takes place.

A *second* contrast is that between archaeology and the social and historical sciences. In archaeology, we never observe processes "before our eyes," in action. Sociology and anthropology, operating mainly in the field of synchronous and contemporary observation, make such "live" observations on processes. History has a substitute. It studies the remains of the operation of processes that do indicate the nature of the process in words. The interpretative task of the archaeologist is thus much more difficult.

A *third* contrast exists between archaeology and the physical sciences. In the former field, humans, or human-containing systems, are the subject of study, while students of the physical sciences study phenomena other than humans. Scientists have thus been able to develop an approach that sees the phenomena studied (objects) as completely separate from the researcher (subject). As a consequence, they can assume objectivity and reproducibility of obervations within a stringently fixed context.

The *last* contrast is one between archaeology and all other disciplines. Archaeology is the only one of them that destroys its own evidence in a substantial way: Whatever feature we do not recognize, we do not register. It thus is discarded forever, and lands on the dump. History keeps its sources and guards them jealously. The other disciplines (except perhaps ethnography) work essentially with replicable observations.

The result for archaeology of these peculiarities may be summarized as follows: The second and the last lead to *fragility and slowness of the feedback cycle that functions as a corrective measure relative to archaeological hypotheses.* The first and the third lead to *a confusion of the various subject–object relationships that play a role in archaeology* and to differences of opinion concerning the nature of these relationships. These two problems seem to run like a red thread throughout the development of archaeology, and they are, in my opinion, responsible for our problems in dealing with morphogenesis conceptually and in relation to archaeological data.

## Framework

As a first step in designing a framework that may help disentangle these problems, we will place ourselves on the "human" side of the epistemological debate so that we may consider phenomena entirely as products of our perception. (Not to prove the point, but to give it some credibility as a useful "trick," we need only look at the development of the history of science, which is so full of examples of the shattering effects of change in perception.)

Next, I argue that man has the capacity to perceive in essentially two dimensions (Figure 23.1): (*a*) simultaneous dimension (perception of space); and (*b*) sequential dimension (perception of time). In both these dimensions, humans essentially distinguish: (*a*) sameness (homogeneity, continuity); and (*b*) contrast (heterogeneity, discontinuity).

It must be noted that sameness and contrast are relative to one another. Perceiving only homogeneity has the same effect as perceiving only heterogeneity: No structure is perceived, no contrast, no phenomena. It is only upon perceiving both in the same dimension that we can distinguish phenomena, that we may separate subject from object, and that we may conceive of time and space as observational dimensions in which both actions and thoughts are independent of one another (Figure 23.2).

Because the two are inseparable, human information-processing always operates on two levels: that of the context (i.e., dimension), which stresses the underlying homogeneity of phenomena, and that of the various phenomena, which stresses heterogeneity. In archaeological terms, we create the "type" on the basis of observation of various phenomena (pots, houses, etc.) and consider the "type" that binds the individual pots, houses, etc., together. Thus "no class can be a member of itself or of the class of nonmembers" (Russell, 1903).

Several consequences of this duality need further consideration in the context of this chapter:

1. The duality allows for the hierarchical nesting of contexts. What serves as a context relative to the level below it may also serve as a phenomenon relative

```
DISCONTINUITIES IN:

SIMULTANEOUS PERCEPTION:   MATTER, SUBSTANCE, BOUNDARY

SEQUENTIAL PERCEPTION:     ENERGY, WORK, TRANSFORMATION

PERCEPTION OF DISCONTINUITIES: INFORMATION, FORM
```

**Figure 23.1.** Modes of perception and resultant concepts.

| NATURE OF THE<br>DIMENSION<br><br>NATURE OF THE<br>PERCEPTION | SIMULTANEOUS | SEQUENTIAL | SIMULTANEOUS and<br>SEQUENTIAL |
|---|---|---|---|
| CONTINUITY | NO PATTERN<br>(SAMENESS) | NO PATTERN<br>(SAMENESS) | NO PATTERN<br>(SAMENESS) |
| DISCONTINUITY | NO PATTERN<br>(CHAOS) | NO PATTERN<br>(CHAOS) | NO PATTERN<br>(CHAOS) |
| CONTINUITY and<br>DISCONTINUITY | FORM and SIZE of<br>SPATIAL ENTITIES<br><br>SPATIAL<br>DIMENSIONS | NATURE and SIZE of<br>TEMPORAL ENTITIES<br><br>TEMPORAL<br>DIMENSIONS | CHANGE<br>MOVEMENT |

**Figure 23.2.** Matrix combining the nature of perceptions and the dimensions in which they occur.

to the level above it. Two examples may illustrate this, and they have been presented in Figures 23.3 and 23.4: (a) "typologies" in the sense of culture–historical archaeology; and (b) "nesting" of hypothetical generalizations concerning human behavior in complex societies in the manner advocated by processual archaeologists. In both cases, the relationships between different levels of the hierarchy need not be functionally or otherwise similar.

2. Hierarchical nesting of a series of contexts between subject and object allows the subject at once distance from and involvement with the object. It is the hierarchical nature of human information-processing that allows the distinction of different objects, of object and subject, of spatial, temporal, and other relations, etc. The more information is processed, the more phenomena, and the more relations between these phenomena that may be distinguished.

3. The nature of the perception of phenomena constrains the nature of the context and vice versa. Thus, we may conclude that in different cultures the hierarchical organization of contexts would differ. As a result, conceptions of space, time, and causality would be dependent upon the cultures in which they occur. Although this is probably valid for cultural aggregates as a whole, the argument may not be used at the level of the individual with the same confidence. "Chance" (randomness) may play a part at that level because it may be responsible for the phenomena first perceived, and thus for the idiosyncratic aspects of the contextual framework developed by an individual.

4. Once a context exists, an individual phenomenon may be checked against it (i.e., perceived), but contexts are not established on the basis of a single observation. As a result of this asymmetry, (a) contexts may not be communicated directly between humans except in the framework of a context of more general nature; (b) more-encompassing contexts cannot be formulated in the terminology of less-encompassing ones, but the opposite is possible and, in fact, common; and (c) different contexts at the same level of generality, which have been induced from different sets of phenomena, are mutually incompatible and at most complementary (e.g., the culture–historical and the processual approaches to archaeology).

## Subject–Object Relationships

With this background in mind, we may now distinguish and describe the four different kinds of subject–object relationships that are relevant (Figure 23.5).

### Subject = Object

Imagine that subject and all possible objects are rolled into one ball of infinitely small size. In such a situation, subject and object are identical and indistinguishable. Nor can the subject distinguish between objects, so that it cannot conceive of any relationships between objects, nor of any dimensions

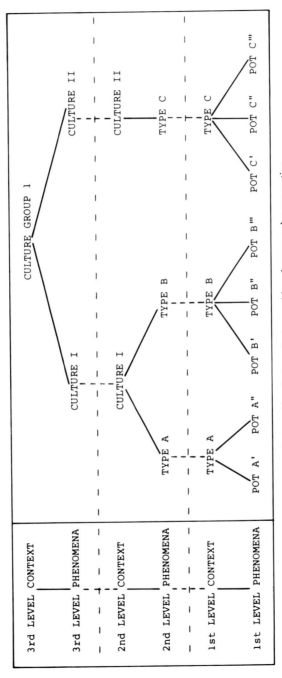

**Figure 23.3.** Culture–historical typologies combine phenomena by summation.

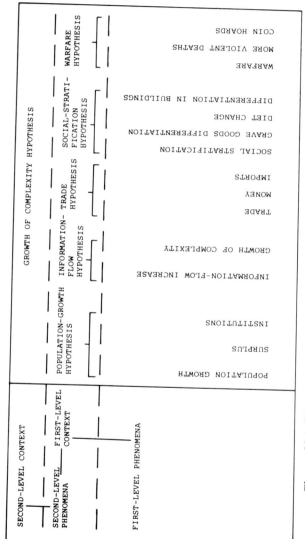

**Figure 23.4.** Hierarchical classifications may also be based on different *fundamenta classificationis* at different levels.

| SUBJECT = OBJECT | SUBJECT ≠ OBJECT | SUBJECT → OBJECT | SUBJECT ⇆ OBJECT |
|---|---|---|---|
| NO DISTINCTION BETWEEN SUBJECT AND OBJECTS | DISTINCTIONS ABSOLUTE BETWEEN SUBJECT AND OBJECTS | SUBJECT AND OBJECT INDEPENDENT ENTITIES | SUBJECT AND OBJECT DEPENDENT ENTITIES |
| NO DISTINCTION BETWEEN OBJECTS | ABSOLUTE DISTINCTION BETWEEN OBJECTS | OBJECT(S) are ABSOLUTE(S) | OBJECT(S) are NOT ABSOLUTE(S) |
|  |  | SUBJECT(S) are NOT ABSOLUTE(S) | SUBJECT(S) are NOT ABSOLUTE(S) |
| NO DIMENSIONS | ABSOLUTE DIMENSIONS | STATISTICAL APPROXIMATION OF ABSOLUTE DIMENSIONS | CONTEXTUAL DIMENSIONS |
| NO CONTEXTS | RELATIONSHIPS between OBJECTS | STATISTICAL EPISTEMOLOGY | CONTEXTUAL EPISTEMOLOGY |
|  | OBJECTIVITY | SUBJECTIVITY | PERCEPTION DEPENDENT on PERCEPTUAL TRANSFORMATION |
|  | REAL, PERMANENT PHENOMENA OUTSIDE SUBJECT | REAL, PERMANENT PHENOMENA OUTSIDE SUBJECT | PHENOMENA PART OF CONTEXT |
|  | UNIVERSALITY PRINCIPLE; INFERENCE = PREDICTION | APPROXIMATE PREDICTIONS POSSIBLE | NO PREDICTION, NO INFERENCE POSSIBLE OUTSIDE CONTEXT |
|  |  |  | NO DISCRETE PHENOMENA |
|  | ISOTROPIC DIMENSIONS | TEMPORAL DIMENSION NONHOMOGENEOUS, ANISOTROPIC | TEMPORAL DIMENSION ANISOTROPIC, NONHOMOGENEOUS, CONTEXTUAL (BIFURCATIONS) |
|  | HOMOGENEOUS DIMENSIONS | SPATIAL DIMENSIONS NONHOMOGENEOUS | SPATIAL DIMENSIONS ANISOTROPIC, NONHOMOGENEOUS, CONTEXTUAL (FIELDS) |

**Figure 23.5.** Four different kinds of subject–object relationships.

(temporal, spatial, or other) or other contexts that may serve as a framework for studying relationships. In short, no distinction of any kind is possible.

## Subject ≠ Object

Whenever subject and object(s) are separate entities, the subject can theoretically achieve all those things that it could not do in the case just outlined, i.e: (*a*) the subject may perceive any number of objects; (*b*) the subject may distinguish and study the relationships between these objects; and (*c*) the subject may, upon studying these relationships, conceive of a (set of) dimension(s) that serve(s) as a framework for such study. (Spatial dimensions are the result of studying phenomena of various sizes and generalizing in such a way that all variability is subsumed.)

The essential characteristic of this case is the absolute nature of subject, object, and subject–object opposition. It does indeed go quite a way beyond their separateness. It assumes the nonexistence of any change in either the subject or the object(s) as a result of observation of the one by the other. This absolute opposition allows the subject to do the following: (*a*) to conceive of a "real world" outside the subject, and thus to strive for "objectivity" in perception and study; (*b*) to assume that "like causes have like effects" (principle of universality) independent of the subject and of the circumstances; (*c*) to conceive of dimensions as absolutes; (*d*) to conceive of dimensions as theoretically homogeneous, so that conceptual tools like interval and ratio scales of measurement may be developed; and to assume that a change in position relative to a dimension may always be compensated for by an equal change in the opposite direction, so that there is no inherent directionality in any dimension (including the temporal and the causal): Dimensions are isotropic.

## Subject → Object

In the third case, subject and object are also independent entities. Moreover, object(s) are conceived of as absolutes, part of the "real world" outside the subject. But perceptions by subjects are not considered absolutes, so that differences in the perception of one and the same (set of) object(s) occur. The result is a "statistical" approach to epistemology, which knows no absolute and independent statements. Instead, it is based on the idea that we have a certain chance to perceive a phenomenon or a dimension in a certain manner. The "average" of such perceptions is considered the best approximation of the "real-world objects." Differences between perceptions are not subject to inquiry. It is considered that they are due to variability extraneous to the subject–object relationship, which cannot and need not be studied. In summary, "subjective" subjects attempt to reconstruct an "intersubjective" image of an "objective" set of phenomena.

In simultaneous perception, this implies that phenomena are perceived as "clusters" or other regularities in distribution, even though they are discrete and absolute in the "real world." The same is true of dimensions. Their manifestation has a degree of "fuzziness" that requires a statistical definition, achieved by means of such techniques as factor analysis or multidimensional scaling. Phenomena as well as dimensions are in this case perceived as nonhomogeneous.

In sequential perception, we have to distinguish between the past and the future. Past phenomena are theoretically perceptible with complete certainty, while our perception of future phenomena may vary and is thus statistical. The temporal dimension may therefore be conceived of as a line from the past to the present that, in the present, is supplanted by a bundle of "half" lines that run toward the future. Each fragment of a line represents a possibility that may come true according to a certain "objective" probability (Von Weizsäcker 1972, 160). Thus, sequential perception is tied to the future (and is thus anisotropic). There is no going back on changes by generating equal changes in the opposite direction.

In relation to perception of the future, the concept of probability is thus essential to a discussion of fundamental concepts. (The place in the bundle of half lines cannot be determined without recourse to probabilities.) Measurement may influence which fragment of a line one hits when testing a hypothesis. Measurement does not therefore so much verify a theory as determine its results. Statistics have a predictive function.

In relation to the perception of the past, probability is not essential. Lacking knowledge may theoretically be obtained by collecting more data. Because that is often very difficult, statistical methods have been used in "predicting the past." Such use is not in keeping with the tenets of the statistical approach. In such cases, statistics have an inferential, not a predictive function (Mellor, Chapter 5 this volume).

Distinction between these two situations is necessary if one is to assess the problems inherent in using the statistical approach in archaeology correctly.

Subject ⇌ Object

The fourth and last case to be discussed is that in which the subject is assumed to be part of a larger structure in which subject and object are interrelated. Thus, the nature of a perception may constrain the nature of the subject's perceptive framework, which may in turn constrain the nature of the perception. Accordingly, the aim of research shifts away from attempting to achieve intersubjective constructs concerning an objective set of phenomena toward study of the relationship between perceptions and perceptive frameworks. The object loses in importance in favor of the perception. The perception is no longer constrained by the object, but by the perceptive framework.

As a result, there are no longer any absolute phenomena or dimensions in simultaneous or sequential perception to be perceived or approximated. Similarly, the principle of universality (like causes have like effects) is no longer valid. Like causes may have unlike effects, or like effects may have unlike causes. There are no set contexts, no set relations between phenomena, no interval or ratio scales of measurement. In their stead should come an appreciation of the nature of the perceptive structure that is the framework for the interrelation of subject and object. Because that structure is "beyond" the subject, it cannot be perceived from "within": The whole cannot be known through the study of its parts and their relations. The appreciation of the nature of the perceptive structure forgoing is, so far, all but nonexistent in the social sciences and humanities; however, a glimpse of the changes that it will bring about may possibly be obtained by considering two related cases in physics.

In the spatial sphere, a similar problem (at a much lower level of generalization) has led to the development of the "field" concept and related theories, in which particles behave according to "force gradients" in which they move (Figure 23.9).

In the temporal sphere, we may use as an illustration the macromodel of thermodynamic interaction ("flow-structure model") developed by Prigogine and his associates (Nicolis and Prigogine 1976, Prigogine 1978, Allen 1980). Both models essentially consider the part as part (i.e., from the perspective of the whole in which it partakes), instead of considering the whole as sum of the parts (i.e., from the perspective of the part). In analysis, therefore, stress is placed upon relations and transformations rather than upon entities in simultaneous or sequential perception. We will develop this theme further in the last part of this chapter.

I hope that this section has encouraged an awareness of the nature and importance of the subject–object relationship in the consideration of any scientific endeavor. The following section will attempt to demonstrate the effect of these cases on archaeological reasoning.

## Subject–Object relationships in archaeology

Before I sketch, in brief paragraphs, the way in which subject–object relationships have constrained archaeological reasoning, it is important to make a few preliminary remarks. The first of these concerns the nature of the subjects and objects in archaeology. Here, we must distinguish the following relationships (Figure 23.6):

   *a.* archaeologist–artifact studied;
   *b.* archaeologist–human studied; and
   *c.* human studied–artifact studied.

The second concerns the development of archaeology. Here, I have chosen a division in stages that does not quite overlap the usual ones. I will distinguish the following phases: (*a*) looking at the artifact; (*b*) looking at the individual; and (*c*)

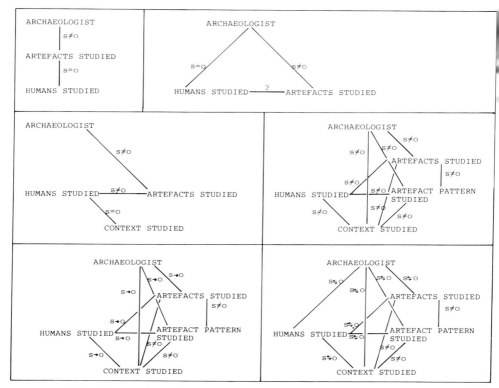

**Figure 23.6.** Different kinds of relationships studied among the archaeologist, the phenomena studied, and past humans.

looking at the system in which humans operate. Evidently, archaeologists have at all times professed to be interested in, and to be concerned with, the study of artifacts, humans, and systems or other contexts. The distinction that we make is dependent upon the operationality of such attempts, rather than upon a statement of aims. In distinguishing and discussing approaches, we must make another reservation: We will not attempt to define "schools" of thought, but rather "platforms": The positions of individual scholars within the discipline differ to such an extent that distinguishing schools demands more space than is available in the present format.

Looking at the Artifact

In the first phase of archaeology, collecting and comparing artifacts and other archaeological phenomena was the main activity (e.g., Thomsen 1837). At one point or other, this led to grouping at different levels ("types" and groups of "types"), thus creating units of perception at a higher level that were homogeneous. In simultaneous perception, these were exemplified by "cultures" in the sense in which Childe used that concept. And in sequential perception they were conceived of as "phases" or "stages" of development (Childe 1950, Rowe 1962). Such units were distinguished on the basis of phenotypical distance between artifacts or, at a higher level, between types. Thus, the spatial and temporal units were relative in nature and dependent upon the phenomena ("cultures" on the distribution of "types" in space and "stages" on their distribution in time).

There were no spatial, temporal, or other dimensions in any absolute sense (cf. Montelius 1904, Hole and Shaw 1967). Indeed, the resistance to the introduction of absolute ($^{14}$C) chronology may well have had something to do with the encompassing nature of the change in perspective required to adopt such an absolute dimension. The absence of such absolute dimensions was closely related to the inadequacy of the explanations for change that were offered: "evolution" for sequential change and "migration" or "diffusion" for spatial change. Migration was particularly telling, as it identifies displacement of artifacts with movement of people. It pointed clearly to an essential aspect of archaeology in this period—the fact that *artifacts, human behavior, and the system in which humans operated often were not distinguished.* Notably, the study of artifacts was regularly confused with the study of past human behavior.

It seems that the three possible subject–object relationships mentioned in the beginning of this section were not always distinguished. Mostly, it appears, artifact analysis was based on the first assumption (archaeologist ≠ artifact studied), while interpretation was based on the third (human studied = artifact studied). Thus, the archaeologist seems to have identified his analytical context (in which the subject ≠ object relation dominated) with his interpretive context (in which the subject = object and the subject ≠ object relations alternated), without recognizing the second (human studied–artifact studied) relationship. Here, subject and object were identified.

A good example of this confusion was the insistence on the objectivity of typology, when the types were clearly the product of subjective judgment (cf. Malmer 1963, Clarke 1968, 38, 522). Similarly, in explaining "typology," Montelius had to resort to his own time and perspective, i.e., by referring to the development of trains that took place in the nineteenth century. Thus, Montelius made use of a subject = object relationship concerning archaeologist–human studied, and of a subject ≠ object relationship concerning archaeologist–artifact studied. Another example is inherent in the "migration" explanation mentioned above. Here, human studied and artifact studied had a subject = object relationship, while archaeologist, artifact, and human studied had a subject ≠ object relationship. Clearly, in this phase in the development of archaeology, there were problems with the intuitively felt difference between the results of artifact studies and human life as it may have been in the past.

Looking at the Individual

In American archaeology, it was the achievement of the developments of the
1960s and early 1970s to have shifted perspective from the artifact to "the
Indian behind it," and to have introduced a clear stress on process. Equally
important was the stress on "being scientific," following strict rules of logic and
attempting replicability (and thus objectivity) of research. Notwithstanding the
fact that in much of the literature from this period the understanding of the
manner in which "science" operates and of various kinds of logic left much to be
desired, the wish to be "scientific" and "objective" seems to have had an
important impact on the development of the discipline. It implies a move
towards a subject $\neq$ object relationship.

One of the consequences was that we are able to distinguish three clear levels
of analysis and theory formulation: (*a*) the lower level, operating between the
artifact and the artifact pattern; (*b*) the middle level, operating between the
artifact pattern and the human activities involved; and (*c*) the higher level,
operating between the humans involved and the structure of which they are
assumed to be a part.

*Microlevel (artifact and artifact pattern).* At this level, I should discuss the
nature of the "raw" data as they come out of the field, that is, the nature of the
individual remains of past human activity (whether these are artifacts or
ecological data or yet other data), the nature of the patterning, and most
important, the nature of the reasoning that brings these together.

The "raw" data are clearly of a physicochemical nature: artifacts, dis-
coloration, pollen, seeds, bones,. etc. Between them and the researcher, the
subject–object relationship is one of absolute distinction, as it is in the "hard"
sciences. It is less easy to define the archaeologist's relationship with the
"human imprint" on these data. Instead of direct "explication" of this aspect
(through identification) as we saw in the last section, we find an attempt to
extend the "objective" approach. Cases in point are the use of technological
artifact research (Keeley 1973, Franken and Kalsbeek 1975, Semenov 1964)
and the use of ethnoarchaeology (e.g., DeBoer and Lathrap, 1979). All are
based on the universality principle. In the former case, the aim is to isolate the
physicochemical variables from the cultural ones through which humans
interact with matter, while in the second case the archaeologist attempts to
achieve an "objective" view of human actions. These developments notwithstanding, it seems to me that "subjective" interpretation still has an
important place at this level.

Artifact patterning of most kinds was also increasingly approached with "objective" aims in mind. Various trends point in that direction, such as objective
typology (e.g., numerical taxonomy), various statistical approaches to spatial
clustering (association analysis, etc.), and ethnoarchaeological research on site
formation (Binford (ed.) Bonnichsen 1973, 1977). In actual practice, however,
many of these techniques are evidently not objective. We have seen in an earlier

section that statistical approaches do not follow the subject ≠ object pattern, but rather a subject → object approach.

This fact introduces complications in the temporal dimension due to the nature of the statistical time conception, and due to the fact that statistics are used inferentially rather than predictively. The exact consequences of this complication are, at present, unknown.

As for ethnoarchaeology, our selection of the ethnographic cases used is often constrained by factors other than the scientific, while the rules for the use of such analogies are rarely followed (e.g., Thompson 1958). Thus, although universalism is the basis of ethnoarchaeological research, such research is not in any way necessarily objective. As a consequence, we have recently seen a growing concern with the bias introduced by using the extant ethnographic record, so often fragmented, as our basis of inference (Wobst 1978).

It seems to be through the reasoning that connects our analyses and that is responsible for the nature of our interpretative models, that "subjectivity" and "identification" keep interfering at this level, perhaps because this phase of our scientific argument is a deductive one. This does not invalidate Binford's argument that it does not matter how we generate a model, provided that its testing is solid, but it does introduce subjectivity (1968).

*Middle level (artifact pattern and human activity).* It may be illustrative to begin this subsection with a discussion of the "polythetic type" concept, introduced by Clarke together with numerical taxonomy (1968). Numerical taxonomy applies a statistical (subject → object) approach to the relationship between archaeologist and artifact (pattern) studied. "Polythetic typology," on the other hand, applies the same statistical subject → object approach to the relationship between past human and artifact patterns. It is based on the argument that although there was a certain "norm" for the manufacture of ancient artifacts, there would be deviations from that norm in any actual society. By presenting numerical taxonomy as a means to reconstruct polythetic types, Clarke thus confused two subject–object relationships.

It would be unfair to hold Clarke responsible for this confusion. Rather, his argument seems typical of a stage in the development of the discipline in which the distinction between the level of human activity and that of artifact (patterns) was being formed. Altogether, we have very little theory at this level (the so-called "middle range theory"), even though many are now stressing the importance of bringing together a body of such "theory" (e.g., Binford 1977).

Typically, however, much of what is brought together refers to the interaction between human and their natural environment: analysis of hunting, fishing, and gathering activities and their concomitant patterning of bone, seeds, artifacts, etc.; analysis of field systems; analysis of the provenience of raw materials, and the subsequent distribution of these materials in a transformed state. In generating such middle range theory, one may be relatively "objective," and may lean rather heavily on physicochemical laws, constants, and the universality principle. Much less well developed are those aspects of theory formation at this level that concern themselves entirely with cultural aspects. One example might be the analysis of decoration on pottery assemblages. Initially, such analysis was confined to ethnoarchaeological studies (e.g., Hardin 1979). Recently, after a number of attempts that did not succeed, decoration has been analyzed for the purpose of relating it to human behavior at a higher level, e.g., at the systems level (cf. Voss 1980, Braun 1980). But analyses at the level of the individual human are lacking in archaeology.

Another example in which the state of the art seems to be similar is that of the determination of activity areas. Ethnoarchaeology was the first area of this development (e.g., Yellen 1977), and statistical approaches were developed for tracing activity areas in the past (e.g., Whallon 1973). However, the link between patterning and human behavior is lacking for archaeological data. Perhaps it is too early to suggest an explanation for the lack of really "cultural" middle range theory. It seems, however, that apart from the brevity of the period during which we devoted attention to the problem, there is another factor responsible. As we move away from materials and the physicochemical world, we move, as it were, away from the object in the form in which it is most clearly opposable to the subject (humans), and we move toward that subject. *Its regularities can only be studied in the context of some knowledge about the workings of human information processing.* It is in that area that we lack any generalization, any "grip." It seems to me that we cannot successfully achieve a corpus of middle range theory until we have filled this gap. That can only happen at a higher level of generalization—where we are no longer concerned with individuals but with large numbers of humans.

*Macrolevel (human activity and its context).* Certainly, this problem is more palpable at the next higher level, where the relationship between the activity of (individual and aggregates of) humans and the context in which these operate is at issue. This relationship was not explicit in much of earlier archaeology and has only been stressed after the introduction of the "systems" approach. Evidently, there are two kinds of context involved, the natural and the cultural. Both led to the subdisciplines "ecological archaeology" and "cultural ecology," respectively. The main inherent difference from our point of view is one that has already been stressed in a different context. The natural environment could be studied more effectively in a subject $\neq$ object framework than could the cultural. Hence the natural environment is much better known than the cultural environment, which requires an adequate approach to the subjectivity problem before any scientific study can take place.

Crosscutting this distinction between natural and cultural context is one that concerns the way in which one looks at that context (Figure 23.9). The interface between human activity and its context may be approached from two vantage points, that of the human(s) and that of the context. Each approach has its own kind of subject–object relationship. The former, based on the study of artifacts, artifact patterns, and human behavior, operates in a subject $\neq$ object framework. In theoretical arguments, that framework is somewhat tenuously maintained by arguing that the humans involved are "others," with a different cultural baggage and that we therefore are able to judge them "objectively" (cf. arguments against cultural relativism or historicism). The other approach, based on a more abstract concept of "context," has fewer "hard" data (i.e., data of a physicochemical nature) to build on, and it attempts to achieve a notably more "cultural" interpretation. It is, thus far, the least explicit in its methodology (in archaeology proper, at least), and thus runs a greater risk of incorporating intuitive (i.e., subject = object) interpretations.

I have the impression from the archaeological literature that this problem has not received much attention, and that *in general, archaeologists have used the first approach.* Some examples may illustrate that thesis. Economic issues, for example, are approached either from a decision-making approach or by studying flows of matter and energy through the system. Both approaches look at individual entities (either the individual humans who are making the decisions or the aggregate of quanta of matter and energy that flow). In the latter case, we do not ask what *structures* the flows; we merely study them as if moving through channels that have been otherwise established.

Similarly, our (i.e., archaeologists') use of the "feedback" concept seems telling. In general systems theory, such feedback is instantaneous—an inherent part of the systemic context used to analyze data. In archaeology, on the other hand, feedback is considered a sequence of events through time that connects a chain of entities by means of a series of exchanges. It is interesting to see how the essential part played in general systems theory by information flows has not been incorporated into archaeological systems approaches that have heavily stressed matter and energy flows. Information, as opposed to matter and energy, is not subject to the laws of conservation, and is thus the only commodity of the three with a solid claim as a structuring element in human interactions.

The first (sum-of-the-parts) approach to the (human) context allows for the use of universalist principles, experiments, ethnoarchaeological data, etc., and entails some degree of functionalism. Moreover, it stresses the dependence of systems on the natural world, often to the point of determinism. It requires isolation of (closed) systems that exchange little or nothing with the outside world. Such systems are considered as aggregates of subsystems. "Society" is conceived of as an aggregate of individuals moving in a context (environment) but without a cohesion of their own. Spatially, this approach favors regional research, if possible of isolated regions (*Siedlungskammer*). And sequentially, the system is perceived either as a point in time (homeostatic system) or changing, as a point moving in a temporal dimension that is conceived as homogeneous and anisotropic (= evolutionary). In the latter case, we speak of morphogenetic systems. Clearly, all these facts point in the direction of considerable use of this (sum-of-the-parts) approach by archaeologists concerned with interpretation at this (uppermost) level.

Last among the topics to be discussed in this section is that of the nature of the dimensions that we have created by looking at the past in the preceding manner.

Clearly, the differences between approaches at various levels are also reflected in the way in which dimensions are used. But, overriding these differences, we have a set of dimensions for "the past" as a whole. This set has also undergone important changes in comparison to the "world view" discussed in the last section. Clearly, the most important of these is the fact that archaeology has introduced *absolute* dimensions, notably in sequential perception ($^{14}C$ dating, absolute chronology, tree-ring research, etc.), but also in simultaneous perception. In the latter, we no longer define our cultural units entirely relative to archaeological remains. More and more, transects are part of our research universe, as are soil maps and other ecological data that, together, enable us to conceive of cultural phenomena as happening *in* an area instead of "being" the area by definition. Perhaps the most important step in that direction is a direct consequence of Binford's insistence upon the fact that humans participate differentially in culture (1965).

### Looking at the System in Which Humans Operate

Recently, attention has been drawn to the need to "consider the larger systems in which separate social units are linked." Core–periphery models (Wallerstein 1975) have come into vogue (Paynter 1980, in press) and now figure alongside cluster–interaction models (Price 1977) and related kinds of models built within a structural–Marxist framework (Friedman and Rowlands, 1977). Others have argued for the introduction of the concept of "perceived environment." A somewhat earlier development began by noting the problems inherent in "feedback–loop explanation" if one wants to transcend the study of the individual homeostatic system (Wright 1969, 1977, Johnson 1973, 1978, 1980). After reading the preceding remarks, it will come as no surprise that many of these pointers in a new direction come from those involved with research at the macrolevel and, to a somewhat lesser degree, from those working at the middle level ("middle range theory"). These groups of archaeologists are the ones directly confronted with the absence of a coherent "cultural" point of view that allows them to study the human input in the interaction between man and his (entire) environment.

Searching, as is required, for a structuring principle "beyond" the humans studied essentially creates a subject $\leftrightarrows$ object relationship between the archaeologist and his context and between man in the past and his environment. The two structures need not be identical and need not even be transformations of one another. As a consequence, this kind of research creates an essential relativity that is inherent and inevitable. Time and place become relative dimensions: They may even turn out to be nonhomogeneous, and they certainly will be anisotropic. The universality principle will no longer be a sufficient basis for comparison or analogy. Rather, we will have to study the context generated by individual cultures as we are studying the impulses that result from those contexts, and we will then proceed by assessing the relationship between context and phenomena.

## Some Conclusions of Part I

Looking back on this brief overview of the different kinds of subject–object relationships *and the part they have played and are playing in archaeology*, we may conclude the following:

1. That each of the approaches taken has in itself been profitable, and in many cases, will continue to be of use.
2. That most of the problems reside in the fact that the relationship between the results and the past has remained unclear, as well as the relationship between those results and the archaeologists involved.
3. That a number of our present problems arise from the fact that our epistemological structure, our theory, and our methodology do not equip us to study the context of human institutions from a cultural perspective.
4. That there has been considerable confusion between different levels of analysis, the topics to be addressed at those levels, and the analytical techniques used to address these problems.
5. That constructing an approach that is directed at some of the problems mentioned will necessarily involve taking a subject ⇌ object position as a basis, and therefore will introduce a considerable degree of relativity in our arguments. It will have to be applied to the highest level first.

## PART II: AN APPROACH TO THE CONTEXT OF HUMAN INSTITUTIONS

### Preamble

The last conclusion of the preceding section may have been thought pessimistic. What is the use of approaching a discipline, or part of a discipline, with a set of tools based on such a shaky, relativistic framework? The answer may be given at two levels, the practical and the theoretical. First, at the practical level, our current approaches to the study of genesis and decay of human institutions have come to a halt as far as overall interpretation is concerned. We cannot study transformations between institutions of varying form before we have a framework within which we can undertake such an operation. At present, we do not even have an accepted basis for comparison between institutions of different character.

Multicausal "systemic" models have at most been able to provide explanations in specific cases through the use of deviation amplification as a concept. Comparative studies of the growth of complexity through this approach have been bogged down. Approaches based on a random interaction model (i.e., a statistical model), such as those drawn from "classical" information theory, have been able to study organizational stages in a theoretical manner and have come up with quite interesting results. These results relate to (*a*) interaction and structuring in small groups; (*b*) the *when* and *how* of organizational responses to the processing of more information; and (*c*) the decay of organizations due to increasing entropy. Such studies, however, have not been able to come up with a *why* for organizational changes, and that is the question we are ultimately asking. At the theoretical level, we must note that in order to achieve interpretation of human institutions, we need to create a frame of reference. As the phenomena are at the level of aggregates of humans, the context needs to be at a level beyond these. Hence, there is no escaping the problems mentioned: We can only interpret "better" at the cost of directly relating the interpretation to our own world view.

If we accept for the moment the need to build an approach to the context of human institutions, the next question is: How can we avoid falling into the pits into which the cultural relativists and historicists have somersaulted with such aplomb? The main reason for their somersault seems to have been that they began to "relativize" without a *context*. Let us take cultural relativism as an example. Here, phenomena within each society were judged within the context that that society offered. As such, they were therefore exempt from judgment against another context—that of the observer. Cultural relativism may be seen as an attempt to create a subject $\neq$ object relationship between anthropologist and cultural context where, up to that point, these two quantities had been tied into a subject = object relationship.

Here, essentially we want to do something different. We want to create a context *over and above* individual cultural contexts, so that we may compare these contexts themselves. To achieve that, we need to choose an explanatory principle that is essentially applicable to all human institutions and societies. We have chosen as such an explanatory principle the nature of information-processing in groups, based on the premise that we need not concern ourselves with individual behavior or with individual trajectories of processed bits of information because what structures human behavior in the long run is a certain nonrandomness in the distribution of all of these individual trajectories.

## A "Flow Structure" Approach

Any approach that is to grapple successfully with the problem of designing a "context" or "structure" within which we can analyze human institutions must fill the following prerequisites:

1. *Self-structuring.* As we wish to design a structure "beyond" human institutions, the structure cannot be structured by humans. It must, in some way or other, be self-structuring.
2. *Contextual.* By the same token, the structure is required to "explain" human institutions, and to be "explained" by the nature of human information-processing. The relationship between the structure and humans must thus be a subject $\rightleftharpoons$ object relationship.

3. *Anisotropic Sequential Perception.* As human sequential perception seems to be anisotropic, always moving from past through present to future, the temporal dimension generated by the interaction between "structure" and humans is necessarily nonisotropic.
4. *Accounting for Growth and Decay.* Nevertheless, the approach should be able to account for both growth and decay in human institutions. Decay cannot, in this construction, be conceived of as the reverse of growth.
5. *Bridging Argument.* If the approach is to be one that can easily be made operational, it should include a bridging argument that ties it to the highest present level of analysis—that of the behavior of human aggregates.

In the following brief sketch of the line of thought followed, I will, *entirely for the sake of argument and elegance*, begin with that bridging argument, even though these ideas were not originally developed in this way.

I shall begin with the nature of human institutions. These may be conceived of as exchange mechanisms and exchange channels, by and through which matter, energy, and information are exchanged. Of these three commodities, the first two are subject to the laws of conservation, and therefore cannot be considered as "structuring." Information, on the other hand, can spread freely, and is therefore the only one of the three that may serve as a link between individuals. It is thus the only potential "structuring" commodity of the three.

The first theoretical framework that comes to mind—communications theory—has traditionally been directed at studying information that moves through channels established and maintained by other means (i.e., telephone cables, etc.). It has thus conceived of the information by means of a random approach. Nonrandomness is message, randomness is noise. The direction of the message was determined by the channel (and thus is outside the bounds of study). This approach could never meet our first prerequisite, i.e., that it be self-structuring. Any random approach is essentially self-*un*structuring because it is subject to the second law of classical thermodynamics: Total entropy within a system grows in the absence of exchanges with the outside.

If the approach we choose is to explain the "why" of structuring as well as the "how," it must be able to account for nonstructured as well as structured situations. This criterion is met by so-called "diffusion–reaction systems" such as those described by Rosen (1979). Here, a potential in an otherwise random situation generates nonrandomness. Were we able to construe or find a self-perpetuating, self-amplifying potential in the homogeneous system, we would have found a self-structuring principle. The potential we are looking for seems to be inherent in our two-level approach to information-processing. Assuming a basic dependency between phenomena and context, an enhanced flow of information would seem to widen the scope of the context. Such widening, in turn, would cause the information flow to grow even more. There is thus a mutual amplifying effect—an effect that could push minor deviations (well within the range of variation in a random situation) progressively further apart so that the natural trend toward growing entropy is reversed. It is an effect, moreover, that does not follow a linear function. The "nesting" of hierarchical contexts we are talking about should, it seems, be seen as a discontinuous process. First, a certain context is "filled" to the point where it encompasses the maximum amount of information that it can handle. At that point, there is a *sudden* breakthrough to a higher-context level. Filling it in turn is at first a rapid process. Slowly but surely, the rate at which it is filled slows until a stagnant point is reached that prepares the system for another jump (cf. Figure 23.7). Except for the infinitesimally brief moments before such a jump, there is thus a potential between the processing capacity of the context and the world outside the subject. It is this potential that generates a flow of information.

So far, information-processing has been described as an individual activity. How should we see this process as a group phenomenon? In a group, it is the shared contexts that permit human communication. These contexts come to be shared by information exchange. They will thus nest as the total amount of information exchanged within a group expands. Thus, the more information a group processes, the more is exchanged, and the higher the potential. The effect on the group can be modeled on the basis of some of the results of "interaction analysis" such as that presented by Mayhew, Levinger, and others, and from a slightly different angle by Johnson in this volume (Mayhew and Levinger 1976, Johnson Chapter 21 this volume). Growing interaction in small groups creates hierarchization because, as more information is processed, this causes higher rates of interaction among some members of the group. Such higher rates in turn push the potential up, and so on. In the end the group is stratified on the basis of

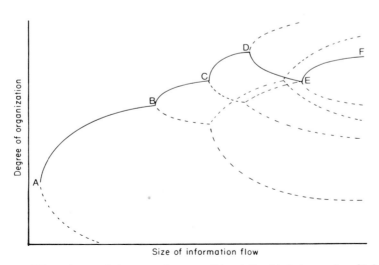

**Figure 23.7.** Bifurcation graph demonstrating a possible relationship between size of information flow and degree of organization in a flow structure. The solid line represents one possible trajectory of the system. The broken lines represent alternative choices that were not made.

amount of information processed per unit time: Those who process most are at the top. To keep their position, they will have to create a special-purpose transmission context. This is done by means of special purpose symboling, specialization, etc. Not everyone at the top interacts with everyone lower down any longer, while those at lower levels may in time come to specialize as well— albeit to a somewhat lesser degree. Structurally, the situation may be visualized as the functioning of a vortex. As long as it is expanding, the vortex will need ever-increasing amounts of information to be processed. This is achieved by exploration, intensification, specialization, etc. As soon as the situation becomes stagnant, the potential decreases, and the structure dissipates (Figure 23.8).

The model that underlies these arguments has been developed in mathematics by Türing (1952), in chemistry by Prigogine and his coworkers (Nicolis and Prigogine 1977, Prigogine 1978), and has recently been applied to the development of urban areas by Allen (1980). It has been discussed in this volume by Allen, Rosen, and Segraves-Whallon, and elsewhere by van der Leeuw (in press). I will therefore refrain from going into any of the details in this chapter. I would, however, like to point to a few of its more salient characteristics.

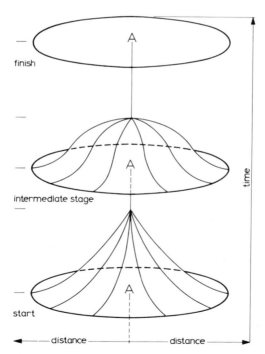

**Figure 23.8.** Information-flow structure going through the stages of (a) growing potential; (b) decreasing potential; and (c) potential spent (Adapted from Abler, Adams, and Gould, 1977.)

1. The model cannot be understood by observation of its parts. The study of the thermodynamic phenomena for which it was originally developed has been undertaken "from below" with as little success as we have had in explaining the growth of complexity in the past.
2. Graphical representation of the process of structuring that takes place leads to the bifurcating graph presented in Figure 23.7. There is a clear implication of both deterministic (line) and the statistical (bifurcating points) elements. As the curve (development within the same organizational level) slows down, any of the oscillations that occur may lead to modification of the system either by the timely invention of a new, more encompassing context level or by the failure to do so and the inherent decay that follows. (Most clearly, the difference with the present approach is summarized by noting that a crisis, generally perceived as the coming together of a number of unexpected and difficult circumstances, may now be seen as a temporary incapacity of the information-processing system to deal with the amount of processing required.)
3. It is important to note that it is impossible to derive knowledge concerning the trajectory of the system from observing it at one point in time. The whole process must be followed in order to know it. Needless to say, this has important consequences for archaeologists. The graph in Figure 23.7 makes this point very clearly: Observation of the system at point $E$ does not betray which one of the many trajectories has been followed on its way to that point.
4. Spatially, an application of this approach leads to the stipulation of fields around points with a different information potential. These fields may be represented by gradients across physical space that are manifest only at those points were material remains indicate differences in the amount and organization of information-processing. There will be no absolute boundaries, only gradients of varying steepness (Figure 23.9).
5. Physical space is, in this approach, not identical to "real space." From the point of view of those participating in one or more institutions, "perceived space" is a much more real thing.
6. Interaction and its intensity may be traced archaeologically in many ways. Enumerating them here would carry us too far. I refer the reader to the publications by Kramer (in press), Feinman (1980), Rice (in press), and van der Leeuw (1981).

## CONCLUSION

The purpose of this chapter has been to present some of the reasons behind my involvement in recent years with the "flow-structure" approach based on Prigogine's work. Primarily, this is the need for a coherent model of human

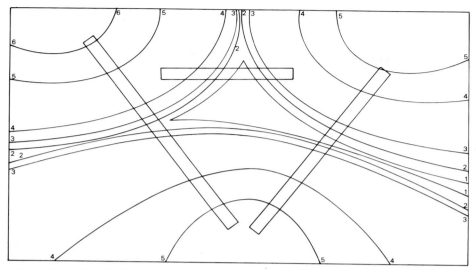

**Figure 23.9.** Hypothetical reconstruction of a field with three highs, made on the basis of data from two transects.

perception and information-processing. Only with such a model in hand may we study what humans do to their environment, to themselves, and to each other. Only such a model may explain the clear negentropic aspects of human culture and its institutions. Designing such a model implies leaving the "objectivist" approach to data, and recognizing the fact that perception is a field of tension between distance from and involvement with the phenomena observed (subject ⇌ object approach). Such a shift in epistemology, in my opinion, does not necessarily imply being "unscientific." On the contrary, it may deepen and widen our insight if we know how it is arrived at, and what its relation is to our own life. That is not to say that we sould condone idiosyncrasy in our discipline, but only to imply that knowing how information-processing affects aggregates of humans may be of help in knowing something about the past.

## ACKNOWLEDGMENTS

    The author would like to take this occasion to thank a number of colleagues publicly who have, directly or indirectly, contributed to the development of the ideas put forward in this paper. Among them are the staff of the Albert Egges van Giffen Instituut voor Pre- en Protohistorie, and notably the participants in the Assendelver Polders Project. Outside Amsterdam, my gratitude goes to Martin Wobst, Bob Whallon and Barbara Segraves-Whallon, Greg Johnson, Henry Wright, Chris Peebles, Margaret Ann Hardin, Colin Renfrew, Ian Hodder, and Bob Paynter in chronological order. Also, while writing, I have profited from discussions with and remarks from Esther Hicks, Bert Voorrips, Klavs Randsborg, and Caroline Steele.

# REFERENCES

Allen, P. M., 1980, The evolutionary paradigm of dissipative structures. (Paper presented at the annual meetings of the American Association for the Advancement of Science, January 1980.)

Binford, L. R., 1965, Archaeological systematics and the study of culture process, *American Antiquity* 31, 203–210.

Binford, L. R., 1968, Archaeological perspectives, in Binford, L. R., S. R. (eds.), *New Perspectives in Archaeology,* Chicago, Aldine, 5–32.

Binford, L. R., (ed.), 1977, *For Theory Building in Archaelogy,* New York, Academic Press.

Bonnichsen, R., 1973, Millie's camp: an experiment in ethnoarchaeology, *World Archaeology* 4, 277–291.

Braun, D. P., 1980, Neolithic regional cooperation, a Midwestern example. (Paper presented at the annual meetings of the Society for American Archaeology, April 1980.)

Childe, V. G., 1950, *Prehistoric Migrations in Europe,* Oslo.

Clarke, D. L., 1968, *Analytical Archaeology,* London, Methuen.

DeBoer, W., and Lathrap, D., 1979, The making and breaking of Shipibo–Conibo ceramics, in Kramer, C. (ed.), *Ethnoarchaeology,* New York, 102–138, Columbia U.P.

Feinman, G., 1980, Changing administrative organization: its effects on ceramic production in prehispanic Oaxaca, Mexico, in Blanton, R., Kowalewski, S., Feinman, G., and Appel, J. (eds.), *Prehispanic Settlement Patterns in the Valley of Oaxaca, Mexico, Volume II, The Central and Southern Regions,* in press.

Franken, H. J., and Kalsbeek, J., 1975, *Potters of a Medieval Village in the Jordan Valley,* Amsterdam, Elsevier.

Friedman, J., and Rowlands, M. (eds.), 1977, *The Evolution of Social Systems,* London, Duckworth.

Hardin, M. A., 1979, The cognitive basis of productivity in a decorative art style: implications of an ethnographic study for archaeologists' taxonomies, in Kramer, C. (ed.), *Ethnoarchaeology,* New York, 75–101, Columbia U.P.

Hole, F., and Shaw, M., 1967, *Computer Analysis of Chronological Seriation,* Houston, Rice University Publications.

Johnson, G. A., 1973, *Local Exchange and Early State Development in Southwestern Iran,* Anthropological Papers, Museum of Anthropology, University of Michigan, Ann Arbor, 51.

Johnson, G. A., 1978, Information sources and the development of decision-making organizations, in Redman, C. L., and others (eds.), *Social Archaeology, Beyond Subsistence and Dating,* New York, 87–112, Academic Press.

Johnson, G. A. 1980, Rank-size convexity and system integration, *Economic Geography.*

Johnson, G. A., in press, *Organizational response to scalar stress.* (Paper presented at the Second TAG Conference, Southampton, December, 1980.

Keeley, L., 1973, Technique and method of microwear studies: a critical review, *World Archaeology* 5, 323–336.

Kramer, C., in press, Variability, complexity and spatial organization in Southwest Asian Settlements, in Van der Leeuw, S. E., (ed.), *Archaeological Approaches to the Study of Complexity,* Amsterdam, I.P.P. (Cinqula VI).

Malmer, M. P., 1963, *Metodproblem inom Jarnalderns Konsthistoria,* Lund, (Acta Archaeologica Lundensia in 8°, vol. 3)

Mayhew, B. H., and Levinger, R. L., 1976, Size and the density of interaction in human aggregates, *American Journal of Sociology* 82, 86–110.

Montelius, O., 1904, *Die Typologische Methode,* Stockholm, author's edition.

Nicolis, G. and Prigogine, I., 1977, *Self-organization in nonequilibrium systems,* New York, Academic Press.

Paynter, R., 1980, *Long distance processes, stratification and settlement pattern,* doctoral dissertation, Department of Anthropology, Massachussetts–Amherst.

Paynter, R., in press, Social complexity in peripheries: problems and models, in Van der Leeuw, S. E. (ed.), *Archaeological Approaches to the Study of Complexity,* Amsterdam, I.P.P. (Cingula VI).

Price, B., 1977, *Shifts in Production and Organization: A Cluster-interaction Model,* Current Anthropology 18, no. 2, pp. 209–34.

Prigogine, I., 1978, Time, structure and fluctuations, *Science* 201, 777–785.

Rice, P. M., in press, Evolution of specialized pottery production: a trial model, *Current Anthropology.*

Rosen, R., 1979, Morphogenesis in biological and social systems, in Renfrew, A. C. and Cooke, K. L. (eds.), *Transformations, Mathematical Approaches to Culture Change,* New York, Academic Press 91–111.

Rowe, J. H., 1962, Worsaae's Law and the use of grave lots for archaeological dating, *American Antiquity* 28, 129–137.

Russell, B., 1903, *Principles of Mathematics,* New York.

Semenov, S. A., 1964, *Prehistoric Technology,* (translated from the Russian), London, Cory, Adams & MacGay.

Thompson, R. H., 1958, *Modern Yucatecan Maya Pottery Making,* Memoir 15, Society for American Archaeology, Salt Lake City.

Thomsen, C., 1837, *Leitfaden zur Nordischen Altertumskunde,* Copenhagen, kgl. Nordiske Oldskrift-Selskab.

Türing, A. M., 1952, The chemical basis of morphogenesis, *Philosophical Transactions of the Royal Society,* B, 237, 5–72.

Van der Leeuw, S. E., in press, Information flows, flow structures and the explanation of change in Archaeology, in Van der Leeuw, S. E. (ed.), *Archaeological Approaches to the Study of Complexity,* Amsterdam, I.P.P. (Cingula VI).

Voss, J. A., 1980, The measurement and evaluation of change in the regional social networks of egalitarian societies: an example from the Neolithic of northwestern Europe. (Paper presented at the annual meetings of the society for American Archaeology, May 3, 1980.)

Von Weizsäcker, C. F., 1972, *Die Einheit der Natur,* München.

Wallerstein, I., 1975, The Modern World System, Capitalist Agriculture and the Origin of the European World Economy in the 16th century, New York, Academic Press.

Whallon, R., 1973, Spatial analysis of occupation floors I: the application of dimensional analysis of variance, *American Antiquity* 38, 266–278.

Wobst, H. M., 1978, The archaeo–ethnology of hunter–gatherers or the tyranny of the thnographic record in archaeology, *American Antiquity* 43, 303–309.

Wright, H. T., 1968, *The Administration of Rural Production in An Early Mesopotamian Town,* Anthropological Papers, University of Michigan, Museum of Anthropology, No. 38, Ann Arbor.

Wright, H. T., 1977, Toward an explanation of the origin of the state, in Hill, J. N. (ed.), *The Explanation of Culture Change,* Albuquerque, School of American Research and University of New Mexico Press.

Yellen, J., 1977, *Archaeological Approaches to the Present,* New York, Academic Press.

# Comment: The Emergence of Structure

*COLIN RENFREW*

It is my feeling that the chapters in Part II of this volume open the way for major new developments in our understanding of the formation of complex societies.

Up to a decade or so ago, one of the principal approaches to this question employed the use of a systems model, laying great stress upon *homeostatic* mechanisms. Change within the system was seen to originate in the response of the system—through mechanisms of negative feedback—to changes in the environment of the system. These might be climatic or ecological or indeed social, if there were significant changes in the organization or behavior of neighboring polities. This focus is reflected in many of the contributions to an interesting seminar held in 1970 and published under the title *The Explanation of Prehistoric Change* (Hill 1977).

A second phase in systems thinking, as applied to early societies, was introduced by a new emphasis upon *positive* feedback. Positive feedback within subsystems and especially positive feedback between subsystems—the multiplier effect—were seen as processes essential to growth, and hence to complexity. This approach was termed by Maruyama "the second cybernetics." He wrote (Maruyama 1963, 66) that:

> The secret of the growth of the city is in the process of deviation amplifying mutual positive feedback networks rather than in the initial condition or in the initial kick. This process rather than the initial condition has generated the complexly structured city. It is

**459**

THEORY AND EXPLANATION
IN ARCHAEOLOGY

in this sense that the deviation-amplifying mutual causal process is called "morphogenesis."

We have now in archaeology, I believe, entered a third phase, where the insights of these two previous phases are seen as valuable, but as incomplete. Under the influence of catastrophe theory, and hence inevitably of the work of Christopher Zeeman (1977), I 1978, 221, wrote citing the preceding passage from Maruyama, a couple of years ago that:

> It is becoming clearer now, however, and despite these words, that the crux of the analysis does in fact lie precisely in that initial condition, which can make that random initial kick so crucially decisive, when in other conditions such a small kick or perturbation would be insignificant, mere noise. For the behaviour is crucially determined by the position of the initial conditions, relative to the (unseen) catastrophe set, which is itself governed by the global topology of the singularity.

This third phase offers several valuable new ingredients, some foreseen in a valuable paper by Rosen (1979), to which Sander E. van der Leeuw referred in Chapter 23 in this volume, and which I know has influenced his thinking.

Catastrophe theory, whose potential application to the field of societal evolution Christopher Zeeman (Chapter 18 this volume) has so elegantly demonstrated for us, offers powerful new insights into the phenomena of sudden change, of discontinuity, and of bifurcation. It is worth remarking that this application, with its analagous use of the cusp catastrophe in relation to decision in the economic field, to biological evolution, and to societal change, could easily find a place within what is often termed general systems theory.

But the potential impact of catastrophe theory upon archaeology is much greater and wider than this. For most archaeologists, this is the first introduction to a framework of thought—that of the branch of mathematics known as topology—where the global behavior of dynamical systems is studied. It involves the careful consideration of the key notion of stability and the use of such potentially helpful concepts as those of attractor surfaces in multidimensional space and, to use Waddington's term (1977, 110), "the epigenetic landscape." It gives new scope to the notion of the "trajectory" of a system, and emphasizes such useful distinctions as those here employed by Zeeman between local and global optima. These things are not special to catastrophe theory but they become part of the necessary mental equipment of anyone seeking to grasp its essentials.

I should interpolate here that any reader approaching this subject for the first time will understandably be vexed at what will seem, coming from an archaeologist, as a massively pretentious dose of jargon, lifted straight from an entirely separate discipline in a manner calculated more to confuse than to illuminate. But it is the opinion of all the authors in Part III that these ideas are important and enlightening to our thinking about processes of change. That being so, it is necessary to use the concepts and hence the terminology of that discipline, whose potential relevance is becoming clear to us. I would claim then that what would be jargon in our own field, if it were irrelevant to it or merely expressing what is already known to us in some new and obscure way, is in fact the means to a valuable extension in our thought.

Peter Allen in his useful chapter (Chapter 19 this volume) has introduced to us a further, relatively new approach, which, although starting with questions in chemistry rather than topology, has much in common with the catastrophe-theory approach to morphogenesis. The lucid demonstration by the "Brussels School" that nonequilibrium systems can have self-organizing properties and that structure can emerge spontaneously (in a sense) from homogeneity (although at the expense of dissipation of energy, a point that avoids the infringement of the second law of thermodynamics) has much to offer us. One aspect that is usefully explored in the discussion of Allen's chapter is the role of stochastic elements in the formation of such structure, for although its general features may be predictable (sometimes with a range of alternatives), its precise form is not. There are points of similarity here, therefore, with the process familiar in simulation studies where stochastic process is introduced by the use of random numbers to determine the specific location of new elements introduced to the system or to fix the initial value of other parameters. It is, however, the generation of successive bifurcations that gives the behavior of the system its greater richness of variety and that is one important element of the process of self-organization, and hence the formation of structure.

In a general sense, these are precisely the problems that face the archaeologist or anthropologist in contemplating the emerging structures and patterned behaviors that together amount to complex society. This relevance to our work was well brought out in the chapter by Barbara Abbott Segraves (Chapter 16 this volume), and is exemplified in Allen's application to urban growth. It is implied also in Johnson's contribution (Chapter 21 this volume), with its persuasive demonstration of the relationship between complexity and size of unit in human societies, tending to the avoidance of stress and of inefficiency in communication. Johnson was careful to point out, however, that while the correlation is a powerful one at the macroscale, it is much less so when a limited size range is examined. This observation is important, since it counteracts any suggestion that simple growth alone can be used in any specific case to predict an increase in complexity through the development of further hierarchical structure. Growth therefore does not automatically generate complexity. Nor does his chapter seek to suggest that there is any necessarily innate tendency toward growth in human society: We cannot simply rely on population increase as some universal "prime mover."

Many archaeologists and anthropologists will feel, not unreasonably, that the investigation of general principles of self-organization cannot tell us very much about human society as such, that the rich network of interpersonal relations of any human society are not to be modeled in what may seem a mechanistic way. Yet there need be no contradiction here. Workers on Maya settlement pattern, for instance, have commented that one organizing principle that may have been used is conformity with the points of the compass. But this expression of human intentionality does not prevent a correspondence with some of the principles of central place theory (Marcus 1973). Likewise, for specific settlement forms, Wheatley (1971) in his book *The Pivot of the Four Quarters* has laid stress on the cognitive factors influencing the layout of Chinese urban centers, without suggesting that they do not at the same time conform to the more general principles postulated by urban geographers.

If structures of new kinds are generated as a result of human interactions, without the necessary intervention of any prior human intention that they be formed, as the perspective of the "Brussels School" implies, there are interesting consequences. For although the human conceptualization of these structures—that is to say the meaning that they have within society—is not a precondition to their formation, it will certainly not long be delayed subsequently. For cognitive archaeologists, therefore, and for those concerned with the interpretations and meanings of things within the society's own patterns of though, interesting new possibilities arise. We should be asking new questions about the range of human intellectual response in forming symbolic concepts to cope cognitively with these emergent structures.

This, I believe, sets the whole current discussion about cognitive archaeology (which arises in part from the background of structural anthropology) upon a new basis. The current tendency within that school of thought is to study "meaning" and cognitive structure primarily in relation to other cognitive structures and symbolic forms and often to examine the coherence of these within some logically consistent thought structure. In the current terminology, this is an "emic" or cognitive approach, which is advocated by its adherents as more interesting and fruitful than the "etic" or operational approach that they see as a feature of much contemporary archaeology, and conceive as preventing it in large measure from recognizing the operation of the human mind and the human ability to give pattern to experience.

Here now we see a new range of questions concerning the interaction of the self-organized structure with the symbolic formulation by which a specific society or culture assimilates that structure to its thought and understanding. The approach thus suggests the possibility of examining more thoroughly the interaction of the "etic" upon the "emic," of the operational upon the cognized. It may suggest a systematic reexamination of the way in which individual societies ascribe meaning to the structures that arise within them.

The interaction is of course a two-way one, and one of the most interesting features of the simulation approach outlined by Doran in his chapter (Chapter 20 this volume) was his recognition of this point and its incorporation within his model.

The approach to the past that seems to be emerging here might well be characterized as yet a further paradigm to add to those that have been discussed in the chapters in this book. It is, however, one that may find it possible to obey Lewis Binford's injunction (Chapter 10 this volume) that ways must be found of relating theory to data, and data to theory, if the paradigm is to have any enduring use in the construction of archaeological understanding, and to avoid the status of a mere exercise in logical self-consistency or of a simple translation of existing ideas into a superficially attractive new terminology. For the theory is concerned with the emergence of pattern, and the search for pattern in the data is a basic concern of the archaeologist. The necessary mediating arguments and concepts must still be forged, as Binford urges. But I felt Johnson's contribution to be a particularly relevant and encouraging one in this respect, in its successful shift in level of approach from the general, in terms of concepts relating to hierarchy, to the particular data, and from the data back to the concepts.

There are then several important elements that may come together to form this new morphogenetic paradigm in archaeology. The first is the concept of "system trajectory," seen not merely in traditional system-theory terms, but in the dynamical sense facilitated by differential topology, including catastrophe theory. The second is the whole approach to self-organizing systems, pioneered by the "Brussels School," which overlaps in some respects with the foregoing. The third is preoccupation with information flow, stressed by van der Leeuw, and cogently set out by Johnson in his chapter in this volume and in earlier publications. The fourth element is computer simulation, if it can be developed to cope with the complexity that we are dealing with in such a way as to escape the inflexibility of so many algorithms: The enthusiasm of Doran gives hope that it can. Finally, as I have suggested before, further work is needed on cognitive aspects of human society in a manner that can be interrelated with the other elements of the developing approach, rather than being content to stand apart, and indeed aloof, from the foregoing approaches as does so much current work in this direction.

Amidst the optimism, it is appropriate however to end upon a note of caution. As Lewis Binford has well said, a paradigm is not an explanation. So far, in applying this new morphogenetic paradigm or its elements to human society, we have not actually explained anything at all. What is on offer is a way of thought that may lead to the formulation of useful and valid explanatory theories, together with some clearly formulated and well-tried methods from neighboring disciplines and a considerable wealth of experience. It would be well to avoid the "oversell" that has obscured the real, but sometimes modest, merits of other paradigmatic approaches in recent years. We may have here, as I am inclined to believe, one of the most fruitful approaches to our general problems currently available. But let no eulogistic incantation about epigenetic landscape and self-organizing systems obscure from us that what we have at present are opportunities, not results. The millennium has not yet come.

# REFERENCES

Hill, J. N. (ed.), 1977, *The Explanation of Prehistoric Change,* Albuquerque, University of New Mexico Press.

Marcus, J., 1973, Territorial organization of the lowland Classic Maya, *Science* 180, 811–816.

Maruyama, M., 1963, The second cybernetics: deviation-amplifying mutual causal processes, *American Scientist* 51, 164–179.

Renfrew, C., 1978, Trajectory discontinuity and morphogenesis, the implications of catastrophe theory for archaeology, *American Antiquity* 43, 203–222.

Rosen, R., 1979, Morphogenesis in biological and social systems, in Renfrew, C., and Cooke, K. L. (eds.), *Transformations: Mathematical Approaches to Culture Change,* New York, Academic Press, 91–111.

Waddington, C. H., 1977, *Tools for Thought,* St. Albans, Paladin.

Wheatley, P., 1971, *The Pivot of the Four Quarters,* Edinburgh, University Press.

Zeeman, E. C., 1977, *Catastrophe Theory: Selected Papers 1972–1977,* New York, Addison-Wesley Publishing Co.

# Subject Index